PETERSON'S

Competitive Colleges®

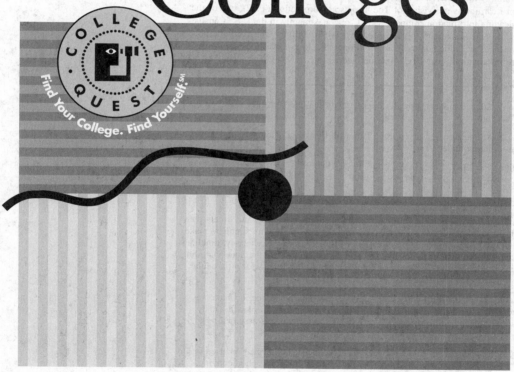

COLLEGE QUEST

Find Your College. Find Yourself.℠

Headed for college? Visit **CollegeQuest**, the premier online resource for expert admission advice, at **petersons.com**

Peterson's
Thomson Learning™

Australia • Canada • Denmark • Japan • Mexico • New Zealand • Philippines
Puerto Rico • Singapore • Spain • United Kingdom • United States

About Peterson's

Founded in 1966, Peterson's, a division of Thomson Learning, is the nation's largest and most respected provider of lifelong learning online resources, software, reference guides, and books. The Education Supersite^{SM} at petersons.com—the Web's most heavily traveled education resource—has searchable databases and interactive tools for contacting U.S.-accredited institutions and programs. CollegeQuest^{SM} (CollegeQuest.com) offers a complete solution for every step of the college decision-making process. GradAdvantage^{TM} (GradAdvantage.org), developed with Educational Testing Service, is the only electronic admissions service capable of sending official graduate test score reports with a candidate's online application. Peterson's serves over 55 million education consumers annually.

Thomson Learning is among the world's largest providers of lifelong learning information. Headquartered in Stamford, CT, with multiple offices worldwide, Thomson Learning is a division of The Thomson Corporation (TTC), one of the world's leading information companies. TTC operates mainly in the U.S., Canada, and the UK and has annual revenues of over US$6 billion. The Corporation's common shares are traded on the Toronto, Montreal, and London stock exchanges. For more information, visit TTC's Internet address at www.thomcorp.com.

Visit Peterson's Education Center on the Internet (World Wide Web) at www.petersons.com

ISSN 0887-0152
ISBN 0-7689-0386-6 (sponsor version)
    0-7689-0385-8 (trade version)

Printed in the United States of America

10 9 8 7 6 5 4 3 2 1

CONTENTS

COMPETITIVE COLLEGES—WHY SHOULD YOU CARE?

Excellent colleges typically take great care in admitting students. For them, selecting the entering class is, as Bill Fitzsimmons, Dean of Undergraduate Admission and Financial Aid at Harvard University, describes it: a process of "sculpting" the best possible class from the pool of qualified applicants. The goal of an admission committee is to bring together a community of students who can learn from one another, each one bringing their own particular talents, skills, and experiences that will contribute to the development of all the others.

Students who have excelled in high school want to go on excelling. They need an educational environment that will push them, test them, help them go beyond their past accomplishments. They require a college that "fits" exactly right, one that will help them develop into what they can uniquely become.

At the start, you'll likely find that everyone's list of "best" colleges is very much alike. Except for adding the most popular regional schools or schools serving an unusual interest or a family's traditional alma mater, your initial list and your classmates' basic lists probably will include the Ivy League schools and one or more of up to a dozen other similarly prestigious colleges and universities. The one quality shared by these schools is prestige. It certainly can be argued that it helps to graduate from a prestigious college. But prestige is a limited and very expensive factor upon which to base one's college choice. In "A New Way to Look at Colleges: How to Discover the Reality Behind the Dream," beginning on page 14, Robert Zemsky identifies twenty-one attributes of a college education that could lead you to a more rational choice. You and we know that there are truly excellent college choices beyond the eight Ivy League schools and a newsstand magazine's designated top schools. One of these "other" college choices could very well be the best fit for your particular requirements and goals.

We make only one assumption in *Competitive Colleges.* This is that the most influential factor in determining your experience on campus is the other students you will find there. In selecting colleges for inclusion in this book, we measure the competitiveness of the admission environment at colleges. This is measured over a meaningful period of time by entering-class statistics, such as GPA, class ranking, and test scores, and the college's acceptance rate. The 394 colleges selected for inclusion in this book routinely attract and admit an above-average share of the nation's high-achieving students.

Selecting a college is a great adventure, and Peterson's wants to guide you in this quest. Peterson's Web site, *CollegeQuest.com*, is a great tool for this. Check us out! We will look for you.

UNDERSTANDING THE COLLEGE ADMISSION PROCESS

BY TED SPENCER, Director of Undergraduate Admissions at the University of Michigan

The process you are about to begin, that of choosing a college, can be very challenging, sometimes frustrating, but most often rewarding. As Director of Admissions at a large, selective university, I would like to provide some basic information about the admission process that should help you get into the college of your choice. Although each competitive college or university has its own distinctive qualities and goals, the process of applying to them is strikingly similar. The following will give you the basic information you need to know to help you plan and apply to college.

GATHERING INFORMATION

How do you get the information you need to choose a college? Although colleges publish volumes of information about themselves that they are willing to mail or give out in person, another way to find out about them is through a guide such as *Peterson's Competitive Colleges.*

The major difference between the college-published materials and *Competitive Colleges* is that the colleges present only the most appealing picture of themselves and are perhaps, then, somewhat less objective. As a student seeking information about college, you should review both the information provided in books like this one and the information sent by the colleges. Your goal should be to use all of the available literature to assist you in developing your list of the top five or ten colleges in which you are interested.

Chances are that if you are a top student and you have taken the PSAT, SAT I, SAT II, ACT, PACT, or AP (Advanced Placement) tests, you will receive a great deal of material directly from many colleges and universities. Colleges purchase lists of names of students taking these exams and then screen the list for students they think will be most successful at their institutions. Some colleges will also automatically mail course catalogs, posters, departmental brochures, and pamphlets, as well as videocassettes. If you do not receive this information but would like a sample, write or call that particular college.

My advice is to take a look at the materials you receive and then use them to help you decide (if you don't already know) about the type of college you would like to attend. Allow the materials to help you narrow your list of top schools by comparing key facts and characteristics.

OTHER HELPFUL SOURCES

Published information about colleges, printed by the colleges, is certainly an important way to narrow your choices. But there are at least five other means of learning more about colleges and universities:

- *High School Counselors.* Although most high school counselors are overburdened, they have established positive relationships with the college representatives in your state as well as with out-of-state universities where large numbers of their students apply. As you attempt to gain more information while narrowing your choice of colleges, the high school counselor can give you a fairly accurate assessment of colleges to which you will have the best chance of gaining admission.

- *Parents.* Because most prospective students and their parents are at that stage in life in which they view issues in different ways, students tend to be reluctant to ask parents' opinions about college choices. However, you may find that parents are very helpful because they often are actively gathering information about the colleges that they feel are best suited for you. And not only do they gather information—you can be sure that they have thoroughly read the piles of literature that colleges have mailed to you. Ask your parents questions about what they have read and also about the colleges from which they graduated. As alumni of schools on your list, parents can be a very valuable resource.

- *College Day/Night/Fairs Visitation.* One of the best ways to help narrow your college choices is to meet with a person representing a college while they are visiting your area or high school. In fact, most admission staff members spend a good portion of the late spring and fall visiting high schools and attending college fairs. In some cases, college fairs feature students, faculty members, and alumni. Before attending one of these sessions, you should prepare a list of questions you would like to ask the representatives. Most students want to know about five major areas: academic preparation, the admission process, financial aid, social life, and job preparation. Most college representatives can be extremely helpful in addressing these questions as well as the many others that you may have. It is then up to you to decide if their answers fit your criteria of the college you are seeking.

- *Alumni.* For many schools, alumni are a very important part of the admission process. In some cases, alumni conduct interviews and even serve as surrogate admission officers, particularly when admission office staff cannot travel. As recent graduates, alumni can talk about their own experience and can give balance to the materials you have received from the college or university.

- *Campus Visits.* Finally, try to schedule a campus visit as part of your information-gathering process. By the time you begin thinking about a campus visit, you should have narrowed down your college shopping list. Hopefully your short list of colleges will have met your personal and educational goals. Before deciding which schools to visit, you should sort the materials into piles of "definitely not interested," "definitely interested," or "could be interested." Next, in an effort to make sure that the reality lives up to the printed viewbook, you should schedule a visit and see firsthand what the college is really like. Most colleges and universities provide daily campus tours to both prospective and admitted students. The tours for prospective students are generally set up to help you answer questions about the following: class size and student-to-teacher ratio;

size of the library, residence halls, and computer centers; registration and faculty advising; and retention, graduation rates, and career placement planning. Since the tours may not cover everything you came prepared to ask about, be sure to ask questions of as many staff, students, and faculty members as possible before leaving the campus.

THE ADMISSION PROCESS

ADMISSION CRITERIA

After you go through the process of selecting a college or narrowing your choices to a few schools, the admission process now focuses on you—your academic record and skills—and judgment will be passed on these pieces of information for admission to a particular school. The first things you should find out about each college on your priority list are the admission criteria—what it takes to get in:

1. Does the college or university require standardized tests—the ACT or SAT I? Do they prefer one or the other, or will they accept either?
2. Do they require SAT II Subject Tests and, if so, which ones?
3. Are Advanced Placement scores accepted and, if so, what are the minimums needed?
4. In terms of grades and class rank, what is the profile of a typical entering student?

It is also important to find out which type of admission notification system the college uses—rolling or deferred admission. On a rolling system, you find out your status within several weeks of applying; with the deferred system, notification is generally made in the spring. For the most part, public universities and colleges use rolling admission and private colleges generally use delayed notification.

THE APPLICATION

The application is the primary vehicle used to introduce yourself to the admission office. As with any introduction, you should try to make a good first impression. The first thing you should do in presenting your application is to find out what the college or university wants from you. This means you should read the application carefully to learn the following:

1. Must the application be typed, or can you print it?
2. Is there an application fee and, if so, how much is it?
3. Is there a deadline and, if so, when is it?
4. What standardized tests are required?
5. Is an essay required?
6. Is an interview required?
7. Can you send letters of recommendation?
8. How long will it take to find out the admission decision?
9. What other things can you do to improve your chances of admission?

My advice is to submit your application early. It does not guarantee admission, but it is much better than submitting it late or near the deadline. Also, don't assume that colleges using rolling admission will always have openings close to their deadlines. Regardless of when you submit it, make sure that the application is legible and that all the information that is requested is provided.

TRANSCRIPTS

While all of the components of the application are extremely important in the admission process, perhaps the single most important item is your transcript because it tells: (1) what courses you took; (2) which courses were college-preparatory and challenging; (3) class rank; and (4) grades and test scores.

- *Required Course Work.* Generally speaking, most colleges look at the high school transcript to see if the applicant followed a college-preparatory track while in high school. So, if you have taken four years of English, math, natural science, social sciences, and foreign language, you are on the right track. Many selective colleges require four years of English; three years each of math, natural science, and social science; and two years of a foreign language. It is also true that some selective colleges believe students who are interested in majoring in math and science need more than the minimum requirements in those areas.
- *Challenging Courses.* As college admission staff members continue to evaluate your transcript, they also look to see how demanding your course load has been during high school. If the high school offered Advanced Placement or Honors courses, the expectation of most selective colleges is that students will have taken seven or more honors classes or four or more AP courses during their four years in high school. However, if you do elect to take challenging courses, it is also important that you make good grades in those courses. Quite often, students ask, "If I take honors and AP courses and get a 'C,' does that count more than getting a 'B' or higher in a strictly college-prep course?" It's a difficult question to answer, because too many C's and B's can outweigh mostly A's. On the other hand, students who take the more challenging courses will be better prepared to take the more rigorous courses in college. Consequently, many colleges will give extra consideration when making their selections to the students who take the more demanding courses.
- *Transcript Trends.* Because the courses you take in high school are such a critical part of the college decision-making process, your performance in those courses indicates to colleges whether you are following an upward or downward trend. Beginning with the ninth grade, admission staff look at your transcript to see if you have started to develop good academic habits. In general, when colleges review your performance in the ninth grade, they are looking to see if you are in the college-preparatory track.

By sophomore year, students should begin choosing more demanding courses and become more involved in extracurricular activities. This will show that you are beginning to learn how to balance your academic and extracurricular commitments. Many admission officers consider the sophomore year to be the most critical and telling year for the student's future success.

The junior year is perhaps the second-most-important year in high school. The grades you earn and the courses you take will help to reinforce the trend you began in your sophomore year. At the end of your junior year, many colleges will know enough about the type of student you are to make their admission decision.

The upward and positive trend must continue, however, during your senior year. Many selective schools do not use senior grades in making their admission decisions. However, almost all do review the final transcript, so your last year needs to show a strong performance to the end. The research shows that students who finish their senior year with strong grades will start their freshman year in college with strong grades.

THE APPLICATION REVIEW PROCESS

WHAT'S NEXT?

At this point, you have done all you can do. So you might as well sit back and relax, if that's possible, and wait for the letters to come in the mail. Hopefully, if you've evaluated all the college materials you were sent earlier and you prepared your application carefully and sent it to several colleges, you will be admitted to either your first, second, or third choice. It may help your peace of mind, however, to know what happens to your application after the materials have been submitted.

Once your application is received by the admission office, it is reviewed, in most cases by noncounseling staff, to determine if you have completed the application properly. If items are missing, you will receive a letter of notification identifying additional information that must be provided. Be sure to send any additional or missing information the college requests back to them as soon as possible. Once your application is complete, it is then ready for the decision process.

READER REVIEW

The process by which the decision is finalized varies from school to school. Most of the private colleges and universities use a system in which each application is read by 2 or more admission staff members. In some cases, faculty members are also readers. If all of the readers agree on the decision, a letter is sent. Under this system, if the readers do not agree, the application will be reviewed by a committee or may be forwarded to an associate dean, dean, or director of admission for the final decision. One advantage to this process is that each applicant is reviewed by several people, thereby eliminating bias.

COMMITTEE REVIEW

At some universities, a committee reviews every application. Under that system, a committee member is assigned a number of applications to present. It is that member's responsibility to prepare background information on each applicant and then present the file to the committee for discussion and a vote. In this process, every applicant is voted on.

COUNSELOR REVIEW

The review process that many selective public institutions use is one in which the counselor responsible for a particular school or geographical territory makes the final decision. In this case, the counselor who makes the admission decision is also the one who identified and recruited the student, thereby lending a more personal tone to the process.

COMPUTER-GENERATED REVIEW

Many large state universities that process nearly 20,000 applications a year have developed computer-generated guidelines to admit their applicants. If applicants meet the required GPA and test scores, they are immediately notified of the decision.

Once the decisions are made using one of these methods, colleges use a variety of ways to notify students. The common methods used are early action or early decision, rolling admission, and deferred admission.

A WORD OF ADVICE

When you start the admission process, do so with the idea of exploring as many college opportunities as you can. From the very beginning, avoid focusing on just one college or, for that matter, one type of college. Look at private, public, large, small, highly selective, selective—in short, a variety of colleges and universities. Take advantage of every available resource, including students, parents, counselors, and college materials, in order to help identify the colleges that will be a great fit for you.

Finally, the most important thing you can do is to build a checklist of what you want out of the college experience and then match your list with one of the many wonderful colleges and universities just waiting for you to enroll.

APPLYING TO PROFESSIONAL COLLEGES FOR ART AND MUSIC

BY THERESA LYNCH BEDOYA, Vice President of Admission and Financial Aid, Maryland Institute, College of Art

The term "competitive" will have a different meaning if you are applying to a professional college specializing in art or music. The goal of selective art and music colleges is to admit students of extraordinary talent. Since you are using this resource as part of your college search, you most likely have distinguished yourself academically. But to gain admission to the music and art colleges listed in this guide, you will also need to be competitive in your achievements in the arts.

ADMISSION CRITERIA

In order to choose the most talented students from those who apply, most professional art and music colleges require evidence of talent, skill, ability, experience, and desire as demonstrated in an audition or by a portfolio of artwork. Each art and music college has expectations and academic requirements particular to the program of study you choose.

Admission will be based upon the review of traditional criteria such as your grade point average, level of course work, test scores, essays, and interviews. However, for most professional colleges, the evaluation of your portfolio or your audition will supersede the review of all other criteria for admission. (Many visual arts colleges even prescreen potential applicants through review of the portfolio prior to application in order to determine eligibility for admission. This process, which occurs early in the senior year, allows students the opportunity to gain valuable guidance early in the admission process. It also creates a more "acceptable" pool of applicants and is the reason that acceptance rates at many visual art colleges appear to be higher than other selective institutions.) In some cases, the evaluation of your talent and academic achievement will be given equal weight.

In contrast, most comprehensive colleges and universities offering majors in art and music will rely on academic criteria to make an admission decision. The portfolio or audition, if required, will play a secondary role. You should take these factors into account when deciding whether to apply to art and music schools or to colleges and universities that offer art and music programs.

PREPARING FOR YOUR PORTFOLIO REVIEW OR AUDITION

If you are interested in the visual arts, you should gain as much studio experience as possible in order to develop a strong portfolio. Take full advantage of your high school art program and enroll in extra Saturday or summer classes or seek private tutoring. Exhibit your artwork when the opportunity is provided. Become better informed as an artist by studying art history and the works of contemporary artists.

If you plan to study music, remember that experience and confidence need to be clearly evident in your audition. Therefore, become involved as much as possible in your own high school music activities as well as local, district, and state youth orchestras, choirs, and performance ensembles. The more you perform and study, the more confident you will be on stage.

Contact the schools to which you are applying early in the process to learn how and when they will receive your portfolio or conduct your audition.

PAYING FOR COLLEGE

BY **DON BETTERTON**, Director of Financial Aid at Princeton University

Regardless of which college a student chooses, higher education requires a major investment of time, energy, and money. By taking advantage of a variety of available resources, most students can bring the education that is right for them within reach.

A NOTE OF ENCOURAGEMENT

While there is no denying that the cost of an education at some competitive colleges can be high, it is important to recognize that, although the rate of increase in costs during the last ten years has outpaced gains in family income, there are more options available to pay for college than ever before.

Many families find it is economically wise to spread costs out over a number of years by borrowing money for college. A significant amount of government money, both federal and state, is available to students. Moreover, colleges themselves have expanded their own student aid efforts considerably. In spite of rapidly increasing costs, most competitive colleges are still able to provide financial aid to all admitted students with demonstrated need.

In addition, many colleges have developed ways to assist families who are not eligible for need-based assistance. These include an increasing number of merit scholarships as well as various forms of parental loans. There also are a number of organizations that give merit awards based on a student's academic record, talent, or special characteristics. Thus, regardless of your family's income, if you are academically qualified and knowledgeable about the many different sources of aid, you should be able to attend the college of your choice.

ESTIMATING COSTS

If you have not yet settled on specific colleges and you would like to begin early financial planning, estimate a budget. By calculating a 5 percent increase on 1999–2000 charges, we can estimate 2000–2001 expenses at a typical competitive college as follows: tuition and fees, about $19,800; room and board, about $6,800; and an allowance for books and miscellaneous

expenses, about $2,050. Thus a rough budget (excluding travel expenses) for the year is $28,650.

IDENTIFYING RESOURCES

There are essentially four sources of funds you can use to pay for college:

1. Money from your parents
2. Need-based scholarships or grants from a college or outside organization
3. Your own contribution from savings, loans, and jobs
4. Assistance unrelated to demonstrated financial need.

All of these are considered by the financial aid office, and the aid "package" given to a student after the parental contribution has been determined usually consists of a combination of scholarships, loans, and campus work.

THE PARENTAL CONTRIBUTION

The financial aid policies of most colleges are based on the assumption that parents should contribute as much as they reasonably can to the educational expenses of their children. The amount of this contribution varies greatly, but almost every family is expected to pay something.

Because there is no limit on aid eligibility based solely on income, the best rule of thumb is *apply for financial aid if there is any reasonable doubt about your ability to meet college costs.* Since it is generally true that applying for financial aid does not affect a student's chances of being admitted, any candidate for admission should apply for aid if his or her family feels they will be unable to pay the entire cost of attendance. (In spite of considerable publicity on the subject, there are still only a handful of competitive colleges that practice need-sensitive admissions.)

Application for aid is made by completing the Free Application for Federal Student Aid (FAFSA). In addition, many competitive colleges will require you to also file a separate form called PROFILE, since they need more detailed information to award their own funds. The financial aid section of a college's admission information booklet will tell you which financial aid application is required, when it should be filed, and whether a separate aid form of the college's own design is also necessary.

Colleges use the same national system (the Federal Methodology) to determine eligibility for federal and state student aid. This process of coming up with an expected contribution from you (the student) and your parents is called "need analysis." The information on the FAFSA—parental and student income and assets, the number of family members, and the number attending college as well as other variables—is analyzed to derive the expected family contribution.

You can estimate how much your parents might be asked to contribute for college by consulting the chart on page 12. (Keep in mind that the actual parental contribution is determined on campus by a financial aid officer, using the national system as a guideline.)

Competitive colleges that also require the PROFILE will have at their disposal information they will analyze in addition to what is reported on the FAFSA. The net result of this further examination (for example, adding the value of the family home to the equation) will usually increase the expected parental contribution compared to the Federal Methodology.

Parental Borrowing

Some families who are judged to have sufficient resources to be able to finance their children's college costs find that lack of cash at any moment prevents them from paying college bills without difficulty. Other families prefer to use less current income by extending their payments over more than four years. In both instances, these families rely on borrowing to assist with college payments. Each year parental loans become a more important form of college financing.

The Federal PLUS program, part of the Federal Family Education Loan Program, is designed to help both aid and non-aid families. It allows parents to pay their share of educational costs by borrowing at a reasonable interest rate, with the backing of the federal government. The 7½–8½ percent loans are available from banks that offer FFEL Stafford Student Loans or directly from the Department of Education through the William D. Ford Direct

Federal Loan Program. Many competitive colleges, state governments, and commercial lenders also have their own parental loan programs patterned along the lines of PLUS. For more information about parental loans, contact a college financial aid office or your state higher education department.

NEED-BASED SCHOLARSHIP OR GRANT ASSISTANCE

Need-based aid is primarily available from federal and state governments and from colleges themselves. It is not necessary for a student to apply directly for a particular scholarship at a college; the financial aid office will match an eligible applicant with the appropriate fund.

The Federal Pell Grant is by far the largest single form of federal student assistance; an estimated 4 million students receive awards annually. Families with incomes of up to $25,000 (higher when other family assets are relatively low) may be eligible for grants ranging from $250 to $3,125.

For state scholarships, students should check with the department of higher education about eligibility requirements. Aid applicants are expected to apply directly to outside organizations for any scholarships for which they may be eligible.

It is particularly important to apply for a Federal Pell Grant and a state scholarship. Application for both Pell and state scholarships is made by checking the appropriate box on the FAFSA. (Aid recipients are required to notify the college financial aid office about outside awards, as colleges take into consideration grants from all sources before assigning scholarships from their own funds.)

THE STUDENT'S OWN CONTRIBUTION

All undergraduates, not only those who apply for financial aid, can assume responsibility for meeting a portion of their college expenses by borrowing, working during the academic year and the summer, and contributing a portion of their savings. Colleges require aid recipients to provide a "self-help" contribution before awarding scholarship money because they believe students should pay a reasonable share of their own educational costs.

Student Loans

Many students will be able to borrow to help pay for college. Colleges administer three loans (all backed by the federal government): the Direct Stafford Loan, FFEL Stafford Loan, and the Federal Perkins Loan. Students must demonstrate financial need to be eligible for either the Direct Stafford or the Perkins Loan.

Note: Rather than providing FFEL Stafford Loans, many colleges have made arrangements to participate in the Direct Stafford Loan Program. As far as the student is concerned, the loan terms are essentially the same.

Summer Employment

All students, whether or not they are receiving financial aid, should plan to work during the summer months. Students can be expected to save from $800 to $1,850 before their freshman year and $1,500 to $2,550 each summer while enrolled in college. It is worthwhile for a student to begin working while in high school to increase the chance of finding summer employment during college vacations.

Term-Time Employment

Colleges have student employment offices that find jobs for students during the school year. Aid recipients on work-study receive priority in placement, but once they have been assisted, non-aid students are helped as well. Some jobs relate closely to academic interests; others should be viewed as a source of income rather than intellectual stimulation. A standard 8- to 12-hour-per-week job does not normally interfere with academic work or extracurricular activities and results in approximately $1,550 to $2,250 in earnings during the year.

Student Savings

Student assets accumulated prior to starting college are available to help pay college bills. The need analysis system expects 35 percent of each year's student savings to go toward college expenses. This source can often be quite substantial, particularly when families have accumulated large sums in the student's name (or in a trust fund with the student as the beneficiary). If you have a choice whether to keep college savings in the parents' name or the student's name, you should realize that the contribution rate on parental assets is 12 percent, compared to 35 percent for the student's savings.

AID NOT REQUIRING NEED AS AN ELIGIBILITY CRITERION

There are scholarships available to students whether or not they are eligible for need-based financial aid. Awards based on merit are given by certain state scholarship programs, and National Merit Scholarship winners usually receive a $2,000 stipend regardless of family financial circumstances. Scholarships and prizes are also awarded by community organizations and other local groups. In addition, some parents receive tuition payments for their children as employment benefits. Most colleges offer merit scholarships to a limited group of highly qualified applicants. The selection of recipients for such awards depends on unusual talent in a specific area or on overall academic excellence. To find out more about qualifying for a merit scholarship, see your high school guidance counselor or consult a scholarship guide, such as Santamaria's *Financial Aids for Higher Education* and *Peterson's College Money Handbook*. You can also search for scholarships on the Internet at http://www.collegequest.com.

The Reserve Officers' Training Corps sponsors an extensive scholarship program that pays for tuition and books and provides an expense allowance of $1500 per school year. The Army, Air Force, and Navy/Marine Corps have ROTC units at many colleges. High school guidance offices have brochures describing ROTC application procedures.

A SIMPLE METHOD FOR ESTIMATING FAMILY CONTRIBUTION

The chart that follows will enable parents to make an approximation of the yearly amount the national financial aid need analysis system will expect them to pay for college.

To use the chart, you need to work with your income, assets, and size of your family. Read the instructions below and enter the proper amounts in the spaces provided.

1. Parents' total income before taxes

   A. Adjusted gross income (equivalent to tax return entry; use actual or estimated) _____A

   B. Nontaxable income (Social Security benefits, child support, welfare, etc.) _____B

   Total Income: A + B _____①

2. Parents' total assets

   C. Total of cash, savings, and checking accounts _____C

   D. Total value of investments (stocks, bonds, real estate other than home, etc.) _____D

   Total Assets: C + D _____②

3. Family size (include student, parents, other dependent children, and other dependents) _____③

Now find the figures on the chart that correspond to your entries in ①, ②, and ③ to determine your approximate expected parental contribution, interpolating as necessary.

4. Estimated parental contribution from chart _____④

If there will be more than one family member in college half-time or more, divide the figure above by the number in college.

5. Estimated parental contribution for each person in college _____⑤

6. Student's savings _____ × .35 = _____⑥

7. Finally, add the estimated parental contribution in ⑤ and the estimated student contribution in ⑥ to arrive at the total estimated family contribution _____⑦

This number can be compared to college costs to determine an approximate level of need.

APPROXIMATE EXPECTED PARENTAL CONTRIBUTION CHART

	Assets					Income Before Taxes				
		$20,000	30,000	40,000	50,000	60,000	70,000	80,000	90,000	100,000
	$20,000									
FAMILY SIZE	3	$220	2,100	3,200	5,400	8,700	11,800	14,800	17,600	20,400
	4	0	1,400	2,000	4,000	7,400	10,500	13,400	15,900	19,300
	5	0	300	1,300	3,000	6,200	9,300	12,200	15,100	18,100
	6	0	0	600	2,100	5,000	7,800	10,800	13,700	16,600
	$30,000									
FAMILY SIZE	3	$220	2,100	3,200	5,400	8,700	11,800	14,800	17,600	20,400
	4	0	1,400	2,000	4,000	7,400	10,500	13,400	15,900	19,300
	5	0	300	1,300	3,000	6,200	9,300	12,200	15,100	18,100
	6	0	0	600	2,100	5,000	7,800	10,800	13,700	16,600
	$40,000									
FAMILY SIZE	3	$220	2,200	3,300	5,600	8,900	11,900	14,900	14,700	21,700
	4	0	1,500	2,100	4,100	7,500	10,700	13,600	16,000	20,400
	5	0	400	1,400	3,100	6,300	9,400	12,300	15,200	18,100
	6	0	0	600	2,200	5,100	8,000	11,000	13,900	16,700
	$50,000									
FAMILY SIZE	3	$600	2,500	3,800	6,200	9,500	12,500	15,500	18,300	21,200
	4	0	1,800	2,400	4,600	8,200	11,300	14,200	16,700	20,000
	5	0	600	1,600	3,500	6,900	10,000	12,900	15,700	18,700
	6	0	0	900	2,500	5,700	8,600	11,600	14,500	17,300
	$60,000									
FAMILY SIZE	3	$800	2,900	4,200	6,700	10,100	13,100	16,000	18,900	21,800
	4	140	2,000	2,700	5,100	8,700	11,900	14,800	17,600	20,600
	5	0	900	1,900	3,900	7,500	10,600	13,500	16,300	19,300
	6	0	0	1,200	2,900	6,300	9,200	12,200	15,100	17,900

					Income Before Taxes					
	Assets	$20,000	30,000	40,000	50,000	60,000	70,000	80,000	90,000	100,000
	$80,000									
FAMILY SIZE	3	$1,400	3,500	5,100	7,800	11,000	14,200	17,100	20,000	22,900
	4	600	2,600	3,400	6,100	9,800	12,900	15,700	18,300	21,600
	5	0	1,400	2,500	4,800	8,600	11,700	14,600	17,400	20,400
	6	0	300	1,700	3,600	7,300	10,200	13,200	16,000	19,100
	$100,000									
FAMILY SIZE	3	$1,800	4,400	6,100	8,900	12,300	15,300	18,200	21,100	24,000
	4	1,200	3,300	4,200	7,200	10,900	14,000	16,800	15,400	22,700
	5	100	1,900	3,200	5,800	9,700	12,800	15,600	18,500	21,500
	6	0	900	2,300	4,400	8,400	11,400	14,400	17,200	20,100
	$120,000									
FAMILY SIZE	3	$2,500	5,300	7,300	10,100	13,400	16,300	19,300	22,300	25,100
	4	1,700	4,100	5,100	8,400	12,100	15,200	18,000	20,600	23,900
	5	600	2,500	4,000	6,900	10,800	13,900	16,600	19,600	22,600
	6	250	1,400	2,900	5,400	9,600	12,500	15,500	18,300	21,200
	$140,000									
FAMILY SIZE	3	$3,200	6,500	8,400	11,200	14,500	17,400	20,400	23,300	26,200
	4	2,300	5,100	6,200	9,500	13,200	16,200	19,100	21,700	25,000
	5	1,200	3,200	4,900	8,100	11,900	15,100	17,900	20,800	23,800
	6	800	1,900	3,700	6,500	10,700	13,600	16,500	19,400	22,400

A New Way to Look at Colleges: How to Discover the Reality Behind the Dream

BY ROBERT ZEMSKY, Professor and Director of the University of Pennsylvania's Institute for Research on Higher Education

If you are at the beginning of the college selection process, opening this volume may be your first serious attempt to find out what's ahead of you. More likely, you are already a veteran who suspects that there is no end to the things people want you to look at before choosing a college. There on your table or desk are books, brochures, magazines, and all the mail that started arriving the day after you registered for the SAT or the ACT. Whether you are a beginner or a veteran, your task is to narrow your choice of colleges and universities to a manageable few, submit your applications, and then make your final choice. My job in the next few pages is to explain how this process works and what you might consider as you get yourself organized to make that decision. Here goes!

WHAT'S REALLY GOING ON?

Choosing a college has become a serious business that annually engulfs high school seniors (and increasingly juniors and sophomores), their families, and friends. Now it is your turn. What do you need to know, and when do you need to know it? What kind of information will really help you make this decision when you are alternately told, "This is the most important choice of your life," and "Don't sweat it. You can always change your mind later." What do you need to know about the colleges and universities you are considering? What do you need to know about yourself? What do you need to know about how you might turn out if you choose one institution instead of another? What will you be like six or seven years after you graduate from that college?

To begin, let's look at the college choice process itself. As colleges have become more expensive, this process has gotten both more complex and more competitive. The basic script goes as follows: consider the colleges and universities to which you might apply, get your credentials in order, take (and score your best on) the right tests, write a compelling admissions essay, and ask the right people to write your recommendations. If you get a chance, go visit the colleges and universities you are considering and check out what goes on in the classroom and laboratory, spend some time in the library, and talk with students and faculty members.

Once your applications are submitted, it will be the institution's turn to go to work. An admissions committee, often composed of faculty members, will read your essays and letters of recommendation, will look at your transcript, will consider if you could make a special contribution to the institution by playing in the orchestra or on the basketball team, and will take into consideration whether or not members of your family are graduates of the institution. Then, they will render judgment. If you are one of the lucky ones, you will get a "fat" envelope on or about March 1. Otherwise, you will get a thin envelope that contains a short but nicely written letter wishing you good luck at some other college or university. At that point, you will be expected to make your decision, choosing from among the colleges and universities that have chosen you.

ON THE OTHER SIDE OF THE SCREEN

All along, a lot of other activities have occurred just out of your sight. The process actually begins when college admissions offices across the country begin their annual search for new applicants. They will buy lists of names of high school students with the kind of interests that their institutions think are important or with given grade point averages or high SAT or ACT scores. You know you are on these lists when you start getting mail, each piece proclaiming the virtues of the mailing institution. (It has been wryly observed that what these mailings have most in common is the impression that at or near the center of every college or university is a body of water that can be best viewed from one of the verdant hills surrounding the campus.) You will be visited in your high school by a seemingly endless stream of assistant deans of admissions, many of them recent graduates of the institutions they represent, each extolling the virtues of their college or university. Once you show an interest—that is, you become an "inquiry"—you will get even more attention, possibly a phone call, certainly more printed material, and most likely a Web site address where you can check out the institution.

Later, if you apply and are admitted, the wooing will begin in earnest with invitations to visit the campus, to talk to faculty members, and to attend local events so you can meet the other students in your area who are considering the institution. At the height of this activity, if not before, you will come to understand that the institution wants you possibly more than you want it! You will discover that the institution is, in fact, selling itself. The admissions officers you have been working with want as many students as possible to consider their institutions. Their job is to get you to apply and, if you are admitted, to persuade you to choose their institution over someone else's.

KNOWING THE MARKET

What's going on? The answer is quite simple: higher education in the United States is a $150-billion-a-year enterprise. Colleges and universities are special institutions devoted to student learning and scholarly research; they are also enterprises that require revenues—in your case, the tuition you will pay. Even the most famous, most prestigious, best-endowed colleges and universities depend on tuition revenue to pay their faculty, operate their facilities, and field their sports teams. No students, no revenue, no institution!

What does this make you? Both a learner and a consumer, both a student and a customer. Each of these roles carries opportunities and responsibilities. As student and learner, you will be responsible for much of what happens to you. In college, even more than in high school, faculty members assume you

want to be there, that you understand that doing the work is the key part of learning. As consumer and customer, you have to know what you want, have to be able to distinguish a quality product from one that looks good but doesn't really measure up. Indeed, as a consumer, you have a special responsibility. The range and quality of products available to you are primarily functions of how good a shopper you (and all the other students choosing a college) are—how informed, how demanding, how ready to say, "I'll take myself elsewhere if what you offer is not what I want, not of the quality I expect, or not offered at a price I can afford."

THE LAW OF PRICE AND DEMAND

Once you understand that the admissions process is also a market process, then the basic rules become clearer. The first is simply that the net price (that is, the tuition minus the financial aid package) an institution charges reflects how many young people like you are likely to apply to and choose that institution. In general, the harder an institution is to get into, the higher the tuition it charges. Most institutions that are truly selective will also be truly expensive. Keep in mind that prestige is the major driver of demand, and what you require from your college may not be exactly what a particular prestigious "brand-name" college has to offer to its students.

You already know that each year a college education gets more expensive, and it has been doing so for a long time. The trend for the last twenty years has been one of constant tuition increases, with college tuition charges increasing faster than almost anything you or your parents are likely to buy—faster than the cost of an automobile, a cable television subscription, a dinner in a restaurant, or a movie ticket.

And why did prices increase? Because the demand for higher education went up. Thirty years ago, most young people went directly to work. Today, most young people first go to college. The surprise is that going to college is not the guarantee of higher salaries and incomes it once was. The figure on the next page charts the incomes of young men ages 25–34 over a twenty-five-year period for three groups: college grads, high school grads, and high school dropouts. The figures are in constant dollars, which means that they are based on what things actually cost in each of the years.

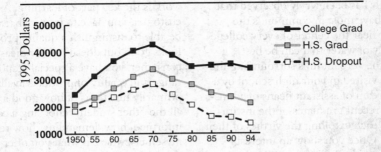

Annual Earnings (Constant Dollars): Men, 25 to 34
Source: Samuel Stringfield, "Attempting to Enhance Students'
Learning Through Innovative Programs," in *School Effectiveness
and School Improvement 6* (1995), p. 68.

These statistics provide an insight that brings us back to the college selection process and why you are reading this guide in the first place. What you and countless high school juniors and seniors before you have figured out is that choosing the right college means selecting the path that will enable you to graduate prepared for the kind of occupation that best suits you, at an income you desire, confident in performing complex tasks, prepared for a lifetime of learning, and strengthened with a coherent system of personal values.

THE RANKINGS

As college has become both more important and more expensive, choosing the right college has become an increasingly contentious as well as uncertain process. No wonder you want more information—information that is unbiased and that meaningfully compares the institutions you are considering with one another. What you want to know is where's the quality, where's the excitement, where's the best. Where do they have what you want? For any other major—and indeed not-so-major— investment or purchase, you could consult a host of guides that report on how well the product fared: how it was used, how it held up, whether or not it met acceptable standards, and what its buyers thought about the product after using it for a while. The first question an experienced consumer would likely ask when confronted with the decision you are about to make

would be, "Where's my *Consumer Reports?*"What you would want to learn about is product reliability and customer satisfaction.

Before you pay all that money, you want to know what you are buying! And that's what the rankings give you. Right? Well, yes and no. What the best-known rankings measure is not quality but the three "Ps": price, prestige, and pedigree. If nothing else frames your college choice, price, prestige, and pedigree are not a bad proxy for quality, although all you are really being told is how hard it is to get into a particular institution.

You also have to be careful with the popular rankings lists. They pretend to be a precision that most of us who study higher education would find laughable if students and parents didn't take the rankings so seriously. There is probably no real differ-ence between a number 1 and a number 10 ranking or between a number 20 and a number 35. Indeed, the rankers' search for precision leads them to constantly change their formulas, which produces results that often defy explanation. In any given year, my own institution, for example, rises or falls six or more places in the rankings. When the news is good, we wonder what we did to suddenly get so much better. When we drop in the rankings, we are equally puzzled as to how we suddenly went so wrong. The answer is that we didn't do anything. We like to think we are constantly improving the quality of our undergraduate education, but we understand that improvement takes time, that our reputation today is likely to be pretty close to our reputation tomorrow or our reputation yesterday. Keep this in mind when a "hot school" tells you it just jumped ten places in the rankings.

FRAMING YOUR CHOICE

So what do you have to go on? You have a lot of good descriptive information about the colleges you are considering, much of it coming from the institutions you are looking at, some of it from the handful of reliable college guides that have well-deserved reputations for doing it right. You will also find what I call the gossip and specialty guides that identify the "best party schools," the "best jock schools," the "best buys," and a limited number of "hidden treasures," colleges that are much better than their competitive rankings suggest.

Then you have the advice and testimony of a host of people who care about you—your friends, parents, perhaps older brothers or sisters or cousins, your high school counselor, and teachers—and who may or may not know very much about what kind of college will work best for you. Talk to these people, listen to what they have to say, but most of all, listen to yourself as you ask your questions and explain what you are looking for in a college. Often, the purpose of good conversation is as much to find out what's on your mind as it is to listen to others.

If at all possible, visit the institutions you are considering. Get the feel and taste of the campus. Attend classes. Talk to students. Wander about on your own—it's the closest thing to a test-drive as you are going to get.

If you get a chance, try to find a sample of more recent graduates of the institution, people roughly ten years older than you. Ask what they are doing now. Do they like their jobs? Do they have the right skills? Did their college education serve them well? What did they learn while in college? How much of it do they remember? How much do they use? What do they wish they had learned but did not? Are they likely to go on for further schooling or to get an advanced degree? Do they see themselves as lifelong learners? Finally, don't be embarrassed to ask them what values are important to them today. College is ultimately about acquiring and testing a set of

values—life perspectives, really—that will shape what you do for a long time to come. Where are you likely to find a sample of recent grads to talk with? Start by asking the admissions office if they have a list of recent grads you can talk to in your area. Often, the development office or the office of alumni affairs is a good source of names as well.

IN SEARCH OF BETTER CONSUMER INFORMATION

My suspicion is that not many of you will take me up on the recommendation to ask recent graduates about their college experiences. You just can't imagine asking somebody these questions, and what would you really do with the answers if you could get them? I am, however, quite serious about the importance of the perspective of the recent graduate. At the Institute for Research on Higher Education, we have used this perspective to begin speculating as to what a really relevant consumers' guide might look like—one that focuses on product value and reliability. And our answer is that one way to choose a college is to ask, "How am I likely to turn out? What am I likely to be doing, say, six years after graduation?" The answer, as you now probably suspect, lies in the experiences of recent graduates of each institution.

Working with the National Center for Postsecondary Improvement and Peterson's, we have begun testing a new way to use the experiences of graduates of an institution as a basis for a new kind of consumer information. Our testing has included random samples of graduates from fifteen colleges and universities from all across the country and all across the market. While only a few of you will actually be considering the colleges and universities that participated in the test, what their graduates told us can assist you as you think about college.

DISTANCE FROM TARGET

When considering colleges and universities, it helps to think about the set of attributes that represents your ideal or target. What you want to know is how close a particular college or university is to that target. Graphically, it helps to think of a bull's-eye—as in, "Of the attributes important to me, how often does College A as opposed to University B hit the bull's-eye?"

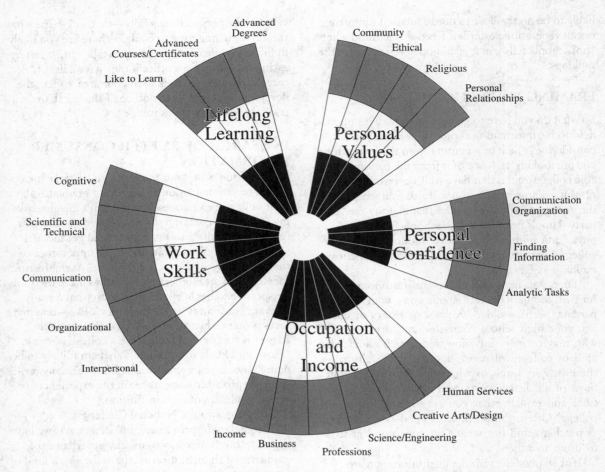

Target: College Attribute Categories

We used the bull's-eye image to help us determine the important questions we wanted to ask recent college graduates. We finally settled on five types of questions that focus on:

- the values recent grads said were important to them now that they had graduated from college
- the complex tasks they felt confident performing
- their current occupations and annual incomes
- the job skills they needed and used at work
- their involvement with lifelong learning

We next identified the key values, performance confidences, occupations, income, work skills, and indications of lifelong learning. The target above

graphically represents these five "type" groupings and their component attributes.

Only colleges and universities are likely to be interested in how their graduates scored on all twenty-one attributes: where their graduates hit the bull's-eye and where their graduates were either in the middle area of the dartboard (not so bad) and where they fell on the outer rim (cause for concern). Potential students, on the other hand, will probably be interested in what areas and how many times a given institution hit the bull's-eye. Using the data from our pilot institutions, we can represent exactly how that information from typical institutions might appear.

ONE "NAME-BRAND" COLLEGE, EIGHT BULL'S-EYES

Below is the list of attributes for which the graduates of a name-brand liberal arts colleges hit the bull's-eye. In all, the graduates of this institution collected eight bull's-eyes.

College A's Areas of High Scores (Bull's-Eyes)

Personal Values	
Importance of Religious Values	●

Personal Confidence (in performing complex tasks)	
Confidence in Analyzing Data/Facts	●

Occupation and Income	
Human Services Occupations	●

Work Skills	
Interpersonal Job Skills	●
Organizational Job Skills	●
Communication Job Skills	●
Scientific and Technical Job Skills	●
Cognitive Job Skills	●

That's the static measure of the college. What you would really like to know is how this college stacks up against the other institutions you are considering in terms of the attributes and characteristics you think are most important. What you really want to do is construct your own rankings, for which *you* get to define what constitutes quality. Suppose, for example, that you are interested primarily in liberal arts colleges and are thinking of a possible career in business, but you also come from a strongly religious background and want your college years to strengthen rather than diminish the importance you attach to your religious values. Imagine that you have narrowed your choice to four liberal arts colleges and wish to rate their graduates against the key categories you have selected: importance of religious values, confidence in performing organizational tasks, business occupation, income, communication job skills, and earning postbaccalaureate credits and certificates. The chart in the next column shows how the four colleges you are considering compared with each other.

Liberal Arts Colleges Compared for First Student

	College A	College B	College C	College D
Personal Values				
Importance of Religious Values	●	◓	○	○
Personal Confidence (in performing complex tasks)				
Confidence in Organizational Tasks	○	●	●	●
Occupation and Income				
Business Occupations	○	●	○	○
Income	○	●	○	○
Work Skills				
Communication Job Skills	●	●	○	○
Lifelong Learning				
Advanced Courses/Certificates	◓	●	●	○

● Bull's-Eye   ○ Average   ◓ Low Scores

How did your four liberal arts colleges compare? On five of the six attributes you chose as important, College B hit the bull's-eye. If your personal ranking of the institutions was a simple score card that reported who got the most bull's-eyes, then College B was the clear winner.

Alas, real choices are seldom that clear-cut. You said religious values were important to you, but the graduates of College B generally reported that religious values are not very important to them. Perhaps religious values were not very important to them as high school seniors; perhaps they became relatively less important to them while in college. We cannot know for sure, but their diminished importance to the graduates of your target college is a reason to pause and look again at the chart.

What about College A? Fewer bull's-eyes but solid in terms of business occupations, OK on income, really good on communication skills. You would find that this college was particularly good in providing its graduates with the work skills they used on the job. How do you choose? Not from these comparisons alone! You will want to visit the schools, get the feel of the campuses, and talk to students and faculty members. Now those conversations will be better informed. You will know what to ask, what to look for. You will feel more comfortable asking these important questions because there are relevant answers.

Let's take another example. We can compare the same four liberal arts colleges, but this time we want to rate them as if you were interested in a possible career in science.

Liberal Arts Colleges Compared for Second Student

	College A	College B	College C	College D
Personal Values				
Importance of Community Values	○	◉	○	○
Importance of Ethical Values	○	○	●	◉
Personal Confidence (in performing complex tasks)				
Confidence in Analytic Tasks	●	●	●	○
Occupation and Income				
Scientific and Engineering Occupations	○	◉	○	◉
Work Skills				
Scientific and Technical Job Skills	●	●	○	◉
Lifelong Learning				
Advanced Degrees	○	◉	●	●

● Bull's-Eye   ○ Average   ◉ Low Scores

Remember, these are the same colleges as were in our first example. Given the change in what we are interested in, however, the top-rated choice now would probably be College C: three bull's-eyes and solid in everything else. The fact that its graduates were not concentrated as much in the sciences as some other colleges might encourage you to extend your search to other liberal arts colleges that scored a bull's-eye for Scientific Occupations. Or you might think that the graduates of this institution go on to advanced degrees, use science and technical skills on the job, and have the kind of attachment to ethical values that you think is important in a world being changed by science and technology. The fact that many of their graduates go on to do things that aren't science related may be a plus, since you may not want to attend a college that specializes in just science and engineering education. Again, the purpose of the

comparisons is not to let a chart make the decision for you but to help you think through what you really want.

These two examples also shed some light on the rankings and their shortcomings. Actually, in the popular rankings publications, the highest-ranked college among the four we have been considering is College D, currently more prestigious and pricier and harder to get into than the other three. In many areas, this institution does a superb job and scores lots of bull's-eyes, but when the criteria for determining the overall ranking of these four colleges were customized, as in our two examples, then other choices emerged.

PUBLIC UNIVERSITIES: CREDIBLE CHOICES AT A GOOD PRICE

We need to also say a word about price. The tuition charged by these private liberal arts colleges ranges from about $16,850 to about $23,250, which raises the possibility of finding a less costly public alternative. You could consider four public institutions in your own state using the same criteria you used for rating the graduates of the four private liberal arts colleges. Let's consider the last example of a student interested in a career in science: the same six criteria now applied to the graduates of four public universities yield the chart on the following page.

Here, Universities C and D have the most bull's-eyes. For this set of ratings criteria, Universities C and D have as many bull's-eyes as the best of the liberal arts colleges. The public universities' most glaring weakness is probably the fact that relatively few of their graduates go on to advanced degrees. My guess is that there is a feeling at these institutions that when you graduate, you are finished in the sense of being ready for the job market.

We could continue with more examples, but the three charts already presented make the basic points I think can help you make your college decisions this year even without access to the new kind of consumer information we are developing.

SCHOLAR, KNOW THYSELF

Knowing how the graduates of a particular college or university turn out is helpful. Armed with that kind of information, you can more easily imagine yourself as

Public Universities Compared for Second Student

	University A	University B	University C	University D
Personal Values				
Importance of Community Values	Average	Bull's-Eye	Average	Bull's-Eye
Importance of Ethical Values	Bull's-Eye	Bull's-Eye	Bull's-Eye	Low Scores
Personal Confidence (in performing complex tasks)				
Confidence in Analytic Tasks	Average	Average	Low Scores	Average
Occupation and Income				
Scientific and Engineering Occupations	Low Scores	Average	Bull's-Eye	Bull's-Eye
Work Skills				
Scientific and Technical Job Skills	Average	Average	Bull's-Eye	Bull's-Eye
Lifelong Learning				
Advanced Degrees	Average	Average	Average	Average

● Bull's-Eye   ○ Average   ○ Low Scores

a graduate of that institution—whether or not what it offers is, in fact, what you are looking for.

Knowing what you want does matter. Understanding what you want and possessing good information about the colleges and universities you are considering means you don't have to depend on the rankings to tell you which are the best institutions. Nor do you need to use a definition of quality that assumes one model fits all. More interesting, and I think more fun, is using your own definition of what constitutes a "best institution" and then applying those criteria to the colleges and universities you are considering. It is not wrong to rank institutions, but it is wrong to rely on someone else's scoring system for determining which is the best place for you.

It would also be wrong to rely on any set of charts or scores to determine the college or university you ought to attend. Having access to the outcomes that characterize the graduates of specific institutions will stimulate purposeful discussion: among those who are searching for the best institution for themselves; between those future college freshmen and their parents, teachers, and guidance counselors; and between the student shopper and recent graduates of the institutions under consideration. In the end, what will likely prove most important is your visit to the campus—but when you arrive, you will know what to ask of whom.

Good luck! I don't envy you the task, but I confess to being a little bit jealous of your ability to chart a course that, if done right, will open the world to you. For our part, we are going to continue to develop more and better consumer information—asking an ever-widening circle of college graduates to report on what they are doing and the kinds of jobs they have, their further education, the values they hold important, and the kinds of tasks they feel confident performing. Starting next year, graduates in the classes of 1992–1994 will have a chance to use the Peterson's Web page to tell us about their experiences since leaving college. And, in about ten years, it will be your turn. So please do us the favor of connecting to CollegeQuest.com sometime in 2010 or 2011 and let us know what happened to you. We will use that information to guide other high school seniors as they travel the road on which you are now embarking.

The work reported herein was supported by the Educational Research and Development Center program, agreement number R309A60001, CFDA 84.309A, as administered by the Office of Educational Research and Improvement (OERI), U.S. Department of Education. The findings and opinions expressed by NCPI do not necessarily reflect the position or policies of OERI or the U.S. Department of Education.

WHAT'S INSIDE AND ONLINE

On pages 26 and 48 you will find brief explanations, in profile format, of the information that is packed into each college's full-page description. A pair of icons appears at the top of these descriptions. When one or both of these icons appears on a college's full-page profile, it is an indication that the college is a partner in one of Peterson's valuable programs, described below, designed to aid college students in the application process.

Colleges with this icon are sponsors of this book. These colleges have arranged for copies of *Peterson's Competitive Colleges* to reach outstanding students.

In an effort to provide you with more convenient ways to apply, many colleges accept common applications. These common applications make it easier for you to apply to several colleges at once. For example, with CollegeQuest eApply at www. CollegeQquest.com, you can apply to more than 1,200 colleges using a single application. You can enter all of your basic biographical and academic information into a personal information manager, which stores the data for use on each new application that you open. This reduces the amount of time you have to spend repeatedly entering information as well as the risk of errors. Once you have completed your applications, you can then print them and mail them, or you can submit them electronically through CollegeQuest's secure connection if the college accepts electronic applications.

COLLEGEQUEST.COM

One of the most comprehensive Web resources for college-bound students can be found at CollegeQquest.com. CollegeQuest provides information and tools that will help you prepare, search, apply, and pay for college. If you are preparing for the SAT or ACT, you will find test dates, valuable test-taking tips, and full-length practice tests that you can download for free. You can search through Peterson's complete college database to find the colleges that best fit your needs and then view in-depth profiles or do a side-by-side comparison of selected colleges. The site will keep you on track with a personal organizer and college calendar that provides general reminders, test dates, and key dates for every college that you add to your personal list. The financial aid section provides a complete overview of how financial aid works, a free scholarship search using Peterson's database of over 800,000 awards, and a family contribution estimator that will help your family calculate how much you will be expected to contribute toward the cost of college. All of these tools are supplemented with informative articles throughout each section, as well as an Advice Center and Expert Forum, where admissions and financial aid experts are available to answer your questions.

PETERSONS.COM

Peterson's publications offer some of the most comprehensive information available to students about all aspects of preparation for higher education. Now petersons.com brings this information together at one central address, offering consistently organized information about educational opportunities at all levels. Hundreds of private schools, camps, study-abroad programs, and graduate schools have their own sites at petersons.com, which permits each to develop a full array of information and communication tools. A searchable database leads users to applicable institutional sites where they will find an overview of the institution. Features include online applications and "instant inquiry" e-mail. Visit petersons.com, the most comprehensive education resource on the Web, brought to you by Peterson's, the world's largest education information and services provider, at www.petersons.com.

SPONSOR LIST

The institutions listed below arranged for copies of *Competitive Colleges* to reach outstanding students—students eager to learn more about top schools. The following icon appears next to each of the names on the list:

Agnes Scott College
Albion College
Albright College
Alfred University
Allegheny College
Alma College
American University
Amherst College
Art Center College of Design
Auburn University
Augustana College (IL)
Babson College
Baldwin-Wallace College
Barnard College
Baylor University
Belmont University
Beloit College
Bennington College
Berry College
Bethel College (MN)
Birmingham-Southern College
Boston College
Boston University
Bowdoin College
Brandeis University
Brown University
Bryn Mawr College
Bucknell University
Buena Vista University
Butler University
Calvin College
Carnegie Mellon University
Carroll College (MT)
The Catholic University of
   America
Central College (IA)
Christian Brothers University
Claremont McKenna College

Clarkson University
Clemson University
College of Insurance
College of Saint Benedict
College of the Atlantic
College of the Holy Cross
The College of Wooster
Colorado State University
Concordia College (MN)
Cooper Union for the
   Advancement of Science
   and Art
Cornell University
Creighton University
Dartmouth College
David Lipscomb University
Davidson College
Denison University
DePaul University
DePauw University
Drake University
Drew University
Eckerd College
Elizabethtown College
Emory University
Eugene Lang College, New
   School University
Fisk University
Florida Institute of Technology
Florida State University
Fordham University
Franklin and Marshall College
Georgetown College (KY)
Georgia Institute of Technology
Gettysburg College
Goucher College
Grove City College
Hamilton College

Hampshire College
Harding University
Harvard University
Harvey Mudd College
Haverford College
Hendrix College
Hillsdale College
Hiram College
Hobart and William Smith
   Colleges
Hofstra University
Illinois College
Illinois Institute of Technology
Illinois Wesleyan University
Iowa State University of Science
   and Technology
John Carroll University
Johns Hopkins University
Juniata College
Kettering University
Knox College
Lafayette College
Lake Forest College
Lawrence University
Lehigh University
Le Moyne College
Linfield College
List College, Jewish Theological
   Seminary of America
Loyola College of Maryland
Loyola University Chicago
Lyon College
Mannes College of Music,
   New School University
Marquette University
Maryville College
Maryville University of
   Saint Louis

Messiah College
Miami University (OH)
Michigan Technological University
Middlebury College
Millsaps College
Mills College
Morehouse College
Mount Holyoke College
Mount Union College
Muhlenberg College
Nebraska Wesleyan University
New Jersey Institute of Technology
New York School of Interior Design
North Carolina School of the Arts
North Central College
Oberlin College
Oglethorpe University
Ohio Northern University
Ohio Wesleyan University
Pacific Lutheran University
Pitzer College
Polytechnic University, Brooklyn Campus
Pomona College
Presbyterian College
Princeton University
Quincy University
Randolph-Macon Woman's College
Reed College
Rensselaer Polytechnic Institute
Rice University
Ripon College
Rochester Institute of Technology
Rockhurst University
St. John's College (MD)
St. John's College (NM)
Saint Joseph's University
St. Lawrence University
Saint Louis University

Saint Mary's College of California
St. Mary's College of Maryland
St. Norbert College
Samford University
Sarah Lawrence College
Shepherd College
Siena College
Simon's Rock College of Bard
Simpson College
Skidmore College
Smith College
Southern Methodist University
Southwestern University
State University of New York at Binghamton
State University of New York at Buffalo
State University of New York College at Geneseo
State University of New York Maritime College
Stevens Institute of Technology
Susquehanna University
Swarthmore College
Sweet Briar College
Syracuse University
Texas A&M University
Transylvania University
Trinity College (CT)
Trinity University
Truman State University
Tulane University
Union College (NY)
Union University
United States Air Force Academy
United States Coast Guard Academy
United States Merchant Marine Academy
United States Military Academy
The University of Alabama in Huntsville
The University of Arizona

University of Cincinnati
University of Colorado at Boulder
University of Dallas
University of Dayton
University of Georgia
University of Illinois at Urbana-Champaign
The University of Iowa
University of Kansas
University of Maryland, College Park
University of Massachusetts Amherst
University of Michigan
University of Minnesota, Twin Cities Campus
University of Redlands
University of Rhode Island
University of Rochester
University of Scranton
University of Southern California
Valparaiso University
Vanderbilt University
Villanova University
Virginia Polytechnic Institute and State University
Wabash College
Wartburg College
Washington & Jefferson College
Washington College
Washington University in St. Louis
Wellesley College
Wells College
Wesleyan College
Wesleyan University
Westminster College
Whitman College
Whittier College
Williams College

Competitive Art and Music Colleges

Art or Music College Name

Setting ■ Public/Private ■ Institutional Control ■ Coed?
City, State

Web site: www.website.com
Contact: Contact name and address
Telephone: Telephone number **Fax:** Fax number
E-mail: E-mail address

 eApply

Academics
- Degrees awarded
- Challenging opportunities and special programs
- Most frequently chosen fields
- Faculty, including student-faculty ratio
- Cooperative programs

Facilities and Resources
- Performance facilities/studio space
- Exhibition halls and galleries
- Library facilities
- Special media collections

Applying
- Required documentation and standardized tests
- Portfolio/audition information
- GPA minimum
- Interviews
- Deadlines

> **S**ponsoring schools are able to submit a brief message in order to highlight special programs or opportunities that are available or to more fully explain their particular commitment to higher education. That message appears in this box.

Getting in Last Year
- Number who applied
- Percent accepted
- Number enrolled (percent)
- Percent h.s. achievers
- Average GPA
- SAT I/ACT performance
- Number of National Merit Scholars
- Number of class presidents
- Number of valedictorians

The Student Body
- How many students on campus and number who are undergrads
- Where they come from
- Percent from in-state
- Who they are:
  —Women and men
  —Ethnic makeup
  —International students

Graduation and After
- Percent graduating in 4, 5, or 6 years
- Percent pursuing further study, with most popular fields, if provided
- Percent with job offers within 6 months
- How many organizations recruit on campus
- Major academic awards won by students

Financial Matters
- Tuition and fees
- Room and board
- Percent of need met
- Average financial aid received per undergraduate

ART CENTER COLLEGE OF DESIGN

SUBURBAN SETTING ■ PRIVATE ■ INDEPENDENT ■ COED
PASADENA, CALIFORNIA

Web site: www.artcenter.edu
Contact: Ms. Kit Baron, Vice President, Student Services, 1700 Lida Street,
Pasadena, CA 91103-1999
Telephone: 626-396-2373 **Fax:** 626-795-0578
E-mail: admissions@artcenter.edu

Since 1930, Art Center College of Design has offered specialized programs for students who desire an advanced and focused education in the visual arts. Students apply directly to one of the 9 majors; each major offers a unique track of studio and liberal arts courses. Majors include advertising, illustration, environmental design, film, fine arts, product design, photography, graphic design, and transportation design. The intensity of focus on one specialization and emphasis on professional-level projects have prepared graduates for prestigious positions throughout the world. Over 200 companies visit the campus each year to recruit graduates for positions. Art Center is a leader in both computer technology and cutting-edge concept development. The goal is to assist students with their personal exploration and, at the same time, prepare them for leadership roles in the art and design community.

Getting in Last Year
1,148 applied
65% were accepted
33 enrolled (4%)
3.10 average high school GPA

The Student Body
1,438 total
1,345 undergraduates
38 home states and territories
69% from California
51 home countries, other than U.S.
39.1% women, 60.9% men
0.9% African American
0.9% American Indian
28% Asian American
9.7% Hispanic American
19.9% international students

Graduation and After
94% had job offers within 6 months
200 organizations recruited on campus

Financial Matters
$18,890 tuition and fees (1999–2000)
50% average percent of need met
$15,460 average financial aid amount received
  per undergraduate (1999–2000 estimated)

Academics

Art Center awards bachelor's and master's **degrees**. Challenging opportunities include advanced placement, accelerated degree programs, and independent study. Special programs include internships and summer session for credit.

The most frequently chosen field is visual/performing arts. A complete listing of majors at Art Center appears in the Majors Index beginning on page 432.

The **faculty** at Art Center has 72 full-time members. The student-faculty ratio is 9:1.

Art Center offers exchange programs with Occidental College and California Institute of Technology. Exchange programs include cross-registration in classes and use of libraries and other facilities.

Facilities and Resources

Art Center's facilities are housed in a contemporary steel and glass structure that affords views of the Los Angeles valleys. Computer graphics equipment includes 60 Silicon Graphics workstations, 115 Macintosh computers, and a range of peripheral hardware and digital and audio equipment. Two galleries house both student work and traveling shows. State-of-the-art photography and industrial design facilities combine traditional equipment with state-of-the-art technology.

173 **computers** are available on campus that provide access to the Internet. The **library** has 73,595 books and 385 subscriptions. Other features are a rare book room, a CD-ROM workstation, and 180 laser discs of rare features, animation, and advertising.

Applying

Art Center requires an essay, a high school transcript, and portfolio, and in some cases SAT I or ACT. It recommends an interview and a minimum high school GPA of 3.0. Application deadline: rolling admissions; 3/1 priority date for financial aid. Deferred admission is possible.

Portfolios are the single most important component of the application. Academic credentials and experience are also weighed heavily. Students apply directly to one major, so the college requires portfolios to focus on that area.

CALIFORNIA INSTITUTE OF THE ARTS

SUBURBAN SETTING ■ PRIVATE ■ INDEPENDENT ■ COED
VALENCIA, CALIFORNIA

Web site: www.calarts.edu
Contact: Mr. Kenneth Young, Director of Admissions, 24700 McBean
   Parkway, Valencia, CA 91355-2340
Telephone: 661-253-7863 or toll-free 800-292-ARTS (in-state),
   800-545-ARTS (out-of-state)
E-mail: admiss@calarts.edu

Academics

Cal Arts awards bachelor's and master's **degrees** and post-bachelor's certificates. Challenging opportunities include advanced placement, student-designed majors, independent study, and a senior project. Special programs include internships and study-abroad.

The most frequently chosen field is visual/performing arts. A complete listing of majors at Cal Arts appears in the Majors Index beginning on page 432.

The **faculty** at Cal Arts has 122 full-time members. The student-faculty ratio is 7:1.

Cal Arts participates in exchange programs with Hochschule der Kimote, Berlin; London Contemporary Dance School; CIRM, Nice, Italy; and the Glasgow School of Art in Scotland.

Facilities and Resources

Cal Arts has 8 major performance spaces for theater, dance, and music, and assigned art studio spaces for art students; sound stages, editing facilities, and studios for film and video students. Other media sources include more than 10,000 music scores, 20,000 musical recordings, 1,200 films, 110,000 slides, and 12,000 exhibition catalogs.

Student rooms are linked to a campus network. 87 **computers** are available on campus that provide access to the Internet. The 2 **libraries** have 95,973 books and 613 subscriptions.

Applying

Cal Arts requires an essay, a high school transcript, and portfolio or audition, and in some cases an interview and recommendations. Application deadline: rolling admissions; 3/2 priority date for financial aid. Deferred admission is possible.

Portfolios and auditions are most important, and essays are very important. Test scores and GPA are not considered.

Getting in Last Year
1,271 applied
40% were accepted
146 enrolled (29%)

The Student Body
1,224 total
804 undergraduates
46 home states and territories
45% from California
41 home countries, other than U.S.
44.3% women, 55.7% men
5.1% African American
1.9% American Indian
8.7% Asian American
8.7% Hispanic American
9.8% international students

Graduation and After
25% pursued further study (25% arts and sciences)
50 organizations recruited on campus
1 Fulbright scholar

Financial Matters
$19,950 tuition and fees (2000–2001)
$5150 room and board
82% average percent of need met
$17,674 average financial aid amount received per undergraduate (1999–2000 estimated)

CLEVELAND INSTITUTE OF MUSIC

URBAN SETTING ■ PRIVATE ■ INDEPENDENT ■ COED
CLEVELAND, OHIO

Web site: www.cim.edu
Contact: Mr. William Fay, Director of Admission, 11021 East Boulevard,
   Cleveland, OH 44106-1776
Telephone: 216-795-3107 **Fax:** 216-791-1530
E-mail: cimadmission@po.cwru.edu

Getting in Last Year
361 applied
29% were accepted
52 enrolled (50%)
55% from top tenth of their h.s. class

The Student Body
369 total
222 undergraduates
37 home states and territories
17% from Ohio
13 home countries, other than U.S.
53.2% women, 46.8% men
1.4% African American
6.8% Asian American
4.1% Hispanic American
14.9% international students

Graduation and After
90% pursued further study (90% arts and
   sciences)

Financial Matters
$18,625 tuition and fees (1999–2000)
$5590 room and board
80% average percent of need met
$14,283 average financial aid amount received
   per undergraduate (1999–2000 estimated)

Academics
Cleveland Institute of Music awards bachelor's, master's, and doctoral **degrees**. Challenging opportunities include advanced placement, accelerated degree programs, and a senior project. Special programs include internships, summer session for credit, off-campus study, and Army and Air Force ROTC.

The most frequently chosen field is visual/performing arts. A complete listing of majors at Cleveland Institute of Music appears in the Majors Index beginning on page 432.

The student-faculty ratio is 7:1.

In 1969, The Cleveland Institute of Music (CIM) and Case Western Reserve University established a Joint Music Program at both the undergraduate and graduate levels. Each institution continues activities peculiar to it: CIM concentrates on the education and training of professionals skilled in the arts of performance, composition, and related musical disciplines, while Case Western Reserve University pursues and develops studies in the fields of music history, musicology, and music education.

Facilities and Resources
Facilities include classrooms, teaching studios, practice rooms, the CIM library, an orchestra library, a specially designed eurhythmics studio, an opera workshop and studio, and a music store. In addition, there are two concert and recital halls, electronic music studios, an annex, and dormitory.

Student rooms are linked to a campus network. 25 **computers** are available on campus that provide access to the Internet. The **library** has 47,500 books and 110 subscriptions. Audiovisual facilities include a sound-recording collection of 18,000 CDs, records, audio- and videotapes, reel-to-reel tapes, laser discs, and CD-ROMs.

Applying
Cleveland Institute of Music requires an essay, SAT I or ACT, a high school transcript, 2 recommendations, and audition. It recommends an interview. Application deadline: 12/1; 2/15 for financial aid. Early and deferred admission are possible.

Acceptance for study is determined by musical talent and achievement. Audition appointments are scheduled by the Admission Office only upon receipt of application.

THE CORCORAN COLLEGE OF ART AND DESIGN

URBAN SETTING ■ PRIVATE ■ INDEPENDENT ■ COED
WASHINGTON, DISTRICT OF COLUMBIA

Web site: www.corcoran.edu
Contact: Ms. Anne E. Bowman, Director of Admissions, 500 17th Street, NW, Washington, DC 20006-4804
Telephone: 202-639-1814 or toll-free 888-CORCORAN (out-of-state) **Fax:** 202-639-1830
E-mail: admofc@corcoran.org

Academics

Corcoran awards bachelor's **degrees**. Challenging opportunities include advanced placement, independent study, and a senior project. Special programs include internships, summer session for credit, and off-campus study.

The most frequently chosen field is visual/performing arts. A complete listing of majors at Corcoran appears in the Majors Index beginning on page 432.

The **faculty** at Corcoran has 29 full-time members, 69% with terminal degrees. The student-faculty ratio is 8:1.

Corcoran participates in the Alliance of Independent Colleges of Art and Design (AICAD) Student Mobility Program. Through the Visual Arts Community Outreach Program (VACOP), students teach art fundamentals in the Washington, DC, metropolitan area. Corcoran is nationally accredited by the National Association of Schools of Art and Design (NASAD).

Facilities and Resources

Corcoran remains one of the few examples of the "museum-art school," maintaining its original relationship with the Corcoran Gallery of Art. Studios are accessible 7 days a week; fine arts majors have semiprivate studios; photography majors have unlimited access to department facilities; graphic design majors have studios in Georgetown and 3 computer labs. Seniors exhibit annually in the Museum's Hemicycle gallery.

45 **computers** are available on campus that provide access to the Internet. The **library** has 20,518 books and 148 subscriptions. Other media resources include computers for word processing and Internet access, televisions, VCRs, and slide projectors.

Applying

Corcoran requires SAT I or ACT, a high school transcript, portfolio, and a minimum high school GPA of 2.5, and in some cases an essay, an interview, and 2 recommendations. It recommends an essay, an interview, 2 recommendations, and a minimum high school GPA of 3.0. Application deadline: rolling admissions; 3/15 priority date for financial aid. Early and deferred admission are possible.

The portfolio is very important relative to all other admission criteria. Writing samples are welcome.

Getting in Last Year

227 applied
58% were accepted
44 enrolled (33%)
16% from top tenth of their h.s. class
2.94 average high school GPA
11% had SAT verbal scores over 600
3% had SAT math scores over 600
22% had ACT scores over 24
3% had SAT verbal scores over 700

The Student Body

425 undergraduates
20 home states and territories
14% from District of Columbia
14 home countries, other than U.S.
68.9% women, 31.1% men
8.2% African American
0.3% American Indian
7.5% Asian American
6.5% Hispanic American
13% international students

Graduation and After

37% graduated in 4 years
7% graduated in 5 years

Financial Matters

$14,140 tuition and fees (1999–2000)
47% average percent of need met
$7670 average financial aid amount received per undergraduate (1999–2000 estimated)

THE CURTIS INSTITUTE OF MUSIC

URBAN SETTING ■ PRIVATE ■ INDEPENDENT ■ COED
PHILADELPHIA, PENNSYLVANIA
Contact: Mr. Christopher Hodges, Admissions Officer, 1726 Locust Street,
Philadelphia, PA 19103-6107
Telephone: 215-893-5262 **Fax:** 215-893-7900

Getting in Last Year
789 applied
6% were accepted

The Student Body
165 total
150 undergraduates
24 home states and territories
22 home countries, other than U.S.

Financial Matters
$795 tuition and fees (1999–2000)

Academics

Curtis awards bachelor's and master's **degrees**. Challenging opportunities include advanced placement and accelerated degree programs. Off-campus study is a special program.

The most frequently chosen field is visual/performing arts. A complete listing of majors at Curtis appears in the Majors Index beginning on page 432.

The **faculty** at Curtis has 80 members.

Students who have completed Curtis' liberal arts requirements may enroll at no cost at the University of Pennsylvania for additional courses not available at Curtis under a reciprocal agreement between the two schools.

Facilities and Resources

Curtis Hall, a 250-seat auditorium with splendid acoustics and facilities for recording, is used for student recitals, alumni and faculty concerts, organ lessons and practice, master classes, school assemblies, orchestra rehearsals, and recording sessions. Curtis Opera Studio, a black-box theater that seats 125, has recording capabilities and is used primarily by the vocal studies department for opera performances, dance and movement classes, rehearsals, and master classes.

The **library** has 70,000 books. The library contains more than 65,000 volumes of music, scores, and books and more than 14,000 recordings, including scholarly editions of the works of 60 composers as well as authoritative editions of the standard repertoire.

Applying

Curtis requires an essay, SAT I, a high school transcript, recommendations, and audition. Application deadline: 1/15. Early admission is possible.

Because the school's enrollment has always been limited to the exceptional candidate, the audition process is extremely competitive.

FASHION INSTITUTE OF TECHNOLOGY

URBAN SETTING ■ PUBLIC ■ STATE AND LOCALLY SUPPORTED ■ COED
NEW YORK, NEW YORK

Web site: www.fitnyc.suny.edu
Contact: Mr. Jim Pidgeon, Director of Admissions, Seventh Avenue at 27th
Street, New York, NY 10001-5992
Telephone: 212-217-7675 or toll-free 800-GOTOFIT (out-of-state) **Fax:**
212-217-7481
E-mail: fitinfo@sfitva.cc.fitsuny.edu

Academics

FIT awards associate, bachelor's, and master's **degrees**. Challenging opportunities
include advanced placement, an honors program, and a senior project. Special programs
include cooperative education, internships, summer session for credit, and study-abroad.

The most frequently chosen fields are trade and industry, business/marketing, and
visual/performing arts. A complete listing of majors at FIT appears in the Majors Index
beginning on page 432.

The **faculty** at FIT has 175 full-time members. The student-faculty ratio is 13:1.

In 1986, FIT established an affiliation with the Politecnico Internazionale della Moda
in Florence, Italy. FIT-sponsored study-abroad programs are available in Australia,
Canada, England, France, Italy, and Spain. Through FIT's membership in the College
Consortium for International Studies, additional semester-abroad opportunities are also
available.

Facilities and Resources

The Fred P. Pomerantz Art and Design Center houses photography studios and
darkrooms, painting and printmaking rooms, a sculpture studio, a graphics laboratory, a
model-making workshop, and a toy design workshop. Student presentations are staged in
the Kate Murphy Amphitheatre. Other facilities include the Marvin Feldman Center, the
800-seat Morris W. and Fannie B. Haft Auditorium, the Quick Response Center, the
Design/Research Lighting Laboratory, and the Peter G. Scotese Computer-Aided
Design and Communications Center.

450 **computers** are available on campus for student use. The **library** has 154,015
books. The library carries an international assortment of sketchbooks, periodicals, slides,
films, and extensive clippings files. Its special collections contain rare books, original
fashion sketches, photographs, and archives. The Shirly Goodman Resource Center
houses the Gladys Marcus Library and the Museum at FIT.

Applying

FIT requires an essay, a high school transcript, and portfolio for art and design
programs. It recommends SAT I or ACT. Application deadline: 1/15; 3/1 priority date
for financial aid. Deferred admission is possible.

Getting in Last Year
3,961 applied
1,103 enrolled
8% from top tenth of their h.s. class
3.3 average high school GPA

The Student Body
10,853 total
10,750 undergraduates
51 home states and territories
83% from New York
70 home countries, other than U.S.
81.2% women, 18.8% men
7.7% African American
0.1% American Indian
12.1% Asian American
10.3% Hispanic American
10.6% international students

Graduation and After
86% had job offers within 6 months
95 organizations recruited on campus

Financial Matters
$3195 resident tuition and fees (1999–2000)
$7475 nonresident tuition and fees (1999–2000)
$7339 room and board

THE JUILLIARD SCHOOL

URBAN SETTING ■ PRIVATE ■ INDEPENDENT ■ COED
NEW YORK, NEW YORK

Web site: www.juilliard.edu
Contact: Ms. Mary K. Gray, Director of Admissions, 60 Lincoln Center
  Plaza, New York, NY 10023-6588
Telephone: 212-799-5000 ext. 223 **Fax:** 212-724-0263
E-mail: webmaster@juilliard.edu

Getting in Last Year
1,755 applied
8% were accepted
94 enrolled (71%)

The Student Body
961 total
665 undergraduates
39 home states and territories
18% from New York
26 home countries, other than U.S.
51.9% women, 48.1% men
12.5% African American
0.2% American Indian
12.5% Asian American
4% Hispanic American
22% international students

Graduation and After
70% graduated in 4 years
3% graduated in 5 years
2% graduated in 6 years

Financial Matters
$16,600 tuition and fees (1999–2000)
$6850 room and board
71% average percent of need met
$15,188 average financial aid amount received
  per undergraduate (1999–2000)

Academics

Juilliard awards bachelor's, master's, and doctoral **degrees**. Challenging opportunities include accelerated degree programs, student-designed majors, and a senior project. Off-campus study is a special program.

The most frequently chosen field is visual/performing arts. A complete listing of majors at Juilliard appears in the Majors Index beginning on page 432.

The Juilliard School, Columbia University, and Barnard College have a cooperative program offering students combined music conservatory and liberal arts education. A joint-degree program offers academically and musically gifted students the opportunity to earn both a Bachelor of Arts and a Master of Music degree in five years.

Another cross-registration program opens individual courses for academic credit at Juilliard to qualified students in the three undergraduate liberal arts schools. Juilliard also maintains a nonformalized and limited exchange with the Royal Academy of Music in London.

Facilities and Resources

Juilliard's modern Lincoln Center home includes 15 two-story rehearsal studios, 84 practice rooms, and 35 teaching studios housing more than 250 Steinway pianos, a large permanent instrument collection, and 28 classrooms. Juilliard features 4 auditoriums: the Juilliard Theater seats 933 people and has a movable ceiling; Paul Recital Hall seats 278; Morse Recital Hall, suitable for various types of performances, seats 200; and the Drama Theater seats 206 and is equipped with a complete theatrical lighting system.

In-house scenery and costume shops produce materials for all of Juilliard's fully staged opera, dance, and drama presentations.

12 **computers** are available on campus for student use. The **library** has 65,000 books and 200 subscriptions. Other media resources include 47,000 performance and study scores, 14,000 musical recordings, and a listening lab. Students have access to the world-wide OCLC database, the latest notation software (Finale), state-of-the-art sequencing software, and Yamaha DX7 synthesizers. Juilliard's archives feature the Ruth Dana Collection of First and Early Editions of Franz Liszt's Piano Music; the Rare Libretto Collection; Leonard Rose's Collection of Cello Music; and several works by Belgian violinist-composer Eugene Ysaye.

Applying

Juilliard requires a high school transcript and audition, and in some cases an essay. Application deadline: 12/1; 3/1 priority date for financial aid. Early admission is possible.

The members of the Juilliard faculty believe personal auditions are the means by which they may best judge talent and potential and consider the audition the most important factor in determining admission status.

Manhattan School of Music

Urban setting ■ Private ■ Independent ■ Coed
New York, New York

Web site: www.msmnyc.edu
Contact: Ms. Lee Cioppa, Director of Admission, 120 Claremont Avenue, New York, NY 10040
Telephone: 212-749-2802 ext. 2 **Fax:** 212-749-3025
E-mail: admission@msmnyc.edu

Academics

MSM awards bachelor's, master's, and doctoral **degrees** and post-bachelor's and post-master's certificates. Challenging opportunities include advanced placement and a senior project. Off-campus study is a special program.

The most frequently chosen field is visual/performing arts. A complete listing of majors at MSM appears in the Majors Index beginning on page 432.

The **faculty** at MSM has 50 full-time members. The student-faculty ratio is 8:1. MSM has a cross-registration program with Barnard College.

Facilities and Resources

Facilities of note at MSM include the 1,000-seat Borden Auditorium, the 250-seat Hubbard Recital Hall (with organ), the 60-seat Pforzheimer Recital Hall, the 35-seat Myers Recital Hall and Recording Studio, and two electronic music studios.

10 **computers** are available on campus that provide access to the Internet. The **library** has 39,684 books and 134 subscriptions.

Applying

MSM requires an essay, a high school transcript, audition, and a minimum high school GPA of 2.0. It recommends SAT I or ACT, an interview, 1 recommendation, and a minimum high school GPA of 3.0. Application deadline: 12/15; 3/15 priority date for financial aid.

Auditions are by far the most important part of the application process. Transcripts and TOEFL scores (for international students) are also very important; essays are somewhat important.

Getting in Last Year

665 applied
33% were accepted
84 enrolled (38%)

The Student Body

818 total
391 undergraduates
40 home states and territories
22% from New York
40 home countries, other than U.S.
46% women, 54% men
3.9% African American
0.3% American Indian
9.2% Asian American
5% Hispanic American
27.6% international students

Graduation and After

43% graduated in 4 years
13% graduated in 5 years
60% pursued further study (60% arts and sciences)
1 Fulbright scholar

Financial Matters

$19,580 tuition and fees (1999–2000)
$5250 room only
60% average percent of need met
$15,915 average financial aid amount received per undergraduate (1998–99)

MANNES COLLEGE OF MUSIC, NEW SCHOOL UNIVERSITY
URBAN SETTING ■ PRIVATE ■ INDEPENDENT ■ COED
NEW YORK, NEW YORK

Web site: www.mannes.edu
Contact: Ms. Emily E. Taxson, Associate Director of Admissions, 150 West 85th Street, New York, NY 10024-4402
Telephone: 212-580-0210 ext. 246 or toll-free 800-292-3040 (out-of-state)
Fax: 212-580-1738
E-mail: mannesadmissions@newschool.edu

Academics
Mannes awards bachelor's and master's **degrees** and post-master's certificates. Challenging opportunities include advanced placement, accelerated degree programs, double majors, and a senior project. Summer session for credit is a special program.

The most frequently chosen field is visual/performing arts. A complete listing of majors at Mannes appears in the Majors Index beginning on page 432.

The **faculty** at Mannes has 25 full-time members. The student-faculty ratio is 8:1.

Mannes students may take liberal arts courses in other New School Divisions: at Eugene Lang College or through the Adult Division. Mannes students will also interact with students at Parsons School of Design or the School of Dramatic Arts.

Facilities and Resources
Mannes is located in a Federal-style building on Manhattan's Upper West Side. The building houses classrooms, practice rooms, offices, a student lounge, and a spacious library with study carrels and a listening room. Two concert halls are available; the larger seats 300, the smaller—suitable for student recitals—seats 50. Additional performance opportunities are available through the use of facilities at the New School's downtown campus.

475 **computers** are available on campus that provide access to the Internet. The 3 **libraries** have 191,789 books and 896 subscriptions.

Applying
Mannes requires a high school transcript, 1 recommendation, and audition. It recommends an interview. Application deadline: 12/15; 3/1 priority date for financial aid. Deferred admission is possible.

Students are required to pass entrance examinations in their major field of study. (Accompanists will be provided for students auditioning in voice and orchestral instruments.) Placement tests in theory, ear training, and dictation are also required.

Founded in 1916 by David and Clara Damrosch Mannes, who were then world renowned as a violin-piano duo, the Mannes College of Music is recognized nationally and internationally as among the finest professional music conservatories. As such, its primary focus is on the training of outstanding young musicians who are preparing for professional careers in performance, unlike college and university music departments, which more often prepare students for careers in fields other than performance. Mannes is also distinguished by a relatively small enrollment that permits the close and supportive environment of a craft shop.

Getting in Last Year
257 applied
31% were accepted
28 enrolled (35%)

The Student Body
323 total
160 undergraduates
24 home states and territories
39% from New York
42 home countries, other than U.S.
4.5% African American
0.6% American Indian
8.9% Asian American
5% Hispanic American
34.6% international students

Graduation and After
45% pursued further study (45% arts and sciences)

Financial Matters
$18,000 tuition and fees (1999–2000)
$6875 room only
52% average percent of need met
$9528 average financial aid amount received per undergraduate (1999–2000 estimated)

MARYLAND INSTITUTE, COLLEGE OF ART

URBAN SETTING ■ PRIVATE ■ INDEPENDENT ■ COED
BALTIMORE, MARYLAND

Web site: www.mica.edu
Contact: Ms. Danielle Salisbury, Director of Undergraduate Admission, 1300
Mount Royal Avenue, Baltimore, MD 21217-4191
Telephone: 410-225-2222 **Fax:** 410-225-2337
E-mail: admissions@mica.edu

Academics

MICA awards bachelor's and master's **degrees** and post-bachelor's certificates. Challenging opportunities include advanced placement, accelerated degree programs, student-designed majors, double majors, independent study, and a senior project. Special programs include internships, summer session for credit, off-campus study, study-abroad, and Army ROTC.

The most frequently chosen field is visual/performing arts. A complete listing of majors at MICA appears in the Majors Index beginning on page 432.

The **faculty** at MICA has 89 full-time members, 87% with terminal degrees. The student-faculty ratio is 10:1.

MICA is a member of the Association of Independent Colleges of Art and Design (AICAD). Through this association qualified Institute students can participate in a semester-long program in Manhattan or can spend up to one year at any of more than 30 member schools across the country and in Canada. MICA also offers study abroad opportunities in England, France, Japan, Italy, the Netherlands, Scotland, Greece, Canada, Israel, and Mexico. MICA participates in an academic exchange program with the nearby Johns Hopkins University, Goucher College, Loyola College, Notre Dame College, the University of Baltimore, and the Peabody Conservatory of Music.

Facilities and Resources

Students have 24-hour access to individual and shared studio space. More than 250,000 square feet of institutional facilities in 6 buildings are dedicated to studio and classroom space, including 9 galleries that total over 5,600 square feet. MICA has a 250-seat auditorium and a state-of-the-art media lecture room with a color projection system, sound and video playback, and multimedia computer projection. Computer classrooms, a 3-D imaging lab, a computerized writing lab, and a digital video facility provide access to more than 235 computers for students in every major.

Student rooms are linked to a campus network. 279 **computers** are available on campus that provide access to the Internet. The **library** has 50,000 books and 305 subscriptions. The Media Resources Collection houses more than 100,000 slides.

Applying

MICA requires an essay, a high school transcript, and art portfolio, and in some cases SAT I or ACT. It recommends an interview and 2 recommendations. Application deadline: 1/15; 3/1 priority date for financial aid. Early and deferred admission are possible.

The portfolio of artwork should demonstrate talent, ability, and experience and is considered very important. Level of course work, GPA, test scores, and essays are also weighed heavily.

Getting in Last Year

1,496 applied
52% were accepted
305 enrolled (39%)
15% from top tenth of their h.s. class
3.3 average high school GPA
41% had SAT verbal scores over 600
26% had SAT math scores over 600
8% had SAT verbal scores over 700
3% had SAT math scores over 700

The Student Body

1,254 total
1,115 undergraduates
47 home states and territories
25% from Maryland
54 home countries, other than U.S.
57% women, 43% men
3.9% African American
0.3% American Indian
5.7% Asian American
4.1% Hispanic American
6.2% international students

Graduation and After

20% pursued further study (14% arts and sciences, 6% education)
30 organizations recruited on campus
1 Fulbright scholar

Financial Matters

$18,710 tuition and fees (1999–2000)
$4400 room only

MASSACHUSETTS COLLEGE OF ART

URBAN SETTING ■ PUBLIC ■ STATE-SUPPORTED ■ COED
BOSTON, MASSACHUSETTS

Web site: www.massart.edu
Contact: Ms. Kay Ransdell, Dean of Admissions, 621 Huntington Avenue, Boston, MA 02115-5882
Telephone: 617-232-1555 ext. 235 **Fax:** 617-566-4034
E-mail: admissions@massart.edu

Getting in Last Year
1,049 applied
47% were accepted
250 enrolled (50%)
16% from top tenth of their h.s. class
3.14 average high school GPA
38% had SAT verbal scores over 600
21% had SAT math scores over 600
7% had SAT verbal scores over 700
3% had SAT math scores over 700

The Student Body
2,371 total
2,266 undergraduates
34 home states and territories
78% from Massachusetts
36 home countries, other than U.S.
63.5% women, 36.5% men
3.3% African American
0.2% American Indian
3.1% Asian American
3.4% Hispanic American
5% international students

Graduation and After
25% graduated in 4 years
20% graduated in 5 years
7% graduated in 6 years
5% pursued further study
8 organizations recruited on campus

Financial Matters
$3808 resident tuition and fees (1999–2000)
$10,668 nonresident tuition and fees (1999–2000)
$7164 room and board
83% average percent of need met
$8440 average financial aid amount received per undergraduate (1999–2000)

Academics
MassArt awards bachelor's and master's **degrees** and post-bachelor's certificates. Challenging opportunities include advanced placement, student-designed majors, double majors, independent study, and a senior project. Special programs include cooperative education, internships, summer session for credit, off-campus study, and study-abroad.

The most frequently chosen fields are visual/performing arts, education, and architecture. A complete listing of majors at MassArt appears in the Majors Index beginning on page 432.

The **faculty** at MassArt has 72 full-time members. The student-faculty ratio is 13:1.

MassArt is a member of the Professional Arts Consortium (ProArts), an association of neighboring Boston colleges (Berklee College of Music, Boston Architectural Center, the Boston Conservatory, Emerson College, and the School of the Museum of Fine Arts) that prepare their students to be professionals in the visual and performing arts and architecture. MassArt participates in the College Academic Program Sharing (CAPS) and the Public College Exchange Program, through which students can cross-register at the majority of Massachusetts state colleges and universities.

MassArt participates in the mobility program of the Association of Independent Colleges of Art and Design (AICAD), coordinates exchange programs with 3 schools in England (The Chelsea School of Art and Design, London; The West Surrey College of Art and Design; The Central Saint Martin's School of Art and Design, London) and has exploratory exchange programs with 2 schools in the Netherlands (the Rietveld Academy, Amsterdam; the Royal Academy of Visual Arts, The Hague), and one with the Universitat de Barcelona in Spain and with the Fachhochschule in Wiesbaden, Germany.

Facilities and Resources
The main Huntington/Bakalar Galleries comprise 9,000 square feet. An additional 30,000 square feet of exhibition space are student programmed. Student studio space totals 250,000 square feet. Performance spaces include the 500-seat main auditorium, an 18,000-square-foot flexible space, an analog/digital sound studio, and a variety of smaller studio spaces for video and interrelated media projects.

250 **computers** are available on campus that provide access to the Internet. The **library** has 757 subscriptions. Other media resources include 700 films, 1,500 videotapes, 100,000 slides, sound recordings, posters, a rare book collection, the Gunn Associate pictorial reference file (90,000 images collected from periodicals between 1939 and 1965), and the College's archives, consisting of manuscripts, artwork, and rare publications.

Applying
MassArt requires an essay, SAT I or ACT, a high school transcript, portfolio, and a minimum high school GPA of 2.9. It recommends recommendations. Application deadline: 3/1; 3/15 priority date for financial aid. Early and deferred admission are possible.

The portfolio should consist of a minimum of 15 recent art works presented in slide format. The portfolio is very important, although transcripts and test scores, as well as motivation and drive shown in a required Statement of Purpose, are also important.

New England Conservatory of Music

Urban Setting ■ Private ■ Independent ■ Coed
Boston, Massachusetts

Web site: www.newenglandconservatory.edu
Contact: Ms. Allison T. Ball, Dean of Enrollment Services, 290 Huntington Avenue, Boston, MA 02115-5000
Telephone: 617-585-1101 **Fax:** 617-585-1115

Academics

NEC awards bachelor's, master's, and doctoral **degrees**. Challenging opportunities include advanced placement and a senior project. Special programs include summer session for credit and off-campus study.

The most frequently chosen field is visual/performing arts. A complete listing of majors at NEC appears in the Majors Index beginning on page 432.

The **faculty** at NEC has 77 full-time members.

NEC participates in a double-degree program with Tufts University. Students in the double-degree program earn a Bachelor of Music degree from NEC and a Bachelor of Arts or Bachelor of Science degree from Tufts University. Cross-registration is also available at Northeastern University and Simmons College.

Facilities and Resources

NEC has more than 150 practice rooms ranging in size from 180 to more than 500 square feet. Most rooms are equipped with Steinway grand pianos, while some hold upright pianos. There are locked practice rooms for percussion, harpsichord, and organ.

9 **computers** are available on campus for student use. The 2 **libraries** have 71,000 books and 260 subscriptions. Other media resources include 110,000 volumes of music, books, sound and video recordings, and microforms. Special collections include early scores and manuscripts.

Applying

NEC requires an essay, SAT I or ACT, a high school transcript, 2 recommendations, and audition. Application deadline: 2/2 priority date for financial aid. Deferred admission is possible.

Audition and/or portfolio review are judged as most important admission criteria.

Getting in Last Year

1,502 applied
49% were accepted
84 enrolled (11%)
3.05 average high school GPA

The Student Body

768 total
398 undergraduates
37 home states and territories
19% from Massachusetts
21 home countries, other than U.S.
49.7% women, 50.3% men
5% African American
0.5% American Indian
7.3% Asian American
4.5% Hispanic American
22.4% international students

Graduation and After

58 organizations recruited on campus

Financial Matters

$19,800 tuition and fees (1999–2000)
$8600 room and board
67% average percent of need met
$14,957 average financial aid amount received per undergraduate (1999–2000 estimated)

NEW YORK SCHOOL OF INTERIOR DESIGN

URBAN SETTING ■ PRIVATE ■ INDEPENDENT ■ COED
NEW YORK, NEW YORK

Web site: www.nysid.edu
Contact: Ms. Lydia Paiste, Admissions Associate, 170 East 70th Street, New York, NY 10021-5110
Telephone: 212-472-1500 ext. 204 or toll-free 800-336-9743 **Fax:** 212-472-1867
E-mail: admissions@nysid.edu

Manhattan, with its world-famous museums, showrooms, and architectural landmarks, is home to the New York School of Interior Design (NYSID). NYSID is a single-major college dedicated solely to the study of interior design. Facilities include a new lighting lab, a computer-aided design (CAD) lab, and an extensive reference library. Many NYSID graduates have gone on to find work in the best design and architectural firms in New York City and around the world. The Bachelor of Fine Arts degree is a FIDER-accredited program.

Getting in Last Year
199 enrolled

The Student Body
706 total
694 undergraduates
17 home states and territories
85% from New York
24 home countries, other than U.S.
85.4% women, 14.6% men

Financial Matters
$16,070 tuition and fees (2000–2001)
60% average percent of need met
$5500 average financial aid amount received per undergraduate (1999–2000)

Academics

NYSID awards associate, bachelor's, and master's **degrees**. Challenging opportunities include advanced placement, independent study, and a senior project. Special programs include internships and summer session for credit. A complete listing of majors at NYSID appears in the Majors Index beginning on page 432.

The student-faculty ratio is 7:1.

Facilities and Resources

Facilities include an extensive design library, materials library of manufacturers' catalogs and samples, a new lighting design laboratory, a computer-aided design (CAD) lab, and gallery spaces that host a variety of exhibitions each year, including the annual student exhibition. NYSID also has a large open studio space.

35 **computers** are available on campus that provide access to the Internet. The **library** has 5,500 books and 90 subscriptions. Other media resources include architecture, art, and interior design videos, collections of rare folios, material samples, and product information.

Applying

NYSID requires an essay, SAT I or ACT, a high school transcript, 2 recommendations, portfolio, and a minimum high school GPA of 2.5, and in some cases an interview. It recommends an interview. Application deadline: rolling admissions; 5/1 priority date for financial aid. Deferred admission is possible.

The quality of an applicant's portfolio is given equal consideration in relation to other admission requirements. Applicants who exhibit exceptional talent or ability are considered for scholarships.

NORTH CAROLINA SCHOOL OF THE ARTS

URBAN SETTING ■ PUBLIC ■ STATE-SUPPORTED ■ COED
WINSTON-SALEM, NORTH CAROLINA

Web site: www.ncarts.edu
Contact: Mrs. Kelye Suzanne Bush, Director of Admissions, 1533 South Main Street, PO Box 12189, Winston-Salem, NC 27127-2188
Telephone: 336-770-3290 **Fax:** 336-770-3370
E-mail: admissions@ncarts.edu

Academics

NCSA awards bachelor's and master's **degrees**. A senior project is a challenging opportunity.

The most frequently chosen field is visual/performing arts. A complete listing of majors at NCSA appears in the Majors Index beginning on page 432.

The **faculty** at NCSA has 122 full-time members. The student-faculty ratio is 8:1.

Facilities and Resources

Facilities include 71 music practice rooms; 27 teaching studios; 3 large rehearsal halls; a 600-seat concert auditorium housing a Kenan Organ and Hamburg and Steinway grand pianos; a 56-seat recital hall; electronic and film music composition studios equipped with state-of-the-art MIDI instruments; and a historic 1,380-seat theater with state-of-the-art stage, electronic, and sound equipment, rehearsal and warm-up rooms, dressing rooms, sound and light projection booths, and orchestra pit.

20 **computers** are available on campus for student use. Other media resources include 40,000 music scores, 36,000 records, CDs, and tapes.

Applying

NCSA requires SAT I or ACT, a high school transcript, 2 recommendations, an audition, and in some cases an essay and an interview. Application deadline: rolling admissions; 3/1 priority date for financial aid.

In addition to the transcripts, test scores, and references, admission to NCSA is based on talent and potential as assessed in an audition before the arts faculty.

The School's mission encompasses not only the performing arts but the moving image and visual arts as well. The relationship between students and their teachers, that of apprentice to master, is the heart of the School. The members of a resident faculty of 100 artists have had successful careers on Broadway, in Hollywood, and as members of great orchestras and dance companies and theaters of the world. School of the Arts alumni have distinguished themselves in such famous places as the Metropolitan Opera, the Houston Ballet, the Great Lakes Theater Festival, the Merce Cunningham Dance Company, Broadway, and Hollywood.

Getting in Last Year
638 applied
46% were accepted
176 enrolled (60%)
16% from top tenth of their h.s. class
3.27 average high school GPA
33% had SAT verbal scores over 600
23% had SAT math scores over 600
45% had ACT scores over 24
4% had SAT verbal scores over 700
2% had SAT math scores over 700

The Student Body
794 total
727 undergraduates
40 home states and territories
48% from North Carolina
16 home countries, other than U.S.
39.1% women, 60.9% men
7.9% African American
0.4% American Indian
2.1% Asian American
2.3% Hispanic American
2.9% international students

Graduation and After
34% graduated in 4 years
2% graduated in 5 years

Financial Matters
$2517 resident tuition and fees (1999–2000)
$11,145 nonresident tuition and fees (1999–2000)
$4462 room and board
61% average percent of need met
$6476 average financial aid amount received per undergraduate (1998–99)

Getting in Last Year
1,617 applied
44% were accepted
371 enrolled (53%)
2.9 average high school GPA
28% had SAT verbal scores over 600
27% had SAT math scores over 600
5% had SAT verbal scores over 700
5% had SAT math scores over 700

The Student Body
2,716 total
2,397 undergraduates
47 home states and territories
52% from New York
65 home countries, other than U.S.
72.3% women, 27.7% men
4.1% African American
0.4% American Indian
17.1% Asian American
7.7% Hispanic American
29.9% international students

Graduation and After
43% graduated in 4 years
10% graduated in 5 years
2% graduated in 6 years
5% pursued further study (5% arts and sciences)
100 organizations recruited on campus

Financial Matters
$21,790 tuition and fees (2000–2001)
65% average percent of need met
$13,782 average financial aid amount received per undergraduate (1999–2000 estimated)

Parsons School of Design, New School University
URBAN SETTING ■ PRIVATE ■ INDEPENDENT ■ COED
NEW YORK, NEW YORK

Web site: www.parsons.edu
Contact: Ms. Nadine M. Bourgeois, Assistant Dean and Director of Admissions, 66 Fifth Avenue, New York, NY 10011-8878
Telephone: 212-229-8910 or toll-free 800-252-0852
E-mail: parsadm@newschool.edu

Academics
Parsons awards associate, bachelor's, and master's **degrees**. Challenging opportunities include advanced placement, accelerated degree programs, an honors program, independent study, and a senior project. Special programs include internships, summer session for credit, off-campus study, and study-abroad.

The most frequently chosen fields are visual/performing arts, communications/communication technologies, and business/marketing. A complete listing of majors at Parsons appears in the Majors Index beginning on page 432.

The **faculty** at Parsons has 26 full-time members. The student-faculty ratio is 12:1.

Students enrich their education by taking part in mobility or exchange programs arranged between Parsons and other art and design colleges. Parsons offers study-abroad opportunities in Israel, the Netherlands, Great Britain, and Sweden. Parsons participates in exchange programs with the 31 schools of the Alliance of Independent Colleges of Art and Design (AICAD). Parsons is also affiliated with a number of two-year schools whose graduates may transfer to Parsons to complete their degrees.

Facilities and Resources
The students at Parsons work within 3 designated buildings that house studios equipped for specific fields of work.

475 **computers** are available on campus that provide access to the Internet. The 3 **libraries** have 191,789 books and 896 subscriptions. Other media resources include visual, printed, and online services and links to the libraries of New York University and Cooper Union for the Advancement of Science and Art. Parsons is also connected to the Smithsonian Collection in Washington, DC.

Applying
Parsons requires SAT I or ACT, a high school transcript, portfolio, home examination, and a minimum high school GPA of 2.0, and in some cases an essay and an interview. It recommends a minimum high school GPA of 3.0. Application deadline: 7/1; 3/1 priority date for financial aid. Early admission is possible.

The portfolio requirement plays a key role in the decision-making process of the admissions committee.

RHODE ISLAND SCHOOL OF DESIGN

URBAN SETTING ■ PRIVATE ■ INDEPENDENT ■ COED
PROVIDENCE, RHODE ISLAND

Web site: www.risd.edu
Contact: Mr. Edward Newhall, Director of Admissions, 2 College Street,
   Providence, RI 02903-2784
Telephone: 401-454-6300 or toll-free 800-364-RISD **Fax:** 401-454-6309
E-mail: admissions@risd.edu

Academics

RISD awards bachelor's, master's, and first-professional **degrees**. Challenging opportunities include advanced placement and a senior project. Special programs include internships, off-campus study, and study-abroad.

The most frequently chosen fields are visual/performing arts and architecture. A complete listing of majors at RISD appears in the Majors Index beginning on page 432.

The **faculty** at RISD has 139 full-time members. The student-faculty ratio is 11:1.

RISD offers cross-registration with neighboring Brown University and participates in the mobility program of the Association of Independent Colleges of Art and Design (AICAD). Students may also consider a unique international study opportunity through the International Exchange Program. RISD currently has exchange agreements with 26 schools in 15 other countries.

Facilities and Resources

RISD's 13-acre urban campus has 40 buildings encompassing one million square feet of space. Each of 17 studio disciplines has its own facility offering studios, classrooms, and specialized facilities such as shops and computer labs. There are 11 galleries on campus available for the exhibition of student work. The 45 galleries in RISD's Museum of Art display selections from the permanent collection of 100,000 works of art, and the Nature Lab contains more than 70,000 items of natural history.

Student rooms are linked to a campus network. 300 **computers** are available on campus that provide access to the Internet. The **library** has 90,000 books and 393 subscriptions. Other media resources include an image collection of 550,000 slides, photos, and clippings.

Applying

RISD requires an essay, SAT I or ACT, a high school transcript, and portfolio, drawing assignments. It recommends 3 recommendations. Application deadline: 2/15; 2/15 priority date for financial aid. Early and deferred admission are possible.

The portfolio should contain 8 to 20 slides of a student's best work. The portfolio is very important in relation to the other criteria, although the application is a combination of all the required elements. For architecture students, the portfolio is less crucial.

Getting in Last Year

2,432 applied
36% were accepted
387 enrolled (44%)
21% from top tenth of their h.s. class
3.20 average high school GPA
49% had SAT verbal scores over 600
52% had SAT math scores over 600
10% had SAT verbal scores over 700
9% had SAT math scores over 700

The Student Body

2,112 total
1,861 undergraduates
51 home states and territories
7% from Rhode Island
52 home countries, other than U.S.
2.1% African American
0.3% American Indian
11% Asian American
4.2% Hispanic American
13.4% international students

Graduation and After

5% pursued further study (5% arts and sciences)
50 organizations recruited on campus
1 Fulbright scholar

Financial Matters

$21,405 tuition and fees (1999–2000)
$6490 room and board

Getting in Last Year
1,603 applied
22% were accepted
133 enrolled (37%)
17% from top tenth of their h.s. class
37% had SAT verbal scores over 600
29% had SAT math scores over 600
10% had SAT verbal scores over 700
6% had SAT math scores over 700
2 valedictorians

The Student Body
851 total
617 undergraduates
27 home states and territories
82% from New Jersey
6 home countries, other than U.S.
57.5% women, 42.5% men
5.3% African American
0.6% American Indian
5.7% Asian American
3.9% Hispanic American
1.1% international students

Graduation and After
80% had job offers within 6 months
500 organizations recruited on campus

Financial Matters
$6052 resident tuition and fees (1999–2000)
$10,982 nonresident tuition and fees (1999–2000)
$6098 room and board
84% average percent of need met
$7817 average financial aid amount received per undergraduate (1999–2000)

RUTGERS, THE STATE UNIVERSITY OF NEW JERSEY, MASON GROSS SCHOOL OF THE ARTS
SMALL-TOWN SETTING ■ PUBLIC ■ STATE-SUPPORTED ■ COED
NEW BRUNSWICK, NEW JERSEY

Web site: www.rutgers.edu
Contact: Ms. Diane Wms. Harris, Associate Director of University Undergraduate Admissions, 65 Davidson Road, Room 202, Piscataway, NJ 08854-8097
Telephone: 732-932-4636 **Fax:** 732-445-0237
E-mail: admissions@asb-ugadm.rutgers.edu

Academics
Rutgers, The State University of New Jersey, Mason Gross School of the Arts awards bachelor's, master's, and doctoral **degrees** (also offers artist diploma). Challenging opportunities include advanced placement, an honors program, and a senior project. Special programs include internships, summer session for credit, off-campus study, study-abroad, and Army and Air Force ROTC.

The most frequently chosen field is visual/performing arts. A complete listing of majors at Rutgers, The State University of New Jersey, Mason Gross School of the Arts appears in the Majors Index beginning on page 432.

The **faculty** at Rutgers, The State University of New Jersey, Mason Gross School of the Arts has 79 full-time members, 97% with terminal degrees. The student-faculty ratio is 6:1.

The Music Department is a full member of the National Association of Schools of Music.

Facilities and Resources
The Music Department presents major concerts in the Nicholas Music Center, Voorhees and Kirkpatrick Chapels, McKinney Hall, and the Marryott Auditorium. There are 10 classrooms, 49 faculty studios, 48 practice rooms, 7 rehearsal rooms, and 5 technical rooms totalling 60,000 square feet. Most of the Fine Arts Department is housed in the Civic Square building, in downtown New Brunswick. The four-story building features drawing, painting, and film and video production studios; computer laboratories; state-of-the-art printmaking facilities; classrooms with high ceilings; storage; soft floors; museum-quality gallery spaces; student lounges; and graduate and undergraduate studios. The sculpture and ceramic facilities are on a campus connected by continually operating buses. Fine Arts space totals more than 70,000 square feet.

Student rooms are linked to a campus network. 1,450 **computers** are available on campus that provide access to online grade reports and the Internet. The 15 **libraries** have 6,362,037 books and 28,934 subscriptions. The library maintains an extensive collection of scholarly journals, books, scores, and recordings. Rutgers, The State University of New Jersey, Mason Gross School of the Arts, has two art libraries: one connected to the Jane Voorhees Zimmeril Museum houses reference works, and the other, the Mable Smith Douglass Library, circulates materials and is the home of the Douglass Women Artist Series and several important archives, including that of *Heresies* magazine. Slide libraries are found at the Mason Gross School of the Arts building and the two libraries. The slide library is currently being digitized.

Applying
Rutgers, The State University of New Jersey, Mason Gross School of the Arts requires SAT I or ACT, a high school transcript, and audition, portfolio, or interview, and in some cases SAT II Subject Tests. Application deadline: 12/15; 3/15 priority date for financial aid. Early and deferred admission are possible.

For Bachelor of Music majors, the audition is the most important criterion for admission. No audition is required for Bachelor of Arts majors. For admission to the Fine Arts department, a substantial portfolio is required. The portfolio is reviewed by the entire faculty. Portfolios help identify innovative thinking and creativity and are very important in the admissions process.

SAN FRANCISCO CONSERVATORY OF MUSIC

URBAN SETTING ■ PRIVATE ■ INDEPENDENT ■ COED
SAN FRANCISCO, CALIFORNIA

Web site: www.sfcm.edu
Contact: Ms. Joan Gordon, Admissions Officer, 1201 Ortega Street, San
    Francisco, CA 94122-4411
Telephone: 415-759-3431 **Fax:** 415-759-3499
E-mail: jog@sfcm.edu

Academics

SFCM awards bachelor's and master's **degrees** and post-master's certificates. Challenging opportunities include advanced placement, accelerated degree programs, double majors, and independent study.

The most frequently chosen field is visual/performing arts. A complete listing of majors at SFCM appears in the Majors Index beginning on page 432.

The **faculty** at SFCM has 26 full-time members, 27% with terminal degrees. The student-faculty ratio is 6:1.

Facilities and Resources

Performance spaces include the 333-seat Hellman Hall and 50-seat Agnes Albert Performance Hall. Hellman Hall is considered one of the finest concert halls of its size in northern California. It also includes one of the few professional recording studios in a Bay Area concert hall. Both halls are available for formal and informal student concerts. Practice rooms are available to enrolled students at no charge. Almost all practice rooms have windows and most overlook the Conservatory courtyard.

7 **computers** are available on campus for student use. The **library** has 33,574 books and 78 subscriptions. The Conservatory Library collection includes video recordings pertinent to music study. These recordings are primarily opera performances, music history lectures, and a collection of Conservatory master classes and concerts.

Applying

SFCM requires SAT I or ACT, a high school transcript, 2 recommendations, and audition. It recommends SAT I. Application deadline: 3/1; 3/1 priority date for financial aid. Early admission is possible.

The audition is the most important criterion used to determine eligibility for admission to the program.

Getting in Last Year

95 applied
64% were accepted
21 enrolled (34%)
3.34 average high school GPA
42% had SAT verbal scores over 600
16% had SAT math scores over 600
8% had SAT math scores over 700

The Student Body

243 total
136 undergraduates
25 home states and territories
65% from California
14 home countries, other than U.S.
53.7% women, 46.3% men
2.3% African American
14.5% Asian American
7.6% Hispanic American
16.8% international students

Graduation and After

76% graduated in 4 years
6% graduated in 5 years
50% pursued further study (45% arts and
    sciences, 5% education)

Financial Matters

$18,670 tuition and fees (1999–2000)
81% average percent of need met
$12,281 average financial aid amount received
    per undergraduate (1998–99)

WESTMINSTER CHOIR COLLEGE OF RIDER UNIVERSITY

SMALL-TOWN SETTING ■ PRIVATE ■ INDEPENDENT ■ COED
PRINCETON, NEW JERSEY

Web site: westminster.rider.edu
Contact: Ms. Monica Thomas Tritto, Assistant Director of Admissions, 101 Walnut Lane, Princeton, NJ 08540-3899
Telephone: 609-921-7144 ext. 103 or toll-free 800-96-CHOIR **Fax:** 609-921-2538
E-mail: wccadmission@rider.edu

Academics

Westminster awards bachelor's and master's **degrees**. Challenging opportunities include advanced placement, an honors program, double majors, independent study, and a senior project. Special programs include internships, summer session for credit, and off-campus study.

The most frequently chosen field is visual/performing arts. A complete listing of majors at Westminster appears in the Majors Index beginning on page 432.

Westminster has a cooperative program with Princeton University permitting limited undergraduate and graduate student cross-registration. For graduate students there is a similar affiliation with Princeton Theological Seminary. An arrangement also exists by which graduates holding the Master of Music degree with a major in sacred music may apply for advanced standing in the doctoral program at Drew University. A cooperative program between Westminster and the New School for Music Study exists for students in the Master of Piano Performance and Pedagogy program.

Facilities and Resources

Westminster performance facilities include the Fine Arts Theater (550 seats), Bristol Hall (350 seats), Williamson Hall (100 seats), Scheide Hall (100 seats), and the Playhouse/Opera Theatre (300 seats).

Student rooms are linked to a campus network. 60 **computers** are available on campus that provide access to the Internet. The **library** has 55,000 books and 160 subscriptions. Special collections include the Erik Routley Hymnology Collection and the archives of the Organ Historical Society. The Westminster Performance Collection contains 420,000 copies of 6,000 titles for study and performances and a single-copy reference of 45,000 individual octavos, the largest collection of its kind.

Applying

Westminster requires an essay, SAT I or ACT, a high school transcript, 2 recommendations, and audition, music examination. It recommends an interview and a minimum high school GPA of 2.5. Application deadline: rolling admissions; 3/1 priority date for financial aid. Early and deferred admission are possible.

Auditions play a very important role in the decision-making process. Westminster accepts applicants based on indicators of musical talent and academic achievement.

COMPETITIVE COLLEGES AND UNIVERSITIES

COLLEGE OR UNIVERSITY NAME

SETTING ■ PUBLIC/PRIVATE ■ INSTITUTIONAL CONTROL ■ COED?
CITY, STATE

Web site: www.website.com
Contact: Contact name and mailing address
Telephone: Telephone number **Fax:** Fax number
E-mail: E-mail address

> **S**ponsoring schools are able to submit a brief message in order to highlight special programs or opportunities that are available or to more fully explain their particular commitment to higher education. That message appears in this box.

Academics

- Degrees awarded
- Most frequently chosen fields
- Faculty, including student-faculty ratio

The Student Body

- How many students on campus and number who are undergrads
- Percent of women and men
- Where students come from
- Percent of students from in-state
- Who they are (international students and ethnic makeup)
- How many students come back for the sophomore year

Facilities and Resources

- Computer resources
- Network, e-mail, and online services
- Library facilities

Campus Life

- Organizations, activities, and student participation
- Fraternities and sororities
- Sports ("m" for men, "w" for women; neither "m" nor "w" means both)

Campus Safety

- Late-night transport/escort service
- Emergency telephone alarm devices
- 24-hour patrols
- Electronically operated residence hall entrances

Applying

- Required documentation and standardized tests
- GPA minimum
- Interviews
- Deadlines

Getting in Last Year
- Number who applied
- Percent accepted
- Number enrolled (percent)
- Percent h.s. achievers
- Average GPA
- SAT I/ACT performance
- Number of National Merit Scholars
- Number of class presidents
- Number of valedictorians

Graduation and After
- Percent graduating in 4, 5, or 6 years
- Percent pursuing further study, with most popular fields, if provided
- Percent with job offers within 6 months
- How many organizations recruit on campus
- Major academic awards won by students

Financial Matters
- Tuition and fees
- Room and board
- Percent of need met
- Average financial aid received per undergraduate

AGNES SCOTT COLLEGE

URBAN SETTING ■ PRIVATE ■ INDEPENDENT RELIGIOUS ■ WOMEN ONLY
DECATUR, GEORGIA

Web site: www.agnesscott.edu
Contact: Ms. Stephanie Balmer, Associate Vice President for Enrollment and
   Director of Admission, 141 East College Avenue, Decatur, GA 30030-3797
Telephone: 404-471-6285 or toll-free 800-868-8602 **Fax:** 404-471-6414
E-mail: admission@agnesscott.edu

Agnes Scott College is committed to a twenty-first century curriculum that emphasizes academic excellence through the liberal arts and sciences and is enhanced by experience-based learning, including internships, collaborative research, independent study, and study abroad. Programs such as the Atlanta Science Center for Women, Atlanta Semester, Global Awareness, and Language Across the Curriculum enrich the Agnes Scott experience. Agnes Scott has had 5 Fulbright scholars in the past 5 years and ranks seventh nationally in the percentage of graduates who earn Ph.D.'s in education and fifteenth in the area of humanities. Atlanta, the South's most dynamic and international city, provides opportunities for fun as well as for internships, community service, and cultural events. In terms of academic quality, personalized attention, financial strength, and a student-governed honor system, a comparable value cannot be found.

Getting in Last Year
688 applied
77% were accepted
241 enrolled (45%)
61% from top tenth of their h.s. class
3.67 average high school GPA
66% had SAT verbal scores over 600
43% had SAT math scores over 600
76% had ACT scores over 24
18% had SAT verbal scores over 700
8% had SAT math scores over 700
12% had ACT scores over 30
9 National Merit Scholars

Graduation and After
46% graduated in 4 years
5% graduated in 5 years
21% pursued further study (5% arts and sciences, 5% law, 2% engineering)
52% had job offers within 6 months
76 organizations recruited on campus

Financial Matters
$16,025 tuition and fees (1999–2000)
$6660 room and board
99% average percent of need met
$16,335 average financial aid amount received per undergraduate (1998–99)

Academics
Agnes Scott awards bachelor's and master's **degrees** and post-bachelor's certificates. Challenging opportunities include advanced placement, accelerated degree programs, student-designed majors, double majors, independent study, a senior project, and Phi Beta Kappa. Special programs include internships, summer session for credit, off-campus study, study-abroad, and Navy and Air Force ROTC.

The most frequently chosen fields are social sciences and history, biological/life sciences, and English. A complete listing of majors at Agnes Scott appears in the Majors Index beginning on page 432.

The **faculty** at Agnes Scott has 75 full-time members, 100% with terminal degrees. The student-faculty ratio is 10:1.

Students of Agnes Scott
The student body totals 887, of whom 879 are undergraduates. Students come from 38 states and territories and 29 other countries. 50% are from Georgia. 4.1% are international students. 19.4% are African American, 0.1% American Indian, 4.6% Asian American, and 2.8% Hispanic American. 82% returned for their sophomore year.

Facilities and Resources
Student rooms are linked to a campus network. 152 **computers** are available on campus that provide access to the Internet. The 2 **libraries** have 204,505 books and 807 subscriptions.

Campus Life
There are 50 active organizations on campus, including a drama/theater group, newspaper, choral group, and marching band. No national or local **sororities**.

Agnes Scott is a member of the NCAA (Division III). **Intercollegiate sports** include basketball, cross-country running, rugby, soccer, softball, swimming, tennis, volleyball.

Campus Safety
Student safety services include shuttle bus service, security systems in apartments, public safety facility, surveillance equipment, late-night transport/escort service, 24-hour emergency telephone alarm devices, and 24-hour patrols by trained security personnel.

Applying
Agnes Scott requires an essay, SAT I or ACT, a high school transcript, and 2 recommendations, and in some cases SAT II Subject Tests. It recommends an interview and a minimum high school GPA of 3.0. Application deadline: 3/1; 3/1 priority date for financial aid. Early and deferred admission are possible.

ALBERTSON COLLEGE OF IDAHO

SMALL-TOWN SETTING ■ PRIVATE ■ INDEPENDENT ■ COED
CALDWELL, IDAHO

Web site: www.acofi.edu
Contact: Mr. Dennis P. Bergvall, Dean of Admissions, 2112 Cleveland
Boulevard, Caldwell, ID 83605-4494
Telephone: 208-459-5305 or toll-free 800-AC-IDAHO **Fax:** 208-454-2077
E-mail: admission@acofi.edu

eAPPLY

Academics

Albertson awards bachelor's **degrees**. Challenging opportunities include advanced placement, accelerated degree programs, student-designed majors, an honors program,
double majors, independent study, and a senior project. Special programs include internships, off-campus study, and study-abroad.

The most frequently chosen fields are biological/life sciences, social sciences and history, and business/marketing. A complete listing of majors at Albertson appears in the
Majors Index beginning on page 432.

The **faculty** at Albertson has 60 members, 90% with terminal degrees. The student-
faculty ratio is 12:1.

Students of Albertson

The student body is made up of 763 undergraduates. 56.6% are women and 43.4% are
men. Students come from 24 states and territories and 7 other countries. 2% are international students. 0.9% are African American, 0.5% American Indian, 4.3% Asian
American, and 3.7% Hispanic American. 73% returned for their sophomore year.

Facilities and Resources

Student rooms are linked to a campus network. 135 **computers** are available on campus
that provide access to online course syllabi, course assignments, course discussion and
the Internet. The 2 **libraries** have 178,719 books and 75,826 subscriptions.

Campus Life

There are 51 active organizations on campus, including a drama/theater group,
newspaper, and choral group. 15% of eligible men and 15% of eligible women are
members of national **fraternities**, national **sororities**, local fraternities, and local sororities.

Albertson is a member of the NAIA. **Intercollegiate sports** (some offering scholarships) include baseball (m), basketball, golf, skiing (downhill), soccer, tennis, volleyball
(w).

Campus Safety

Student safety services include late-night transport/escort service, 24-hour emergency
telephone alarm devices, 24-hour patrols by trained security personnel, student patrols,
and electronically operated dormitory entrances.

Applying

Albertson requires an essay, SAT I or ACT, a high school transcript, and 1 recommendation. It recommends an interview. Application deadline: 6/1; 2/15 priority date for
financial aid. Early and deferred admission are possible.

Getting in Last Year
887 applied
83% were accepted
211 enrolled (29%)
33% from top tenth of their h.s. class
3.6 average high school GPA
37% had SAT verbal scores over 600
36% had SAT math scores over 600
58% had ACT scores over 24
11% had SAT verbal scores over 700
7% had SAT math scores over 700
15% had ACT scores over 30
10 National Merit Scholars
26 valedictorians

Graduation and After
22% pursued further study
60% had job offers within 6 months
15 organizations recruited on campus

Financial Matters
$16,280 tuition and fees (1999–2000)
$4200 room and board
78% average percent of need met
$11,734 average financial aid amount received
per undergraduate (1999–2000 estimated)

ALBION COLLEGE

SMALL-TOWN SETTING ■ PRIVATE ■ INDEPENDENT RELIGIOUS ■ COED
ALBION, MICHIGAN

Web site: www.albion.edu
Contact: Ms. Sharon P. Crawford, Director of Admission, 611 East Porter
Street, Albion, MI 48224
Telephone: 517-629-0600 or toll-free 800-858-6770
E-mail: admissions@albion.edu

Academics

Albion awards bachelor's **degrees**. Challenging opportunities include advanced placement, student-designed majors, an honors program, a senior project, Phi Beta Kappa, and Sigma Xi. Special programs include internships, summer session for credit, off-campus study, and study-abroad.

The most frequently chosen fields are business/marketing, biological/life sciences, and social sciences and history. A complete listing of majors at Albion appears in the Majors Index beginning on page 432.

The **faculty** at Albion has 110 full-time members. The student-faculty ratio is 14:1.

Students of Albion

The student body is made up of 1,425 undergraduates. 53.9% are women and 46.1% are men. Students come from 33 states and territories. 84% are from Michigan. 0.4% are international students. 2.8% are African American, 0.5% American Indian, 2.1% Asian American, and 1.1% Hispanic American. 84% returned for their sophomore year.

Facilities and Resources

Student rooms are linked to a campus network. 500 **computers** are available on campus that provide access to the Internet. The **library** has 400,000 books and 900 subscriptions.

Campus Life

There are 122 active organizations on campus, including a drama/theater group, newspaper, radio station, choral group, and marching band. 45% of eligible men and 44% of eligible women are members of national **fraternities** and national **sororities**.

Albion is a member of the NCAA (Division III). **Intercollegiate sports** include baseball (m), basketball, cross-country running, football (m), golf, soccer, softball (w), swimming, tennis, track and field, volleyball.

Campus Safety

Student safety services include late-night transport/escort service, 24-hour emergency telephone alarm devices, 24-hour patrols by trained security personnel, student patrols, and electronically operated dormitory entrances.

Applying

Albion requires SAT I or ACT, a high school transcript, and 1 recommendation, and in some cases an interview. It recommends an essay and a minimum high school GPA of 3.0. Application deadline: 5/1; 2/15 priority date for financial aid. Early and deferred admission are possible.

As a national liberal arts college, Albion College is a select place for select people. The College is especially good at preparing people for admission to the best graduate and professional schools across the country. The acceptance rate for medical schools is more than 80% each year, and for law schools, the acceptance rate is nearly 100% for students with a GPA of at least 3.2 when they apply. Students looking for special distinction should apply to the Honors Institute. A strong $150-million endowment allows the College to offer superior academic and recreational facilities. Not everyone should attend Albion College to prepare for graduate and professional school. To find out if they are among the select few who should, students should visit the Web site (http://www.albion.edu) and then visit the campus.

Getting in Last Year
1,413 applied
84% were accepted
409 enrolled (35%)
37% from top tenth of their h.s. class
3.60 average high school GPA
44% had SAT verbal scores over 600
46% had SAT math scores over 600
64% had ACT scores over 24
13% had SAT verbal scores over 700
10% had SAT math scores over 700
14% had ACT scores over 30
6 National Merit Scholars
17 class presidents
21 valedictorians

Graduation and After
72% graduated in 4 years
2% graduated in 5 years
2% graduated in 6 years
Graduates pursuing further study: 35% arts
and sciences, 15% medicine, 13% law
69% had job offers within 6 months
36 organizations recruited on campus

Financial Matters
$18,160 tuition and fees (1999–2000)
$5220 room and board
97% average percent of need met
$16,429 average financial aid amount received
per undergraduate (1999–2000)

ALBRIGHT COLLEGE

SUBURBAN SETTING ■ PRIVATE ■ INDEPENDENT RELIGIOUS ■ COED
READING, PENNSYLVANIA

Web site: www.albright.edu
Contact: Mr. Gregory E. Eichhorn, Dean of Admission, 13th and Bern Sts,
  PO Box 15234, Reading, PA 19612-5234
Telephone: 610-921-7512 or toll-free 800-252-1856 **Fax:** 610-921-7294
E-mail: albright@alb.edu

Academics

Albright awards bachelor's **degrees**. Challenging opportunities include advanced placement, accelerated degree programs, student-designed majors, an honors program, and a
senior project. Special programs include internships, summer session for credit, and off-
campus study.

The most frequently chosen fields are business/marketing, psychology, and social
sciences and history. A complete listing of majors at Albright appears in the Majors Index
beginning on page 432.

The **faculty** at Albright has 79 full-time members, 95% with terminal degrees. The
student-faculty ratio is 13:1.

Students of Albright

The student body is made up of 1,581 undergraduates. 57.2% are women and 42.8% are
men. Students come from 26 states and territories and 21 other countries. 70% are from
Pennsylvania. 4.6% are international students. 6.9% are African American, 0.2%
American Indian, 2.5% Asian American, and 2.6% Hispanic American. 89% returned for
their sophomore year.

Facilities and Resources

Student rooms are linked to a campus network. 225 **computers** are available on campus
that provide access to the Internet. The **library** has 199,408 books and 875 subscriptions.

Campus Life

There are 70 active organizations on campus, including a drama/theater group,
newspaper, radio station, and choral group. 24% of eligible men and 23% of eligible
women are members of national **fraternities** and national **sororities**.

Albright is a member of the NCAA (Division III). **Intercollegiate sports** include
badminton (w), baseball (m), basketball, cross-country running, field hockey (w), football
(m), golf (m), ice hockey (m), lacrosse (m), rugby, soccer, softball (w), swimming, tennis,
track and field, volleyball, wrestling (m).

Campus Safety

Student safety services include late-night transport/escort service, 24-hour emergency
telephone alarm devices, 24-hour patrols by trained security personnel, student patrols,
and electronically operated dormitory entrances.

Applying

Albright requires an essay, SAT I or ACT, a high school transcript, and 2 recommendations. It recommends SAT II Subject Tests and an interview. Application deadline: 2/15;
3/1 priority date for financial aid. Early and deferred admission are possible.

I t used to be acceptable to
enter college undecided about a
major; in fact, it was expected.
But things have changed, and today
there is more pressure on students
to choose a major as soon as they
walk on campus. Pressure doesn't
lead to wise decisions, so Albright
has developed a program, the Alpha
Program, specially designed for the
undecided student. Through a
structured package of academic
guidance, peer support, special
events, and career counseling, the
Alpha Program helps students to
choose not only the right major, but
also the right career and the right
future.

Getting in Last Year
1,752 applied
86% were accepted
393 enrolled (26%)
20% from top tenth of their h.s. class
3.38 average high school GPA
17% had SAT verbal scores over 600
18% had SAT math scores over 600
2% had SAT verbal scores over 700
2% had SAT math scores over 700
8 valedictorians

Graduation and After
52% graduated in 4 years
6% graduated in 5 years
1% graduated in 6 years
32% pursued further study (12% arts and
  sciences, 9% law, 5% business)
39% had job offers within 6 months
40 organizations recruited on campus

Financial Matters
$19,460 tuition and fees (1999–2000)
$5780 room and board
88% average percent of need met
$16,605 average financial aid amount received
  per undergraduate (1999–2000)

ALFRED UNIVERSITY

RURAL SETTING ■ PRIVATE ■ INDEPENDENT ■ COED
ALFRED, NEW YORK

Web site: www.alfred.edu
Contact: Katherine M. McCarthy, Director of Admissions, Alumni Hall, Alfred, NY 14802-1205
Telephone: 607-871-2115 or toll-free 800-541-9229 **Fax:** 607-871-2198
E-mail: admwww@alfred.edu

A lfred University has just completed a tremendous 6-year building campaign. Seven buildings have been built or renovated to enhance the academic, cultural, and social lives of University students. New academic programs include athletic training, materials science and engineering, and a B.A. in the fine arts. While the University is committed to offering more opportunities and better facilities to students, it is also committed to holding the line on costs.

Getting in Last Year
1,954 applied
81% were accepted
543 enrolled (34%)
23% from top tenth of their h.s. class
35% had SAT verbal scores over 600
33% had SAT math scores over 600
7% had SAT verbal scores over 700
5% had SAT math scores over 700
15 National Merit Scholars

Graduation and After
49% graduated in 4 years
17% graduated in 5 years
2% graduated in 6 years
22% pursued further study
71% had job offers within 6 months
79 organizations recruited on campus

Financial Matters
$19,074 tuition and fees (1999–2000)
$7174 room and board
95% average percent of need met
$22,350 average financial aid amount received per undergraduate (1999–2000)

Academics

Alfred awards bachelor's, master's, and doctoral **degrees**. Challenging opportunities include advanced placement, accelerated degree programs, student-designed majors, an honors program, double majors, independent study, a senior project, and Sigma Xi. Special programs include cooperative education, internships, summer session for credit, off-campus study, study-abroad, and Army ROTC.

The most frequently chosen fields are engineering/engineering technologies, business/marketing, and psychology. A complete listing of majors at Alfred appears in the Majors Index beginning on page 432.

The **faculty** at Alfred has 172 full-time members, 90% with terminal degrees. The student-faculty ratio is 12:1.

Students of Alfred

The student body totals 2,437, of whom 2,113 are undergraduates. 50% are women and 50% are men. Students come from 37 states and territories and 11 other countries. 68% are from New York. 1.2% are international students. 3.4% are African American, 0.4% American Indian, 1.7% Asian American, and 3.9% Hispanic American. 85% returned for their sophomore year.

Facilities and Resources

Student rooms are linked to a campus network. 322 **computers** are available on campus that provide access to the Internet. The 2 **libraries** have 330,522 books and 1,722 subscriptions.

Campus Life

There are 90 active organizations on campus, including a drama/theater group, newspaper, radio station, television station, and choral group. 20% of eligible men and 11% of eligible women are members of national **fraternities**, national **sororities**, local fraternities, and local sororities.

Alfred is a member of the NCAA (Division III). **Intercollegiate sports** include basketball, cross-country running, equestrian sports, football (m), golf, lacrosse, skiing (cross-country), skiing (downhill), soccer, softball (w), swimming, tennis, track and field, volleyball (w).

Campus Safety

Student safety services include late-night transport/escort service, 24-hour emergency telephone alarm devices, and student patrols.

Applying

Alfred requires an essay, SAT I or ACT, a high school transcript, and 1 recommendation, and in some cases an interview and portfolio. It recommends SAT II: Writing Test and an interview. Application deadline: 2/1. Early and deferred admission are possible.

ALLEGHENY COLLEGE

SMALL-TOWN SETTING ■ PRIVATE ■ INDEPENDENT RELIGIOUS ■ COED
MEADVILLE, PENNSYLVANIA

Web site: www.alleg.edu
Contact: Ms. Megan K. Murphy, Director of Admissions, 520 North Main
Street, Box 5, Meadville, PA 16335
Telephone: 814-332-4351 or toll-free 800-521-5293 **Fax:** 814-337-0431
E-mail: admiss@admin.alleg.edu

Academics

Allegheny awards bachelor's **degrees**. Challenging opportunities include advanced
placement, accelerated degree programs, student-designed majors, double majors,
independent study, a senior project, and Phi Beta Kappa. Special programs include
internships, off-campus study, study-abroad, and Army ROTC.

The most frequently chosen fields are social sciences and history, psychology, and
biological/life sciences. A complete listing of majors at Allegheny appears in the Majors
Index beginning on page 432.

The **faculty** at Allegheny has 131 full-time members, 92% with terminal degrees.
The student-faculty ratio is 14:1.

Students of Allegheny

The student body is made up of 1,886 undergraduates. 53.1% are women and 46.9% are
men. Students come from 38 states and territories and 17 other countries. 61% are from
Pennsylvania. 1.1% are international students. 2.4% are African American, 0.5%
American Indian, 1.4% Asian American, and 1.3% Hispanic American. 81% returned for
their sophomore year.

Facilities and Resources

Student rooms are linked to a campus network. 210 **computers** are available on campus
that provide access to the Internet. The **library** has 259,064 books and 1,265 subscriptions.

Campus Life

There are 100 active organizations on campus, including a drama/theater group,
newspaper, radio station, television station, and choral group. 18% of eligible men and
28% of eligible women are members of national **fraternities** and national **sororities**.

Allegheny is a member of the NCAA (Division III). **Intercollegiate sports** include
baseball (m), basketball, cross-country running, football (m), golf (m), ice hockey (m),
lacrosse, rugby (m), soccer, softball (w), swimming, tennis, track and field, volleyball.

Campus Safety

Student safety services include local police patrol, late-night transport/escort service,
24-hour emergency telephone alarm devices, 24-hour patrols by trained security personnel, and student patrols.

Applying

Allegheny requires an essay, SAT I or ACT, a high school transcript, and 2 recommendations. It recommends SAT II Subject Tests and an interview. Application deadline: 2/15;
2/15 for financial aid. Early and deferred admission are possible.

One of America's oldest
colleges, Allegheny stands
out today for the breadth
of the skills and understandings
consistently developed in its
students: superior professional
capabilities, from writing to
leadership to problem solving; skills
for managing everyday life;
important social abilities; talents for
responsible citizenship; and values
clarification. Students are actively
engaged in learning through small
and dynamic classes, hands-on
laboratories, original research
projects, and collaborations with
faculty. All students complete a
substantial creative or research
project in the senior year, proving
their abilities to complete a major
assignment, work independently,
analyze and synthesize, and write
and speak persuasively.

Getting in Last Year
3,013 applied
75% were accepted
565 enrolled (25%)
37% from top tenth of their h.s. class
3.64 average high school GPA
52% had SAT verbal scores over 600
55% had SAT math scores over 600
66% had ACT scores over 24
9% had SAT verbal scores over 700
8% had SAT math scores over 700
8% had ACT scores over 30
11 National Merit Scholars
24 valedictorians

Graduation and After
63% graduated in 4 years
11% graduated in 5 years
1% graduated in 6 years
Graduates pursuing further study: 15% arts
and sciences, 7% law, 4% medicine
60% had job offers within 6 months
59 organizations recruited on campus

Financial Matters
$20,690 tuition and fees (1999–2000)
$4970 room and board
96% average percent of need met
$17,415 average financial aid amount received
per undergraduate (1999–2000 estimated)

ALMA COLLEGE

SMALL-TOWN SETTING ■ PRIVATE ■ INDEPENDENT RELIGIOUS ■ COED
ALMA, MICHIGAN

Web site: www.alma.edu
Contact: Acting Director of Admissions, Admissions Office, Alma, MI 48801-1599
Telephone: 517-463-7139 or toll-free 800-321-ALMA **Fax:** 517-463-7057
E-mail: admissions@alma.edu

Alma's undergraduates thrive on challenging academic programs in a supportive, small-college atmosphere. The College is committed to a value-added liberal arts curriculum with opportunities for one-on-one research and publication with faculty members whose first priority is teaching. Students enjoy small classes in modern facilities, including the new McIntyre Center for Exercise and Health Science. Alma College offers excellent preparation for professional careers in business, law, medicine, the arts, and a wide range of other fields.

Getting in Last Year
1,366 applied
83% were accepted
335 enrolled (30%)
37% from top tenth of their h.s. class
3.60 average high school GPA
65% had ACT scores over 24
10% had ACT scores over 30
24 valedictorians

Graduation and After
30% pursued further study (12% arts and sciences, 3% engineering, 3% law)
69% had job offers within 6 months
25 organizations recruited on campus

Financial Matters
$15,142 tuition and fees (1999–2000)
$5460 room and board
90% average percent of need met
$13,635 average financial aid amount received per undergraduate (1999–2000 estimated)

Academics

Alma awards bachelor's **degrees**. Challenging opportunities include advanced placement, accelerated degree programs, student-designed majors, an honors program, double majors, independent study, a senior project, and Phi Beta Kappa. Special programs include internships, summer session for credit, off-campus study, study-abroad, and Army ROTC.

The most frequently chosen fields are business/marketing, biological/life sciences, and health professions and related sciences. A complete listing of majors at Alma appears in the Majors Index beginning on page 432.

The **faculty** at Alma has 90 full-time members, 90% with terminal degrees. The student-faculty ratio is 15:1.

Students of Alma

The student body is made up of 1,383 undergraduates. 57.4% are women and 42.6% are men. Students come from 19 states and territories and 12 other countries. 95% are from Michigan. 0.4% are international students. 1.8% are African American, 0.7% American Indian, 0.4% Asian American, and 1.7% Hispanic American. 89% returned for their sophomore year.

Facilities and Resources

Student rooms are linked to a campus network. 469 **computers** are available on campus that provide access to the Internet. The **library** has 223,446 books and 1,178 subscriptions.

Campus Life

There are 113 active organizations on campus, including a drama/theater group, newspaper, radio station, choral group, and marching band. 23% of eligible men and 23% of eligible women are members of national **fraternities**, national **sororities**, local fraternities, and local sororities.

Alma is a member of the NCAA (Division III). **Intercollegiate sports** include baseball (m), basketball, cross-country running, football (m), golf, soccer, softball (w), swimming, tennis, track and field, volleyball (w).

Campus Safety

Student safety services include 24-hour emergency telephone alarm devices and 24-hour patrols by trained security personnel.

Applying

Alma requires SAT I or ACT, a high school transcript, 2 recommendations, and a minimum high school GPA of 2.0, and in some cases an interview. It recommends an essay and ACT. Application deadline: rolling admissions; 2/15 priority date for financial aid. Early and deferred admission are possible.

AMERICAN UNIVERSITY
SUBURBAN SETTING ■ PRIVATE ■ INDEPENDENT RELIGIOUS ■ COED
WASHINGTON, DISTRICT OF COLUMBIA

Web site: www.american.edu
Contact: Ms. Sharon Alson, Director of Admissions, 4400 Massachusetts
    Avenue, NW, Washington, DC 20016-8001
Telephone: 202-885-6000 **Fax:** 202-885-6014
E-mail: afa@american.edu

 eAPPLY

Academics
AU awards associate, bachelor's, master's, doctoral, and first-professional **degrees**. Challenging opportunities include advanced placement, accelerated degree programs, student-designed majors, an honors program, double majors, independent study, a senior project, Phi Beta Kappa, and Sigma Xi. Special programs include cooperative education, internships, summer session for credit, off-campus study, study-abroad, and Army and Air Force ROTC.

The most frequently chosen fields are social sciences and history, business/marketing, and communications/communication technologies. A complete listing of majors at AU appears in the Majors Index beginning on page 432.

The **faculty** at AU has 463 full-time members, 91% with terminal degrees. The student-faculty ratio is 14:1.

Students of AU
The student body totals 10,894, of whom 5,533 are undergraduates. 60.4% are women and 39.6% are men. Students come from 53 states and territories and 130 other countries. 15% are from District of Columbia. 13.2% are international students. 6.8% are African American, 0.4% American Indian, 3.4% Asian American, and 4.9% Hispanic American. 85% returned for their sophomore year.

Facilities and Resources
Student rooms are linked to a campus network. 200 **computers** are available on campus that provide access to the Internet. The 2 **libraries** have 700,000 books and 3,600 subscriptions.

Campus Life
There are 94 active organizations on campus, including a drama/theater group, newspaper, radio station, television station, choral group, and marching band. 20% of eligible men and 25% of eligible women are members of national **fraternities** and national **sororities**.

AU is a member of the NCAA (Division I). **Intercollegiate sports** (some offering scholarships) include basketball, cross-country running, field hockey (w), golf (m), lacrosse (w), soccer, swimming, tennis, track and field, volleyball (w), wrestling (m).

Campus Safety
Student safety services include late-night transport/escort service, 24-hour emergency telephone alarm devices, 24-hour patrols by trained security personnel, and electronically operated dormitory entrances.

Applying
AU requires an essay, SAT I or ACT, a high school transcript, 3 recommendations, writing sample, and a minimum high school GPA of 2.0. It recommends SAT II Subject Tests, an interview, and a minimum high school GPA of 3.0. Application deadline: 2/1; 3/1 priority date for financial aid. Early and deferred admission are possible.

Getting in Last Year
7,754 applied
72% were accepted
1,203 enrolled (21%)
24% from top tenth of their h.s. class
3.19 average high school GPA
53% had SAT verbal scores over 600
42% had SAT math scores over 600
66% had ACT scores over 24
13% had SAT verbal scores over 700
7% had SAT math scores over 700
3% had ACT scores over 30

Graduation and After
61% graduated in 4 years
5% graduated in 5 years
1% graduated in 6 years
50% pursued further study
200 organizations recruited on campus

Financial Matters
$20,373 tuition and fees (1999–2000)
$7982 room and board
74% average percent of need met
$19,470 average financial aid amount received
    per undergraduate (1999–2000)

AMHERST COLLEGE

SMALL-TOWN SETTING ■ PRIVATE ■ INDEPENDENT ■ COED
AMHERST, MASSACHUSETTS

Web site: www.amherst.edu
Contact: Mr. Thomas Parker, Dean of Admission and Financial Aid, PO Box 5000, Amherst, MA 01002
Telephone: 413-542-2328 **Fax:** 413-542-2040
E-mail: admissions@amherst.edu

Getting in Last Year
5,198 applied
19% were accepted
422 enrolled (42%)
87% from top tenth of their h.s. class
93% had SAT verbal scores over 600
93% had SAT math scores over 600
97% had ACT scores over 24
54% had SAT verbal scores over 700
53% had SAT math scores over 700
58% had ACT scores over 30
84 National Merit Scholars
49 valedictorians

Graduation and After
88% graduated in 4 years
8% graduated in 5 years
30% pursued further study
63% had job offers within 6 months
65 organizations recruited on campus
1 Rhodes scholar

Financial Matters
$25,259 tuition and fees (1999–2000)
$6560 room and board
100% average percent of need met
$22,705 average financial aid amount received per undergraduate (1999–2000)

Academics

Amherst College awards bachelor's **degrees**. Challenging opportunities include student-designed majors, an honors program, double majors, independent study, a senior project, Phi Beta Kappa, and Sigma Xi. Special programs include off-campus study and study-abroad.

The most frequently chosen fields are social sciences and history, English, and foreign language/literature. A complete listing of majors at Amherst College appears in the Majors Index beginning on page 432.

The **faculty** at Amherst College has 179 full-time members, 94% with terminal degrees. The student-faculty ratio is 9:1.

Students of Amherst College

The student body is made up of 1,664 undergraduates. Students come from 52 states and territories and 29 other countries. 14% are from Massachusetts. 3.5% are international students. 6.4% are African American, 0.3% American Indian, 12% Asian American, and 6.6% Hispanic American. 97% returned for their sophomore year.

Facilities and Resources

Student rooms are linked to a campus network. 123 **computers** are available on campus that provide access to the Internet. The 6 **libraries** have 866,452 books and 5,053 subscriptions.

Campus Life

There are 100 active organizations on campus, including a drama/theater group, newspaper, radio station, and choral group. No national or local **fraternities** or **sororities.**

Amherst College is a member of the NCAA (Division III). **Intercollegiate sports** include baseball (m), basketball, crew, cross-country running, equestrian sports, fencing, field hockey (w), football (m), golf, ice hockey, lacrosse, rugby, sailing, skiing (downhill), soccer, softball (w), squash, swimming, tennis, track and field, volleyball, water polo.

Campus Safety

Student safety services include late-night transport/escort service, 24-hour emergency telephone alarm devices, 24-hour patrols by trained security personnel, student patrols, and electronically operated dormitory entrances.

Applying

Amherst College requires an essay, SAT I or ACT, 3 SAT II Subject Tests, a high school transcript, and 3 recommendations. It recommends SAT II: Writing Test. Application deadline: 12/31; 2/1 priority date for financial aid. Deferred admission is possible.

AUBURN UNIVERSITY

SMALL-TOWN SETTING ■ PUBLIC ■ STATE-SUPPORTED ■ COED
AUBURN UNIVERSITY, ALABAMA

Web site: www.auburn.edu
Contact: Dr. John Fletcher, Acting Assistant Vice President of Enrollment
Management, 202 Mary Martin Hall, Auburn University, AL 36849-0001
Telephone: 334-844-4080 or toll-free 800-AUBURN9 (in-state)
E-mail: admissions@mail.auburn.edu

Academics

Auburn awards bachelor's, master's, doctoral, and first-professional **degrees** and post-master's certificates. Challenging opportunities include advanced placement, accelerated degree programs, an honors program, double majors, independent study, a senior project, and Sigma Xi. Special programs include cooperative education, internships, summer session for credit, study-abroad, and Army, Navy and Air Force ROTC.

The most frequently chosen fields are business/marketing, engineering/engineering technologies, and education. A complete listing of majors at Auburn appears in the Majors Index beginning on page 432.

The **faculty** at Auburn has 1,146 full-time members, 90% with terminal degrees. The student-faculty ratio is 16:1.

Students of Auburn

The student body totals 22,120, of whom 18,669 are undergraduates. 47.7% are women and 52.3% are men. Students come from 53 states and territories and 51 other countries. 69% are from Alabama. 0.6% are international students. 6.8% are African American, 0.6% American Indian, 1.2% Asian American, and 0.8% Hispanic American. 81% returned for their sophomore year.

Facilities and Resources

Student rooms are linked to a campus network. 600 **computers** are available on campus that provide access to the Internet. The 3 **libraries** have 2,380,000 books and 19,410 subscriptions.

Campus Life

There are 300 active organizations on campus, including a drama/theater group, newspaper, radio station, television station, choral group, and marching band. 17% of eligible men and 27% of eligible women are members of national **fraternities** and national **sororities**.

Auburn is a member of the NCAA (Division I). **Intercollegiate sports** (some offering scholarships) include baseball (m), basketball, cross-country running, football (m), golf, gymnastics (w), soccer (w), softball (w), swimming, tennis, track and field, volleyball (w).

Campus Safety

Student safety services include late-night transport/escort service, 24-hour emergency telephone alarm devices, 24-hour patrols by trained security personnel, and electronically operated dormitory entrances.

Applying

Auburn requires SAT I or ACT, a high school transcript, and a minimum high school GPA of 2.0, and in some cases a minimum high school GPA of 3.0. Application deadline: 9/1; 4/15 priority date for financial aid. Early and deferred admission are possible.

Auburn University provides outstanding, economically accessible instruction to its undergraduate, graduate, and professional students. Programs in agriculture, life sciences, engineering, architecture, pharmacy, and veterinary medicine are especially well known. Auburn consistently produces alumni who are leaders in business and service industries and is among the top 10 in providing NASA astronauts. Despite the diversity of offerings and the emphasis on academic excellence, Auburn is best known for providing activities for every interest in its friendly, welcoming, small-town environment.

Getting in Last Year

10,542 applied
88% were accepted
3,692 enrolled (40%)
24% from top tenth of their h.s. class
3.08 average high school GPA
23% had SAT verbal scores over 600
28% had SAT math scores over 600
42% had ACT scores over 24
4% had SAT verbal scores over 700
4% had SAT math scores over 700
8% had ACT scores over 30
34 National Merit Scholars

Graduation and After

30% graduated in 4 years
28% graduated in 5 years
8% graduated in 6 years
35% pursued further study (9% business, 6% medicine, 5% arts and sciences)
75% had job offers within 6 months
75 organizations recruited on campus

Financial Matters

$2955 resident tuition and fees (1999–2000)
$8745 nonresident tuition and fees (1999–2000)
56% average percent of need met
$5233 average financial aid amount received per undergraduate (1999–2000 estimated)

AUGUSTANA COLLEGE
SUBURBAN SETTING ■ PRIVATE ■ INDEPENDENT RELIGIOUS ■ COED
ROCK ISLAND, ILLINOIS

Web site: www.augustana.edu
Contact: Mr. Martin Sauer, Director of Admissions, 639 38th Street, Rock Island, IL 61201-2296
Telephone: 309-794-7341 or toll-free 800-798-8100 **Fax:** 309-794-7431
E-mail: admissions@augustana.edu

Academics
Augie awards bachelor's **degrees**. Challenging opportunities include advanced placement, accelerated degree programs, an honors program, double majors, independent study, a senior project, and Phi Beta Kappa. Special programs include cooperative education, internships, summer session for credit, and study-abroad.

The most frequently chosen fields are biological/life sciences, business/marketing, and health professions and related sciences. A complete listing of majors at Augie appears in the Majors Index beginning on page 432.

The **faculty** at Augie has 141 full-time members, 89% with terminal degrees. The student-faculty ratio is 13:1.

Students of Augie
The student body is made up of 2,209 undergraduates. 58.9% are women and 41.1% are men. Students come from 26 states and territories. 87% are from Illinois. 0.4% are international students. 3.4% are African American, 0.2% American Indian, 2.4% Asian American, and 2.5% Hispanic American. 83% returned for their sophomore year.

Facilities and Resources
Student rooms are linked to a campus network. 450 **computers** are available on campus that provide access to the Internet. The 4 **libraries** have 227,357 books and 1,870 subscriptions.

Campus Life
There are 109 active organizations on campus, including a drama/theater group, newspaper, radio station, and choral group. 36% of eligible men and 40% of eligible women are members of local **fraternities** and local **sororities**.

Augie is a member of the NCAA (Division III). **Intercollegiate sports** include baseball (m), basketball, cross-country running, football (m), golf, soccer, softball (w), swimming, tennis, track and field, volleyball, wrestling (m).

Campus Safety
Student safety services include late-night transport/escort service, 24-hour emergency telephone alarm devices, 24-hour patrols by trained security personnel, and electronically operated dormitory entrances.

Applying
Augie requires SAT I or ACT and a high school transcript, and in some cases an essay, an interview, and 2 recommendations. Application deadline: rolling admissions; 4/1 priority date for financial aid. Deferred admission is possible.

Augustana College seeks to develop in students the characteristics of liberally educated persons: clarity of thought and expression, curiosity, fair-mindedness, appreciation for the arts and cultural diversity, intellectual honesty, and a considered set of personal values and commitments. Students combine exploration of the arts, sciences, and humanities with in-depth study in their major field(s), guided by an excellent, committed faculty; they grow personally and socially through participation in wide extracurricular and cocurricular opportunities on one of the most beautiful campuses in the country. Special features include innovative interdisciplinary first-year course sequences, foreign study, and internships—both domestic and international.

Getting in Last Year
2,293 applied
80% were accepted
565 enrolled (31%)
33% from top tenth of their h.s. class
3.5 average high school GPA
68% had ACT scores over 24
12% had ACT scores over 30

Graduation and After
33% pursued further study (20% arts and sciences, 5% medicine, 3% business)
64% had job offers within 6 months
166 organizations recruited on campus

Financial Matters
$17,187 tuition and fees (1999–2000)
$5037 room and board
87% average percent of need met
$13,518 average financial aid amount received per undergraduate (1999–2000)

Augustana College

Urban setting ■ Private ■ Independent Religious ■ Coed
Sioux Falls, South Dakota

Web site: www.augie.edu
Contact: Robert Preloger, Vice President for Enrollment, 2001 South Summit Avenue, Sioux Falls, SD 57197
Telephone: 605-336-5518 ext. 5504 or toll-free 800-727-2844 **Fax:** 605-336-5518
E-mail: info@inst.augie.edu

Academics

Augustana awards bachelor's and master's **degrees**. Challenging opportunities include advanced placement, accelerated degree programs, student-designed majors, an honors program, double majors, independent study, and a senior project. Special programs include cooperative education, internships, summer session for credit, off-campus study, and study-abroad.

The most frequently chosen fields are education, health professions and related sciences, and business/marketing. A complete listing of majors at Augustana appears in the Majors Index beginning on page 432.

The **faculty** at Augustana has 118 full-time members, 90% with terminal degrees. The student-faculty ratio is 12:1.

Students of Augustana

The student body totals 1,774, of whom 1,728 are undergraduates. 64.6% are women and 35.4% are men. Students come from 27 states and territories and 10 other countries. 49% are from South Dakota. 1.6% are international students. 0.6% are African American, 0.4% American Indian, 0.6% Asian American, and 0.2% Hispanic American. 80% returned for their sophomore year.

Facilities and Resources

Student rooms are linked to a campus network. 250 **computers** are available on campus that provide access to the Internet. The 2 **libraries** have 295,470 books and 1,568 subscriptions.

Campus Life

There are 50 active organizations on campus, including a drama/theater group, newspaper, radio station, and choral group. 2% of eligible women are members of local **fraternities** and local **sororities**.

Augustana is a member of the NCAA (Division II). **Intercollegiate sports** (some offering scholarships) include baseball (m), basketball, cross-country running, football (m), golf, soccer (w), softball (w), tennis, track and field, volleyball (w), wrestling (m).

Campus Safety

Student safety services include late-night transport/escort service, 24-hour emergency telephone alarm devices, 24-hour patrols by trained security personnel, and electronically operated dormitory entrances.

Applying

Augustana requires SAT I or ACT, a high school transcript, 1 recommendation, and a minimum high school GPA of 2.5. It recommends an interview. Application deadline: 8/1; 3/1 priority date for financial aid. Early and deferred admission are possible.

Getting in Last Year
1,445 applied
86% were accepted
483 enrolled (39%)
27% from top tenth of their h.s. class
3.55 average high school GPA
36% had SAT verbal scores over 600
48% had SAT math scores over 600
57% had ACT scores over 24
12% had SAT verbal scores over 700
12% had SAT math scores over 700
7% had ACT scores over 30
38 valedictorians

Graduation and After
46% graduated in 4 years
12% graduated in 5 years
3% graduated in 6 years
Graduates pursuing further study: 10% arts and sciences, 3% medicine, 2% education
90% had job offers within 6 months
50 organizations recruited on campus

Financial Matters
$14,754 tuition and fees (2000–2001)
$4260 room and board
98% average percent of need met
$13,487 average financial aid amount received per undergraduate (1999–2000)

AUSTIN COLLEGE

SUBURBAN SETTING ■ PRIVATE ■ INDEPENDENT RELIGIOUS ■ COED
SHERMAN, TEXAS

Web site: www.austinc.edu
Contact: Ms. Nan Massingill, Vice President for Institutional Enrollment, 900
    North Grand Avenue, Sherman, TX 75090-4400
Telephone: 903-813-3000 or toll-free 800-442-5363
E-mail: admissions@austinc.edu

Getting in Last Year

1,003 applied
78% were accepted
324 enrolled (41%)
61% from top tenth of their h.s. class
58% had SAT verbal scores over 600
53% had SAT math scores over 600
80% had ACT scores over 24
16% had SAT verbal scores over 700
13% had SAT math scores over 700
31% had ACT scores over 30
5 National Merit Scholars
14 valedictorians

Graduation and After

57% graduated in 4 years
5% graduated in 5 years
2% graduated in 6 years
36% pursued further study
45% had job offers within 6 months
18 organizations recruited on campus
1 Fulbright scholar

Financial Matters

$15,219 tuition and fees (2000–2001)
$5891 room and board
90% average percent of need met
$15,654 average financial aid amount received
    per undergraduate (1999–2000)

Academics

AC awards bachelor's and master's **degrees**. Challenging opportunities include advanced placement, accelerated degree programs, student-designed majors, an honors program, double majors, independent study, and a senior project. Special programs include internships, summer session for credit, off-campus study, and study-abroad.

The most frequently chosen fields are area/ethnic studies, biological/life sciences, and social sciences and history. A complete listing of majors at AC appears in the Majors Index beginning on page 432.

The **faculty** at AC has 79 full-time members, 96% with terminal degrees. The student-faculty ratio is 13:1.

Students of AC

The student body totals 1,257, of whom 1,233 are undergraduates. 54% are women and 46% are men. Students come from 25 states and territories and 14 other countries. 93% are from Texas. 1.8% are international students. 4.5% are African American, 0.7% American Indian, 7.9% Asian American, and 6.4% Hispanic American. 83% returned for their sophomore year.

Facilities and Resources

Student rooms are linked to a campus network. 122 **computers** are available on campus that provide access to the Internet. The **library** has 156,268 books and 7,971 subscriptions.

Campus Life

There are 45 active organizations on campus, including a drama/theater group, newspaper, and choral group. 33% of eligible men and 30% of eligible women are members of local **fraternities** and local **sororities**.

AC is a member of the NCAA (Division III). **Intercollegiate sports** include baseball (m), basketball, cross-country running, football (m), golf, soccer, swimming, tennis, track and field, volleyball (w).

Campus Safety

Student safety services include late-night transport/escort service, 24-hour emergency telephone alarm devices, 24-hour patrols by trained security personnel, and electronically operated dormitory entrances.

Applying

AC requires an essay, SAT I or ACT, a high school transcript, and 2 recommendations, and in some cases an interview. It recommends an interview and a minimum high school GPA of 3.0. Application deadline: 8/15; 4/1 priority date for financial aid. Early and deferred admission are possible.

BABSON COLLEGE

SUBURBAN SETTING ■ PRIVATE ■ INDEPENDENT ■ COED
BABSON PARK, MASSACHUSETTS

Web site: www.babson.edu
Contact: Ms. Amy Reuben, Acting Dean of Undergraduate Admission, Office
of Undergraduate Admissions, Mustard Hall, Babson Park, MA 02457-0310
Telephone: 781-239-5522 or toll-free 800-488-3696 **Fax:** 781-239-4006
E-mail: ugradadmission@babson.edu

  eAPPLY

Academics

Babson awards bachelor's and master's **degrees**. Challenging opportunities include
advanced placement, student-designed majors, freshman honors college, an honors
program, independent study, and a senior project. Special programs include internships,
summer session for credit, off-campus study, study-abroad, and Army, Navy and Air
Force ROTC.

The most frequently chosen field is business/marketing. A complete listing of majors
at Babson appears in the Majors Index beginning on page 432.

The **faculty** at Babson has 159 full-time members. The student-faculty ratio is 11:1.

Students of Babson

The student body totals 3,431, of whom 1,701 are undergraduates. 35.6% are women
and 64.4% are men. Students come from 40 states and territories and 70 other countries.
62% are from Massachusetts. 19.4% are international students. 2% are African
American, 0.3% American Indian, 6% Asian American, and 4% Hispanic American.
90% returned for their sophomore year.

Facilities and Resources

Student rooms are linked to a campus network. 350 **computers** are available on campus
that provide access to the Internet. The 2 **libraries** have 90,543 books and 1,510
subscriptions.

Campus Life

There are 37 active organizations on campus, including a drama/theater group,
newspaper, radio station, and choral group. 10% of eligible men and 10% of eligible
women are members of national **fraternities** and national **sororities**.

Babson is a member of the NCAA (Division III). **Intercollegiate sports** include
baseball (m), basketball, cross-country running, field hockey (w), golf (m), ice hockey
(m), lacrosse, rugby, sailing, skiing (downhill), soccer, softball (w), squash, swimming,
tennis, volleyball.

Campus Safety

Student safety services include late-night transport/escort service, 24-hour emergency
telephone alarm devices, and 24-hour patrols by trained security personnel.

Applying

Babson requires an essay, SAT I or ACT, a high school transcript, and 2 recommendations. It recommends an interview. Application deadline: 2/1; 2/15 for financial aid.
Deferred admission is possible.

Babson is committed to being an international leader in management education. Through a balanced and rigorous program of management and liberal arts courses, the College educates students who are capable of initiating, managing, and implementing change. With an enrollment of approximately 1,600 undergraduates, Babson offers students the opportunity to participate in class discussions and other activities. Through more than 50 organizations and clubs and 20 student-run businesses, students play a role in shaping campus life. Babson's 370-acre residential campus is located 14 miles west of Boston, where students can take advantage of many social and career exploration opportunities.

Getting in Last Year
2,582 applied
45% were accepted
414 enrolled (35%)
29% from top tenth of their h.s. class
43% had SAT verbal scores over 600
51% had SAT math scores over 600
3% had SAT verbal scores over 700
15% had SAT math scores over 700
18 class presidents

Graduation and After
2% pursued further study (2% law)
95% had job offers within 6 months
479 organizations recruited on campus

Financial Matters
$21,952 tuition and fees (2000–2001 estimated)
$8746 room and board
99% average percent of need met
$16,903 average financial aid amount received per undergraduate (1999–2000 estimated)

BALDWIN-WALLACE COLLEGE

SUBURBAN SETTING ■ PRIVATE ■ INDEPENDENT RELIGIOUS ■ COED
BEREA, OHIO

Web site: www.bw.edu
Contact: Mrs. Julie Baker, Director of Undergraduate Admission, 275
    Eastland Road, Berea, OH 44017-2088
Telephone: 440-826-2222 or toll-free 877-BWAPPLY (in-state) **Fax:**
    440-826-3830
E-mail: admission@bw.edu

Academics

B-W awards bachelor's and master's **degrees**. Challenging opportunities include
advanced placement, accelerated degree programs, student-designed majors, an honors
program, double majors, independent study, and a senior project. Special programs
include internships, summer session for credit, off-campus study, study-abroad, and
Army and Air Force ROTC.

The most frequently chosen fields are business/marketing, education, and social sciences and history. A complete listing of majors at B-W appears in the Majors Index
beginning on page 432.

The **faculty** at B-W has 166 full-time members, 73% with terminal degrees. The
student-faculty ratio is 13:1.

Students of B-W

The student body totals 4,646, of whom 4,002 are undergraduates. 61.3% are women
and 38.7% are men. Students come from 34 states and territories. 93% are from Ohio.
0.4% are international students. 4.2% are African American, 0.2% American Indian, 1%
Asian American, and 1% Hispanic American. 86% returned for their sophomore year.

Facilities and Resources

Student rooms are linked to a campus network. 350 **computers** are available on campus
that provide access to the Internet. The 3 **libraries** have 160,000 books and 2,494
subscriptions.

Campus Life

There are 140 active organizations on campus, including a drama/theater group,
newspaper, radio station, and choral group. 17% of eligible men and 25% of eligible
women are members of national **fraternities** and national **sororities**.

B-W is a member of the NCAA (Division III). **Intercollegiate sports** include
baseball (m), basketball, cross-country running, football (m), golf, soccer, softball (w),
swimming, tennis, track and field, volleyball (w), wrestling (m).

Campus Safety

Student safety services include late-night transport/escort service, 24-hour emergency
telephone alarm devices, 24-hour patrols by trained security personnel, student patrols,
and electronically operated dormitory entrances.

Applying

B-W requires an essay, SAT I or ACT, a high school transcript, 1 recommendation, and a
minimum high school GPA of 2.0. It recommends an interview and a minimum high
school GPA of 3.0. Application deadline: rolling admissions; 9/1 for financial aid, with a
5/1 priority date. Deferred admission is possible.

Founded in 1845,
Baldwin-Wallace was among
the first colleges to admit
students without regard to race or
gender. That spirit of inclusiveness
and innovation continues today. The
academic program, rooted in the
liberal arts yet balanced by
abundant opportunities for career
exploration and application, is
designed to prepare students to
make a living . . . and a life worth
living. It's a program committed to
quality and distinguished by a
personalized approach to learning
that celebrates each student.
"Quality education with a personal
touch" is more than a slogan at
B-W. It's a statement of purpose. It
is Baldwin-Wallace.

Getting in Last Year
2,115 applied
81% were accepted
714 enrolled (41%)
30% from top tenth of their h.s. class
3.4 average high school GPA
37% had SAT verbal scores over 600
38% had SAT math scores over 600
50% had ACT scores over 24
4% had SAT verbal scores over 700
7% had SAT math scores over 700
5% had ACT scores over 30

Graduation and After
65% graduated in 4 years
9% graduated in 5 years
2% graduated in 6 years
Graduates pursuing further study: 4% arts and
    sciences, 3% business, 3% law
80% had job offers within 6 months
120 organizations recruited on campus

Financial Matters
$15,340 tuition and fees (2000–2001)
$5460 room and board
98% average percent of need met
$11,828 average financial aid amount received
    per undergraduate (1999–2000)

BARD COLLEGE

RURAL SETTING ■ PRIVATE ■ INDEPENDENT ■ COED
ANNANDALE-ON-HUDSON, NEW YORK

Web site: www.bard.edu
Contact: Ms. Mary Inga Backlund, Director of Admissions,
Annandale-on-Hudson, NY 12504
Telephone: 914-758-7472 **Fax:** 914-758-5208
E-mail: admission@bard.edu

eAPPLY

Academics

Bard awards bachelor's, master's, and doctoral **degrees**. Challenging opportunities include advanced placement, accelerated degree programs, student-designed majors, double majors, independent study, and a senior project. Special programs include internships, off-campus study, and study-abroad.

The most frequently chosen fields are visual/performing arts, social sciences and history, and foreign language/literature. A complete listing of majors at Bard appears in the Majors Index beginning on page 432.

The **faculty** at Bard has 106 full-time members. The student-faculty ratio is 9:1.

Students of Bard

The student body totals 1,427, of whom 1,233 are undergraduates. 58.2% are women and 41.8% are men. Students come from 50 states and territories and 47 other countries. 28% are from New York. 5.6% are international students. 2.2% are African American, 0.3% American Indian, 3.2% Asian American, and 3.9% Hispanic American. 83% returned for their sophomore year.

Facilities and Resources

Student rooms are linked to a campus network. 135 **computers** are available on campus that provide access to the Internet. The 4 **libraries** have 260,000 books and 1,075 subscriptions.

Campus Life

There are 60 active organizations on campus, including a drama/theater group, newspaper, radio station, and choral group. No national or local **fraternities** or **sororities**.

Bard is a member of the NCAA (Division III) and NAIA. **Intercollegiate sports** include basketball, cross-country running, fencing, rugby, soccer, squash, tennis, volleyball.

Campus Safety

Student safety services include late-night transport/escort service, 24-hour emergency telephone alarm devices, 24-hour patrols by trained security personnel, student patrols, and electronically operated dormitory entrances.

Applying

Bard requires an essay, a high school transcript, and 3 recommendations, and in some cases an interview. It recommends SAT I or ACT, an interview, and a minimum high school GPA of 3.0. Application deadline: 1/15; 3/15 for financial aid, with a 2/15 priority date. Early and deferred admission are possible.

Getting in Last Year
2,508 applied
47% were accepted
335 enrolled (28%)
60% from top tenth of their h.s. class
3.50 average high school GPA
74% had SAT verbal scores over 600
58% had SAT math scores over 600
92% had ACT scores over 24
30% had SAT verbal scores over 700
17% had SAT math scores over 700
14% had ACT scores over 30
1 National Merit Scholar
12 class presidents
13 valedictorians

Graduation and After
51% graduated in 4 years
12% graduated in 5 years
3% graduated in 6 years
55% pursued further study (43% arts and sciences, 5% law, 3% business)
198 organizations recruited on campus
1 Fulbright scholar

Financial Matters
$24,000 tuition and fees (1999–2000)
$7220 room and board
85% average percent of need met
$19,325 average financial aid amount received per undergraduate (1999–2000 estimated)

BARNARD COLLEGE
URBAN SETTING ■ PRIVATE ■ INDEPENDENT ■ WOMEN ONLY
NEW YORK, NEW YORK

Web site: www.barnard.edu
Contact: Ms. Doris Davis, Dean of Admissions, 3009 Broadway, New York, NY 10027
Telephone: 212-854-2014 **Fax:** 212-854-6220
E-mail: admissions@barnard.edu

Barnard is a small, select liberal arts college for women. Its superb faculty, about half of whom are women, are leading scholars as well as accessible and dedicated teachers. Barnard's unique affiliation with Columbia University, which is just across the street, gives students a vast selection of courses and extracurricular activities, Division I athletic competition, and a fully coeducational social life. Adding immeasurably to a Barnard education is its location in New York City, where students have access to thousands of internships and unparalleled cultural, intellectual, and social resources.

Getting in Last Year
3,883 applied
37% were accepted
558 enrolled (39%)
74% from top tenth of their h.s. class
3.81 average high school GPA
86% had SAT verbal scores over 600
84% had SAT math scores over 600
93% had ACT scores over 24
32% had SAT verbal scores over 700
20% had SAT math scores over 700
30% had ACT scores over 30
2 National Merit Scholars

Graduation and After
66% graduated in 4 years
11% graduated in 5 years
5% graduated in 6 years
22% pursued further study (6% arts and sciences, 5% medicine, 4% law)
67% had job offers within 6 months
106 organizations recruited on campus
1 Fulbright scholar

Financial Matters
$22,316 tuition and fees (1999–2000)
$9084 room and board
100% average percent of need met
$21,706 average financial aid amount received per undergraduate (1999–2000)

Academics
Barnard awards bachelor's **degrees**. Challenging opportunities include advanced placement, accelerated degree programs, student-designed majors, an honors program, double majors, independent study, a senior project, Phi Beta Kappa, and Sigma Xi. Special programs include internships, off-campus study, and study-abroad.

The most frequently chosen fields are social sciences and history, English, and psychology. A complete listing of majors at Barnard appears in the Majors Index beginning on page 432.

The **faculty** at Barnard has 178 full-time members, 93% with terminal degrees. The student-faculty ratio is 11:1.

Students of Barnard
The student body is made up of 2,318 undergraduates. Students come from 49 states and territories and 25 other countries. 37% are from New York. 3% are international students. 4.3% are African American, 0.3% American Indian, 22.9% Asian American, and 5.8% Hispanic American. 95% returned for their sophomore year.

Facilities and Resources
Student rooms are linked to a campus network. 150 **computers** are available on campus that provide access to the Internet. The **library** has 198,020 books and 900 subscriptions.

Campus Life
There are 100 active organizations on campus, including a drama/theater group, newspaper, radio station, television station, choral group, and marching band. No national or local **sororities**.

Barnard is a member of the NCAA (Division I). **Intercollegiate sports** include archery, basketball, crew, cross-country running, equestrian sports, fencing, field hockey, ice hockey, lacrosse, rugby, sailing, skiing (downhill), soccer, softball, squash, swimming, tennis, track and field, volleyball.

Campus Safety
Student safety services include 4 permanent security posts, late-night transport/escort service, 24-hour emergency telephone alarm devices, and 24-hour patrols by trained security personnel.

Applying
Barnard requires an essay, SAT II: Writing Test, SAT I and SAT II or ACT, a high school transcript, and 3 recommendations. It recommends an interview. Application deadline: 1/15; 2/1 for financial aid. Early and deferred admission are possible.

BARTLESVILLE WESLEYAN COLLEGE

SMALL-TOWN SETTING ■ PRIVATE ■ INDEPENDENT RELIGIOUS ■ COED
BARTLESVILLE, OKLAHOMA

Web site: www.bwc.edu
Contact: Mr. Marty Carver, Director of Enrollment Services, 2201 Silver
  Lake Road, Bartlesville, OK 74006-6299
Telephone: 918-335-6219 or toll-free 800-468-6292 (in-state) **Fax:**
  918-335-6229
E-mail: admissions@bwc.edu

eAPPLY

Academics

BWC awards associate and bachelor's **degrees**. Challenging opportunities include
advanced placement, student-designed majors, independent study, and a senior project.
Special programs include cooperative education, internships, summer session for credit,
and off-campus study. A complete listing of majors at BWC appears in the Majors Index
beginning on page 432.

Students of BWC

The student body is made up of 603 undergraduates. Students come from 28 states and
territories and 7 other countries. 54% are from Oklahoma. 70% returned for their
sophomore year.

Facilities and Resources

Student rooms are linked to a campus network. 30 **computers** are available on campus
that provide access to the Internet. The **library** has 124,722 books and 300 subscriptions.

Campus Life

There are 10 active organizations on campus, including a newspaper and choral group.
No national or local **fraternities** or **sororities**.

  BWC is a member of the NAIA and NCCAA. **Intercollegiate sports** (some offering
scholarships) include baseball (m), basketball, golf (m), soccer, softball (w), volleyball (w).

Campus Safety

Student safety services include 24-hour emergency telephone alarm devices, 24-hour
patrols by trained security personnel, and electronically operated dormitory entrances.

Applying

BWC requires SAT I or ACT, a high school transcript, and recommendations. It recommends a minimum high school GPA of 2.0. Application deadline: rolling admissions;
3/31 priority date for financial aid. Early and deferred admission are possible.

Getting in Last Year
489 applied
66% were accepted
30% from top tenth of their h.s. class
3.59 average high school GPA
32% had SAT verbal scores over 600
19% had SAT math scores over 600
38% had ACT scores over 24
2% had SAT verbal scores over 700
4% had SAT math scores over 700
3% had ACT scores over 30
1 National Merit Scholar

Graduation and After
**10% pursued further study (6% theology, 2%
  arts and sciences, 1% business)**

Financial Matters
$9200 tuition and fees (2000–2001)
$4600 room and board
55% average percent of need met
**$6466 average financial aid amount received
  per undergraduate (1999–2000 estimated)**

BATES COLLEGE
SUBURBAN SETTING ■ PRIVATE ■ INDEPENDENT ■ COED
LEWISTON, MAINE

Web site: www.bates.edu
Contact: Mr. Wylie L. Mitchell, Dean of Admissions, 23 Campus Avenue, Lewiston, ME 04240-6028
Telephone: 207-786-6000 **Fax:** 207-786-6025
E-mail: admissions@bates.edu

Getting in Last Year
3,860 applied
33% were accepted
479 enrolled (38%)
62% from top tenth of their h.s. class
90% had SAT verbal scores over 600
92% had SAT math scores over 600
30% had SAT verbal scores over 700
29% had SAT math scores over 700

Graduation and After
79% graduated in 4 years
4% graduated in 5 years
1% graduated in 6 years
17% pursued further study
75 organizations recruited on campus

Financial Matters
$31,400 comprehensive fee (1999–2000)
100% average percent of need met
$20,487 average financial aid amount received per undergraduate (1999–2000 estimated)

Academics
Bates awards bachelor's **degrees**. Challenging opportunities include advanced placement, accelerated degree programs, student-designed majors, an honors program, double majors, independent study, a senior project, and Phi Beta Kappa. Special programs include internships, off-campus study, and study-abroad.

The most frequently chosen fields are social sciences and history, biological/life sciences, and psychology. A complete listing of majors at Bates appears in the Majors Index beginning on page 432.

The **faculty** at Bates has 165 full-time members. The student-faculty ratio is 10:1.

Students of Bates
The student body is made up of 1,706 undergraduates. Students come from 48 states and territories and 46 other countries. 11% are from Maine. 4.3% are international students. 2.2% are African American, 0.1% American Indian, 4% Asian American, and 1.4% Hispanic American. 92% returned for their sophomore year.

Facilities and Resources
Student rooms are linked to a campus network. 758 **computers** are available on campus that provide access to the Internet. The **library** has 547,220 books and 1,715 subscriptions.

Campus Life
There are 71 active organizations on campus, including a drama/theater group, newspaper, radio station, television station, and choral group. No national or local **fraternities** or **sororities**.

Bates is a member of the NCAA (Division III). **Intercollegiate sports** include badminton, baseball (m), basketball, crew, cross-country running, equestrian sports, fencing, field hockey (w), football (m), golf, ice hockey, lacrosse, rugby, sailing, skiing (cross-country), skiing (downhill), soccer, softball (w), squash, swimming, tennis, track and field, volleyball, water polo.

Campus Safety
Student safety services include late-night transport/escort service, 24-hour emergency telephone alarm devices, 24-hour patrols by trained security personnel, student patrols, and electronically operated dormitory entrances.

Applying
Bates requires an essay, a high school transcript, and 3 recommendations. It recommends an interview. Application deadline: 1/15; 1/15 for financial aid. Early and deferred admission are possible.

BAYLOR UNIVERSITY

URBAN SETTING ■ PRIVATE ■ INDEPENDENT RELIGIOUS ■ COED
WACO, TEXAS

Web site: www.baylor.edu
Contact: Ms. Teri Tippit, Director of Recruitment, PO Box 97056, Waco, TX
76798-7056
Telephone: 254-710-3435 or toll-free 800-BAYLOR U **Fax:** 254-710-3436
E-mail: admissions_office@baylor.edu

Academics

Baylor awards bachelor's, master's, doctoral, and first-professional **degrees**. Challenging opportunities include advanced placement, accelerated degree programs, student-designed majors, an honors program, double majors, a senior project, Phi Beta Kappa, and Sigma Xi. Special programs include internships, summer session for credit, study-abroad, and Air Force ROTC. A complete listing of majors at Baylor appears in the Majors Index beginning on page 432.

The **faculty** at Baylor has 650 full-time members, 78% with terminal degrees. The student-faculty ratio is 18:1.

Students of Baylor

The student body totals 13,334, of whom 11,472 are undergraduates. 57.9% are women and 42.1% are men. Students come from 50 states and territories and 75 other countries. 82% are from Texas. 1.7% are international students. 5.8% are African American, 0.5% American Indian, 5.3% Asian American, and 7.5% Hispanic American. 82% returned for their sophomore year.

Facilities and Resources

Student rooms are linked to a campus network. 1,000 **computers** are available on campus that provide access to the Internet. The 9 **libraries** have 1,500,000 books and 20,555 subscriptions.

Campus Life

There are 269 active organizations on campus, including a drama/theater group, newspaper, radio station, television station, choral group, and marching band. 20% of eligible men and 30% of eligible women are members of national **fraternities**, national **sororities**, local fraternities, and local sororities.

Baylor is a member of the NCAA (Division I). **Intercollegiate sports** (some offering scholarships) include badminton, baseball (m), basketball, crew, cross-country running, fencing, football (m), golf, lacrosse, rugby, sailing, soccer, softball (w), tennis, track and field, volleyball.

Campus Safety

Student safety services include bicycle patrols, late-night transport/escort service, 24-hour emergency telephone alarm devices, 24-hour patrols by trained security personnel, and electronically operated dormitory entrances.

Applying

Baylor requires an essay, SAT I or ACT, and a high school transcript. It recommends an interview. Application deadline: rolling admissions; 3/1 priority date for financial aid. Early and deferred admission are possible.

As a selective Baptist university, Baylor is committed to educating the whole student, mind, body, and spirit. Each student enjoys the individual attention of a dedicated faculty, the options afforded by a comprehensive range of challenging academic programs, and a supporting environment that fosters intellectual, social, and spiritual growth. Baylor's strong core curriculum, based on the liberal arts, crosses all majors and emphasizes analytical skills and ethical practices. With competitive financial assistance packages, Baylor strives to help families from all financial backgrounds achieve their dreams of the best education possible. Students should visit Baylor and discover why it is frequently cited as a best value.

Getting in Last Year
7,209 applied
87% were accepted
2,772 enrolled (44%)
38% from top tenth of their h.s. class
39% had SAT verbal scores over 600
46% had SAT math scores over 600
54% had ACT scores over 24
9% had SAT verbal scores over 700
9% had SAT math scores over 700
9% had ACT scores over 30
51 National Merit Scholars

Graduation and After
39% graduated in 4 years
24% graduated in 5 years
4% graduated in 6 years
265 organizations recruited on campus
1 Fulbright scholar

Financial Matters
$11,938 tuition and fees (2000–2001)
$5238 room and board
69% average percent of need met
$8805 average financial aid amount received
per undergraduate (1999–2000)

eAPPLY

Getting in Last Year
887 applied
95% were accepted
329 enrolled (39%)
28% from top tenth of their h.s. class
3.4 average high school GPA
39% had SAT verbal scores over 600
43% had SAT math scores over 600
46% had ACT scores over 24
7% had SAT verbal scores over 700
8% had SAT math scores over 700
5% had ACT scores over 30
6 National Merit Scholars
1 class president
16 valedictorians

Graduation and After
35% graduated in 4 years
17% graduated in 5 years
1% graduated in 6 years
Graduates pursuing further study: 5% arts and
    sciences, 2% business, 2% law
75% had job offers within 6 months
42 organizations recruited on campus

Financial Matters
$12,650 tuition and fees (1999–2000)
$3940 room and board

BELLARMINE COLLEGE

SUBURBAN SETTING ■ PRIVATE ■ INDEPENDENT RELIGIOUS ■ COED
LOUISVILLE, KENTUCKY

Web site: www.bellarmine.edu
Contact: Mr. Timothy A. Sturgeon, Dean of Admission, 2001 Newburg Road,
    Louisville, KY 40205-0671
Telephone: 502-452-8131 or toll-free 800-274-4723 ext. 8131 **Fax:**
    502-452-8002
E-mail: admissions@bellarmine.edu

Academics
Bellarmine awards bachelor's and master's **degrees**. Challenging opportunities include advanced placement, accelerated degree programs, student-designed majors, an honors program, double majors, independent study, and a senior project. Special programs include internships, summer session for credit, off-campus study, study-abroad, and Army and Air Force ROTC.

The most frequently chosen fields are business/marketing, health professions and related sciences, and social sciences and history. A complete listing of majors at Bellarmine appears in the Majors Index beginning on page 432.

The **faculty** at Bellarmine has 101 full-time members, 79% with terminal degrees. The student-faculty ratio is 14:1.

Students of Bellarmine
The student body totals 2,880, of whom 2,373 are undergraduates. 64.1% are women and 35.9% are men. Students come from 19 states and territories and 12 other countries. 69% are from Kentucky. 0.8% are international students. 3.4% are African American, 0.2% American Indian, 1.3% Asian American, and 1.3% Hispanic American. 83% returned for their sophomore year.

Facilities and Resources
Student rooms are linked to a campus network. 160 **computers** are available on campus that provide access to the Internet. The **library** has 97,737 books and 401 subscriptions.

Campus Life
There are 45 active organizations on campus, including a drama/theater group, newspaper, and choral group. 3% of eligible men and 3% of eligible women are members of national **fraternities** and national **sororities**.

Bellarmine is a member of the NCAA (Division II). **Intercollegiate sports** (some offering scholarships) include baseball (m), basketball, cross-country running, field hockey (w), golf, soccer, softball (w), tennis, track and field, volleyball (w).

Campus Safety
Student safety services include 24-hour locked residence hall entrances, security cameras, late-night transport/escort service, 24-hour emergency telephone alarm devices, and 24-hour patrols by trained security personnel.

Applying
Bellarmine requires an essay, SAT I or ACT, a high school transcript, recommendations, and a minimum high school GPA of 2.5. It recommends an interview. Application deadline: 8/15; 3/1 priority date for financial aid. Early and deferred admission are possible.

BELMONT UNIVERSITY

URBAN SETTING ■ PRIVATE ■ INDEPENDENT RELIGIOUS ■ COED
NASHVILLE, TENNESSEE

Web site: www.belmont.edu
Contact: Dr. Kathryn Baugher, Dean of Enrollment Services, 1900 Belmont
Boulevard, Nashville, TN 37212
Telephone: 615-460-6785 or toll-free 800-56E-NROL **Fax:** 615-460-5434
E-mail: buadmission@mail.belmont.edu

  eAPPLY

Academics

Belmont awards bachelor's and master's **degrees** and post-bachelor's certificates. Challenging opportunities include advanced placement, accelerated degree programs, student-designed majors, an honors program, double majors, independent study, and a senior project. Special programs include cooperative education, internships, summer session for credit, study-abroad, and Army ROTC.

The most frequently chosen fields are visual/performing arts, business/marketing, and health professions and related sciences. A complete listing of majors at Belmont appears in the Majors Index beginning on page 432.

The **faculty** at Belmont has 195 full-time members. The student-faculty ratio is 10:1.

Students of Belmont

The student body totals 3,026, of whom 2,521 are undergraduates. 61.2% are women and 38.8% are men. Students come from 48 states and territories and 12 other countries. 63% are from Tennessee. 1.3% are international students. 3.1% are African American, 0.5% American Indian, 1.5% Asian American, and 1.2% Hispanic American. 76% returned for their sophomore year.

Facilities and Resources

Student rooms are linked to a campus network. 250 **computers** are available on campus that provide access to the Internet. The **library** has 166,194 books and 1,381 subscriptions.

Campus Life

There are 52 active organizations on campus, including a drama/theater group, newspaper, radio station, television station, and choral group. 6% of eligible men and 8% of eligible women are members of national **fraternities**, national **sororities**, local fraternities, and local sororities.

Belmont is a member of the NCAA (Division I). **Intercollegiate sports** (some offering scholarships) include baseball (m), basketball, cross-country running, golf, soccer, softball (w), tennis, track and field, volleyball (w).

Campus Safety

Student safety services include late-night transport/escort service, 24-hour emergency telephone alarm devices, 24-hour patrols by trained security personnel, and electronically operated dormitory entrances.

Applying

Belmont requires an essay, SAT I or ACT, a high school transcript, recommendations, resume of activities, and a minimum high school GPA of 3.0, and in some cases an interview. Application deadline: 8/1; 3/1 priority date for financial aid. Deferred admission is possible.

Belmont University brings together the best of liberal arts and professional education, providing an academically challenging education in a Christian community. Located in Nashville on the former Belle Monte estate, Belmont offers a campus rich in heritage that also has the conveniences and advantages of one of the fastest-growing cities in the nation. Belmont students benefit from an education marked by personal attention from professors; special academic opportunities, such as the Belmont University Research Symposium, studies abroad, and the honors program; and outstanding internship opportunities in many areas, including business, health care, education, communication arts, and the music industry.

Getting in Last Year
1,130 applied
78% were accepted
507 enrolled (57%)
26% from top tenth of their h.s. class
3.43 average high school GPA
35% had SAT verbal scores over 600
32% had SAT math scores over 600
60% had ACT scores over 24
3% had SAT verbal scores over 700
4% had SAT math scores over 700
8% had ACT scores over 30
18 valedictorians

Graduation and After
33% graduated in 4 years
10% graduated in 5 years
20% pursued further study
160 organizations recruited on campus

Financial Matters
$11,600 tuition and fees (1999–2000)
$5000 room and board
86% average percent of need met
$11,764 average financial aid amount received
per undergraduate (1999–2000 estimated)

BELOIT COLLEGE

SMALL-TOWN SETTING ■ PRIVATE ■ INDEPENDENT ■ COED
BELOIT, WISCONSIN

Web site: www.beloit.edu
Contact: Mr. James Zielinski, Director of Admissions, 700 College Street,
Beloit, WI 53511-5596
Telephone: 608-363-2500 or toll-free 800-356-0751 **Fax:** 608-363-2075
E-mail: admiss@beloit.edu

Academics

Beloit awards bachelor's **degrees**. Challenging opportunities include advanced placement, student-designed majors, double majors, independent study, a senior project, and Phi Beta Kappa. Special programs include internships, summer session for credit, off-campus study, and study-abroad.

The most frequently chosen fields are social sciences and history, visual/performing arts, and English. A complete listing of majors at Beloit appears in the Majors Index beginning on page 432.

The **faculty** at Beloit has 91 full-time members, 97% with terminal degrees. The student-faculty ratio is 11:1.

Students of Beloit

The student body is made up of 1,223 undergraduates. 58.3% are women and 41.7% are men. Students come from 49 states and territories and 52 other countries. 22% are from Wisconsin. 10.7% are international students. 4.5% are African American, 0.4% American Indian, 3.5% Asian American, and 3.9% Hispanic American. 93% returned for their sophomore year.

Facilities and Resources

Student rooms are linked to a campus network. 152 **computers** are available on campus that provide access to the Internet. The **library** has 243,779 books and 980 subscriptions.

Campus Life

There are 100 active organizations on campus, including a drama/theater group, newspaper, radio station, television station, and choral group. 15% of eligible men and 5% of eligible women are members of national **fraternities** and local **sororities**.

Beloit is a member of the NCAA (Division III). **Intercollegiate sports** include baseball (m), basketball, cross-country running, fencing, football (m), golf (m), ice hockey (m), lacrosse, soccer, softball (w), swimming, tennis, track and field, volleyball (w).

Campus Safety

Student safety services include late-night transport/escort service, 24-hour emergency telephone alarm devices, and 24-hour patrols by trained security personnel.

Applying

Beloit requires an essay, SAT I or ACT, a high school transcript, and 1 recommendation, and in some cases an interview. It recommends an interview. Application deadline: rolling admissions; 2/1 for financial aid. Early and deferred admission are possible.

Getting in Last Year
1,495 applied
67% were accepted
302 enrolled (30%)
40% from top tenth of their h.s. class
3.5 average high school GPA
67% had SAT verbal scores over 600
50% had SAT math scores over 600
75% had ACT scores over 24
21% had SAT verbal scores over 700
11% had SAT math scores over 700
25% had ACT scores over 30
4 National Merit Scholars
3 class presidents
12 valedictorians

Graduation and After
55% graduated in 4 years
10% graduated in 5 years
2% graduated in 6 years
30% pursued further study (20% arts and sciences, 5% medicine, 3% business)
70% had job offers within 6 months

Financial Matters
$20,440 tuition and fees (1999–2000)
$4628 room and board
100% average percent of need met
$16,256 average financial aid amount received per undergraduate (1998–99)

BENNINGTON COLLEGE

SMALL-TOWN SETTING ■ PRIVATE ■ INDEPENDENT ■ COED
BENNINGTON, VERMONT

Web site: www.bennington.edu
Contact: Mr. Deane Bogardus, Director of Admissions, Bennington, VT
  05201-9993
Telephone: 802-440-4312 or toll-free 800-833-6845
E-mail: admissions@bennington.edu

Academics

Bennington awards bachelor's and master's **degrees** and post-bachelor's certificates. Challenging opportunities include student-designed majors, independent study, and a senior project. Special programs include internships, off-campus study, and study-abroad.

The most frequently chosen fields are visual/performing arts, interdisciplinary studies, and English. A complete listing of majors at Bennington appears in the Majors Index beginning on page 432.

The **faculty** at Bennington has 58 full-time members, 81% with terminal degrees. The student-faculty ratio is 7:1.

Students of Bennington

The student body totals 571, of whom 447 are undergraduates. 70% are women and 30% are men. Students come from 37 states and territories and 10 other countries. 8% are from Vermont. 8.9% are international students. 1.6% are African American, 0.2% American Indian, 1.6% Asian American, and 1.6% Hispanic American. 78% returned for their sophomore year.

Facilities and Resources

Student rooms are linked to a campus network. 60 **computers** are available on campus that provide access to the Internet. The 3 **libraries** have 119,804 books and 600 subscriptions.

Campus Life

There are 20 active organizations on campus, including a drama/theater group, newspaper, radio station, and choral group. No national or local **fraternities** or **sororities**.

Intercollegiate sports include soccer.

Campus Safety

Student safety services include late-night transport/escort service, 24-hour emergency telephone alarm devices, and 24-hour patrols by trained security personnel.

Applying

Bennington requires an essay, SAT I or ACT, a high school transcript, and 2 recommendations. It recommends an interview. Application deadline: 1/1; 3/1 priority date for financial aid. Early and deferred admission are possible.

A Bennington education imparts more than a body of knowledge or an excellent liberal arts education. It imparts an approach to life—the belief that the way to get things done is to do them. The College was founded more than 6 decades ago on the premise that people learn best by pursuing that which most interests them and by working closely with teachers who are themselves actively engaged in their fields. Self-directedness is central; the power of the Bennington experience has everything to do with the role students have in shaping their education, and the result is lifelong confidence, adaptability, and independence of mind.

Getting in Last Year
524 applied
83% were accepted
142 enrolled (33%)
34% from top tenth of their h.s. class
3.5 average high school GPA
66% had SAT verbal scores over 600
31% had SAT math scores over 600
10% had SAT verbal scores over 700
4% had SAT math scores over 700

Graduation and After
35% graduated in 4 years
6% graduated in 5 years
2% graduated in 6 years

Financial Matters
$22,500 tuition and fees (1999–2000)
$5650 room and board
77% average percent of need met
$17,610 average financial aid amount received
  per undergraduate (1999–2000)

BEREA COLLEGE

SMALL-TOWN SETTING ■ PRIVATE ■ INDEPENDENT ■ COED
BEREA, KENTUCKY

Web site: www.berea.edu
Contact: Mr. Joseph Bagnoli, Director of Admissions, CPO 2220, Berea, KY 40404
Telephone: 606-986-9341 ext. 5083 or toll-free 800-326-5948
E-mail: admissions@berea.edu

Getting in Last Year
1,751 applied
34% were accepted
423 enrolled (71%)
58% from top tenth of their h.s. class
3.47 average high school GPA
26% had SAT verbal scores over 600
20% had SAT math scores over 600
46% had ACT scores over 24
3% had SAT verbal scores over 700
2% had SAT math scores over 700
3% had ACT scores over 30

Graduation and After
38% graduated in 4 years
12% graduated in 5 years
2% graduated in 6 years
75 organizations recruited on campus

Financial Matters
$199 fees (1999–2000)
$3686 room and board
89% average percent of need met
$19,042 average financial aid amount received per undergraduate (1999–2000)

Academics
Berea awards bachelor's **degrees**. Challenging opportunities include advanced placement, student-designed majors, double majors, independent study, and a senior project. Special programs include internships, summer session for credit, off-campus study, and study-abroad.

The most frequently chosen fields are business/marketing, social sciences and history, and home economics/vocational home economics. A complete listing of majors at Berea appears in the Majors Index beginning on page 432.

The **faculty** at Berea has 122 full-time members, 91% with terminal degrees. The student-faculty ratio is 11:1.

Students of Berea
The student body is made up of 1,522 undergraduates. 57% are women and 43% are men. Students come from 42 states and territories. 48% are from Kentucky. 11.9% are African American, 0.3% American Indian, 1.6% Asian American, and 0.7% Hispanic American. 79% returned for their sophomore year.

Facilities and Resources
145 **computers** are available on campus that provide access to the Internet. The 3 **libraries** have 322,626 books and 1,662 subscriptions.

Campus Life
There are 93 active organizations on campus, including a drama/theater group, newspaper, and choral group. No national or local **fraternities** or **sororities**.

Berea is a member of the NAIA. **Intercollegiate sports** include baseball (m), basketball, cross-country running, golf (m), soccer, softball (w), swimming, tennis, track and field, volleyball (w).

Campus Safety
Student safety services include crime prevention programs, late-night transport/escort service, 24-hour emergency telephone alarm devices, 24-hour patrols by trained security personnel, and electronically operated dormitory entrances.

Applying
Berea requires an essay, SAT I or ACT, a high school transcript, and financial aid application, and in some cases an interview. It recommends 2 recommendations. Application deadline: 4/15; 2/1 priority date for financial aid. Early admission is possible.

BERRY COLLEGE

SMALL-TOWN SETTING ■ PRIVATE ■ INDEPENDENT RELIGIOUS ■ COED
MOUNT BERRY, GEORGIA

Web site: www.berry.edu
Contact: Mr. George Gaddie, Dean of Admissions, PO Box 490159, Mount
    Berry, GA 30149-0159
Telephone: 706-236-2215 or toll-free 800-237-7942 **Fax:** 706-290-2178
E-mail: admissions@berry.edu

  eAPPLY

Academics
Berry awards bachelor's and master's **degrees**. Challenging opportunities include
advanced placement, accelerated degree programs, student-designed majors, an honors
program, double majors, independent study, and a senior project. Special programs
include cooperative education, internships, summer session for credit, and study-abroad.
A complete listing of majors at Berry appears in the Majors Index beginning on page
432.
    The student-faculty ratio is 12:1.

Students of Berry
The student body totals 2,086, of whom 1,896 are undergraduates. 61.8% are women
and 38.2% are men. Students come from 30 states and territories and 20 other countries.
84% are from Georgia. 1.1% are international students. 1.4% are African American,
0.4% American Indian, 0.9% Asian American, and 1.4% Hispanic American. 80%
returned for their sophomore year.

Facilities and Resources
Student rooms are linked to a campus network. 100 **computers** are available on campus
that provide access to the Internet. The 2 **libraries** have 255,284 books and 1,418
subscriptions.

Campus Life
There are 71 active organizations on campus, including a drama/theater group,
newspaper, television station, and choral group. No national or local **fraternities** or
sororities.
    Berry is a member of the NAIA. **Intercollegiate sports** (some offering scholarships)
include baseball (m), basketball, crew, cross-country running, equestrian sports, golf (m),
rugby (m), soccer, tennis, track and field.

Campus Safety
Student safety services include late-night transport/escort service, 24-hour emergency
telephone alarm devices, and 24-hour patrols by trained security personnel.

Applying
Berry requires SAT I or ACT and a high school transcript. Application deadline: 7/28;
4/1 priority date for financial aid. Early and deferred admission are possible.

Berry College is an independent, coeducational college with fully accredited arts, sciences, and professional programs as well as specialized graduate programs in education and business administration. The College serves humanity by inspiring and educating students regardless of their economic status and emphasizes a comprehensive educational program committed to high academic standards, Christian values, and practical work experiences. The campus is an unusually beautiful environment with approximately 28,000 acres of land. Fields, forests, lakes, and mountains provide scenic beauty in a protected natural setting. The College is located in Rome, Georgia, 65 miles northwest of Atlanta and 65 miles south of Chattanooga.

Getting in Last Year
1,953 applied
68% were accepted
378 enrolled (29%)
3.64 average high school GPA
48% had SAT verbal scores over 600
46% had SAT math scores over 600
64% had ACT scores over 24
9% had SAT verbal scores over 700
7% had SAT math scores over 700
11% had ACT scores over 30
5 National Merit Scholars
12 valedictorians

Graduation and After
31% pursued further study
99% had job offers within 6 months
103 organizations recruited on campus

Financial Matters
$11,550 tuition and fees (1999–2000)
$5272 room and board
96% average percent of need met
$11,100 average financial aid amount received
    per undergraduate (1999–2000 estimated)

BETHEL COLLEGE
SUBURBAN SETTING ■ PRIVATE ■ INDEPENDENT RELIGIOUS ■ COED
ST. PAUL, MINNESOTA

Web site: www.bethel.edu
Contact: Mr. John C. Lassen, Director of Admissions, 3900 Bethel Drive, St. Paul, MN 55112
Telephone: 651-638-6436 or toll-free 800-255-8706 ext. 6242 **Fax:** 651-635-1490
E-mail: bcoll-admit@bethel.edu

Bethel College provides academic excellence in a dynamic Christian environment. *U.S. News & World Report* has recognized Bethel as eighth overall among liberal arts colleges in the Midwest. What makes Bethel outstanding are its excellent students, expert faculty, and dedicated staff. Bethel is committed to providing a high-quality liberal arts education to prepare tomorrow's leaders to make a difference in their community, the church, and the world.

Getting in Last Year
1,526 applied
81% were accepted
519 enrolled (42%)
30% from top tenth of their h.s. class
44% had SAT verbal scores over 600
39% had SAT math scores over 600
48% had ACT scores over 24
6% had SAT verbal scores over 700
8% had SAT math scores over 700
7% had ACT scores over 30

Graduation and After
65% graduated in 4 years
6% graduated in 5 years
3% graduated in 6 years

Financial Matters
$15,335 tuition and fees (1999–2000)
$5410 room and board
83% average percent of need met
$12,726 average financial aid amount received per undergraduate (1999–2000 estimated)

Academics
Bethel awards associate, bachelor's, and master's **degrees**. Challenging opportunities include advanced placement, student-designed majors, freshman honors college, an honors program, double majors, independent study, and a senior project. Special programs include internships, summer session for credit, off-campus study, study-abroad, and Army, Navy and Air Force ROTC.

The most frequently chosen fields are health professions and related sciences, business/marketing, and interdisciplinary studies. A complete listing of majors at Bethel appears in the Majors Index beginning on page 432.

The **faculty** at Bethel has 134 full-time members, 72% with terminal degrees. The student-faculty ratio is 16:1.

Students of Bethel
The student body totals 2,983, of whom 2,721 are undergraduates. 63.4% are women and 36.6% are men. Students come from 38 states and territories. 72% are from Minnesota. 1.5% are African American, 0.3% American Indian, 2.7% Asian American, and 1% Hispanic American. 83% returned for their sophomore year.

Facilities and Resources
Student rooms are linked to a campus network. 305 **computers** are available on campus that provide access to the Internet. The **library** has 150,203 books and 3,449 subscriptions.

Campus Life
Active organizations on campus include a drama/theater group, newspaper, radio station, television station, and choral group. No national or local **fraternities** or **sororities**.

Bethel is a member of the NCAA (Division III). **Intercollegiate sports** include baseball (m), basketball, cross-country running, football (m), golf (m), ice hockey, soccer, softball (w), tennis, track and field, volleyball.

Campus Safety
Student safety services include late-night transport/escort service, 24-hour emergency telephone alarm devices, 24-hour patrols by trained security personnel, student patrols, and electronically operated dormitory entrances.

Applying
Bethel requires an essay, SAT I, ACT or PSAT, a high school transcript, and 2 recommendations, and in some cases an interview. It recommends an interview. Application deadline: 6/1; 4/15 priority date for financial aid. Deferred admission is possible.

BIRMINGHAM-SOUTHERN COLLEGE

URBAN SETTING ■ PRIVATE ■ INDEPENDENT RELIGIOUS ■ COED
BIRMINGHAM, ALABAMA

Web site: www.bsc.edu
Contact: Ms. DeeDee Barnes Bruns, Dean of Admission and Financial Aid,
  Box 549008, Birmingham, AL 35254
Telephone: 205-226-4696 or toll-free 800-523-5793 **Fax:** 205-226-3074
E-mail: admissions@bsc.edu

Academics

Birmingham-Southern awards bachelor's and master's **degrees**. Challenging opportunities include advanced placement, accelerated degree programs, student-designed majors, an honors program, double majors, independent study, a senior project, and Phi Beta Kappa. Special programs include internships, summer session for credit, off-campus study, study-abroad, and Army and Air Force ROTC.

The most frequently chosen fields are business/marketing, interdisciplinary studies, and English. A complete listing of majors at Birmingham-Southern appears in the Majors Index beginning on page 432.

The **faculty** at Birmingham-Southern has 95 full-time members, 94% with terminal degrees. The student-faculty ratio is 13:1.

Students of Birmingham-Southern

The student body totals 1,528, of whom 1,453 are undergraduates. 59.9% are women and 40.1% are men. Students come from 28 states and territories. 77% are from Alabama. 0.6% are international students. 11.9% are African American, 0.7% American Indian, 3.8% Asian American, and 0.3% Hispanic American. 80% returned for their sophomore year.

Facilities and Resources

Student rooms are linked to a campus network. 156 **computers** are available on campus that provide access to the Internet. The **library** has 270,296 books and 1,032 subscriptions.

Campus Life

There are 70 active organizations on campus, including a drama/theater group, newspaper, and choral group. 62% of eligible men and 65% of eligible women are members of national **fraternities** and national **sororities**.

Birmingham-Southern is a member of the NCAA (Division I) and NAIA. **Intercollegiate sports** (some offering scholarships) include baseball (m), basketball (m), cross-country running, soccer, tennis, volleyball (w).

Campus Safety

Student safety services include late-night transport/escort service, 24-hour emergency telephone alarm devices, 24-hour patrols by trained security personnel, and electronically operated dormitory entrances.

Applying

Birmingham-Southern requires an essay, SAT I or ACT, a high school transcript, 1 recommendation, and a minimum high school GPA of 2.0, and in some cases an interview. Application deadline: rolling admissions; 3/1 priority date for financial aid. Early and deferred admission are possible.

The College continues to be recognized as one of the nation's leading liberal arts colleges by *National Review, U.S. News & World Report,* and *Money* magazine. Special features of the curriculum are the Interim Term and the Honors Program, as well as undergraduate research, the Leadership Studies Program, service learning opportunities, and international study programs. The Interim Term (January) provides an opportunity for independent study, foreign and domestic trips, and internships with government and private organizations. The College has been recognized for its outstanding track record of graduate admission to medical, law, and graduate schools and job placement.

Getting in Last Year
867 applied
95% were accepted
337 enrolled (41%)
34% from top tenth of their h.s. class
3.22 average high school GPA
51% had SAT verbal scores over 600
50% had SAT math scores over 600
74% had ACT scores over 24
14% had SAT verbal scores over 700
9% had SAT math scores over 700
19% had ACT scores over 30
13 National Merit Scholars
11 valedictorians

Graduation and After
39% pursued further study (13% arts and sciences, 8% business, 7% medicine)
29 organizations recruited on campus

Financial Matters
$15,498 tuition and fees (1999–2000)
$5460 room and board
84% average percent of need met
$8521 average financial aid amount received per undergraduate (1999–2000)

BOSTON COLLEGE

SUBURBAN SETTING ■ PRIVATE ■ INDEPENDENT RELIGIOUS ■ COED
CHESTNUT HILL, MASSACHUSETTS

Web site: www.bc.edu
Contact: Mr. John L. Mahoney Jr., Director of Undergraduate Admission, 140 Commonwealth Avenue, Devlin Hall 208, Chestnut Hill, MA 02167-3809
Telephone: 617-552-3100 or toll-free 800-360-2522 **Fax:** 617-552-0798
E-mail: ugadmis@bc.edu

Boston College is a school with international stature strengthened by the more than 450-year tradition of Jesuit education, which emphasizes rigorous academic development grounded in the arts and sciences and a commitment to the development of the whole person. Through opportunities to participate in honors programs, research with faculty members, independent study, study abroad, and service learning, students are challenged to fulfill their potential as scholars. With artistic, cultural, service, social, religious, and athletic opportunities that abound on campus and throughout the city of Boston, students are challenged to fulfill their potential as caring, thoughtful individuals and future leaders in society.

Getting in Last Year
19,746 applied
35% were accepted
2,284 enrolled (33%)
62% from top tenth of their h.s. class
71% had SAT verbal scores over 600
78% had SAT math scores over 600
18% had SAT verbal scores over 700
24% had SAT math scores over 700
7 National Merit Scholars

Graduation and After
81% graduated in 4 years
3% graduated in 5 years
1% graduated in 6 years
16% pursued further study (5% law, 4% arts and sciences, 4% business)
14 Fulbright scholars

Financial Matters
$22,256 tuition and fees (1999–2000)
$8250 room and board

Academics
BC awards bachelor's, master's, doctoral, and first-professional **degrees** and post-master's certificates (also offers continuing education program with significant enrollment not reflected in profile). Challenging opportunities include advanced placement, accelerated degree programs, student-designed majors, freshman honors college, an honors program, double majors, independent study, and Phi Beta Kappa. Special programs include internships, summer session for credit, off-campus study, study-abroad, and Army, Navy and Air Force ROTC.

The most frequently chosen fields are business/marketing, social sciences and history, and education. A complete listing of majors at BC appears in the Majors Index beginning on page 432.

The **faculty** at BC has 631 full-time members. The student-faculty ratio is 14:1.

Students of BC
The student body totals 13,765, of whom 9,190 are undergraduates. 52.8% are women and 47.2% are men. Students come from 53 states and territories and 63 other countries. 27% are from Massachusetts. 2.4% are international students. 4.4% are African American, 0.4% American Indian, 8.2% Asian American, and 5.2% Hispanic American. 94% returned for their sophomore year.

Facilities and Resources
Student rooms are linked to a campus network. 200 **computers** are available on campus that provide access to the Internet. The 7 **libraries** have 1,590,964 books and 18,300 subscriptions.

Campus Life
There are 140 active organizations on campus, including a drama/theater group, newspaper, radio station, television station, choral group, and marching band. No national or local **fraternities** or **sororities**.

BC is a member of the NCAA (Division I). **Intercollegiate sports** (some offering scholarships) include baseball (m), basketball, crew, cross-country running, fencing, field hockey (w), football (m), golf, ice hockey, lacrosse, rugby, sailing, skiing (downhill), soccer, softball (w), swimming, tennis, track and field, volleyball (w), water polo (m), wrestling (m).

Campus Safety
Student safety services include late-night transport/escort service, 24-hour emergency telephone alarm devices, 24-hour patrols by trained security personnel, and electronically operated dormitory entrances.

Applying
BC requires an essay, SAT II: Writing Test, SAT I and SAT II or ACT, a high school transcript, and 2 recommendations. Application deadline: 1/15; 2/1 priority date for financial aid. Early and deferred admission are possible.

BOSTON UNIVERSITY
URBAN SETTING ■ PRIVATE ■ INDEPENDENT ■ COED
BOSTON, MASSACHUSETTS

Web site: www.bu.edu
Contact: Ms. Kelly A. Walter, Director of Undergraduate Admissions, 121
Bay State Road, Boston, MA 02215
Telephone: 617-353-2300 **Fax:** 617-353-9695
E-mail: admissions@bu.edu

Academics
Boston University awards bachelor's, master's, doctoral, and first-professional **degrees** and post-master's certificates. Challenging opportunities include advanced placement, accelerated degree programs, student-designed majors, an honors program, double majors, independent study, a senior project, Phi Beta Kappa, and Sigma Xi. Special programs include cooperative education, internships, summer session for credit, off-campus study, study-abroad, and Army, Navy and Air Force ROTC.

The most frequently chosen fields are social sciences and history, communications/communication technologies, and business/marketing. A complete listing of majors at Boston University appears in the Majors Index beginning on page 432.

The **faculty** at Boston University has 2,312 full-time members, 83% with terminal degrees. The student-faculty ratio is 13:1.

Students of Boston University
The student body totals 28,487, of whom 18,018 are undergraduates. 58.3% are women and 41.7% are men. Students come from 54 states and territories and 105 other countries. 23% are from Massachusetts. 7.9% are international students. 3.1% are African American, 0.4% American Indian, 12.2% Asian American, and 5.5% Hispanic American. 85% returned for their sophomore year.

Facilities and Resources
Student rooms are linked to a campus network. 500 **computers** are available on campus that provide access to research and educational networks and the Internet. The 19 **libraries** have 2,100,000 books and 28,535 subscriptions.

Campus Life
There are 365 active organizations on campus, including a drama/theater group, newspaper, radio station, television station, choral group, and marching band. 3% of eligible men and 4% of eligible women are members of national **fraternities** and national **sororities**.

Boston University is a member of the NCAA (Division I). **Intercollegiate sports** (some offering scholarships) include badminton, basketball, crew, cross-country running, equestrian sports, fencing, field hockey (w), golf, gymnastics, ice hockey, lacrosse, rugby, sailing, skiing (downhill), soccer, softball, swimming, table tennis, tennis, track and field, volleyball, water polo (w), wrestling (m).

Campus Safety
Student safety services include security personnel at residence hall entrances, self-defense education, well-lit sidewalks, late-night transport/escort service, 24-hour emergency telephone alarm devices, 24-hour patrols by trained security personnel, and electronically operated dormitory entrances.

Applying
Boston University requires an essay, SAT I or ACT, a high school transcript, and 2 recommendations, and in some cases SAT II Subject Tests, SAT II: Writing Test, an interview, and audition, portfolio. It recommends a minimum high school GPA of 3.0. Application deadline: 1/1; 2/15 priority date for financial aid. Early and deferred admission are possible.

Boston University (BU) has 10 undergraduate schools and colleges with more than 130 programs of study in areas as diverse as biochemistry, theater arts, physical therapy, elementary education, and broadcast journalism. Students can customize their own major, either through the Boston University Collaborative Degree Program or the University Professors Program. BU has an international student body, with students from every state and more than 100 countries. In addition, opportunities to study abroad exist on almost every continent, so students can easily add an international component to their education.

Getting in Last Year
28,090 applied
55% were accepted
4,225 enrolled (27%)
55% from top tenth of their h.s. class
3.49 average high school GPA
72% had SAT verbal scores over 600
75% had SAT math scores over 600
93% had ACT scores over 24
19% had SAT verbal scores over 700
20% had SAT math scores over 700
26% had ACT scores over 30
49 National Merit Scholars
139 valedictorians

Graduation and After
55% graduated in 4 years
11% graduated in 5 years
2% graduated in 6 years
25% pursued further study
400 organizations recruited on campus
2 Fulbright scholars

Financial Matters
$24,100 tuition and fees (1999–2000)
$8130 room and board
93% average percent of need met
$21,654 average financial aid amount received per undergraduate (1999–2000)

BOWDOIN COLLEGE

SMALL-TOWN SETTING ■ PRIVATE ■ INDEPENDENT ■ COED
BRUNSWICK, MAINE

Web site: www.bowdoin.edu
Contact: Dr. Richard E. Steele, Dean of Admissions, 5000 College Station,
   Brunswick, ME 04011-8441
Telephone: 207-725-3100 **Fax:** 207-725-3101
E-mail: admissions-lit@polar.bowdoin.edu

Academics

Bowdoin awards bachelor's **degrees**. Challenging opportunities include advanced placement, accelerated degree programs, student-designed majors, double majors,
independent study, and Phi Beta Kappa. Special programs include off-campus study and
study-abroad.

The most frequently chosen fields are social sciences and history, biological/life sciences, and foreign language/literature. A complete listing of majors at Bowdoin appears
in the Majors Index beginning on page 432.

The **faculty** at Bowdoin has 113 full-time members, 97% with terminal degrees. The
student-faculty ratio is 10:1.

Students of Bowdoin

The student body is made up of 1,608 undergraduates. 51.7% are women and 48.3% are
men. Students come from 50 states and territories and 32 other countries. 16% are from
Maine. 2.2% are international students. 2.1% are African American, 0.4% American
Indian, 6.9% Asian American, and 2.8% Hispanic American. 94% returned for their
sophomore year.

Facilities and Resources

Student rooms are linked to a campus network. 210 **computers** are available on campus
that provide access to the Internet. The 6 **libraries** have 888,377 books and 2,272
subscriptions.

Campus Life

There are 87 active organizations on campus, including a drama/theater group,
newspaper, radio station, television station, and choral group. No national or local
fraternities or **sororities**.

Bowdoin is a member of the NCAA (Division III). **Intercollegiate sports** include
baseball (m), basketball, cross-country running, field hockey (w), football (m), golf, ice
hockey, lacrosse, sailing, skiing (cross-country), skiing (downhill), soccer, softball (w),
squash, swimming, tennis, track and field, volleyball (w).

Campus Safety

Student safety services include self-defense education, whistle program, late-night
transport/escort service, 24-hour emergency telephone alarm devices, 24-hour patrols by
trained security personnel, student patrols, and electronically operated dormitory
entrances.

Applying

Bowdoin requires an essay, SAT I, a high school transcript, and 3 recommendations. It
recommends an interview. Application deadline: 1/1; 2/15 priority date for financial aid.
Early and deferred admission are possible.

One current Bowdoin senior comments, "While I was studying off campus, there were so many things I missed about Bowdoin: the remarkable sense of community, the depth and excellence of the faculty, the energy and intelligence of the student body, and the unsurpassable beauty of Maine. . . . At Bowdoin, we are encouraged to be creative, to think for ourselves, and to challenge everything we hear." Bowdoin is just 25 minutes from Portland, Maine's largest city, and 3 miles from the ocean. Because of the location, Bowdoin students have incredible research opportunities as well as an open invitation to explore the outdoors.

Getting in Last Year
3,942 applied
32% were accepted
464 enrolled (37%)
77% from top tenth of their h.s. class
92% had SAT verbal scores over 600
91% had SAT math scores over 600
44% had SAT verbal scores over 700
38% had SAT math scores over 700
18 National Merit Scholars
42 valedictorians

Graduation and After
85% graduated in 4 years
4% graduated in 5 years
1% graduated in 6 years
20% pursued further study (8% arts and sciences, 4% law, 4% medicine)
70% had job offers within 6 months
50 organizations recruited on campus
6 Fulbright scholars

Financial Matters
$24,955 tuition and fees (1999–2000)
$6520 room and board
100% average percent of need met
$19,647 average financial aid amount received
   per undergraduate (1998–99)

BRADLEY UNIVERSITY
URBAN SETTING ■ PRIVATE ■ INDEPENDENT ■ COED
PEORIA, ILLINOIS

Web site: www.bradley.edu
Contact: Ms. Nickie Roberson, Director of Admissions, 1501 West Bradley
Avenue, Peoria, IL 61625-0002
Telephone: 309-677-1000 or toll-free 800-447-6460
E-mail: admissions@bradley.edu

Academics
Bradley awards bachelor's and master's **degrees**. Challenging opportunities include
advanced placement, accelerated degree programs, student-designed majors, an honors
program, double majors, independent study, and a senior project. Special programs
include cooperative education, internships, summer session for credit, off-campus study,
study-abroad, and Army ROTC.

The most frequently chosen fields are business/marketing, engineering/engineering
technologies, and communications/communication technologies. A complete listing of
majors at Bradley appears in the Majors Index beginning on page 432.

The **faculty** at Bradley has 323 full-time members, 83% with terminal degrees. The
student-faculty ratio is 14:1.

Students of Bradley
The student body totals 5,837, of whom 4,961 are undergraduates. 53.9% are women
and 46.1% are men. Students come from 43 states and territories and 35 other countries.
81% are from Illinois. 1.7% are international students. 4.1% are African American, 0.3%
American Indian, 1.8% Asian American, and 1.8% Hispanic American. 84% returned for
their sophomore year.

Facilities and Resources
Student rooms are linked to a campus network. 2,000 **computers** are available on
campus that provide access to the Internet. The **library** has 508,011 books and 2,013
subscriptions.

Campus Life
There are 220 active organizations on campus, including a drama/theater group,
newspaper, radio station, and choral group. 41% of eligible men and 28% of eligible
women are members of national **fraternities** and national **sororities**.

Bradley is a member of the NCAA (Division I). **Intercollegiate sports** (some offering scholarships) include baseball (m), basketball, cross-country running, fencing, golf,
ice hockey (m), soccer, softball (w), swimming, table tennis, tennis, track and field (w),
volleyball (w).

Campus Safety
Student safety services include late-night transport/escort service, 24-hour emergency
telephone alarm devices, 24-hour patrols by trained security personnel, and electronically operated dormitory entrances.

Applying
Bradley requires SAT I or ACT, a high school transcript, and a minimum high school
GPA of 2.0. It recommends an essay, an interview, recommendations, and a minimum
high school GPA of 3.0. Application deadline: rolling admissions; 3/1 priority date for
financial aid. Early and deferred admission are possible.

Getting in Last Year
4,545 applied
81% were accepted
1,079 enrolled (29%)
31% from top tenth of their h.s. class
44% had SAT verbal scores over 600
56% had SAT math scores over 600
70% had ACT scores over 24
10% had SAT verbal scores over 700
12% had SAT math scores over 700
14% had ACT scores over 30
17 National Merit Scholars
50 valedictorians

Graduation and After
Graduates pursuing further study: 5% arts and
sciences, 2% law
97% had job offers within 6 months
324 organizations recruited on campus

Financial Matters
$13,960 tuition and fees (1999–2000)
$5300 room and board
90% average percent of need met
$11,112 average financial aid amount received
per undergraduate (1999–2000)

BRANDEIS UNIVERSITY

SUBURBAN SETTING ■ PRIVATE ■ INDEPENDENT ■ COED
WALTHAM, MASSACHUSETTS

Web site: www.brandeis.edu
Contact: Mr. Michael Kalafatas, Director of Admissions, 415 South Street, Waltham, MA 02254-9110
Telephone: 781-736-3500 or toll-free 800-622-0622 (out-of-state) **Fax:** 781-736-3536
E-mail: sendinfo@brandeis.edu

Academics

Brandeis awards bachelor's, master's, and doctoral **degrees** and post-bachelor's certificates. Challenging opportunities include advanced placement, accelerated degree programs, student-designed majors, an honors program, double majors, independent study, a senior project, and Phi Beta Kappa. Special programs include internships, summer session for credit, off-campus study, study-abroad, and Army and Air Force ROTC.

The most frequently chosen fields are social sciences and history, biological/life sciences, and psychology. A complete listing of majors at Brandeis appears in the Majors Index beginning on page 432.

The **faculty** at Brandeis has 316 full-time members, 98% with terminal degrees. The student-faculty ratio is 9:1.

Students of Brandeis

The student body totals 4,527, of whom 3,112 are undergraduates. 56.3% are women and 43.7% are men. Students come from 45 states and territories and 50 other countries. 41% are from Massachusetts. 5.3% are international students. 1.9% are African American, 0.3% American Indian, 9.7% Asian American, and 2.5% Hispanic American. 92% returned for their sophomore year.

Facilities and Resources

Student rooms are linked to a campus network. 100 **computers** are available on campus that provide access to educational software and the Internet. The 3 **libraries** have 1,060,323 books and 6,000 subscriptions.

Campus Life

There are 211 active organizations on campus, including a drama/theater group, newspaper, radio station, television station, and choral group. No national or local **fraternities** or **sororities**.

Brandeis is a member of the NCAA (Division III). **Intercollegiate sports** include baseball (m), basketball, crew, cross-country running, fencing, field hockey (w), golf (m), ice hockey (m), lacrosse, rugby, sailing, skiing (downhill), soccer, softball (w), swimming, tennis, track and field, volleyball (w).

Campus Safety

Student safety services include late-night transport/escort service, 24-hour emergency telephone alarm devices, 24-hour patrols by trained security personnel, and electronically operated dormitory entrances.

Applying

Brandeis requires an essay, SAT I and SAT II or ACT, a high school transcript, and 2 recommendations. It recommends an interview and a minimum high school GPA of 3.0. Application deadline: 1/31; 1/31 priority date for financial aid. Deferred admission is possible.

Brandeis's top-ranked faculty members focus on teaching undergraduates and are accessible to students during classes, during office hours, and even at home. Students become involved in cutting-edge faculty research at the Volen Center for Complex Systems—studying the brain's cognitive processes—and throughout the University. Brandeis has an ideal location on the commuter rail 9 miles west of Boston, state-of-the-art sports facilities, and internships that complement interests in law, medicine, government, finance, the media, public service, and the arts. Brandeis offers broad, renewable financial aid for domestic and international students, including both need- and merit-based scholarships that cover up to 75% of tuition.

Getting in Last Year
5,792 applied
52% were accepted
794 enrolled (27%)
63% from top tenth of their h.s. class
3.5 average high school GPA
84% had SAT verbal scores over 600
83% had SAT math scores over 600
30% had SAT verbal scores over 700
33% had SAT math scores over 700
23 National Merit Scholars

Graduation and After
74% graduated in 4 years
4% graduated in 5 years
1% graduated in 6 years
Graduates pursuing further study: 8% arts and sciences, 8% law, 3% medicine
200 organizations recruited on campus
1 Fulbright scholar

Financial Matters
$25,174 tuition and fees (1999–2000)
$7040 room and board
92% average percent of need met
$19,589 average financial aid amount received per undergraduate (1999–2000 estimated)

Brigham Young University

Suburban setting ■ Private ■ Independent Religious ■ Coed
Provo, Utah

Web site: www.byu.edu
Contact: Mr. Erlend D. Peterson, Dean of Admissions and Records, Provo, UT 84602-1001
Telephone: 801-378-2539 **Fax:** 801-378-4264
E-mail: admissions@byu.edu

Academics

BYU awards bachelor's, master's, doctoral, and first-professional **degrees**. Challenging opportunities include advanced placement, accelerated degree programs, freshman honors college, an honors program, double majors, independent study, a senior project, and Sigma Xi. Special programs include cooperative education, internships, summer session for credit, off-campus study, study-abroad, and Army and Air Force ROTC.

The most frequently chosen fields are social sciences and history, education, and business/marketing. A complete listing of majors at BYU appears in the Majors Index beginning on page 432.

The **faculty** at BYU has 1,395 full-time members, 81% with terminal degrees. The student-faculty ratio is 20:1.

Students of BYU

The student body totals 32,731, of whom 30,037 are undergraduates. 53.3% are women and 46.7% are men. Students come from 53 states and territories and 107 other countries. 29% are from Utah. 3% are international students. 0.3% are African American, 0.6% American Indian, 2.3% Asian American, and 2.2% Hispanic American. 87% returned for their sophomore year.

Facilities and Resources

Student rooms are linked to a campus network. 1,800 **computers** are available on campus that provide access to the Internet. The 3 **libraries** have 2,500,849 books and 16,029 subscriptions.

Campus Life

There are 140 active organizations on campus, including a drama/theater group, newspaper, radio station, television station, choral group, and marching band. No national or local **fraternities** or **sororities**.

BYU is a member of the NCAA (Division I). **Intercollegiate sports** (some offering scholarships) include baseball (m), basketball, cross-country running, football (m), golf, gymnastics, lacrosse (m), racquetball, rugby (m), soccer, softball (w), swimming, tennis, track and field, volleyball, wrestling (m).

Campus Safety

Student safety services include late-night transport/escort service, 24-hour emergency telephone alarm devices, 24-hour patrols by trained security personnel, and electronically operated dormitory entrances.

Applying

BYU requires an essay, ACT, a high school transcript, an interview, and 1 recommendation. Application deadline: 2/15; 4/15 priority date for financial aid. Early and deferred admission are possible.

Getting in Last Year

8,078 applied
64% were accepted
4,857 enrolled (94%)
54% from top tenth of their h.s. class
3.74 average high school GPA
88% had ACT scores over 24
25% had ACT scores over 30
133 National Merit Scholars

Graduation and After

24% graduated in 4 years
18% graduated in 5 years
26% graduated in 6 years
23% pursued further study
79% had job offers within 6 months
600 organizations recruited on campus
2 Fulbright scholars

Financial Matters

$2830 tuition and fees (1999–2000)
$4454 room and board

BROWN UNIVERSITY

Urban setting ■ Private ■ Independent ■ Coed
Providence, Rhode Island

Web site: www.brown.edu
Contact: Mr. Michael Goldberger, Director of Admission, Box 1876, Providence, RI 02912
Telephone: 401-863-2378 **Fax:** 401-863-9300
E-mail: admission_undergraduate@brown.edu

Brown is a university/college with a renowned faculty that teaches students in both the undergraduate college and the graduate school. The unique, nonrestrictive curriculum allows students freedom in selecting their courses, and they may choose their concentration from 83 areas, complete a double major, or pursue an independent concentration. The 140-acre campus is set in a residential neighborhood (National Historic District) and features state-of-the-art computing facilities and an athletics complex. A real sense of community exists on campus, as every student has an academic adviser, and there are several peer counselors in the residence halls.

Getting in Last Year
14,756 applied
17% were accepted
1,388 enrolled (55%)
86% from top tenth of their h.s. class
86% had SAT verbal scores over 600
92% had SAT math scores over 600
94% had ACT scores over 24
54% had SAT verbal scores over 700
54% had SAT math scores over 700
51% had ACT scores over 30
159 valedictorians

Graduation and After
80% graduated in 4 years
10% graduated in 5 years
3% graduated in 6 years
30% pursued further study (10% arts and sciences, 10% law, 9% medicine)
60% had job offers within 6 months
400 organizations recruited on campus
1 Rhodes, 14 Fulbright scholars

Financial Matters
$25,186 tuition and fees (1999–2000)
$7094 room and board
100% average percent of need met
$20,655 average financial aid amount received per undergraduate (1999–2000)

Academics
Brown awards bachelor's, master's, doctoral, and first-professional **degrees**. Challenging opportunities include advanced placement, accelerated degree programs, student-designed majors, an honors program, double majors, independent study, a senior project, Phi Beta Kappa, and Sigma Xi. Special programs include internships, summer session for credit, off-campus study, study-abroad, and Army ROTC.

The most frequently chosen fields are social sciences and history, liberal arts/general studies, and biological/life sciences. A complete listing of majors at Brown appears in the Majors Index beginning on page 432.

The **faculty** at Brown has 704 full-time members, 98% with terminal degrees. The student-faculty ratio is 8:1.

Students of Brown
The student body totals 7,758, of whom 6,108 are undergraduates. 52.7% are women and 47.3% are men. Students come from 52 states and territories and 72 other countries. 4% are from Rhode Island. 6.6% are international students. 5.9% are African American, 0.4% American Indian, 14.4% Asian American, and 5.8% Hispanic American. 96% returned for their sophomore year.

Facilities and Resources
Student rooms are linked to a campus network. 400 **computers** are available on campus that provide access to the Internet. The 7 **libraries** have 3,000,000 books and 17,000 subscriptions.

Campus Life
There are 240 active organizations on campus, including a drama/theater group, newspaper, radio station, television station, choral group, and marching band. 10% of eligible men and 2% of eligible women are members of national **fraternities**, national **sororities**, and coed fraternity.

Brown is a member of the NCAA (Division I). **Intercollegiate sports** include badminton, baseball (m), basketball, crew, cross-country running, equestrian sports, fencing, field hockey (w), football (m), golf, gymnastics (w), ice hockey, lacrosse, rugby, sailing, skiing (cross-country), skiing (downhill), soccer, softball (w), squash, swimming, tennis, track and field, volleyball, water polo, wrestling (m).

Campus Safety
Student safety services include late-night transport/escort service, 24-hour emergency telephone alarm devices, 24-hour patrols by trained security personnel, and electronically operated dormitory entrances.

Applying
Brown requires an essay, SAT I and SAT II or ACT, a high school transcript, and 2 recommendations. Application deadline: 1/1; 3/1 for financial aid. Early and deferred admission are possible.

BRYN MAWR COLLEGE

SUBURBAN SETTING ■ PRIVATE ■ INDEPENDENT ■ WOMEN ONLY
BRYN MAWR, PENNSYLVANIA

Web site: www.brynmawr.edu
Contact: Ms. Nancy Monnich, Director of Admissions and Financial Aid, 101
   North Merion Avenue, Bryn Mawr, PA 19010
Telephone: 610-526-5152 or toll-free 800-BMC-1885 (out-of-state)
E-mail: admissions@brynmawr.edu

 eAPPLY

Academics

Bryn Mawr awards bachelor's, master's, and doctoral **degrees**. Challenging opportunities include advanced placement, accelerated degree programs, student-designed majors, an honors program, double majors, independent study, and Sigma Xi. Special programs include summer session for credit, off-campus study, study-abroad, and Air Force ROTC.

The most frequently chosen fields are health professions and related sciences, social sciences and history, and biological/life sciences. A complete listing of majors at Bryn Mawr appears in the Majors Index beginning on page 432.

The **faculty** at Bryn Mawr has 126 full-time members, 98% with terminal degrees. The student-faculty ratio is 10:1.

Students of Bryn Mawr

The student body totals 1,779, of whom 1,316 are undergraduates. Students come from 49 states and territories and 48 other countries. 18% are from Pennsylvania. 7.5% are international students. 4.2% are African American, 0.1% American Indian, 16.6% Asian American, and 2.7% Hispanic American. 90% returned for their sophomore year.

Facilities and Resources

Student rooms are linked to a campus network. 175 **computers** are available on campus that provide access to the Internet. The 4 **libraries** have 1,040,758 books and 3,759 subscriptions.

Campus Life

There are 100 active organizations on campus, including a drama/theater group, newspaper, and choral group. No national or local **sororities**.

Bryn Mawr is a member of the NCAA (Division III). **Intercollegiate sports** include badminton, basketball, crew, cross-country running, fencing, field hockey, ice hockey, lacrosse, rugby, soccer, swimming, tennis, track and field, volleyball.

Campus Safety

Student safety services include shuttle bus service, awareness programs, late-night transport/escort service, 24-hour emergency telephone alarm devices, 24-hour patrols by trained security personnel, and electronically operated dormitory entrances.

Applying

Bryn Mawr requires an essay, SAT I and SAT II or ACT, a high school transcript, and 3 recommendations. It recommends an interview. Application deadline: 1/15; 1/15 for financial aid. Early and deferred admission are possible.

Bryn Mawr, founded in 1885 to offer women the challenging education then available only to men, remains a place where women succeed beyond all stereotypical notions of "suitability." Women major in the sciences and mathematics 3 to 5 times more often than the national average (29 times the national average in physics), and Bryn Mawr ranks first in the nation in the percentage of undergraduates who earn a Ph.D. in the humanities and fourth in all fields. Close relationships with faculty members praised for their teaching and known for their scholarship foster an education that is active and enjoyable.

Getting in Last Year
1,596 applied
59% were accepted
321 enrolled (34%)
61% from top tenth of their h.s. class
82% had SAT verbal scores over 600
78% had SAT math scores over 600
89% had ACT scores over 24
35% had SAT verbal scores over 700
18% had SAT math scores over 700
39% had ACT scores over 30
11 National Merit Scholars
20 valedictorians

Graduation and After
73% graduated in 4 years
4% graduated in 5 years
Graduates pursuing further study: 20% arts and sciences, 3% law, 2% medicine
52% had job offers within 6 months
60 organizations recruited on campus
1 Fulbright scholar

Financial Matters
$23,360 tuition and fees (1999–2000)
$8100 room and board
100% average percent of need met
$20,802 average financial aid amount received per undergraduate (1998–99)

BUCKNELL UNIVERSITY

SMALL-TOWN SETTING ■ PRIVATE ■ INDEPENDENT ■ COED
LEWISBURG, PENNSYLVANIA

Web site: www.bucknell.edu
Contact: Mr. Mark D. Davies, Dean of Admissions, Lewisburg, PA 17837
Telephone: 570-577-1101 **Fax:** 570-577-3760
E-mail: admissions@bucknell.edu

Since 1846, scholars have come together at Bucknell to ask questions and explore answers. Bucknell professors enjoy national reputations, and Bucknell students are known for their intelligence and vitality. Together, they explore a wide-ranging curriculum that includes the arts, humanities, social sciences, sciences, education, business administration, and engineering. Beginning with first-year foundation seminars, students and faculty learn to respect each other through lively classroom discussions and through collaboration in research and scholarly papers. In the supportive atmosphere of Bucknell, each person makes full use of the present and finds exciting possibilities for the future.

Getting in Last Year
7,011 applied
44% were accepted
886 enrolled (29%)
54% from top tenth of their h.s. class
63% had SAT verbal scores over 600
75% had SAT math scores over 600
10% had SAT verbal scores over 700
18% had SAT math scores over 700

Graduation and After
83% graduated in 4 years
3% graduated in 5 years
Graduates pursuing further study: 12% arts
and sciences, 3% engineering, 3% law
96% had job offers within 6 months
101 organizations recruited on campus
1 Fulbright scholar

Financial Matters
$22,881 tuition and fees (1999–2000)
$5469 room and board
100% average percent of need met
$17,241 average financial aid amount received
per undergraduate (1999–2000 estimated)

Academics

Bucknell awards bachelor's and master's **degrees**. Challenging opportunities include advanced placement, student-designed majors, an honors program, double majors, independent study, a senior project, Phi Beta Kappa, and Sigma Xi. Special programs include internships, summer session for credit, off-campus study, study-abroad, and Army ROTC.

The most frequently chosen fields are social sciences and history, business/marketing, and engineering/engineering technologies. A complete listing of majors at Bucknell appears in the Majors Index beginning on page 432.

The **faculty** at Bucknell has 280 full-time members, 94% with terminal degrees. The student-faculty ratio is 12:1.

Students of Bucknell

The student body totals 3,560, of whom 3,403 are undergraduates. 48.5% are women and 51.5% are men. Students come from 46 states and territories and 33 other countries. 35% are from Pennsylvania. 1.6% are international students. 3.2% are African American, 0.3% American Indian, 4.1% Asian American, and 2.8% Hispanic American. 94% returned for their sophomore year.

Facilities and Resources

Student rooms are linked to a campus network. 350 **computers** are available on campus that provide access to the Internet. The **library** has 432,730 books and 2,789 subscriptions.

Campus Life

There are 135 active organizations on campus, including a drama/theater group, newspaper, radio station, and choral group. 51% of eligible men and 57% of eligible women are members of national **fraternities**, national **sororities**, and local sororities.

Bucknell is a member of the NCAA (Division I). **Intercollegiate sports** include baseball (m), basketball, crew, cross-country running, equestrian sports, fencing (m), field hockey (w), football (m), golf, gymnastics (w), ice hockey (m), lacrosse, rugby, skiing (downhill), soccer, softball (w), swimming, tennis, track and field, volleyball, water polo, wrestling (m).

Campus Safety

Student safety services include well-lit pathways, self-defense education, safety/security orientation, late-night transport/escort service, 24-hour emergency telephone alarm devices, 24-hour patrols by trained security personnel, and student patrols.

Applying

Bucknell requires an essay, SAT I or ACT, a high school transcript, recommendations, and a minimum high school GPA of 2.5. It recommends an interview. Application deadline: 1/1; 1/1 for financial aid. Deferred admission is possible.

Buena Vista University

Small-town setting ■ Private ■ Independent Religious ■ Coed
Storm Lake, Iowa

Web site: www.bvu.edu
Contact: Ms. Louise Cummings-Simmons, Director of Admissions, 610 West
Fourth Street, Storm Lake, IA 50588
Telephone: 712-749-2351 or toll-free 800-383-9600
E-mail: admissions@bvu.edu

  eApply

Academics

BVU awards bachelor's and master's **degrees**. Challenging opportunities include advanced placement, student-designed majors, freshman honors college, an honors program, double majors, independent study, and a senior project. Special programs include internships, summer session for credit, off-campus study, and study-abroad.

The most frequently chosen fields are business/marketing, education, and protective services/public administration. A complete listing of majors at BVU appears in the Majors Index beginning on page 432.

The **faculty** at BVU has 81 full-time members, 58% with terminal degrees. The student-faculty ratio is 16:1.

Students of BVU

The student body totals 1,399, of whom 1,283 are undergraduates. 49% are women and 51% are men. Students come from 15 states and territories and 6 other countries. 86% are from Iowa. 1.8% are international students. 0.3% are African American, 0.1% American Indian, 1.1% Asian American, and 1.2% Hispanic American. 80% returned for their sophomore year.

Facilities and Resources

Student rooms are linked to a campus network. 400 **computers** are available on campus that provide access to the Internet. The **library** has 124,645 books and 841 subscriptions.

Campus Life

There are 50 active organizations on campus, including a drama/theater group, newspaper, radio station, television station, choral group, and marching band. No national or local **fraternities** or **sororities**.

BVU is a member of the NCAA (Division III). **Intercollegiate sports** include baseball (m), basketball, cross-country running, football (m), golf, soccer, softball (w), swimming, tennis, track and field, volleyball (w), wrestling (m).

Campus Safety

Student safety services include night security patrols, late-night transport/escort service, 24-hour emergency telephone alarm devices, and electronically operated dormitory entrances.

Applying

BVU requires SAT I or ACT, a high school transcript, and recommendations, and in some cases an essay and an interview. It recommends a minimum high school GPA of 3.0. Application deadline: 6/1; 6/1 priority date for financial aid. Early and deferred admission are possible.

Buena Vista University's students are given the opportunity to excel through a student-professor ratio of 15:1, sophisticated technology and facilities, innovative academic programs, and career and graduate school placement services. Students can view the world through exchange programs with schools in Japan and Taiwan and January Interim programs in Europe, Australia, and other locations. They meet national and international leaders and performers on campus through the Academic & Cultural Events Series. Located in America's heartland, Buena Vista's lakeside campus offers a peaceful environment in a progressive college town.

Getting in Last Year
1,117 applied
86% were accepted
325 enrolled (34%)
15% from top tenth of their h.s. class
3.30 average high school GPA
37% had ACT scores over 24
3% had ACT scores over 30
15 valedictorians

Graduation and After
39% graduated in 4 years
9% graduated in 5 years
1% graduated in 6 years
15% pursued further study (2% arts and sciences, 2% business, 1% medicine)
95% had job offers within 6 months
50 organizations recruited on campus

Financial Matters
$15,751 tuition and fees (1999–2000)
$4507 room and board
97% average percent of need met
$16,257 average financial aid amount received per undergraduate (1999–2000 estimated)

Getting in Last Year
3,116 applied
86% were accepted
863 enrolled (32%)
41% from top tenth of their h.s. class
3.55 average high school GPA
40% had SAT verbal scores over 600
46% had SAT math scores over 600
69% had ACT scores over 24
7% had SAT verbal scores over 700
8% had SAT math scores over 700
14% had ACT scores over 30
4 National Merit Scholars
49 valedictorians

Graduation and After
39% graduated in 4 years
18% graduated in 5 years
4% graduated in 6 years
Graduates pursuing further study: 7% arts and sciences, 3% law, 3% medicine
66% had job offers within 6 months

Financial Matters
$17,360 tuition and fees (1999–2000)
$5850 room and board
82% average percent of need met
$12,212 average financial aid amount received per undergraduate (1998–99)

BUTLER UNIVERSITY
URBAN SETTING ■ PRIVATE ■ INDEPENDENT ■ COED
INDIANAPOLIS, INDIANA

Web site: www.butler.edu
Contact: Mr. William Preble, Director of Admissions, 4600 Sunset Avenue, Indianapolis, IN 46208-3485
Telephone: 317-940-8100 ext. 8124 or toll-free 888-940-8100 **Fax:** 317-940-8150
E-mail: admission@butler.edu

Academics
Butler awards associate, bachelor's, master's, and first-professional **degrees** and post-bachelor's certificates. Challenging opportunities include advanced placement, accelerated degree programs, an honors program, double majors, independent study, a senior project, and Sigma Xi. Special programs include cooperative education, internships, summer session for credit, off-campus study, study-abroad, and Army and Air Force ROTC.

The most frequently chosen fields are business/marketing, health professions and related sciences, and education. A complete listing of majors at Butler appears in the Majors Index beginning on page 432.

The **faculty** at Butler has 247 full-time members, 79% with terminal degrees. The student-faculty ratio is 14:1.

Students of Butler
The student body totals 4,147, of whom 3,294 are undergraduates. 61.7% are women and 38.3% are men. Students come from 41 states and territories and 38 other countries. 61% are from Indiana. 1.6% are international students. 4% are African American, 0.4% American Indian, 1.9% Asian American, and 1% Hispanic American. 82% returned for their sophomore year.

Facilities and Resources
Student rooms are linked to a campus network. 240 **computers** are available on campus that provide access to the Internet. The 2 **libraries** have 2,359 subscriptions.

Campus Life
There are 100 active organizations on campus, including a drama/theater group, newspaper, radio station, television station, choral group, and marching band. 31% of eligible men and 35% of eligible women are members of national **fraternities** and national **sororities**.

Butler is a member of the NCAA (Division I). **Intercollegiate sports** (some offering scholarships) include baseball (m), basketball, crew, cross-country running, football (m), golf, ice hockey (m), lacrosse (m), rugby (m), soccer, softball (w), swimming, tennis, track and field, volleyball (w).

Campus Safety
Student safety services include late-night transport/escort service, 24-hour emergency telephone alarm devices, 24-hour patrols by trained security personnel, and electronically operated dormitory entrances.

Applying
Butler requires an essay, SAT I or ACT, and a high school transcript, and in some cases an interview and audition. It recommends SAT II Subject Tests. Application deadline: 8/15; 3/1 priority date for financial aid. Deferred admission is possible.

California Institute of Technology

Suburban setting ■ Private ■ Independent ■ Coed
Pasadena, California

Web site: www.caltech.edu
Contact: Ms. Charlene Liebau, Director of Admissions, 1200 East California
    Boulevard, Pasadena, CA 91125-0001
Telephone: 626-395-6341 or toll-free 800-568-8324 **Fax:** 626-683-3026
E-mail: ugadmissions@caltech.edu

Academics

Caltech awards bachelor's, master's, and doctoral **degrees**. Challenging opportunities
include student-designed majors and Sigma Xi. Special programs include internships,
off-campus study, and Army and Air Force ROTC.

The most frequently chosen fields are engineering/engineering technologies, physical sciences, and biological/life sciences. A complete listing of majors at Caltech appears
in the Majors Index beginning on page 432.

Students of Caltech

The student body totals 1,889, of whom 907 are undergraduates. 30% are women and
70% are men. Students come from 39 states and territories and 33 other countries. 43%
are from California. 8.8% are international students. 1.1% are African American, 0.2%
American Indian, 24.3% Asian American, and 5.3% Hispanic American. 96% returned
for their sophomore year.

Facilities and Resources

Student rooms are linked to a campus network. 600 **computers** are available on campus
that provide access to the Internet. The 11 **libraries** have 550,325 books and 3,449
subscriptions.

Campus Life

There are 85 active organizations on campus, including a drama/theater group,
newspaper, and choral group. No national or local **fraternities** or **sororities**.

Caltech is a member of the NCAA (Division III). **Intercollegiate sports** include
baseball (m), basketball, cross-country running, fencing, golf, ice hockey (m), soccer,
swimming, tennis, track and field, volleyball (w), water polo.

Campus Safety

Student safety services include late-night transport/escort service, 24-hour emergency
telephone alarm devices, and 24-hour patrols by trained security personnel.

Applying

Caltech requires an essay, SAT I, SAT II Subject Tests, SAT II: Writing Test, SAT II
subject test in math and either physics, chemistry, or biology, a high school transcript,
and 3 recommendations. Application deadline: 1/1; 1/15 priority date for financial aid.
Early and deferred admission are possible.

Getting in Last Year

2,894 applied
18% were accepted
234 enrolled (45%)
100% from top tenth of their h.s. class
98% had SAT verbal scores over 600
100% had SAT math scores over 600
76% had SAT verbal scores over 700
97% had SAT math scores over 700
58 National Merit Scholars
93 valedictorians

Graduation and After

71% graduated in 4 years
12% graduated in 5 years
3% graduated in 6 years
Graduates pursuing further study: 26% arts
    and sciences, 20% engineering, 3% medicine
176 organizations recruited on campus

Financial Matters

$19,476 tuition and fees (1999–2000)
$6000 room and board
100% average percent of need met
$16,798 average financial aid amount received
    per undergraduate (1998–99)

CALIFORNIA POLYTECHNIC STATE UNIVERSITY, SAN LUIS OBISPO

SMALL-TOWN SETTING ■ PUBLIC ■ STATE-SUPPORTED ■ COED
SAN LUIS OBISPO, CALIFORNIA

Web site: www.calpoly.edu
Contact: Mr. James Maraviglia, Director of Admissions and Evaluations, San Luis Obispo, CA 93407
Telephone: 805-756-2311 **Fax:** 805-756-5400
E-mail: admprosp@calpoly.edu

Academics

Cal Poly State University awards bachelor's and master's **degrees**. Challenging opportunities include advanced placement, an honors program, double majors, independent study, a senior project, and Sigma Xi. Special programs include cooperative education, internships, summer session for credit, off-campus study, study-abroad, and Army ROTC.

The most frequently chosen fields are engineering/engineering technologies, agriculture, and business/marketing. A complete listing of majors at Cal Poly State University appears in the Majors Index beginning on page 432.

The **faculty** at Cal Poly State University has 668 full-time members, 94% with terminal degrees. The student-faculty ratio is 20:1.

Students of Cal Poly State University

The student body totals 16,470, of whom 15,503 are undergraduates. 44.2% are women and 55.8% are men. Students come from 48 states and territories and 41 other countries. 97% are from California. 0.5% are international students. 1.3% are African American, 1.3% American Indian, 11% Asian American, and 11.4% Hispanic American. 87% returned for their sophomore year.

Facilities and Resources

Student rooms are linked to a campus network. 1,880 **computers** are available on campus that provide access to the Internet. The **library** has 621,062 books and 4,917 subscriptions.

Campus Life

There are 360 active organizations on campus, including a drama/theater group, newspaper, radio station, choral group, and marching band. 11% of eligible men and 7% of eligible women are members of national **fraternities**, national **sororities**, local fraternities, and local sororities.

Cal Poly State University is a member of the NCAA (Division I). **Intercollegiate sports** (some offering scholarships) include baseball (m), basketball, cross-country running, equestrian sports, football (m), golf (m), gymnastics (w), soccer, softball (w), swimming, tennis, track and field, volleyball (w), wrestling (m).

Campus Safety

Student safety services include late-night transport/escort service, 24-hour emergency telephone alarm devices, 24-hour patrols by trained security personnel, student patrols, and electronically operated dormitory entrances.

Applying

Cal Poly State University requires SAT I or ACT and a high school transcript. Application deadline: 11/30; 3/2 priority date for financial aid. Early admission is possible.

CALVIN COLLEGE

SUBURBAN SETTING ■ PRIVATE ■ INDEPENDENT RELIGIOUS ■ COED
GRAND RAPIDS, MICHIGAN

eAPPLY

Web site: www.calvin.edu
Contact: Mr. Dale D. Kuiper, Director of Admissions, 3201 Burton Street, SE, Grand Rapids, MI 49546-4388
Telephone: 616-957-6106 or toll-free 800-668-0122
E-mail: admissions@calvin.edu

Academics

Calvin awards bachelor's and master's **degrees** and post-bachelor's certificates. Challenging opportunities include advanced placement, student-designed majors, an honors program, double majors, independent study, and a senior project. Special programs include cooperative education, internships, summer session for credit, off-campus study, study-abroad, and Army ROTC.

The most frequently chosen fields are business/marketing, education, and social sciences and history. A complete listing of majors at Calvin appears in the Majors Index beginning on page 432.

The **faculty** at Calvin has 273 full-time members, 78% with terminal degrees. The student-faculty ratio is 16:1.

Students of Calvin

The student body totals 4,264, of whom 4,218 are undergraduates. 55.4% are women and 44.6% are men. Students come from 44 states and territories and 31 other countries. 57% are from Michigan. 6.9% are international students. 0.9% are African American, 0.2% American Indian, 1.8% Asian American, and 1.1% Hispanic American. 85% returned for their sophomore year.

Facilities and Resources

Student rooms are linked to a campus network. 659 **computers** are available on campus that provide access to the Internet. The **library** has 2,721 subscriptions.

Campus Life

There are 40 active organizations on campus, including a drama/theater group, newspaper, radio station, and choral group. No national or local **fraternities** or **sororities**.

Calvin is a member of the NCAA (Division III). **Intercollegiate sports** include baseball (m), basketball, cross-country running, golf, ice hockey (m), lacrosse, soccer, softball (w), swimming, tennis, track and field, volleyball.

Campus Safety

Student safety services include crime prevention programs, crime alert bulletins, late-night transport/escort service, 24-hour emergency telephone alarm devices, 24-hour patrols by trained security personnel, student patrols, and electronically operated dormitory entrances.

Applying

Calvin requires an essay, SAT I or ACT, a high school transcript, 1 recommendation, and a minimum high school GPA of 2.5. It recommends ACT. Application deadline: 8/15; 2/15 priority date for financial aid. Deferred admission is possible.

> **C**alvin College is a place where knowledge and faith can grow—where students prepare to take their individual place in God's world. On Calvin's spacious campus, students, faculty, and staff form a community of supportive, committed people who savor the joyful task of serving God through intellectual curiosity, spirited interaction, and conscientious work. More than 4,000 students from throughout the U.S. and many other countries find Calvin to be an ideal place for thinking, questing people who are committed to a lifetime of service in today's world.

Getting in Last Year
1,971 applied
99% were accepted
1,061 enrolled (55%)
26% from top tenth of their h.s. class
3.49 average high school GPA
47% had SAT verbal scores over 600
47% had SAT math scores over 600
70% had ACT scores over 24
13% had SAT verbal scores over 700
13% had SAT math scores over 700
15% had ACT scores over 30
20 National Merit Scholars
41 valedictorians

Graduation and After
46% graduated in 4 years
20% graduated in 5 years
2% graduated in 6 years
Graduates pursuing further study: 7% arts and sciences, 5% education, 2% medicine
72% had job offers within 6 months
154 organizations recruited on campus

Financial Matters
$13,420 tuition and fees (1999–2000)
$4675 room and board
86% average percent of need met
$10,350 average financial aid amount received per undergraduate (1999–2000 estimated)

 **eApply**

Getting in Last Year
2,151 applied
81% were accepted
542 enrolled (31%)
20% from top tenth of their h.s. class
3.3 average high school GPA
24% had SAT verbal scores over 600
25% had SAT math scores over 600
40% had ACT scores over 24
3% had SAT verbal scores over 700
4% had SAT math scores over 700
5% had ACT scores over 30
7 valedictorians

Graduation and After
53% graduated in 4 years
5% graduated in 5 years
2% graduated in 6 years
15% pursued further study (8% arts and sciences, 4% law, 2% medicine)
87% had job offers within 6 months

Financial Matters
$16,000 tuition and fees (1999–2000)
$4900 room and board
$14,406 average financial aid amount received per undergraduate (1999–2000)

CAPITAL UNIVERSITY
SUBURBAN SETTING ■ PRIVATE ■ INDEPENDENT RELIGIOUS ■ COED
COLUMBUS, OHIO

Web site: www.capital.edu
Contact: Mrs. Kimberly V. Ebbrecht, Director of Admission, 2199 East Main Street, Columbus, OH 43209-2394
Telephone: 614-236-6101 or toll-free 800-289-6289 **Fax:** 614-236-6926
E-mail: admissions@capital.edu

Academics
Capital awards bachelor's, master's, and first-professional **degrees**. Challenging opportunities include advanced placement, student-designed majors, double majors, and independent study. Special programs include internships, summer session for credit, off-campus study, study-abroad, and Army ROTC.

The most frequently chosen fields are business/marketing, education, and health professions and related sciences. A complete listing of majors at Capital appears in the Majors Index beginning on page 432.

The **faculty** at Capital has 181 full-time members, 68% with terminal degrees. The student-faculty ratio is 14:1.

Students of Capital
The student body totals 4,039, of whom 2,807 are undergraduates. 63.4% are women and 36.6% are men. Students come from 21 states and territories and 8 other countries. 92% are from Ohio. 1% are international students. 15.8% are African American, 0.4% American Indian, 0.7% Asian American, and 1.1% Hispanic American. 74% returned for their sophomore year.

Facilities and Resources
Student rooms are linked to a campus network. 100 **computers** are available on campus that provide access to the Internet. The **library** has 175,709 books and 893 subscriptions.

Campus Life
There are 60 active organizations on campus, including a drama/theater group, newspaper, radio station, television station, and choral group. 25% of eligible men and 25% of eligible women are members of national **fraternities**, national **sororities**, local fraternities, and local sororities.

Capital is a member of the NCAA (Division III). **Intercollegiate sports** include baseball (m), basketball, cross-country running, football (m), golf, soccer, softball (w), tennis, volleyball (w), wrestling (m).

Campus Safety
Student safety services include late-night transport/escort service, 24-hour patrols by trained security personnel, and electronically operated dormitory entrances.

Applying
Capital requires SAT I or ACT, a high school transcript, 1 recommendation, and a minimum high school GPA of 2.5, and in some cases an essay and audition. It recommends an interview. Application deadline: 4/15; 2/15 priority date for financial aid. Deferred admission is possible.

CARLETON COLLEGE

SMALL-TOWN SETTING ■ PRIVATE ■ INDEPENDENT ■ COED
NORTHFIELD, MINNESOTA

Web site: www.carleton.edu
Contact: Mr. Paul Thiboutot, Dean of Admissions, One North College
Street, Northfield, MN 55057-4001
Telephone: 507-646-4190 or toll-free 800-995-2275 **Fax:** 507-646-4526
E-mail: admissions@acs.carleton.edu

eAPPLY

Academics

Carleton awards bachelor's **degrees**. Challenging opportunities include advanced placement, accelerated degree programs, student-designed majors, double majors, independent study, a senior project, Phi Beta Kappa, and Sigma Xi. Special programs include internships, off-campus study, and study-abroad.

The most frequently chosen fields are social sciences and history, physical sciences, and biological/life sciences. A complete listing of majors at Carleton appears in the Majors Index beginning on page 432.

The **faculty** at Carleton has 178 full-time members, 96% with terminal degrees. The student-faculty ratio is 10:1.

Students of Carleton

The student body is made up of 1,905 undergraduates. 53.3% are women and 46.7% are men. Students come from 50 states and territories and 15 other countries. 22% are from Minnesota. 1.5% are international students. 2.9% are African American, 0.4% American Indian, 8.9% Asian American, and 3.4% Hispanic American. 95% returned for their sophomore year.

Facilities and Resources

Student rooms are linked to a campus network. 363 **computers** are available on campus that provide access to the Internet. The 2 **libraries** have 514,029 books and 1,505 subscriptions.

Campus Life

There are 122 active organizations on campus, including a drama/theater group, newspaper, radio station, and choral group. No national or local **fraternities** or **sororities**.

Carleton is a member of the NCAA (Division III). **Intercollegiate sports** include baseball (m), basketball, crew, cross-country running, fencing, field hockey (w), football (m), golf, ice hockey, lacrosse, rugby, skiing (cross-country), skiing (downhill), soccer, softball (w), swimming, tennis, track and field, volleyball, water polo, wrestling (m).

Campus Safety

Student safety services include late-night transport/escort service, 24-hour emergency telephone alarm devices, 24-hour patrols by trained security personnel, student patrols, and electronically operated dormitory entrances.

Applying

Carleton requires an essay, SAT I or ACT, a high school transcript, and 2 recommendations. It recommends SAT II Subject Tests, SAT II: Writing Test, and an interview. Application deadline: 1/15; 2/1 for financial aid, with a 1/15 priority date. Early and deferred admission are possible.

Getting in Last Year
3,457 applied
46% were accepted
510 enrolled (32%)
61% from top tenth of their h.s. class
92% had SAT verbal scores over 600
89% had SAT math scores over 600
99% had ACT scores over 24
51% had SAT verbal scores over 700
41% had SAT math scores over 700
54% had ACT scores over 30
85 National Merit Scholars
45 valedictorians

Graduation and After
81% graduated in 4 years
6% graduated in 5 years
1% graduated in 6 years
17% pursued further study (12% arts and
    sciences, 2% medicine, 1% education)
63% had job offers within 6 months
60 organizations recruited on campus
4 Fulbright scholars

Financial Matters
$23,469 tuition and fees (1999–2000)
$4761 room and board
100% average percent of need met
$18,824 average financial aid amount received
    per undergraduate (1999–2000)

CARNEGIE MELLON UNIVERSITY

URBAN SETTING ■ PRIVATE ■ INDEPENDENT ■ COED
PITTSBURGH, PENNSYLVANIA

Web site: www.cmu.edu
Contact: Mr. Michael Steidel, Director of Admissions, 5000 Forbes Avenue, Pittsburgh, PA 15213-3891
Telephone: 412-268-2082 **Fax:** 412-268-7838
E-mail: undergraduate-admissions@andrew.cmu.edu

First envisioned by steel magnate and philanthropist Andrew Carnegie, Carnegie Mellon University has steadily built upon its foundations of excellence and innovation to become one of America's leading universities. Carnegie Mellon's unique approach to education—giving students opportunities to become experts in their chosen fields while studying a broad range of course work across disciplines—will help students become leaders and problem solvers today *and* tomorrow. The University offers more than 70 majors and minors across 6 undergraduate colleges. Whether students are interested in creating the technology of tomorrow or getting their break on Broadway, a Carnegie Mellon education can take them there.

Academics

CMU awards bachelor's, master's, and doctoral **degrees** and post-bachelor's and post-master's certificates. Challenging opportunities include advanced placement, accelerated degree programs, student-designed majors, an honors program, double majors, independent study, a senior project, Phi Beta Kappa, and Sigma Xi. Special programs include cooperative education, internships, summer session for credit, off-campus study, study-abroad, and Army, Navy and Air Force ROTC.

The most frequently chosen fields are engineering/engineering technologies, visual/performing arts, and business/marketing. A complete listing of majors at CMU appears in the Majors Index beginning on page 432.

The **faculty** at CMU has 1,042 full-time members. The student-faculty ratio is 6:1.

Students of CMU

The student body totals 8,436, of whom 5,262 are undergraduates. 36% are women and 64% are men. Students come from 52 states and territories and 54 other countries. 24% are from Pennsylvania. 8.7% are international students. 3.5% are African American, 0.5% American Indian, 19.5% Asian American, and 4.8% Hispanic American. 92% returned for their sophomore year.

Facilities and Resources

Student rooms are linked to a campus network. 364 **computers** are available on campus that provide access to the Internet. The 3 **libraries** have 922,337 books and 5,272 subscriptions.

Campus Life

There are 100 active organizations on campus, including a drama/theater group, newspaper, radio station, choral group, and marching band. 13% of eligible men and 9% of eligible women are members of national **fraternities**, national **sororities**, and local sororities.

CMU is a member of the NCAA (Division III). **Intercollegiate sports** include baseball (m), basketball, crew, cross-country running, fencing, football (m), golf (m), ice hockey (m), lacrosse, riflery (m), rugby (m), skiing (cross-country), soccer, swimming, tennis, track and field, volleyball.

Campus Safety

Student safety services include late-night transport/escort service, 24-hour emergency telephone alarm devices, 24-hour patrols by trained security personnel, and electronically operated dormitory entrances.

Applying

CMU requires an essay, SAT II Subject Tests, SAT I or ACT, a high school transcript, and 1 recommendation, and in some cases SAT II: Writing Test and portfolio, audition. It recommends an interview. Application deadline: 1/1; 2/15 priority date for financial aid. Early and deferred admission are possible.

Getting in Last Year
14,114 applied
38% were accepted
1,254 enrolled (24%)
67% from top tenth of their h.s. class
3.61 average high school GPA
77% had SAT verbal scores over 600
90% had SAT math scores over 600
92% had ACT scores over 24
29% had SAT verbal scores over 700
57% had SAT math scores over 700
45% had ACT scores over 30

Graduation and After
58% graduated in 4 years
14% graduated in 5 years
3% graduated in 6 years
20% pursued further study (9% arts and sciences, 7% engineering, 2% medicine)
945 organizations recruited on campus

Financial Matters
$22,300 tuition and fees (1999–2000)
$6810 room and board
78% average percent of need met
$15,789 average financial aid amount received per undergraduate (1999–2000)

CARROLL COLLEGE

SMALL-TOWN SETTING ■ PRIVATE ■ INDEPENDENT RELIGIOUS ■ COED
HELENA, MONTANA

Web site: www.carroll.edu
Contact: Ms. Candace A. Cain, Director of Admission, 1601 North Benton
   Avenue, Helena, MT 59625-0002
Telephone: 406-447-4384 or toll-free 800-99-ADMIT **Fax:** 406-447-4533
E-mail: enroll@carroll.edu

Academics

Carroll awards associate and bachelor's **degrees**. Challenging opportunities include advanced placement, accelerated degree programs, student-designed majors, freshman honors college, an honors program, double majors, independent study, and a senior project. Special programs include cooperative education, internships, summer session for credit, and study-abroad. A complete listing of majors at Carroll appears in the Majors Index beginning on page 432.

The **faculty** at Carroll has 77 full-time members. The student-faculty ratio is 12:1.

Students of Carroll

The student body is made up of 1,243 undergraduates. 58.9% are women and 41.1% are men. Students come from 28 states and territories and 10 other countries. 71% are from Montana. 2.7% are international students. 0.8% are American Indian, 0.9% Asian American, and 1.9% Hispanic American. 80% returned for their sophomore year.

Facilities and Resources

Student rooms are linked to a campus network. 76 **computers** are available on campus that provide access to the Internet. The 2 **libraries** have 86,889 books and 607 subscriptions.

Campus Life

There are 35 active organizations on campus, including a drama/theater group, newspaper, radio station, and choral group. No national or local **fraternities** or **sororities**.

Carroll is a member of the NAIA. **Intercollegiate sports** (some offering scholarships) include basketball, football (m), golf (w), soccer (w), swimming, volleyball (w).

Campus Safety

Student safety services include late-night transport/escort service.

Applying

Carroll requires an essay, SAT I or ACT, a high school transcript, 1 recommendation, and a minimum high school GPA of 2.0, and in some cases SAT II Subject Tests, SAT II: Writing Test, and an interview. It recommends an interview and a minimum high school GPA of 3.0. Application deadline: 6/1; 3/1 priority date for financial aid. Early and deferred admission are possible.

The Carroll College motto, "Not for school, but for life," guides students as they develop their intellectual, spiritual, and social potential through an outstanding liberal arts education highlighted by diverse curricula and student-oriented faculty members. Given the College's low student-faculty ratio, students are recognized as important individuals and provided the opportunity to play a significant role in their own educational development. Located in Montana's capital city, Carroll's campus is framed by historic and modern facilities. Nestled midway between Glacier and Yellowstone National Parks in some of the world's most beautiful wilderness and recreational areas, Carroll is an ideal setting in which to live and learn.

Getting in Last Year
608 applied
91% were accepted
245 enrolled (44%)
26% from top tenth of their h.s. class
3.39 average high school GPA
27% had SAT verbal scores over 600
25% had SAT math scores over 600
53% had ACT scores over 24
4% had SAT verbal scores over 700
4% had SAT math scores over 700
7% had ACT scores over 30
17 valedictorians

Graduation and After
29% graduated in 4 years
13% graduated in 5 years
2% graduated in 6 years
28% pursued further study (9% arts and sciences, 4% business, 4% law)
66% had job offers within 6 months
95 organizations recruited on campus

Financial Matters
$11,778 tuition and fees (1999–2000)
$4716 room and board
91% average percent of need met
$11,670 average financial aid amount received per undergraduate (1998–99)

eAPPLY

CASE WESTERN RESERVE UNIVERSITY

URBAN SETTING ■ PRIVATE ■ INDEPENDENT ■ COED
CLEVELAND, OHIO

Web site: www.cwru.edu
Contact: Mr. William T. Conley, Dean of Undergraduate Admission, 10900 Euclid Avenue, Cleveland, OH 44106
Telephone: 216-368-4450
E-mail: admission@po.cwru.edu

Getting in Last Year

4,380 applied
72% were accepted
766 enrolled (24%)
67% from top tenth of their h.s. class
75% had SAT verbal scores over 600
84% had SAT math scores over 600
90% had ACT scores over 24
32% had SAT verbal scores over 700
46% had SAT math scores over 700
45% had ACT scores over 30

Graduation and After

46% graduated in 4 years
22% graduated in 5 years
4% graduated in 6 years
34% pursued further study (9% engineering, 8% medicine, 6% arts and sciences)
211 organizations recruited on campus

Financial Matters

$20,260 tuition and fees (2000–2001)
$5815 room and board
96% average percent of need met
$18,549 average financial aid amount received per undergraduate (1999–2000)

Academics

CWRU awards bachelor's, master's, doctoral, and first-professional **degrees**. Challenging opportunities include advanced placement, accelerated degree programs, student-designed majors, an honors program, double majors, independent study, a senior project, Phi Beta Kappa, and Sigma Xi. Special programs include cooperative education, internships, summer session for credit, off-campus study, study-abroad, and Army and Air Force ROTC.

The most frequently chosen fields are engineering/engineering technologies, social sciences and history, and biological/life sciences. A complete listing of majors at CWRU appears in the Majors Index beginning on page 432.

The **faculty** at CWRU has 553 full-time members, 95% with terminal degrees. The student-faculty ratio is 8:1.

Students of CWRU

The student body totals 9,300, of whom 3,380 are undergraduates. 40% are women and 60% are men. Students come from 54 states and territories and 34 other countries. 61% are from Ohio. 3.3% are international students. 4.8% are African American, 0.2% American Indian, 13.1% Asian American, and 2% Hispanic American. 92% returned for their sophomore year.

Facilities and Resources

Student rooms are linked to a campus network. 100 **computers** are available on campus that provide access to software library, CD-ROM databases and the Internet. The 7 **libraries** have 14,520 subscriptions.

Campus Life

There are 100 active organizations on campus, including a drama/theater group, newspaper, radio station, choral group, and marching band. 32% of eligible men and 16% of eligible women are members of national **fraternities**, national **sororities**, and local sororities.

CWRU is a member of the NCAA (Division III). **Intercollegiate sports** include archery, badminton, baseball (m), basketball, crew, cross-country running, fencing, football (m), golf (m), ice hockey, skiing (downhill), soccer, softball (w), swimming, tennis, track and field, volleyball, wrestling (m).

Campus Safety

Student safety services include crime prevention programs, late-night transport/escort service, 24-hour emergency telephone alarm devices, 24-hour patrols by trained security personnel, student patrols, and electronically operated dormitory entrances.

Applying

CWRU requires an essay, SAT I or ACT, a high school transcript, and 1 recommendation. It recommends SAT II Subject Tests and an interview. Application deadline: 2/1; 4/15 for financial aid, with a 2/1 priority date. Early and deferred admission are possible.

The Catholic University of America

URBAN SETTING ■ PRIVATE ■ INDEPENDENT RELIGIOUS ■ COED
WASHINGTON, DISTRICT OF COLUMBIA

  eAPPLY

Web site: www.cua.edu
Contact: Mr. John Dolan, Dean of Enrollment Management, Cardinal Station
Post Office, Washington, DC 20064
Telephone: 202-319-5305 or toll-free 800-673-2772 (out-of-state) **Fax:**
202-319-6533
E-mail: cua-admissions@cua.edu

Academics

CUA awards bachelor's, master's, doctoral, and first-professional **degrees** and post-master's certificates. Challenging opportunities include advanced placement, accelerated degree programs, student-designed majors, freshman honors college, an honors program, a senior project, Phi Beta Kappa, and Sigma Xi. Special programs include internships, summer session for credit, off-campus study, study-abroad, and Army, Navy and Air Force ROTC.

The most frequently chosen fields are architecture, social sciences and history, and engineering/engineering technologies. A complete listing of majors at CUA appears in the Majors Index beginning on page 432.

The **faculty** at CUA has 365 full-time members, 97% with terminal degrees. The student-faculty ratio is 10:1.

Students of CUA

The student body totals 5,597, of whom 2,557 are undergraduates. 53.8% are women and 46.2% are men. Students come from 50 states and territories and 48 other countries. 6% are from District of Columbia. 4.8% are international students. 7.6% are African American, 0.3% American Indian, 4.6% Asian American, and 4.9% Hispanic American. 85% returned for their sophomore year.

Facilities and Resources

Student rooms are linked to a campus network. 450 **computers** are available on campus that provide access to the Internet. The 8 **libraries** have 1,430,000 books and 10,945 subscriptions.

Campus Life

There are 84 active organizations on campus, including a drama/theater group, newspaper, radio station, and choral group. 1% of eligible men and 1% of eligible women are members of national **fraternities**, national **sororities**, and local sororities.

CUA is a member of the NCAA (Division III). **Intercollegiate sports** include baseball (m), basketball, cross-country running, field hockey (w), football (m), lacrosse, soccer, softball (w), swimming, tennis, track and field, volleyball (w).

Campus Safety

Student safety services include controlled access of academic buildings, late-night transport/escort service, 24-hour emergency telephone alarm devices, 24-hour patrols by trained security personnel, and electronically operated dormitory entrances.

Applying

CUA requires an essay, SAT I or ACT, a high school transcript, and 1 recommendation. It recommends SAT II Subject Tests and SAT II: Writing Test. Application deadline: 2/15; 2/15 for financial aid, with a 1/15 priority date. Early and deferred admission are possible.

The Catholic University of America, situated on 155 residential, tree-lined acres in Washington, D.C., offers the beauty of a traditional collegiate campus and the excitement of the nation's capital. Catholic University, founded by the U.S. Catholic bishops, is the national university of the Catholic church. Catholic University is a valuable resource for employers looking to fill top internships. Undergraduates work in congressional offices, executive agencies, professional associations, research institutes, lobbying groups, and media organizations. Overseas programs include internships with the British and Irish parliaments. At Catholic University, undergraduate students can apply to six schools: arts and sciences, which includes politics, business, communications, premed, and prelaw; architecture and planning; engineering; music; nursing; and philosophy.

Getting in Last Year
2,604 applied
88% were accepted
797 enrolled (35%)
27% from top tenth of their h.s. class
3.30 average high school GPA
44% had SAT verbal scores over 600
39% had SAT math scores over 600
61% had ACT scores over 24
10% had SAT verbal scores over 700
7% had SAT math scores over 700
15% had ACT scores over 30

Graduation and After
33% pursued further study (10% arts and
sciences, 7% engineering, 6% law)
88% had job offers within 6 months
160 organizations recruited on campus

Financial Matters
$18,972 tuition and fees (1999–2000)
$7765 room and board
88% average percent of need met
$15,801 average financial aid amount received
per undergraduate (1998–99)

Getting in Last Year
1,814 applied
74% were accepted
722 enrolled (54%)
36% from top tenth of their h.s. class
3.59 average high school GPA
49% had SAT verbal scores over 600
44% had SAT math scores over 600
68% had ACT scores over 24
10% had SAT verbal scores over 700
9% had SAT math scores over 700
14% had ACT scores over 30
14 National Merit Scholars
85 valedictorians

Graduation and After
59% graduated in 4 years
6% graduated in 5 years
1% graduated in 6 years
Graduates pursuing further study: 4% theology, 2% medicine, 2% arts and sciences
96% had job offers within 6 months
230 organizations recruited on campus

Financial Matters
$10,740 tuition and fees (1999–2000)
$4788 room and board
40% average percent of need met
$9452 average financial aid amount received per undergraduate (1998–99)

CEDARVILLE COLLEGE
RURAL SETTING ■ PRIVATE ■ INDEPENDENT RELIGIOUS ■ COED
CEDARVILLE, OHIO

Web site: www.cedarville.edu
Contact: Mr. Roscoe Smith, Director of Admissions, PO Box 601, Cedarville, OH 45314-0601
Telephone: 937-766-7700 or toll-free 800-CEDARVILLE **Fax:** 937-766-7575
E-mail: admiss@cedarville.edu

Academics
Cedarville awards associate and bachelor's **degrees**. Challenging opportunities include advanced placement, accelerated degree programs, an honors program, double majors, independent study, and a senior project. Special programs include internships, summer session for credit, study-abroad, and Army and Air Force ROTC.

The most frequently chosen fields are education, philosophy, and business/marketing. A complete listing of majors at Cedarville appears in the Majors Index beginning on page 432.

The **faculty** at Cedarville has 158 full-time members, 63% with terminal degrees. The student-faculty ratio is 17:1.

Students of Cedarville
The student body is made up of 2,762 undergraduates. 54.6% are women and 45.4% are men. Students come from 54 states and territories. 0.4% are international students. 0.7% are African American, 0.2% American Indian, 1% Asian American, and 0.7% Hispanic American. 86% returned for their sophomore year.

Facilities and Resources
Student rooms are linked to a campus network. 1,700 **computers** are available on campus that provide access to software packages and the Internet. The **library** has 133,891 books and 2,878 subscriptions.

Campus Life
There are 55 active organizations on campus, including a drama/theater group, newspaper, radio station, and choral group. No national or local **fraternities** or **sororities**.

Cedarville is a member of the NAIA and NCCAA. **Intercollegiate sports** (some offering scholarships) include baseball (m), basketball, cross-country running, golf (m), soccer, softball (w), tennis, track and field, volleyball (w).

Campus Safety
Student safety services include late-night transport/escort service, 24-hour emergency telephone alarm devices, 24-hour patrols by trained security personnel, and student patrols.

Applying
Cedarville requires an essay, SAT I or ACT, a high school transcript, 2 recommendations, and a minimum high school GPA of 3.0, and in some cases an interview. Application deadline: rolling admissions; 3/1 priority date for financial aid. Early and deferred admission are possible.

Centenary College of Louisiana

SUBURBAN SETTING ■ PRIVATE ■ INDEPENDENT RELIGIOUS ■ COED
SHREVEPORT, LOUISIANA

Web site: www.centenary.edu
Contact: Mr. J. Timothy Martin, Dean of Enrollment Management, 2911 Centenary Blvd, PO Box 41188, Shreveport, LA 71134-1188
Telephone: 318-869-5131 or toll-free 800-234-4448 **Fax:** 318-869-5005
E-mail: jtmartin@centenary.edu

eAPPLY

Academics

Centenary awards bachelor's and master's **degrees**. Challenging opportunities include advanced placement, student-designed majors, an honors program, double majors, independent study, and a senior project. Special programs include internships, summer session for credit, off-campus study, study-abroad, and Army ROTC.

The most frequently chosen fields are business/marketing, social sciences and history, and biological/life sciences. A complete listing of majors at Centenary appears in the Majors Index beginning on page 432.

The **faculty** at Centenary has 70 full-time members, 91% with terminal degrees. The student-faculty ratio is 12:1.

Students of Centenary

The student body totals 1,020, of whom 878 are undergraduates. 59.2% are women and 40.8% are men. Students come from 32 states and territories and 7 other countries. 62% are from Louisiana. 2% are international students. 6.1% are African American, 1% American Indian, 1.4% Asian American, and 2.5% Hispanic American. 75% returned for their sophomore year.

Facilities and Resources

186 **computers** are available on campus that provide access to the Internet. The 2 **libraries** have 181,000 books and 1,190 subscriptions.

Campus Life

There are 34 active organizations on campus, including a drama/theater group, newspaper, radio station, and choral group. 27% of eligible men and 27% of eligible women are members of national **fraternities** and national **sororities**.

Centenary is a member of the NCAA (Division I). **Intercollegiate sports** (some offering scholarships) include baseball (m), basketball, crew, cross-country running, golf, gymnastics (w), riflery, sailing, soccer, softball (w), tennis, volleyball (w).

Campus Safety

Student safety services include late-night transport/escort service, 24-hour emergency telephone alarm devices, 24-hour patrols by trained security personnel, and electronically operated dormitory entrances.

Applying

Centenary requires an essay, SAT I or ACT, a high school transcript, 1 recommendation, and a minimum high school GPA of 2.0, and in some cases SAT II Subject Tests. It recommends an interview and class rank. Application deadline: 3/1; 2/15 priority date for financial aid. Early and deferred admission are possible.

Getting in Last Year
727 applied
83% were accepted
269 enrolled (44%)
35% from top tenth of their h.s. class
30% had SAT verbal scores over 600
35% had SAT math scores over 600
60% had ACT scores over 24
10% had SAT verbal scores over 700
5% had SAT math scores over 700
11% had ACT scores over 30

Graduation and After
37% graduated in 4 years
12% graduated in 5 years
2% graduated in 6 years
51% had job offers within 6 months
40 organizations recruited on campus

Financial Matters
$14,600 tuition and fees (2000–2001 estimated)
$4500 room and board
84% average percent of need met
$10,512 average financial aid amount received per undergraduate (1999–2000)

CENTRAL COLLEGE

SMALL-TOWN SETTING ■ PRIVATE ■ INDEPENDENT RELIGIOUS ■ COED
PELLA, IOWA

Web site: www.central.edu
Contact: John Olsen, Vice President of Admission and Student Enrollment
  Services, 812 University Street, Pella, IA 50219-1999
Telephone: 515-628-7600 or toll-free 800-458-5503 **Fax:** 515-628-5316
E-mail: admissions@central.edu

Academics

Central awards bachelor's **degrees**. Challenging opportunities include advanced placement, student-designed majors, freshman honors college, an honors program, and a senior project. Special programs include internships, summer session for credit, off-campus study, and study-abroad.

The most frequently chosen fields are English, business/marketing, and communications/communication technologies. A complete listing of majors at Central appears in the Majors Index beginning on page 432.

The **faculty** at Central has 86 full-time members, 88% with terminal degrees. The student-faculty ratio is 13:1.

Students of Central

The student body is made up of 1,301 undergraduates. 55.7% are women and 44.3% are men. Students come from 37 states and territories and 17 other countries. 81% are from Iowa. 0.9% are international students. 0.4% are African American, 0.2% American Indian, 0.6% Asian American, and 1.2% Hispanic American. 82% returned for their sophomore year.

Facilities and Resources

Student rooms are linked to a campus network. 168 **computers** are available on campus that provide access to the Internet. The 4 **libraries** have 198,000 books and 924 subscriptions.

Campus Life

There are 72 active organizations on campus, including a drama/theater group, newspaper, radio station, and choral group. 15% of eligible men and 7% of eligible women are members of local **fraternities** and local **sororities**.

Central is a member of the NCAA (Division III). **Intercollegiate sports** include baseball (m), basketball, cross-country running, football (m), golf, soccer, softball (w), tennis, track and field, volleyball (w), wrestling (m).

Campus Safety

Student safety services include late-night transport/escort service, 24-hour emergency telephone alarm devices, student patrols, and electronically operated dormitory entrances.

Applying

Central requires SAT I or ACT and a high school transcript, and in some cases an essay, an interview, and 3 recommendations. It recommends an interview and a minimum high school GPA of 2.0. Application deadline: rolling admissions; 3/1 priority date for financial aid. Early and deferred admission are possible.

"**C**hallenging yet supportive" describes Central College in Pella, Iowa. Students establish one-to-one relationships with their professors, while a curriculum focusing on mind, body, and spirit engages students and prepares them for a career or graduate school. More than 98% of Central's May 1999 graduates either accepted professional employment or enrolled in a graduate school of their choice within 6 months of graduation. Study-abroad opportunities provide eye-opening experiences for students, and nearly 50% of Central's graduates study overseas in one of the College's 8 international programs.

Getting in Last Year
1,191 applied
85% were accepted
404 enrolled (40%)
21% from top tenth of their h.s. class
3.41 average high school GPA
30% had SAT verbal scores over 600
44% had SAT math scores over 600
48% had ACT scores over 24
4% had SAT verbal scores over 700
9% had SAT math scores over 700
6% had ACT scores over 30
11 valedictorians

Graduation and After
57% graduated in 4 years
6% graduated in 5 years
20% pursued further study (10% arts and
  sciences, 5% medicine, 2% business)
94% had job offers within 6 months
68 organizations recruited on campus

Financial Matters
$14,186 tuition and fees (1999–2000)
$4944 room and board
90% average percent of need met
$13,978 average financial aid amount received
  per undergraduate (1999–2000)

CENTRE COLLEGE

SMALL-TOWN SETTING ■ PRIVATE ■ INDEPENDENT RELIGIOUS ■ COED
DANVILLE, KENTUCKY

Web site: www.centre.edu
Contact: Mr. J. Carey Thompson, Dean of Admission and Finacial Aid, 600 West Walnut Street, Danville, KY 40422-1394
Telephone: 606-238-5350 or toll-free 800-423-6236 **Fax:** 606-238-5373
E-mail: admission@centre.edu

Academics

Centre awards bachelor's **degrees**. Challenging opportunities include advanced placement, student-designed majors, double majors, independent study, a senior project, and Phi Beta Kappa. Special programs include internships, off-campus study, study-abroad, and Army and Air Force ROTC.

The most frequently chosen fields are social sciences and history, English, and biological/life sciences. A complete listing of majors at Centre appears in the Majors Index beginning on page 432.

The **faculty** at Centre has 91 full-time members, 91% with terminal degrees. The student-faculty ratio is 10:1.

Students of Centre

The student body is made up of 1,022 undergraduates. 51% are women and 49% are men. Students come from 39 states and territories and 7 other countries. 65% are from Kentucky. 0.9% are international students. 2.9% are African American, 0.1% American Indian, 0.7% Asian American, and 0.5% Hispanic American. 87% returned for their sophomore year.

Facilities and Resources

Student rooms are linked to a campus network. 150 **computers** are available on campus that provide access to the Internet. The 2 **libraries** have 265,000 books and 850 subscriptions.

Campus Life

There are 70 active organizations on campus, including a drama/theater group, newspaper, and choral group. 60% of eligible men and 65% of eligible women are members of national **fraternities** and national **sororities**.

Centre is a member of the NCAA (Division III). **Intercollegiate sports** include baseball (m), basketball, cross-country running, field hockey (w), football (m), golf, soccer, softball (w), swimming, tennis, track and field, volleyball (w).

Campus Safety

Student safety services include late-night transport/escort service, 24-hour emergency telephone alarm devices, 24-hour patrols by trained security personnel, and electronically operated dormitory entrances.

Applying

Centre requires an essay, SAT I or ACT, a high school transcript, and 1 recommendation. It recommends SAT II: Writing Test and an interview. Application deadline: 2/1; 3/1 for financial aid. Early and deferred admission are possible.

Getting in Last Year

1,142 applied
86% were accepted
250 enrolled (26%)
50% from top tenth of their h.s. class
3.68 average high school GPA
65% had SAT verbal scores over 600
65% had SAT math scores over 600
91% had ACT scores over 24
21% had SAT verbal scores over 700
18% had SAT math scores over 700
27% had ACT scores over 30
6 National Merit Scholars
22 valedictorians

Graduation and After

68% graduated in 4 years
5% graduated in 5 years
40% pursued further study (21% arts and sciences, 9% law, 5% medicine)
70% had job offers within 6 months
25 organizations recruited on campus
1 Rhodes, 1 Fulbright scholar

Financial Matters

$21,350 comprehensive fee (1999–2000)
100% average percent of need met
$15,120 average financial aid amount received per undergraduate (1999–2000)

CHAPMAN UNIVERSITY

SUBURBAN SETTING ■ PRIVATE ■ INDEPENDENT RELIGIOUS ■ COED
ORANGE, CALIFORNIA

Web site: www.chapman.edu
Contact: Mr. Michael O. Drummy, Associate Dean for Enrollment Services and Chief Admission Officer, One University Drive, Orange, CA 92866
Telephone: 714-997-6711 or toll-free 888-CUAPPLY **Fax:** 714-997-6713
E-mail: admit@chapman.edu

Academics

Chapman awards bachelor's, master's, and first-professional **degrees**. Challenging opportunities include advanced placement, accelerated degree programs, an honors program, double majors, independent study, and a senior project. Special programs include cooperative education, internships, summer session for credit, study-abroad, and Army and Air Force ROTC. A complete listing of majors at Chapman appears in the Majors Index beginning on page 432.

The **faculty** at Chapman has 204 full-time members, 78% with terminal degrees. The student-faculty ratio is 13:1.

Students of Chapman

The student body totals 3,897, of whom 2,594 are undergraduates. 56.4% are women and 43.6% are men. Students come from 38 states and territories and 29 other countries. 3% are international students. 3.6% are African American, 1.3% American Indian, 8.3% Asian American, and 23.4% Hispanic American. 84% returned for their sophomore year.

Facilities and Resources

200 **computers** are available on campus that provide access to the Internet. The 2 **libraries** have 203,915 books and 2,121 subscriptions.

Campus Life

There are 65 active organizations on campus, including a drama/theater group, newspaper, radio station, and choral group. 10% of eligible men and 15% of eligible women are members of national **fraternities** and national **sororities**.

Chapman is a member of the NCAA (Division III). **Intercollegiate sports** include baseball (m), basketball, crew, cross-country running, football (m), golf, lacrosse, soccer, softball (w), swimming (w), tennis, track and field (w), volleyball (w), water polo.

Campus Safety

Student safety services include full safety education program, late-night transport/escort service, 24-hour emergency telephone alarm devices, and 24-hour patrols by trained security personnel.

Applying

Chapman requires an essay, SAT I or ACT, a high school transcript, 1 recommendation, and a minimum high school GPA of 2.5. It recommends SAT II Subject Tests, an interview, and a minimum high school GPA of 3.0. Application deadline: 1/31; 3/1 priority date for financial aid. Early and deferred admission are possible.

CHRISTENDOM COLLEGE

RURAL SETTING ■ PRIVATE ■ INDEPENDENT RELIGIOUS ■ COED
FRONT ROYAL, VIRGINIA

Web site: www.christendom.edu
Contact: Mr. Paul Heisler, Director of Admissions, 134 Christendom Drive, Front Royal, VA 22630-5103
Telephone: 540-636-2900 ext. 290 or toll-free 800-877-5456 ext. 290 **Fax:** 540-636-1655
E-mail: admissions@christendom.edu

eApply

Academics

Christendom awards associate, bachelor's, and master's **degrees**. Challenging opportunities include advanced placement, accelerated degree programs, double majors, and a senior project. Special programs include cooperative education, internships, summer session for credit, and study-abroad.

The most frequently chosen fields are social sciences and history, philosophy, and English. A complete listing of majors at Christendom appears in the Majors Index beginning on page 432.

The **faculty** at Christendom has 21 full-time members, 71% with terminal degrees. The student-faculty ratio is 12:1.

Students of Christendom

The student body totals 344, of whom 259 are undergraduates. 53.3% are women and 46.7% are men. Students come from 48 states and territories and 4 other countries. 21% are from Virginia. 3.5% are international students. 0.8% are African American, 1.9% Asian American, and 2.3% Hispanic American. 84% returned for their sophomore year.

Facilities and Resources

17 **computers** are available on campus that provide access to the Internet. The **library** has 61,787 books and 249 subscriptions.

Campus Life

There are 15 active organizations on campus, including a drama/theater group, newspaper, and choral group. No national or local **fraternities** or **sororities**.

Intercollegiate sports include baseball (m), basketball, soccer.

Campus Safety

Student safety services include night patrols by trained security personnel, late-night transport/escort service, and 24-hour emergency telephone alarm devices.

Applying

Christendom requires an essay, SAT I or ACT, a high school transcript, and 2 recommendations. It recommends an interview and a minimum high school GPA of 3.0. Application deadline: rolling admissions; 4/1 priority date for financial aid. Early admission is possible.

Getting in Last Year
162 applied
85% were accepted
74 enrolled (54%)
30% from top tenth of their h.s. class
3.45 average high school GPA
63% had SAT verbal scores over 600
48% had SAT math scores over 600
78% had ACT scores over 24
30% had SAT verbal scores over 700
12% had SAT math scores over 700
6% had ACT scores over 30

Graduation and After
45% graduated in 4 years
4% graduated in 5 years
2% graduated in 6 years
20% pursued further study (8% arts and sciences, 6% theology, 4% law)
80% had job offers within 6 months
4 organizations recruited on campus

Financial Matters
$11,530 tuition and fees (2000–2001)
$4570 room and board
90% average percent of need met
$9085 average financial aid amount received per undergraduate (1999–2000)

CHRISTIAN BROTHERS UNIVERSITY

URBAN SETTING ■ PRIVATE ■ INDEPENDENT RELIGIOUS ■ COED
MEMPHIS, TENNESSEE

Web site: www.cbu.edu
Contact: Ms. Courtney Fee, Dean of Admission, 650 East Parkway South, Memphis, TN 38104
Telephone: 901-321-3205 or toll-free 800-288-7576 **Fax:** 901-321-3202
E-mail: admissions@cbu.edu

Christian Brothers University is located in the center of the friendly Southern city of Memphis, Tennessee. Situated on a beautiful 70-acre campus, Christian Brothers University encourages a true sense of excellence and achievement that embodies the history and the tradition of the Christian Brothers. CBU offers a low student-faculty ratio and is known for the high academic caliber of its students and the caring commitment of its faculty. At Christian Brothers University, students "dream no little dreams." Outstanding acceptance rates for medical and law school students, along with a high graduate placement rate, ensure that CBU's graduates are prepared for the future.

Getting in Last Year
859 applied
77% were accepted
245 enrolled (37%)
28% from top tenth of their h.s. class
3.47 average high school GPA
25% had SAT verbal scores over 600
28% had SAT math scores over 600
58% had ACT scores over 24
8% had SAT math scores over 700
13% had ACT scores over 30

Graduation and After
30% pursued further study
85.7% had job offers within 6 months
211 organizations recruited on campus

Financial Matters
$13,490 tuition and fees (1999–2000)
$3950 room and board

Academics
CBU awards bachelor's and master's **degrees**. Challenging opportunities include advanced placement, accelerated degree programs, an honors program, double majors, and a senior project. Special programs include internships, summer session for credit, off-campus study, study-abroad, and Army, Navy and Air Force ROTC.

The most frequently chosen fields are business/marketing, engineering/engineering technologies, and psychology. A complete listing of majors at CBU appears in the Majors Index beginning on page 432.

The **faculty** at CBU has 117 full-time members. The student-faculty ratio is 13:1.

Students of CBU
The student body totals 1,992, of whom 1,598 are undergraduates. 52.6% are women and 47.4% are men. Students come from 27 states and territories and 44 other countries. 72% are from Tennessee. 7.4% are international students. 21.1% are African American, 0.3% American Indian, 2.8% Asian American, and 1.8% Hispanic American. 73% returned for their sophomore year.

Facilities and Resources
Student rooms are linked to a campus network. 280 **computers** are available on campus that provide access to online class listings, e-mail, course assignments and the Internet. The **library** has 100,000 books and 537 subscriptions.

Campus Life
There are 23 active organizations on campus, including a drama/theater group, newspaper, and choral group. 24% of eligible men and 20% of eligible women are members of national **fraternities**, national **sororities**, and local sororities.

CBU is a member of the NCAA (Division II). **Intercollegiate sports** (some offering scholarships) include baseball (m), basketball, cross-country running, golf (m), soccer, softball (w), tennis, volleyball (w).

Campus Safety
Student safety services include late-night transport/escort service, 24-hour emergency telephone alarm devices, 24-hour patrols by trained security personnel, student patrols, and electronically operated dormitory entrances.

Applying
CBU requires an essay, SAT I or ACT, a high school transcript, and a minimum high school GPA of 2.25, and in some cases recommendations. It recommends an interview. Application deadline: 8/23; 3/15 priority date for financial aid. Early and deferred admission are possible.

CLAREMONT McKENNA COLLEGE

SMALL-TOWN SETTING ■ PRIVATE ■ INDEPENDENT ■ COED
CLAREMONT, CALIFORNIA

Web site: www.mckenna.edu
Contact: Mr. Richard C. Vos, Vice President/Dean of Admission and
Financial Aid, 890 Columbia Avenue, Claremont, CA 91711
Telephone: 909-621-8088
E-mail: admission@mckenna.edu

  eAPPLY

Academics

CMC awards bachelor's **degrees**. Challenging opportunities include advanced placement, accelerated degree programs, student-designed majors, an honors program, double majors, independent study, a senior project, Phi Beta Kappa, and Sigma Xi. Special programs include internships, off-campus study, study-abroad, and Army, Navy and Air Force ROTC.

The most frequently chosen fields are social sciences and history, interdisciplinary studies, and psychology. A complete listing of majors at CMC appears in the Majors Index beginning on page 432.

The **faculty** at CMC has 120 full-time members. The student-faculty ratio is 8:1.

Students of CMC

The student body is made up of 1,016 undergraduates. 44.5% are women and 55.5% are men. Students come from 40 states and territories and 22 other countries. 63% are from California. 3.3% are international students. 4.3% are African American, 0.2% American Indian, 16.8% Asian American, and 13.2% Hispanic American. 96% returned for their sophomore year.

Facilities and Resources

Student rooms are linked to a campus network. 162 **computers** are available on campus that provide access to the Internet. The 4 **libraries** have 2,028,793 books and 6,028 subscriptions.

Campus Life

There are 280 active organizations on campus, including a drama/theater group, newspaper, radio station, and choral group. No national or local **fraternities** or **sororities**.

CMC is a member of the NCAA (Division III). **Intercollegiate sports** include badminton, baseball (m), basketball, cross-country running, football (m), golf (m), lacrosse, rugby, skiing (downhill), soccer, softball (w), swimming, tennis, track and field, volleyball, water polo.

Campus Safety

Student safety services include late-night transport/escort service, 24-hour emergency telephone alarm devices, 24-hour patrols by trained security personnel, student patrols, and electronically operated dormitory entrances.

Applying

CMC requires an essay, SAT I or ACT, a high school transcript, 2 recommendations, and a minimum high school GPA of 3.0. It recommends SAT II Subject Tests and an interview. Application deadline: 1/15; 2/1 for financial aid. Early and deferred admission are possible.

Claremont McKenna College (CMC) offers a traditional liberal arts education with a twist: within the context of a liberal arts curriculum, CMC focuses on economics, government, and international relations as it prepares students for leadership in business, government, and other professions. CMC's enrollment of approximately 1,000 students ensures a personalized educational experience. However, with 4 other colleges—Harvey Mudd, Pitzer, Pomona, and Scripps—and 2 graduate schools right next door, CMC students also have access to the academic, intellectual, social, and athletic resources typical of a medium-sized university.

Getting in Last Year
2,827 applied
28% were accepted
252 enrolled (32%)
78% from top tenth of their h.s. class
3.87 average high school GPA
88% had SAT verbal scores over 600
88% had SAT math scores over 600
44% had SAT verbal scores over 700
47% had SAT math scores over 700
19 National Merit Scholars
3 class presidents
27 valedictorians

Graduation and After
81% graduated in 4 years
2% graduated in 5 years
24% pursued further study (11% law, 6% arts and sciences, 2% business)
64% had job offers within 6 months
100 organizations recruited on campus
1 Fulbright scholar

Financial Matters
$20,760 tuition and fees (1999–2000)
$7060 room and board
100% average percent of need met
$18,980 average financial aid amount received per undergraduate (1999–2000)

eApply

Getting in Last Year
692 applied
78% were accepted
188 enrolled (35%)
23% from top tenth of their h.s. class
3.40 average high school GPA
13% had SAT verbal scores over 600
16% had SAT math scores over 600
59% had ACT scores over 24
3% had SAT math scores over 700
2% had ACT scores over 30
2 valedictorians

Graduation and After
40% graduated in 4 years
16% graduated in 5 years
1% graduated in 6 years
29% pursued further study (2% business, 2% education)
59% had job offers within 6 months
18 organizations recruited on campus

Financial Matters
$13,586 tuition and fees (1999–2000)
$5082 room and board
100% average percent of need met
$11,423 average financial aid amount received per undergraduate (1999–2000)

CLARKE COLLEGE
URBAN SETTING ■ PRIVATE ■ INDEPENDENT RELIGIOUS ■ COED
DUBUQUE, IOWA

Web site: www.clarke.edu
Contact: Mr. John D. Foley, Director of Admissions, 1550 Clarke Drive, Dubuque, IA 52001-3198
Telephone: 319-588-6316 or toll-free 800-383-2345 **Fax:** 319-588-6789
E-mail: admissions@clarke.edu

Academics
Clarke awards associate, bachelor's, and master's **degrees**. Challenging opportunities include advanced placement, student-designed majors, an honors program, double majors, independent study, and a senior project. Special programs include cooperative education, internships, summer session for credit, off-campus study, and study-abroad.

The most frequently chosen fields are health professions and related sciences, business/marketing, and computer/information sciences. A complete listing of majors at Clarke appears in the Majors Index beginning on page 432.

The **faculty** at Clarke has 87 full-time members, 75% with terminal degrees. The student-faculty ratio is 9:1.

Students of Clarke
The student body totals 1,283, of whom 1,120 are undergraduates. 66.4% are women and 33.6% are men. Students come from 27 states and territories and 13 other countries. 59% are from Iowa. 2.7% are international students. 1.2% are African American, 0.2% American Indian, 0.2% Asian American, and 3.3% Hispanic American. 77% returned for their sophomore year.

Facilities and Resources
Student rooms are linked to a campus network. 184 **computers** are available on campus that provide access to the Internet. The **library** has 115,562 books and 936 subscriptions.

Campus Life
There are 63 active organizations on campus, including a drama/theater group, newspaper, radio station, and choral group. No national or local **fraternities** or **sororities**.

Clarke is a member of the NCAA (Division III). **Intercollegiate sports** include baseball (m), basketball, cross-country running, golf, skiing (downhill), soccer, softball (w), tennis, volleyball.

Campus Safety
Student safety services include late-night transport/escort service, 24-hour emergency telephone alarm devices, 24-hour patrols by trained security personnel, and electronically operated dormitory entrances.

Applying
Clarke requires SAT I or ACT, a high school transcript, rank in upper 50% of high school class, minimum ACT score of 21 or minimum SAT score of 1000, and a minimum high school GPA of 2.0, and in some cases an interview. Application deadline: rolling admissions; 4/15 priority date for financial aid. Deferred admission is possible.

CLARKSON UNIVERSITY

SMALL-TOWN SETTING ■ PRIVATE ■ INDEPENDENT ■ COED
POTSDAM, NEW YORK

   eAPPLY

Web site: www.clarkson.edu
Contact: Mr. Brian T. Grant, Director of Enrollment Operations, Holcroft
House, Potsdam, NY 13699
Telephone: 315-268-6479 or toll-free 800-527-6577 **Fax:** 315-268-7647
E-mail: admission@clarkson.edu

Academics

Clarkson awards bachelor's, master's, and doctoral **degrees**. Challenging opportunities
include advanced placement, accelerated degree programs, student-designed majors, an
honors program, double majors, independent study, a senior project, and Sigma Xi.
Special programs include cooperative education, internships, summer session for credit,
off-campus study, study-abroad, and Army and Air Force ROTC.

The most frequently chosen fields are engineering/engineering technologies, busi-
ness/marketing, and interdisciplinary studies. A complete listing of majors at Clarkson
appears in the Majors Index beginning on page 432.

The **faculty** at Clarkson has 153 full-time members, 92% with terminal degrees. The
student-faculty ratio is 16:1.

Students of Clarkson

The student body totals 2,902, of whom 2,581 are undergraduates. 26.7% are women
and 73.3% are men. Students come from 36 states and territories and 28 other countries.
72% are from New York. 2.9% are international students. 2.8% are African American,
0.6% American Indian, 2.4% Asian American, and 1.6% Hispanic American. 85%
returned for their sophomore year.

Facilities and Resources

Student rooms are linked to a campus network. 199 **computers** are available on campus
that provide access to the Internet. The **library** has 237,251 books and 1,705 subscriptions.

Campus Life

There are 39 active organizations on campus, including a drama/theater group,
newspaper, radio station, and television station. 15% of eligible men and 17% of eligible
women are members of national **fraternities**, national **sororities**, and local fraternities.

Clarkson is a member of the NCAA (Division III). **Intercollegiate sports** (some offering scholarships) include baseball (m), basketball, cross-country running, golf (m), ice
hockey, lacrosse, rugby (m), skiing (cross-country), skiing (downhill), soccer, swimming,
tennis, volleyball (w).

Campus Safety

Student safety services include late-night transport/escort service, 24-hour emergency
telephone alarm devices, 24-hour patrols by trained security personnel, and electronically operated dormitory entrances.

Applying

Clarkson requires SAT I or ACT, a high school transcript, and 1 recommendation. It
recommends SAT II Subject Tests and an interview. Application deadline: 3/15; 3/1
priority date for financial aid. Early and deferred admission are possible.

> **C**larkson is a blend of vivid
> contrasts—high-powered
> academics in a cooperative
> and friendly community, technically
> oriented students who enjoy people,
> and a location that serves as a
> gateway to outstanding outdoor
> recreational opportunities and
> numerous social and cultural
> activities at 3 other area colleges.
> Clarkson's students are described as
> hard-working, outgoing, energized
> team players; the academic
> programs as relevant, flexible, and
> nationally respected; and the
> teachers as approachable, concerned,
> accomplished, and inspiring. Clarkson
> alumni, students, and faculty share
> an exceptionally strong bond and
> the lifetime benefits that come from
> a global network of personal and
> professional ties.

Getting in Last Year
2,568 applied
83% were accepted
707 enrolled (33%)
39% from top tenth of their h.s. class
3.31 average high school GPA
39% had SAT verbal scores over 600
61% had SAT math scores over 600
7% had SAT verbal scores over 700
13% had SAT math scores over 700
6 National Merit Scholars
22 valedictorians

Graduation and After
16% pursued further study (6% engineering,
6% arts and sciences, 3% business)
97% had job offers within 6 months
167 organizations recruited on campus

Financial Matters
$20,225 tuition and fees (1999–2000)
$7484 room and board
87% average percent of need met
$14,647 average financial aid amount received
per undergraduate (1998–99)

eApply

CLARK UNIVERSITY
URBAN SETTING ■ PRIVATE ■ INDEPENDENT ■ COED
WORCESTER, MASSACHUSETTS

Web site: www.clarku.edu

Contact: Mr. Harold M. Wingood, Dean of Admissions, 950 Main Street, Worcester, MA 01610-1477

Telephone: 508-793-7431 or toll-free 800-GO-CLARK (out-of-state)

E-mail: admissions@admissions.clark.edu

Academics
Clark awards bachelor's, master's, and doctoral **degrees** and post-bachelor's and post-master's certificates. Challenging opportunities include advanced placement, accelerated degree programs, student-designed majors, an honors program, double majors, independent study, a senior project, and Phi Beta Kappa. Special programs include internships, summer session for credit, off-campus study, study-abroad, and Army and Air Force ROTC.

The most frequently chosen fields are social sciences and history, psychology, and biological/life sciences. A complete listing of majors at Clark appears in the Majors Index beginning on page 432.

The **faculty** at Clark has 150 full-time members, 99% with terminal degrees. The student-faculty ratio is 12:1.

Students of Clark
The student body totals 3,003, of whom 2,182 are undergraduates. 59.7% are women and 40.3% are men. Students come from 40 states and territories and 63 other countries. 41% are from Massachusetts. 11% are international students. 3.4% are African American, 0.1% American Indian, 3.9% Asian American, and 3% Hispanic American. 87% returned for their sophomore year.

Facilities and Resources
Student rooms are linked to a campus network. 100 **computers** are available on campus that provide access to online course support and the Internet. The 5 **libraries** have 3,593 subscriptions.

Campus Life
There are 74 active organizations on campus, including a drama/theater group, newspaper, radio station, television station, and choral group. No national or local **fraternities** or **sororities**.

Clark is a member of the NCAA (Division III). **Intercollegiate sports** include baseball (m), basketball, crew, cross-country running, field hockey (w), lacrosse (m), soccer, softball (w), swimming, tennis, volleyball (w), wrestling (w).

Campus Safety
Student safety services include late-night transport/escort service, 24-hour emergency telephone alarm devices, 24-hour patrols by trained security personnel, student patrols, and electronically operated dormitory entrances.

Applying
Clark requires an essay, SAT II: Writing Test, SAT I or ACT, and a high school transcript. It recommends SAT II Subject Tests, an interview, 2 recommendations, and a minimum high school GPA of 3.0. Application deadline: 2/1; 2/1 priority date for financial aid. Early and deferred admission are possible.

CLEMSON UNIVERSITY

SMALL-TOWN SETTING ■ PUBLIC ■ STATE-SUPPORTED ■ COED
CLEMSON, SOUTH CAROLINA

Web site: www.clemson.edu
Contact: Mrs. Audrey Bodell, Assistant Director of Admissions, 105 Sikes
   Hall, PO Box 345124, Clemson, SC 29634
Telephone: 864-656-2287 **Fax:** 864-656-2464
E-mail: cuadmissions@clemson.edu

Academics

Clemson awards bachelor's, master's, and doctoral **degrees**. Challenging opportunities include advanced placement, accelerated degree programs, an honors program, double majors, a senior project, and Sigma Xi. Special programs include cooperative education, internships, summer session for credit, study-abroad, and Army and Air Force ROTC.

The most frequently chosen fields are business/marketing, engineering/engineering technologies, and education. A complete listing of majors at Clemson appears in the Majors Index beginning on page 432.

The **faculty** at Clemson has 935 full-time members, 87% with terminal degrees. The student-faculty ratio is 16:1.

Students of Clemson

The student body totals 16,982, of whom 13,526 are undergraduates. 45.4% are women and 54.6% are men. Students come from 52 states and territories. 69% are from South Carolina. 0.7% are international students. 7.7% are African American, 0.2% American Indian, 1.4% Asian American, and 0.9% Hispanic American. 84% returned for their sophomore year.

Facilities and Resources

Student rooms are linked to a campus network. 1,000 **computers** are available on campus that provide access to the Internet. The 2 **libraries** have 1,648,741 books and 5,978 subscriptions.

Campus Life

There are 260 active organizations on campus, including a drama/theater group, newspaper, radio station, choral group, and marching band. 20% of eligible men and 20% of eligible women are members of national **fraternities** and national **sororities**.

Clemson is a member of the NCAA (Division I). **Intercollegiate sports** (some offering scholarships) include baseball (m), basketball, bowling, crew, cross-country running, equestrian sports, fencing, field hockey, football (m), golf (m), lacrosse, riflery, rugby, sailing, skiing (cross-country), skiing (downhill), soccer, swimming, tennis, track and field, volleyball (w), weight lifting.

Campus Safety

Student safety services include late-night transport/escort service, 24-hour emergency telephone alarm devices, 24-hour patrols by trained security personnel, and electronically operated dormitory entrances.

Applying

Clemson requires SAT I or ACT and a high school transcript, and in some cases SAT II Subject Tests. It recommends an essay, an interview, and recommendations. Application deadline: 5/1; 4/1 priority date for financial aid. Early and deferred admission are possible.

> **C**lemson's honors program, known as Calhoun College, is designed for academically talented students who wish to cultivate a lifelong love of learning and to prepare for lives as leaders and change-agents. The honors experience includes a core of interdisciplinary courses and opportunities for independent research. Under the administration of Calhoun College, the Dixon Fellows Program helps prepare students to compete for prestigious postgraduate scholarships such as Rhodes, Marshall, Truman, and Fulbright. Housing for 300 Calhoun scholars is available in Holmes Hall, located in the heart of Clemson's beautiful campus.

Getting in Last Year
9,501 applied
68% were accepted
2,891 enrolled (45%)
34% from top tenth of their h.s. class
3.54 average high school GPA
33% had SAT verbal scores over 600
46% had SAT math scores over 600
67% had ACT scores over 24
5% had SAT verbal scores over 700
10% had SAT math scores over 700
15% had ACT scores over 30
22 National Merit Scholars
126 valedictorians

Graduation and After
37% graduated in 4 years
30% graduated in 5 years
6% graduated in 6 years
85% had job offers within 6 months
392 organizations recruited on campus

Financial Matters
$3470 resident tuition and fees (1999–2000)
$9456 nonresident tuition and fees (1999–2000)
$4122 room and board
82% average percent of need met
$7123 average financial aid amount received per undergraduate (1999–2000)

Getting in Last Year
1,176 applied
82% were accepted
328 enrolled (34%)
27% from top tenth of their h.s. class
3.56 average high school GPA
42% had SAT verbal scores over 600
27% had SAT math scores over 600
54% had ACT scores over 24
4% had SAT verbal scores over 700
7% had ACT scores over 30
12 valedictorians

Graduation and After
53% graduated in 4 years
8% graduated in 5 years
1% graduated in 6 years
Graduates pursuing further study: 8% business, 5% law, 3% arts and sciences
98% had job offers within 6 months
88 organizations recruited on campus

Financial Matters
$17,540 tuition and fees (1999–2000)
$5020 room and board
95% average percent of need met
$18,048 average financial aid amount received per undergraduate (1999–2000 estimated)

COE COLLEGE
URBAN SETTING ■ PRIVATE ■ INDEPENDENT RELIGIOUS ■ COED
CEDAR RAPIDS, IOWA

Web site: www.coe.edu
Contact: Mr. Dennis Trotter, Vice President of Admission and Financial Aid, 1220 1st Avenue, NE, Cedar Rapids, IA 52402-5070
Telephone: 319-399-8500 or toll-free 877-225-5263 **Fax:** 319-399-8816
E-mail: admission@coe.edu

Academics
Coe awards bachelor's and master's **degrees**. Challenging opportunities include advanced placement, accelerated degree programs, student-designed majors, freshman honors college, an honors program, double majors, independent study, a senior project, and Phi Beta Kappa. Special programs include internships, summer session for credit, off-campus study, study-abroad, and Army and Air Force ROTC.

The most frequently chosen fields are business/marketing, social sciences and history, and visual/performing arts. A complete listing of majors at Coe appears in the Majors Index beginning on page 432.

The **faculty** at Coe has 73 full-time members, 92% with terminal degrees. The student-faculty ratio is 12:1.

Students of Coe
The student body totals 1,304, of whom 1,246 are undergraduates. 54% are women and 46% are men. Students come from 35 states and territories and 16 other countries. 57% are from Iowa. 4.1% are international students. 2.5% are African American, 0.1% American Indian, 1.2% Asian American, and 1.4% Hispanic American. 80% returned for their sophomore year.

Facilities and Resources
Student rooms are linked to a campus network. 165 **computers** are available on campus that provide access to the Internet. The 2 **libraries** have 149,888 books and 881 subscriptions.

Campus Life
There are 65 active organizations on campus, including a drama/theater group, newspaper, radio station, and choral group. 24% of eligible men and 15% of eligible women are members of national **fraternities** and national **sororities**.

Coe is a member of the NCAA (Division III). **Intercollegiate sports** include baseball (m), basketball, cross-country running, football (m), golf, soccer, softball (w), swimming, tennis, track and field, volleyball (w), wrestling (m).

Campus Safety
Student safety services include late-night transport/escort service, 24-hour emergency telephone alarm devices, 24-hour patrols by trained security personnel, and electronically operated dormitory entrances.

Applying
Coe requires an essay, SAT I or ACT, a high school transcript, and 1 recommendation. It recommends an interview and a minimum high school GPA of 3.0. Application deadline: 3/1; 3/1 priority date for financial aid. Early and deferred admission are possible.

COLBY COLLEGE

SMALL-TOWN SETTING ■ PRIVATE ■ INDEPENDENT ■ COED
WATERVILLE, MAINE

Web site: www.colby.edu
Contact: Mr. Parker J. Beverage, Dean of Admissions and Financial Aid,
Office of Admissions and Financial Aid, 4800 Mayflower Hill, Waterville,
ME 04901-8848
Telephone: 207-872-3168 or toll-free 800-723-3032 **Fax:** 207-872-3474
E-mail: admissions@colby.edu

eAPPLY

Academics

Colby awards bachelor's **degrees**. Challenging opportunities include advanced placement, student-designed majors, an honors program, double majors, independent study, a
senior project, and Phi Beta Kappa. Special programs include internships, off-campus
study, study-abroad, and Army ROTC.

The most frequently chosen fields are social sciences and history, biological/life sciences, and English. A complete listing of majors at Colby appears in the Majors Index
beginning on page 432.

The **faculty** at Colby has 147 full-time members. The student-faculty ratio is 11:1.

Students of Colby

The student body is made up of 1,764 undergraduates. 51.6% are women and 48.4% are
men. Students come from 46 states and territories and 52 other countries. 11% are from
Maine. 4.1% are international students. 2.6% are African American, 0.2% American
Indian, 4.8% Asian American, and 2.4% Hispanic American. 91% returned for their
sophomore year.

Facilities and Resources

Student rooms are linked to a campus network. 276 **computers** are available on campus
that provide access to the Internet. The 3 **libraries** have 591,845 books and 2,390
subscriptions.

Campus Life

There are 90 active organizations on campus, including a drama/theater group,
newspaper, radio station, and choral group. No national or local **fraternities** or **sororities**.

Colby is a member of the NCAA (Division III). **Intercollegiate sports** include
badminton, baseball (m), basketball, crew, cross-country running, equestrian sports, fencing, field hockey (w), football (m), golf, ice hockey, lacrosse, rugby, sailing, skiing (cross-
country), skiing (downhill), soccer, softball (w), squash, swimming, tennis, track and field,
volleyball, water polo.

Campus Safety

Student safety services include campus lighting, student emergency response team, late-
night transport/escort service, 24-hour emergency telephone alarm devices, 24-hour
patrols by trained security personnel, and electronically operated dormitory entrances.

Applying

Colby requires an essay, SAT I or ACT, a high school transcript, and 2 recommendations. It recommends an interview. Application deadline: 1/15; 2/1 for financial aid.
Deferred admission is possible.

Getting in Last Year

4,363 applied
33% were accepted
489 enrolled (34%)
52% from top tenth of their h.s. class
82% had SAT verbal scores over 600
83% had SAT math scores over 600
96% had ACT scores over 24
23% had SAT verbal scores over 700
26% had SAT math scores over 700
33% had ACT scores over 30
9 valedictorians

Graduation and After

84% graduated in 4 years
5% graduated in 5 years
Graduates pursuing further study: 12% arts
and sciences, 2% law, 1% medicine
80% had job offers within 6 months
55 organizations recruited on campus

Financial Matters

$31,580 comprehensive fee (1999–2000)
100% average percent of need met
$20,100 average financial aid amount received
per undergraduate (1999–2000 estimated)

eAPPLY

Getting in Last Year
5,590 applied
42% were accepted
750 enrolled (32%)
66% from top tenth of their h.s. class
3.39 average high school GPA
78% had SAT verbal scores over 600
82% had SAT math scores over 600
87% had ACT scores over 24
19% had SAT verbal scores over 700
20% had SAT math scores over 700
67% had ACT scores over 30
31 valedictorians

Graduation and After
85% graduated in 4 years
3% graduated in 5 years
14% pursued further study (5% arts and sciences, 4% law, 4% medicine)
79% had job offers within 6 months
109 organizations recruited on campus

Financial Matters
$24,750 tuition and fees (1999–2000)
$6330 room and board
98% average percent of need met
$21,543 average financial aid amount received per undergraduate (1999–2000 estimated)

COLGATE UNIVERSITY
RURAL SETTING ■ PRIVATE ■ INDEPENDENT ■ COED
HAMILTON, NEW YORK

Web site: www.colgate.edu
Contact: Ms. Mary F. Hill, Dean of Admission, 13 Oak Drive, Hamilton, NY 13346-1386
Telephone: 315-228-7401 **Fax:** 315-228-7544
E-mail: admission@mail.colgate.edu

Academics
Colgate awards bachelor's and master's **degrees**. Challenging opportunities include advanced placement, student-designed majors, an honors program, double majors, independent study, a senior project, and Phi Beta Kappa. Special programs include off-campus study, study-abroad, and Army ROTC.

The most frequently chosen fields are social sciences and history, biological/life sciences, and English. A complete listing of majors at Colgate appears in the Majors Index beginning on page 432.

The **faculty** at Colgate has 230 full-time members, 98% with terminal degrees. The student-faculty ratio is 10:1.

Students of Colgate
The student body totals 2,876, of whom 2,868 are undergraduates. 51.7% are women and 48.3% are men. Students come from 44 states and territories and 29 other countries. 32% are from New York. 2.4% are international students. 4.6% are African American, 0.5% American Indian, 5.6% Asian American, and 3.7% Hispanic American. 98% returned for their sophomore year.

Facilities and Resources
Student rooms are linked to a campus network. 400 **computers** are available on campus that provide access to software applications and the Internet. The 2 **libraries** have 600,000 books and 2,250 subscriptions.

Campus Life
There are 100 active organizations on campus, including a drama/theater group, newspaper, radio station, television station, choral group, and marching band. 33% of eligible men and 31% of eligible women are members of national **fraternities**, national **sororities**, and local fraternities.

Colgate is a member of the NCAA (Division I). **Intercollegiate sports** include baseball (m), basketball, crew, cross-country running, equestrian sports, fencing, field hockey (w), football (m), golf, ice hockey, lacrosse, rugby, sailing, skiing (downhill), soccer, softball (w), squash, swimming, tennis, track and field, volleyball, water polo, wrestling.

Campus Safety
Student safety services include late-night transport/escort service, 24-hour emergency telephone alarm devices, 24-hour patrols by trained security personnel, student patrols, and electronically operated dormitory entrances.

Applying
Colgate requires an essay, SAT I with 3 SAT II Subject Tests (including SAT II: Writing Test) or ACT, a high school transcript, and 3 recommendations. Application deadline: 1/15; 2/1 for financial aid. Early and deferred admission are possible.

COLLEGE OF INSURANCE

URBAN SETTING ■ PRIVATE ■ INDEPENDENT ■ COED
NEW YORK, NEW YORK

Web site: www.tci.edu
Contact: Ms. Theresa C. Marro, Director of Admissions, 101 Murray Street, New York, NY 10007
Telephone: 212-815-9232 or toll-free 800-356-5146 **Fax:** 212-964-3381
E-mail: admissions@tci.edu

Academics

College of Insurance awards associate, bachelor's, and master's **degrees**. Challenging opportunities include advanced placement and a senior project. Special programs include cooperative education, summer session for credit, and off-campus study.

The most frequently chosen field is business/marketing. A complete listing of majors at College of Insurance appears in the Majors Index beginning on page 432.

The **faculty** at College of Insurance has 10 full-time members, 100% with terminal degrees. The student-faculty ratio is 11:1.

Students of College of Insurance

The student body totals 357, of whom 270 are undergraduates. 52.6% are women and 47.4% are men. 82% are from New York. 13% are international students. 18.1% are African American, 10% Asian American, and 9.6% Hispanic American. 72% returned for their sophomore year.

Facilities and Resources

19 **computers** are available on campus that provide access to the Internet. The 2 **libraries** have 418 subscriptions.

Campus Life

Active organizations on campus include a newspaper. College of Insurance has national **fraternities**.

This institution has no intercollegiate sports.

Campus Safety

Student safety services include 24-hour emergency telephone alarm devices and 24-hour patrols by trained security personnel.

Applying

College of Insurance requires an essay, SAT I or ACT, a high school transcript, an interview, and a minimum high school GPA of 2.5. It recommends recommendations. Application deadline: 5/1. Deferred admission is possible.

> **T**he College of Insurance is a fully accredited institution that is sponsored by more than 300 companies in the insurance and financial services industry. The College of Insurance is centrally located in the heart of the financial district, within walking distance of the World Trade Center, SoHo, Chinatown, and the South Street Seaport. The College is housed in an award-winning, self-contained building with dormitories on the top 4 floors. The College of Insurance offers qualified students the opportunity to participate in a unique cooperative work-study program.

Getting in Last Year

56 applied
71% were accepted
13 enrolled (33%)
35% from top tenth of their h.s. class
25% had SAT verbal scores over 600
62% had SAT math scores over 600
6% had SAT verbal scores over 700
18% had SAT math scores over 700

Graduation and After

30% graduated in 4 years
20% graduated in 5 years
95% had job offers within 6 months
30 organizations recruited on campus

Financial Matters

$14,612 tuition and fees (1999–2000)
$7900 room and board
97% average percent of need met
$16,715 average financial aid amount received per undergraduate (1998–99)

The College of New Jersey

Suburban setting ■ Public ■ State-supported ■ Coed
Ewing, New Jersey

Web site: www.tcnj.edu
Contact: Ms. Lisa Angeloni, Director of Admissions, Admission Office, PO Box 7718, Ewing, NJ 08628
Telephone: 609-771-2131 or toll-free 800-624-0967 **Fax:** 609-637-5174
E-mail: admiss@vm.tcnj.edu

Getting in Last Year

5,755 applied
55% were accepted
1,209 enrolled (38%)
57% from top tenth of their h.s. class
3.25 average high school GPA
54% had SAT verbal scores over 600
65% had SAT math scores over 600
10% had SAT verbal scores over 700
14% had SAT math scores over 700
31 valedictorians

Graduation and After

59% graduated in 4 years
19% graduated in 5 years
1% graduated in 6 years
25% pursued further study (8% education, 7% arts and sciences, 6% business)
65% had job offers within 6 months
265 organizations recruited on campus

Financial Matters

$5685 resident tuition and fees (1999–2000)
$9002 nonresident tuition and fees (1999–2000)
$6330 room and board
$6000 average financial aid amount received per undergraduate (1998–99)

Academics

TCNJ awards bachelor's and master's **degrees**. Challenging opportunities include advanced placement, an honors program, double majors, independent study, and a senior project. Special programs include internships, summer session for credit, off-campus study, study-abroad, and Army and Air Force ROTC.

The most frequently chosen fields are education, business/marketing, and English. A complete listing of majors at TCNJ appears in the Majors Index beginning on page 432.

The **faculty** at TCNJ has 328 full-time members, 88% with terminal degrees. The student-faculty ratio is 12:1.

Students of TCNJ

The student body totals 6,747, of whom 5,930 are undergraduates. 59.6% are women and 40.4% are men. Students come from 20 states and territories and 13 other countries. 96% are from New Jersey. 0.2% are international students. 6.1% are African American, 0.2% American Indian, 4.7% Asian American, and 5.4% Hispanic American. 93% returned for their sophomore year.

Facilities and Resources

Student rooms are linked to a campus network. 800 **computers** are available on campus that provide access to the Internet. The **library** has 520,000 books and 4,700 subscriptions.

Campus Life

There are 150 active organizations on campus, including a drama/theater group, newspaper, radio station, and choral group. 20% of eligible men and 20% of eligible women are members of national **fraternities**, national **sororities**, local fraternities, and local sororities.

TCNJ is a member of the NCAA (Division III). **Intercollegiate sports** include baseball (m), basketball, cross-country running, field hockey (w), football (m), golf (m), lacrosse (w), soccer, softball (w), swimming, tennis, track and field, wrestling (m).

Campus Safety

Student safety services include late-night transport/escort service, 24-hour emergency telephone alarm devices, 24-hour patrols by trained security personnel, student patrols, and electronically operated dormitory entrances.

Applying

TCNJ requires an essay, SAT I, SAT II: Writing Test, a high school transcript, and a minimum high school GPA of 2.0, and in some cases an interview. Application deadline: 2/15; 6/1 for financial aid, with a 3/1 priority date. Early and deferred admission are possible.

COLLEGE OF SAINT BENEDICT

COORDINATE WITH SAINT JOHN'S UNIVERSITY (MN)

SMALL-TOWN SETTING ■ PRIVATE ■ INDEPENDENT RELIGIOUS ■ WOMEN ONLY
SAINT JOSEPH, MINNESOTA

Web site: www.csbsju.edu
Contact: Ms. Mary Milbert, Dean of Admissions, 37 South College Avenue,
Saint Joseph, MN 56374-2091
Telephone: 320-363-5308 or toll-free 800-544-1489 **Fax:** 320-363-5010
E-mail: admissions@csbsju.edu

Academics

St. Ben's awards bachelor's **degrees**. Challenging opportunities include advanced placement, accelerated degree programs, student-designed majors, an honors program,
double majors, independent study, and a senior project. Special programs include internships, off-campus study, study-abroad, and Army ROTC.

The most frequently chosen fields are business/marketing, health professions and
related sciences, and social sciences and history. A complete listing of majors at St. Ben's
appears in the Majors Index beginning on page 432.

The **faculty** at St. Ben's has 126 full-time members, 77% with terminal degrees. The
student-faculty ratio is 13:1.

Students of St. Ben's

The student body is made up of 2,000 undergraduates. Students come from 30 states and
territories and 17 other countries. 87% are from Minnesota. 3.1% are international
students. 0.6% are African American, 0.3% American Indian, 1.7% Asian American, and
1.1% Hispanic American. 89% returned for their sophomore year.

Facilities and Resources

Student rooms are linked to a campus network. 350 **computers** are available on campus
that provide access to the Internet. The 3 **libraries** have 726,844 books and 8,564
subscriptions.

Campus Life

There are 80 active organizations on campus, including a drama/theater group,
newspaper, radio station, and choral group. No national or local **sororities**.

St. Ben's is a member of the NCAA (Division III). **Intercollegiate sports** include
basketball, crew, cross-country running, golf, gymnastics, lacrosse, rugby, skiing (cross-
country), soccer, softball, swimming, tennis, track and field, volleyball.

Campus Safety

Student safety services include well-lit pathways, late-night transport/escort service, 24-
hour emergency telephone alarm devices, 24-hour patrols by trained security personnel,
student patrols, and electronically operated dormitory entrances.

Applying

St. Ben's requires an essay, SAT I or ACT, and a high school transcript, and in some cases
recommendations. It recommends an interview and a minimum high school GPA of 2.8.
Application deadline: rolling admissions; 4/1 priority date for financial aid. Early and
deferred admission are possible.

The College of Saint
Benedict and Saint John's
University are 2 of just 5
Catholic colleges that are recognized
as national liberal arts institutions.
Their mission is to foster learning,
leadership, and wisdom for a
lifetime. This is achieved through a
unified curriculum stressing open
inquiry, intellectual challenge,
cooperative scholarship, service
learning, and artistic creativity; an
emphasis on the personal growth of
women and men through separate
residence halls, student development
programming, athletics, and
leadership opportunities; an
experience of Benedictine values,
including the formation of community
built on respect for individual
persons; and an entry into a
heritage of leadership and service.

Getting in Last Year
1,159 applied
88% were accepted
515 enrolled (50%)
36% from top tenth of their h.s. class
3.7 average high school GPA
42% had SAT verbal scores over 600
38% had SAT math scores over 600
60% had ACT scores over 24
7% had SAT verbal scores over 700
3% had SAT math scores over 700
8% had ACT scores over 30

Graduation and After
67% graduated in 4 years
6% graduated in 5 years
1% graduated in 6 years
14% pursued further study (8% arts and sciences, 3% medicine, 2% law)
84% had job offers within 6 months
85 organizations recruited on campus

Financial Matters
$16,441 tuition and fees (1999–2000)
$5040 room and board
91% average percent of need met
$14,488 average financial aid amount received
per undergraduate (1999–2000 estimated)

eAPPLY

Getting in Last Year
826 applied
37% were accepted
300 enrolled (97%)
33% from top tenth of their h.s. class
3.52 average high school GPA
50% had SAT verbal scores over 600
35% had SAT math scores over 600
52% had ACT scores over 24
5% had SAT verbal scores over 700
5% had SAT math scores over 700
7% had ACT scores over 30
14 valedictorians

Graduation and After
39% graduated in 4 years
7% graduated in 5 years
2% graduated in 6 years
38% pursued further study (35% arts and
    sciences, 2% medicine)
61.8% had job offers within 6 months
4 organizations recruited on campus

Financial Matters
$15,510 tuition and fees (1999–2000)
$4760 room and board
80% average percent of need met
$11,602 average financial aid amount received
    per undergraduate (1999–2000 estimated)

THE COLLEGE OF ST. SCHOLASTICA
SUBURBAN SETTING ■ PRIVATE ■ INDEPENDENT RELIGIOUS ■ COED
DULUTH, MINNESOTA

Web site: www.css.edu
Contact: Mr. Brian Dalton, Vice President for Enrollment Management, 1200
    Kenwood Avenue, Duluth, MN 55811-4199
Telephone: 218-723-6053 or toll-free 800-447-5444 **Fax:** 218-723-6290
E-mail: admissions@css.edu

Academics
St. Scholastica awards bachelor's and master's **degrees**. Challenging opportunities
include advanced placement, student-designed majors, an honors program, independent
study, and a senior project. Special programs include internships, summer session for
credit, off-campus study, study-abroad, and Army and Air Force ROTC.

The most frequently chosen fields are health professions and related sciences,
biological/life sciences, and parks and recreation. A complete listing of majors at St.
Scholastica appears in the Majors Index beginning on page 432.

The **faculty** at St. Scholastica has 110 full-time members, 49% with terminal
degrees. The student-faculty ratio is 13:1.

Students of St. Scholastica
The student body totals 2,079, of whom 1,429 are undergraduates. 73.7% are women
and 26.3% are men. Students come from 23 states and territories and 9 other countries.
87% are from Minnesota. 0.6% are international students. 0.9% are African American,
1.5% American Indian, 1.1% Asian American, and 0.6% Hispanic American. 83%
returned for their sophomore year.

Facilities and Resources
Student rooms are linked to a campus network. 158 **computers** are available on campus
that provide access to the Internet. The 2 **libraries** have 118,703 books and 759
subscriptions.

Campus Life
There are 45 active organizations on campus, including a drama/theater group,
newspaper, and choral group. No national or local **fraternities** or **sororities**.

St. Scholastica is a member of the NCAA (Division III) and NAIA. **Intercollegiate
sports** include baseball (m), basketball, cross-country running, ice hockey (m), soccer,
softball (w), tennis, volleyball (w).

Campus Safety
Student safety services include student door monitor at night, late-night transport/escort
service, 24-hour emergency telephone alarm devices, 24-hour patrols by trained security
personnel, and electronically operated dormitory entrances.

Applying
St. Scholastica requires SAT I or ACT and a high school transcript, and in some cases an
interview and a minimum high school GPA of 2.0. It recommends an essay, PSAT, an
interview, and recommendations. Application deadline: rolling admissions; 3/15 priority
date for financial aid. Early and deferred admission are possible.

COLLEGE OF THE ATLANTIC

SMALL-TOWN SETTING ■ PRIVATE ■ INDEPENDENT ■ COED
BAR HARBOR, MAINE

Web site: www.coa.edu
Contact: Mr. David Mahoney, Director of Admission and Financial Aid, 105
Eden Street, Bar Harbor, ME 04609-1198
Telephone: 207-288-5015 ext. 233 or toll-free 800-528-0025 **Fax:**
207-288-4126
E-mail: inquiry@ecology.coa.edu

Academics

COA awards bachelor's and master's **degrees**. Challenging opportunities include advanced placement, accelerated degree programs, student-designed majors, independent study, and a senior project. Special programs include cooperative education, internships, off-campus study, and study-abroad.

The most frequently chosen field is liberal arts/general studies. A complete listing of majors at COA appears in the Majors Index beginning on page 432.

The **faculty** at COA has 19 full-time members. The student-faculty ratio is 4:1.

Students of COA

The student body totals 293, of whom 288 are undergraduates. 66.3% are women and 33.7% are men. Students come from 38 states and territories and 9 other countries. 21% are from Maine. 0.4% are African American, 0.4% American Indian, 1.1% Asian American, and 0.7% Hispanic American. 93% returned for their sophomore year.

Facilities and Resources

Student rooms are linked to a campus network. 42 **computers** are available on campus that provide access to the Internet. The 2 **libraries** have 33,032 books.

Campus Life

There are 12 active organizations on campus, including a drama/theater group, newspaper, and choral group. No national or local **fraternities** or **sororities**.
Intercollegiate sports include soccer.

Campus Safety

Student safety services include late-night transport/escort service, 24-hour emergency telephone alarm devices, and 24-hour patrols by trained security personnel.

Applying

COA requires an essay, a high school transcript, and 3 recommendations, and in some cases an interview. It recommends SAT I and SAT II or ACT, an interview, and a minimum high school GPA of 3.0. Application deadline: 3/1; 2/15 priority date for financial aid. Early and deferred admission are possible.

College of the Atlantic integrates student qualities of intellectual rigor, self-motivation, independence, and passion for the environment with institutional characteristics of self-designed concentrations of study, small seminar-style classes, and an abundance of supplementary fieldwork, allowing students the opportunity to combine areas of academic interest with the interdisciplinary liberal arts exploration of human ecology. At a college where questioning ideas and seeking relationships are encouraged, faculty members work along with students as they develop individualized programs of study, which enable them to address ecological problems from multiple perspectives. This personalized approach to education combined with practical experience in problem solving allows students to develop important skills necessary to make meaningful contributions to society.

Getting in Last Year
234 applied
73% were accepted
73 enrolled (43%)
28% from top tenth of their h.s. class
3.74 average high school GPA
71% had SAT verbal scores over 600
42% had SAT math scores over 600
67% had ACT scores over 24
21% had SAT verbal scores over 700
8% had SAT math scores over 700
8% had ACT scores over 30
8 National Merit Scholars
4 class presidents
1 valedictorian

Graduation and After
58% graduated in 4 years
10% graduated in 5 years
7% pursued further study (2% arts and sciences, 2% education, 2% law)
75% had job offers within 6 months

Financial Matters
$19,485 tuition and fees (1999–2000)
$5220 room and board
89% average percent of need met
$15,771 average financial aid amount received per undergraduate (1999–2000 estimated)

COLLEGE OF THE HOLY CROSS

SUBURBAN SETTING ■ PRIVATE ■ INDEPENDENT RELIGIOUS ■ COED
WORCESTER, MASSACHUSETTS

Web site: www.holycross.edu
Contact: Ms. Ann Bowe McDermott, Director of Admissions, 1 College
Street, Worcester, MA 01610-2395
Telephone: 508-793-2443 or toll-free 800-442-2421
E-mail: admissions@holycross.edu

In a college world of shrinking resources and growing class enrollments, Holy Cross continues to fully support and refine its 150-year-old mission as a completely undergraduate Jesuit liberal arts college. An example of that commitment to open intellectual discourse is the popular First Year Program. Every one of the course offerings is taught by a faculty member, and the average class size is 15 students. The Jesuit nature of the community ensures that all its members recognize the importance of service to others and the need for social justice in daily affairs.

Academics

Holy Cross awards bachelor's **degrees**. Challenging opportunities include advanced placement, accelerated degree programs, student-designed majors, an honors program, double majors, independent study, a senior project, Phi Beta Kappa, and Sigma Xi. Special programs include internships, off-campus study, study-abroad, and Army, Navy and Air Force ROTC.

The most frequently chosen fields are social sciences and history, English, and psychology. A complete listing of majors at Holy Cross appears in the Majors Index beginning on page 432.

The **faculty** at Holy Cross has 221 full-time members, 94% with terminal degrees. The student-faculty ratio is 13:1.

Students of Holy Cross

The student body is made up of 2,801 undergraduates. 52.4% are women and 47.6% are men. Students come from 49 states and territories. 33% are from Massachusetts. 0.8% are international students. 2.6% are African American, 0.1% American Indian, 2.8% Asian American, and 4.7% Hispanic American. 94% returned for their sophomore year.

Facilities and Resources

Student rooms are linked to a campus network. 175 **computers** are available on campus that provide access to the Internet. The 3 **libraries** have 548,492 books and 1,689 subscriptions.

Campus Life

There are 85 active organizations on campus, including a drama/theater group, newspaper, radio station, choral group, and marching band. No national or local **fraternities** or **sororities**.

Holy Cross is a member of the NCAA (Division I). **Intercollegiate sports** include baseball (m), basketball, crew, cross-country running, field hockey (w), football (m), golf (m), ice hockey, lacrosse, sailing, soccer, softball (w), swimming, tennis, track and field, volleyball (w).

Campus Safety

Student safety services include late-night transport/escort service, 24-hour emergency telephone alarm devices, 24-hour patrols by trained security personnel, and electronically operated dormitory entrances.

Applying

Holy Cross requires an essay, SAT II: Writing Test, SAT I and SAT II or ACT, a high school transcript, and 2 recommendations. It recommends an interview. Application deadline: 1/15; 2/1 priority date for financial aid. Early and deferred admission are possible.

Getting in Last Year
4,834 applied
44% were accepted
722 enrolled (34%)
54% from top tenth of their h.s. class
71% had SAT verbal scores over 600
73% had SAT math scores over 600
16% had SAT verbal scores over 700
17% had SAT math scores over 700

Graduation and After
91% graduated in 4 years
2% graduated in 5 years
15% pursued further study (6% arts and sciences, 4% law, 1% business)
77 organizations recruited on campus
6 Fulbright scholars

Financial Matters
$23,815 tuition and fees (2000–2001)
$7540 room and board
100% average percent of need met
$17,236 average financial aid amount received per undergraduate (1999–2000)

THE COLLEGE OF WILLIAM AND MARY

SMALL-TOWN SETTING ■ PUBLIC ■ STATE-SUPPORTED ■ COED
WILLIAMSBURG, VIRGINIA

Web site: www.wm.edu
Contact: Ms. Virginia Carey, Dean of Admission, Office of Admission, PO
  Box 8795, Williamsburg, VA 23187-8795
Telephone: 757-221-4223 **Fax:** 757-221-1242
E-mail: admiss@facstaff.wm.edu

eAPPLY

Academics

William and Mary awards bachelor's, master's, doctoral, and first-professional **degrees**. Challenging opportunities include advanced placement, accelerated degree programs, student-designed majors, an honors program, double majors, independent study, a senior project, Phi Beta Kappa, and Sigma Xi. Special programs include summer session for credit, study-abroad, and Army ROTC.

The most frequently chosen fields are social sciences and history, business/marketing, and biological/life sciences. A complete listing of majors at William and Mary appears in the Majors Index beginning on page 432.

The **faculty** at William and Mary has 575 full-time members, 92% with terminal degrees. The student-faculty ratio is 12:1.

Students of William and Mary

The student body totals 7,553, of whom 5,552 are undergraduates. 57.6% are women and 42.4% are men. Students come from 50 states and territories and 52 other countries. 64% are from Virginia. 1.3% are international students. 4.4% are African American, 0.4% American Indian, 6.7% Asian American, and 2.8% Hispanic American. 95% returned for their sophomore year.

Facilities and Resources

Student rooms are linked to a campus network. 300 **computers** are available on campus that provide access to the Internet. The 10 **libraries** have 1,956,624 books and 11,462 subscriptions.

Campus Life

There are 300 active organizations on campus, including a drama/theater group, newspaper, radio station, television station, and choral group. 32% of eligible men and 24% of eligible women are members of national **fraternities** and national **sororities**.

William and Mary is a member of the NCAA (Division I). **Intercollegiate sports** (some offering scholarships) include baseball (m), basketball, cross-country running, field hockey (w), football (m), golf, gymnastics, lacrosse (w), soccer, swimming, tennis, track and field, volleyball (w).

Campus Safety

Student safety services include late-night transport/escort service, 24-hour emergency telephone alarm devices, 24-hour patrols by trained security personnel, student patrols, and electronically operated dormitory entrances.

Applying

William and Mary requires an essay, SAT I or ACT, and a high school transcript, and in some cases an interview. It recommends SAT II Subject Tests, SAT II: Writing Test, and 1 recommendation. Application deadline: 1/5; 3/15 for financial aid, with a 2/15 priority date. Early and deferred admission are possible.

Getting in Last Year
6,878 applied
45% were accepted
1,301 enrolled (42%)
74% from top tenth of their h.s. class
3.90 average high school GPA
83% had SAT verbal scores over 600
81% had SAT math scores over 600
100% had ACT scores over 24
34% had SAT verbal scores over 700
26% had SAT math scores over 700
71% had ACT scores over 30
13 National Merit Scholars
33 class presidents
117 valedictorians

Graduation and After
78% graduated in 4 years
8% graduated in 5 years
2% graduated in 6 years
Graduates pursuing further study: 13% arts
  and sciences, 7% law, 6% medicine
47% had job offers within 6 months
150 organizations recruited on campus
2 Rhodes, 1 Fulbright scholar

Financial Matters
$4610 resident tuition and fees (1999–2000)
$16,434 nonresident tuition and fees (1999–
  2000)
$4897 room and board
89% average percent of need met
$7965 average financial aid amount received
  per undergraduate (1999–2000 estimated)

The College of Wooster

SMALL-TOWN SETTING ■ PRIVATE ■ INDEPENDENT RELIGIOUS ■ COED
WOOSTER, OHIO

Web site: www.wooster.edu
Contact: Ms. Carol D. Wheatley, Director of Admissions, 1189 Beall Avenue, Wooster, OH 44691-2363
Telephone: 330-263-2270 ext. 2118 or toll-free 800-877-9905 **Fax:** 330-263-2621
E-mail: admissions@wooster.edu

Wooster's curriculum provides students the breadth that is to be found in hundreds of course offerings and the depth that comes from 47 majors and programs of study. Small classes and an accessible faculty committed to teaching undergraduates ensure individual attention for every student. A First-Year Seminar in Critical Inquiry links advising with teaching in a small seminar setting, while senior-year students work one-on-one with a faculty member on an Independent Study Project, a concept that was introduced into Wooster's curriculum 50 years ago. Wooster is one of the very few colleges that requires independent research of every student.

Getting in Last Year
2,195 applied
79% were accepted
513 enrolled (30%)
64% from top tenth of their h.s. class
3.50 average high school GPA
51% had SAT verbal scores over 600
50% had SAT math scores over 600
78% had ACT scores over 24
14% had SAT verbal scores over 700
12% had SAT math scores over 700
15% had ACT scores over 30
8 National Merit Scholars
25 valedictorians

Graduation and After
Graduates pursuing further study: 11% law, 9% education, 7% medicine
87% had job offers within 6 months
26 organizations recruited on campus
1 Fulbright scholar

Financial Matters
$20,530 tuition and fees (1999–2000)
$5420 room and board
100% average percent of need met
$17,365 average financial aid amount received per undergraduate (1999–2000)

Academics
Wooster awards bachelor's **degrees**. Challenging opportunities include advanced placement, student-designed majors, double majors, independent study, a senior project, Phi Beta Kappa, and Sigma Xi. Special programs include internships, summer session for credit, off-campus study, and study-abroad.

The most frequently chosen fields are social sciences and history, English, and biological/life sciences. A complete listing of majors at Wooster appears in the Majors Index beginning on page 432.

The **faculty** at Wooster has 123 full-time members, 93% with terminal degrees. The student-faculty ratio is 13:1.

Students of Wooster
The student body is made up of 1,709 undergraduates. 52.8% are women and 47.2% are men. Students come from 46 states and territories and 29 other countries. 56% are from Ohio. 7.7% are international students. 4.4% are African American, 0.1% American Indian, 1.7% Asian American, and 0.8% Hispanic American. 80% returned for their sophomore year.

Facilities and Resources
Student rooms are linked to a campus network. 192 **computers** are available on campus that provide access to the Internet. The 3 **libraries** have 934,376 books and 3,746 subscriptions.

Campus Life
There are 81 active organizations on campus, including a drama/theater group, newspaper, radio station, choral group, and marching band. 15% of eligible men and 12% of eligible women are members of local **fraternities**, local **sororities**, and coed fraternity.

Wooster is a member of the NCAA (Division III). **Intercollegiate sports** include badminton, baseball (m), basketball, cross-country running, field hockey (w), football (m), golf (m), ice hockey (m), lacrosse, rugby, soccer, softball (w), swimming, tennis, track and field, volleyball.

Campus Safety
Student safety services include late-night transport/escort service, 24-hour emergency telephone alarm devices, 24-hour patrols by trained security personnel, student patrols, and electronically operated dormitory entrances.

Applying
Wooster requires an essay, SAT I or ACT, a high school transcript, and 2 recommendations. It recommends an interview. Application deadline: 2/15; 2/15 priority date for financial aid. Early and deferred admission are possible.

THE COLORADO COLLEGE

URBAN SETTING ■ PRIVATE ■ INDEPENDENT ■ COED
COLORADO SPRINGS, COLORADO

Web site: www.coloradocollege.edu

Contact: Mr. Terrance K. Swenson, Dean of Admission and Financial Aid, 14 East Cache la Poudre, 900 Block North Cascade, West, Colorado Springs, CO 80903-3294

Telephone: 719-389-6344 or toll-free 800-542-7214 **Fax:** 719-389-6816

E-mail: admission@coloradocollege.edu

eAPPLY

Academics

CC awards bachelor's and master's **degrees** (master's degree in education only). Challenging opportunities include advanced placement, student-designed majors, an honors program, double majors, independent study, a senior project, and Phi Beta Kappa. Special programs include cooperative education, summer session for credit, off-campus study, study-abroad, and Army ROTC.

The most frequently chosen fields are social sciences and history, biological/life sciences, and English. A complete listing of majors at CC appears in the Majors Index beginning on page 432.

The **faculty** at CC has 166 full-time members, 97% with terminal degrees. The student-faculty ratio is 11:1.

Students of CC

The student body totals 1,964, of whom 1,941 are undergraduates. 55.5% are women and 44.5% are men. Students come from 50 states and territories and 31 other countries. 28% are from Colorado. 2.1% are international students. 1.9% are African American, 0.8% American Indian, 3.3% Asian American, and 5.7% Hispanic American. 93% returned for their sophomore year.

Facilities and Resources

Student rooms are linked to a campus network. 190 **computers** are available on campus that provide access to the Internet. The 3 **libraries** have 650,000 books and 2,312 subscriptions.

Campus Life

There are 80 active organizations on campus, including a drama/theater group, newspaper, radio station, and choral group. 13% of eligible men and 18% of eligible women are members of national **fraternities** and national **sororities**.

CC is a member of the NCAA (Division III). **Intercollegiate sports** (some offering scholarships) include basketball, cross-country running, equestrian sports, field hockey, football (m), ice hockey, lacrosse, rugby, skiing (downhill), soccer, softball (w), swimming, tennis, track and field, volleyball, water polo.

Campus Safety

Student safety services include whistle program, late-night transport/escort service, 24-hour emergency telephone alarm devices, 24-hour patrols by trained security personnel, and electronically operated dormitory entrances.

Applying

CC requires an essay, SAT I or ACT, a high school transcript, and 3 recommendations. Application deadline: 1/15; 2/15 for financial aid. Deferred admission is possible.

Getting in Last Year
3,644 applied
55% were accepted
483 enrolled (24%)
42% from top tenth of their h.s. class
3.80 average high school GPA
69% had SAT verbal scores over 600
71% had SAT math scores over 600
85% had ACT scores over 24
19% had SAT verbal scores over 700
18% had SAT math scores over 700
24% had ACT scores over 30
22 National Merit Scholars
38 valedictorians

Graduation and After
71% graduated in 4 years
7% graduated in 5 years
1% graduated in 6 years
Graduates pursuing further study: 16% arts and sciences, 5% law, 5% medicine
68 organizations recruited on campus

Financial Matters
$21,822 tuition and fees (1999–2000)
$5568 room and board
93% average percent of need met
$18,764 average financial aid amount received per undergraduate (1999–2000)

---

www.petersons.com

 **eAPPLY**

COLORADO SCHOOL OF MINES
SMALL-TOWN SETTING ■ PUBLIC ■ STATE-SUPPORTED ■ COED
GOLDEN, COLORADO

Web site: www.mines.edu
Contact: Mr. Bill Young, Director of Enrollment Management, Weaver Towers-1811 Elm Street, Golden, CO 80401-1842
Telephone: 303-273-3227 or toll-free 800-446-9488 (out-of-state) **Fax:** 303-273-3509
E-mail: admit@mines.edu

Getting in Last Year
1,984 applied
76% were accepted
566 enrolled (38%)
57% from top tenth of their h.s. class
3.80 average high school GPA
45% had SAT verbal scores over 600
80% had SAT math scores over 600
87% had ACT scores over 24
10% had SAT verbal scores over 700
23% had SAT math scores over 700
24% had ACT scores over 30
77 class presidents
77 valedictorians

Graduation and After
22% graduated in 4 years
29% graduated in 5 years
4% graduated in 6 years
15% pursued further study (11% engineering, 1% arts and sciences, 1% business)
85% had job offers within 6 months
169 organizations recruited on campus

Financial Matters
$5211 resident tuition and fees (1999–2000)
$15,311 nonresident tuition and fees (1999–2000)
$4920 room and board
100% average percent of need met
$10,195 average financial aid amount received per undergraduate (1998–99)

Academics
CSM awards bachelor's, master's, and doctoral **degrees**. Challenging opportunities include advanced placement, accelerated degree programs, an honors program, double majors, a senior project, and Sigma Xi. Special programs include cooperative education, internships, summer session for credit, study-abroad, and Army ROTC.

The most frequently chosen fields are engineering/engineering technologies, mathematics, and physical sciences. A complete listing of majors at CSM appears in the Majors Index beginning on page 432.

The **faculty** at CSM has 191 full-time members, 98% with terminal degrees. The student-faculty ratio is 16:1.

Students of CSM
The student body totals 3,202, of whom 2,473 are undergraduates. 24.2% are women and 75.8% are men. Students come from 51 states and territories and 28 other countries. 79% are from Colorado. 3.8% are international students. 1.3% are African American, 0.9% American Indian, 5% Asian American, and 7% Hispanic American. 88% returned for their sophomore year.

Facilities and Resources
Student rooms are linked to a campus network. The **library** has 260,000 books and 2,000 subscriptions.

Campus Life
There are 95 active organizations on campus, including a drama/theater group, newspaper, choral group, and marching band. 20% of eligible men and 20% of eligible women are members of national **fraternities** and national **sororities**.

CSM is a member of the NCAA (Division II). **Intercollegiate sports** (some offering scholarships) include baseball (m), basketball, cross-country running, football (m), golf (m), skiing (downhill) (m), soccer (m), softball (w), swimming, tennis, track and field, volleyball (w), wrestling (m).

Campus Safety
Student safety services include 24-hour emergency telephone alarm devices and 24-hour patrols by trained security personnel.

Applying
CSM requires SAT I or ACT and a high school transcript, and in some cases an essay, an interview, and recommendations. It recommends rank in upper one-third of high school class. Application deadline: 6/1; 3/1 priority date for financial aid. Deferred admission is possible.

COLORADO STATE UNIVERSITY

URBAN SETTING ■ PUBLIC ■ STATE-SUPPORTED ■ COED
FORT COLLINS, COLORADO

Web site: www.colostate.edu
Contact: Ms. Mary Ontiveros, Director of Admissions, Spruce Hall, Fort Collins, CO 80523-0015
Telephone: 970-491-6909
E-mail: admissions@vines.colostate.edu

Academics

Colorado State awards bachelor's, master's, doctoral, and first-professional **degrees**. Challenging opportunities include advanced placement, accelerated degree programs, student-designed majors, an honors program, double majors, a senior project, Phi Beta Kappa, and Sigma Xi. Special programs include cooperative education, internships, summer session for credit, off-campus study, study-abroad, and Army and Air Force ROTC.

The most frequently chosen fields are business/marketing, engineering/engineering technologies, and agriculture. A complete listing of majors at Colorado State appears in the Majors Index beginning on page 432.

The **faculty** at Colorado State has 979 full-time members, 92% with terminal degrees. The student-faculty ratio is 20:1.

Students of Colorado State

The student body totals 22,782, of whom 18,800 are undergraduates. 51.6% are women and 48.4% are men. Students come from 55 states and territories and 49 other countries. 80% are from Colorado. 1.1% are international students. 1.7% are African American, 1.2% American Indian, 2.9% Asian American, and 5.6% Hispanic American. 82% returned for their sophomore year.

Facilities and Resources

Student rooms are linked to a campus network. 3,500 **computers** are available on campus that provide access to the Internet. The 4 **libraries** have 1,068,962 books and 21,255 subscriptions.

Campus Life

There are 300 active organizations on campus, including a drama/theater group, newspaper, radio station, choral group, and marching band. 11% of eligible men and 12% of eligible women are members of national **fraternities**, national **sororities**, local fraternities, and local sororities.

Colorado State is a member of the NCAA (Division I). **Intercollegiate sports** (some offering scholarships) include basketball, cross-country running, football (m), golf, softball (w), swimming (w), tennis (w), track and field, volleyball (w).

Campus Safety

Student safety services include late-night transport/escort service, 24-hour emergency telephone alarm devices, 24-hour patrols by trained security personnel, student patrols, and electronically operated dormitory entrances.

Applying

Colorado State requires SAT I or ACT and a high school transcript. It recommends an essay and recommendations. Application deadline: 7/1; 3/1 priority date for financial aid. Deferred admission is possible.

Colorado State's scenic location, at the base of the Rocky Mountain foothills, provides the perfect background for intellectual and personal growth. Students describe the University as providing "an academically challenging and rigorous curriculum in a supportive environment," a place where they can feel at ease to be themselves and are encouraged to develop their own unique talents. In addition to nearly 100 programs of study, students can enhance their education through the Honors Program, study abroad, and many opportunities for hands-on experience, including undergraduate research, an extensive network of internships, and volunteer/community service. Colorado State students graduate with the confidence that their education will make a difference.

Getting in Last Year
10,465 applied
77% were accepted
3,137 enrolled (39%)
25% from top tenth of their h.s. class
3.5 average high school GPA
27% had SAT verbal scores over 600
33% had SAT math scores over 600
57% had ACT scores over 24
4% had SAT verbal scores over 700
5% had SAT math scores over 700
7% had ACT scores over 30
14 National Merit Scholars
100 valedictorians

Graduation and After
501 organizations recruited on campus

Financial Matters
$3062 resident tuition and fees (1999–2000)
$10,748 nonresident tuition and fees (1999–2000)
$5200 room and board
82% average percent of need met
$6929 average financial aid amount received per undergraduate (1998–99)

COLORADO TECHNICAL UNIVERSITY

SUBURBAN SETTING ■ PRIVATE ■ PROPRIETARY ■ COED
COLORADO SPRINGS, COLORADO

Web site: www.colotechu.edu
Contact: Mr. Bill Somners, Admissions Manager, 4435 North Chestnut Street, Colorado Springs, CO 80907-3896
Telephone: 719-598-0200 **Fax:** 719-598-3740
E-mail: cotechcs@iex.net

Academics

Colorado Tech awards associate, bachelor's, master's, and doctoral **degrees**. Challenging opportunities include advanced placement, accelerated degree programs, double majors, independent study, and a senior project. Special programs include cooperative education, internships, summer session for credit, and Army ROTC.

The most frequently chosen fields are engineering/engineering technologies and computer/information sciences. A complete listing of majors at Colorado Tech appears in the Majors Index beginning on page 432.

The **faculty** at Colorado Tech has 28 full-time members, 43% with terminal degrees. The student-faculty ratio is 25:1.

Students of Colorado Tech

The student body totals 1,764, of whom 1,124 are undergraduates. 24.2% are women and 75.8% are men. 1% are international students. 8.2% are African American, 0.5% American Indian, 2.6% Asian American, and 0.7% Hispanic American. 51% returned for their sophomore year.

Facilities and Resources

110 **computers** are available on campus that provide access to the Internet. The **library** has 14,200 books and 340 subscriptions.

Campus Life

There are 7 active organizations on campus. No national or local **fraternities** or **sororities**.

This institution has no intercollegiate sports.

Campus Safety

Student safety services include late-night transport/escort service and 24-hour emergency telephone alarm devices.

Applying

Colorado Tech requires (in some cases) an essay, ACT ASSET tests in English and math, and a high school transcript. It recommends SAT I or ACT, an interview, and a minimum high school GPA of 3.0. Application deadline: rolling admissions. Deferred admission is possible.

COLUMBIA UNIVERSITY, COLUMBIA COLLEGE

URBAN SETTING ■ PRIVATE ■ INDEPENDENT ■ COED
NEW YORK, NEW YORK

Web site: www.columbia.edu
Contact: Mr. Eric Furda, Director of Undergraduate Admissions, 1130
    Amsterdam Avenue MC 2807, New York, NY 10027
Telephone: 212-854-2522 **Fax:** 212-854-1209
E-mail: ugrad-admiss@columbia.edu

Academics

Columbia College awards bachelor's **degrees**. Challenging opportunities include
advanced placement, student-designed majors, an honors program, a senior project, and
Phi Beta Kappa. Special programs include internships, summer session for credit, off-
campus study, and study-abroad. A complete listing of majors at Columbia appears in the
Majors Index beginning on page 432.

The **faculty** at Columbia has 632 full-time members. The student-faculty ratio is 7:1.

Students of Columbia College

The student body is made up of 3,913 undergraduates. Students come from 49 states and
territories and 39 other countries. 96% returned for their sophomore year.

Facilities and Resources

Student rooms are linked to a campus network. 400 **computers** are available on campus
that provide access to the Internet. The 21 **libraries** have 6,800,000 books and 66,000
subscriptions.

Campus Life

Active organizations on campus include a drama/theater group, newspaper, radio station,
television station, choral group, and marching band. 19% of eligible men and 25% of
eligible women are members of national **fraternities**, national **sororities**, and coed
fraternities.

Columbia is a member of the NCAA (Division I). **Intercollegiate sports** include
archery, badminton, baseball (m), basketball, crew, cross-country running, equestrian
sports, fencing, field hockey (w), football (m), golf (m), ice hockey (m), lacrosse,
racquetball, riflery, rugby, sailing, soccer, softball (w), squash, swimming, table tennis,
tennis, track and field, volleyball, water polo, wrestling (m).

Campus Safety

Student safety services include 24-hour ID check at door, late-night transport/escort
service, 24-hour emergency telephone alarm devices, and 24-hour patrols by trained
security personnel.

Applying

Columbia requires an essay, SAT II Subject Tests, SAT II: Writing Test, SAT I or ACT, a
high school transcript, and 3 recommendations. It recommends an interview. Application
deadline: 1/1; 2/10 for financial aid. Early and deferred admission are possible.

Getting in Last Year
13,013 applied
14% were accepted
964 enrolled (55%)
83% from top tenth of their h.s. class

Graduation and After
80% pursued further study
1 Rhodes, 2 Marshall, 12 Fulbright scholars

Financial Matters
$24,974 tuition and fees (1999–2000)
$7732 room and board
100% average percent of need met
$21,365 average financial aid amount received
    per undergraduate (1999–2000)

COLUMBIA UNIVERSITY, THE FU FOUNDATION SCHOOL OF ENGINEERING AND APPLIED SCIENCE

URBAN SETTING ■ PRIVATE ■ INDEPENDENT ■ COED
NEW YORK, NEW YORK

Web site: www.columbia.edu
Contact: Mr. Eric Furda, Director of Undergraduate Admissions, 1130 Amsterdam Avenue MC 2807, New York, NY 10027
Telephone: 212-854-2522 **Fax:** 212-854-1209
E-mail: ugrad-admiss@columbia.edu

Academics

Columbia SEAS awards bachelor's, master's, and doctoral **degrees**. Challenging opportunities include advanced placement, accelerated degree programs, and an honors program. Special programs include internships, summer session for credit, and study-abroad. A complete listing of majors at Columbia SEAS appears in the Majors Index beginning on page 432.

The **faculty** at Columbia SEAS has 108 full-time members. The student-faculty ratio is 5:1.

Students of Columbia SEAS

The student body is made up of 1,248 undergraduates. Students come from 44 states and territories and 31 other countries. 89% returned for their sophomore year.

Facilities and Resources

Student rooms are linked to a campus network. 400 **computers** are available on campus that provide access to the Internet. The 21 **libraries** have 6,800,000 books and 66,000 subscriptions.

Campus Life

Active organizations on campus include a drama/theater group, newspaper, radio station, television station, choral group, and marching band. 19% of eligible men and 25% of eligible women are members of national **fraternities**, national **sororities**, and coed fraternities.

Columbia SEAS is a member of the NCAA (Division I). **Intercollegiate sports** include archery, badminton, baseball (m), basketball, crew, cross-country running, equestrian sports, fencing, field hockey (w), football (m), golf (m), ice hockey (m), lacrosse, riflery, rugby, sailing, soccer, softball (w), squash, swimming, table tennis, tennis, track and field, volleyball, water polo, wrestling (m).

Campus Safety

Student safety services include 24-hour ID check at door, late-night transport/escort service, 24-hour emergency telephone alarm devices, and 24-hour patrols by trained security personnel.

Applying

Columbia SEAS requires an essay, SAT II Subject Tests, SAT II: Writing Test, SAT I or ACT, a high school transcript, and 3 recommendations. It recommends an interview and a minimum high school GPA of 3.0. Application deadline: 1/1; 2/10 for financial aid. Early and deferred admission are possible.

CONCORDIA COLLEGE

SUBURBAN SETTING ■ PRIVATE ■ INDEPENDENT RELIGIOUS ■ COED
MOORHEAD, MINNESOTA

Web site: www.cord.edu
Contact: Mr. Scott E. Ellingson, Interim Director of Admissions, 901 8th
Street South, Moorhead, MN 56562
Telephone: 218-299-3004 or toll-free 800-699-9897 **Fax:** 218-299-3947
E-mail: admissions@cord.edu

Academics

Concordia awards bachelor's **degrees**. Challenging opportunities include advanced
placement, an honors program, double majors, independent study, and a senior project.
Special programs include cooperative education, internships, summer session for credit,
off-campus study, study-abroad, and Army and Air Force ROTC.

The most frequently chosen fields are education, business/marketing, and biological/
life sciences. A complete listing of majors at Concordia appears in the Majors Index
beginning on page 432.

The **faculty** at Concordia has 183 full-time members, 72% with terminal degrees.
The student-faculty ratio is 14:1.

Students of Concordia

The student body is made up of 2,913 undergraduates. 63.3% are women and 36.7% are
men. Students come from 37 states and territories and 34 other countries. 61% are from
Minnesota. 3.6% are international students. 0.4% are African American, 0.3% American
Indian, 1.6% Asian American, and 0.6% Hispanic American. 79% returned for their
sophomore year.

Facilities and Resources

Student rooms are linked to a campus network. 185 **computers** are available on campus
that provide access to the Internet. The **library** has 300,000 books and 1,440 subscriptions.

Campus Life

There are 80 active organizations on campus, including a drama/theater group,
newspaper, radio station, television station, and choral group. 4% of eligible men and 4%
of eligible women are members of local **fraternities**, local **sororities**, and local coed
fraternity.

Concordia is a member of the NCAA (Division III). **Intercollegiate sports** include
baseball (m), basketball, cross-country running, football (m), golf, ice hockey, skiing
(cross-country) (w), soccer, softball (w), swimming (w), tennis, track and field, volleyball,
wrestling (m).

Campus Safety

Student safety services include well-lit campus, 24-hour locked wing doors, late-night
transport/escort service, 24-hour emergency telephone alarm devices, 24-hour patrols by
trained security personnel, and student patrols.

Applying

Concordia requires SAT I or ACT, a high school transcript, and 2 recommendations. It
recommends an interview. Application deadline: rolling admissions. Early and deferred
admission are possible.

Identified by *U.S. News & World Report* as a National Liberal Arts College, Concordia is distinctive as one of the largest in that group, offering more than 80 majors. Academic programs that blend liberal arts and career preparation and an extensive off-campus cooperative education program help students meet career goals. The college is also noted for the friendliness of the student body and both the safety and opportunities of a small city environment. As a result of extraordinary donor support, the college has a reputation for high quality yet has maintained a tuition level below that of comparable colleges.

Getting in Last Year
2,112 applied
88% were accepted
797 enrolled (43%)
29% from top tenth of their h.s. class
45% had SAT verbal scores over 600
43% had SAT math scores over 600
53% had ACT scores over 24
7% had SAT verbal scores over 700
3% had SAT math scores over 700
10% had ACT scores over 30
5 National Merit Scholars

Graduation and After
18% pursued further study (6% arts and sciences, 3% medicine, 2% business)
75% had job offers within 6 months
60 organizations recruited on campus

Financial Matters
$14,020 tuition and fees (2000–2001)
$3900 room and board
100% average percent of need met
$11,209 average financial aid amount received
per undergraduate (1999–2000 estimated)

eApply

Getting in Last Year
3,700 applied
39% were accepted
477 enrolled (33%)
56% from top tenth of their h.s. class
73% had SAT verbal scores over 600
72% had SAT math scores over 600
81% had ACT scores over 24
21% had SAT verbal scores over 700
17% had SAT math scores over 700
26% had ACT scores over 30
2 National Merit Scholars
11 valedictorians

Graduation and After
Graduates pursuing further study: 17% arts and sciences, 5% law, 2% medicine
84 organizations recruited on campus

Financial Matters
$30,595 comprehensive fee (1999–2000)
100% average percent of need met
$21,186 average financial aid amount received per undergraduate (1999–2000 estimated)

CONNECTICUT COLLEGE
SUBURBAN SETTING ■ PRIVATE ■ INDEPENDENT ■ COED
NEW LONDON, CONNECTICUT

Web site: www.camel.conncoll.edu
Contact: Mr. Lee A. Coffin, Dean of Admissions, 270 Mohegan Avenue, New London, CT 06320-4196
Telephone: 860-439-2202 **Fax:** 860-439-4301
E-mail: admit@conncoll.edu

Academics
Connecticut awards bachelor's and master's **degrees**. Challenging opportunities include advanced placement, accelerated degree programs, student-designed majors, an honors program, double majors, independent study, a senior project, and Phi Beta Kappa. Special programs include internships, summer session for credit, off-campus study, and study-abroad. A complete listing of majors at Connecticut appears in the Majors Index beginning on page 432.

The **faculty** at Connecticut has 157 full-time members, 78% with terminal degrees. The student-faculty ratio is 11:1.

Students of Connecticut
The student body totals 1,820, of whom 1,764 are undergraduates. 57.1% are women and 42.9% are men. Students come from 38 states and territories and 51 other countries. 25% are from Connecticut. 7.6% are international students. 3.5% are African American, 0.3% American Indian, 2.4% Asian American, and 2.7% Hispanic American. 91% returned for their sophomore year.

Facilities and Resources
Student rooms are linked to a campus network. 150 **computers** are available on campus that provide access to the Internet. The 2 **libraries** have 938,566 books and 2,357 subscriptions.

Campus Life
There are 75 active organizations on campus, including a drama/theater group, newspaper, radio station, and choral group. No national or local **fraternities** or **sororities**.

Connecticut is a member of the NCAA (Division III). **Intercollegiate sports** include basketball, crew, cross-country running, equestrian sports, field hockey (w), golf, ice hockey, lacrosse, rugby, sailing, skiing (downhill), soccer, squash, swimming, tennis, track and field, volleyball (w).

Campus Safety
Student safety services include late-night transport/escort service, 24-hour emergency telephone alarm devices, 24-hour patrols by trained security personnel, and electronically operated dormitory entrances.

Applying
Connecticut requires an essay, ACT or 3 SAT II Subject Tests (including SAT II: Writing Test), a high school transcript, 2 recommendations, and a minimum high school GPA of 2.0. It recommends SAT I and an interview. Application deadline: 1/15; 1/15 for financial aid. Deferred admission is possible.

COOPER UNION FOR THE ADVANCEMENT OF SCIENCE AND ART

URBAN SETTING ■ PRIVATE ■ INDEPENDENT ■ COED
NEW YORK, NEW YORK

Web site: www.cooper.edu
Contact: Mr. Richard Bory, Dean of Admissions and Records and Registrar, 30 Cooper Square, New York, NY 10003-7120
Telephone: 212-353-4120 **Fax:** 212-353-4342
E-mail: admission@cooper.edu

Academics

Cooper Union awards bachelor's and master's **degrees**. Challenging opportunities include advanced placement, student-designed majors, an honors program, independent study, and a senior project. Special programs include internships, summer session for credit, off-campus study, and study-abroad.

The most frequently chosen fields are engineering/engineering technologies, visual/performing arts, and architecture. A complete listing of majors at Cooper Union appears in the Majors Index beginning on page 432.

The **faculty** at Cooper Union has 53 full-time members, 75% with terminal degrees. The student-faculty ratio is 7:1.

Students of Cooper Union

The student body totals 907, of whom 870 are undergraduates. 34.4% are women and 65.6% are men. Students come from 33 states and territories. 63% are from New York. 10% are international students. 5% are African American, 0.4% American Indian, 25.2% Asian American, and 7.7% Hispanic American. 92% returned for their sophomore year.

Facilities and Resources

Student rooms are linked to a campus network. 200 **computers** are available on campus that provide access to the Internet. The **library** has 97,000 books and 370 subscriptions.

Campus Life

There are 68 active organizations on campus, including a drama/theater group and newspaper. 20% of eligible men and 10% of eligible women are members of national **fraternities** and national **sororities**.

Intercollegiate sports include basketball (m), soccer (m), table tennis, tennis, volleyball.

Campus Safety

Student safety services include security guards, 24-hour emergency telephone alarm devices, and 24-hour patrols by trained security personnel.

Applying

Cooper Union requires SAT I or ACT, a high school transcript, and a minimum high school GPA of 2.0, and in some cases an essay, SAT II Subject Tests, 3 recommendations, and portfolio, home examination. It recommends a minimum high school GPA of 3.0. Application deadline: 5/1 for financial aid, with a 4/15 priority date. Early and deferred admission are possible.

Each of Cooper Union's schools—Art, Architecture, Engineering—adheres strongly to preparation for its profession within a design-centered, problem-solving philosophy of education in a tuition-free environment. A rigorous curriculum and group projects reinforce this unique atmosphere in higher education and are factors in *Money* magazine's decision to name Cooper Union "In a Class by Itself."

Getting in Last Year
2,216 applied
13% were accepted
186 enrolled (64%)
80% from top tenth of their h.s. class
3.4 average high school GPA

Graduation and After
57% graduated in 4 years
17% graduated in 5 years
3% graduated in 6 years
43% pursued further study (15% engineering, 14% arts and sciences, 6% law)
98% had job offers within 6 months
80 organizations recruited on campus
2 Fulbright scholars

Financial Matters
All students are awarded full tuition scholarships
92% average percent of need met

 **eAPPLY**

CORNELL COLLEGE

SMALL-TOWN SETTING ■ PRIVATE ■ INDEPENDENT RELIGIOUS ■ COED
MOUNT VERNON, IOWA

Web site: www.cornell-iowa.edu
Contact: Ms. Florence Hines, Dean of Admission and Financial Assistance,
600 First Street West, Mount Vernon, IA 52314-1098
Telephone: 319-895-4477 or toll-free 800-747-1112 **Fax:** 319-895-4451
E-mail: admissions@cornell-iowa.edu

Getting in Last Year
1,102 applied
72% were accepted
269 enrolled (34%)
31% from top tenth of their h.s. class
3.44 average high school GPA
44% had SAT verbal scores over 600
43% had SAT math scores over 600
68% had ACT scores over 24
7% had SAT verbal scores over 700
5% had SAT math scores over 700
13% had ACT scores over 30
1 National Merit Scholar

Graduation and After
56% graduated in 4 years
2% graduated in 5 years
1% graduated in 6 years
27 organizations recruited on campus

Financial Matters
$18,995 tuition and fees (1999–2000)
$5140 room and board
85% average percent of need met
$17,500 average financial aid amount received
per undergraduate (1999–2000 estimated)

Academics

Cornell awards bachelor's **degrees**. Challenging opportunities include advanced placement, student-designed majors, double majors, independent study, a senior project, and Phi Beta Kappa. Special programs include internships, off-campus study, and study-abroad.

The most frequently chosen fields are social sciences and history, biological/life sciences, and psychology. A complete listing of majors at Cornell appears in the Majors Index beginning on page 432.

The **faculty** at Cornell has 69 full-time members, 94% with terminal degrees.

Students of Cornell

The student body is made up of 965 undergraduates. 59% are women and 41% are men. Students come from 40 states and territories and 10 other countries. 26% are from Iowa. 1.7% are international students. 2.3% are African American, 1.1% American Indian, 1.5% Asian American, and 2.5% Hispanic American. 80% returned for their sophomore year.

Facilities and Resources

Student rooms are linked to a campus network. 105 **computers** are available on campus that provide access to the Internet. The **library** has 865 subscriptions.

Campus Life

There are 76 active organizations on campus, including a drama/theater group, newspaper, radio station, and choral group. 32% of eligible men and 32% of eligible women are members of local **fraternities** and local **sororities**.

Cornell is a member of the NCAA (Division III). **Intercollegiate sports** include baseball (m), basketball, cross-country running, football (m), golf, soccer, softball (w), tennis, track and field, volleyball, wrestling (m).

Campus Safety

Student safety services include 24-hour emergency telephone alarm devices and 24-hour patrols by trained security personnel.

Applying

Cornell requires an essay, SAT I or ACT, a high school transcript, 1 recommendation, and a minimum high school GPA of 2.5. It recommends an interview. Application deadline: 2/1; 3/1 priority date for financial aid. Early and deferred admission are possible.

CORNELL UNIVERSITY

SMALL-TOWN SETTING ■ PRIVATE ■ INDEPENDENT ■ COED
ITHACA, NEW YORK

Web site: www.cornell.edu
Contact: Ms. Doris Davis, Associate Provost of Admissions and Financial Aid,
    410 Thurston Avenue, Ithaca, NY 14850
Telephone: 607-255-3316 **Fax:** 607-255-0659
E-mail: admissions@cornell.edu

Academics

Cornell awards bachelor's, master's, doctoral, and first-professional **degrees**. Challenging opportunities include advanced placement, accelerated degree programs, student-designed majors, an honors program, double majors, independent study, a senior project, Phi Beta Kappa, and Sigma Xi. Special programs include cooperative education, internships, summer session for credit, off-campus study, study-abroad, and Army, Navy and Air Force ROTC.

The most frequently chosen fields are engineering/engineering technologies, agriculture, and business/marketing. A complete listing of majors at Cornell appears in the Majors Index beginning on page 432.

The **faculty** at Cornell has 1,588 full-time members, 90% with terminal degrees. The student-faculty ratio is 11:1.

Students of Cornell

The student body totals 19,021, of whom 13,669 are undergraduates. Students come from 56 states and territories and 81 other countries. 45% are from New York. 7.2% are international students. 4.5% are African American, 0.5% American Indian, 16.5% Asian American, and 5.9% Hispanic American. 93% returned for their sophomore year.

Facilities and Resources

Student rooms are linked to a campus network. The 18 **libraries** have 6,260,779 books and 61,941 subscriptions.

Campus Life

There are 400 active organizations on campus, including a drama/theater group, newspaper, radio station, choral group, and marching band. 22% of eligible men and 19% of eligible women are members of national **fraternities**, national **sororities**, and local fraternities.

Cornell is a member of the NCAA (Division I). **Intercollegiate sports** include baseball (m), basketball, crew, cross-country running, equestrian sports (w), fencing (w), field hockey (w), football (m), golf (m), gymnastics (w), ice hockey, lacrosse, soccer, softball (w), squash, swimming, tennis, track and field, volleyball (w), wrestling (m).

Campus Safety

Student safety services include escort service, late-night transport/escort service, 24-hour emergency telephone alarm devices, 24-hour patrols by trained security personnel, and electronically operated dormitory entrances.

Applying

Cornell requires an essay, SAT I or ACT, a high school transcript, and 1 recommendation, and in some cases SAT II Subject Tests, SAT II: Writing Test, and an interview. Application deadline: 1/1; 2/14 for financial aid. Early and deferred admission are possible.

Cornell University, an Ivy League land-grant school located in central New York, is home to 13,500 undergraduates pursuing studies in more than 70 majors found in the University's 7 small to midsized undergraduate colleges: Agriculture & Life Sciences; Architecture, Art & Planning; Arts & Sciences; Engineering; Hotel Administration; Human Ecology; and Industrial & Labor Relations. Students come from all 50 states and many other countries. Cornell's special features include a world-renowned faculty; an outstanding undergraduate research program; 17 libraries; superb research and teaching facilities; a large, diverse study-abroad program; more than 500 student organizations; more than 30 varsity sports; and a graduation rate close to 90%.

Getting in Last Year
19,949 applied
33% were accepted
3,136 enrolled (48%)
80% from top tenth of their h.s. class
83% had SAT verbal scores over 600
91% had SAT math scores over 600
34% had SAT verbal scores over 700
54% had SAT math scores over 700
47 National Merit Scholars

Graduation and After
81% graduated in 4 years
8% graduated in 5 years
2% graduated in 6 years
32% pursued further study
66% had job offers within 6 months
500 organizations recruited on campus
1 Marshall, 9 Fulbright scholars

Financial Matters
$23,848 tuition and fees (1999–2000)
$7827 room and board
100% average percent of need met
$18,700 average financial aid amount received
    per undergraduate (1999–2000 estimated)

CREIGHTON UNIVERSITY
URBAN SETTING ■ PRIVATE ■ INDEPENDENT RELIGIOUS ■ COED
OMAHA, NEBRASKA

Web site: www.creighton.edu
Contact: Mr. Dennis J. O'Driscoll, Director of Admissions, 2500 California
   Plaza, Omaha, NE 68178-0001
Telephone: 402-280-2703 or toll-free 800-282-5835 **Fax:** 402-280-2685
E-mail: admissions@creighton.edu

With the goal of providing educational excellence to a greater number of students, Creighton University expanded its scholarship offerings in 1999. A Creighton education is within the reach of many students through need-based financial aid and performance-based scholarships. Creighton has numerous University and endowed academic scholarships, ranging from $1000 to full tuition, fees, and room stipends. Outstanding academic achievement and leadership are rewarded with a variety of awards in the Colleges of Arts and Sciences and Business Administration and the School of Nursing. ROTC Scholarship Supplements are granted to Advance Designee Army and Air Force scholarship winners. Creighton is a Center for Excellence for the Army ROTC, with scholarship supplements available to nursing students.

Academics
Creighton awards associate, bachelor's, master's, doctoral, and first-professional **degrees.** Challenging opportunities include advanced placement, accelerated degree programs, an honors program, double majors, independent study, and a senior project. Special programs include internships, summer session for credit, study-abroad, and Army and Air Force ROTC.

The most frequently chosen fields are health professions and related sciences, business/marketing, and biological/life sciences. A complete listing of majors at Creighton appears in the Majors Index beginning on page 432.

The **faculty** at Creighton has 1,438 members. The student-faculty ratio is 14:1.

Students of Creighton
The student body totals 6,325, of whom 3,976 are undergraduates. 58.2% are women and 41.8% are men. Students come from 48 states and territories and 58 other countries. 46% are from Nebraska. 4.3% are international students. 3.2% are African American, 0.6% American Indian, 11.8% Asian American, and 3.1% Hispanic American. 85% returned for their sophomore year.

Facilities and Resources
Student rooms are linked to a campus network.

Campus Life
There are 130 active organizations on campus, including a drama/theater group, newspaper, radio station, television station, and choral group. 29% of eligible men and 30% of eligible women are members of national **fraternities** and national **sororities.**

Creighton is a member of the NCAA (Division I). **Intercollegiate sports** (some offering scholarships) include baseball (m), basketball, crew (w), cross-country running, golf, soccer, softball (w), tennis, volleyball (w).

Campus Safety
Student safety services include late-night transport/escort service, 24-hour emergency telephone alarm devices, 24-hour patrols by trained security personnel, student patrols, and electronically operated dormitory entrances.

Applying
Creighton requires SAT I or ACT, a high school transcript, 1 recommendation, and a minimum high school GPA of 2.75. It recommends an essay. Application deadline: 8/1; 5/15 priority date for financial aid. Deferred admission is possible.

Getting in Last Year
3,112 applied
91% were accepted
834 enrolled (29%)
41% from top tenth of their h.s. class
3.67 average high school GPA
41% had SAT verbal scores over 600
46% had SAT math scores over 600
71% had ACT scores over 24
8% had SAT verbal scores over 700
11% had SAT math scores over 700
18% had ACT scores over 30

Graduation and After
58% graduated in 4 years
13% graduated in 5 years
1% graduated in 6 years
101 organizations recruited on campus

Financial Matters
$14,132 tuition and fees (1999–2000)
$5446 room and board
89% average percent of need met
$13,169 average financial aid amount received
   per undergraduate (1999–2000)

DARTMOUTH COLLEGE

RURAL SETTING ■ PRIVATE ■ INDEPENDENT ■ COED
HANOVER, NEW HAMPSHIRE

Web site: www.dartmouth.edu
Contact: Mr. Karl M. Furstenberg, Dean of Admissions and Financial Aid,
6016 McNutt Hall, Hanover, NH 03755
Telephone: 603-646-2875
E-mail: admissions.office@dartmouth.edu

  eAPPLY

Academics

Dartmouth awards bachelor's, master's, doctoral, and first-professional **degrees**. Challenging opportunities include advanced placement, accelerated degree programs, student-designed majors, an honors program, double majors, independent study, a senior project, Phi Beta Kappa, and Sigma Xi. Special programs include internships, summer session for credit, off-campus study, study-abroad, and Army ROTC.

The most frequently chosen fields are social sciences and history, biological/life sciences, and English. A complete listing of majors at Dartmouth appears in the Majors Index beginning on page 432.

The **faculty** at Dartmouth has 439 full-time members, 96% with terminal degrees. The student-faculty ratio is 9:1.

Students of Dartmouth

The student body totals 5,344, of whom 4,057 are undergraduates. 47.9% are women and 52.1% are men. Students come from 52 states and territories and 47 other countries. 3% are from New Hampshire. 4% are international students. 5.4% are African American, 2.1% American Indian, 9.8% Asian American, and 5.1% Hispanic American. 98% returned for their sophomore year.

Facilities and Resources

Student rooms are linked to a campus network. 122 **computers** are available on campus that provide access to the Internet. The 9 **libraries** have 2,261,911 books and 20,043 subscriptions.

Campus Life

There are 250 active organizations on campus, including a drama/theater group, newspaper, radio station, television station, choral group, and marching band. 41% of eligible men and 28% of eligible women are members of national **fraternities**, national **sororities**, local fraternities, local sororities, and coed fraternities.

Dartmouth is a member of the NCAA (Division I). **Intercollegiate sports** include baseball (m), basketball, crew, cross-country running, equestrian sports, fencing, field hockey (w), football (m), golf, gymnastics, ice hockey, lacrosse, rugby, sailing, skiing (cross-country), skiing (downhill), soccer, softball (w), squash, swimming, tennis, track and field, volleyball, water polo, wrestling (m).

Campus Safety

Student safety services include late-night transport/escort service, 24-hour emergency telephone alarm devices, 24-hour patrols by trained security personnel, and student patrols.

Applying

Dartmouth requires an essay, SAT I and SAT II or ACT, a high school transcript, and 2 recommendations. It recommends an interview. Application deadline: 1/1; 2/1 for financial aid. Early and deferred admission are possible.

From Daniel Webster to Dr. Seuss, Dartmouth College has empowered talented individuals to explore the life of the mind, to engage the world, and to build community. Members of the tightly knit student body profess an uncommon love for their alma mater. This dynamic group of women and men find common ground in intellectual pursuits and an appreciation of diversity. Dartmouth supports these core values with university-level resources that enable exceptional undergraduates to collaborate with distinguished faculty members and to work in cutting-edge research facilities.

Getting in Last Year
10,259 applied
21% were accepted
1,054 enrolled (49%)
87% from top tenth of their h.s. class
95% had SAT verbal scores over 600
95% had SAT math scores over 600
65% had SAT verbal scores over 700
66% had SAT math scores over 700
53 National Merit Scholars
196 valedictorians

Graduation and After
87% graduated in 4 years
6% graduated in 5 years
1% graduated in 6 years
20% pursued further study
215 organizations recruited on campus
5 Fulbright scholars

Financial Matters
$24,884 tuition and fees (1999–2000)
$6390 room and board
100% average percent of need met
$23,331 average financial aid amount received
per undergraduate (1999–2000)

David Lipscomb University

URBAN SETTING ■ PRIVATE ■ INDEPENDENT RELIGIOUS ■ COED
NASHVILLE, TENNESSEE

Web site: www.lipscomb.edu
Contact: Mr. Scott Gilman, Director of Admissions, 3901 Granny White
  Pike, Nashville, TN 37204-3951
Telephone: 615-269-1776 or toll-free 800-333-4358 ext. 1776 **Fax:**
  615-269-1804
E-mail: admissions@dlu.edu

---

ounded in 1891, Lipscomb is a distinctly Christian university with a sterling academic reputation. More than 100 major programs of study are offered. Lipscomb's 21st-century campuswide fiber-optic network provides PC connections in every residence hall, residence hall lobby lab, and many other locations for Internet access to resources worldwide. Lipscomb University is a beautiful, quiet place with a special atmosphere that encourages learning. Nashville is one of the most exciting cities in the South. Its wide range of cultural and career opportunities enhances the academic program and each student's potential for employment following graduation.

Academics

Lipscomb University awards bachelor's, master's, and first-professional **degrees**. Challenging opportunities include advanced placement, accelerated degree programs, an honors program, double majors, independent study, and a senior project. Special programs include internships, summer session for credit, study-abroad, and Army and Air Force ROTC.

The most frequently chosen fields are business/marketing, education, and communications/communication technologies. A complete listing of majors at Lipscomb University appears in the Majors Index beginning on page 432.

The **faculty** at Lipscomb University has 94 full-time members, 85% with terminal degrees.

Students of Lipscomb University

The student body totals 2,504, of whom 2,317 are undergraduates. 56% are women and 44% are men. Students come from 40 states and territories and 38 other countries. 64% are from Tennessee. 1.4% are international students. 3.9% are African American, 0.3% American Indian, 1.1% Asian American, and 0.4% Hispanic American. 79% returned for their sophomore year.

Facilities and Resources

Student rooms are linked to a campus network. 232 **computers** are available on campus that provide access to the Internet.

Campus Life

There are 60 active organizations on campus, including a drama/theater group, newspaper, radio station, and choral group. 15% of eligible men and 20% of eligible women are members of local **fraternities** and local **sororities**.

Lipscomb University is a member of the NAIA. **Intercollegiate sports** (some offering scholarships) include baseball (m), basketball, cross-country running, golf, soccer, softball (w), tennis, volleyball (w).

Campus Safety

Student safety services include late-night transport/escort service, 24-hour emergency telephone alarm devices, 24-hour patrols by trained security personnel, and electronically operated dormitory entrances.

Applying

Lipscomb University requires SAT I or ACT, a high school transcript, 2 recommendations, and a minimum high school GPA of 2.25. It recommends an essay and an interview. Application deadline: rolling admissions; 2/28 priority date for financial aid. Early admission is possible.

Getting in Last Year
1,598 applied
93% were accepted
598 enrolled (40%)
26% from top tenth of their h.s. class
3.17 average high school GPA
32% had SAT verbal scores over 600
35% had SAT math scores over 600
47% had ACT scores over 24
6% had SAT verbal scores over 700
5% had SAT math scores over 700
10% had ACT scores over 30
1 National Merit Scholar
23 valedictorians

Graduation and After
31% graduated in 4 years
16% graduated in 5 years
3% graduated in 6 years
271 organizations recruited on campus

Financial Matters
$9689 tuition and fees (1999–2000)
$4344 room and board

Davidson College

  eAPPLY

SMALL-TOWN SETTING ■ PRIVATE ■ INDEPENDENT RELIGIOUS ■ COED
DAVIDSON, NORTH CAROLINA

Web site: www.davidson.edu
Contact: Dr. Nancy J. Cable, Dean of Admission and Financial Aid, PO Box
1719, Davidson, NC 28036-1719
Telephone: 704-892-2230 or toll-free 800-768-0380 **Fax:** 704-892-2016
E-mail: admission@davidson.edu

Academics

Davidson awards bachelor's **degrees**. Challenging opportunities include advanced placement, accelerated degree programs, student-designed majors, an honors program, double majors, independent study, a senior project, and Phi Beta Kappa. Special programs include off-campus study, study-abroad, and Army and Air Force ROTC.

The most frequently chosen fields are social sciences and history, biological/life sciences, and English. A complete listing of majors at Davidson appears in the Majors Index beginning on page 432.

The **faculty** at Davidson has 152 full-time members, 97% with terminal degrees. The student-faculty ratio is 11:1.

Students of Davidson

The student body is made up of 1,652 undergraduates. Students come from 46 states and territories and 37 other countries. 19% are from North Carolina. 3.1% are international students. 5% are African American, 0.3% American Indian, 1.9% Asian American, and 2.4% Hispanic American. 97% returned for their sophomore year.

Facilities and Resources

Student rooms are linked to a campus network. 130 **computers** are available on campus that provide access to the Internet. The 2 **libraries** have 395,794 books and 2,829 subscriptions.

Campus Life

There are 100 active organizations on campus, including a drama/theater group, newspaper, radio station, and choral group. 55% of eligible men and 65% of eligible women are members of national **fraternities** and women's eating houses.

Davidson is a member of the NCAA (Division I). **Intercollegiate sports** (some offering scholarships) include baseball (m), basketball, crew, cross-country running, fencing, field hockey (w), football (m), golf (m), lacrosse, rugby (m), sailing, soccer, swimming, tennis, track and field, volleyball (w), wrestling (m).

Campus Safety

Student safety services include late-night transport/escort service, 24-hour emergency telephone alarm devices, 24-hour patrols by trained security personnel, and electronically operated dormitory entrances.

Applying

Davidson requires an essay, SAT I or ACT, a high school transcript, and 4 recommendations. It recommends SAT II Subject Tests, SAT II: Writing Test, and an interview. Application deadline: 1/2; 2/15 priority date for financial aid. Early and deferred admission are possible.

Davidson College is one of the nation's premier academic institutions, a college of the liberal arts and sciences respected for its intellectual vigor, the high quality of its faculty and students, and the achievements of its alumni. It is distinguished by its strong honor system, close interaction between professors and students, an environment that encourages both intellectual growth and community service, and a commitment to international education. Davidson places great value on student participation in extracurricular activities, intercollegiate athletics, and intramural sports. Nearby Charlotte, North Carolina, offers students the cultural, international, and internship opportunities of a major metropolitan center.

Getting in Last Year
2,824 applied
38% were accepted
455 enrolled (42%)
74% from top tenth of their h.s. class
81% had SAT verbal scores over 600
83% had SAT math scores over 600
35% had SAT verbal scores over 700
30% had SAT math scores over 700

Graduation and After
89% graduated in 4 years
3% graduated in 5 years
68% had job offers within 6 months
90 organizations recruited on campus
1 Rhodes, 2 Fulbright scholars

Financial Matters
$22,228 tuition and fees (1999–2000)
$6340 room and board
98% average percent of need met
$13,889 average financial aid amount received per undergraduate (1998–99)

DEEP SPRINGS COLLEGE
RURAL SETTING ■ PRIVATE ■ INDEPENDENT ■ MEN ONLY
DEEP SPRINGS, CALIFORNIA

Web site: www.deepsprings.edu
Contact: Dr. L. Jackson Newell, President, HC 72, Box 45001, Deep Springs, CA, via, Dyer, NV 89010-9803
Telephone: 760-872-2000
E-mail: apcom@deepsprings.edu

Academics
Deep Springs College awards associate **degrees**. Challenging opportunities include accelerated degree programs, student-designed majors, freshman honors college, an honors program, and independent study. Special programs include cooperative education, internships, and summer session for credit.

The most frequently chosen field is liberal arts/general studies. A complete listing of majors at Deep Springs College appears in the Majors Index beginning on page 432.

The **faculty** at Deep Springs College has 4 full-time members, 100% with terminal degrees. The student-faculty ratio is 3:1.

Students of Deep Springs College
The student body is made up of 24 undergraduates. Students come from 14 states and territories. 12% are from California.

Facilities and Resources
6 **computers** are available on campus that provide access to the Internet. The **library** has 20,000 books and 60 subscriptions.

Campus Life
Active organizations on campus include a drama/theater group and choral group. No national or local **fraternities**.

This institution has no intercollegiate sports.

Applying
Deep Springs College requires an essay, SAT I and SAT II or ACT, a high school transcript, an interview, and recommendations. Application deadline: 11/15.

DENISON UNIVERSITY
SMALL-TOWN SETTING ■ PRIVATE ■ INDEPENDENT ■ COED
GRANVILLE, OHIO

Web site: www.denison.edu
Contact: Ms. Pennie Miller, Communications Coordinator, Box H, Granville, OH 43023
Telephone: 740-587-6618 or toll-free 800-DENISON
E-mail: admissions@denison.edu

eAPPLY

Academics
Denison awards bachelor's **degrees**. Challenging opportunities include advanced placement, student-designed majors, an honors program, double majors, independent study, a senior project, Phi Beta Kappa, and Sigma Xi. Special programs include cooperative education, internships, off-campus study, and study-abroad.

The most frequently chosen fields are social sciences and history, biological/life sciences, and visual/performing arts. A complete listing of majors at Denison appears in the Majors Index beginning on page 432.

The **faculty** at Denison has 167 full-time members, 98% with terminal degrees. The student-faculty ratio is 12:1.

Students of Denison
The student body is made up of 2,089 undergraduates. 54.8% are women and 45.2% are men. Students come from 45 states and territories and 30 other countries. 43% are from Ohio. 4.2% are international students. 4.4% are African American, 0.2% American Indian, 2.4% Asian American, and 1.5% Hispanic American. 84% returned for their sophomore year.

Facilities and Resources
Student rooms are linked to a campus network. 400 **computers** are available on campus that provide access to the Internet. The **library** has 339,644 books and 1,208 subscriptions.

Campus Life
There are 86 active organizations on campus, including a drama/theater group, newspaper, radio station, television station, and choral group. 30% of eligible men and 32% of eligible women are members of national **fraternities** and national **sororities**.

Denison is a member of the NCAA (Division III). **Intercollegiate sports** include baseball (m), basketball, crew (m), cross-country running, equestrian sports, field hockey (w), football (m), golf (m), ice hockey (m), lacrosse, riflery, rugby, sailing, skiing (downhill), soccer, softball (w), squash, swimming, tennis, track and field, volleyball (w).

Campus Safety
Student safety services include late-night transport/escort service, 24-hour emergency telephone alarm devices, 24-hour patrols by trained security personnel, and electronically operated dormitory entrances.

Applying
Denison requires an essay, SAT I or ACT, a high school transcript, and 2 recommendations. It recommends SAT II Subject Tests and an interview. Application deadline: 2/1; 2/15 priority date for financial aid. Early and deferred admission are possible.

Denison University, a 4-year, highly selective, national, residential liberal arts college for men and women, located in Granville, Ohio, is known for its curricular innovation and unique faculty-student learning partnerships. Students may choose from 42 academic majors and concentrations and 9 preprofessional programs or design their own programs of study while living on the beautiful 1,200-acre hillside campus. Founded in 1831, Denison has more than 25,500 alumni and an endowment of more than $324 million.

Getting in Last Year
2,991 applied
69% were accepted
587 enrolled (29%)
52% from top tenth of their h.s. class
3.50 average high school GPA
51% had SAT verbal scores over 600
59% had SAT math scores over 600
85% had ACT scores over 24
11% had SAT verbal scores over 700
12% had SAT math scores over 700
24% had ACT scores over 30
16 National Merit Scholars
29 class presidents
31 valedictorians

Graduation and After
22% pursued further study (8% arts and sciences, 5% medicine, 4% law)
72% had job offers within 6 months
60 organizations recruited on campus

Financial Matters
$22,210 tuition and fees (2000–2001)
$6300 room and board
98% average percent of need met
$9772 average financial aid amount received per undergraduate (1999–2000 estimated)

DePaul University

URBAN SETTING ■ PRIVATE ■ INDEPENDENT RELIGIOUS ■ COED
CHICAGO, ILLINOIS

Web site: www.depaul.edu
Contact: Mr. Ray Kennelley, Dean of Admission, 1 East Jackson Boulevard, Chicago, IL 60604-2287
Telephone: 312-362-8300 or toll-free 800-4DE-PAUL (out-of-state)
E-mail: admitdpu@wppost.depaul.edu

DePaul is an urban university offering over 100 undergraduate and graduate programs. A private Catholic institution founded by the Vincentian order in 1898, today DePaul reflects a wide diversity of ethnic, religious, and economic backgrounds. DePaul students study in a great city with unlimited opportunities for professional experience before graduation. Students are active participants in projects and organizations working to meet the needs of the city. DePaul continues to emphasize teaching ability as a priority for faculty selection.

Getting in Last Year
6,050 applied
78% were accepted
1,750 enrolled (37%)
19% from top tenth of their h.s. class
3.3 average high school GPA
38% had SAT verbal scores over 600
35% had SAT math scores over 600
48% had ACT scores over 24
8% had SAT verbal scores over 700
4% had SAT math scores over 700
6% had ACT scores over 30
40 National Merit Scholars

Graduation and After
38% graduated in 4 years
14% graduated in 5 years
5% graduated in 6 years
1000 organizations recruited on campus

Financial Matters
$14,700 tuition and fees (1999–2000)
$6300 room and board

Academics

DePaul awards bachelor's, master's, doctoral, and first-professional **degrees** and post-bachelor's and post-master's certificates. Challenging opportunities include advanced placement, accelerated degree programs, student-designed majors, freshman honors college, an honors program, independent study, and a senior project. Special programs include cooperative education, internships, summer session for credit, study-abroad, and Army ROTC.

The most frequently chosen fields are business/marketing, liberal arts/general studies, and social sciences and history. A complete listing of majors at DePaul appears in the Majors Index beginning on page 432.

The **faculty** at DePaul has 581 full-time members. The student-faculty ratio is 15:1.

Students of DePaul

The student body totals 19,549, of whom 11,776 are undergraduates. 58.9% are women and 41.1% are men. Students come from 50 states and territories and 44 other countries. 85% are from Illinois. 1.7% are international students. 12.2% are African American, 0.3% American Indian, 8.7% Asian American, and 12.5% Hispanic American. 84% returned for their sophomore year.

Facilities and Resources

Student rooms are linked to a campus network. 850 **computers** are available on campus that provide access to the Internet. The 3 **libraries** have 759,569 books and 16,465 subscriptions.

Campus Life

There are 120 active organizations on campus, including a drama/theater group, newspaper, and radio station. 3% of eligible men and 3% of eligible women are members of national **fraternities** and national **sororities**.

DePaul is a member of the NCAA (Division I). **Intercollegiate sports** (some offering scholarships) include basketball, cross-country running, golf, riflery, soccer, softball (w), tennis, track and field, volleyball (w).

Campus Safety

Student safety services include late-night transport/escort service, 24-hour emergency telephone alarm devices, 24-hour patrols by trained security personnel, and electronically operated dormitory entrances.

Applying

DePaul requires SAT I or ACT, a high school transcript, 1 recommendation, and a minimum high school GPA of 2.0, and in some cases an interview, audition, and a minimum high school GPA of 3.0. It recommends a minimum high school GPA of 3.0. Application deadline: rolling admissions; 4/1 priority date for financial aid. Early and deferred admission are possible.

DePauw University

Small-town setting ■ Private ■ Independent Religious ■ Coed
Greencastle, Indiana

Web site: www.depauw.edu
Contact: Mr. Larry West, Director of Admission, 101 East Seminary Street,
Greencastle, IN 46135-0037
Telephone: 765-658-4006 or toll-free 800-447-2495 **Fax:** 765-658-4007
E-mail: admissions@depauw.edu

eApply

Academics

DePauw awards bachelor's **degrees**. Challenging opportunities include advanced placement, student-designed majors, an honors program, double majors, independent study, a
senior project, Phi Beta Kappa, and Sigma Xi. Special programs include internships, off-
campus study, study-abroad, and Army and Air Force ROTC.

The most frequently chosen fields are social sciences and history, communications/
communication technologies, and English. A complete listing of majors at DePauw appears in the Majors Index beginning on page 432.

The **faculty** at DePauw has 188 full-time members, 93% with terminal degrees. The
student-faculty ratio is 11:1.

Students of DePauw

The student body is made up of 2,216 undergraduates. 56.3% are women and 43.7% are
men. Students come from 47 states and territories and 15 other countries. 57% are from
Indiana. 0.8% are international students. 6.1% are African American, 0.1% American
Indian, 1.5% Asian American, and 2.7% Hispanic American. 84% returned for their
sophomore year.

Facilities and Resources

Student rooms are linked to a campus network. 185 **computers** are available on campus
that provide access to the Internet. The 4 **libraries** have 247,587 books and 1,387
subscriptions.

Campus Life

There are 65 active organizations on campus, including a drama/theater group,
newspaper, radio station, television station, and choral group. 57% of eligible men and
54% of eligible women are members of national **fraternities**, national **sororities**, and
local sororities.

DePauw is a member of the NCAA (Division III). **Intercollegiate sports** include
baseball (m), basketball, cross-country running, field hockey (w), football (m), golf, soccer, softball (w), swimming, tennis, track and field, volleyball (w).

Campus Safety

Student safety services include late-night transport/escort service, 24-hour emergency
telephone alarm devices, 24-hour patrols by trained security personnel, and electronically operated dormitory entrances.

Applying

DePauw requires an essay, SAT I or ACT, a high school transcript, and 1 recommendation. It recommends an interview and a minimum high school GPA of 3.0. Application deadline: 2/1; 2/15 priority date for financial aid. Early and deferred admission
are possible.

DePauw University
provides a traditional
education in the arts and
sciences in both the College of
Liberal Arts and the School of Music,
complemented by one of the largest
internship programs in the nation.
Extensive internship opportunities
exist in business, science, the arts,
and news media as well as in
professional and not-for-profit
organizations nationally and
internationally. Honors programs are
offered in classics, management,
media, and science. DePauw offers
large university facilities with small
classes; the average class size is
18. Ample opportunities are
available for students to personalize
education and engage in
collaborative research with
professors. There are extensive
opportunities for international study,
and more than half of DePauw's
students volunteer for community
service each year.

Getting in Last Year
2,687 applied
67% were accepted
581 enrolled (32%)
49% from top tenth of their h.s. class
3.66 average high school GPA
45% had SAT verbal scores over 600
49% had SAT math scores over 600
78% had ACT scores over 24
8% had SAT verbal scores over 700
8% had SAT math scores over 700
15% had ACT scores over 30
10 National Merit Scholars
28 valedictorians

Graduation and After
72% graduated in 4 years
5% graduated in 5 years
1% graduated in 6 years
25% pursued further study (9% medicine, 7%
law, 5% arts and sciences)
82% had job offers within 6 months
52 organizations recruited on campus

Financial Matters
$19,730 tuition and fees (1999–2000)
$6080 room and board
100% average percent of need met
$17,960 average financial aid amount received
per undergraduate (1999–2000)

eApply

Getting in Last Year
3,434 applied
64% were accepted
620 enrolled (28%)
47% from top tenth of their h.s. class
54% had SAT verbal scores over 600
46% had SAT math scores over 600
11% had SAT verbal scores over 700
6% had SAT math scores over 700
18 National Merit Scholars
9 class presidents
19 valedictorians

Graduation and After
75% graduated in 4 years
4% graduated in 5 years
Graduates pursuing further study: 7% arts and sciences, 4% law, 2% education
98% had job offers within 6 months
23 organizations recruited on campus

Financial Matters
$24,450 tuition and fees (2000–2001)
$6450 room and board
94% average percent of need met
$20,228 average financial aid amount received per undergraduate (1999–2000)

DICKINSON COLLEGE

SUBURBAN SETTING ■ PRIVATE ■ INDEPENDENT ■ COED
CARLISLE, PENNSYLVANIA

Web site: www.dickinson.edu
Contact: Mr. Christopher Seth Allen, Director of Admissions, PO Box 1773, Carlisle, PA 17013-2896
Telephone: 717-245-1231 or toll-free 800-644-1773 **Fax:** 717-245-1231
E-mail: admit@dickinson.edu

Academics

Dickinson awards bachelor's **degrees**. Challenging opportunities include advanced placement, accelerated degree programs, student-designed majors, double majors, independent study, a senior project, and Phi Beta Kappa. Special programs include internships, summer session for credit, off-campus study, study-abroad, and Army ROTC.

The most frequently chosen fields are social sciences and history, foreign language/literature, and English. A complete listing of majors at Dickinson appears in the Majors Index beginning on page 432.

The **faculty** at Dickinson has 154 full-time members, 90% with terminal degrees. The student-faculty ratio is 13:1.

Students of Dickinson

The student body is made up of 2,067 undergraduates. 60.3% are women and 39.7% are men. Students come from 42 states and territories and 18 other countries. 44% are from Pennsylvania. 1% are international students. 1.2% are African American, 0.1% American Indian, 2.9% Asian American, and 2% Hispanic American. 89% returned for their sophomore year.

Facilities and Resources

Student rooms are linked to a campus network. 350 **computers** are available on campus that provide access to the Internet.

Campus Life

There are 129 active organizations on campus, including a drama/theater group, newspaper, radio station, and choral group. 45% of eligible men and 39% of eligible women are members of national **fraternities**, national **sororities**, local fraternities, and local sororities.

Dickinson is a member of the NCAA (Division III). **Intercollegiate sports** include baseball (m), basketball, cross-country running, equestrian sports, fencing, field hockey (w), football (m), golf, ice hockey (m), lacrosse, skiing (downhill), soccer, softball (w), squash, swimming, tennis, track and field, volleyball, wrestling (m).

Campus Safety

Student safety services include late-night transport/escort service, 24-hour emergency telephone alarm devices, 24-hour patrols by trained security personnel, student patrols, and electronically operated dormitory entrances.

Applying

Dickinson requires an essay, a high school transcript, and 2 recommendations. It recommends SAT II Subject Tests, SAT I and SAT II or ACT, an interview, and a minimum high school GPA of 3.0. Application deadline: 2/1; 2/1 priority date for financial aid. Early and deferred admission are possible.

DRAKE UNIVERSITY

SUBURBAN SETTING ■ PRIVATE ■ INDEPENDENT ■ COED
DES MOINES, IOWA

Web site: www.drake.edu
Contact: Mr. Thomas F. Willoughby, Dean of Admission, 2507 University
   Avenue, Des Moines, IA 50311-4516
Telephone: 515-271-3181 or toll-free 800-44DRAKE **Fax:** 515-271-2831
E-mail: admitinfo@acad.drake.edu

  eAPPLY

Academics

Drake awards bachelor's, master's, doctoral, and first-professional **degrees**. Challenging opportunities include advanced placement, student-designed majors, an honors program, double majors, independent study, a senior project, and Phi Beta Kappa. Special programs include cooperative education, internships, summer session for credit, off-campus study, study-abroad, and Army and Air Force ROTC.

The most frequently chosen fields are business/marketing, health professions and related sciences, and communications/communication technologies. A complete listing of majors at Drake appears in the Majors Index beginning on page 432.

The **faculty** at Drake has 262 full-time members, 94% with terminal degrees. The student-faculty ratio is 14:1.

Students of Drake

The student body totals 4,646, of whom 3,234 are undergraduates. 59.3% are women and 40.7% are men. Students come from 46 states and territories and 50 other countries. 42% are from Iowa. 5.5% are international students. 3.3% are African American, 0.5% American Indian, 3.7% Asian American, and 1.5% Hispanic American. 82% returned for their sophomore year.

Facilities and Resources

Student rooms are linked to a campus network. 1,081 **computers** are available on campus that provide access to the Internet. The 2 **libraries** have 553,569 books and 2,284 subscriptions.

Campus Life

There are 140 active organizations on campus, including a drama/theater group, newspaper, radio station, television station, choral group, and marching band. 32% of eligible men and 30% of eligible women are members of national **fraternities** and national **sororities**.

Drake is a member of the NCAA (Division I). **Intercollegiate sports** (some offering scholarships) include basketball, crew (w), cross-country running, football (m), golf (m), ice hockey (m), rugby, soccer, softball (w), swimming, tennis, track and field, volleyball.

Campus Safety

Student safety services include 24-hour desk attendants in residence halls, late-night transport/escort service, 24-hour emergency telephone alarm devices, and 24-hour patrols by trained security personnel.

Applying

Drake requires SAT I or ACT, a high school transcript, 1 recommendation, and a minimum high school GPA of 2.5, and in some cases PCAT for pharmacy transfers. It recommends an essay and an interview. Application deadline: rolling admissions; 3/1 priority date for financial aid. Early and deferred admission are possible.

Drake University maximizes the potential of its students with a unique set of advantages. It is big enough to offer more than 70 undergraduate academic programs, 140 organizations, and a community of students from around the world. Yet Drake's exceptional faculty and academic and extracurricular options are highly accessible to students beginning their first year of college. Drake's location in Des Moines, Iowa's capital, offers numerous professional internships; 70% of Drake's undergraduates have at least one. Drake is affordable; 95% of its students receive financial assistance. It is a great value, too—95% of Drake's graduates get career positions or enter graduate school within 6 months of graduating.

Getting in Last Year

2,388 applied
90% were accepted
676 enrolled (31%)
34% from top tenth of their h.s. class
3.55 average high school GPA
39% had SAT verbal scores over 600
49% had SAT math scores over 600
67% had ACT scores over 24
10% had SAT verbal scores over 700
9% had SAT math scores over 700
14% had ACT scores over 30
10 National Merit Scholars

Graduation and After

48% graduated in 4 years
10% graduated in 5 years
6% graduated in 6 years
21% pursued further study (13% arts and
   sciences, 4% law, 2% business)
93.3% had job offers within 6 months
110 organizations recruited on campus

Financial Matters

$16,580 tuition and fees (1999–2000)
$4870 room and board
83% average percent of need met
$14,149 average financial aid amount received
   per undergraduate (1999–2000)

DREW UNIVERSITY

SUBURBAN SETTING ■ PRIVATE ■ INDEPENDENT RELIGIOUS ■ COED
MADISON, NEW JERSEY

Web site: www.drew.edu
Contact: Mr. Roberto Noya, Dean of Admissions for the College of Liberal
    Arts, 36 Madison Avenue, Madison, NJ 07940-1493
Telephone: 973-408-3739 **Fax:** 973-408-3036
E-mail: cadm@drew.edu

On a forested campus 30 miles from Manhattan, inspiring professors offer students experiential learning opportunities that help them connect the traditions of the liberal arts to the world of work and the global community. Faculty members employ technology creatively in teaching the arts and sciences. Students at Drew take advantage of remarkable internship opportunities in the New York metropolitan area and many off-campus study opportunities, including semesters in New York on art, theater, the United Nations, and Wall Street; semesters in London and Brussels; and Drew International Seminars throughout the world.

Getting in Last Year
2,400 applied
75% were accepted
407 enrolled (23%)
44% from top tenth of their h.s. class
57% had SAT verbal scores over 600
52% had SAT math scores over 600
18% had SAT verbal scores over 700
14% had SAT math scores over 700
15 National Merit Scholars

Graduation and After
74% graduated in 4 years
2% graduated in 5 years
1% graduated in 6 years
27% pursued further study (19% arts and
  sciences, 5% medicine, 3% law)

Financial Matters
$23,008 tuition and fees (1999–2000)
$6564 room and board
90% average percent of need met
$20,137 average financial aid amount received
  per undergraduate (1999–2000 estimated)

Academics
Drew awards bachelor's, master's, doctoral, and first-professional **degrees** and post-bachelor's certificates. Challenging opportunities include advanced placement, accelerated degree programs, student-designed majors, double majors, independent study, a senior project, and Phi Beta Kappa. Special programs include internships, summer session for credit, off-campus study, and study-abroad.

The most frequently chosen fields are social sciences and history, psychology, and English. A complete listing of majors at Drew appears in the Majors Index beginning on page 432.

The **faculty** at Drew has 117 full-time members, 93% with terminal degrees. The student-faculty ratio is 11:1.

Students of Drew
The student body totals 2,381, of whom 1,485 are undergraduates. 57.6% are women and 42.4% are men. Students come from 42 states and territories and 11 other countries. 57% are from New Jersey. 1.2% are international students. 3.7% are African American, 0.4% American Indian, 6.1% Asian American, and 5.2% Hispanic American. 87% returned for their sophomore year.

Facilities and Resources
Student rooms are linked to a campus network. The **library** has 462,498 books and 2,257 subscriptions.

Campus Life
There are 50 active organizations on campus, including a drama/theater group, newspaper, radio station, television station, and choral group. No national or local **fraternities** or **sororities**.

Drew is a member of the NCAA (Division III). **Intercollegiate sports** include baseball (m), basketball, cross-country running, equestrian sports, fencing, field hockey (w), lacrosse, soccer, softball (w), swimming, tennis.

Campus Safety
Student safety services include late-night transport/escort service, 24-hour emergency telephone alarm devices, 24-hour patrols by trained security personnel, and electronically operated dormitory entrances.

Applying
Drew requires an essay, SAT I or ACT, a high school transcript, and 2 recommendations. It recommends SAT I and an interview. Application deadline: 2/15; 3/1 for financial aid. Deferred admission is possible.

DRURY UNIVERSITY

URBAN SETTING ■ PRIVATE ■ INDEPENDENT ■ COED
SPRINGFIELD, MISSOURI

Web site: www.drury.edu
Contact: Mr. Michael Thomas, Director of Admissions, 900 North Benton, Springfield, MO 65802
Telephone: 417-873-7205 or toll-free 800-922-2274 (in-state) **Fax:** 417-866-3873
E-mail: druryad@drury.edu

Academics

Drury awards bachelor's and master's **degrees** (also offers evening program with significant enrollment not reflected in profile). Challenging opportunities include advanced placement, accelerated degree programs, student-designed majors, freshman honors college, an honors program, double majors, independent study, and a senior project. Special programs include internships, summer session for credit, off-campus study, study-abroad, and Army ROTC. A complete listing of majors at Drury appears in the Majors Index beginning on page 432.

The **faculty** at Drury has 118 full-time members, 90% with terminal degrees. The student-faculty ratio is 12:1.

Students of Drury

The student body totals 1,760, of whom 1,431 are undergraduates. 53.2% are women and 46.8% are men. 80% are from Missouri. 4.2% are international students. 0.7% are African American, 0.6% American Indian, 1.8% Asian American, and 1.4% Hispanic American. 80% returned for their sophomore year.

Facilities and Resources

Student rooms are linked to a campus network. 95 **computers** are available on campus that provide access to the Internet. The 2 **libraries** have 164,457 books and 1,101 subscriptions.

Campus Life

There are 48 active organizations on campus, including a drama/theater group, newspaper, radio station, television station, and choral group. 35% of eligible men and 35% of eligible women are members of national **fraternities** and national **sororities**.

Drury is a member of the NCAA (Division II). **Intercollegiate sports** (some offering scholarships) include basketball (m), golf (m), soccer, swimming, tennis, volleyball (w).

Campus Safety

Student safety services include late-night transport/escort service, 24-hour emergency telephone alarm devices, 24-hour patrols by trained security personnel, student patrols, and electronically operated dormitory entrances.

Applying

Drury requires an essay, SAT I or ACT, a high school transcript, and 1 recommendation. It recommends an interview. Application deadline: rolling admissions; 3/15 priority date for financial aid. Deferred admission is possible.

Getting in Last Year

994 applied
91% were accepted
364 enrolled (40%)
27% from top tenth of their h.s. class
3.54 average high school GPA
68% had ACT scores over 24
18% had ACT scores over 30
7 National Merit Scholars

Graduation and After

43% graduated in 4 years
8% graduated in 5 years
2% graduated in 6 years
26% pursued further study
69% had job offers within 6 months

Financial Matters

$10,695 tuition and fees (1999–2000)
$4130 room and board
84% average percent of need met
$7983 average financial aid amount received per undergraduate (1999–2000)

eAPPLY

Getting in Last Year
13,407 applied
28% were accepted
1,630 enrolled (43%)
88% from top tenth of their h.s. class
89% had SAT verbal scores over 600
93% had SAT math scores over 600
96% had ACT scores over 24
49% had SAT verbal scores over 700
61% had SAT math scores over 700
62% had ACT scores over 30
216 valedictorians

Graduation and After
87% graduated in 4 years
5% graduated in 5 years
25% pursued further study (9% medicine, 8% law, 7% arts and sciences)
45% had job offers within 6 months
210 organizations recruited on campus
1 Rhodes, 12 Fulbright scholars

Financial Matters
$24,751 tuition and fees (1999–2000)
$7088 room and board
100% average percent of need met
$18,593 average financial aid amount received per undergraduate (1998–99)

DUKE UNIVERSITY

SUBURBAN SETTING ■ PRIVATE ■ INDEPENDENT RELIGIOUS ■ COED
DURHAM, NORTH CAROLINA

Web site: www.duke.edu
Contact: Mr. Christoph Guttentag, Director of Admissions, Durham, NC 27708-0586
Telephone: 919-684-3214 **Fax:** 919-684-8941
E-mail: askduke@admiss.duke.edu

Academics

Duke awards bachelor's, master's, doctoral, and first-professional **degrees**. Challenging opportunities include advanced placement, accelerated degree programs, student-designed majors, an honors program, a senior project, Phi Beta Kappa, and Sigma Xi. Special programs include internships, summer session for credit, off-campus study, study-abroad, and Army, Navy and Air Force ROTC.

The most frequently chosen fields are social sciences and history, biological/life sciences, and engineering/engineering technologies. A complete listing of majors at Duke appears in the Majors Index beginning on page 432.

The **faculty** at Duke has 2,168 full-time members, 95% with terminal degrees. The student-faculty ratio is 8:1.

Students of Duke

The student body totals 11,811, of whom 6,368 are undergraduates. 48% are women and 52% are men. Students come from 52 states and territories and 77 other countries. 12% are from North Carolina. 3.7% are international students. 8.9% are African American, 0.4% American Indian, 12.9% Asian American, and 4.4% Hispanic American. 97% returned for their sophomore year.

Facilities and Resources

Student rooms are linked to a campus network. 600 **computers** are available on campus that provide access to the Internet. The 12 **libraries** have 4,645,050 books and 33,003 subscriptions.

Campus Life

There are 350 active organizations on campus, including a drama/theater group, newspaper, radio station, television station, choral group, and marching band. 29% of eligible men and 42% of eligible women are members of national **fraternities** and national **sororities**.

Duke is a member of the NCAA (Division I). **Intercollegiate sports** (some offering scholarships) include baseball (m), basketball, crew, cross-country running, equestrian sports, fencing, field hockey, football, golf, ice hockey, lacrosse, racquetball, rugby, sailing, skiing (cross-country), skiing (downhill), soccer, softball, swimming, tennis, track and field, volleyball, water polo, wrestling (m).

Campus Safety

Student safety services include late-night transport/escort service, 24-hour emergency telephone alarm devices, 24-hour patrols by trained security personnel, and electronically operated dormitory entrances.

Applying

Duke requires an essay, SAT I or ACT, a high school transcript, and 3 recommendations, and in some cases SAT II Subject Tests and SAT II: Writing Test. It recommends an interview, audition tape for applicants with outstanding dance, dramatic, or musical talent; slides of artwork, and a minimum high school GPA of 3.0. Application deadline: 1/2; 2/1 for financial aid. Early and deferred admission are possible.

Earlham College

SMALL-TOWN SETTING ■ PRIVATE ■ INDEPENDENT RELIGIOUS ■ COED
RICHMOND, INDIANA

Web site: www.earlham.edu
Contact: Director of Admissions, 801 National Road West, Richmond, IN 47374
Telephone: 765-983-1200 or toll-free 800-327-5426 **Fax:** 765-983-1560
E-mail: admission@earlham.edu

eAPPLY

Academics

Earlham awards bachelor's **degrees**. Challenging opportunities include advanced placement, accelerated degree programs, student-designed majors, double majors, independent study, a senior project, and Phi Beta Kappa. Special programs include internships, off-campus study, and study-abroad.

The most frequently chosen fields are biological/life sciences, social sciences and history, and interdisciplinary studies. A complete listing of majors at Earlham appears in the Majors Index beginning on page 432.

The **faculty** at Earlham has 75 full-time members, 99% with terminal degrees. The student-faculty ratio is 11:1.

Students of Earlham

The student body totals 1,191, of whom 1,123 are undergraduates. 56.5% are women and 43.5% are men. Students come from 48 states and territories and 22 other countries. 32% are from Indiana. 4% are international students. 8.3% are African American, 0.4% American Indian, 2.5% Asian American, and 2% Hispanic American. 87% returned for their sophomore year.

Facilities and Resources

Student rooms are linked to a campus network. 128 **computers** are available on campus that provide access to the Internet. The 2 **libraries** have 375,000 books and 1,188 subscriptions.

Campus Life

There are 64 active organizations on campus, including a drama/theater group, newspaper, radio station, and choral group. No national or local **fraternities** or **sororities**.

Earlham is a member of the NCAA (Division III). **Intercollegiate sports** include baseball (m), basketball, cross-country running, equestrian sports, field hockey (w), football (m), lacrosse, rugby (m), soccer, tennis, track and field, volleyball.

Campus Safety

Student safety services include late-night transport/escort service, 24-hour emergency telephone alarm devices, 24-hour patrols by trained security personnel, student patrols, and electronically operated dormitory entrances.

Applying

Earlham requires an essay, SAT I or ACT, a high school transcript, 2 recommendations, and a minimum high school GPA of 3.0. It recommends SAT I and an interview. Application deadline: 2/15; 3/1 priority date for financial aid. Early and deferred admission are possible.

Getting in Last Year

1,038 applied
84% were accepted
296 enrolled (34%)
12% from top tenth of their h.s. class
3.30 average high school GPA
51% had SAT verbal scores over 600
39% had SAT math scores over 600
61% had ACT scores over 24
17% had SAT verbal scores over 700
8% had SAT math scores over 700
11% had ACT scores over 30
3 National Merit Scholars
3 valedictorians

Graduation and After

61% graduated in 4 years
9% graduated in 5 years
23% pursued further study (9% arts and sciences, 5% medicine, 3% education)
73% had job offers within 6 months
65 organizations recruited on campus
1 Fulbright scholar

Financial Matters

$20,256 tuition and fees (1999–2000)
$4810 room and board
94% average percent of need met
$19,624 average financial aid amount received per undergraduate (1999–2000 estimated)

ECKERD COLLEGE

SUBURBAN SETTING ■ PRIVATE ■ INDEPENDENT RELIGIOUS ■ COED
ST. PETERSBURG, FLORIDA

Web site: www.eckerd.edu
Contact: Dr. Richard R. Hallin, Dean of Admissions, 4200 54th Avenue South, St. Petersburg, FL 33711
Telephone: 727-864-8331 or toll-free 800-456-9009 **Fax:** 727-866-2304
E-mail: admissions@eckerd.edu

The Eckerd campus is a peaceful, tropical setting bordering Tampa Bay and the Gulf of Mexico. Students feel very secure in the suburban environment and have easy access to the cultural, social, and recreational opportunities of the Tampa Bay metropolitan area. Classes are small. Independent study and study-abroad experiences are encouraged. Almost all students live on campus, where a sense of community flourishes. Students enjoy a great deal of freedom in their social lives and in the design of their academic programs. Volunteer service is extensive, since the Eckerd Honor Code encourages students to be "givers" rather than "takers."

Getting in Last Year
1,783 applied
76% were accepted
403 enrolled (30%)
26% from top tenth of their h.s. class
3.24 average high school GPA
37% had SAT verbal scores over 600
42% had SAT math scores over 600
61% had ACT scores over 24
7% had SAT verbal scores over 700
6% had SAT math scores over 700
8% had ACT scores over 30
12 National Merit Scholars
25 class presidents
25 valedictorians

Graduation and After
54% graduated in 4 years
3% graduated in 5 years
1% graduated in 6 years
25% pursued further study
45% had job offers within 6 months
175 organizations recruited on campus

Financial Matters
$18,220 tuition and fees (1999–2000)
$4960 room and board
85% average percent of need met
$16,000 average financial aid amount received per undergraduate (1999–2000 estimated)

Academics
Eckerd awards bachelor's **degrees**. Challenging opportunities include advanced placement, accelerated degree programs, student-designed majors, an honors program, double majors, independent study, a senior project, and Sigma Xi. Special programs include internships, summer session for credit, off-campus study, study-abroad, and Army and Air Force ROTC.

The most frequently chosen fields are biological/life sciences, business/marketing, and social sciences and history. A complete listing of majors at Eckerd appears in the Majors Index beginning on page 432.

The **faculty** at Eckerd has 96 full-time members, 94% with terminal degrees. The student-faculty ratio is 14:1.

Students of Eckerd
The student body is made up of 1,530 undergraduates. 54.8% are women and 45.2% are men. Students come from 49 states and territories and 55 other countries. 30% are from Florida. 12.4% are international students. 2.6% are African American, 0.2% American Indian, 1% Asian American, and 3.5% Hispanic American. 77% returned for their sophomore year.

Facilities and Resources
Student rooms are linked to a campus network. 144 **computers** are available on campus that provide access to the Internet. The **library** has 150,923 books and 3,009 subscriptions.

Campus Life
There are 50 active organizations on campus, including a drama/theater group, newspaper, radio station, and choral group. No national or local **fraternities** or **sororities**.

Eckerd is a member of the NCAA (Division II). **Intercollegiate sports** (some offering scholarships) include baseball (m), basketball, cross-country running (w), golf (m), sailing, soccer, softball (w), swimming, tennis, volleyball.

Campus Safety
Student safety services include late-night transport/escort service, 24-hour emergency telephone alarm devices, 24-hour patrols by trained security personnel, student patrols, and electronically operated dormitory entrances.

Applying
Eckerd requires an essay, SAT I or ACT, a high school transcript, and 1 recommendation. It recommends SAT II Subject Tests, SAT II: Writing Test, an interview, and a minimum high school GPA of 3.0. Application deadline: rolling admissions; 4/1 priority date for financial aid. Early and deferred admission are possible.

ELIZABETHTOWN COLLEGE

SMALL-TOWN SETTING ■ PRIVATE ■ INDEPENDENT RELIGIOUS ■ COED
ELIZABETHTOWN, PENNSYLVANIA

eAPPLY

Web site: www.etown.edu
Contact: W. Kent Barnds, Director of Admissions, 1 Alpha Drive,
    Elizabethtown, PA 17022-2298
Telephone: 717-361-1400 **Fax:** 717-361-1365
E-mail: admissions@acad.etown.edu

Academics

E-town awards bachelor's **degrees**. Challenging opportunities include advanced placement, double majors, independent study, and a senior project. Special programs include
internships, summer session for credit, off-campus study, and study-abroad.

The most frequently chosen fields are business/marketing, education, and health
professions and related sciences. A complete listing of majors at E-town appears in the
Majors Index beginning on page 432.

The **faculty** at E-town has 103 full-time members, 84% with terminal degrees. The
student-faculty ratio is 12:1.

Students of E-town

The student body is made up of 1,778 undergraduates. 65.2% are women and 34.8% are
men. Students come from 26 states and territories and 25 other countries. 68% are from
Pennsylvania. 84% returned for their sophomore year.

Facilities and Resources

Student rooms are linked to a campus network. 100 **computers** are available on campus
that provide access to the Internet. The 2 **libraries** have 141,357 books and 1,108
subscriptions.

Campus Life

There are 80 active organizations on campus, including a drama/theater group,
newspaper, radio station, television station, and choral group. No national or local
fraternities or **sororities**.

E-town is a member of the NCAA (Division III). **Intercollegiate sports** include
baseball (m), basketball, cross-country running, field hockey (w), golf (m), lacrosse, soccer, softball (w), swimming, tennis, track and field, volleyball, wrestling (m).

Campus Safety

Student safety services include self-defense workshops, crime prevention program, late-
night transport/escort service, 24-hour emergency telephone alarm devices, 24-hour
patrols by trained security personnel, and student patrols.

Applying

E-town requires an essay, SAT I or ACT, a high school transcript, 2 recommendations,
and a minimum high school GPA of 2.0, and in some cases an interview. It recommends
an interview and a minimum high school GPA of 3.0. Application deadline: rolling
admissions; 3/15 priority date for financial aid. Early and deferred admission are possible.

Elizabethtown College is exceeding expectations for personal attention, experiential learning, and combining the liberal arts with professional programs. The College is located in south-central Pennsylvania, near Hershey and Harrisburg, the state capital. Faculty members put student learning first and take pride in mentoring. Diverse opportunities, great facilities, collaborative research, internships, and the College's residential environment provide the perfect atmosphere for experiential learning. Athletes excel within nationally competitive programs. Musical ensembles and theater groups perform throughout the region, and students are leaders in more than 80 clubs and organizations. The College offers 40 majors and 60 minors. Elizabethtown allows graduates to distinguish themselves to employers and graduate schools.

Getting in Last Year
2,219 applied
78% were accepted
504 enrolled (29%)
29% from top tenth of their h.s. class
29% had SAT verbal scores over 600
33% had SAT math scores over 600
40% had ACT scores over 24
3% had SAT verbal scores over 700
3% had SAT math scores over 700
9% had ACT scores over 30
8 class presidents
9 valedictorians

Graduation and After
60% graduated in 4 years
7% graduated in 5 years
28% pursued further study
33 organizations recruited on campus

Financial Matters
$18,220 tuition and fees (1999–2000)
$5380 room and board
90% average percent of need met
$15,036 average financial aid amount received
    per undergraduate (1999–2000)

EMORY UNIVERSITY

SUBURBAN SETTING ■ PRIVATE ■ INDEPENDENT RELIGIOUS ■ COED
ATLANTA, GEORGIA

Web site: www.emory.edu
Contact: Mr. Daniel C. Walls, Dean of Admission, Boisfeuillet Jones Center–
  Office of Admissions, Atlanta, GA 30322-1100
Telephone: 404-727-6036 or toll-free 800-727-6036
E-mail: admiss@unix.cc.emory.edu

Academics

Emory awards bachelor's, master's, doctoral, and first-professional **degrees** (enrollment figures include Emory University, Oxford College; application data for main campus only). Challenging opportunities include advanced placement, accelerated degree programs, an honors program, double majors, a senior project, Phi Beta Kappa, and Sigma Xi. Special programs include internships, summer session for credit, off-campus study, study-abroad, and Air Force ROTC.

The most frequently chosen fields are psychology, business/marketing, and biological/life sciences. A complete listing of majors at Emory appears in the Majors Index beginning on page 432.

The **faculty** at Emory has 1,848 full-time members, 100% with terminal degrees. The student-faculty ratio is 7:1.

Students of Emory

The student body totals 11,294, of whom 6,215 are undergraduates. 55.1% are women and 44.9% are men. Students come from 49 states and territories and 44 other countries. 20% are from Georgia. 2.4% are international students. 9.6% are African American, 0.2% American Indian, 15.2% Asian American, and 3.1% Hispanic American. 94% returned for their sophomore year.

Facilities and Resources

Student rooms are linked to a campus network. 600 **computers** are available on campus that provide access to the Internet. The 8 **libraries** have 2,300,000 books and 24,687 subscriptions.

Campus Life

There are 200 active organizations on campus, including a drama/theater group, newspaper, radio station, television station, and choral group. 33% of eligible men and 33% of eligible women are members of national **fraternities** and national **sororities**.

Emory is a member of the NCAA (Division III). **Intercollegiate sports** include badminton, baseball (m), basketball, bowling, crew, cross-country running, fencing, field hockey (w), golf (m), ice hockey (m), lacrosse (m), racquetball, rugby (m), sailing, soccer, softball (w), swimming, tennis, track and field, volleyball, wrestling (m).

Campus Safety

Student safety services include late-night transport/escort service, 24-hour emergency telephone alarm devices, 24-hour patrols by trained security personnel, and student patrols.

Applying

Emory requires an essay, SAT I or ACT, a high school transcript, and 1 recommendation. It recommends SAT II Subject Tests and a minimum high school GPA of 3.0. Application deadline: 1/15; 4/1 for financial aid, with a 2/15 priority date. Early and deferred admission are possible.

Selective and innovative, with an emphasis on excellent teaching, Emory University seeks students with serious intellectual and professional interests. Emory is located 5 miles northeast of downtown Atlanta. Of the 11,000 students enrolled at Emory, more than 6,000 are undergraduates from every region of the US and more than 40 other nations. Emory offers a broad-based liberal arts program that includes more than 50 majors. Many student organizations encourage widespread involvement in campus life. Oxford College of Emory University, a small-campus option, is located 40 miles east of the Atlanta campus and enrolls 600 students in a 2-year program that is part of a 4-year program.

Getting in Last Year
9,850 applied
43% were accepted
1,520 enrolled (36%)
81% from top tenth of their h.s. class
3.7 average high school GPA
83% had SAT verbal scores over 600
85% had SAT math scores over 600
99% had ACT scores over 24
23% had SAT verbal scores over 700
26% had SAT math scores over 700
30% had ACT scores over 30
59 National Merit Scholars

Graduation and After
75% graduated in 4 years
6% graduated in 5 years
2% graduated in 6 years
74% pursued further study (25% medicine,
  22% law, 20% arts and sciences)
200 organizations recruited on campus
1 Rhodes, 7 Fulbright scholars

Financial Matters
$23,130 tuition and fees (1999–2000)
$7750 room and board
99% average percent of need met
$19,873 average financial aid amount received
  per undergraduate (1999–2000)

EUGENE LANG COLLEGE, NEW SCHOOL UNIVERSITY

URBAN SETTING ■ PRIVATE ■ INDEPENDENT ■ COED
NEW YORK, NEW YORK

Web site: www.newschool.edu
Contact: Ms. Jennifer Fondiller, Director of Admissions, 65 West 11th Street, New York, NY 10011-8601
Telephone: 212-229-5665
E-mail: lang@newschool.edu

 eAPPLY

Academics

Eugene Lang College awards bachelor's **degrees**. Challenging opportunities include accelerated degree programs, independent study, and a senior project. Special programs include internships, summer session for credit, off-campus study, and study-abroad.

The most frequently chosen field is liberal arts/general studies. A complete listing of majors at Eugene Lang College appears in the Majors Index beginning on page 432.

The **faculty** at Eugene Lang College has 14 full-time members. The student-faculty ratio is 10:1.

Students of Eugene Lang College

The student body is made up of 520 undergraduates. 67.9% are women and 32.1% are men. Students come from 41 states and territories and 20 other countries. 41% are from New York. 5% are international students. 6.7% are African American, 0.8% American Indian, 5.2% Asian American, and 10.8% Hispanic American. 73% returned for their sophomore year.

Facilities and Resources

475 **computers** are available on campus that provide access to the Internet. The 3 **libraries** have 191,789 books and 896 subscriptions.

Campus Life

There are 10 active organizations on campus, including a drama/theater group, newspaper, and choral group. No national or local **fraternities** or **sororities**.

This institution has no intercollegiate sports.

Campus Safety

Student safety services include 24-hour desk attendants in residence halls, 24-hour emergency telephone alarm devices, and electronically operated dormitory entrances.

Applying

Eugene Lang College requires an essay, SAT I or ACT or 4 SAT II Subject Tests, a high school transcript, an interview, 2 recommendations, and a minimum high school GPA of 2.0. It recommends a minimum high school GPA of 3.0. Application deadline: 2/1; 3/1 priority date for financial aid. Early and deferred admission are possible.

Eugene Lang College offers students of diverse backgrounds the opportunity to design their own program of study within one of 5 interdisciplinary liberal arts concentrations in the social sciences and the humanities. Students discuss and debate issues in small seminar courses that are never larger than 15 students. They enrich their programs with internships in a wide variety of areas, such as media and publishing, community service, and education, and they can pursue a dual degree at one of the University's 5 other divisions. The Greenwich Village location makes all the cultural treasures of the city—museums, libraries, dance, music, and theater—a distinct part of the campus.

Getting in Last Year
718 applied
54% were accepted
110 enrolled (28%)
24% from top tenth of their h.s. class
3.00 average high school GPA
74% had SAT verbal scores over 600
28% had SAT math scores over 600
22% had SAT verbal scores over 700
4% had SAT math scores over 700
3 class presidents
2 valedictorians

Graduation and After
20% graduated in 4 years
16% graduated in 5 years
4% graduated in 6 years
82% had job offers within 6 months

Financial Matters
$19,915 tuition and fees (1999–2000)
$9005 room and board
69% average percent of need met
$14,861 average financial aid amount received per undergraduate (1999–2000 estimated)

eAPPLY

Getting in Last Year
6,457 applied
61% were accepted
837 enrolled (21%)
22% from top tenth of their h.s. class
3.3 average high school GPA
35% had SAT verbal scores over 600
43% had SAT math scores over 600
4% had SAT verbal scores over 700
5% had SAT math scores over 700
13 National Merit Scholars
26 class presidents
5 valedictorians

Graduation and After
78% graduated in 4 years
3% graduated in 5 years
18% pursued further study (5% arts and sciences, 5% law, 5% medicine)
72% had job offers within 6 months
130 organizations recruited on campus
4 Fulbright scholars

Financial Matters
$20,435 tuition and fees (1999–2000)
$7380 room and board
77% average percent of need met
$14,460 average financial aid amount received per undergraduate (1999–2000)

FAIRFIELD UNIVERSITY
SUBURBAN SETTING ■ PRIVATE ■ INDEPENDENT RELIGIOUS ■ COED
FAIRFIELD, CONNECTICUT

Web site: www.fairfield.edu
Contact: Ms. Mary Spiegel, Director of Admission, 1073 North Benson Road, Fairfield, CT 06430-5195
Telephone: 203-254-4100 **Fax:** 203-254-4199
E-mail: admis@fair1.fairfield.edu

Academics
Fairfield awards bachelor's and master's **degrees** and post-master's certificates. Challenging opportunities include advanced placement, freshman honors college, an honors program, double majors, independent study, a senior project, and Phi Beta Kappa. Special programs include internships, summer session for credit, study-abroad, and Army ROTC.

The most frequently chosen fields are business/marketing, social sciences and history, and English. A complete listing of majors at Fairfield appears in the Majors Index beginning on page 432.

The **faculty** at Fairfield has 209 full-time members, 92% with terminal degrees. The student-faculty ratio is 13:1.

Students of Fairfield
The student body totals 5,127, of whom 4,064 are undergraduates. 52.6% are women and 47.4% are men. Students come from 34 states and territories and 34 other countries. 27% are from Connecticut. 1.5% are international students. 2.9% are African American, 0.1% American Indian, 2.6% Asian American, and 3.7% Hispanic American. 89% returned for their sophomore year.

Facilities and Resources
Student rooms are linked to a campus network. 140 **computers** are available on campus that provide access to the Internet. The **library** has 482,475 books and 1,881 subscriptions.

Campus Life
There are 100 active organizations on campus, including a drama/theater group, newspaper, radio station, television station, and choral group. No national or local **fraternities** or **sororities**.

Fairfield is a member of the NCAA (Division I). **Intercollegiate sports** (some offering scholarships) include baseball (m), basketball, crew, cross-country running, equestrian sports, field hockey (w), football (m), golf, ice hockey (m), lacrosse, soccer, softball (w), swimming, tennis, volleyball (w).

Campus Safety
Student safety services include bicycle patrols by security staff, late-night transport/escort service, 24-hour emergency telephone alarm devices, 24-hour patrols by trained security personnel, and electronically operated dormitory entrances.

Applying
Fairfield requires SAT I or ACT, a high school transcript, 1 recommendation, rank in upper 40% of high school class, and a minimum high school GPA of 3.0. It recommends SAT II Subject Tests and an interview. Application deadline: 2/1; 2/15 priority date for financial aid. Early and deferred admission are possible.

FISK UNIVERSITY

URBAN SETTING ■ PRIVATE ■ INDEPENDENT RELIGIOUS ■ COED
NASHVILLE, TENNESSEE

Web site: www.fisk.edu
Contact: Mr. Anthony E. Jones, Director of Admissions, 1000 17th Avenue
  North, Nashville, TN 37208-3051
Telephone: 615-329-8665 or toll-free 800-443-FISK
E-mail: lcampbel@dubois.fisk.edu

  eAPPLY

Academics

Fisk awards bachelor's and master's **degrees**. Challenging opportunities include advanced placement, student-designed majors, an honors program, a senior project, and Phi Beta Kappa. Special programs include cooperative education, internships, off-campus study, and Army and Air Force ROTC.

The most frequently chosen fields are psychology, business/marketing, and biological/life sciences. A complete listing of majors at Fisk appears in the Majors Index beginning on page 432.

The **faculty** at Fisk has 63 full-time members, 70% with terminal degrees. The student-faculty ratio is 12:1.

Students of Fisk

The student body totals 886, of whom 812 are undergraduates. 71.7% are women and 28.3% are men. Students come from 41 states and territories and 3 other countries. 29% are from Tennessee. 2.1% are international students. 97.8% are African American and 0.1% Asian American. 88% returned for their sophomore year.

Facilities and Resources

Student rooms are linked to a campus network. 40 **computers** are available on campus that provide access to the Internet. The **library** has 202,636 books and 380 subscriptions.

Campus Life

There are 55 active organizations on campus, including a drama/theater group, newspaper, radio station, and choral group. 25% of eligible men and 35% of eligible women are members of national **fraternities** and national **sororities**.

Fisk is a member of the NCAA (Division III). **Intercollegiate sports** include baseball (m), basketball, cross-country running, tennis, track and field, volleyball (w).

Campus Safety

Student safety services include late-night transport/escort service and 24-hour patrols by trained security personnel.

Applying

Fisk requires an essay, SAT I or ACT, a high school transcript, 2 recommendations, medical history, and a minimum high school GPA of 2.0. It recommends SAT II Subject Tests. Application deadline: 6/15; 2/15 priority date for financial aid. Early admission is possible.

Since its founding in 1866, Fisk University has stood as a proud symbol of achievement, becoming the first historically African-American college granted a chapter of Phi Beta Kappa honor society. The University remains committed first to teaching, involving both its faculty and its most advanced students in original research, to the liberal arts, and to the preparation of leaders. In proportion to its enrollment, more Fisk graduates achieve the PhD than the African-American graduates of any other college or university in the country. Fisk's liberal arts education has served as a strong foundation for alumni who have excelled professionally, including renowned historian John Hope Franklin; Nikki Giovanni, poet and author; the Honorable John Lewis, U.S. Representative (GA); David Levering Lewis, Pulitzer Prize winner and historian at Princeton University; Dr. Carol Surles, President of Texas Woman's University; and Hazel O'Leary, former U.S. Secretary of Energy.

Getting in Last Year
730 applied
97% were accepted
262 enrolled (37%)
18% from top tenth of their h.s. class
3.03 average high school GPA
5% had SAT verbal scores over 600
6% had SAT math scores over 600
12% had ACT scores over 24
12 class presidents
2 valedictorians

Graduation and After
40% graduated in 4 years
10% graduated in 5 years
2% graduated in 6 years
24% pursued further study (11% arts and
  sciences, 5% dentistry, 5% law)
63 organizations recruited on campus

Financial Matters
$8770 tuition and fees (1999–2000)
$4930 room and board
75% average percent of need met
$12,500 average financial aid amount received
  per undergraduate (1999–2000 estimated)

FLORIDA INSTITUTE OF TECHNOLOGY

SMALL-TOWN SETTING ■ PRIVATE ■ INDEPENDENT ■ COED
MELBOURNE, FLORIDA

Web site: www.fit.edu
Contact: Ms. Judi Marino, Director of Undergraduate Admissions, 150 West University Boulevard, Melbourne, FL 32901-6975
Telephone: 321-674-8030 or toll-free 800-348-4636 (in-state), 800-888-4348 (out-of-state) **Fax:** 321-723-9468
E-mail: admissions@fit.edu

Florida Institute of Technology is proud to announce the opening of the F. W. Olin Engineering Complex and the F. W. Olin Life Sciences Building. These two facilities offer the best and newest in laboratory, computer, and research equipment and opportunities. The university broke ground in January 2000 for the Clemente Sports and Recreation Complex. This is a first-class facility that will greatly improve students' opportunities for social, athletic, and recreational activities. The facility is scheduled to be open for use by the beginning of classes in fall 2001.

Getting in Last Year
1,939 applied
79% were accepted
395 enrolled (26%)
27% from top tenth of their h.s. class
3.36 average high school GPA
31% had SAT verbal scores over 600
42% had SAT math scores over 600
60% had ACT scores over 24
5% had SAT verbal scores over 700
6% had SAT math scores over 700
9% had ACT scores over 30

Graduation and After
32% graduated in 4 years
15% graduated in 5 years
2% graduated in 6 years
Graduates pursuing further study: 12% engineering, 7% arts and sciences, 2% business
75% had job offers within 6 months
96 organizations recruited on campus

Financial Matters
$17,300 tuition and fees (1999–2000)
$5270 room and board
83% average percent of need met
$16,220 average financial aid amount received per undergraduate (1998–99)

Academics

Florida Tech awards associate, bachelor's, master's, and doctoral **degrees** and post-bachelor's certificates. Challenging opportunities include advanced placement, accelerated degree programs, a senior project, and Sigma Xi. Special programs include cooperative education, internships, summer session for credit, and Army ROTC.

The most frequently chosen fields are engineering/engineering technologies, biological/life sciences, and trade and industry. A complete listing of majors at Florida Tech appears in the Majors Index beginning on page 432.

The **faculty** at Florida Tech has 160 full-time members. The student-faculty ratio is 12:1.

Students of Florida Tech

The student body totals 4,178, of whom 1,933 are undergraduates. 30.8% are women and 69.2% are men. Students come from 49 states and territories and 82 other countries. 38% are from Florida. 27.6% are international students. 4.8% are African American, 0.3% American Indian, 2.5% Asian American, and 5.2% Hispanic American. 76% returned for their sophomore year.

Facilities and Resources

Student rooms are linked to a campus network. 600 **computers** are available on campus that provide access to the Internet. The **library** has 3,967 subscriptions.

Campus Life

There are 83 active organizations on campus, including a drama/theater group, newspaper, television station, and marching band. 17% of eligible men and 13% of eligible women are members of national **fraternities**, national **sororities**, and local sororities.

Florida Tech is a member of the NCAA (Division II). **Intercollegiate sports** (some offering scholarships) include baseball (m), basketball, crew, cross-country running, soccer (m), softball (w), volleyball (w).

Campus Safety

Student safety services include self-defense education, late-night transport/escort service, 24-hour emergency telephone alarm devices, and 24-hour patrols by trained security personnel.

Applying

Florida Tech requires SAT I or ACT, a high school transcript, and a minimum high school GPA of 2.5, and in some cases a minimum high school GPA of 3.0. It recommends an essay, an interview, and a minimum high school GPA of 2.8. Application deadline: rolling admissions; 3/15 priority date for financial aid. Early and deferred admission are possible.

FLORIDA STATE UNIVERSITY

SUBURBAN SETTING ■ PUBLIC ■ STATE-SUPPORTED ■ COED
TALLAHASSEE, FLORIDA

Web site: www.fsu.edu
Contact: Office of Admissions, 2500 University Center, Building A,
Tallahassee, FL 32306-2400
Telephone: 850-644-6200 **Fax:** 850-644-0197
E-mail: admissions@admin.fsu.edu

eAPPLY

Academics

Florida State awards associate, bachelor's, master's, doctoral, and first-professional **degrees** and post-bachelor's and post-master's certificates. Challenging opportunities include advanced placement, accelerated degree programs, an honors program, double majors, independent study, a senior project, Phi Beta Kappa, and Sigma Xi. Special programs include cooperative education, internships, summer session for credit, off-campus study, study-abroad, and Army, Navy and Air Force ROTC.

The most frequently chosen fields are business/marketing, social sciences and history, and education. A complete listing of majors at Florida State appears in the Majors Index beginning on page 432.

The **faculty** at Florida State has 1,008 full-time members, 89% with terminal degrees.

Students of Florida State

The student body totals 32,878, of whom 25,965 are undergraduates. 55.5% are women and 44.5% are men. Students come from 51 states and territories and 134 other countries. 80% are from Florida. 1.1% are international students. 12.3% are African American, 0.4% American Indian, 2.6% Asian American, and 7.6% Hispanic American. 85% returned for their sophomore year.

Facilities and Resources

Student rooms are linked to a campus network. The 7 **libraries** have 2,263,257 books and 15,511 subscriptions.

Campus Life

There are 301 active organizations on campus, including a drama/theater group, newspaper, radio station, television station, choral group, and marching band. 7% of eligible men and 8% of eligible women are members of national **fraternities**, national **sororities**, local fraternities, and local sororities.

Florida State is a member of the NCAA (Division I). **Intercollegiate sports** (some offering scholarships) include baseball (m), basketball, crew (w), cross-country running, football (m), golf, soccer (w), softball (w), swimming, tennis, track and field, volleyball (w).

Campus Safety

Student safety services include late-night transport/escort service, 24-hour emergency telephone alarm devices, 24-hour patrols by trained security personnel, and electronically operated dormitory entrances.

Applying

Florida State requires SAT I or ACT and a high school transcript, and in some cases audition. It recommends an essay and a minimum high school GPA of 3.0. Application deadline: 3/3; 2/15 priority date for financial aid. Early admission is possible.

Florida State University is one of the nation's most popular universities, enrolling students from all 50 states and over 100 countries. Its diverse student population participates in a Liberal Studies Program that has been nationally recognized for its effectiveness in fostering a spirit of free inquiry into humane values and for developing strong written analytical skills. Home of the National High Magnetic Field Laboratory, the Supercomputer Computations Institute, and other internationally acclaimed research centers, Florida State is one of only 88 institutions in the Research I category as classified by the Carnegie Foundation for the Advancement of Teaching. FSU invites students to explore the state of their future, Florida State University.

Getting in Last Year
21,159 applied
64% were accepted
4,937 enrolled (36%)
47% from top tenth of their h.s. class
3.55 average high school GPA
33% had SAT verbal scores over 600
34% had SAT math scores over 600
46% had ACT scores over 24
6% had SAT verbal scores over 700
5% had SAT math scores over 700
7% had ACT scores over 30
97 National Merit Scholars

Graduation and After
38% graduated in 4 years
22% graduated in 5 years
4% graduated in 6 years
35% pursued further study
926 organizations recruited on campus
2 Fulbright scholars

Financial Matters
$2196 resident tuition and fees (1999–2000)
$9184 nonresident tuition and fees (1999–2000)
$4952 room and board
29% average percent of need met
$3127 average financial aid amount received per undergraduate (1999–2000)

FORDHAM UNIVERSITY

URBAN SETTING ■ PRIVATE ■ INDEPENDENT RELIGIOUS ■ COED
NEW YORK, NEW YORK

Web site: www.fordham.edu
Contact: Mr. John W. Buckley, Dean of Admission, East Fordham Road, New York, NY 10458
Telephone: 718-817-4000 or toll-free 800-FORDHAM **Fax:** 718-367-9404
E-mail: ad_buckley@lars.fordham.edu

Fordham, New York City's Jesuit university, offers a distinctive educational experience, including the rigors of a 450-year Jesuit tradition in education, in the "capital of the world." Fordham has 2 New York City residential campuses—Rose Hill and Lincoln Center. A distinguished faculty of scholars, 94 percent of whom hold Ph.D.'s or other terminal degrees, are committed to the development of each student's fullest potential. The low student-faculty ratio of 10:1 and the small average class size of 17 ensure individualized support. Fordham offers more than 75 majors, more than 125 athletic and extracurricular activities, and a successful internship program in the world's most competitive market.

Getting in Last Year
8,600 applied
62% were accepted
1,584 enrolled (30%)
29% from top tenth of their h.s. class
3.51 average high school GPA
44% had SAT verbal scores over 600
35% had SAT math scores over 600
72% had ACT scores over 24
9% had SAT verbal scores over 700
4% had SAT math scores over 700
11% had ACT scores over 30
20 valedictorians

Graduation and After
60% graduated in 4 years
7% graduated in 5 years
1% graduated in 6 years
25% pursued further study (7% arts and sciences, 6% law, 5% business)
90% had job offers within 6 months
500 organizations recruited on campus
1 Marshall scholar

Financial Matters
$19,660 tuition and fees (1999–2000)
$6480 room and board
75% average percent of need met
$16,351 average financial aid amount received per undergraduate (1998–99)

Academics

Fordham awards bachelor's, master's, doctoral, and first-professional **degrees** (branch locations: an 85-acre campus at Rose Hill and an 8-acre campus at Lincoln Center). Challenging opportunities include advanced placement, accelerated degree programs, student-designed majors, an honors program, double majors, independent study, a senior project, Phi Beta Kappa, and Sigma Xi. Special programs include internships, summer session for credit, off-campus study, study-abroad, and Army, Navy and Air Force ROTC.

The most frequently chosen fields are social sciences and history, business/marketing, and communications/communication technologies. A complete listing of majors at Fordham appears in the Majors Index beginning on page 432.

The **faculty** at Fordham has 594 full-time members. The student-faculty ratio is 10:1.

Students of Fordham

The student body totals 13,551, of whom 6,578 are undergraduates. 59% are women and 41% are men. Students come from 48 states and territories and 38 other countries. 66% are from New York. 1.3% are international students. 5.1% are African American, 0.2% American Indian, 4.4% Asian American, and 12.5% Hispanic American. 88% returned for their sophomore year.

Facilities and Resources

Student rooms are linked to a campus network. 617 **computers** are available on campus that provide access to the Internet. The 5 **libraries** have 1,870,513 books and 12,022 subscriptions.

Campus Life

Active organizations on campus include a drama/theater group, newspaper, radio station, choral group, and marching band. No national or local **fraternities** or **sororities**.

Fordham is a member of the NCAA (Division I). **Intercollegiate sports** (some offering scholarships) include baseball (m), basketball, crew, cross-country running, equestrian sports, football (m), golf (m), ice hockey (m), lacrosse, rugby, soccer, softball (w), squash (m), swimming, tennis, track and field, volleyball (w), water polo (m).

Campus Safety

Student safety services include late-night transport/escort service, 24-hour emergency telephone alarm devices, 24-hour patrols by trained security personnel, student patrols, and electronically operated dormitory entrances.

Applying

Fordham requires an essay, SAT I or ACT, a high school transcript, and 1 recommendation, and in some cases an interview. It recommends SAT II Subject Tests, an interview, and a minimum high school GPA of 3.0. Application deadline: 2/1; 2/1 priority date for financial aid. Early and deferred admission are possible.

FRANKLIN AND MARSHALL COLLEGE

SUBURBAN SETTING ■ PRIVATE ■ INDEPENDENT ■ COED
LANCASTER, PENNSYLVANIA

Web site: www.fandm.edu
Contact: Gregory Goldsmith, Director of Admissions, PO Box 3003,
  Lancaster, PA 17604-3003
Telephone: 717-291-3953 **Fax:** 717-291-4389
E-mail: admission@fandm.edu

Academics

F&M awards bachelor's **degrees**. Challenging opportunities include advanced place-ment, accelerated degree programs, student-designed majors, an honors program, double majors, independent study, a senior project, Phi Beta Kappa, and Sigma Xi. Special programs include internships, summer session for credit, off-campus study, and study-abroad.

The most frequently chosen fields are social sciences and history, business/marketing, and English. A complete listing of majors at F&M appears in the Majors Index beginning on page 432.

The **faculty** at F&M has 161 full-time members, 95% with terminal degrees. The student-faculty ratio is 11:1.

Students of F&M

The student body is made up of 1,864 undergraduates. 50.3% are women and 49.7% are men. Students come from 39 states and territories and 46 other countries. 41% are from Pennsylvania. 6.4% are international students. 3.2% are African American, 0.2% American Indian, 3.7% Asian American, and 2.9% Hispanic American. 96% returned for their sophomore year.

Facilities and Resources

Student rooms are linked to a campus network. 70 **computers** are available on campus that provide access to the Internet. The 2 **libraries** have 311,928 books and 1,596 subscriptions.

Campus Life

There are 120 active organizations on campus, including a drama/theater group, newspaper, radio station, television station, and choral group. No national or local **fraternities** or **sororities**.

F&M is a member of the NCAA (Division III). **Intercollegiate sports** include baseball (m), basketball, crew, cross-country running, fencing, field hockey (w), football (m), golf, ice hockey (m), lacrosse, rugby, soccer, softball (w), squash, swimming, tennis, track and field, volleyball, wrestling (m).

Campus Safety

Student safety services include residence hall security, connected by campus security to city police and fire company, late-night transport/escort service, 24-hour emergency telephone alarm devices, 24-hour patrols by trained security personnel, and electroni-cally operated dormitory entrances.

Applying

F&M requires an essay, a high school transcript, and 2 recommendations, and in some cases SAT I or ACT. It recommends an interview. Application deadline: 2/1; 2/1 for financial aid. Early and deferred admission are possible.

Franklin & Marshall is an institution that typifies the concept of liberal learning. Whether the course is in theater or physics, classes are small, engagement is high, and discussion dominates over lecture. Beginning with the First Year Seminar, students at Franklin & Marshall are repeatedly invited to participate actively in intellectual investigation at a high level. Graduates consistently testify to the quality of an F&M education as mental preparation for life.

Getting in Last Year
3,927 applied
50% were accepted
516 enrolled (26%)
64% from top tenth of their h.s. class
64% had SAT verbal scores over 600
73% had SAT math scores over 600
19% had SAT verbal scores over 700
21% had SAT math scores over 700
6 National Merit Scholars
21 valedictorians

Graduation and After
72% graduated in 4 years
5% graduated in 5 years
1% graduated in 6 years
Graduates pursuing further study: 15% arts and sciences, 8% law, 6% medicine
62% had job offers within 6 months
64 organizations recruited on campus

Financial Matters
$23,720 tuition and fees (1999–2000)
$5730 room and board
100% average percent of need met
$17,860 average financial aid amount received per undergraduate (1999–2000)

eAPPLY

FURMAN UNIVERSITY
SUBURBAN SETTING ■ PRIVATE ■ INDEPENDENT ■ COED
GREENVILLE, SOUTH CAROLINA

Web site: www.furman.edu
Contact: Mr. David R. O'Cain, Director of Admissions, 3300 Poinsett
    Highway, Greenville, SC 29613
Telephone: 864-294-2034 **Fax:** 864-294-3127
E-mail: admissions@furman.edu

Academics
Furman awards bachelor's and master's **degrees**. Challenging opportunities include
advanced placement, accelerated degree programs, student-designed majors, double
majors, independent study, a senior project, and Phi Beta Kappa. Special programs
include cooperative education, internships, summer session for credit, study-abroad, and
Army ROTC.

The most frequently chosen fields are social sciences and history, business/marketing,
and education. A complete listing of majors at Furman appears in the Majors Index
beginning on page 432.

The **faculty** at Furman has 200 full-time members, 96% with terminal degrees. The
student-faculty ratio is 12:1.

Students of Furman
The student body totals 3,453, of whom 2,840 are undergraduates. 54.8% are women
and 45.2% are men. Students come from 45 states and territories. 34% are from South
Carolina. 1% are international students. 5.5% are African American, 0.1% American
Indian, 1.8% Asian American, and 1% Hispanic American. 92% returned for their
sophomore year.

Facilities and Resources
Student rooms are linked to a campus network. 250 **computers** are available on campus
that provide access to the Internet. The 3 **libraries** have 339,415 books and 2,464
subscriptions.

Campus Life
There are 128 active organizations on campus, including a drama/theater group,
newspaper, radio station, choral group, and marching band. 30% of eligible men and
35% of eligible women are members of national **fraternities** and national **sororities**.

Furman is a member of the NCAA (Division I). **Intercollegiate sports** (some offering scholarships) include baseball (m), basketball, crew, cross-country running, fencing,
football (m), golf, ice hockey (m), rugby, soccer, softball (w), swimming, tennis, track and
field, volleyball, weight lifting.

Campus Safety
Student safety services include late-night transport/escort service, 24-hour emergency
telephone alarm devices, 24-hour patrols by trained security personnel, student patrols,
and electronically operated dormitory entrances.

Applying
Furman requires an essay, SAT I or ACT, and a high school transcript, and in some cases
SAT II Subject Tests. It recommends 2 recommendations and a minimum high school
GPA of 3.0. Application deadline: 2/1; 2/1 priority date for financial aid. Early admission
is possible.

GEORGETOWN COLLEGE

SUBURBAN SETTING ■ PRIVATE ■ INDEPENDENT RELIGIOUS ■ COED
GEORGETOWN, KENTUCKY

  eAPPLY

Web site: www.georgetowncollege.edu
Contact: Ms. Dana Hall, Interim Director of Admissions, 400 East College
Street, Georgetown, KY 40324-1696
Telephone: 502-863-8009 or toll-free 800-788-9985
E-mail: admissions@georgetowncollege.edu

Academics

Georgetown awards bachelor's and master's **degrees**. Challenging opportunities include advanced placement, accelerated degree programs, student-designed majors, and a senior project. Special programs include cooperative education, internships, summer session for credit, off-campus study, study-abroad, and Army and Air Force ROTC.

The most frequently chosen fields are biological/life sciences, business/marketing, and psychology. A complete listing of majors at Georgetown appears in the Majors Index beginning on page 432.

The **faculty** at Georgetown has 87 full-time members, 90% with terminal degrees. The student-faculty ratio is 13:1.

Students of Georgetown

The student body totals 1,672, of whom 1,338 are undergraduates. 57.8% are women and 42.2% are men. Students come from 26 states and territories and 5 other countries. 84% are from Kentucky. 0.5% are international students. 2.5% are African American, 0.1% American Indian, 0.1% Asian American, and 0.2% Hispanic American. 78% returned for their sophomore year.

Facilities and Resources

Student rooms are linked to a campus network. 150 **computers** are available on campus that provide access to the Internet. The 2 **libraries** have 139,940 books and 1,105 subscriptions.

Campus Life

There are 97 active organizations on campus, including a drama/theater group, newspaper, radio station, and choral group. 33% of eligible men and 35% of eligible women are members of national **fraternities**, national **sororities**, and local fraternities.

Georgetown is a member of the NAIA. **Intercollegiate sports** (some offering scholarships) include baseball (m), basketball, cross-country running, football (m), golf, soccer, softball (w), tennis, volleyball (w).

Campus Safety

Student safety services include late-night transport/escort service and 24-hour patrols by trained security personnel.

Applying

Georgetown requires an essay, SAT I or ACT, a high school transcript, and a minimum high school GPA of 2.5, and in some cases an interview and recommendations. It recommends ACT. Application deadline: 7/1; 2/15 priority date for financial aid.

> **G**eorgetown College distinguishes itself from many other small liberal arts colleges across the nation by offering a combination of a rigorous and respected academic program, a wealth of opportunities for leadership and involvement in extracurricular activities, and a strong commitment to Christian values and principles. While there is no shortage of schools that possess any one of these characteristics, institutions that combine any two of these qualities are less common. By placing all three side by side at unique levels and combinations, Georgetown provides a special framework that fosters intellectual, social, and spiritual growth.

Getting in Last Year
810 applied
89% were accepted
340 enrolled (47%)
38% from top tenth of their h.s. class
3.53 average high school GPA
25% had SAT verbal scores over 600
33% had SAT math scores over 600
53% had ACT scores over 24
3% had SAT verbal scores over 700
5% had SAT math scores over 700
8% had ACT scores over 30
33 valedictorians

Graduation and After
40 organizations recruited on campus
1 Fulbright scholar

Financial Matters
$12,390 tuition and fees (2000–2001)
$4600 room and board
93% average percent of need met
$11,821 average financial aid amount received per undergraduate (1999–2000 estimated)

Georgetown University

Urban setting ■ Private ■ Independent Religious ■ Coed
Washington, District of Columbia

Web site: www.georgetown.edu
Contact: Mr. Charles A. Deacon, Dean of Undergraduate Admissions, 37th and O Street, NW, Washington, DC 20057
Telephone: 202-687-3600 **Fax:** 202-687-6660

Getting in Last Year
13,244 applied
23% were accepted
1,498 enrolled (50%)
78% from top tenth of their h.s. class
85% had SAT verbal scores over 600
85% had SAT math scores over 600
91% had ACT scores over 24
44% had SAT verbal scores over 700
42% had SAT math scores over 700
46% had ACT scores over 30
60 class presidents
114 valedictorians

Graduation and After
84% graduated in 4 years
5% graduated in 5 years
1% graduated in 6 years
20% pursued further study (7% arts and sciences, 6% law, 6% medicine)
75% had job offers within 6 months
327 organizations recruited on campus

Financial Matters
$23,295 tuition and fees (1999–2000)
$8693 room and board
100% average percent of need met
$19,048 average financial aid amount received per undergraduate (1999–2000 estimated)

Academics

Georgetown awards bachelor's, master's, doctoral, and first-professional **degrees**. Challenging opportunities include advanced placement, student-designed majors, an honors program, double majors, independent study, a senior project, Phi Beta Kappa, and Sigma Xi. Special programs include internships, summer session for credit, off-campus study, study-abroad, and Army, Navy and Air Force ROTC.

The most frequently chosen fields are social sciences and history, business/marketing, and English. A complete listing of majors at Georgetown appears in the Majors Index beginning on page 432.

The **faculty** at Georgetown has 622 full-time members. The student-faculty ratio is 12:1.

Students of Georgetown

The student body totals 12,498, of whom 6,361 are undergraduates. 54.4% are women and 45.6% are men. Students come from 52 states and territories and 84 other countries. 1% are from District of Columbia. 6.5% are international students. 6% are African American, 0.2% American Indian, 8.8% Asian American, and 5.5% Hispanic American. 97% returned for their sophomore year.

Facilities and Resources

Student rooms are linked to a campus network. 360 **computers** are available on campus that provide access to the Internet. The 7 **libraries** have 2,363,790 books and 27,379 subscriptions.

Campus Life

There are 111 active organizations on campus, including a drama/theater group, newspaper, radio station, and choral group. No national or local **fraternities** or **sororities**.

Georgetown is a member of the NCAA (Division I). **Intercollegiate sports** (some offering scholarships) include baseball (m), basketball, crew, cross-country running, field hockey (w), football (m), golf (m), ice hockey (m), lacrosse, rugby (m), sailing, soccer, swimming, tennis, track and field, volleyball (w).

Campus Safety

Student safety services include late-night transport/escort service, 24-hour emergency telephone alarm devices, 24-hour patrols by trained security personnel, and electronically operated dormitory entrances.

Applying

Georgetown requires an essay, SAT I or ACT, a high school transcript, an interview, and 2 recommendations. It recommends SAT II Subject Tests and SAT II: Writing Test. Application deadline: 1/10; 2/1 priority date for financial aid. Early and deferred admission are possible.

THE GEORGE WASHINGTON UNIVERSITY

URBAN SETTING ■ PRIVATE ■ INDEPENDENT ■ COED
WASHINGTON, DISTRICT OF COLUMBIA

Web site: www.gwu.edu
Contact: Dr. Kathryn M. Napper, Director of Admission, Office of
  Undergraduate Admissions, Washington, DC 20052
Telephone: 202-994-6040 or toll-free 800-447-3765
E-mail: gwadm@gwis2.circ.gwu.edu

eAPPLY

Academics

GW awards associate, bachelor's, master's, doctoral, and first-professional **degrees** and post-bachelor's and post-master's certificates. Challenging opportunities include advanced placement, accelerated degree programs, student-designed majors, an honors program, double majors, independent study, a senior project, Phi Beta Kappa, and Sigma Xi. Special programs include cooperative education, internships, summer session for credit, off-campus study, study-abroad, and Army, Navy and Air Force ROTC.

The most frequently chosen fields are social sciences and history, business/marketing, and psychology. A complete listing of majors at GW appears in the Majors Index beginning on page 432.

The **faculty** at GW has 739 full-time members, 93% with terminal degrees.

Students of GW

The student body totals 20,346, of whom 8,695 are undergraduates. 55.9% are women and 44.1% are men. Students come from 55 states and territories and 101 other countries. 8% are from District of Columbia. 6.4% are international students. 7% are African American, 0.4% American Indian, 10.4% Asian American, and 5% Hispanic American. 92% returned for their sophomore year.

Facilities and Resources

Student rooms are linked to a campus network. 550 **computers** are available on campus that provide access to the Internet. The 3 **libraries** have 1,841,842 books and 14,729 subscriptions.

Campus Life

There are 208 active organizations on campus, including a drama/theater group, newspaper, radio station, television station, choral group, and marching band. 16% of eligible men and 14% of eligible women are members of national **fraternities** and national **sororities**.

GW is a member of the NCAA (Division I). **Intercollegiate sports** (some offering scholarships) include baseball (m), basketball, crew, cross-country running, golf (m), gymnastics (w), soccer, swimming, tennis, volleyball (w), water polo (m).

Campus Safety

Student safety services include late-night transport/escort service, 24-hour emergency telephone alarm devices, 24-hour patrols by trained security personnel, and electronically operated dormitory entrances.

Applying

GW requires an essay, SAT I or ACT, a high school transcript, and 2 recommendations, and in some cases SAT II Subject Tests. It recommends SAT I, SAT II: Writing Test, and an interview. Application deadline: 2/1; 2/1 priority date for financial aid. Early and deferred admission are possible.

Getting in Last Year
14,326 applied
49% were accepted
2,120 enrolled (30%)
47% from top tenth of their h.s. class
63% had SAT verbal scores over 600
63% had SAT math scores over 600
80% had ACT scores over 24
15% had SAT verbal scores over 700
12% had SAT math scores over 700
16% had ACT scores over 30
36 National Merit Scholars

Graduation and After
58% graduated in 4 years
7% graduated in 5 years
1% graduated in 6 years
21% pursued further study (7% arts and sciences, 6% law, 4% medicine)
88 organizations recruited on campus
1 Marshall, 4 Fulbright scholars

Financial Matters
$23,375 tuition and fees (1999–2000)
$8210 room and board
92% average percent of need met
$20,900 average financial aid amount received per undergraduate (1998–99)

GEORGIA INSTITUTE OF TECHNOLOGY

URBAN SETTING ■ PUBLIC ■ STATE-SUPPORTED ■ COED
ATLANTA, GEORGIA

Web site: www.gatech.edu
Contact: Ms. Deborah Smith, Director of Admissions, 225 North Avenue, NW, Atlanta, GA 30332-0320
Telephone: 404-894-4154 **Fax:** 404-894-9511
E-mail: admissions@success.gatech.edu

eorgia Tech is ranked third overall and first among public engineering schools, thirty-second among business schools, and tenth among public institutions in overall reputation by *U.S. News & World Report. Money* magazine ranks Tech as the second-best buy among science/technology schools. Tech consistently ranks in the top 5 among public colleges in the percentage of National Merit and National Achievement Scholars and has the largest voluntary cooperative education program in America. Tech's low cost, focus on experiential education, and reputation with graduate schools and employers ensure students receive the greatest return on their educational investment.

Academics

Georgia Tech awards bachelor's, master's, and doctoral **degrees**. Challenging opportunities include advanced placement, accelerated degree programs, student-designed majors, an honors program, double majors, independent study, a senior project, and Sigma Xi. Special programs include cooperative education, internships, summer session for credit, off-campus study, study-abroad, and Army, Navy and Air Force ROTC.

The most frequently chosen fields are engineering/engineering technologies, business/marketing, and computer/information sciences. A complete listing of majors at Georgia Tech appears in the Majors Index beginning on page 432.

The **faculty** at Georgia Tech has 709 full-time members, 94% with terminal degrees. The student-faculty ratio is 14:1.

Students of Georgia Tech

The student body totals 14,074, of whom 10,256 are undergraduates. 29.2% are women and 70.8% are men. Students come from 52 states and territories and 82 other countries. 67% are from Georgia. 4.1% are international students. 8.6% are African American, 0.2% American Indian, 12.5% Asian American, and 2.7% Hispanic American. 88% returned for their sophomore year.

Facilities and Resources

Student rooms are linked to a campus network. 1,450 **computers** are available on campus that provide access to the Internet.

Campus Life

There are 280 active organizations on campus, including a drama/theater group, newspaper, radio station, choral group, and marching band. 25% of eligible men and 25% of eligible women are members of national **fraternities** and national **sororities**.

Georgia Tech is a member of the NCAA (Division I). **Intercollegiate sports** (some offering scholarships) include baseball (m), basketball, cross-country running, football (m), golf (m), ice hockey (m), lacrosse, rugby (m), softball (w), swimming (m), tennis, track and field, volleyball (w), wrestling (m).

Campus Safety

Student safety services include late-night transport/escort service, 24-hour emergency telephone alarm devices, 24-hour patrols by trained security personnel, student patrols, and electronically operated dormitory entrances.

Applying

Georgia Tech requires an essay, SAT I or ACT, and a high school transcript, and in some cases SAT II Subject Tests. It recommends SAT I. Application deadline: 1/15; 3/1 priority date for financial aid. Early admission is possible.

Getting in Last Year
7,579 applied
69% were accepted
2,320 enrolled (45%)
60% from top tenth of their h.s. class
3.70 average high school GPA
68% had SAT verbal scores over 600
89% had SAT math scores over 600
16% had SAT verbal scores over 700
34% had SAT math scores over 700
91 National Merit Scholars

Graduation and After
28% graduated in 4 years
33% graduated in 5 years
7% graduated in 6 years
20% pursued further study
70% had job offers within 6 months
800 organizations recruited on campus

Financial Matters
$3108 resident tuition and fees (1999–2000)
$10,350 nonresident tuition and fees (1999–2000)
$5118 room and board
72% average percent of need met
$5890 average financial aid amount received per undergraduate (1999–2000)

GETTYSBURG COLLEGE

SMALL-TOWN SETTING ■ PRIVATE ■ INDEPENDENT RELIGIOUS ■ COED
GETTYSBURG, PENNSYLVANIA

Web site: www.gettysburg.edu
Contact: Ms. Gail Sweezey, Director of Admissions, Gettysburg, PA
17325-1483
Telephone: 717-337-6100 or toll-free 800-431-0803 **Fax:** 717-337-6008
E-mail: admiss@gettysburg.edu

  eAPPLY

Academics

Gettysburg College awards bachelor's **degrees**. Challenging opportunities include advanced placement, accelerated degree programs, student-designed majors, an honors program, double majors, independent study, a senior project, and Phi Beta Kappa. Special programs include internships, off-campus study, and study-abroad.

The most frequently chosen fields are business/marketing, social sciences and history, and biological/life sciences. A complete listing of majors at Gettysburg College appears in the Majors Index beginning on page 432.

The **faculty** at Gettysburg College has 161 full-time members, 88% with terminal degrees. The student-faculty ratio is 11:1.

Students of Gettysburg College

The student body is made up of 2,182 undergraduates. 51.3% are women and 48.7% are men. Students come from 40 states and territories and 25 other countries. 71% are from Pennsylvania. 1.6% are international students. 1.4% are African American, 0.2% American Indian, 1.3% Asian American, and 1.2% Hispanic American. 87% returned for their sophomore year.

Facilities and Resources

Student rooms are linked to a campus network. 250 **computers** are available on campus that provide access to the Internet. The 3 **libraries** have 326,328 books and 1,414 subscriptions.

Campus Life

There are 60 active organizations on campus, including a drama/theater group, newspaper, radio station, television station, choral group, and marching band. 42% of eligible men and 38% of eligible women are members of national **fraternities** and national **sororities**.

Gettysburg College is a member of the NCAA (Division III). **Intercollegiate sports** include baseball (m), basketball, cross-country running, field hockey (w), football (m), golf, ice hockey (m), lacrosse, rugby (m), soccer, softball (w), swimming, tennis, track and field, volleyball (w), wrestling (m).

Campus Safety

Student safety services include late-night transport/escort service, 24-hour emergency telephone alarm devices, 24-hour patrols by trained security personnel, and electronically operated dormitory entrances.

Applying

Gettysburg College requires an essay, SAT I or ACT, a high school transcript, 1 recommendation, and a minimum high school GPA of 2.0. It recommends an interview and a minimum high school GPA of 3.0. Application deadline: 3/15 for financial aid, with a 2/15 priority date. Early and deferred admission are possible.

As the twenty-first century dawns, higher education faces a new world of change and challenge. Revolutionary advances in technology, unprecedented access to information, a rich diversity of perspectives, and frequent calls to social action demand more from a liberal arts education than ever before. Leading colleges must respond with innovative programs, appropriate resources, and exceptional teaching. At Gettysburg College, we are committed to preparing our students for the opportunities of this changing world. Our founding principles embrace a rigorous liberal arts education that fosters a global perspective, a spirit of collaboration, a dedication to public service, and an enriching campus life. We believe that this approach to education instills in Gettysburg College students a lifelong desire for learning, a drive for discovery and contribution, and a compassionate respect for others and our world.

Getting in Last Year
3,871 applied
68% were accepted
689 enrolled (26%)
3.50 average high school GPA
43% had SAT verbal scores over 600
48% had SAT math scores over 600
6% had SAT verbal scores over 700
6% had SAT math scores over 700

Graduation and After
74% graduated in 4 years
4% graduated in 5 years
Graduates pursuing further study: 9% arts and sciences, 7% law, 6% education
64% had job offers within 6 months
51 organizations recruited on campus
1 Fulbright scholar

Financial Matters
$24,032 tuition and fees (1999–2000)
$5644 room and board
100% average percent of need met
$19,800 average financial aid amount received per undergraduate (1998–99)

Getting in Last Year
574 applied
95% were accepted
226 enrolled (41%)
27% from top tenth of their h.s. class
3.38 average high school GPA
40% had SAT verbal scores over 600
38% had SAT math scores over 600
16% had SAT verbal scores over 700
10% had SAT math scores over 700
8 National Merit Scholars
11 valedictorians

Graduation and After
39% graduated in 4 years
19% graduated in 5 years
4% graduated in 6 years
40% pursued further study (15% arts and sciences, 11% medicine, 5% business)
40 organizations recruited on campus

Financial Matters
$13,140 tuition and fees (2000–2001 estimated)
$4640 room and board
92% average percent of need met
$12,974 average financial aid amount received per undergraduate (1999–2000)

GOSHEN COLLEGE
SMALL-TOWN SETTING ■ PRIVATE ■ INDEPENDENT RELIGIOUS ■ COED
GOSHEN, INDIANA

Web site: www.goshen.edu
Contact: Ms. Marty Kelley, Director of Admissions, 1700 South Main Street, Goshen, IN 46526-4794
Telephone: 219-535-7535 or toll-free 800-348-7422 **Fax:** 219-535-7609
E-mail: admissions@goshen.edu

Academics
Goshen awards bachelor's **degrees**. Challenging opportunities include advanced placement, accelerated degree programs, student-designed majors, freshman honors college, an honors program, double majors, independent study, and a senior project. Special programs include cooperative education, internships, summer session for credit, off-campus study, and study-abroad.

The most frequently chosen fields are business/marketing, education, and health professions and related sciences. A complete listing of majors at Goshen appears in the Majors Index beginning on page 432.

The **faculty** at Goshen has 73 full-time members. The student-faculty ratio is 12:1.

Students of Goshen
The student body is made up of 1,084 undergraduates. 57% are women and 43% are men. Students come from 38 states and territories and 34 other countries. 52% are from Indiana. 9.5% are international students. 2.1% are African American, 1.5% Asian American, and 2.5% Hispanic American. 81% returned for their sophomore year.

Facilities and Resources
Student rooms are linked to a campus network. 143 **computers** are available on campus that provide access to online services and the Internet. The 3 **libraries** have 121,500 books and 750 subscriptions.

Campus Life
There are 26 active organizations on campus, including a drama/theater group, newspaper, radio station, television station, and choral group. No national or local **fraternities** or **sororities**.

Goshen is a member of the NAIA. **Intercollegiate sports** (some offering scholarships) include baseball (m), basketball, cross-country running, golf (m), soccer, softball (w), tennis, track and field, volleyball (w).

Campus Safety
Student safety services include late-night transport/escort service, 24-hour emergency telephone alarm devices, and 24-hour patrols by trained security personnel.

Applying
Goshen requires SAT I or ACT, a high school transcript, an interview, 2 recommendations, rank in upper 50% of high school class, minimum SAT score of 920, and a minimum high school GPA of 2.0. It recommends an essay. Application deadline: rolling admissions; 3/1 priority date for financial aid. Early and deferred admission are possible.

GOUCHER COLLEGE

SUBURBAN SETTING ■ PRIVATE ■ INDEPENDENT ■ COED
BALTIMORE, MARYLAND

Web site: www.goucher.edu
Contact: Mr. Carlton E. Surbeck III, Director of Admissions, 1021 Dulaney
    Valley Road, Baltimore, MD 21204-2794
Telephone: 410-337-6100 or toll-free 800-GOUCHER **Fax:** 410-337-6354
E-mail: admission@goucher.edu

Academics
Goucher awards bachelor's and master's **degrees**. Challenging opportunities include advanced placement, accelerated degree programs, student-designed majors, an honors program, double majors, independent study, a senior project, and Phi Beta Kappa. Special programs include internships, off-campus study, and study-abroad.

The most frequently chosen fields are biological/life sciences, English, and visual/performing arts. A complete listing of majors at Goucher appears in the Majors Index beginning on page 432.

The **faculty** at Goucher has 78 full-time members, 97% with terminal degrees. The student-faculty ratio is 11:1.

Students of Goucher
The student body totals 1,706, of whom 1,137 are undergraduates. 72.7% are women and 27.3% are men. Students come from 43 states and territories and 21 other countries. 41% are from Maryland. 2.3% are international students. 7.8% are African American, 0.2% American Indian, 3.2% Asian American, and 2.8% Hispanic American. 82% returned for their sophomore year.

Facilities and Resources
Student rooms are linked to a campus network. 96 **computers** are available on campus that provide access to the Internet. The **library** has 295,593 books and 1,138 subscriptions.

Campus Life
There are 40 active organizations on campus, including a drama/theater group, newspaper, and choral group. No national or local **fraternities** or **sororities**.

Goucher is a member of the NCAA (Division III). **Intercollegiate sports** include basketball, cross-country running, equestrian sports, field hockey (w), lacrosse, soccer, swimming, tennis, volleyball (w).

Campus Safety
Student safety services include late-night transport/escort service, 24-hour emergency telephone alarm devices, and 24-hour patrols by trained security personnel.

Applying
Goucher requires an essay, SAT I or ACT, a high school transcript, 3 recommendations, and a minimum high school GPA of 2.0. It recommends SAT II Subject Tests, SAT II: Writing Test, an interview, and a minimum high school GPA of 3.0. Application deadline: 2/1; 2/15 priority date for financial aid. Early and deferred admission are possible.

A strong commitment to excellence in liberal arts education has been a hallmark of Goucher since 1885. Goucher's core curriculum in the liberal arts is complemented by independent study, study abroad, and an extensive internship program. The College has played a leading role in integrating information technology in all subject areas. Goucher is located 8 miles north of Baltimore and an hour from Washington, D.C.

Getting in Last Year
2,078 applied
85% were accepted
303 enrolled (17%)
27% from top tenth of their h.s. class
3.11 average high school GPA
53% had SAT verbal scores over 600
38% had SAT math scores over 600
65% had ACT scores over 24
12% had SAT verbal scores over 700
6% had SAT math scores over 700
16% had ACT scores over 30
6 valedictorians

Graduation and After
59% graduated in 4 years
9% graduated in 5 years
2% graduated in 6 years
25% pursued further study (15% arts and sciences, 4% medicine, 3% business)
84% had job offers within 6 months
17 organizations recruited on campus

Financial Matters
$20,485 tuition and fees (1999–2000)
$7380 room and board
100% average percent of need met
$15,700 average financial aid amount received per undergraduate (1998–99)

Getting in Last Year
1,757 applied
67% were accepted
325 enrolled (28%)
46% from top tenth of their h.s. class
81% had SAT verbal scores over 600
84% had SAT math scores over 600
95% had ACT scores over 24
40% had SAT verbal scores over 700
32% had SAT math scores over 700
50% had ACT scores over 30
30 National Merit Scholars
33 valedictorians

Graduation and After
76% graduated in 4 years
7% graduated in 5 years
33% pursued further study
55% had job offers within 6 months
52 organizations recruited on campus

Financial Matters
$19,460 tuition and fees (1999–2000)
$5600 room and board
100% average percent of need met
$17,122 average financial aid amount received
    per undergraduate (1999–2000 estimated)

GRINNELL COLLEGE

SMALL-TOWN SETTING ■ PRIVATE ■ INDEPENDENT ■ COED
GRINNELL, IOWA

Web site: www.grinnell.edu
Contact: Mr. Thomas Crady, Vice President for Student Services, PO Box
    805, Grinnell, IA 50112-0807
Telephone: 515-269-3600 or toll-free 800-247-0113 **Fax:** 515-269-4800
E-mail: askgrin@grinnell.edu

Academics

Grinnell College awards bachelor's **degrees**. Challenging opportunities include
advanced placement, accelerated degree programs, student-designed majors, double
majors, independent study, and Phi Beta Kappa. Special programs include internships,
off-campus study, and study-abroad.

The most frequently chosen fields are social sciences and history, biological/life sciences, and English. A complete listing of majors at Grinnell College appears in the
Majors Index beginning on page 432.

The **faculty** at Grinnell College has 133 full-time members, 91% with terminal
degrees.

Students of Grinnell College

The student body is made up of 1,335 undergraduates. 55.3% are women and 44.7% are
men. Students come from 50 states and territories and 47 other countries. 14% are from
Iowa. 7.8% are international students. 2.8% are African American, 0.3% American
Indian, 4.8% Asian American, and 4.4% Hispanic American. 92% returned for their
sophomore year.

Facilities and Resources

Student rooms are linked to a campus network. 281 **computers** are available on campus
that provide access to the Internet. The 3 **libraries** have 267,257 books and 3,100
subscriptions.

Campus Life

There are 127 active organizations on campus, including a drama/theater group,
newspaper, radio station, and choral group. No national or local **fraternities** or **sororities**.

Grinnell College is a member of the NCAA (Division III). **Intercollegiate sports**
include baseball (m), basketball, cross-country running, football (m), golf, soccer, softball
(w), swimming, tennis, track and field, volleyball (w).

Campus Safety

Student safety services include late-night transport/escort service, 24-hour emergency
telephone alarm devices, 24-hour patrols by trained security personnel, student patrols,
and electronically operated dormitory entrances.

Applying

Grinnell College requires an essay, SAT I or ACT, a high school transcript, and 2 recommendations. It recommends an interview. Application deadline: 1/20; 2/1 for financial
aid. Early and deferred admission are possible.

GROVE CITY COLLEGE

SMALL-TOWN SETTING ■ PRIVATE ■ INDEPENDENT RELIGIOUS ■ COED
GROVE CITY, PENNSYLVANIA

Web site: www.gcc.edu
Contact: Mr. Jeffrey C. Mincey, Director of Admissions, 100 Campus Drive,
  Grove City, PA 16127-2104
Telephone: 724-458-2100 **Fax:** 724-458-3395
E-mail: admissions@gcc.edu

Academics

Grove City awards bachelor's and master's **degrees**. Challenging opportunities include advanced placement, student-designed majors, double majors, independent study, a senior project, and Sigma Xi. Special programs include internships, summer session for credit, and study-abroad.

The most frequently chosen fields are business/marketing, biological/life sciences, and education. A complete listing of majors at Grove City appears in the Majors Index beginning on page 432.

The **faculty** at Grove City has 113 full-time members, 75% with terminal degrees. The student-faculty ratio is 20:1.

Students of Grove City

The student body totals 2,324, of whom 2,313 are undergraduates. 49.2% are women and 50.8% are men. Students come from 46 states and territories and 11 other countries. 56% are from Pennsylvania. 0.9% are international students. 0.4% are African American, 0.6% Asian American, and 0.2% Hispanic American. 91% returned for their sophomore year.

Facilities and Resources

Student rooms are linked to a campus network. 142 **computers** are available on campus that provide access to the Internet. The **library** has 158,000 books.

Campus Life

There are 123 active organizations on campus, including a drama/theater group, newspaper, radio station, choral group, and marching band. 9% of eligible men and 19% of eligible women are members of local **fraternities** and local **sororities**.

Grove City is a member of the NCAA (Division III). **Intercollegiate sports** include baseball (m), basketball, cross-country running, football (m), golf, soccer, softball (w), swimming, tennis, track and field, volleyball (w), water polo.

Campus Safety

Student safety services include monitored women's residence hall entrances, late-night transport/escort service, 24-hour emergency telephone alarm devices, 24-hour patrols by trained security personnel, student patrols, and electronically operated dormitory entrances.

Applying

Grove City requires an essay, SAT I or ACT, a high school transcript, and 2 recommendations. It recommends an interview. Application deadline: 2/15; 4/15 for financial aid. Early and deferred admission are possible.

> **G**rove City is a nationally acclaimed 4-year private Christian college of liberal arts and sciences. From its founding days, the College has endeavored to give young people the best in liberal and scientific education at the lowest possible cost and, in keeping with this historic policy, still maintain one of the lowest tuitions of an independent, high-quality college. J. Howard Pew, one of the guiding spirits in building Grove City College, stated that the College's "prime responsibility is to inculcate in the minds and hearts of youth those Christian, moral, and ethical principles without which our country cannot long endure." These principles have been part of the dynamic motivation of Grove City College.

Getting in Last Year
2,163 applied
44% were accepted
587 enrolled (61%)
59% from top tenth of their h.s. class
3.70 average high school GPA
68% had SAT verbal scores over 600
73% had SAT math scores over 600
83% had ACT scores over 24
18% had SAT verbal scores over 700
17% had SAT math scores over 700
21% had ACT scores over 30
13 National Merit Scholars
76 valedictorians

Graduation and After
68% graduated in 4 years
7% graduated in 5 years
18% pursued further study (11% arts and
  sciences, 2% education, 2% medicine)
92% had job offers within 6 months
120 organizations recruited on campus

Financial Matters
$7506 tuition and fees (1999–2000)
$4048 room and board
77% average percent of need met
$3310 average financial aid amount received
  per undergraduate (1999–2000 estimated)

eAPPLY

Getting in Last Year
1,227 applied
76% were accepted
223 enrolled (24%)
16% from top tenth of their h.s. class
3.27 average high school GPA
51% had SAT verbal scores over 600
37% had SAT math scores over 600
63% had ACT scores over 24
17% had SAT verbal scores over 700
5% had SAT math scores over 700
12% had ACT scores over 30
8 National Merit Scholars
4 class presidents
10 valedictorians

Graduation and After
Graduates pursuing further study: 14% arts
   and sciences, 4% business, 2% law
50% had job offers within 6 months
115 organizations recruited on campus

Financial Matters
$16,970 tuition and fees (2000–2001)
$5610 room and board
93% average percent of need met
$14,420 average financial aid amount received
   per undergraduate (1999–2000 estimated)

GUILFORD COLLEGE
SUBURBAN SETTING ■ PRIVATE ■ INDEPENDENT RELIGIOUS ■ COED
GREENSBORO, NORTH CAROLINA

Web site: www.guilford.edu

Contact: Mr. Randy Doss, Dean of Enrollment, 5800 West Friendly Avenue,
   Greensboro, NC 27410-4173

Telephone: 336-316-2100 or toll-free 800-992-7759 **Fax:** 336-316-2954

E-mail: admission@guilford.edu

Academics
Guilford awards bachelor's **degrees**. Challenging opportunities include advanced placement, accelerated degree programs, student-designed majors, an honors program,
double majors, independent study, and a senior project. Special programs include internships, summer session for credit, off-campus study, study-abroad, and Army and Air
Force ROTC.

The most frequently chosen fields are social sciences and history, business/marketing,
and psychology. A complete listing of majors at Guilford appears in the Majors Index
beginning on page 432.

The **faculty** at Guilford has 89 full-time members, 90% with terminal degrees. The
student-faculty ratio is 13:1.

Students of Guilford
The student body is made up of 1,245 undergraduates. 54.4% are women and 45.6% are
men. Students come from 42 states and territories and 30 other countries. 25% are from
North Carolina. 2.7% are international students. 6.9% are African American, 0.8%
American Indian, 1.1% Asian American, and 3.1% Hispanic American. 78% returned for
their sophomore year.

Facilities and Resources
Student rooms are linked to a campus network. 150 **computers** are available on campus
that provide access to the Internet. The **library** has 250,000 books and 1,059 subscriptions.

Campus Life
There are 46 active organizations on campus, including a drama/theater group,
newspaper, radio station, and choral group. No national or local **fraternities** or **sororities**.

Guilford is a member of the NCAA (Division III). **Intercollegiate sports** include
baseball (m), basketball, bowling, cross-country running, football (m), golf (m), lacrosse,
rugby, soccer, tennis, track and field, volleyball.

Campus Safety
Student safety services include late-night transport/escort service, 24-hour emergency
telephone alarm devices, 24-hour patrols by trained security personnel, student patrols,
and electronically operated dormitory entrances.

Applying
Guilford requires an essay, SAT I or ACT, a high school transcript, 2 recommendations,
and a minimum high school GPA of 2.0. It recommends an interview and a minimum
high school GPA of 3.0. Application deadline: 2/15; 3/1 priority date for financial aid.
Early and deferred admission are possible.

Gustavus Adolphus College

SMALL-TOWN SETTING ■ PRIVATE ■ INDEPENDENT RELIGIOUS ■ COED
ST. PETER, MINNESOTA

Web site: www.gustavus.edu
Contact: Mr. Mark H. Anderson, Dean of Admission, 800 West College
 Avenue, St. Peter, MN 56082-1498
Telephone: 507-933-7676 or toll-free 800-GUSTAVU(S)
E-mail: admission@gac.edu

Academics

Gustavus awards bachelor's **degrees**. Challenging opportunities include advanced placement, accelerated degree programs, student-designed majors, an honors program, double majors, independent study, a senior project, Phi Beta Kappa, and Sigma Xi. Special programs include cooperative education, internships, summer session for credit, off-campus study, study-abroad, and Army ROTC.

The most frequently chosen fields are social sciences and history, business/marketing, and biological/life sciences. A complete listing of majors at Gustavus appears in the Majors Index beginning on page 432.

The **faculty** at Gustavus has 170 full-time members, 88% with terminal degrees. The student-faculty ratio is 13:1.

Students of Gustavus

The student body is made up of 2,543 undergraduates. 55.4% are women and 44.6% are men. Students come from 42 states and territories and 17 other countries. 77% are from Minnesota. 1.5% are international students. 1% are African American, 0.2% American Indian, 2.9% Asian American, and 0.6% Hispanic American. 91% returned for their sophomore year.

Facilities and Resources

Student rooms are linked to a campus network. 250 **computers** are available on campus that provide access to the Internet. The 5 **libraries** have 254,086 books and 1,752 subscriptions.

Campus Life

There are 85 active organizations on campus, including a drama/theater group, newspaper, radio station, and choral group. 20% of eligible men and 25% of eligible women are members of local **fraternities** and local **sororities**.

Gustavus is a member of the NCAA (Division III). **Intercollegiate sports** include baseball (m), basketball, cross-country running, football (m), golf, gymnastics (w), ice hockey, lacrosse (m), rugby, skiing (cross-country), soccer, softball (w), swimming, tennis, track and field, volleyball.

Campus Safety

Student safety services include late-night transport/escort service, 24-hour emergency telephone alarm devices, 24-hour patrols by trained security personnel, and electronically operated dormitory entrances.

Applying

Gustavus requires an essay, SAT I or ACT, a high school transcript, and 2 recommendations. It recommends an interview. Application deadline: 4/1; 2/15 priority date for financial aid. Early and deferred admission are possible.

Getting in Last Year
1,993 applied
79% were accepted
654 enrolled (42%)
35% from top tenth of their h.s. class
3.61 average high school GPA
52% had SAT verbal scores over 600
62% had SAT math scores over 600
71% had ACT scores over 24
19% had SAT verbal scores over 700
14% had SAT math scores over 700
16% had ACT scores over 30
8 National Merit Scholars
50 valedictorians

Graduation and After
72% graduated in 4 years
3% graduated in 5 years
36% pursued further study (13% arts and
 sciences, 7% business, 5% law)
92% had job offers within 6 months

Financial Matters
$17,430 tuition and fees (1999–2000)
$4320 room and board
90% average percent of need met
$13,459 average financial aid amount received
 per undergraduate (1999–2000 estimated)

HAMILTON COLLEGE

RURAL SETTING ■ PRIVATE ■ INDEPENDENT ■ COED
CLINTON, NEW YORK

Web site: www.hamilton.edu
Contact: Mr. Richard M. Fuller, Dean of Admission and Financial Aid, 198 College Hill Road, Clinton, NY 13323-1296
Telephone: 315-859-4421 or toll-free 800-843-2655 **Fax:** 315-859-4457
E-mail: admission@hamilton.edu

Chartered in 1812, Hamilton is the third oldest college in New York State, and is named in honor of U.S. statesman Alexander Hamilton. The College is a highly selective, residential community offering students a rigorous liberal arts curriculum for the 21st century. Students are challenged to think, write, and speak critically, creatively, and analytically so that upon graduation they will distinguish themselves in both their professions and their communities. Renowned for its beautiful campus in the foothills of the Adirondack Mountains, Hamilton offers a strong sense of community; highly qualified, often internationally recognized, faculty members; and state-of-the-art facilities.

Getting in Last Year
3,909 applied
42% were accepted
500 enrolled (30%)
48% from top tenth of their h.s. class
71% had SAT verbal scores over 600
69% had SAT math scores over 600
14% had SAT verbal scores over 700
15% had SAT math scores over 700
10 National Merit Scholars
7 valedictorians

Graduation and After
81% graduated in 4 years
4% graduated in 5 years
1% graduated in 6 years
15% pursued further study
90% had job offers within 6 months
32 organizations recruited on campus

Financial Matters
$25,050 tuition and fees (1999–2000)
$6200 room and board
99% average percent of need met
$19,490 average financial aid amount received per undergraduate (1999–2000 estimated)

Academics
Hamilton awards bachelor's **degrees**. Challenging opportunities include advanced placement, accelerated degree programs, student-designed majors, double majors, independent study, a senior project, Phi Beta Kappa, and Sigma Xi. Special programs include internships, off-campus study, study-abroad, and Army and Air Force ROTC.

The most frequently chosen fields are social sciences and history, English, and visual/performing arts. A complete listing of majors at Hamilton appears in the Majors Index beginning on page 432.

The **faculty** at Hamilton has 167 full-time members, 93% with terminal degrees. The student-faculty ratio is 9:1.

Students of Hamilton
The student body is made up of 1,740 undergraduates. 49.4% are women and 50.6% are men. Students come from 41 states and territories and 33 other countries. 43% are from New York. 3.1% are international students. 3.1% are African American, 0.2% American Indian, 3.6% Asian American, and 3.9% Hispanic American. 92% returned for their sophomore year.

Facilities and Resources
Student rooms are linked to a campus network. 200 **computers** are available on campus that provide access to the Internet. The 4 **libraries** have 890,591 books and 3,585 subscriptions.

Campus Life
There are 80 active organizations on campus, including a drama/theater group, newspaper, radio station, and choral group. 29% of eligible men and 12% of eligible women are members of national **fraternities**, local **sororities**, and private society.

Hamilton is a member of the NCAA (Division III). **Intercollegiate sports** include baseball (m), basketball, crew, cross-country running, fencing, field hockey (w), football (m), golf, ice hockey, lacrosse, rugby, sailing, skiing (downhill), soccer, softball (w), squash, swimming, tennis, track and field, volleyball, water polo.

Campus Safety
Student safety services include student safety program, late-night transport/escort service, 24-hour emergency telephone alarm devices, 24-hour patrols by trained security personnel, and electronically operated dormitory entrances.

Applying
Hamilton requires an essay, SAT I or ACT, a high school transcript, 1 recommendation, and sample of expository prose. It recommends an interview. Application deadline: 1/15; 2/1 for financial aid. Early and deferred admission are possible.

Hamline University

Urban setting ■ Private ■ Independent Religious ■ Coed
St. Paul, Minnesota

Web site: www.hamline.edu
Contact: Mr. Steven Bjork, Director of Undergraduate Admission, 1536
   Hewitt Avenue C1930, St. Paul, MN 55104-1284
Telephone: 651-523-2207 or toll-free 800-753-9753 **Fax:** 651-523-2458
E-mail: cla-admis@gw.hamline.edu

 eApply

Academics

Hamline awards bachelor's, master's, doctoral, and first-professional **degrees**. Challenging opportunities include advanced placement, student-designed majors, an honors program, double majors, independent study, a senior project, and Phi Beta Kappa. Special programs include cooperative education, internships, summer session for credit, off-campus study, study-abroad, and Air Force ROTC.

The most frequently chosen fields are social sciences and history, business/marketing, and psychology. A complete listing of majors at Hamline appears in the Majors Index beginning on page 432.

The **faculty** at Hamline has 154 full-time members, 88% with terminal degrees. The student-faculty ratio is 14:1.

Students of Hamline

The student body totals 3,111, of whom 1,833 are undergraduates. 66% are women and 34% are men. Students come from 27 states and territories and 34 other countries. 79% are from Minnesota. 2.8% are international students. 3.1% are African American, 0.5% American Indian, 3.4% Asian American, and 1.1% Hispanic American. 83% returned for their sophomore year.

Facilities and Resources

Student rooms are linked to a campus network. 236 **computers** are available on campus that provide access to the Internet. The 2 **libraries** have 445,902 books and 3,803 subscriptions.

Campus Life

There are 75 active organizations on campus, including a drama/theater group, newspaper, and choral group. 5% of eligible women are members of local **sororities** and an international dining club.

Hamline is a member of the NCAA (Division III). **Intercollegiate sports** include baseball (m), basketball, cross-country running, football (m), gymnastics (w), ice hockey (m), soccer, softball (w), swimming, tennis, track and field, volleyball (w).

Campus Safety

Student safety services include late-night transport/escort service, 24-hour emergency telephone alarm devices, 24-hour patrols by trained security personnel, student patrols, and electronically operated dormitory entrances.

Applying

Hamline requires an essay, SAT I or ACT, a high school transcript, and 2 recommendations. It recommends an interview. Application deadline: rolling admissions; 5/1 priority date for financial aid. Early and deferred admission are possible.

Getting in Last Year

1,230 applied
83% were accepted
421 enrolled (41%)
29% from top tenth of their h.s. class
3.41 average high school GPA
57% had SAT verbal scores over 600
35% had SAT math scores over 600
55% had ACT scores over 24
11% had SAT verbal scores over 700
5% had SAT math scores over 700
7% had ACT scores over 30
6 National Merit Scholars
16 valedictorians

Graduation and After

58% graduated in 4 years
1% graduated in 5 years
1% graduated in 6 years
26% pursued further study (14% arts and sciences, 5% law, 4% education)
71% had job offers within 6 months
1 Fulbright scholar

Financial Matters

$15,798 tuition and fees (1999–2000)
$5291 room and board
73% average percent of need met
$15,205 average financial aid amount received per undergraduate (1999–2000 estimated)

Getting in Last Year
991 applied
74% were accepted
307 enrolled (42%)
14% from top tenth of their h.s. class
3.1 average high school GPA
27% had SAT verbal scores over 600
29% had SAT math scores over 600
37% had ACT scores over 24
6% had SAT verbal scores over 700
4% had SAT math scores over 700
6% had ACT scores over 30
6 class presidents
6 valedictorians

Graduation and After
50% graduated in 4 years
14% graduated in 5 years
30% pursued further study (8% law, 7% arts and sciences, 3% business)
75% had job offers within 6 months
30 organizations recruited on campus

Financial Matters
$16,531 tuition and fees (1999–2000)
$5898 room and board
87% average percent of need met
$12,638 average financial aid amount received per undergraduate (1999–2000 estimated)

HAMPDEN-SYDNEY COLLEGE
RURAL SETTING ■ PRIVATE ■ INDEPENDENT RELIGIOUS ■ MEN ONLY
HAMPDEN-SYDNEY, VIRGINIA

Web site: www.hsc.edu
Contact: Ms. Anita H. Garland, Dean of Admissions, PO Box 667, Hampden-Sydney, VA 23943-0667
Telephone: 804-223-6120 or toll-free 800-755-0733 **Fax:** 804-223-6346
E-mail: hsapp@tiger.hsc.edu

Academics
Hampden-Sydney awards bachelor's **degrees**. Challenging opportunities include advanced placement, accelerated degree programs, an honors program, double majors, independent study, a senior project, Phi Beta Kappa, and Sigma Xi. Special programs include internships, summer session for credit, off-campus study, study-abroad, and Army ROTC.

The most frequently chosen fields are social sciences and history, business/marketing, and psychology. A complete listing of majors at Hampden-Sydney appears in the Majors Index beginning on page 432.

The **faculty** at Hampden-Sydney has 62 full-time members, 94% with terminal degrees. The student-faculty ratio is 13:1.

Students of Hampden-Sydney
The student body is made up of 996 undergraduates. Students come from 34 states and territories and 3 other countries. 60% are from Virginia. 0.3% are international students. 3.6% are African American, 0.2% American Indian, 0.7% Asian American, and 1% Hispanic American. 80% returned for their sophomore year.

Facilities and Resources
Student rooms are linked to a campus network. 140 **computers** are available on campus that provide access to the Internet. The **library** has 219,221 books and 948 subscriptions.

Campus Life
There are 29 active organizations on campus, including a drama/theater group, newspaper, radio station, and choral group. 37% of eligible undergraduates are members of national **fraternities**.

Hampden-Sydney is a member of the NCAA (Division III). **Intercollegiate sports** include baseball, basketball, cross-country running, football, golf, lacrosse, rugby, soccer, tennis, volleyball, water polo.

Campus Safety
Student safety services include 24-hour emergency telephone alarm devices and 24-hour patrols by trained security personnel.

Applying
Hampden-Sydney requires an essay, SAT I or ACT, a high school transcript, 2 recommendations, and a minimum high school GPA of 2.0. It recommends SAT II Subject Tests, SAT II: Writing Test, an interview, and a minimum high school GPA of 3.0. Application deadline: 3/1; 3/1 priority date for financial aid. Early admission is possible.

HAMPSHIRE COLLEGE

RURAL SETTING ■ PRIVATE ■ INDEPENDENT ■ COED
AMHERST, MASSACHUSETTS

Web site: www.hampshire.edu
Contact: Ms. Audrey Smith, Director of Admissions, 839 West Street,
Amherst, MA 01002
Telephone: 413-559-5471 **Fax:** 413-559-5631
E-mail: admissions@hampshire.edu

eAPPLY

Academics

Hampshire awards bachelor's **degrees**. Challenging opportunities include advanced placement, student-designed majors, independent study, and a senior project. Special programs include internships, off-campus study, and study-abroad. A complete listing of majors at Hampshire appears in the Majors Index beginning on page 432.

The **faculty** at Hampshire has 85 full-time members. The student-faculty ratio is 12:1.

Students of Hampshire

The student body is made up of 1,172 undergraduates. Students come from 50 states and territories and 31 other countries. 17% are from Massachusetts. 4.6% are international students. 3.5% are African American, 0.2% American Indian, 3.9% Asian American, and 2.9% Hispanic American. 77% returned for their sophomore year.

Facilities and Resources

Student rooms are linked to a campus network. 125 **computers** are available on campus that provide access to the Internet. The **library** has 120,918 books and 760 subscriptions.

Campus Life

There are 75 active organizations on campus, including a drama/theater group, newspaper, television station, and choral group. No national or local **fraternities** or **sororities**.

Hampshire is a member of the NSCAA. **Intercollegiate sports** include basketball, fencing, soccer.

Campus Safety

Student safety services include late-night transport/escort service, 24-hour emergency telephone alarm devices, 24-hour patrols by trained security personnel, and student patrols.

Applying

Hampshire requires an essay, a high school transcript, and 2 recommendations. It recommends an interview. Application deadline: 2/1; 2/1 priority date for financial aid. Early and deferred admission are possible.

Hampshire College's bold, innovative approach to the liberal arts creates an academic atmosphere that energizes students to work hard and grow tremendously, both personally and intellectually. Students have the freedom to design an individualized course of study in a graduate school–like environment, culminating in original final projects such as science or social science research, academic study, or a body of work in writing, performing, visual, or media arts. Students work closely with faculty mentors, often integrating different disciplines. Independent thinking is expected. Hampshire students and faculty agree: if you incorporate what you love into your education, you will love your education.

Getting in Last Year
1,774 applied
61% were accepted
295 enrolled (27%)
22% from top tenth of their h.s. class
3.29 average high school GPA
79% had SAT verbal scores over 600
52% had SAT math scores over 600
89% had ACT scores over 24
36% had SAT verbal scores over 700
12% had SAT math scores over 700
47% had ACT scores over 30

Graduation and After
38% graduated in 4 years
16% graduated in 5 years
1% graduated in 6 years
1 Fulbright scholar

Financial Matters
$25,400 tuition and fees (1999–2000)
$6622 room and board
100% average percent of need met
$21,500 average financial aid amount received per undergraduate (1999–2000 estimated)

HARDING UNIVERSITY

SMALL-TOWN SETTING ■ PRIVATE ■ INDEPENDENT RELIGIOUS ■ COED
SEARCY, ARKANSAS

Web site: www.harding.edu
Contact: Mr. Mike Williams, Assistant Vice President of Admissions, Box 11255, Searcy, AR 72149-0001
Telephone: 501-279-4407 or toll-free 800-477-4407 **Fax:** 501-279-4865
E-mail: admissions@harding.edu

Located in the beautiful foothills of the Ozark Mountains, Harding is one of America's more highly regarded private universities. At Harding, students build lifetime friendships and, upon graduation, are highly recruited. Harding's Christian environment and challenging academic program develop students who can compete and succeed. Whether on the main campus or in the international studies program in Italy, Greece, England, or Australia, students find Harding to be a caring and serving family. From Missouri flood relief to working with orphans in Haiti or farmers in Kenya, hundreds of Harding students serve others worldwide each year.

Getting in Last Year
1,552 applied
80% were accepted
940 enrolled (76%)
35% from top tenth of their h.s. class
3.3 average high school GPA
50% had ACT scores over 24
13% had ACT scores over 30
13 National Merit Scholars
45 valedictorians

Graduation and After
29% graduated in 4 years
21% graduated in 5 years
5% graduated in 6 years
25% pursued further study (9% education, 7% arts and sciences, 3% business)
90% had job offers within 6 months
240 organizations recruited on campus

Financial Matters
$8472 tuition and fees (1999–2000)
$4250 room and board
75% average percent of need met
$8349 average financial aid amount received per undergraduate (1999–2000)

Academics

Harding awards bachelor's and master's **degrees**. Challenging opportunities include advanced placement, accelerated degree programs, student-designed majors, freshman honors college, an honors program, and a senior project. Special programs include cooperative education, internships, summer session for credit, study-abroad, and Army ROTC.

The most frequently chosen fields are business/marketing, education, and health professions and related sciences. A complete listing of majors at Harding appears in the Majors Index beginning on page 432.

The **faculty** at Harding has 203 full-time members, 70% with terminal degrees. The student-faculty ratio is 17:1.

Students of Harding

The student body totals 3,976, of whom 3,752 are undergraduates. 55.1% are women and 44.9% are men. Students come from 50 states and territories and 34 other countries. 26% are from Arkansas. 4.1% are international students. 4.1% are African American, 1.3% American Indian, 0.6% Asian American, and 1.5% Hispanic American. 76% returned for their sophomore year.

Facilities and Resources

140 **computers** are available on campus that provide access to the Internet. The 2 **libraries** have 489,291 books and 1,330 subscriptions.

Campus Life

There are 52 active organizations on campus, including a drama/theater group, newspaper, radio station, choral group, and marching band. 56% of eligible men and 46% of eligible women are members of local **fraternities** and local **sororities**.

Harding is a member of the NCAA (Division II). **Intercollegiate sports** (some offering scholarships) include baseball (m), basketball, cross-country running, football (m), golf (m), soccer, tennis, track and field, volleyball (w).

Campus Safety

Student safety services include 24-hour emergency telephone alarm devices and 24-hour patrols by trained security personnel.

Applying

Harding requires SAT I or ACT, a high school transcript, an interview, and 2 recommendations. Application deadline: 7/1. Early and deferred admission are possible.

HARVARD UNIVERSITY

URBAN SETTING ■ PRIVATE ■ INDEPENDENT ■ COED
CAMBRIDGE, MASSACHUSETTS

Web site: www.harvard.edu
Contact: Office of Admissions and Financial Aid, Byerly Hall, 8 Garden
  Street, Cambridge, MA 02138
Telephone: 617-495-1551
E-mail: college@harvard.edu

Academics

Harvard awards bachelor's, master's, doctoral, and first-professional **degrees**. Challenging opportunities include advanced placement, accelerated degree programs, student-designed majors, an honors program, a senior project, Phi Beta Kappa, and Sigma Xi. Special programs include summer session for credit, off-campus study, and Army, Navy and Air Force ROTC. A complete listing of majors at Harvard appears in the Majors Index beginning on page 432.

The **faculty** at Harvard has 1,705 full-time members, 99% with terminal degrees. The student-faculty ratio is 8:1.

Students of Harvard

The student body totals 17,606, of whom 6,684 are undergraduates. 46.3% are women and 53.7% are men. Students come from 53 states and territories and 93 other countries. 6.9% are international students. 7.9% are African American, 0.7% American Indian, 17.4% Asian American, and 7.7% Hispanic American. 97% returned for their sophomore year.

Facilities and Resources

Student rooms are linked to a campus network. The 91 **libraries** have 13,400,000 books and 97,568 subscriptions.

Campus Life

There are 250 active organizations on campus, including a drama/theater group, newspaper, radio station, choral group, and marching band. 99% of eligible men and 99% of eligible women are members of "House" system.

Harvard is a member of the NCAA (Division I). **Intercollegiate sports** include baseball (m), basketball, crew, cross-country running, fencing, field hockey (w), football (m), golf, ice hockey, lacrosse, sailing, skiing (cross-country), skiing (downhill), soccer, softball (w), squash, swimming, tennis, track and field, volleyball, water polo, wrestling (m).

Campus Safety

Student safety services include required and optional safety courses, late-night transport/escort service, 24-hour emergency telephone alarm devices, 24-hour patrols by trained security personnel, and electronically operated dormitory entrances.

Applying

Harvard requires an essay, SAT II Subject Tests, SAT I or ACT, a high school transcript, an interview, and 2 recommendations. Application deadline: 1/1; 2/1 priority date for financial aid. Deferred admission is possible.

Harvard and Radcliffe, the coeducational undergraduate colleges of Harvard University, offer a curriculum of 3,000 courses, the world's largest university library, a state-of-the-art Science Center, art museums, athletic facilities, and a comprehensive housing system. Excellence and diversity are the hallmarks of the experience. Students come from all 50 states and many other countries and from all educational, ethnic, and economic backgrounds. Students choose from more than 40 academic fields and pursue more than 250 different extracurricular activities. The admission process is rigorous. The committee considers academic achievement, extracurricular strengths, and personal qualities. Harvard and Radcliffe offer need-based financial aid.

Getting in Last Year
18,161 applied
11% were accepted
95% from top tenth of their h.s. class
370 National Merit Scholars

Graduation and After
86% graduated in 4 years
9% graduated in 5 years
2% graduated in 6 years
2 Rhodes, 7 Marshall scholars

Financial Matters
$24,407 tuition and fees (1999–2000)
$7757 room and board
100% average percent of need met
$22,010 average financial aid amount received
  per undergraduate (1998–99)

HARVEY MUDD COLLEGE

SUBURBAN SETTING ■ PRIVATE ■ INDEPENDENT ■ COED
CLAREMONT, CALIFORNIA

Web site: www.hmc.edu
Contact: Mr. Deren Finks, Vice President, Dean of Admissions and Financial
Aid, 301 East 12th Street, Claremont, CA 91711-5994
Telephone: 909-621-8011 **Fax:** 909-607-7046
E-mail: admission@hmc.edu

Harvey Mudd College (HMC) educates leaders in math, science, and engineering while maintaining an emphasis in the humanities and social sciences. As a member of the Claremont Colleges, HMC augments the benefits of a small, residential college with the advantages and resources of a much larger institution. Research is required; last year, more than $2 million was spent on undergraduate research, the highest of any US undergraduate institution. From studying chaos theory to participating in intramural and varsity sports, from real-world clinic research to improv comedy, students at Mudd are passionate about what they do.

Getting in Last Year
1,642 applied
33% were accepted
170 enrolled (32%)
87% from top tenth of their h.s. class
97% had SAT verbal scores over 600
100% had SAT math scores over 600
62% had SAT verbal scores over 700
98% had SAT math scores over 700
39 National Merit Scholars
24 valedictorians

Graduation and After
73% graduated in 4 years
4% graduated in 5 years
1% graduated in 6 years
36% pursued further study
90% had job offers within 6 months
72 organizations recruited on campus
1 Rhodes scholar

Financial Matters
$22,083 tuition and fees (1999–2000)
$8017 room and board
100% average percent of need met
$17,616 average financial aid amount received per undergraduate (1999–2000)

Academics

Harvey Mudd awards bachelor's and master's **degrees**. Challenging opportunities include advanced placement, student-designed majors, double majors, and a senior project. Special programs include cooperative education, internships, off-campus study, study-abroad, and Army and Air Force ROTC.

The most frequently chosen fields are engineering/engineering technologies, protective services/public administration, and computer/information sciences. A complete listing of majors at Harvey Mudd appears in the Majors Index beginning on page 432.

The **faculty** at Harvey Mudd has 75 full-time members, 100% with terminal degrees. The student-faculty ratio is 9:1.

Students of Harvey Mudd

The student body totals 709, of whom 703 are undergraduates. 26.7% are women and 73.3% are men. Students come from 43 states and territories and 15 other countries. 46% are from California. 2.6% are international students. 0.6% are African American, 0.3% American Indian, 23.3% Asian American, and 3.7% Hispanic American. 96% returned for their sophomore year.

Facilities and Resources

Student rooms are linked to a campus network. 200 **computers** are available on campus that provide access to the Internet. The 2 **libraries** have 1,381,108 books and 4,321 subscriptions.

Campus Life

There are 80 active organizations on campus, including a drama/theater group, newspaper, radio station, and choral group. No national or local **fraternities** or **sororities**.

Harvey Mudd is a member of the NCAA (Division III). **Intercollegiate sports** include baseball (m), basketball, cross-country running, football (m), golf (m), soccer, softball (w), swimming, tennis, track and field, volleyball (w), water polo.

Campus Safety

Student safety services include late-night transport/escort service, 24-hour emergency telephone alarm devices, and 24-hour patrols by trained security personnel.

Applying

Harvey Mudd requires an essay, SAT I, SAT II Subject Tests, SAT II: Writing Test, SAT II Subject Test in math, third SAT II Subject Test, a high school transcript, and 3 recommendations. It recommends an interview. Application deadline: 1/15; 2/1 for financial aid. Deferred admission is possible.

HASTINGS COLLEGE

SMALL-TOWN SETTING ■ PRIVATE ■ INDEPENDENT RELIGIOUS ■ COED
HASTINGS, NEBRASKA

Web site: www.hastings.edu
Contact: Mr. Michael Karloff, Director of Admissions, 800 North Turner
Avenue, Hastings, NE 68901-7696
Telephone: 402-461-7316 or toll-free 800-532-7642 **Fax:** 402-461-7490
E-mail: admissions@hastings.edu

eAPPLY

Academics

Hastings awards bachelor's and master's **degrees**. Challenging opportunities include advanced placement, student-designed majors, double majors, independent study, and a senior project. Special programs include internships, summer session for credit, off-campus study, and study-abroad.

The most frequently chosen fields are education, business/marketing, and psychology. A complete listing of majors at Hastings appears in the Majors Index beginning on page 432.

The **faculty** at Hastings has 69 full-time members, 68% with terminal degrees. The student-faculty ratio is 13:1.

Students of Hastings

The student body totals 1,148, of whom 1,118 are undergraduates. 52.9% are women and 47.1% are men. Students come from 28 states and territories and 6 other countries. 78% are from Nebraska. 1% are international students. 1.2% are African American, 0.4% American Indian, 0.3% Asian American, and 1.7% Hispanic American. 75% returned for their sophomore year.

Facilities and Resources

Student rooms are linked to a campus network. 120 **computers** are available on campus that provide access to the Internet. The **library** has 123,512 books and 583 subscriptions.

Campus Life

There are 60 active organizations on campus, including a drama/theater group, newspaper, radio station, television station, choral group, and marching band. 20% of eligible men and 32% of eligible women are members of local **fraternities** and local **sororities**.

Hastings is a member of the NAIA. **Intercollegiate sports** (some offering scholarships) include baseball (m), basketball, cross-country running, football (m), golf, soccer, softball (w), tennis, track and field, volleyball (w).

Campus Safety

Student safety services include late-night transport/escort service, 24-hour emergency telephone alarm devices, student patrols, and electronically operated dormitory entrances.

Applying

Hastings requires SAT I or ACT, a high school transcript, counselor's recommendation, and a minimum high school GPA of 2.0, and in some cases an essay, an interview, and 2 recommendations. Application deadline: 8/1; 9/1 for financial aid, with a 5/1 priority date.

Getting in Last Year

1,098 applied
86% were accepted
288 enrolled (30%)
24% from top tenth of their h.s. class
28% had SAT verbal scores over 600
26% had SAT math scores over 600
47% had ACT scores over 24
3% had SAT verbal scores over 700
8% had SAT math scores over 700
9% had ACT scores over 30
1 National Merit Scholar
31 class presidents
22 valedictorians

Graduation and After

44% graduated in 4 years
13% graduated in 5 years
1% graduated in 6 years
17% pursued further study (10% arts and sciences, 1% education, 1% law)
71.5% had job offers within 6 months
18 organizations recruited on campus

Financial Matters

$12,418 tuition and fees (1999–2000)
$3986 room and board
77% average percent of need met
$10,292 average financial aid amount received per undergraduate (1999–2000)

HAVERFORD COLLEGE

SUBURBAN SETTING ■ PRIVATE ■ INDEPENDENT ■ COED
HAVERFORD, PENNSYLVANIA

Web site: www.haverford.edu
Contact: Ms. Delsie Z. Phillips, Director of Admissions, 370 Lancaster
Avenue, Haverford, PA 19041-1392
Telephone: 610-896-1350 **Fax:** 610-896-1338
E-mail: admitme@haverford.edu

Haverford is a liberal arts college of 1,100 students located 10 miles outside of Philadelphia. Academic rigor, integrity, and concern for others form the foundation of Haverford's approach to education. Aspects such as a student-run Honor Code, a sense of Quaker heritage, and a cooperative program with Bryn Mawr College, Swarthmore College, and the University of Pennsylvania mark Haverford as unique. Students thrive in part because classes are small and extracurricular commitment is expected and because the community is passionate about learning, understanding, and making sound and thoughtful judgments.

Getting in Last Year
2,650 applied
33% were accepted
302 enrolled (35%)
76% from top tenth of their h.s. class
85% had SAT verbal scores over 600
84% had SAT math scores over 600
47% had SAT verbal scores over 700
39% had SAT math scores over 700

Graduation and After
19% pursued further study (8% arts and sciences, 6% medicine, 5% law)
67% had job offers within 6 months
119 organizations recruited on campus
1 Fulbright scholar

Financial Matters
$23,780 tuition and fees (1999–2000)
$7620 room and board
100% average percent of need met
$19,984 average financial aid amount received per undergraduate (1999–2000 estimated)

Academics

Haverford awards bachelor's **degrees**. Challenging opportunities include advanced placement, accelerated degree programs, student-designed majors, double majors, independent study, a senior project, and Phi Beta Kappa. Special programs include off-campus study and study-abroad.

The most frequently chosen fields are social sciences and history, biological/life sciences, and English. A complete listing of majors at Haverford appears in the Majors Index beginning on page 432.

The **faculty** at Haverford has 102 full-time members, 97% with terminal degrees. The student-faculty ratio is 9:1.

Students of Haverford

The student body is made up of 1,118 undergraduates. 52.8% are women and 47.2% are men. Students come from 47 states and territories and 27 other countries. 20% are from Pennsylvania. 2.5% are international students. 5.3% are African American, 0.2% American Indian, 8.8% Asian American, and 5.2% Hispanic American. 95% returned for their sophomore year.

Facilities and Resources

Student rooms are linked to a campus network. 76 **computers** are available on campus that provide access to the Internet. The 6 **libraries** have 386,891 books and 2,715 subscriptions.

Campus Life

There are 50 active organizations on campus, including a drama/theater group, newspaper, radio station, and choral group. No national or local **fraternities** or **sororities**.

Haverford is a member of the NCAA (Division III). **Intercollegiate sports** include baseball (m), basketball, crew, cross-country running, fencing, field hockey (w), golf, lacrosse, soccer, softball (w), squash, tennis, track and field, volleyball (w), wrestling (m).

Campus Safety

Student safety services include late-night transport/escort service, 24-hour emergency telephone alarm devices, and 24-hour patrols by trained security personnel.

Applying

Haverford requires an essay, SAT II Subject Tests, SAT II: Writing Test, SAT I or ACT, a high school transcript, and 2 recommendations. It recommends an interview. Application deadline: 1/15; 1/31 for financial aid. Early and deferred admission are possible.

HENDRIX COLLEGE

SUBURBAN SETTING ■ PRIVATE ■ INDEPENDENT RELIGIOUS ■ COED
CONWAY, ARKANSAS

Web site: www.hendrix.edu
Contact: Mr. Rock Jones, Vice President for Enrollment, 1600 Washington
Avenue, Conway, AR 72032
Telephone: 501-450-1362 or toll-free 800-277-9017 **Fax:** 501-450-3843
E-mail: adm@hendrix.edu

Academics

Hendrix awards bachelor's **degrees**. Challenging opportunities include advanced placement, student-designed majors, an honors program, double majors, independent study, a senior project, and Phi Beta Kappa. Special programs include internships, off-campus study, study-abroad, and Army ROTC.

The most frequently chosen fields are social sciences and history, biological/life sciences, and psychology. A complete listing of majors at Hendrix appears in the Majors Index beginning on page 432.

The **faculty** at Hendrix has 80 full-time members, 99% with terminal degrees. The student-faculty ratio is 14:1.

Students of Hendrix

The student body totals 1,147, of whom 1,143 are undergraduates. 54.2% are women and 45.8% are men. Students come from 39 states and territories and 10 other countries. 68% are from Arkansas. 1% are international students. 5.2% are African American, 0.5% American Indian, 3.6% Asian American, and 1.6% Hispanic American. 86% returned for their sophomore year.

Facilities and Resources

Student rooms are linked to a campus network. 75 **computers** are available on campus that provide access to the Internet. The **library** has 146,294 books and 704 subscriptions.

Campus Life

There are 54 active organizations on campus, including a drama/theater group, newspaper, radio station, and choral group. No national or local **fraternities** or **sororities**.

Hendrix is a member of the NCAA (Division III). **Intercollegiate sports** include baseball (m), basketball, cross-country running, golf, rugby (m), soccer, softball (w), swimming, tennis, track and field, volleyball (w).

Campus Safety

Student safety services include late-night transport/escort service, 24-hour emergency telephone alarm devices, 24-hour patrols by trained security personnel, and electronically operated dormitory entrances.

Applying

Hendrix requires an essay, SAT I or ACT, and a high school transcript, and in some cases an interview and 1 recommendation. Application deadline: rolling admissions; 2/16 priority date for financial aid. Early and deferred admission are possible.

A small college located at the foothills of the Ozark Mountains 30 miles from Little Rock, Hendrix is a nationally recognized liberal arts college that prepares students for the finest professional and graduate schools in the country. The College enrolls 1,150 students who are taught by a faculty of 80 professors, all of whom have PhDs or appropriate terminal degrees in their fields. Most students complete an undergraduate research project, and many study abroad while at Hendrix. Eighty-five percent of Hendrix students live on campus, fostering an intimate community in which students and faculty members interact in all aspects of campus life.

Getting in Last Year
962 applied
88% were accepted
369 enrolled (44%)
45% from top tenth of their h.s. class
3.70 average high school GPA
70% had SAT verbal scores over 600
62% had SAT math scores over 600
84% had ACT scores over 24
24% had SAT verbal scores over 700
19% had SAT math scores over 700
32% had ACT scores over 30
24 National Merit Scholars
27 valedictorians

Graduation and After
52% graduated in 4 years
5% graduated in 5 years
1% graduated in 6 years
Graduates pursuing further study: 13% arts and sciences, 10% medicine, 5% law
60.7% had job offers within 6 months
76 organizations recruited on campus

Financial Matters
$11,615 tuition and fees (1999–2000)
$4415 room and board
89% average percent of need met
$11,601 average financial aid amount received per undergraduate (1999–2000)

HILLSDALE COLLEGE

SMALL-TOWN SETTING ■ PRIVATE ■ INDEPENDENT ■ COED
HILLSDALE, MICHIGAN

Web site: www.hillsdale.edu
Contact: Mr. Jeffrey S. Lantis, Director of Admissions, 33 East College
    Street, Hillsdale, MI 49242-1298
Telephone: 517-437-7341 ext. 2327 **Fax:** 517-437-0190
E-mail: admissions@ac.hillsdale.edu

Academics

Hillsdale awards bachelor's **degrees**. Challenging opportunities include advanced placement, accelerated degree programs, an honors program, double majors, independent study, and a senior project. Special programs include internships, summer session for credit, study-abroad, and Army, Navy and Air Force ROTC.

The most frequently chosen fields are business/marketing, social sciences and history, and biological/life sciences. A complete listing of majors at Hillsdale appears in the Majors Index beginning on page 432.

The **faculty** at Hillsdale has 96 full-time members, 89% with terminal degrees. The student-faculty ratio is 11:1.

Students of Hillsdale

The student body is made up of 1,167 undergraduates. 51.8% are women and 48.2% are men. Students come from 47 states and territories and 10 other countries. 51% are from Michigan. 90% returned for their sophomore year.

Facilities and Resources

150 **computers** are available on campus that provide access to the Internet. The 4 **libraries** have 180,000 books and 19,200 subscriptions.

Campus Life

There are 45 active organizations on campus, including a drama/theater group, newspaper, and choral group. 35% of eligible men and 45% of eligible women are members of national **fraternities** and national **sororities**.

Hillsdale is a member of the NCAA (Division II). **Intercollegiate sports** (some offering scholarships) include baseball (m), basketball, cross-country running, equestrian sports (w), football (m), golf (m), ice hockey (m), lacrosse (m), soccer, softball (w), swimming, tennis, track and field, volleyball (w).

Campus Safety

Student safety services include late-night transport/escort service, 24-hour emergency telephone alarm devices, 24-hour patrols by trained security personnel, and electronically operated dormitory entrances.

Applying

Hillsdale requires an essay, SAT I or ACT, a high school transcript, 1 recommendation, and a minimum high school GPA of 3.1, and in some cases an interview. It recommends SAT II Subject Tests, SAT II: Writing Test, and an interview. Application deadline: rolling admissions; 3/15 priority date for financial aid. Early and deferred admission are possible.

Located in south-central Michigan, Hillsdale College provides a value-based liberal arts education grounded in the Judeo-Christian heritage and the traditions of the Western world. The refusal of government funding is what makes Hillsdale unique. The College's fierce independence is critical to the level and type of educational excellence Hillsdale is able to provide.

Getting in Last Year
1,008 applied
84% were accepted
323 enrolled (38%)
40% from top tenth of their h.s. class
3.55 average high school GPA
63% had SAT verbal scores over 600
53% had SAT math scores over 600
72% had ACT scores over 24
23% had SAT verbal scores over 700
12% had SAT math scores over 700
23% had ACT scores over 30
11 National Merit Scholars
20 valedictorians

Graduation and After
52% graduated in 4 years
18% graduated in 5 years
Graduates pursuing further study: 7% arts and sciences, 5% business, 5% law
97% had job offers within 6 months
44 organizations recruited on campus
1 Fulbright scholar

Financial Matters
$13,460 tuition and fees (1999–2000)
$5630 room and board
76% average percent of need met
$13,524 average financial aid amount received per undergraduate (1998–99)

Hiram College

RURAL SETTING ■ PRIVATE ■ INDEPENDENT RELIGIOUS ■ COED
HIRAM, OHIO

Web site: www.hiram.edu
Contact: Mr. Monty L. Curtis, Vice President for Admission and College
Relations, Box 96, Hiram, OH 44234-0067
Telephone: 330-569-5169 or toll-free 800-362-5280 **Fax:** 330-569-5944
E-mail: admission@hiram.edu

Academics

Hiram awards bachelor's **degrees**. Challenging opportunities include advanced placement, accelerated degree programs, student-designed majors, double majors, a senior
project, and Phi Beta Kappa. Special programs include internships, summer session for
credit, and study-abroad.

The most frequently chosen fields are social sciences and history, business/marketing,
and biological/life sciences. A complete listing of majors at Hiram appears in the Majors
Index beginning on page 432.

The **faculty** at Hiram has 66 full-time members, 97% with terminal degrees. The
student-faculty ratio is 12:1.

Students of Hiram

The student body is made up of 1,204 undergraduates. 55.1% are women and 44.9% are
men. Students come from 23 states and territories and 19 other countries. 79% are from
Ohio. 1.8% are international students. 8.9% are African American, 0.2% American
Indian, 1% Asian American, and 1.5% Hispanic American. 81% returned for their
sophomore year.

Facilities and Resources

Student rooms are linked to a campus network. The **library** has 177,282 books and 908
subscriptions.

Campus Life

There are 90 active organizations on campus, including a drama/theater group,
newspaper, radio station, and choral group. Hiram has vegetarian co-op.

Hiram is a member of the NCAA (Division III). **Intercollegiate sports** include
baseball (m), basketball, cross-country running, equestrian sports, football (m), golf,
rugby, sailing, soccer, softball (w), swimming, table tennis, tennis, track and field, volleyball (w).

Campus Safety

Student safety services include late-night transport/escort service, 24-hour emergency
telephone alarm devices, 24-hour patrols by trained security personnel, and electronically operated dormitory entrances.

Applying

Hiram requires an essay, SAT I or ACT, a high school transcript, and 2 recommendations, and in some cases an interview. It recommends an interview and 3 recommendations. Application deadline: 3/15; 2/15 priority date for financial aid. Early and deferred
admission are possible.

Hiram's 12-3 academic
calendar is unique among
colleges and universities.
Each 15-week semester combines a
comprehensive 12-week session of
3 courses with an intensive, 3-week
immersion in a single seminar either
on or off campus. Hiram
supplements classroom study
through career-oriented internships
and an extensive and distinctive
study-abroad program that takes
Hiram students all over the world.
More than 50% of Hiram students
participate, and all courses are
taught by Hiram faculty members
and are a regular part of the
curriculum. Hiram recently opened a
new $6.2-million science hall.

Getting in Last Year
760 applied
86% were accepted
286 enrolled (44%)
32% from top tenth of their h.s. class
3.40 average high school GPA
42% had SAT verbal scores over 600
39% had SAT math scores over 600
49% had ACT scores over 24
10% had SAT verbal scores over 700
8% had SAT math scores over 700
8% had ACT scores over 30
13 valedictorians

Graduation and After
52% graduated in 4 years
6% graduated in 5 years
53% had job offers within 6 months
24 organizations recruited on campus

Financial Matters
$17,710 tuition and fees (1999–2000)
$6024 room and board

Hobart and William Smith Colleges

Small-town setting ■ Private ■ Independent ■ Coed
Geneva, New York

Web site: www.hws.edu
Contact: Ms. Mara O'Laughlin, Director of Admissions, Geneva, NY 14456-3397
Telephone: 315-781-3472 or toll-free 800-245-0100 **Fax:** 315-781-5471
E-mail: hoadm@hws.edu

As models of interdisciplinary teaching and learning, Hobart and William Smith have long brought together the traditional and the innovative in the design and implementation of general curricula. The Colleges provide a distinguished program in the liberal arts within a coordinate system that establishes equality between men and women. Nearly two thirds of Hobart and William Smith students study abroad in one of nearly 30 locales. Numerous opportunities for internships are provided. Small classes, a dedicated faculty, and extensive opportunities for independent and off-campus study contribute to a climate that is academically rigorous.

Getting in Last Year
2,634 applied
75% were accepted
503 enrolled (26%)
25% from top tenth of their h.s. class
3.25 average high school GPA
36% had SAT verbal scores over 600
37% had SAT math scores over 600
4% had SAT verbal scores over 700
3% had SAT math scores over 700
8 National Merit Scholars
9 class presidents
5 valedictorians

Graduation and After
70% graduated in 4 years
12% graduated in 5 years
1% graduated in 6 years
30% pursued further study (14% arts and sciences, 5% medicine, 4% law)
70% had job offers within 6 months
48 organizations recruited on campus

Financial Matters
$24,342 tuition and fees (1999–2000)
$6882 room and board
89% average percent of need met
$21,368 average financial aid amount received per undergraduate (1998–99)

Academics
HWS awards bachelor's **degrees**. Challenging opportunities include advanced placement, accelerated degree programs, student-designed majors, an honors program, double majors, independent study, a senior project, and Phi Beta Kappa. Special programs include internships, off-campus study, and study-abroad.

The most frequently chosen fields are social sciences and history, English, and psychology. A complete listing of majors at HWS appears in the Majors Index beginning on page 432.

The **faculty** at HWS has 134 full-time members, 96% with terminal degrees. The student-faculty ratio is 13:1.

Students of HWS
The student body is made up of 1,830 undergraduates. 52.2% are women and 47.8% are men. Students come from 40 states and territories and 19 other countries. 50% are from New York. 1.5% are international students. 5.7% are African American, 0.2% American Indian, 2.1% Asian American, and 3.7% Hispanic American. 88% returned for their sophomore year.

Facilities and Resources
Student rooms are linked to a campus network. 146 **computers** are available on campus that provide access to the Internet. The 2 **libraries** have 340,185 books and 1,562 subscriptions.

Campus Life
There are 60 active organizations on campus, including a drama/theater group, newspaper, radio station, and choral group. 19% of eligible men are members of national **fraternities**.

HWS is a member of the NCAA (Division III). **Intercollegiate sports** include basketball, crew, cross-country running, field hockey (w), football (m), golf (m), ice hockey, lacrosse, rugby, sailing, skiing (downhill), soccer, squash, swimming (w), tennis.

Campus Safety
Student safety services include late-night transport/escort service, 24-hour emergency telephone alarm devices, 24-hour patrols by trained security personnel, and electronically operated dormitory entrances.

Applying
HWS requires an essay, SAT I or ACT, a high school transcript, and 2 recommendations. It recommends SAT II Subject Tests and an interview. Application deadline: 2/1; 3/15 for financial aid, with a 2/15 priority date. Early and deferred admission are possible.

Hofstra University

SUBURBAN SETTING ■ PRIVATE ■ INDEPENDENT ■ COED
HEMPSTEAD, NEW YORK

Web site: www.hofstra.edu
Contact: Ms. Mary Beth Carey, Executive Dean of Enrollment Management,
100 Hofstra University, Hempstead, NY 11549
Telephone: 516-463-6700 or toll-free 800-HOFSTRA **Fax:** 516-560-7660
E-mail: hofstra@hofstra.edu

Academics
Hofstra awards associate, bachelor's, master's, doctoral, and first-professional **degrees** and post-bachelor's certificates. Challenging opportunities include advanced placement, accelerated degree programs, student-designed majors, an honors program, double majors, independent study, a senior project, and Phi Beta Kappa. Special programs include internships, summer session for credit, study-abroad, and Army ROTC.

The most frequently chosen fields are business/marketing, psychology, and communications/communication technologies. A complete listing of majors at Hofstra appears in the Majors Index beginning on page 432.

The **faculty** at Hofstra has 489 full-time members, 88% with terminal degrees. The student-faculty ratio is 13:1.

Students of Hofstra
The student body totals 13,141, of whom 9,300 are undergraduates. 54.1% are women and 45.9% are men. Students come from 44 states and territories. 89% are from New York. 7.8% are African American, 0.2% American Indian, 4.5% Asian American, and 5.8% Hispanic American. 78% returned for their sophomore year.

Facilities and Resources
Student rooms are linked to a campus network. 350 **computers** are available on campus that provide access to the Internet. The 2 **libraries** have 1,400,000 books and 7,017 subscriptions.

Campus Life
There are 120 active organizations on campus, including a drama/theater group, newspaper, radio station, television station, and choral group. 10% of eligible men and 10% of eligible women are members of national **fraternities**, national **sororities**, local fraternities, and local sororities.

Hofstra is a member of the NCAA (Division I). **Intercollegiate sports** (some offering scholarships) include baseball (m), basketball, cross-country running, field hockey (w), football (m), golf (m), lacrosse, soccer, softball (w), tennis, volleyball (w), wrestling (m).

Campus Safety
Student safety services include security booths at each residence hall, late-night transport/escort service, 24-hour emergency telephone alarm devices, 24-hour patrols by trained security personnel, student patrols, and electronically operated dormitory entrances.

Applying
Hofstra requires SAT I or ACT, a high school transcript, and 1 recommendation, and in some cases an essay and an interview. It recommends SAT II Subject Tests. Application deadline: rolling admissions; 2/15 priority date for financial aid. Early and deferred admission are possible.

Founded in 1935, Hofstra University has grown to be recognized both nationally and internationally by its resources, academic offerings, accreditations, conferences, and cultural events. Hofstra's undergraduate education places great emphasis on the role of the student in the life of the University. Hofstra also offers graduate programs in business, education, liberal arts, and law. Students have easy access to the theater and cultural life of New York City yet have a learning environment on Long Island on a 240-acre campus that is also an accredited arboretum and museum.

Getting in Last Year
8,997 applied
82% were accepted
1,906 enrolled (26%)
12% from top tenth of their h.s. class
3.0 average high school GPA
21% had SAT verbal scores over 600
22% had SAT math scores over 600
54% had ACT scores over 24
3% had SAT verbal scores over 700
3% had SAT math scores over 700
7% had ACT scores over 30
17 valedictorians

Graduation and After
42% graduated in 4 years
16% graduated in 5 years
4% graduated in 6 years
190 organizations recruited on campus

Financial Matters
$14,512 tuition and fees (1999–2000)
$7060 room and board
$7839 average financial aid amount received
per undergraduate (1999–2000 estimated)

eAPPLY

Getting in Last Year
2,089 applied
89% were accepted
755 enrolled (41%)
37% from top tenth of their h.s. class
3.64 average high school GPA
41% had SAT verbal scores over 600
49% had SAT math scores over 600
10% had SAT verbal scores over 700
12% had SAT math scores over 700
15 National Merit Scholars
18 valedictorians

Graduation and After
52% graduated in 4 years
15% graduated in 5 years
2% graduated in 6 years
27% pursued further study (17% arts and
   sciences, 2% engineering, 2% law)
54 organizations recruited on campus

Financial Matters
$16,024 tuition and fees (1999–2000)
$5030 room and board
96% average percent of need met
$14,227 average financial aid amount received
   per undergraduate (1999–2000)

HOPE COLLEGE
SMALL-TOWN SETTING ■ PRIVATE ■ INDEPENDENT RELIGIOUS ■ COED
HOLLAND, MICHIGAN

Web site: www.hope.edu
Contact: Office of Admissions, 69 East 10th Street, PO Box 9000, Holland,
   MI 49422-9000
Telephone: 616-395-7850 or toll-free 800-968-7850 **Fax:** 616-395-7130
E-mail: admissions@hope.edu

Academics
Hope awards bachelor's **degrees**. Challenging opportunities include advanced place-ment, student-designed majors, double majors, a senior project, Phi Beta Kappa, and Sigma Xi. Special programs include internships, summer session for credit, off-campus study, and study-abroad.

The most frequently chosen fields are business/marketing, biological/life sciences, and English. A complete listing of majors at Hope appears in the Majors Index beginning on page 432.

The **faculty** at Hope has 204 full-time members, 82% with terminal degrees. The student-faculty ratio is 14:1.

Students of Hope
The student body is made up of 2,943 undergraduates. 59.8% are women and 40.2% are men. Students come from 36 states and territories and 27 other countries. 77% are from Michigan. 1.4% are international students. 0.9% are African American, 0.2% American Indian, 1.5% Asian American, and 1.5% Hispanic American. 87% returned for their sophomore year.

Facilities and Resources
Student rooms are linked to a campus network. 260 **computers** are available on campus that provide access to the Internet. The 2 **libraries** have 318,386 books and 1,945 subscriptions.

Campus Life
There are 67 active organizations on campus, including a drama/theater group, newspaper, radio station, and choral group. 9% of eligible men and 10% of eligible women are members of local **fraternities** and local **sororities**.

Hope is a member of the NCAA (Division III). **Intercollegiate sports** include baseball (m), basketball, cross-country running, football (m), golf, ice hockey (m), lacrosse (m), soccer, softball (w), swimming, tennis, track and field, volleyball, water polo.

Campus Safety
Student safety services include late-night transport/escort service, 24-hour emergency telephone alarm devices, 24-hour patrols by trained security personnel, and electroni-cally operated dormitory entrances.

Applying
Hope requires an essay, SAT I or ACT, and a high school transcript, and in some cases 1 recommendation. It recommends an interview. Application deadline: rolling admissions; 2/15 priority date for financial aid. Early and deferred admission are possible.

HOUGHTON COLLEGE

RURAL SETTING ■ PRIVATE ■ INDEPENDENT RELIGIOUS ■ COED
HOUGHTON, NEW YORK

Web site: www.houghton.edu
Contact: Mr. Timothy Fuller, Vice President for Enrollment, PO Box 128, Houghton, NY 14744
Telephone: 716-567-9353 or toll-free 800-777-2556 **Fax:** 716-567-9522
E-mail: admission@houghton.edu

Academics

Houghton awards associate and bachelor's **degrees**. Challenging opportunities include advanced placement, an honors program, double majors, independent study, and a senior project. Special programs include internships, summer session for credit, off-campus study, study-abroad, and Army ROTC.

The most frequently chosen fields are liberal arts/general studies, business/marketing, and education. A complete listing of majors at Houghton appears in the Majors Index beginning on page 432.

The **faculty** at Houghton has 78 full-time members, 85% with terminal degrees. The student-faculty ratio is 14:1.

Students of Houghton

The student body is made up of 1,380 undergraduates. 63% are women and 37% are men. Students come from 37 states and territories and 27 other countries. 64% are from New York. 4.6% are international students. 2.8% are African American, 0.5% American Indian, 0.7% Asian American, and 1% Hispanic American. 82% returned for their sophomore year.

Facilities and Resources

Student rooms are linked to a campus network. 130 **computers** are available on campus that provide access to the Internet. The **library** has 217,618 books and 3,027 subscriptions.

Campus Life

There are 50 active organizations on campus, including a drama/theater group, newspaper, radio station, and choral group. No national or local **fraternities** or **sororities**.

Houghton is a member of the NAIA. **Intercollegiate sports** (some offering scholarships) include basketball, cross-country running, field hockey (w), soccer, track and field, volleyball (w).

Campus Safety

Student safety services include phone connection to security patrols, late-night transport/escort service, 24-hour patrols by trained security personnel, and electronically operated dormitory entrances.

Applying

Houghton requires an essay, SAT I or ACT, a high school transcript, 1 recommendation, and pastoral recommendation. It recommends an interview and a minimum high school GPA of 2.5. Application deadline: rolling admissions; 3/1 priority date for financial aid. Early and deferred admission are possible.

Getting in Last Year

1,030 applied
89% were accepted
294 enrolled (32%)
35% from top tenth of their h.s. class
3.19 average high school GPA
46% had SAT verbal scores over 600
39% had SAT math scores over 600
63% had ACT scores over 24
9% had SAT verbal scores over 700
7% had SAT math scores over 700
13% had ACT scores over 30
8 class presidents
16 valedictorians

Graduation and After

48% graduated in 4 years
15% graduated in 5 years
2% graduated in 6 years
25% pursued further study
69% had job offers within 6 months
26 organizations recruited on campus

Financial Matters

$15,140 tuition and fees (2000–2001 estimated)
$5400 room and board
76% average percent of need met
$12,340 average financial aid amount received per undergraduate (1998–99)

ILLINOIS COLLEGE

SMALL-TOWN SETTING ■ PRIVATE ■ INDEPENDENT RELIGIOUS ■ COED
JACKSONVILLE, ILLINOIS

Web site: www.ic.edu
Contact: Gale Vaughn, Director of Enrollment, 1101 West College Avenue,
  Jacksonville, IL 62650-2299
Telephone: 217-245-3030 or toll-free 888-595-3030
E-mail: admissions@hilltop.ic.edu

Academics

IC awards bachelor's **degrees**. Challenging opportunities include advanced placement, accelerated degree programs, double majors, independent study, a senior project, and Phi Beta Kappa. Special programs include internships, summer session for credit, and study-abroad. A complete listing of majors at IC appears in the Majors Index beginning on page 432.

The **faculty** at IC has 55 full-time members. The student-faculty ratio is 14:1.

Students of IC

The student body is made up of 899 undergraduates. 55.6% are women and 44.4% are men. Students come from 14 states and territories and 5 other countries. 97% are from Illinois. 0.7% are international students. 2% are African American, 0.2% American Indian, 0.7% Asian American, and 0.9% Hispanic American. 93% returned for their sophomore year.

Facilities and Resources

Student rooms are linked to a campus network. 77 **computers** are available on campus that provide access to the Internet. The **library** has 143,500 books and 620 subscriptions.

Campus Life

There are 72 active organizations on campus, including a drama/theater group, newspaper, television station, and choral group. 17% of eligible men and 17% of eligible women are members of Greek literary societies.

IC is a member of the NCAA (Division III). **Intercollegiate sports** include baseball (m), basketball, cross-country running, football (m), golf, soccer, softball (w), tennis, track and field, volleyball (w), wrestling (m).

Campus Safety

Student safety services include late-night transport/escort service, 24-hour emergency telephone alarm devices, 24-hour patrols by trained security personnel, and electronically operated dormitory entrances.

Applying

IC requires SAT I or ACT, a high school transcript, and 2 recommendations, and in some cases an essay. It recommends an interview. Application deadline: 8/15; 4/15 priority date for financial aid. Early admission is possible.

Getting in Last Year
1,050 applied
77% were accepted
240 enrolled (30%)
21% from top tenth of their h.s. class
3.2 average high school GPA
22% had SAT verbal scores over 600
43% had SAT math scores over 600
42% had ACT scores over 24
7% had SAT math scores over 700
6% had ACT scores over 30
1 National Merit Scholar
12 valedictorians

Graduation and After
44% graduated in 4 years
12% graduated in 5 years
2% graduated in 6 years
Graduates pursuing further study: 5% business, 5% law, 3% dentistry

Financial Matters
$10,200 tuition and fees (1999–2000)
$4500 room and board
91% average percent of need met
$10,043 average financial aid amount received per undergraduate (1998–99)

ILLINOIS INSTITUTE OF TECHNOLOGY

URBAN SETTING ■ PRIVATE ■ INDEPENDENT ■ COED
CHICAGO, ILLINOIS

Web site: www.iit.edu
Contact: Mr. Terry Miller, Associate Dean of Undergrduate Admission, 10 West 33rd Street PH101, Chicago, IL 60616-3793
Telephone: 312-567-3025 or toll-free 800-448-2329 (out-of-state) **Fax:** 312-567-6939
E-mail: admission@iit.edu

Academics

IIT awards bachelor's, master's, doctoral, and first-professional **degrees** and post-bachelor's certificates. Challenging opportunities include advanced placement, accelerated degree programs, double majors, a senior project, and Sigma Xi. Special programs include cooperative education, internships, summer session for credit, study-abroad, and Army, Navy and Air Force ROTC.

The most frequently chosen fields are engineering/engineering technologies, architecture, and computer/information sciences. A complete listing of majors at IIT appears in the Majors Index beginning on page 432.

The **faculty** at IIT has 280 full-time members, 97% with terminal degrees. The student-faculty ratio is 12:1.

Students of IIT

The student body totals 6,062, of whom 1,706 are undergraduates. 25.6% are women and 74.4% are men. Students come from 48 states and territories and 50 other countries. 66% are from Illinois. 16.5% are international students. 7.8% are African American, 0.3% American Indian, 14.4% Asian American, and 7% Hispanic American. 84% returned for their sophomore year.

Facilities and Resources

Student rooms are linked to a campus network. 450 **computers** are available on campus that provide access to the Internet. The 6 **libraries** have 733,933 books and 3,500 subscriptions.

Campus Life

There are 75 active organizations on campus, including a drama/theater group, newspaper, and radio station. 15% of eligible men and 10% of eligible women are members of national **fraternities** and local **sororities**.

IIT is a member of the NAIA. **Intercollegiate sports** (some offering scholarships) include baseball (m), basketball, cross-country running, swimming, volleyball (w).

Campus Safety

Student safety services include late-night transport/escort service, 24-hour emergency telephone alarm devices, 24-hour patrols by trained security personnel, and electronically operated dormitory entrances.

Applying

IIT requires SAT I or ACT, a high school transcript, 1 recommendation, and a minimum high school GPA of 3.0, and in some cases an essay and an interview. It recommends SAT II Subject Tests. Application deadline: rolling admissions. Deferred admission is possible.

Located in the heart of Chicago, one of the world's great cities, IIT is an ideal place to study architecture, engineering, science, premed, and prelaw. Cutting-edge programs include architectural engineering and environmental engineering. IIT students get jobs! Faculty members are first-rate and accessible. Nobel Laureate Leon Lederman teaches freshman physics. Research, internship, and co-op opportunities abound. Athletics, clubs, and the recreational opportunities offered by a bowling alley and radio station are popular. On-campus housing is guaranteed. IIT offers need-based financial aid and a generous scholarship program.

Getting in Last Year
2,866 applied
65% were accepted
278 enrolled (15%)
52% from top tenth of their h.s. class
3.75 average high school GPA
69% had SAT verbal scores over 600
86% had SAT math scores over 600
87% had ACT scores over 24
21% had SAT verbal scores over 700
40% had SAT math scores over 700
30% had ACT scores over 30

Graduation and After
66% pursued further study
117 organizations recruited on campus

Financial Matters
$17,600 tuition and fees (1999–2000)
$5250 room and board
97% average percent of need met
$18,080 average financial aid amount received per undergraduate (1999–2000 estimated)

ILLINOIS WESLEYAN UNIVERSITY

SUBURBAN SETTING ■ PRIVATE ■ INDEPENDENT ■ COED
BLOOMINGTON, ILLINOIS

Web site: www.iwu.edu
Contact: Mr. James R. Ruoti, Dean of Admissions, PO Box 2900,
Bloomington, IL 61702-2900
Telephone: 309-556-3031 or toll-free 800-332-2498 **Fax:** 309-556-3411
E-mail: iwuadmit@titan.iwu.edu

Academics

IWU awards bachelor's **degrees**. Challenging opportunities include advanced placement, student-designed majors, an honors program, double majors, independent study, and Sigma Xi. Special programs include cooperative education, internships, summer session for credit, off-campus study, study-abroad, and Army ROTC.

The most frequently chosen fields are business/marketing, social sciences and history, and visual/performing arts. A complete listing of majors at IWU appears in the Majors Index beginning on page 432.

The **faculty** at IWU has 150 full-time members, 93% with terminal degrees. The student-faculty ratio is 13:1.

Students of IWU

The student body is made up of 2,091 undergraduates. 56.3% are women and 43.7% are men. Students come from 38 states and territories and 25 other countries. 88% are from Illinois. 2.2% are international students. 3.3% are African American, 3.6% Asian American, and 1.7% Hispanic American. 91% returned for their sophomore year.

Facilities and Resources

Student rooms are linked to a campus network. 445 **computers** are available on campus that provide access to the Internet. The **library** has 271,577 books and 11,577 subscriptions.

Campus Life

There are 130 active organizations on campus, including a drama/theater group, newspaper, radio station, television station, and choral group. 38% of eligible men and 32% of eligible women are members of national **fraternities** and national **sororities**.

IWU is a member of the NCAA (Division III). **Intercollegiate sports** include baseball (m), basketball, cross-country running, football (m), golf, sailing, soccer, softball (w), swimming, tennis, track and field, volleyball (w).

Campus Safety

Student safety services include student/administration security committee, late-night transport/escort service, 24-hour emergency telephone alarm devices, 24-hour patrols by trained security personnel, and student patrols.

Applying

IWU requires an essay, SAT I or ACT, a high school transcript, and a minimum high school GPA of 2.0. It recommends an interview, 3 recommendations, and a minimum high school GPA of 3.0. Application deadline: 3/1; 3/1 for financial aid. Early and deferred admission are possible.

Illinois Wesleyan University (IWU) students are encouraged to pursue multiple interests simultaneously—a philosophy in keeping with the spirit and value of a broad liberal arts education. A student majoring in music and biology put it this way: "At IWU, it's possible to double major and graduate in 4 years. Other campuses told me it would take 5 years." IWU is prepared for the 21st century, with a $23-million state-of-the-art library on the drawing board, renovated residence halls, and recent construction completed on a natural science center, an intercollegiate athletics and student recreation center, a student residence hall, and a Center for Liberal Arts.

Getting in Last Year
2,565 applied
64% were accepted
553 enrolled (34%)
46% from top tenth of their h.s. class
58% had SAT verbal scores over 600
67% had SAT math scores over 600
91% had ACT scores over 24
18% had SAT verbal scores over 700
21% had SAT math scores over 700
22% had ACT scores over 30
12 National Merit Scholars

Graduation and After
71% graduated in 4 years
5% graduated in 5 years
1% graduated in 6 years
28% pursued further study (18% arts and sciences, 4% law, 3% medicine)
68% had job offers within 6 months
76 organizations recruited on campus

Financial Matters
$20,410 tuition and fees (2000–2001)
$5150 room and board
99% average percent of need met
$15,664 average financial aid amount received per undergraduate (1999–2000 estimated)

Iowa State University of Science and Technology

Suburban setting ■ Public ■ State-supported ■ Coed
Ames, Iowa

Web site: www.iastate.edu
Contact: Mr. Phil Caffrey, Associate Director for Freshman Admissions, 100 Alumni Hall, Ames, IA 50011-2010
Telephone: 515-294-5836 or toll-free 800-262-3810 **Fax:** 515-294-2592
E-mail: admissions@iastate.edu

Academics
Iowa State awards bachelor's, master's, doctoral, and first-professional **degrees** and post-master's certificates. Challenging opportunities include advanced placement, accelerated degree programs, student-designed majors, freshman honors college, an honors program, double majors, independent study, a senior project, Phi Beta Kappa, and Sigma Xi. Special programs include cooperative education, internships, summer session for credit, off-campus study, study-abroad, and Army, Navy and Air Force ROTC.

The most frequently chosen fields are business/marketing, engineering/engineering technologies, and agriculture. A complete listing of majors at Iowa State appears in the Majors Index beginning on page 432.

The **faculty** at Iowa State has 1,435 full-time members, 94% with terminal degrees. The student-faculty ratio is 14:1.

Students of Iowa State
The student body totals 26,110, of whom 21,503 are undergraduates. 44.7% are women and 55.3% are men. Students come from 53 states and territories and 86 other countries. 83% are from Iowa. 4.9% are international students. 2.7% are African American, 0.4% American Indian, 2.5% Asian American, and 1.4% Hispanic American. 84% returned for their sophomore year.

Facilities and Resources
Student rooms are linked to a campus network. 2,400 **computers** are available on campus that provide access to e-mail, network services and the Internet. The 2 **libraries** have 2,167,294 books and 22,455 subscriptions.

Campus Life
There are 513 active organizations on campus, including a drama/theater group, newspaper, radio station, television station, choral group, and marching band. 16% of eligible men and 16% of eligible women are members of national **fraternities**, national **sororities**, local fraternities, and local sororities.

Iowa State is a member of the NCAA (Division I). **Intercollegiate sports** (some offering scholarships) include baseball (m), basketball, cross-country running, football (m), golf, gymnastics (w), soccer (w), softball (w), swimming, tennis (w), track and field, volleyball (w), wrestling (m).

Campus Safety
Student safety services include crime prevention programs, threat assessment team, motor vehicle help van, late-night transport/escort service, 24-hour emergency telephone alarm devices, 24-hour patrols by trained security personnel, student patrols, and electronically operated dormitory entrances.

Applying
Iowa State requires SAT I or ACT, a high school transcript, and rank in upper 50% of high school class. Application deadline: 8/21; 3/1 priority date for financial aid. Early and deferred admission are possible.

Iowa State has a national and international reputation for academic excellence, offering more than 100 majors in 7 undergraduate colleges. Known for technology (the first electronic digital computer and fax technology were both developed there), Iowa State was named one of the "most wired" college campuses—students have 24-hour access to more than 1,600 computer workstations, instant e-mail accounts, personal Web page space, and Internet access from every residence hall room. Out-of-class activities, leadership opportunities, and excellent job placement rates, together with a top-notch faculty and challenging in-class work, add up to an outstanding college experience.

Getting in Last Year
12,172 applied
88% were accepted
4,085 enrolled (38%)
25% from top tenth of their h.s. class
3.46 average high school GPA
48% had SAT verbal scores over 600
60% had SAT math scores over 600
57% had ACT scores over 24
19% had SAT verbal scores over 700
23% had SAT math scores over 700
11% had ACT scores over 30
116 National Merit Scholars

Graduation and After
22% graduated in 4 years
32% graduated in 5 years
7% graduated in 6 years
Graduates pursuing further study: 58% arts and sciences, 15% engineering, 7% medicine
76% had job offers within 6 months
1000 organizations recruited on campus

Financial Matters
$3132 resident tuition and fees (2000–2001)
$9974 nonresident tuition and fees (2000–2001)
$4171 room and board
100% average percent of need met
$6032 average financial aid amount received per undergraduate (1998–99)

JAMES MADISON UNIVERSITY

SMALL-TOWN SETTING ■ PUBLIC ■ STATE-SUPPORTED ■ COED
HARRISONBURG, VIRGINIA

Web site: www.jmu.edu
Contact: Ms. Laika Tamny, Associate Director of Admission, Office of Admission, Sonner Hall MSC 0101, Harrisonburg, VA 22807
Telephone: 540-568-6147 **Fax:** 540-568-3332
E-mail: gotojmu@jmu.edu

Getting in Last Year
12,980 applied
65% were accepted
3,039 enrolled (36%)
33% from top tenth of their h.s. class
3.53 average high school GPA
35% had SAT verbal scores over 600
42% had SAT math scores over 600
3% had SAT verbal scores over 700
4% had SAT math scores over 700

Graduation and After
62% graduated in 4 years
17% graduated in 5 years
1% graduated in 6 years
74% had job offers within 6 months
208 organizations recruited on campus

Financial Matters
$3926 resident tuition and fees (1999–2000)
$9532 nonresident tuition and fees (1999–2000)
$5182 room and board
74% average percent of need met
$5036 average financial aid amount received per undergraduate (1998–99)

Academics

JMU awards bachelor's, master's, and doctoral **degrees** (also offers specialist in education degree). Challenging opportunities include advanced placement, accelerated degree programs, freshman honors college, an honors program, double majors, independent study, and a senior project. Special programs include internships, summer session for credit, study-abroad, and Army ROTC.

The most frequently chosen fields are business/marketing, social sciences and history, and psychology. A complete listing of majors at JMU appears in the Majors Index beginning on page 432.

The **faculty** at JMU has 642 full-time members, 82% with terminal degrees. The student-faculty ratio is 18:1.

Students of JMU

The student body totals 15,223, of whom 14,156 are undergraduates. 57.1% are women and 42.9% are men. Students come from 49 states and territories and 51 other countries. 71% are from Virginia. 1.5% are international students. 4.8% are African American, 0.2% American Indian, 4.2% Asian American, and 1.7% Hispanic American. 90% returned for their sophomore year.

Facilities and Resources

Student rooms are linked to a campus network. 500 **computers** are available on campus that provide access to the Internet.

Campus Life

There are 270 active organizations on campus, including a drama/theater group, newspaper, radio station, choral group, and marching band. 14% of eligible men and 17% of eligible women are members of national **fraternities** and national **sororities**.

JMU is a member of the NCAA (Division I). **Intercollegiate sports** (some offering scholarships) include archery, baseball (m), basketball, cross-country running, fencing (w), field hockey (w), football (m), golf, gymnastics, lacrosse (w), soccer, swimming, tennis, track and field, volleyball (w), wrestling (m).

Campus Safety

Student safety services include lighted pathways, late-night transport/escort service, 24-hour emergency telephone alarm devices, 24-hour patrols by trained security personnel, student patrols, and electronically operated dormitory entrances.

Applying

JMU requires an essay, SAT I or ACT, a high school transcript, and English proficiency for international students, and in some cases SAT II Subject Tests. It recommends SAT I and a minimum high school GPA of 3.0. Application deadline: 1/15; 2/15 for financial aid.

JOHN BROWN UNIVERSITY

SMALL-TOWN SETTING ■ PRIVATE ■ INDEPENDENT RELIGIOUS ■ COED
SILOAM SPRINGS, ARKANSAS

Web site: www.jbu.edu
Contact: Ms. Karyn Byrne, Application Coordinator, 200 West University
Street, Siloam Springs, AR 72761-2121
Telephone: 501-524-7454 or toll-free 877-JBU-INFO **Fax:** 501-524-4196
E-mail: jbuinfo@acc.jbu.edu

eAPPLY

Academics

JBU awards associate, bachelor's, and master's **degrees**. Challenging opportunities
include advanced placement, freshman honors college, an honors program, double
majors, independent study, and a senior project. Special programs include internships,
study-abroad, and Army ROTC.

The most frequently chosen fields are business/marketing, education, and
philosophy. A complete listing of majors at JBU appears in the Majors Index beginning
on page 432.

The **faculty** at JBU has 77 full-time members, 68% with terminal degrees. The student-faculty ratio is 16:1.

Students of JBU

The student body totals 1,517, of whom 1,421 are undergraduates. 51.7% are women
and 48.3% are men. Students come from 43 states and territories and 33 other countries.
32% are from Arkansas. 8.8% are international students. 1.4% are African American,
0.9% American Indian, 0.6% Asian American, and 2.3% Hispanic American. 80%
returned for their sophomore year.

Facilities and Resources

Student rooms are linked to a campus network. 75 **computers** are available on campus
that provide access to the Internet. The 5 **libraries** have 93,190 books and 1,580
subscriptions.

Campus Life

There are 20 active organizations on campus, including a drama/theater group,
newspaper, radio station, television station, and choral group. No national or local
fraternities or **sororities**.

JBU is a member of the NAIA. **Intercollegiate sports** (some offering scholarships)
include basketball, soccer (m), swimming, tennis, volleyball (w).

Campus Safety

Student safety services include late-night transport/escort service, 24-hour emergency
telephone alarm devices, and 24-hour patrols by trained security personnel.

Applying

JBU requires an essay, SAT I or ACT, a high school transcript, 2 recommendations, and
a minimum high school GPA of 3.0. It recommends an interview. Application deadline:
3/1; 3/1 priority date for financial aid. Deferred admission is possible.

Getting in Last Year

629 applied
80% were accepted
271 enrolled (54%)
24% from top tenth of their h.s. class
3.49 average high school GPA
32% had SAT verbal scores over 600
36% had SAT math scores over 600
51% had ACT scores over 24
9% had SAT verbal scores over 700
8% had SAT math scores over 700
9% had ACT scores over 30
2 National Merit Scholars
11 class presidents
21 valedictorians

Graduation and After

31% graduated in 4 years
13% graduated in 5 years
3% graduated in 6 years
28% pursued further study (11% business,
9% education, 2% law)
84% had job offers within 6 months
50 organizations recruited on campus

Financial Matters

$11,492 tuition and fees (2000–2001)
$4478 room and board
60% average percent of need met
$9323 average financial aid amount received
per undergraduate (1999–2000)

John Carroll University

SUBURBAN SETTING ■ PRIVATE ■ INDEPENDENT RELIGIOUS ■ COED
UNIVERSITY HEIGHTS, OHIO

Web site: www.jcu.edu
Contact: Mr. Thomas P. Fanning, Director of Admission, 20700 North Park
Boulevard, University Heights, OH 44118-4581
Telephone: 216-397-4294 **Fax:** 216-397-3098
E-mail: admission@jcu.edu

John Carroll University, founded in 1886, is one of 28 Catholic colleges and universities operated in the United States by the Society of Jesus. In the Jesuit tradition of leadership, faith, and service, John Carroll provides its students with a rigorous education rooted in the liberal arts and focused on questions of moral and ethical values. John Carroll offers more than 85 student organizations, community volunteer service opportunities, and academic honor societies to foster leadership activities outside the classroom.

Getting in Last Year
2,612 applied
88% were accepted
834 enrolled (36%)
26% from top tenth of their h.s. class
3.27 average high school GPA
37% had SAT verbal scores over 600
39% had SAT math scores over 600
48% had ACT scores over 24
6% had SAT verbal scores over 700
4% had SAT math scores over 700
4% had ACT scores over 30
10 National Merit Scholars
34 valedictorians

Graduation and After
61% graduated in 4 years
13% graduated in 5 years
1% graduated in 6 years
27% pursued further study (19% arts and
sciences, 4% law, 2% medicine)
64% had job offers within 6 months
280 organizations recruited on campus
1 Fulbright scholar

Financial Matters
$16,384 tuition and fees (2000–2001)
$6128 room and board
88% average percent of need met
$13,230 average financial aid amount received
per undergraduate (1999–2000)

Academics
John Carroll awards bachelor's and master's **degrees**. Challenging opportunities include advanced placement, accelerated degree programs, student-designed majors, an honors program, double majors, independent study, and a senior project. Special programs include cooperative education, internships, summer session for credit, off-campus study, study-abroad, and Army ROTC.

The most frequently chosen fields are business/marketing, social sciences and history, and communications/communication technologies. A complete listing of majors at John Carroll appears in the Majors Index beginning on page 432.

The **faculty** at John Carroll has 234 full-time members, 86% with terminal degrees.

Students of John Carroll
The student body totals 4,389, of whom 3,527 are undergraduates. 52.8% are women and 47.2% are men. Students come from 34 states and territories and 17 other countries. 73% are from Ohio. 0.1% are international students. 3.8% are African American, 0.2% American Indian, 2.9% Asian American, and 1.9% Hispanic American. 88% returned for their sophomore year.

Facilities and Resources
Student rooms are linked to a campus network. 210 **computers** are available on campus that provide access to the Internet. The **library** has 606,000 books and 1,859 subscriptions.

Campus Life
There are 87 active organizations on campus, including a drama/theater group, newspaper, radio station, and choral group. 32% of eligible men and 35% of eligible women are members of local **fraternities** and local **sororities**.

John Carroll is a member of the NCAA (Division III). **Intercollegiate sports** include baseball (m), basketball, crew, football (m), golf (m), ice hockey (m), lacrosse, rugby, sailing, skiing (downhill), soccer, softball (w), swimming, tennis, track and field, volleyball, wrestling (m).

Campus Safety
Student safety services include late-night transport/escort service, 24-hour emergency telephone alarm devices, and 24-hour patrols by trained security personnel.

Applying
John Carroll requires SAT I or ACT, a high school transcript, and 1 recommendation, and in some cases an interview. It recommends an essay, SAT II Subject Tests, and an interview. Application deadline: 2/1; 3/1 priority date for financial aid. Early and deferred admission are possible.

Johns Hopkins University

URBAN SETTING ■ PRIVATE ■ INDEPENDENT ■ COED
BALTIMORE, MARYLAND

Web site: www.jhu.edu
Contact: Mr. Paul White, Director of Undergraduate Admissions, 140
Garland Hall, 3400 North Charles Street, Baltimore, MD 21218-2699
Telephone: 410-516-8171 **Fax:** 410-516-6025
E-mail: gotojhu@jhu.edu

Academics

Johns Hopkins awards bachelor's, master's, and doctoral **degrees**. Challenging opportunities include advanced placement, accelerated degree programs, student-designed majors, an honors program, double majors, independent study, a senior project, Phi Beta Kappa, and Sigma Xi. Special programs include cooperative education, internships, summer session for credit, off-campus study, study-abroad, and Army and Air Force ROTC. A complete listing of majors at Johns Hopkins appears in the Majors Index beginning on page 432.

The **faculty** at Johns Hopkins has 373 full-time members, 99% with terminal degrees. The student-faculty ratio is 10:1.

Students of Johns Hopkins

The student body totals 5,293, of whom 3,924 are undergraduates. 41.1% are women and 58.9% are men. Students come from 55 states and territories and 47 other countries. 14% are from Maryland. 8% are international students. 5.9% are African American, 0.1% American Indian, 18.6% Asian American, and 2.4% Hispanic American. 97% returned for their sophomore year.

Facilities and Resources

Student rooms are linked to a campus network. 405 **computers** are available on campus that provide access to the Internet. The 7 **libraries** have 6,769,920 books and 19,827 subscriptions.

Campus Life

There are 180 active organizations on campus, including a drama/theater group, newspaper, radio station, and choral group. 35% of eligible men and 40% of eligible women are members of national **fraternities** and national **sororities**.

Johns Hopkins is a member of the NCAA (Division III). **Intercollegiate sports** (some offering scholarships) include baseball (m), basketball, crew, cross-country running, fencing, field hockey (w), football (m), ice hockey (m), lacrosse, riflery, rugby (m), soccer, squash (w), swimming, tennis, track and field, volleyball (w), water polo, wrestling (m).

Campus Safety

Student safety services include late-night transport/escort service, 24-hour emergency telephone alarm devices, 24-hour patrols by trained security personnel, student patrols, and electronically operated dormitory entrances.

Applying

Johns Hopkins requires an essay, SAT II: Writing Test, SAT I and SAT II or ACT, a high school transcript, and 1 recommendation, and in some cases SAT II Subject Tests. It recommends an interview. Application deadline: 1/1; 2/15 for financial aid, with a 2/1 priority date. Early and deferred admission are possible.

The Krieger School of Arts and Sciences and the Whiting School of Engineering are the heart of a small but unusually diverse coeducational university. Johns Hopkins was founded in 1876 as the first true American university modeled after the European research university. With a favorable student-faculty ratio, most classes are small and give students an excellent opportunity for advanced studies and creative investigation.

Getting in Last Year
9,496 applied
33% were accepted
1,018 enrolled (32%)
73% from top tenth of their h.s. class
3.9 average high school GPA
84% had SAT verbal scores over 600
92% had SAT math scores over 600
96% had ACT scores over 24
42% had SAT verbal scores over 700
59% had SAT math scores over 700
54% had ACT scores over 30
48 National Merit Scholars
117 valedictorians

Graduation and After
84% graduated in 4 years
4% graduated in 5 years
1% graduated in 6 years
70% pursued further study (22% medicine, 13% arts and sciences, 13% engineering)
34% had job offers within 6 months
125 organizations recruited on campus

Financial Matters
$23,660 tuition and fees (1999–2000)
$7870 room and board
95% average percent of need met
$22,436 average financial aid amount received per undergraduate (1999–2000)

JUNIATA COLLEGE

SMALL-TOWN SETTING ■ PRIVATE ■ INDEPENDENT RELIGIOUS ■ COED
HUNTINGDON, PENNSYLVANIA

Web site: www.juniata.edu
Contact: Ms. Michelle Bartol, Director of Admissions, 1700 Moore Street,
    Huntingdon, PA 16652-2119
Telephone: 814-641-3432 or toll-free 877-JUNIATA **Fax:** 814-641-3100
E-mail: info@juniata.edu

Academics

Juniata awards bachelor's **degrees**. Challenging opportunities include advanced placement, student-designed majors, freshman honors college, an honors program, double
majors, and independent study. Special programs include internships, summer session for
credit, off-campus study, and study-abroad.

The most frequently chosen fields are education, biological/life sciences, and social
sciences and history. A complete listing of majors at Juniata appears in the Majors Index
beginning on page 432.

The **faculty** at Juniata has 86 full-time members, 92% with terminal degrees. The
student-faculty ratio is 13:1.

Students of Juniata

The student body is made up of 1,268 undergraduates. 55.8% are women and 44.2% are
men. Students come from 32 states and territories and 21 other countries. 76% are from
Pennsylvania. 3% are international students. 0.6% are African American, 0.2% American
Indian, 1% Asian American, and 0.6% Hispanic American. 86% returned for their
sophomore year.

Facilities and Resources

Student rooms are linked to a campus network. 150 **computers** are available on campus
that provide access to the Internet. The **library** has 208,000 books and 1,000 subscriptions.

Campus Life

There are 65 active organizations on campus, including a drama/theater group,
newspaper, radio station, and choral group. No national or local **fraternities** or **sororities**.

Juniata is a member of the NCAA (Division III). **Intercollegiate sports** include
baseball (m), basketball, cross-country running, equestrian sports, field hockey (w),
football (m), golf, lacrosse, rugby, skiing (downhill), soccer, softball (w), swimming (w),
tennis (w), track and field, volleyball, wrestling.

Campus Safety

Student safety services include late-night transport/escort service, 24-hour emergency
telephone alarm devices, 24-hour patrols by trained security personnel, and student
patrols.

Applying

Juniata requires an essay, SAT I or ACT, a high school transcript, 1 recommendation,
and a minimum high school GPA of 3.0. It recommends an interview. Application
deadline: 3/15; 3/1 priority date for financial aid. Early and deferred admission are possible.

Students who can be described as intelligent, independent, creative, determined, friendly, active, or unique; students who rise to academic challenges; those who are intrigued by environments rich with lakes, mountains, fresh air, and natural beauty; those who are hungry to discover who they are and what they are capable of—these students owe it to themselves to consider Juniata College. At Juniata, students will have the opportunity to explore their interests and prepare for a useful life and a successful career. Juniata's traditions include excellence in academics, small classes, a close-knit community, a familylike atmosphere, and many surprises, including Mountain Day.

Getting in Last Year
1,133 applied
85% were accepted
327 enrolled (34%)
37% from top tenth of their h.s. class
3.63 average high school GPA
32% had SAT verbal scores over 600
39% had SAT math scores over 600
5% had SAT verbal scores over 700
6% had SAT math scores over 700
10 valedictorians

Graduation and After
62% graduated in 4 years
5% graduated in 5 years
1% graduated in 6 years
33% pursued further study (19% arts and
  sciences, 4% business, 4% medicine)
64% had job offers within 6 months
17 organizations recruited on campus

Financial Matters
$19,360 tuition and fees (2000–2001)
$5290 room and board
97% average percent of need met
$16,697 average financial aid amount received
  per undergraduate (1999–2000)

Kalamazoo College

SUBURBAN SETTING ■ PRIVATE ■ INDEPENDENT RELIGIOUS ■ COED
KALAMAZOO, MICHIGAN

Web site: www.kzoo.edu
Contact: Mrs. Munselle Pientka, Records Manager, Mandelle Hall, 1200
Academy Street, Kalamazoo, MI 49006-3295
Telephone: 616-337-7166 or toll-free 800-253-3602
E-mail: admission@kzoo.edu

eAPPLY

Academics

K-College awards bachelor's **degrees**. Challenging opportunities include advanced placement, double majors, independent study, a senior project, Phi Beta Kappa, and Sigma Xi. Special programs include cooperative education, internships, off-campus study, study-abroad, and Army ROTC.

The most frequently chosen fields are biological/life sciences, social sciences and history, and business/marketing. A complete listing of majors at K-College appears in the Majors Index beginning on page 432.

The **faculty** at K-College has 90 full-time members, 90% with terminal degrees. The student-faculty ratio is 14:1.

Students of K-College

The student body is made up of 1,367 undergraduates. Students come from 42 states and territories and 14 other countries. 70% are from Michigan. 1.7% are international students. 3.3% are African American, 0.1% American Indian, 4.5% Asian American, and 1.5% Hispanic American. 89% returned for their sophomore year.

Facilities and Resources

Student rooms are linked to a campus network. 80 **computers** are available on campus that provide access to the Internet. The 2 **libraries** have 305,874 books and 1,311 subscriptions.

Campus Life

There are 50 active organizations on campus, including a drama/theater group, newspaper, radio station, and choral group. No national or local **fraternities** or **sororities**.

K-College is a member of the NCAA (Division III). **Intercollegiate sports** include baseball (m), basketball, cross-country running, football (m), golf, soccer, softball (w), swimming, tennis, volleyball (w).

Campus Safety

Student safety services include late-night transport/escort service, 24-hour emergency telephone alarm devices, 24-hour patrols by trained security personnel, and electronically operated dormitory entrances.

Applying

K-College requires an essay, SAT I or ACT, a high school transcript, and 2 recommendations. It recommends an interview and a minimum high school GPA of 3.0. Application deadline: 2/1; 2/15 priority date for financial aid. Deferred admission is possible.

Getting in Last Year
1,410 applied
77% were accepted
370 enrolled (34%)
47% from top tenth of their h.s. class
3.69 average high school GPA
64% had SAT verbal scores over 600
59% had SAT math scores over 600
92% had ACT scores over 24
17% had SAT verbal scores over 700
12% had SAT math scores over 700
24% had ACT scores over 30
10 National Merit Scholars
20 valedictorians

Graduation and After
37% pursued further study (6% medicine, 4% arts and sciences, 2% law)
23 organizations recruited on campus

Financial Matters
$19,188 tuition and fees (1999–2000)
$5787 room and board
$15,408 average financial aid amount received per undergraduate (1999–2000)

Getting in Last Year
618 applied
84% were accepted
194 enrolled (37%)
37% from top tenth of their h.s. class
3.36 average high school GPA
17% had SAT verbal scores over 600
21% had SAT math scores over 600
34% had ACT scores over 24
4% had SAT verbal scores over 700
4% had SAT math scores over 700
4% had ACT scores over 30
1 National Merit Scholar
10 valedictorians

Graduation and After
31% graduated in 4 years
4% graduated in 5 years
30% pursued further study (15% arts and sciences, 4% business, 4% medicine)
97% had job offers within 6 months
16 organizations recruited on campus

Financial Matters
$10,020 tuition and fees (1999–2000)
$4770 room and board

KENTUCKY WESLEYAN COLLEGE
SUBURBAN SETTING ■ PRIVATE ■ INDEPENDENT RELIGIOUS ■ COED
OWENSBORO, KENTUCKY

Web site: www.kwc.edu
Contact: Mr. Pat Fawcett, Dean of Admission, 3000 Frederica Street, PO Box 1039, Owensboro, KY 42302-1039
Telephone: 270-926-3111 ext. 5145 or toll-free 800-999-0592 (in-state), 270-999-0592 (out-of-state) **Fax:** 502-926-3196
E-mail: admission@kwc.edu

Academics
Kentucky Wesleyan awards bachelor's **degrees**. Challenging opportunities include advanced placement, student-designed majors, double majors, independent study, and a senior project. Special programs include internships, summer session for credit, off-campus study, and study-abroad.

The most frequently chosen fields are business/marketing, health professions and related sciences, and education. A complete listing of majors at Kentucky Wesleyan appears in the Majors Index beginning on page 432.

The **faculty** at Kentucky Wesleyan has 44 full-time members. The student-faculty ratio is 15:1.

Students of Kentucky Wesleyan
The student body is made up of 747 undergraduates. 57% are women and 43% are men. Students come from 8 states and territories and 6 other countries. 1.3% are international students. 4.8% are African American. 74% returned for their sophomore year.

Facilities and Resources
Student rooms are linked to a campus network. 55 **computers** are available on campus that provide access to the Internet. The **library** has 74,066 books and 462 subscriptions.

Campus Life
There are 40 active organizations on campus, including a drama/theater group, newspaper, radio station, and choral group. 14% of eligible men and 33% of eligible women are members of national **fraternities** and national **sororities**.

Kentucky Wesleyan is a member of the NCAA (Division II). **Intercollegiate sports** (some offering scholarships) include baseball (m), basketball, football (m), golf, soccer, softball (w), tennis, volleyball (w).

Campus Safety
Student safety services include 12-hour patrols by trained security personnel and late-night transport/escort service.

Applying
Kentucky Wesleyan requires an essay, SAT I or ACT, and a high school transcript, and in some cases recommendations. It recommends recommendations. Application deadline: 8/21; 3/1 priority date for financial aid. Early and deferred admission are possible.

KENYON COLLEGE

RURAL SETTING ■ PRIVATE ■ INDEPENDENT ■ COED
GAMBIER, OHIO

Web site: www.kenyon.edu
Contact: Mr. John W. Anderson, Dean of Admissions, Office of Admissions, Gambier, OH 43022-9623
Telephone: 740-427-5776 or toll-free 800-848-2468 **Fax:** 740-427-5770
E-mail: admissions@kenyon.edu

 eAPPLY

Academics

Kenyon awards bachelor's **degrees**. Challenging opportunities include advanced placement, accelerated degree programs, student-designed majors, an honors program, double majors, independent study, a senior project, and Phi Beta Kappa. Special programs include internships, off-campus study, and study-abroad.

The most frequently chosen fields are social sciences and history, English, and psychology. A complete listing of majors at Kenyon appears in the Majors Index beginning on page 432.

The **faculty** at Kenyon has 131 full-time members, 96% with terminal degrees. The student-faculty ratio is 11:1.

Students of Kenyon

The student body is made up of 1,588 undergraduates. 55.9% are women and 44.1% are men. Students come from 48 states and territories. 22% are from Ohio. 1% are international students. 3.8% are African American, 3.4% Asian American, and 2.8% Hispanic American. 91% returned for their sophomore year.

Facilities and Resources

Student rooms are linked to a campus network. 225 **computers** are available on campus that provide access to commercial databases and the Internet. The 2 **libraries** have 362,474 books and 2,590 subscriptions.

Campus Life

There are 136 active organizations on campus, including a drama/theater group, newspaper, radio station, and choral group. 37% of eligible men and 3% of eligible women are members of national **fraternities**, national **sororities**, local fraternities, and local sororities.

Kenyon is a member of the NCAA (Division III). **Intercollegiate sports** include baseball (m), basketball, cross-country running, field hockey (w), football (m), golf (m), lacrosse, soccer, softball (w), swimming, tennis, track and field, volleyball (w).

Campus Safety

Student safety services include late-night transport/escort service, 24-hour emergency telephone alarm devices, 24-hour patrols by trained security personnel, and student patrols.

Applying

Kenyon requires an essay, SAT I or ACT, a high school transcript, 1 recommendation, and a minimum high school GPA of 2.0. It recommends an interview and a minimum high school GPA of 3.0. Application deadline: 2/1; 2/15 for financial aid. Early and deferred admission are possible.

Getting in Last Year
2,420 applied
68% were accepted
459 enrolled (28%)
50% from top tenth of their h.s. class
3.63 average high school GPA
80% had SAT verbal scores over 600
65% had SAT math scores over 600
92% had ACT scores over 24
36% had SAT verbal scores over 700
21% had SAT math scores over 700
40% had ACT scores over 30
34 National Merit Scholars
1 class president
24 valedictorians

Graduation and After
77% graduated in 4 years
5% graduated in 5 years
25% pursued further study (10% arts and sciences, 5% law, 3% medicine)
89% had job offers within 6 months
65 organizations recruited on campus

Financial Matters
$24,590 tuition and fees (1999–2000)
$4160 room and board
96% average percent of need met
$18,626 average financial aid amount received per undergraduate (1998–99)

KETTERING UNIVERSITY

SUBURBAN SETTING ■ PRIVATE ■ INDEPENDENT ■ COED
FLINT, MICHIGAN

Web site: www.kettering.edu
Contact: Mr. Rawlan Lillard II, Director of Admissions, 1700 West Third
Avenue, Flint, MI 48504-4898
Telephone: 810-762-7865 or toll-free 800-955-4464 ext. 7865 (in-state),
800-955-4464 (out-of-state) **Fax:** 810-762-9837
E-mail: admissions@kettering.edu

Academics

Kettering/GMI awards bachelor's and master's **degrees**. Challenging opportunities
include advanced placement, accelerated degree programs, double majors, independent
study, and a senior project. Special programs include cooperative education, internships,
and study-abroad.

The most frequently chosen fields are engineering/engineering technologies, busi-
ness/marketing, and mathematics. A complete listing of majors at Kettering/GMI appears in the Majors Index beginning on page 432.

The **faculty** at Kettering/GMI has 139 full-time members, 83% with terminal
degrees. The student-faculty ratio is 9:1.

Students of Kettering/GMI

The student body totals 3,166, of whom 2,553 are undergraduates. Students come from
48 states and territories and 18 other countries. 60% are from Michigan. 5.5% are international students. 6.9% are African American, 0.2% American Indian, 4.3% Asian
American, and 1.6% Hispanic American. 85% returned for their sophomore year.

Facilities and Resources

Student rooms are linked to a campus network. 300 **computers** are available on campus
that provide access to the Internet. The 2 **libraries** have 94,738 books and 540 subscriptions.

Campus Life

There are 40 active organizations on campus, including a drama/theater group,
newspaper, radio station, and choral group. 50% of eligible men and 50% of eligible
women are members of national **fraternities** and national **sororities**.

Intercollegiate sports include ice hockey (m), soccer (m), volleyball (m).

Campus Safety

Student safety services include late-night transport/escort service, 24-hour emergency
telephone alarm devices, 24-hour patrols by trained security personnel, and electronically operated dormitory entrances.

Applying

Kettering/GMI requires an essay, SAT I or ACT, a high school transcript, and a
minimum high school GPA of 3.0. It recommends SAT II Subject Tests and an interview.
Application deadline: rolling admissions; 2/14 priority date for financial aid. Deferred
admission is possible.

Kettering University,
formerly GMI Engineering
and Management Institute,
is America's premier co-op
university. Kettering University
continues the long tradition of
academic excellence in engineering,
science, math, and business
management. Kettering's goal is to
provide students with top-notch
classroom instruction and
career-directed co-op work
experience in business and industry,
giving students the opportunity for
a head start in a career. The unique
5-year, fully cooperative education
program has students alternating
12-week academic terms on campus
with 12-week terms of paid work
experience with a co-op employer.
With a placement rate of nearly
100%, Kettering University
graduates are in high demand at
America's leading corporations and
have the credentials for admittance
into the nation's top graduate and
professional schools.

Getting in Last Year
1,616 applied
75% were accepted
525 enrolled (43%)
33% from top tenth of their h.s. class
3.50 average high school GPA
42% had SAT verbal scores over 600
70% had SAT math scores over 600
75% had ACT scores over 24
9% had SAT verbal scores over 700
19% had SAT math scores over 700
12% had ACT scores over 30
18 valedictorians

Graduation and After
33% pursued further study (17% business,
 10% engineering, 4% arts and sciences)
98% had job offers within 6 months
550 organizations recruited on campus

Financial Matters
$14,775 tuition and fees (1999–2000)
$4020 room and board
76% average percent of need met
$5465 average financial aid amount received
 per undergraduate (1999–2000 estimated)

King College

SUBURBAN SETTING ■ PRIVATE ■ INDEPENDENT RELIGIOUS ■ COED
BRISTOL, TENNESSEE

Web site: www.king.edu
Contact: Ms. Mindy Clark, Director of Admissions, 1350 King College Road, Bristol, TN 37620-2699
Telephone: 423-652-4861 or toll-free 800-362-0014 **Fax:** 423-652-4727
E-mail: admissions@king.edu

Academics

King awards bachelor's **degrees**. Challenging opportunities include advanced placement, accelerated degree programs, an honors program, double majors, independent study, and a senior project. Special programs include internships, summer session for credit, off-campus study, study-abroad, and Army ROTC.

The most frequently chosen fields are social sciences and history, English, and biological/life sciences. A complete listing of majors at King appears in the Majors Index beginning on page 432.

The **faculty** at King has 36 full-time members, 69% with terminal degrees. The student-faculty ratio is 10:1.

Students of King

The student body is made up of 587 undergraduates. 59.5% are women and 40.5% are men. Students come from 27 states and territories and 29 other countries. 43% are from Tennessee. 7.5% are international students. 2.3% are African American, 0.4% Asian American, and 1% Hispanic American. 74% returned for their sophomore year.

Facilities and Resources

Student rooms are linked to a campus network. 50 **computers** are available on campus that provide access to the Internet. The **library** has 95,136 books and 605 subscriptions.

Campus Life

There are 29 active organizations on campus, including a drama/theater group, newspaper, and choral group. No national or local **fraternities** or **sororities**. King is a member of the NAIA. **Intercollegiate sports** (some offering scholarships) include baseball (m), basketball, golf (m), soccer, tennis, volleyball (w).

Campus Safety

Student safety services include late-night transport/escort service.

Applying

King requires an essay, SAT I or ACT, a high school transcript, and a minimum high school GPA of 2.4, and in some cases an interview and recommendations. It recommends an interview and recommendations. Application deadline: rolling admissions; 3/1 priority date for financial aid. Early and deferred admission are possible.

Getting in Last Year
428 applied
79% were accepted
133 enrolled (39%)
34% from top tenth of their h.s. class
3.19 average high school GPA
32% had SAT verbal scores over 600
29% had SAT math scores over 600
39% had ACT scores over 24
9% had SAT verbal scores over 700
8% had SAT math scores over 700
6% had ACT scores over 30

Graduation and After
31% graduated in 4 years
8% graduated in 5 years
1% graduated in 6 years
31% pursued further study
65% had job offers within 6 months
15 organizations recruited on campus

Financial Matters
$10,750 tuition and fees (1999–2000)
$3850 room and board
77% average percent of need met
$11,005 average financial aid amount received per undergraduate (1999–2000)

KNOX COLLEGE

SMALL-TOWN SETTING ■ PRIVATE ■ INDEPENDENT ■ COED
GALESBURG, ILLINOIS

Web site: www.knox.edu
Contact: Mr. Paul Steenis, Director of Admissions, Admission Office, Box K-148, Galesburg, IL 61401
Telephone: 309-341-7100 or toll-free 800-678-KNOX **Fax:** 309-341-7070
E-mail: admission@knox.edu

For more than 150 years, Knox College has offered students the chance to work closely with distinguished teachers. Knox provides a superior liberal arts program with special strengths in the sciences and creative arts. A college of exceptional diversity, Knox enjoys an open, easygoing campus culture that allows students to take charge of their own lives and to flourish; students can go anywhere with a Knox degree. Knox is eleventh among liberal arts colleges in the percentage of graduates who earn math/science PhDs and thirtieth in the percentage of graduates who become business executives.

Getting in Last Year
1,357 applied
75% were accepted
300 enrolled (30%)
46% from top tenth of their h.s. class
59% had SAT verbal scores over 600
55% had SAT math scores over 600
76% had ACT scores over 24
20% had SAT verbal scores over 700
14% had SAT math scores over 700
21% had ACT scores over 30
8 National Merit Scholars
10 valedictorians

Graduation and After
64% graduated in 4 years
3% graduated in 5 years
2% graduated in 6 years
35% pursued further study (20% arts and sciences, 6% medicine, 5% law)
61% had job offers within 6 months
68 organizations recruited on campus

Financial Matters
$21,174 tuition and fees (2000–2001)
$5436 room and board
100% average percent of need met
$17,686 average financial aid amount received per undergraduate (1999–2000 estimated)

Academics

Knox awards bachelor's **degrees.** Challenging opportunities include advanced placement, student-designed majors, an honors program, double majors, independent study, a senior project, Phi Beta Kappa, and Sigma Xi. Special programs include internships, off-campus study, and study-abroad.

The most frequently chosen fields are social sciences and history, biological/life sciences, and visual/performing arts. A complete listing of majors at Knox appears in the Majors Index beginning on page 432.

The **faculty** at Knox has 99 full-time members, 92% with terminal degrees. The student-faculty ratio is 12:1.

Students of Knox

The student body is made up of 1,220 undergraduates. 55.2% are women and 44.8% are men. Students come from 47 states and territories and 40 other countries. 56% are from Illinois. 11.1% are international students. 3.3% are African American, 0.5% American Indian, 5.2% Asian American, and 3.2% Hispanic American. 88% returned for their sophomore year.

Facilities and Resources

Student rooms are linked to a campus network. 130 **computers** are available on campus that provide access to software applications and the Internet. The 3 **libraries** have 169,661 books.

Campus Life

There are 75 active organizations on campus, including a drama/theater group, newspaper, radio station, and choral group. 33% of eligible men and 12% of eligible women are members of national **fraternities** and national **sororities.**

Knox is a member of the NCAA (Division III). **Intercollegiate sports** include baseball (m), basketball, cross-country running, football (m), golf, soccer, softball (w), swimming, tennis, track and field, volleyball (w), wrestling (m).

Campus Safety

Student safety services include late-night transport/escort service, 24-hour emergency telephone alarm devices, and 24-hour patrols by trained security personnel.

Applying

Knox requires an essay, SAT I or ACT, a high school transcript, and 2 recommendations. It recommends an interview. Application deadline: 2/15; 3/1 priority date for financial aid. Early and deferred admission are possible.

LAFAYETTE COLLEGE

SUBURBAN SETTING ■ PRIVATE ■ INDEPENDENT RELIGIOUS ■ COED
EASTON, PENNSYLVANIA

Web site: www.lafayette.edu
Contact: Ms. Carol Rowlands, Director of Admissions, Easton, PA
  18042-1798
Telephone: 610-330-5100 **Fax:** 610-330-5355
E-mail: admissions@lafayette.edu

  eAPPLY

Academics

Lafayette awards bachelor's **degrees**. Challenging opportunities include advanced placement, accelerated degree programs, student-designed majors, an honors program, Phi Beta Kappa, and Sigma Xi. Special programs include internships, summer session for credit, off-campus study, study-abroad, and Army ROTC.

The most frequently chosen fields are social sciences and history, engineering/engineering technologies, and biological/life sciences. A complete listing of majors at Lafayette appears in the Majors Index beginning on page 432.

The **faculty** at Lafayette has 183 full-time members, 99% with terminal degrees. The student-faculty ratio is 11:1.

Students of Lafayette

The student body is made up of 2,283 undergraduates. 48.1% are women and 51.9% are men. Students come from 41 states and territories and 53 other countries. 29% are from Pennsylvania. 2.8% are international students. 2.7% are African American, 0.2% American Indian, 0.9% Asian American, and 1.1% Hispanic American. 93% returned for their sophomore year.

Facilities and Resources

Student rooms are linked to a campus network. 400 **computers** are available on campus that provide access to the Internet. The 2 **libraries** have 494,000 books and 1,837 subscriptions.

Campus Life

There are 200 active organizations on campus, including a drama/theater group, newspaper, radio station, and choral group. 36% of eligible men and 70% of eligible women are members of national **fraternities**, national **sororities**, and social dorms.

Lafayette is a member of the NCAA (Division I). **Intercollegiate sports** include baseball (m), basketball, crew, cross-country running, equestrian sports, fencing, field hockey (w), football (m), golf (m), ice hockey (m), lacrosse, rugby, skiing (downhill), soccer, softball (w), squash (m), swimming, tennis, track and field, volleyball (w), weight lifting, wrestling (m).

Campus Safety

Student safety services include late-night transport/escort service, 24-hour emergency telephone alarm devices, 24-hour patrols by trained security personnel, student patrols, and electronically operated dormitory entrances.

Applying

Lafayette requires an essay, SAT I, SAT II Subject Tests, a high school transcript, and 1 recommendation. It recommends SAT II: Writing Test and an interview. Application deadline: 1/1; 2/1 for financial aid. Early and deferred admission are possible.

Lafayette College has achieved a unique niche in American higher education: liberal arts and engineering programs in a small-college setting. Lafayette offers small classes, interdisciplinary first-year seminars, and student-faculty collaborative research on a residential campus located in eastern Pennsylvania close to New York and Philadelphia.

Getting in Last Year
4,429 applied
48% were accepted
582 enrolled (27%)
51% from top tenth of their h.s. class
55% had SAT verbal scores over 600
75% had SAT math scores over 600
11% had SAT verbal scores over 700
20% had SAT math scores over 700
4 National Merit Scholars

Graduation and After
78% graduated in 4 years
4% graduated in 5 years
Graduates pursuing further study: 12% arts and sciences, 8% engineering, 6% law
250 organizations recruited on campus

Financial Matters
$22,929 tuition and fees (1999–2000)
$7106 room and board
95% average percent of need met
$19,556 average financial aid amount received per undergraduate (1999–2000)

eAPPLY

LAKE FOREST COLLEGE

SUBURBAN SETTING ■ PRIVATE ■ INDEPENDENT ■ COED
LAKE FOREST, ILLINOIS

Web site: www.lfc.edu
Contact: Mr. William G. Motzer Jr., Director of Admissions, 555 North
 Sheridan Road, Lake Forest, IL 60045-2399
Telephone: 847-735-5000 or toll-free 800-828-4751 **Fax:** 847-735-6271
E-mail: admissions@lfc.edu

Lake Forest College is situated in the remarkably beautiful community of Lake Forest, Illinois' safest city, with a population of more than 5,000. Chicago is located just 30 miles south of the campus, where students enhance their liberal arts education through the world-renowned resources of this great city. Over 80% of LFC students strengthen their education through domestic and international internships, practicums, and the College's extensive study-abroad program. On campus, the distinguished faculty offers students high-quality teaching and the unique opportunity to conduct independent research. Students enjoy the tree-lined campus near the shore of Lake Michigan.

Academics

Lake Forest awards bachelor's and master's **degrees**. Challenging opportunities include advanced placement, accelerated degree programs, student-designed majors, freshman honors college, an honors program, double majors, independent study, a senior project, Phi Beta Kappa, and Sigma Xi. Special programs include internships, summer session for credit, off-campus study, and study-abroad.

The most frequently chosen fields are social sciences and history, business/marketing, and interdisciplinary studies. A complete listing of majors at Lake Forest appears in the Majors Index beginning on page 432.

The **faculty** at Lake Forest has 81 full-time members, 94% with terminal degrees. The student-faculty ratio is 12:1.

Students of Lake Forest

The student body totals 1,254, of whom 1,241 are undergraduates. 57.4% are women and 42.6% are men. Students come from 44 states and territories and 46 other countries. 50% are from Illinois. 7.1% are international students. 6.4% are African American, 0.3% American Indian, 4.6% Asian American, and 3.1% Hispanic American. 74% returned for their sophomore year.

Facilities and Resources

Student rooms are linked to a campus network. 120 **computers** are available on campus that provide access to the Internet. The 2 **libraries** have 285,006 books and 1,111 subscriptions.

Campus Life

There are 103 active organizations on campus, including a drama/theater group, newspaper, radio station, and choral group. 18% of eligible men and 14% of eligible women are members of national **fraternities**, local fraternities, and local **sororities**.

Lake Forest is a member of the NCAA (Division III). **Intercollegiate sports** include baseball (m), basketball, cross-country running, fencing, football (m), ice hockey, lacrosse, rugby (m), soccer, softball (w), swimming, tennis, volleyball, water polo (m).

Campus Safety

Student safety services include late-night transport/escort service, 24-hour emergency telephone alarm devices, 24-hour patrols by trained security personnel, and student patrols.

Applying

Lake Forest requires an essay, SAT I or ACT, a high school transcript, 2 recommendations, and graded paper. It recommends an interview. Application deadline: 3/1; 3/1 priority date for financial aid. Early and deferred admission are possible.

Getting in Last Year
1,296 applied
77% were accepted
341 enrolled (34%)
24% from top tenth of their h.s. class
3.3 average high school GPA
37% had SAT verbal scores over 600
33% had SAT math scores over 600
61% had ACT scores over 24
7% had SAT verbal scores over 700
4% had SAT math scores over 700
8% had ACT scores over 30
1 National Merit Scholar
17 class presidents
6 valedictorians

Graduation and After
55% graduated in 4 years
8% graduated in 5 years
21% pursued further study (8% arts and sciences, 5% law, 3% medicine)
89% had job offers within 6 months
79 organizations recruited on campus
1 Fulbright scholar

Financial Matters
$21,190 tuition and fees (2000–2001)
$5000 room and board
100% average percent of need met
$17,152 average financial aid amount received per undergraduate (1999–2000 estimated)

La Salle University

URBAN SETTING ■ PRIVATE ■ INDEPENDENT RELIGIOUS ■ COED
PHILADELPHIA, PENNSYLVANIA

Web site: www.lasalle.edu
Contact: Mr. Robert G. Voss, Acting Dean of Admission and Financial Aid,
1900 West Olney Avenue, Philadelphia, PA 19141-1199
Telephone: 215-951-1500 or toll-free 800-328-1910 **Fax:** 215-951-1656
E-mail: admiss@lasalle.edu

eApply

Academics

La Salle awards associate, bachelor's, master's, and doctoral **degrees**. Challenging
opportunities include advanced placement, accelerated degree programs, student-
designed majors, freshman honors college, an honors program, double majors,
independent study, and a senior project. Special programs include cooperative education,
internships, summer session for credit, off-campus study, and Army and Air Force
ROTC. A complete listing of majors at La Salle appears in the Majors Index beginning
on page 432.

The **faculty** at La Salle has 182 full-time members. The student-faculty ratio is 17:1.

Students of La Salle

The student body totals 5,655, of whom 3,970 are undergraduates. 57.1% are women
and 42.9% are men. Students come from 29 states and territories. 68% are from
Pennsylvania. 0.6% are international students. 12% are African American, 0.1%
American Indian, 2.6% Asian American, and 4.5% Hispanic American. 89% returned for
their sophomore year.

Facilities and Resources

Student rooms are linked to a campus network. 350 **computers** are available on campus
that provide access to the Internet. The **library** has 365,000 books and 1,700 subscriptions.

Campus Life

There are 115 active organizations on campus, including a drama/theater group,
newspaper, radio station, television station, and choral group. 15% of eligible men and
13% of eligible women are members of national **fraternities**, national **sororities**, local
fraternities, and local sororities.

La Salle is a member of the NCAA (Division I) and NAIA. **Intercollegiate sports**
(some offering scholarships) include baseball (m), basketball, crew, cross-country running, field hockey (w), football (m), golf, lacrosse (w), soccer, softball (w), swimming, tennis, track and field, volleyball (w).

Campus Safety

Student safety services include late-night transport/escort service, 24-hour emergency
telephone alarm devices, 24-hour patrols by trained security personnel, student patrols,
and electronically operated dormitory entrances.

Applying

La Salle requires an essay, SAT I or ACT, a high school transcript, and 1 recommendation. It recommends an interview. Application deadline: 4/1; 3/15 priority date for
financial aid. Early and deferred admission are possible.

LAWRENCE UNIVERSITY

SMALL-TOWN SETTING ■ PRIVATE ■ INDEPENDENT ■ COED
APPLETON, WISCONSIN

Web site: www.lawrence.edu
Contact: Mr. Steven T. Syverson, Dean of Admissions and Financial Aid, PO Box 599, Appleton, WI 54912-0599
Telephone: 920-832-6500 or toll-free 800-227-0982 **Fax:** 920-832-6782
E-mail: excel@lawrence.edu

Lawrence University is committed to the development of intellect and talent, the acquisition of knowledge and understanding, and the cultivation of judgment and values. Independence and creativity are highly prized, with more than half of the students participating in off-campus programs and some 90% pursuing independent study with individual faculty members. Music, art, and the sciences, as well as the traditional liberal arts areas within the humanities and social sciences, are significant strengths within the curriculum. Bright, motivated, curious, and talented students excel at Lawrence.

Getting in Last Year
1,348 applied
81% were accepted
327 enrolled (30%)
49% from top tenth of their h.s. class
3.62 average high school GPA
70% had SAT verbal scores over 600
70% had SAT math scores over 600
86% had ACT scores over 24
23% had SAT verbal scores over 700
23% had SAT math scores over 700
27% had ACT scores over 30
19 valedictorians

Graduation and After
57% graduated in 4 years
13% graduated in 5 years
2% graduated in 6 years
27% pursued further study (20% arts and sciences, 4% medicine, 3% law)
59% had job offers within 6 months
25 organizations recruited on campus
1 Fulbright scholar

Financial Matters
$21,012 tuition and fees (1999–2000)
$4697 room and board
100% average percent of need met
$19,124 average financial aid amount received per undergraduate (1999–2000)

Academics

Lawrence awards bachelor's **degrees**. Challenging opportunities include advanced placement, student-designed majors, double majors, independent study, a senior project, and Phi Beta Kappa. Special programs include internships, off-campus study, and study-abroad.

The most frequently chosen fields are social sciences and history, biological/life sciences, and psychology. A complete listing of majors at Lawrence appears in the Majors Index beginning on page 432.

The **faculty** at Lawrence has 123 full-time members, 89% with terminal degrees. The student-faculty ratio is 11:1.

Students of Lawrence

The student body is made up of 1,246 undergraduates. 54.3% are women and 45.7% are men. Students come from 45 states and territories and 35 other countries. 53% are from Wisconsin. 6.5% are international students. 1.1% are African American, 0.3% American Indian, 3.2% Asian American, and 1.4% Hispanic American. 85% returned for their sophomore year.

Facilities and Resources

Student rooms are linked to a campus network. 140 **computers** are available on campus that provide access to the Internet. The **library** has 367,112 books and 1,346 subscriptions.

Campus Life

There are 130 active organizations on campus, including a drama/theater group, newspaper, radio station, and choral group. 35% of eligible men and 20% of eligible women are members of national **fraternities** and national **sororities**.

Lawrence is a member of the NCAA (Division III). **Intercollegiate sports** include baseball (m), basketball, crew, cross-country running, fencing, football (m), golf (m), ice hockey (m), lacrosse, rugby (w), soccer, softball (w), swimming, tennis, track and field, volleyball (w), wrestling (m).

Campus Safety

Student safety services include evening patrols by trained security personnel, late-night transport/escort service, 24-hour emergency telephone alarm devices, student patrols, and electronically operated dormitory entrances.

Applying

Lawrence requires an essay, SAT I or ACT, a high school transcript, 2 recommendations, and audition for music program. It recommends an interview and a minimum high school GPA of 3.0. Application deadline: 1/15; 3/1 priority date for financial aid. Early and deferred admission are possible.

LEHIGH UNIVERSITY

SUBURBAN SETTING ■ PRIVATE ■ INDEPENDENT ■ COED
BETHLEHEM, PENNSYLVANIA

Web site: www.lehigh.edu
Contact: Mrs. Lorna Hunter, Dean of Admissions and Financial Aid, 27
   Memorial Drive West, Bethlehem, PA 18015-3094
Telephone: 610-758-3100 **Fax:** 610-758-4361
E-mail: inado@lehigh.edu

  eAPPLY

Academics

Lehigh awards bachelor's, master's, and doctoral **degrees** and post-master's certificates. Challenging opportunities include advanced placement, accelerated degree programs, an honors program, double majors, independent study, a senior project, Phi Beta Kappa, and Sigma Xi. Special programs include cooperative education, internships, summer session for credit, off-campus study, study-abroad, and Army ROTC.

The most frequently chosen fields are engineering/engineering technologies, business/marketing, and social sciences and history. A complete listing of majors at Lehigh appears in the Majors Index beginning on page 432.

The **faculty** at Lehigh has 391 full-time members, 99% with terminal degrees. The student-faculty ratio is 12:1.

Students of Lehigh

The student body totals 6,359, of whom 4,605 are undergraduates. 40.2% are women and 59.8% are men. Students come from 52 states and territories and 46 other countries. 32% are from Pennsylvania. 4.4% are international students. 3.2% are African American, 0.2% American Indian, 5% Asian American, and 3.1% Hispanic American. 93% returned for their sophomore year.

Facilities and Resources

Student rooms are linked to a campus network. 463 **computers** are available on campus that provide access to the Internet. The 2 **libraries** have 1,176,028 books and 5,797 subscriptions.

Campus Life

There are 130 active organizations on campus, including a drama/theater group, newspaper, radio station, television station, choral group, and marching band. 41% of eligible men and 43% of eligible women are members of national **fraternities** and national **sororities**.

Lehigh is a member of the NCAA (Division I). **Intercollegiate sports** (some offering scholarships) include baseball (m), basketball, bowling, crew, cross-country running, equestrian sports, field hockey (w), football, golf (m), ice hockey (m), lacrosse, riflery, rugby (m), skiing (downhill), soccer, softball (w), squash (m), swimming, tennis, track and field, volleyball, wrestling (m).

Campus Safety

Student safety services include late-night transport/escort service, 24-hour emergency telephone alarm devices, 24-hour patrols by trained security personnel, student patrols, and electronically operated dormitory entrances.

Applying

Lehigh requires SAT I or ACT, a high school transcript, 1 recommendation, and graded writing sample. It recommends an essay, SAT II Subject Tests, and an interview. Application deadline: 1/1; 2/1 for financial aid, with a 1/15 priority date. Early and deferred admission are possible.

Lehigh University is a comprehensive national university located on a spectacular 1600-acre campus in Bethlehem, Pennsylvania. The University comprises 3 undergraduate colleges—Arts and Sciences, Business and Economics, and Engineering and Applied Sciences; a graduate school; and a graduate-level College of Education. Since its founding in 1865, Lehigh's philosophy has been to prepare young people for a rewarding and successful life. The hallmarks of a Lehigh education are close student-faculty interaction and experiential learning both inside and outside the classroom.

Getting in Last Year
8,853 applied
48% were accepted
1,078 enrolled (25%)
56% from top tenth of their h.s. class
51% had SAT verbal scores over 600
74% had SAT math scores over 600
8% had SAT verbal scores over 700
17% had SAT math scores over 700
11 National Merit Scholars

Graduation and After
26% pursued further study
64% had job offers within 6 months
382 organizations recruited on campus

Financial Matters
$23,150 tuition and fees (1999–2000)
$6630 room and board
95% average percent of need met
$18,100 average financial aid amount received
   per undergraduate (1999–2000 estimated)

LE MOYNE COLLEGE

SUBURBAN SETTING ■ PRIVATE ■ INDEPENDENT RELIGIOUS ■ COED
SYRACUSE, NEW YORK

Web site: www.lemoyne.edu
Contact: Director of Admission, 1419 Salt Spring Road, Syracuse, NY 13214-1399
Telephone: 315-445-4300 or toll-free 800-333-4733 **Fax:** 315-445-4711
E-mail: admsoffc@maple.lemoyne.edu

Academics

Le Moyne awards bachelor's and master's **degrees** and post-bachelor's certificates. Challenging opportunities include advanced placement, accelerated degree programs, an honors program, double majors, independent study, and a senior project. Special programs include internships, summer session for credit, off-campus study, study-abroad, and Army and Air Force ROTC.

The most frequently chosen fields are business/marketing, psychology, and social sciences and history. A complete listing of majors at Le Moyne appears in the Majors Index beginning on page 432.

The **faculty** at Le Moyne has 126 full-time members, 92% with terminal degrees. The student-faculty ratio is 14:1.

Students of Le Moyne

The student body totals 3,116, of whom 2,387 are undergraduates. 58.3% are women and 41.7% are men. Students come from 24 states and territories and 7 other countries. 94% are from New York. 0.1% are international students. 3.7% are African American, 1% American Indian, 0.9% Asian American, and 3.1% Hispanic American. 84% returned for their sophomore year.

Facilities and Resources

Student rooms are linked to a campus network. 225 **computers** are available on campus that provide access to the Internet. The **library** has 231,283 books and 1,710 subscriptions.

Campus Life

There are 70 active organizations on campus, including a drama/theater group, newspaper, radio station, and choral group. No national or local **fraternities** or **sororities**.

Le Moyne is a member of the NCAA (Division II). **Intercollegiate sports** (some offering scholarships) include baseball (m), basketball, cross-country running, golf (m), lacrosse, soccer, softball (w), swimming, tennis, volleyball (w).

Campus Safety

Student safety services include campus watch, self-defense education, lighted pathways, closed circuit TV monitors, late-night transport/escort service, 24-hour emergency telephone alarm devices, 24-hour patrols by trained security personnel, and electronically operated dormitory entrances.

Applying

Le Moyne requires an essay, SAT I or ACT, a high school transcript, and 2 recommendations. It recommends an interview. Application deadline: 3/1; 2/1 priority date for financial aid. Early and deferred admission are possible.

Le Moyne is a coeducational, residential, comprehensive liberal arts college founded in the Jesuit tradition of academic excellence. That powerful tradition, ever-present in Le Moyne's strong academic programs, caring faculty, and reassuring Jesuit presence, emphasizes developing every student's abilities to think clearly and communicate well to help them deal effectively in the real world. There is a strong focus on advisement, career counseling, and career-enhancing internships. Currently ranked as one of the best regional liberal arts college in the North by *U.S. News & World Report,* Le Moyne has consistently received national recognition for outstanding quality and value.

Getting in Last Year
2,275 applied
80% were accepted
473 enrolled (26%)
15% from top tenth of their h.s. class
2.71 average high school GPA
21% had SAT verbal scores over 600
20% had SAT math scores over 600
37% had ACT scores over 24
3% had SAT verbal scores over 700
2% had SAT math scores over 700
4% had ACT scores over 30
3 National Merit Scholars
2 valedictorians

Graduation and After
68% graduated in 4 years
4% graduated in 5 years
1% graduated in 6 years
Graduates pursuing further study: 19% arts and sciences, 8% education, 5% medicine
65% had job offers within 6 months
70 organizations recruited on campus

Financial Matters
$14,980 tuition and fees (1999–2000)
$6320 room and board
85% average percent of need met
$12,578 average financial aid amount received per undergraduate (1999–2000)

LeTourneau University

Suburban setting ■ Private ■ Independent Religious ■ Coed
Longview, Texas

Web site: www.letu.edu
Contact: Mr. Rodney Stanford, Director of Admissions, PO Box 7001,
Admissions Office, Longview, TX 75607-7001
Telephone: 903-233-3400 or toll-free 800-759-8811 **Fax:** 903-233-3411
E-mail: admissions@letu.edu

eApply

Academics

LeTourneau awards associate, bachelor's, and master's **degrees**. Challenging opportunities include advanced placement, double majors, independent study, and a senior project. Special programs include cooperative education, internships, summer session for credit, and off-campus study.

The most frequently chosen fields are engineering/engineering technologies, business/marketing, and biological/life sciences. A complete listing of majors at LeTourneau appears in the Majors Index beginning on page 432.

The **faculty** at LeTourneau has 59 full-time members, 71% with terminal degrees. The student-faculty ratio is 15:1.

Students of LeTourneau

The student body totals 2,805, of whom 2,523 are undergraduates. 46.8% are women and 53.2% are men. Students come from 49 states and territories and 24 other countries. 50% are from Texas. 1.8% are international students. 12.8% are African American, 0.6% American Indian, 1% Asian American, and 5.9% Hispanic American. 79% returned for their sophomore year.

Facilities and Resources

Student rooms are linked to a campus network. 120 **computers** are available on campus that provide access to the Internet. The **library** has 260,000 books and 600 subscriptions.

Campus Life

There are 22 active organizations on campus, including a drama/theater group, newspaper, and choral group. 8% of eligible men and 3% of eligible women are members of 3 societies for men, 1 society for women.

LeTourneau is a member of the NCAA (Division III) and NCCAA. **Intercollegiate sports** include baseball (m), basketball, cross-country running, golf, soccer, softball (w), tennis, volleyball (w).

Campus Safety

Student safety services include late-night transport/escort service, 24-hour emergency telephone alarm devices, 24-hour patrols by trained security personnel, and electronically operated dormitory entrances.

Applying

LeTourneau requires an essay, SAT I or ACT, a high school transcript, 2 recommendations, and a minimum high school GPA of 2.5, and in some cases an interview. Application deadline: 8/1; 2/15 priority date for financial aid. Early and deferred admission are possible.

Getting in Last Year
953 applied
85% were accepted
263 enrolled (33%)
27% from top tenth of their h.s. class
3.50 average high school GPA
41% had SAT verbal scores over 600
54% had SAT math scores over 600
60% had ACT scores over 24
13% had SAT verbal scores over 700
18% had SAT math scores over 700
14% had ACT scores over 30
6 National Merit Scholars
11 valedictorians

Graduation and After
32% graduated in 4 years
16% graduated in 5 years
2% graduated in 6 years
91% had job offers within 6 months
60 organizations recruited on campus

Financial Matters
$12,240 tuition and fees (2000–2001)
$5250 room and board
84% average percent of need met
$11,748 average financial aid amount received
    per undergraduate (1999–2000 estimated)

eApply

Getting in Last Year
3,008 applied
69% were accepted
512 enrolled (25%)
42% from top tenth of their h.s. class
68% had SAT verbal scores over 600
59% had SAT math scores over 600
81% had ACT scores over 24
20% had SAT verbal scores over 700
12% had SAT math scores over 700
25% had ACT scores over 30
13 National Merit Scholars
20 valedictorians

Graduation and After
56% graduated in 4 years
9% graduated in 5 years
1% graduated in 6 years
23% pursued further study (10% arts and sciences, 2% business, 2% education)
28 organizations recruited on campus

Financial Matters
$20,326 tuition and fees (1999–2000)
$6458 room and board
84% average percent of need met
$19,060 average financial aid amount received per undergraduate (1999–2000)

LEWIS & CLARK COLLEGE
SUBURBAN SETTING ■ PRIVATE ■ INDEPENDENT ■ COED
PORTLAND, OREGON

Web site: www.lclark.edu
Contact: Mr. Michael Sexton, Dean of Admissions, 0615 SW Palatine Hill Road, Portland, OR 97219-7899
Telephone: 503-768-7040 or toll-free 800-444-4111 **Fax:** 503-768-7055
E-mail: admissions@lclark.edu

Academics
L & C awards bachelor's, master's, and first-professional **degrees**. Challenging opportunities include advanced placement, accelerated degree programs, student-designed majors, an honors program, double majors, independent study, a senior project, and Phi Beta Kappa. Special programs include internships, summer session for credit, off-campus study, and study-abroad.

The most frequently chosen fields are social sciences and history, biological/life sciences, and visual/performing arts. A complete listing of majors at L & C appears in the Majors Index beginning on page 432.

The **faculty** at L & C has 184 full-time members, 93% with terminal degrees. The student-faculty ratio is 13:1.

Students of L & C
The student body totals 3,203, of whom 1,742 are undergraduates. 59.1% are women and 40.9% are men. Students come from 48 states and territories and 34 other countries. 27% are from Oregon. 5.3% are international students. 1% are African American, 0.7% American Indian, 7% Asian American, and 2.5% Hispanic American. 80% returned for their sophomore year.

Facilities and Resources
Student rooms are linked to a campus network. The 2 **libraries** have 7,326 subscriptions.

Campus Life
There are 100 active organizations on campus, including a drama/theater group, newspaper, radio station, television station, and choral group. No national or local **fraternities** or **sororities**.

L & C is a member of the NCAA (Division III). **Intercollegiate sports** include baseball (m), basketball, crew, cross-country running, football (m), golf, lacrosse, rugby, soccer, softball (w), swimming, tennis, track and field, volleyball (w).

Campus Safety
Student safety services include late-night transport/escort service, 24-hour emergency telephone alarm devices, 24-hour patrols by trained security personnel, student patrols, and electronically operated dormitory entrances.

Applying
L & C requires an essay, SAT I or ACT or academic portfolio, a high school transcript, 2 recommendations, and a minimum high school GPA of 2.0, and in some cases 4 recommendations and portfolio applicants must submit samples of graded work. It recommends an interview and a minimum high school GPA of 3.0. Application deadline: 2/1; 3/1 priority date for financial aid. Early and deferred admission are possible.

LINFIELD COLLEGE

SMALL-TOWN SETTING ■ PRIVATE ■ INDEPENDENT RELIGIOUS ■ COED
McMINNVILLE, OREGON

  eAPPLY

Web site: www.linfield.edu
Contact: Mr. Ernest Sandlin, Director of Admissions, 900 SE Baker Street,
McMinnville, OR 97128-6894
Telephone: 503-434-2489 or toll-free 800-640-2287 **Fax:** 503-434-2472
E-mail: admissions@linfield.edu

Academics

Linfield awards bachelor's **degrees**. Challenging opportunities include advanced placement, accelerated degree programs, an honors program, independent study, and a senior
project. Special programs include cooperative education, internships, summer session for
credit, off-campus study, study-abroad, and Air Force ROTC.

The most frequently chosen fields are business/marketing, health professions and
related sciences, and social sciences and history. A complete listing of majors at Linfield
appears in the Majors Index beginning on page 432.

The **faculty** at Linfield has 108 full-time members, 95% with terminal degrees. The
student-faculty ratio is 13:1.

Students of Linfield

The student body is made up of 1,550 undergraduates. 55.2% are women and 44.8% are
men. Students come from 30 states and territories and 23 other countries. 56% are from
Oregon. 3.5% are international students. 1.5% are African American, 0.8% American
Indian, 6.3% Asian American, and 2.5% Hispanic American. 80% returned for their
sophomore year.

Facilities and Resources

Student rooms are linked to a campus network. 180 **computers** are available on campus
that provide access to the Internet. The **library** has 155,663 books and 1,294 subscriptions.

Campus Life

There are 60 active organizations on campus, including a drama/theater group,
newspaper, radio station, and choral group. 29% of eligible men and 27% of eligible
women are members of national **fraternities**, national **sororities**, local fraternities, and
local sororities.

Linfield is a member of the NCAA (Division III). **Intercollegiate sports** include
baseball (m), basketball, cross-country running, football (m), golf, lacrosse (w), soccer,
softball (w), swimming, tennis, track and field, volleyball (w).

Campus Safety

Student safety services include late-night transport/escort service, 24-hour emergency
telephone alarm devices, 24-hour patrols by trained security personnel, and student
patrols.

Applying

Linfield requires an essay, SAT I or ACT, a high school transcript, and 2 recommendations. It recommends an interview. Application deadline: 2/15; 2/1 priority date for
financial aid. Deferred admission is possible.

> "**W**henever two people meet, there is the opportunity both to teach and to learn . . . and it is never clear who the teacher will be."—Dr. Vivian Bull, Linfield President. Surrounded by opportunities for collaborative learning in intimate settings, Linfield students and faculty members mentor each other toward paths of success. With round-trip airfare paid, nearly 50 percent of Linfield students open doors with an international experience. Students are also encouraged to participate in the award-winning theater and music programs, challenging internship opportunities, nationally competitive athletic programs, many clubs and organizations on campus, and lectures by world-renowned guest speakers.

Getting in Last Year

1,608 applied
92% were accepted
399 enrolled (27%)
30% from top tenth of their h.s. class
3.5 average high school GPA
27% had SAT verbal scores over 600
26% had SAT math scores over 600
28% had ACT scores over 24
3% had SAT verbal scores over 700
3% had SAT math scores over 700
12 class presidents
28 valedictorians

Graduation and After

57% graduated in 4 years
5% graduated in 5 years
1% graduated in 6 years
12% pursued further study (5% arts and sciences, 2% business, 2% medicine)
85% had job offers within 6 months
10 organizations recruited on campus

Financial Matters

$17,720 tuition and fees (1999–2000)
$5300 room and board
87% average percent of need met
$14,800 average financial aid amount received
per undergraduate (1999–2000)

LIST COLLEGE, JEWISH THEOLOGICAL SEMINARY OF AMERICA

URBAN SETTING ■ PRIVATE ■ INDEPENDENT RELIGIOUS ■ COED
NEW YORK, NEW YORK

Web site: www.jtsa.edu
Contact: Ms. Reena Gold, Assistant Director of Admissions, Room 614 Schiff, 3080 Broadway, New York, NY 10027-4649
Telephone: 212-678-8832 **Fax:** 212-678-8947
E-mail: regold@jtsa.edu

The List College of Jewish Studies of the Jewish Theological Seminary offers students an opportunity to earn 2 bachelor's degrees simultaneously. Students pursue one degree in a specific major of Jewish study at List College and another in the liberal arts major of their choice at Columbia University's School of General Studies or Barnard College. In small classes, students receive personal attention from faculty members while they enjoy the warm, supportive community at List College and the exciting, diverse campus life at Columbia or Barnard.

Getting in Last Year
138 applied
63% were accepted
48 enrolled (55%)
39% from top tenth of their h.s. class
3.75 average high school GPA
78% had SAT verbal scores over 600
74% had SAT math scores over 600
90% had ACT scores over 24
30% had SAT verbal scores over 700
11% had SAT math scores over 700
30% had ACT scores over 30

Graduation and After
60% pursued further study

Financial Matters
$8720 tuition and fees (1999–2000)
$5000 room only
75% average percent of need met

Academics
List College awards bachelor's, master's, and doctoral **degrees** (double bachelor's degree with Barnard College, Columbia University). Challenging opportunities include advanced placement, student-designed majors, freshman honors college, an honors program, double majors, and a senior project. Special programs include internships, summer session for credit, off-campus study, and study-abroad.

The most frequently chosen field is philosophy. A complete listing of majors at List College appears in the Majors Index beginning on page 432.

Students of List College
The student body totals 574, of whom 175 are undergraduates. 57.1% are women and 42.9% are men. Students come from 22 states and territories and 3 other countries. 33% are from New York. 86% returned for their sophomore year.

Facilities and Resources
Student rooms are linked to a campus network. 20 **computers** are available on campus that provide access to the Internet. The **library** has 271,000 books and 720 subscriptions.

Campus Life
Active organizations on campus include a drama/theater group, newspaper, radio station, and choral group. No national or local **fraternities** or **sororities**.

This institution has no intercollegiate sports.

Campus Safety
Student safety services include late-night transport/escort service, 24-hour emergency telephone alarm devices, 24-hour patrols by trained security personnel, and electronically operated dormitory entrances.

Applying
List College requires an essay, SAT II: Writing Test, SAT I and SAT II or ACT, a high school transcript, and 2 recommendations. It recommends an interview and a minimum high school GPA of 3.0. Application deadline: 2/15; 3/1 for financial aid. Early and deferred admission are possible.

LOUISIANA STATE UNIVERSITY AND AGRICULTURAL AND MECHANICAL COLLEGE

URBAN SETTING ■ PUBLIC ■ STATE-SUPPORTED ■ COED
BATON ROUGE, LOUISIANA

Web site: www.lsu.edu
Contact: Interim Director of Admissions, 110 Thomas Boyd Hall, Baton Rouge, LA 70803-3103
Telephone: 225-388-1175 **Fax:** 225-388-4433
E-mail: lsuadmit@lsu.edu

Academics

LSU awards bachelor's, master's, doctoral, and first-professional **degrees** and post-master's certificates. Challenging opportunities include advanced placement, accelerated degree programs, student-designed majors, freshman honors college, an honors program, double majors, independent study, a senior project, Phi Beta Kappa, and Sigma Xi. Special programs include cooperative education, internships, summer session for credit, off-campus study, study-abroad, and Army, Navy and Air Force ROTC.

The most frequently chosen fields are business/marketing, engineering/engineering technologies, and education. A complete listing of majors at LSU appears in the Majors Index beginning on page 432.

The **faculty** at LSU has 1,294 full-time members, 79% with terminal degrees. The student-faculty ratio is 21:1.

Students of LSU

The student body totals 30,966, of whom 25,911 are undergraduates. 52.9% are women and 47.1% are men. Students come from 51 states and territories and 107 other countries. 91% are from Louisiana. 2.9% are international students. 9.2% are African American, 0.4% American Indian, 3.9% Asian American, and 2.4% Hispanic American. 83% returned for their sophomore year.

Facilities and Resources

Student rooms are linked to a campus network. 5,000 **computers** are available on campus that provide access to e-mail and the Internet. The 8 **libraries** have 17,975 subscriptions.

Campus Life

There are 269 active organizations on campus, including a drama/theater group, newspaper, radio station, television station, choral group, and marching band. 10% of eligible men and 15% of eligible women are members of national **fraternities** and national **sororities**.

LSU is a member of the NCAA (Division I). **Intercollegiate sports** (some offering scholarships) include baseball (m), basketball, cross-country running, football (m), golf, gymnastics (w), soccer (w), softball (w), swimming, tennis, track and field, volleyball (w).

Campus Safety

Student safety services include self-defense education, crime prevention programs, late-night transport/escort service, 24-hour emergency telephone alarm devices, 24-hour patrols by trained security personnel, and electronically operated dormitory entrances.

Applying

LSU requires SAT I or ACT, a high school transcript, and a minimum high school GPA of 2.3, and in some cases SAT I and SAT II or ACT, 1 recommendation, and minimum ACT score of 17 or SAT I score of 830. Application deadline: 5/1; 4/1 priority date for financial aid. Early admission is possible.

Getting in Last Year

9,661 applied
82% were accepted
5,187 enrolled (65%)
25% from top tenth of their h.s. class
3.19 average high school GPA
46% had ACT scores over 24
7% had ACT scores over 30
38 National Merit Scholars
148 valedictorians

Graduation and After

1300 organizations recruited on campus

Financial Matters

$2881 resident tuition and fees (1999–2000)
$7081 nonresident tuition and fees (1999–2000)
$4220 room and board
73% average percent of need met
$5876 average financial aid amount received per undergraduate (1998–99)

LOYOLA COLLEGE IN MARYLAND

URBAN SETTING ■ PRIVATE ■ INDEPENDENT RELIGIOUS ■ COED
BALTIMORE, MARYLAND

Web site: www.loyola.edu
Contact: Mr. William Bossemeyer, Dean of Admissions, 4501 North Charles Street, Baltimore, MD 21210-2699
Telephone: 410-617-2000 ext. 2252 or toll-free 800-221-9107 Ext. 2252 (in-state) **Fax:** 410-617-2176

> Traditional academic standards are central to Jesuit education. Loyola's curriculum is rigorous, and the faculty's expectations for students are high. The aim is to challenge students and to try to develop their skills and abilities. Hard work is required for a good education, and Loyola is interested in admitting students who have been ambitious in their course selection in high school and who have shown that they can do well in academic work.

Getting in Last Year
6,129 applied
66% were accepted
940 enrolled (23%)
29% from top tenth of their h.s. class
3.4 average high school GPA
51% had SAT verbal scores over 600
56% had SAT math scores over 600
10% had SAT verbal scores over 700
8% had SAT math scores over 700

Graduation and After
70% had job offers within 6 months
265 organizations recruited on campus

Financial Matters
$18,830 tuition and fees (2000–2001)
$7600 room and board
98% average percent of need met
$13,625 average financial aid amount received per undergraduate (1999–2000)

Academics

Loyola awards bachelor's, master's, and doctoral **degrees** and post-bachelor's and post-master's certificates. Challenging opportunities include advanced placement, accelerated degree programs, an honors program, double majors, independent study, a senior project, and Phi Beta Kappa. Special programs include internships, summer session for credit, off-campus study, study-abroad, and Army and Air Force ROTC. A complete listing of majors at Loyola appears in the Majors Index beginning on page 432.

The student-faculty ratio is 14:1.

Students of Loyola

The student body totals 6,263, of whom 3,377 are undergraduates. 55.4% are women and 44.6% are men. 1.4% are international students. 4.7% are African American, 0.1% American Indian, 1.7% Asian American, and 1.7% Hispanic American.

Facilities and Resources

Student rooms are linked to a campus network. 236 **computers** are available on campus that provide access to the Internet. The **library** has 347,158 books and 2,081 subscriptions.

Campus Life

Active organizations on campus include a drama/theater group, newspaper, and choral group. No national or local **fraternities** or **sororities**.

Loyola is a member of the NCAA (Division I).

Campus Safety

Student safety services include late-night transport/escort service, 24-hour emergency telephone alarm devices, 24-hour patrols by trained security personnel, and electronically operated dormitory entrances.

Applying

Loyola requires an essay, SAT I, and a high school transcript. It recommends an interview. Application deadline: 1/15; 2/1 for financial aid. Early and deferred admission are possible.

LOYOLA UNIVERSITY CHICAGO

URBAN SETTING ■ PRIVATE ■ INDEPENDENT RELIGIOUS ■ COED
CHICAGO, ILLINOIS

Web site: www.luc.edu
Contact: Ms. Victoria Valle, Director of Admissions, 820 North Michigan
   Avenue, Chicago, IL 60611-2196
Telephone: 312-915-6500 or toll-free 800-262-2373
E-mail: admission@luc.edu

 eAPPLY

Academics

Loyola awards bachelor's, master's, doctoral, and first-professional **degrees** (also offers adult part-time program with significant enrollment not reflected in profile). Challenging opportunities include advanced placement, accelerated degree programs, an honors program, Phi Beta Kappa, and Sigma Xi. Special programs include internships, summer session for credit, off-campus study, study-abroad, and Army, Navy and Air Force ROTC.

The most frequently chosen fields are business/marketing, psychology, and social sciences and history. A complete listing of majors at Loyola appears in the Majors Index beginning on page 432.

The **faculty** at Loyola has 610 full-time members, 97% with terminal degrees. The student-faculty ratio is 11:1.

Students of Loyola

The student body totals 13,359, of whom 7,596 are undergraduates. 64.1% are women and 35.9% are men. Students come from 50 states and territories. 72% are from Illinois. 1.3% are international students. 8.4% are African American, 0.1% American Indian, 12.5% Asian American, and 8.8% Hispanic American. 81% returned for their sophomore year.

Facilities and Resources

Student rooms are linked to a campus network. 318 **computers** are available on campus that provide access to the Internet. The 4 **libraries** have 1,500,000 books and 11,114 subscriptions.

Campus Life

There are 136 active organizations on campus, including a drama/theater group, newspaper, radio station, and choral group. 8% of eligible men and 7% of eligible women are members of national **fraternities** and national **sororities**.

Loyola is a member of the NCAA (Division I). **Intercollegiate sports** (some offering scholarships) include basketball, cross-country running, golf, soccer, softball (w), track and field, volleyball.

Campus Safety

Student safety services include late-night transport/escort service, 24-hour emergency telephone alarm devices, 24-hour patrols by trained security personnel, and electronically operated dormitory entrances.

Applying

Loyola requires an essay, SAT I or ACT, and a high school transcript. It recommends an interview. Application deadline: 4/1; 3/1 priority date for financial aid. Early admission is possible.

Chicago offers an ideal environment to enrich students' academic experience, with its world-class museums and performing arts; professional sports; culturally rich diversity; and international headquarters for media, commerce, medicine, and banking. Loyola's partnership with the city of Chicago adds an extra dimension—vast resources for internships, fieldwork, and independent exploration—rare in universities of Loyola's affiliation (Jesuit, Catholic), size (medium), and ranking (national research university). Extraordinary resources include a distinguished and dedicated faculty (97% with the PhD) teaching classes averaging 25 students while mentoring new students' living and learning experience on Loyola's residential lakefront campus on Chicago's north shore.

Getting in Last Year

5,698 applied
78% were accepted
1,067 enrolled (24%)
30% from top tenth of their h.s. class
43% had SAT verbal scores over 600
40% had SAT math scores over 600
59% had ACT scores over 24
9% had SAT verbal scores over 700
8% had SAT math scores over 700
9% had ACT scores over 30
13 valedictorians

Financial Matters

$18,310 tuition and fees (1999–2000)
$7006 room and board
87% average percent of need met
$17,834 average financial aid amount received
   per undergraduate (1999–2000)

eApply

Getting in Last Year
1,694 applied
87% were accepted
608 enrolled (41%)
35% from top tenth of their h.s. class
3.58 average high school GPA
49% had SAT verbal scores over 600
55% had SAT math scores over 600
66% had ACT scores over 24
14% had SAT verbal scores over 700
17% had SAT math scores over 700
18% had ACT scores over 30
11 class presidents
44 valedictorians

Graduation and After
70% graduated in 4 years
6% graduated in 5 years
25% pursued further study (11% arts and sciences, 3% medicine, 2% law)
63% had job offers within 6 months
102 organizations recruited on campus

Financial Matters
$17,290 tuition and fees (1999–2000)
$3810 room and board
88% average percent of need met
$14,316 average financial aid amount received per undergraduate (1999–2000 estimated)

LUTHER COLLEGE
SMALL-TOWN SETTING ■ PRIVATE ■ INDEPENDENT RELIGIOUS ■ COED
DECORAH, IOWA

Web site: www.luther.edu
Contact: Dr. David Sallee, Vice President for Enrollment Management, 700 College Drive, Decorah, IA 52101-1045
Telephone: 319-387-1287 or toll-free 800-458-8437 **Fax:** 319-387-2159
E-mail: admissions@luther.edu

Academics
Luther awards bachelor's **degrees**. Challenging opportunities include advanced placement, student-designed majors, an honors program, double majors, independent study, a senior project, and Phi Beta Kappa. Special programs include internships, summer session for credit, off-campus study, and study-abroad.

The most frequently chosen fields are biological/life sciences, visual/performing arts, and business/marketing. A complete listing of majors at Luther appears in the Majors Index beginning on page 432.

The **faculty** at Luther has 171 full-time members, 83% with terminal degrees. The student-faculty ratio is 13:1.

Students of Luther
The student body is made up of 2,550 undergraduates. 59.1% are women and 40.9% are men. Students come from 35 states and territories and 40 other countries. 38% are from Iowa. 5.2% are international students. 0.8% are African American, 0.1% American Indian, 1% Asian American, and 0.8% Hispanic American. 86% returned for their sophomore year.

Facilities and Resources
Student rooms are linked to a campus network. 325 **computers** are available on campus that provide access to the Internet. The **library** has 330,160 books and 1,063 subscriptions.

Campus Life
There are 102 active organizations on campus, including a drama/theater group, newspaper, radio station, and choral group. 9% of eligible men and 10% of eligible women are members of national **fraternities**, local fraternities, and local **sororities**.

Luther is a member of the NCAA (Division III). **Intercollegiate sports** include baseball (m), basketball, cross-country running, football (m), golf, soccer, softball (w), swimming, tennis, track and field, volleyball (w), wrestling (m).

Campus Safety
Student safety services include late-night transport/escort service, 24-hour emergency telephone alarm devices, 24-hour patrols by trained security personnel, and electronically operated dormitory entrances.

Applying
Luther requires an essay, SAT I or ACT, a high school transcript, and 1 recommendation. It recommends an interview. Application deadline: 3/1 priority date for financial aid. Early and deferred admission are possible.

LYON COLLEGE

SMALL-TOWN SETTING ■ PRIVATE ■ INDEPENDENT RELIGIOUS ■ COED
BATESVILLE, ARKANSAS

Web site: www.lyon.edu
Contact: Ms. Kristine Penix, Director of Admissions, PO Box 2317,
  Batesville, AR 72503-2317
Telephone: 870-698-4250 or toll-free 800-423-2542 **Fax:** 870-698-4622
E-mail: admissions@lyon.edu

  eAPPLY

Academics

Lyon awards bachelor's **degrees**. Challenging opportunities include advanced placement, student-designed majors, independent study, and a senior project. Special programs include internships, summer session for credit, and study-abroad.

The most frequently chosen fields are social sciences and history, biological/life sciences, and English. A complete listing of majors at Lyon appears in the Majors Index beginning on page 432.

The **faculty** at Lyon has 42 full-time members, 93% with terminal degrees. The student-faculty ratio is 10:1.

Students of Lyon

The student body is made up of 462 undergraduates. 58.4% are women and 41.6% are men. Students come from 22 states and territories and 21 other countries. 83% are from Arkansas. 7.4% are international students. 4.1% are African American, 1.1% American Indian, 0.9% Asian American, and 1.3% Hispanic American. 74% returned for their sophomore year.

Facilities and Resources

66 **computers** are available on campus that provide access to the Internet. The **library** has 138,674 books and 964 subscriptions.

Campus Life

There are 27 active organizations on campus, including a drama/theater group, newspaper, and choral group. 19% of eligible men and 34% of eligible women are members of national **fraternities**, national **sororities**, and local sororities.

Lyon is a member of the NCAA (Division II) and NAIA. **Intercollegiate sports** (some offering scholarships) include baseball (m), basketball, cross-country running, golf, soccer, tennis, volleyball (w).

Campus Safety

Student safety services include late-night transport/escort service and 24-hour patrols by trained security personnel.

Applying

Lyon requires an essay, SAT I or ACT, a high school transcript, and 1 recommendation. It recommends an interview and a minimum high school GPA of 2.25. Application deadline: rolling admissions; 2/15 priority date for financial aid. Early and deferred admission are possible.

Lyon's powerful sense of community, commitment to honor, and dedication to the education of the total person make it a place where students grow in remarkable ways. Located in the beautiful foothills of the Ozark Mountains, Lyon offers access to talented teacher-scholars as part of a stimulating academic community organized around a residential house system. A strong endowment supports a challenging academic program and exceptional opportunities in such areas as study abroad and student research. Lyon students are noted for their enthusiasm, involvement, and high acceptance rates into graduate and professional schools.

Getting in Last Year
470 applied
81% were accepted
145 enrolled (38%)
43% from top tenth of their h.s. class
3.72 average high school GPA
37% had SAT verbal scores over 600
37% had SAT math scores over 600
70% had ACT scores over 24
9% had SAT verbal scores over 700
6% had SAT math scores over 700
17% had ACT scores over 30
16 valedictorians

Graduation and After
37% graduated in 4 years
7% graduated in 5 years
1% graduated in 6 years
27% pursued further study (7% medicine, 6% arts and sciences, 5% law)
48% had job offers within 6 months
5 organizations recruited on campus

Financial Matters
$10,622 tuition and fees (1999–2000)
$4703 room and board
95% average percent of need met
$11,633 average financial aid amount received per undergraduate (1999–2000 estimated)

eAPPLY

Getting in Last Year
3,161 applied
53% were accepted
460 enrolled (27%)
59% from top tenth of their h.s. class
85% had SAT verbal scores over 600
81% had SAT math scores over 600
95% had ACT scores over 24
38% had SAT verbal scores over 700
23% had SAT math scores over 700
45% had ACT scores over 30
39 National Merit Scholars
29 valedictorians

Graduation and After
69% graduated in 4 years
7% graduated in 5 years
3% graduated in 6 years
18% pursued further study (12% arts and sciences, 3% law, 3% medicine)
65% had job offers within 6 months
100 organizations recruited on campus
1 Marshall, 3 Fulbright scholars

Financial Matters
$20,688 tuition and fees (1999–2000)
$5760 room and board
100% average percent of need met
$16,006 average financial aid amount received per undergraduate (1999–2000 estimated)

MACALESTER COLLEGE
URBAN SETTING ■ PRIVATE ■ INDEPENDENT RELIGIOUS ■ COED
ST. PAUL, MINNESOTA

Web site: www.macalester.edu
Contact: Mr. Lorne T. Robinson, Dean of Admissions and Financial Aid, 1600 Grand Avenue, St. Paul, MN 55105-1899
Telephone: 651-696-6357 or toll-free 800-231-7974 **Fax:** 651-696-6724
E-mail: admissions@macalester.edu

Academics
Mac awards bachelor's **degrees**. Challenging opportunities include advanced placement, student-designed majors, an honors program, double majors, independent study, a senior project, and Phi Beta Kappa. Special programs include cooperative education, internships, off-campus study, study-abroad, and Navy and Air Force ROTC.

The most frequently chosen fields are social sciences and history, biological/life sciences, and psychology. A complete listing of majors at Mac appears in the Majors Index beginning on page 432.

The **faculty** at Mac has 147 full-time members, 93% with terminal degrees. The student-faculty ratio is 11:1.

Students of Mac
The student body is made up of 1,835 undergraduates. 58.1% are women and 41.9% are men. Students come from 50 states and territories and 81 other countries. 38% are from Minnesota. 11.2% are international students. 4.1% are African American, 0.4% American Indian, 5.2% Asian American, and 2.7% Hispanic American. 90% returned for their sophomore year.

Facilities and Resources
Student rooms are linked to a campus network. 291 **computers** are available on campus that provide access to the Internet. The **library** has 390,025 books and 1,703 subscriptions.

Campus Life
There are 70 active organizations on campus, including a drama/theater group, newspaper, radio station, television station, and choral group. No national or local **fraternities** or **sororities**.

Mac is a member of the NCAA (Division III). **Intercollegiate sports** include baseball (m), basketball, crew, cross-country running, fencing, football (m), golf, ice hockey (m), rugby, skiing (cross-country), soccer, softball (w), swimming, tennis, track and field, volleyball, water polo.

Campus Safety
Student safety services include late-night transport/escort service, 24-hour emergency telephone alarm devices, 24-hour patrols by trained security personnel, and electronically operated dormitory entrances.

Applying
Mac requires an essay, SAT I or ACT, a high school transcript, and 3 recommendations. It recommends SAT II Subject Tests and an interview. Application deadline: 1/15; 2/8 priority date for financial aid. Early and deferred admission are possible.

MARIETTA COLLEGE

SMALL-TOWN SETTING ■ PRIVATE ■ INDEPENDENT ■ COED
MARIETTA, OHIO

Web site: www.marietta.edu
Contact: Ms. Marke Vickers, Director of Admission, 215 Fifth Street,
Marietta, OH 45750-4000
Telephone: 740-376-4600 or toll-free 800-331-7896 **Fax:** 740-376-8888
E-mail: admit@marietta.edu

eAPPLY

Academics

Marietta awards associate, bachelor's, and master's **degrees**. Challenging opportunities
include advanced placement, accelerated degree programs, student-designed majors, an
honors program, double majors, independent study, a senior project, and Phi Beta
Kappa. Special programs include internships, summer session for credit, off-campus
study, and study-abroad.

The most frequently chosen fields are liberal arts/general studies, business/market-
ing, and education. A complete listing of majors at Marietta appears in the Majors Index
beginning on page 432.

The **faculty** at Marietta has 75 full-time members, 84% with terminal degrees. The
student-faculty ratio is 12:1.

Students of Marietta

The student body totals 1,214, of whom 1,153 are undergraduates. 51.2% are women
and 48.8% are men. Students come from 35 states and territories and 11 other countries.
50% are from Ohio. 5.6% are international students. 2.6% are African American, 0.7%
American Indian, 0.7% Asian American, and 1.1% Hispanic American. 69% returned for
their sophomore year.

Facilities and Resources

Student rooms are linked to a campus network. 200 **computers** are available on campus
that provide access to the Internet. The **library** has 146,970 books and 1,500 subscriptions.

Campus Life

There are 67 active organizations on campus, including a drama/theater group,
newspaper, radio station, television station, and choral group. 20% of eligible men and
22% of eligible women are members of national **fraternities**, national **sororities**, and
local sororities.

Marietta is a member of the NCAA (Division III). **Intercollegiate sports** include
baseball (m), basketball, crew, football (m), golf, lacrosse (m), soccer, softball (w), tennis,
volleyball (w).

Campus Safety

Student safety services include late-night transport/escort service, 24-hour emergency
telephone alarm devices, 24-hour patrols by trained security personnel, student patrols,
and electronically operated dormitory entrances.

Applying

Marietta requires an essay, SAT I or ACT, a high school transcript, 2 recommendations,
and a minimum high school GPA of 2.0. It recommends SAT II Subject Tests, an
interview, and a minimum high school GPA of 3.0. Application deadline: 4/15; 3/1 priority date for financial aid. Early and deferred admission are possible.

Getting in Last Year
1,065 applied
92% were accepted
302 enrolled (31%)
24% from top tenth of their h.s. class
3.2 average high school GPA
28% had SAT verbal scores over 600
31% had SAT math scores over 600
46% had ACT scores over 24
2% had SAT verbal scores over 700
3% had SAT math scores over 700
7% had ACT scores over 30

Graduation and After
45% graduated in 4 years
8% graduated in 5 years
1% graduated in 6 years
22% pursued further study
77% had job offers within 6 months
23 organizations recruited on campus

Financial Matters
$17,510 tuition and fees (1999–2000)
$4970 room and board
91% average percent of need met
$15,800 average financial aid amount received
per undergraduate (1999–2000)

eAPPLY

Getting in Last Year
308 applied
80% were accepted
93 enrolled (38%)
31% from top tenth of their h.s. class
3.20 average high school GPA
71% had SAT verbal scores over 600
37% had SAT math scores over 600
24% had SAT verbal scores over 700
8% had SAT math scores over 700

Graduation and After
31% graduated in 4 years
5% graduated in 5 years
2% graduated in 6 years

Financial Matters
$19,560 tuition and fees (2000–2001)
$6750 room and board
89% average percent of need met
$19,450 average financial aid amount received
    per undergraduate (1999–2000)

MARLBORO COLLEGE
RURAL SETTING ■ PRIVATE ■ INDEPENDENT ■ COED
MARLBORO, VERMONT

Web site: www.marlboro.edu
Contact: Ms. Katherine S. Hallas, Director of Admissions, PO Box A, South Road, Marlboro, VT 05344
Telephone: 802-257-4333 ext. 237 or toll-free 800-343-0049 (out-of-state)
Fax: 802-257-4154
E-mail: admissions@marlboro.edu

Academics

Marlboro awards bachelor's and master's **degrees**. Challenging opportunities include advanced placement, accelerated degree programs, student-designed majors, double majors, independent study, and a senior project. Special programs include internships, off-campus study, and study-abroad.

The most frequently chosen fields are visual/performing arts, social sciences and history, and biological/life sciences. A complete listing of majors at Marlboro appears in the Majors Index beginning on page 432.

The **faculty** at Marlboro has 33 full-time members. The student-faculty ratio is 7:1.

Students of Marlboro

The student body is made up of 290 undergraduates. 58.6% are women and 41.4% are men. Students come from 32 states and territories and 5 other countries. 18% are from Vermont. 2.1% are international students. 1% are African American, 0.7% American Indian, 1.4% Asian American, and 2.1% Hispanic American. 78% returned for their sophomore year.

Facilities and Resources

Student rooms are linked to a campus network. 42 **computers** are available on campus that provide access to the Internet. The **library** has 54,289 books and 250 subscriptions.

Campus Life

There are 25 active organizations on campus, including a drama/theater group, newspaper, and choral group. No national or local **fraternities** or **sororities**.

Intercollegiate sports include skiing (downhill), soccer.

Campus Safety

Student safety services include 24-hour emergency telephone alarm devices.

Applying

Marlboro requires an essay, SAT I or ACT, a high school transcript, an interview, 1 recommendation, and graded expository essay. It recommends SAT II Subject Tests and a minimum high school GPA of 3.0. Application deadline: 3/1; 3/1 priority date for financial aid. Early and deferred admission are possible.

MARQUETTE UNIVERSITY

URBAN SETTING ■ PRIVATE ■ INDEPENDENT RELIGIOUS ■ COED
MILWAUKEE, WISCONSIN

Web site: www.marquette.edu
Contact: Mr. Raymond A. Brown, Dean of Admissions, PO Box 1881,
Milwaukee, WI 53201-1881
Telephone: 414-288-7302 or toll-free 800-222-6544
E-mail: go2marquette@marquette.edu

  eAPPLY

Academics

Marquette awards associate, bachelor's, master's, doctoral, and first-professional **degrees**. Challenging opportunities include advanced placement, accelerated degree programs, student-designed majors, an honors program, double majors, independent study, a senior project, Phi Beta Kappa, and Sigma Xi. Special programs include cooperative education, internships, summer session for credit, off-campus study, study-abroad, and Army, Navy and Air Force ROTC.

The most frequently chosen fields are business/marketing, engineering/engineering technologies, and health professions and related sciences. A complete listing of majors at Marquette appears in the Majors Index beginning on page 432.

The **faculty** at Marquette has 538 full-time members, 90% with terminal degrees. The student-faculty ratio is 14:1.

Students of Marquette

The student body totals 10,780, of whom 7,437 are undergraduates. 54% are women and 46% are men. Students come from 54 states and territories and 62 other countries. 46% are from Wisconsin. 2.4% are international students. 4.8% are African American, 0.3% American Indian, 4.2% Asian American, and 3.7% Hispanic American. 88% returned for their sophomore year.

Facilities and Resources

Student rooms are linked to a campus network. 1,000 **computers** are available on campus that provide access to the Internet. The 3 **libraries** have 1,154,337 books and 9,225 subscriptions.

Campus Life

There are 156 active organizations on campus, including a drama/theater group, newspaper, radio station, television station, and choral group. 9% of eligible men and 8% of eligible women are members of national **fraternities** and national **sororities**.

Marquette is a member of the NCAA (Division I). **Intercollegiate sports** (some offering scholarships) include baseball (m), basketball, crew, cross-country running, football (m), golf (m), ice hockey (m), lacrosse (m), rugby, sailing, skiing (downhill), soccer, softball (w), swimming, tennis, track and field, volleyball, wrestling (m).

Campus Safety

Student safety services include 24-hour desk attendants in residence halls, late-night transport/escort service, 24-hour emergency telephone alarm devices, 24-hour patrols by trained security personnel, and student patrols.

Applying

Marquette requires an essay, SAT I or ACT, a high school transcript, and a minimum high school GPA of 2.0. It recommends an interview, 1 recommendation, and a minimum high school GPA of 3.0. Application deadline: rolling admissions. Deferred admission is possible.

Getting in Last Year

6,925 applied
84% were accepted
1,718 enrolled (30%)
36% from top tenth of their h.s. class
40% had SAT verbal scores over 600
44% had SAT math scores over 600
72% had ACT scores over 24
7% had SAT verbal scores over 700
8% had SAT math scores over 700
14% had ACT scores over 30
75 valedictorians

Graduation and After

49% graduated in 4 years
19% graduated in 5 years
2% graduated in 6 years
30% pursued further study
66% had job offers within 6 months
400 organizations recruited on campus

Financial Matters

$17,336 tuition and fees (1999–2000)
$6086 room and board
87% average percent of need met
$15,461 average financial aid amount received per undergraduate (1999–2000 estimated)

MARYVILLE COLLEGE

SUBURBAN SETTING ■ PRIVATE ■ INDEPENDENT RELIGIOUS ■ COED
MARYVILLE, TENNESSEE

Web site: www.maryvillecollege.edu
Contact: Ms. Linda L. Moore, Administrative Assistant of Admissions, 502
East Lamar Alexander Parkway, Maryville, TN 37804-5907
Telephone: 865-981-8092 or toll-free 800-597-2687 **Fax:** 865-981-8005
E-mail: admissions@maryvillecollege.edu

One of the South's best colleges, Maryville's emphasis is on education for the individual. Students are guided in the development of a personal plan for intellectual, social, and spiritual growth grounded in a strong liberal arts curriculum supported by a rich array of experiential learning opportunities, including internships, study abroad, service learning, and the College's distinctive outdoor adventure program, Mountain Challenge. A Presbyterian (U.S.A.) college, Maryville is located in the foothills of east Tennessee near Great Smoky Mountain National Park.

Getting in Last Year
1,744 applied
81% were accepted
313 enrolled (22%)
23% from top tenth of their h.s. class
3.49 average high school GPA
31% had SAT verbal scores over 600
31% had SAT math scores over 600
51% had ACT scores over 24
5% had SAT verbal scores over 700
1% had SAT math scores over 700
5% had ACT scores over 30
6 valedictorians

Graduation and After
35% graduated in 4 years
12% graduated in 5 years
2% graduated in 6 years
18% pursued further study (11% arts and sciences, 3% law, 2% business)
62% had job offers within 6 months
80 organizations recruited on campus

Financial Matters
$16,025 tuition and fees (1999–2000)
$5080 room and board
100% average percent of need met
$15,168 average financial aid amount received per undergraduate (1999–2000 estimated)

Academics
MC awards bachelor's **degrees**. Challenging opportunities include advanced placement, student-designed majors, an honors program, double majors, independent study, and a senior project. Special programs include internships, summer session for credit, off-campus study, and study-abroad.

The most frequently chosen fields are education, business/marketing, and social sciences and history. A complete listing of majors at MC appears in the Majors Index beginning on page 432.

The **faculty** at MC has 63 full-time members, 86% with terminal degrees. The student-faculty ratio is 13:1.

Students of MC
The student body is made up of 1,001 undergraduates. 56% are women and 44% are men. Students come from 30 states and territories and 11 other countries. 70% are from Tennessee. 2.9% are international students. 4.8% are African American, 0.3% American Indian, 1.6% Asian American, and 1.3% Hispanic American. 73% returned for their sophomore year.

Facilities and Resources
Student rooms are linked to a campus network. 62 **computers** are available on campus that provide access to the Internet. The 2 **libraries** have 672 subscriptions.

Campus Life
There are 50 active organizations on campus, including a drama/theater group, newspaper, and choral group. No national or local **fraternities** or **sororities**.

MC is a member of the NCAA (Division III). **Intercollegiate sports** include baseball (m), basketball, equestrian sports, football (m), soccer, softball (w), volleyball (w).

Campus Safety
Student safety services include late-night transport/escort service, 24-hour emergency telephone alarm devices, 24-hour patrols by trained security personnel, and electronically operated dormitory entrances.

Applying
MC requires SAT I or ACT, a high school transcript, and a minimum high school GPA of 2.5, and in some cases an essay, an interview, and recommendations. It recommends a minimum high school GPA of 3.0. Application deadline: 3/1; 3/1 priority date for financial aid. Early and deferred admission are possible.

MARYVILLE UNIVERSITY OF SAINT LOUIS

SUBURBAN SETTING ■ PRIVATE ■ INDEPENDENT ■ COED
ST. LOUIS, MISSOURI

Web site: www.maryville.edu
Contact: Dr. Martha Wade, Vice President of Admissions and Enrollment Management, 13550 Conway Road, St. Louis, MO 63141-7299
Telephone: 314-529-9350 or toll-free 800-627-9855 **Fax:** 314-529-9927
E-mail: admissions@maryville.edu

Academics

Maryville awards bachelor's and master's **degrees**. Challenging opportunities include advanced placement, accelerated degree programs, freshman honors college, an honors program, double majors, independent study, and a senior project. Special programs include cooperative education, internships, summer session for credit, off-campus study, study-abroad, and Army ROTC.

The most frequently chosen fields are business/marketing, health professions and related sciences, and psychology. A complete listing of majors at Maryville appears in the Majors Index beginning on page 432.

The **faculty** at Maryville has 92 full-time members, 63% with terminal degrees. The student-faculty ratio is 13:1.

Students of Maryville

The student body totals 3,060, of whom 2,530 are undergraduates. 71.4% are women and 28.6% are men. Students come from 15 states and territories and 38 other countries. 92% are from Missouri. 4.8% are international students. 5.3% are African American, 0.4% American Indian, 1.6% Asian American, and 0.9% Hispanic American. 73% returned for their sophomore year.

Facilities and Resources

Student rooms are linked to a campus network. 260 **computers** are available on campus that provide access to the Internet. The **library** has 125,950 books and 1,558 subscriptions.

Campus Life

There are 33 active organizations on campus, including a drama/theater group, newspaper, and choral group. No national or local **fraternities** or **sororities**.

Maryville is a member of the NCAA (Division III). **Intercollegiate sports** include baseball (m), basketball, cross-country running, golf, soccer, softball (w), tennis, volleyball (w).

Campus Safety

Student safety services include video security system in residence halls, self-defense and education programs, late-night transport/escort service, 24-hour emergency telephone alarm devices, 24-hour patrols by trained security personnel, and electronically operated dormitory entrances.

Applying

Maryville requires SAT I or ACT, a high school transcript, and a minimum high school GPA of 2.5, and in some cases an essay, an interview, recommendations, and audition, portfolio. Application deadline: 8/15; 4/1 priority date for financial aid. Early and deferred admission are possible.

Maryville University of Saint Louis is committed to integrating the liberal arts with professional education by providing innovative and interactive programs with the business, education, health care, cultural, and arts communities it serves. Academic programs are grounded in the humanizing values and ideals that move and guide society—all in the spirit of the liberal arts. In addition, these programs provide opportunities for students to perfect their skills in settings beyond the classroom, gain self-confidence, and profit from the energy of experience.

Getting in Last Year

653 applied
80% were accepted
221 enrolled (42%)
27% from top tenth of their h.s. class
3.39 average high school GPA
18% had SAT verbal scores over 600
22% had SAT math scores over 600
43% had ACT scores over 24
9% had SAT math scores over 700
6% had ACT scores over 30
3 valedictorians

Graduation and After

54% graduated in 4 years
5% graduated in 5 years
3% graduated in 6 years
70 organizations recruited on campus

Financial Matters

$12,280 tuition and fees (1999–2000)
$5400 room and board
68% average percent of need met
$10,279 average financial aid amount received per undergraduate (1999–2000 estimated)

eAPPLY

Getting in Last Year
4,405 applied
56% were accepted
837 enrolled (34%)
46% from top tenth of their h.s. class
3.67 average high school GPA
60% had SAT verbal scores over 600
51% had SAT math scores over 600
10% had SAT verbal scores over 700
6% had SAT math scores over 700
1 National Merit Scholar
12 valedictorians

Graduation and After
64% graduated in 4 years
9% graduated in 5 years
1% graduated in 6 years
18% pursued further study (8% arts and sciences, 4% medicine, 2% education)
70% had job offers within 6 months
64 organizations recruited on campus

Financial Matters
$3204 resident tuition and fees (1999–2000)
$9634 nonresident tuition and fees (1999–2000)
$5298 room and board
54% average percent of need met
$4690 average financial aid amount received per undergraduate (1999–2000 estimated)

MARY WASHINGTON COLLEGE
SMALL-TOWN SETTING ■ PUBLIC ■ STATE-SUPPORTED ■ COED
FREDERICKSBURG, VIRGINIA

Web site: www.mwc.edu
Contact: Dr. Martin A. Wilder Jr., Vice President for Admissions and Financial Aid, 1301 College Avenue, Fredericksburg, VA 22401-5358
Telephone: 540-654-2000 or toll-free 800-468-5614
E-mail: admit@mwc.edu

Academics
Mary Washington awards bachelor's and master's **degrees**. Challenging opportunities include advanced placement, accelerated degree programs, student-designed majors, double majors, independent study, a senior project, and Phi Beta Kappa. Special programs include cooperative education, internships, summer session for credit, and study-abroad.

The most frequently chosen fields are social sciences and history, liberal arts/general studies, and business/marketing. A complete listing of majors at Mary Washington appears in the Majors Index beginning on page 432.

The **faculty** at Mary Washington has 180 full-time members, 83% with terminal degrees. The student-faculty ratio is 17:1.

Students of Mary Washington
The student body totals 4,000, of whom 3,965 are undergraduates. 69% are women and 31% are men. Students come from 44 states and territories and 7 other countries. 74% are from Virginia. 0.4% are international students. 4.2% are African American, 0.2% American Indian, 3.4% Asian American, and 2.4% Hispanic American. 83% returned for their sophomore year.

Facilities and Resources
Student rooms are linked to a campus network. 230 **computers** are available on campus that provide access to the Internet. The **library** has 335,061 books and 1,715 subscriptions.

Campus Life
There are 96 active organizations on campus, including a drama/theater group, newspaper, radio station, and choral group. No national or local **fraternities** or **sororities**.

Mary Washington is a member of the NCAA (Division III). **Intercollegiate sports** include baseball (m), basketball, crew, cross-country running, equestrian sports, field hockey (w), lacrosse, rugby, soccer, softball (w), swimming, tennis, track and field, volleyball.

Campus Safety
Student safety services include self-defense and safety classes, late-night transport/escort service, 24-hour emergency telephone alarm devices, 24-hour patrols by trained security personnel, student patrols, and electronically operated dormitory entrances.

Applying
Mary Washington requires an essay, SAT I or ACT, and a high school transcript. It recommends SAT II Subject Tests. Application deadline: 2/1; 3/1 for financial aid. Deferred admission is possible.

MASSACHUSETTS INSTITUTE OF TECHNOLOGY

URBAN SETTING ■ PRIVATE ■ INDEPENDENT ■ COED
CAMBRIDGE, MASSACHUSETTS

Web site: web.mit.edu
Contact: Ms. Marilee Jones, Dean of Admissions, 77 Massachusetts Avenue,
 Cambridge, MA 02139-4307
Telephone: 617-253-4791
E-mail: mitfrosh@mit.edu

Academics

MIT awards bachelor's, master's, and doctoral **degrees**. Challenging opportunities include advanced placement, accelerated degree programs, student-designed majors, a senior project, Phi Beta Kappa, and Sigma Xi. Special programs include cooperative education, internships, summer session for credit, off-campus study, and Army, Navy and Air Force ROTC.

The most frequently chosen fields are engineering/engineering technologies, computer/information sciences, and biological/life sciences. A complete listing of majors at MIT appears in the Majors Index beginning on page 432.

The **faculty** at MIT has 1,189 full-time members.

Students of MIT

The student body totals 9,972, of whom 4,300 are undergraduates. 41.1% are women and 58.9% are men. Students come from 53 states and territories and 81 other countries. 10% are from Massachusetts. 8.3% are international students. 6.3% are African American, 2% American Indian, 27.7% Asian American, and 10.5% Hispanic American. 98% returned for their sophomore year.

Facilities and Resources

Student rooms are linked to a campus network. 950 **computers** are available on campus that provide access to the Internet. The 12 **libraries** have 2,532,175 books and 18,359 subscriptions.

Campus Life

There are 326 active organizations on campus, including a drama/theater group, newspaper, radio station, television station, choral group, and marching band. 50% of eligible men and 25% of eligible women are members of national **fraternities**, national **sororities**, and local fraternities.

MIT is a member of the NCAA (Division III). **Intercollegiate sports** include baseball (m), basketball, crew, cross-country running, fencing, field hockey (w), football (m), golf (m), gymnastics, ice hockey, lacrosse, riflery, rugby, sailing, skiing (cross-country), skiing (downhill), soccer, softball (w), squash (m), swimming, tennis, track and field, volleyball, water polo, wrestling (m).

Campus Safety

Student safety services include late-night transport/escort service, 24-hour emergency telephone alarm devices, 24-hour patrols by trained security personnel, student patrols, and electronically operated dormitory entrances.

Applying

MIT requires an essay, SAT II Subject Tests, SAT I or ACT, a high school transcript, an interview, and 2 recommendations. Application deadline: 1/1; 1/11 priority date for financial aid. Deferred admission is possible.

Getting in Last Year

9,136 applied
19% were accepted
1,048 enrolled (60%)
95% from top tenth of their h.s. class
93% had SAT verbal scores over 600
100% had SAT math scores over 600
99% had ACT scores over 24
58% had SAT verbal scores over 700
88% had SAT math scores over 700
78% had ACT scores over 30
133 National Merit Scholars
55 class presidents
218 valedictorians

Graduation and After

81% graduated in 4 years
9% graduated in 5 years
2% graduated in 6 years
Graduates pursuing further study: 16% engineering, 11% arts and sciences, 7% medicine
41% had job offers within 6 months
700 organizations recruited on campus

Financial Matters

$25,000 tuition and fees (1999–2000)
$6900 room and board
100% average percent of need met
$23,445 average financial aid amount received per undergraduate (1998–99)

MESSIAH COLLEGE

SMALL-TOWN SETTING ■ PRIVATE ■ INDEPENDENT RELIGIOUS ■ COED
GRANTHAM, PENNSYLVANIA

Web site: www.messiah.edu
Contact: Mr. William G. Strausbaugh, Dean for Enrollment Management,
One College Avenue, Grantham, PA 17027-0800
Telephone: 717-691-6000 or toll-free 800-382-1349 (in-state), 800-233-4220
(out-of-state) **Fax:** 717-796-5374
E-mail: admiss@messiah.edu

> **M**essiah College provides an education that is both rigorously academic and unapologetically Christian. The learning process is characterized by lively student-faculty interaction that actively integrates faith issues with academic content. Messiah offers a strategically located campus, impressive academic and residence life facilities, and over 50 majors and 50 minors in the applied and liberal arts and sciences. Students pursue extracurricular interests in 18 intercollegiate sports, ministries, service learning areas, music ensembles, and scores of other activities. A multifaceted internship program provides career experience for students before they graduate. After graduation 96% of graduates report employment/voluntary service or enrollment in graduate school within 6 months.

Academics

Messiah College awards bachelor's **degrees**. Challenging opportunities include advanced placement, accelerated degree programs, student-designed majors, freshman honors college, an honors program, double majors, independent study, and a senior project. Special programs include internships, summer session for credit, off-campus study, and study-abroad.

The most frequently chosen fields are education, business/marketing, and health professions and related sciences. A complete listing of majors at Messiah College appears in the Majors Index beginning on page 432.

The **faculty** at Messiah College has 141 full-time members, 77% with terminal degrees. The student-faculty ratio is 15:1.

Students of Messiah College

The student body is made up of 2,735 undergraduates. 61.6% are women and 38.4% are men. Students come from 39 states and territories and 22 other countries. 51% are from Pennsylvania. 1.7% are international students. 1.3% are African American, 0.2% American Indian, 1.4% Asian American, and 1.5% Hispanic American. 86% returned for their sophomore year.

Facilities and Resources

Student rooms are linked to a campus network. 299 **computers** are available on campus that provide access to the Internet. The **library** has 233,732 books and 1,316 subscriptions.

Campus Life

There are 60 active organizations on campus, including a drama/theater group, newspaper, radio station, and choral group. No national or local **fraternities** or **sororities**.

Messiah College is a member of the NCAA (Division III). **Intercollegiate sports** include baseball (m), basketball, cross-country running, field hockey (w), golf (m), lacrosse, soccer, softball (w), tennis, track and field, volleyball (w), wrestling (m).

Campus Safety

Student safety services include bicycle patrols, late-night transport/escort service, 24-hour emergency telephone alarm devices, 24-hour patrols by trained security personnel, student patrols, and electronically operated dormitory entrances.

Applying

Messiah College requires an essay, SAT I or ACT, a high school transcript, and 2 recommendations. It recommends an interview and a minimum high school GPA of 3.0. Application deadline: rolling admissions; 4/1 priority date for financial aid. Early and deferred admission are possible.

Getting in Last Year
2,088 applied
81% were accepted
678 enrolled (40%)
34% from top tenth of their h.s. class
3.68 average high school GPA
47% had SAT verbal scores over 600
44% had SAT math scores over 600
68% had ACT scores over 24
10% had SAT verbal scores over 700
9% had SAT math scores over 700
20% had ACT scores over 30
13 National Merit Scholars
43 valedictorians

Graduation and After
66% graduated in 4 years
4% graduated in 5 years
1% graduated in 6 years
8% pursued further study (5% arts and sciences, 2% education, 1% medicine)
89% had job offers within 6 months
453 organizations recruited on campus

Financial Matters
$15,096 tuition and fees (1999–2000)
$5580 room and board
75% average percent of need met
$11,909 average financial aid amount received per undergraduate (1999–2000)

MIAMI UNIVERSITY

SMALL-TOWN SETTING ■ PUBLIC ■ STATE-RELATED ■ COED
OXFORD, OHIO

Web site: www.muohio.edu
Contact: Dr. James S. McCoy, Associate Vice President for Enrollment Services, Oxford, OH 45056
Telephone: 513-529-2531 **Fax:** 513-529-1550
E-mail: admission@muohio.edu

Academics

Miami University awards bachelor's, master's, and doctoral **degrees** and post-master's certificates. Challenging opportunities include advanced placement, student-designed majors, an honors program, double majors, independent study, a senior project, Phi Beta Kappa, and Sigma Xi. Special programs include cooperative education, internships, summer session for credit, off-campus study, study-abroad, and Army, Navy and Air Force ROTC.

The most frequently chosen fields are business/marketing, education, and social sciences and history. A complete listing of majors at Miami University appears in the Majors Index beginning on page 432.

The **faculty** at Miami University has 772 full-time members, 81% with terminal degrees. The student-faculty ratio is 18:1.

Students of Miami University

The student body totals 16,575, of whom 15,288 are undergraduates. 55.1% are women and 44.9% are men. Students come from 49 states and territories and 70 other countries. 73% are from Ohio. 0.5% are international students. 3.7% are African American, 0.4% American Indian, 1.7% Asian American, and 1.7% Hispanic American. 90% returned for their sophomore year.

Facilities and Resources

Student rooms are linked to a campus network. 1,000 **computers** are available on campus that provide access to the Internet. The 4 **libraries** have 2,190,506 books.

Campus Life

There are 350 active organizations on campus, including a drama/theater group, newspaper, radio station, television station, choral group, and marching band. 24% of eligible men and 27% of eligible women are members of national **fraternities** and national **sororities**.

Miami University is a member of the NCAA (Division I). **Intercollegiate sports** (some offering scholarships) include archery, baseball (m), basketball, cross-country running, equestrian sports, fencing, field hockey (w), football (m), golf (m), gymnastics, ice hockey (m), lacrosse (m), racquetball, rugby (m), sailing, soccer, softball (w), swimming, tennis, track and field, volleyball, wrestling (m).

Campus Safety

Student safety services include late-night transport/escort service, 24-hour emergency telephone alarm devices, 24-hour patrols by trained security personnel, student patrols, and electronically operated dormitory entrances.

Applying

Miami University requires SAT I or ACT and a high school transcript. It recommends an essay and 1 recommendation. Application deadline: 1/31; 2/15 priority date for financial aid.

Miami University is acclaimed for an "unusually strong commitment to undergraduate teaching" by *U.S. News & World Report's America's Best Colleges* and is considered one of only 21 "Best Buy" public institutions, offering "remarkable educational opportunities at a relatively modest cost," by *Fiske Guide to Colleges 2000*. Also noteworthy are Miami's honors program that combines seminar-style courses, research and creative projects, community service, and an honors residence hall; its many research opportunities for undergraduates; and its high rate of students accepted at professional schools. Miami is among the top 10 US universities for the number of students studying abroad.

Getting in Last Year
11,993 applied
79% were accepted
3,605 enrolled (38%)
32% from top tenth of their h.s. class
45% had SAT verbal scores over 600
57% had SAT math scores over 600
76% had ACT scores over 24
7% had SAT verbal scores over 700
10% had SAT math scores over 700
12% had ACT scores over 30
38 National Merit Scholars
180 valedictorians

Graduation and After
63% graduated in 4 years
16% graduated in 5 years
2% graduated in 6 years
Graduates pursuing further study: 14% arts and sciences, 7% law, 7% medicine
550 organizations recruited on campus
1 Marshall scholar

Financial Matters
$6112 resident tuition and fees (1999–2000)
$12,766 nonresident tuition and fees (1999–2000)
$5330 room and board
74% average percent of need met
$5889 average financial aid amount received per undergraduate (1999–2000)

MICHIGAN STATE UNIVERSITY

SUBURBAN SETTING ■ PUBLIC ■ STATE-SUPPORTED ■ COED
EAST LANSING, MICHIGAN

Web site: www.msu.edu
Contact: Dr. Gordon Stanley, Assistant to the Provost for Enrollment and
Director of Admissions, East Lansing, MI 48824-1020
Telephone: 517-355-8332 **Fax:** 517-353-1647
E-mail: admis@msu.edu

Getting in Last Year
22,623 applied
71% were accepted
6,716 enrolled (42%)
23% from top tenth of their h.s. class
3.44 average high school GPA
30% had SAT verbal scores over 600
37% had SAT math scores over 600
52% had ACT scores over 24
7% had SAT verbal scores over 700
9% had SAT math scores over 700
7% had ACT scores over 30
150 National Merit Scholars
100 valedictorians

Graduation and After
32% graduated in 4 years
29% graduated in 5 years
6% graduated in 6 years
20% pursued further study
80% had job offers within 6 months
620 organizations recruited on campus
3 Fulbright scholars

Financial Matters
$5590 resident tuition and fees (1999–2000)
$12,992 nonresident tuition and fees (1999–2000)
$4298 room and board
88% average percent of need met
$7142 average financial aid amount received per undergraduate (1999–2000 estimated)

Academics

Michigan State awards bachelor's, master's, doctoral, and first-professional **degrees**. Challenging opportunities include advanced placement, accelerated degree programs, student-designed majors, freshman honors college, an honors program, double majors, independent study, a senior project, Phi Beta Kappa, and Sigma Xi. Special programs include cooperative education, internships, summer session for credit, off-campus study, study-abroad, and Army and Air Force ROTC.

The most frequently chosen fields are business/marketing, social sciences and history, and engineering/engineering technologies. A complete listing of majors at Michigan State appears in the Majors Index beginning on page 432.

The **faculty** at Michigan State has 2,309 full-time members, 95% with terminal degrees. The student-faculty ratio is 18:1.

Students of Michigan State

The student body totals 43,038, of whom 33,966 are undergraduates. 53.3% are women and 46.7% are men. Students come from 54 states and territories and 85 other countries. 94% are from Michigan. 2.1% are international students. 8.7% are African American, 0.6% American Indian, 4% Asian American, and 2.4% Hispanic American. 87% returned for their sophomore year.

Facilities and Resources

Student rooms are linked to a campus network. 1,800 **computers** are available on campus that provide access to the Internet. The 16 **libraries** have 4,194,445 books.

Campus Life

There are 350 active organizations on campus, including a drama/theater group, newspaper, radio station, television station, choral group, and marching band. 8% of eligible men and 8% of eligible women are members of national **fraternities** and national **sororities**.

Michigan State is a member of the NCAA (Division I). **Intercollegiate sports** (some offering scholarships) include baseball (m), basketball, crew (w), cross-country running, equestrian sports, field hockey (w), football (m), golf, gymnastics, ice hockey (m), lacrosse (m), soccer (m), softball (w), swimming, tennis, track and field, volleyball (w), wrestling (m).

Campus Safety

Student safety services include self-defense workshops, late-night transport/escort service, 24-hour emergency telephone alarm devices, and 24-hour patrols by trained security personnel.

Applying

Michigan State requires SAT I or ACT and a high school transcript. Application deadline: 7/30; 6/30 for financial aid, with a 2/21 priority date. Deferred admission is possible.

Michigan Technological University

SMALL-TOWN SETTING ■ PUBLIC ■ STATE-SUPPORTED ■ COED
HOUGHTON, MICHIGAN

Web site: www.mtu.edu
Contact: Ms. Nancy Rehling, Director of Undergraduate Admissions, 1400
  Townsend Drive, Houghton, MI 49931-1295
Telephone: 906-487-2335 **Fax:** 906-487-3343
E-mail: mtu4u@mtu.edu

Academics

Michigan Tech awards associate, bachelor's, master's, and doctoral **degrees**. Challenging opportunities include advanced placement, student-designed majors, double majors, a senior project, and Sigma Xi. Special programs include cooperative education, summer session for credit, off-campus study, study-abroad, and Army and Air Force ROTC.

The most frequently chosen fields are engineering/engineering technologies, business/marketing, and computer/information sciences. A complete listing of majors at Michigan Tech appears in the Majors Index beginning on page 432.

The **faculty** at Michigan Tech has 366 full-time members, 88% with terminal degrees. The student-faculty ratio is 16:1.

Students of Michigan Tech

The student body totals 6,321, of whom 5,661 are undergraduates. 26.8% are women and 73.2% are men. Students come from 43 states and territories and 63 other countries. 81% are from Michigan. 4.7% are international students. 2.2% are African American, 1% American Indian, 1.1% Asian American, and 0.7% Hispanic American. 82% returned for their sophomore year.

Facilities and Resources

Student rooms are linked to a campus network. 1,146 **computers** are available on campus that provide access to the Internet. The **library** has 5,149 subscriptions.

Campus Life

There are 145 active organizations on campus, including a drama/theater group, newspaper, radio station, and choral group. 85% of eligible men and 15% of eligible women are members of national **fraternities**, national **sororities**, local fraternities, and local sororities.

Michigan Tech is a member of the NCAA (Division II). **Intercollegiate sports** (some offering scholarships) include basketball, cross-country running, fencing, football (m), ice hockey, racquetball, riflery, skiing (cross-country), skiing (downhill), soccer, squash, swimming, table tennis, tennis, track and field, volleyball (w), water polo.

Campus Safety

Student safety services include late-night transport/escort service, 24-hour emergency telephone alarm devices, and 24-hour patrols by trained security personnel.

Applying

Michigan Tech requires a high school transcript. It recommends SAT I or ACT and an interview. Application deadline: rolling admissions; 2/21 priority date for financial aid. Deferred admission is possible.

Michigan Tech is recognized as one of the nation's leading universities for undergraduate and graduate education in science and engineering. MTU's state-of-the-art campus is located near Lake Superior in Michigan's beautiful Upper Peninsula. *Money Guide* ranks Michigan Tech among the top 10 scientific and technical universities in the nation, and *U.S. News & World Report* includes Michigan Tech with the top 50 best values among national universities. MTU is one of Michigan's 4 nationally recognized research universities.

Getting in Last Year
2,689 applied
94% were accepted
1,155 enrolled (45%)
34% from top tenth of their h.s. class
3.51 average high school GPA
46% had SAT verbal scores over 600
64% had SAT math scores over 600
69% had ACT scores over 24
10% had SAT verbal scores over 700
17% had SAT math scores over 700
13% had ACT scores over 30
7 National Merit Scholars
63 valedictorians

Graduation and After
22% graduated in 4 years
32% graduated in 5 years
9% graduated in 6 years
20% pursued further study
91% had job offers within 6 months
183 organizations recruited on campus

Financial Matters
$4491 resident tuition and fees (1999–2000)
$10,704 nonresident tuition and fees (1999–2000)
$4726 room and board
79% average percent of need met
$6397 average financial aid amount received per undergraduate (1999–2000 estimated)

MIDDLEBURY COLLEGE

SMALL-TOWN SETTING ■ PRIVATE ■ INDEPENDENT ■ COED
MIDDLEBURY, VERMONT

Web site: www.middlebury.edu
Contact: Mr. John Hanson, Director of Admissions, Emma Willard House,
Middlebury, VT 05753-6002
Telephone: 802-443-3000 **Fax:** 802-443-2056
E-mail: admissions@middlebury.edu

Academics

Middlebury awards bachelor's, master's, and doctoral **degrees**. Challenging opportunities include advanced placement, accelerated degree programs, student-designed majors, an honors program, double majors, independent study, and Phi Beta Kappa. Special programs include internships, summer session for credit, off-campus study, and study-abroad.

The most frequently chosen fields are social sciences and history, English, and foreign language/literature. A complete listing of majors at Middlebury appears in the Majors Index beginning on page 432.

The **faculty** at Middlebury has 218 full-time members, 92% with terminal degrees. The student-faculty ratio is 10:1.

Students of Middlebury

The student body totals 2,270, of whom 2,265 are undergraduates. 50.9% are women and 49.1% are men. Students come from 50 states and territories and 71 other countries. 5% are from Vermont. 7.3% are international students. 2.5% are African American, 0.5% American Indian, 4.1% Asian American, and 5% Hispanic American. 96% returned for their sophomore year.

Facilities and Resources

Student rooms are linked to a campus network. 200 **computers** are available on campus that provide access to the Internet. The 4 **libraries** have 774,993 books and 1,923 subscriptions.

Campus Life

There are 100 active organizations on campus, including a drama/theater group, newspaper, radio station, and choral group. Middlebury has social houses, commons system.

Middlebury is a member of the NCAA (Division III). **Intercollegiate sports** include baseball (m), basketball, cross-country running, field hockey (w), football (m), golf, ice hockey, lacrosse, skiing (cross-country), skiing (downhill), soccer, squash (w), swimming, tennis, track and field, volleyball (w).

Campus Safety

Student safety services include late-night transport/escort service and student patrols.

Literary study, global understanding based on language proficiency and cultural knowledge, environmental studies grounded in science, language study and pedagogy, instruction by leading faculty members and scholars, application of learning to the real world—these elements form the academic core of excellence at this 200-year-old institution. The beautiful campus has a new state-of-the-art interdisciplinary science facility, a contemporary arts center, sophisticated computer networks, multimedia workstations for language study, comprehensive libraries with global connections, and outstanding athletic facilities, including a ski area and golf course. To attend Middlebury is to have a lifetime of opportunities, made possible by one of the world's foremost liberal arts colleges.

Getting in Last Year
4,869 applied
26% were accepted
524 enrolled (42%)
72% from top tenth of their h.s. class
96% had SAT verbal scores over 600
94% had SAT math scores over 600
56% had SAT verbal scores over 700
46% had SAT math scores over 700

Graduation and After
80% graduated in 4 years
6% graduated in 5 years
1% graduated in 6 years
12% pursued further study (3% arts and sciences, 2% law, 1% medicine)
65 organizations recruited on campus

Financial Matters
$31,790 comprehensive fee (1999–2000)
100% average percent of need met
$23,538 average financial aid amount received per undergraduate (1999–2000 estimated)

MILLIKIN UNIVERSITY

SUBURBAN SETTING ■ PRIVATE ■ INDEPENDENT RELIGIOUS ■ COED
DECATUR, ILLINOIS

Web site: www.millikin.edu
Contact: Mr. Lin Stoner, Dean of Admission, 1184 West Main Street,
   Decatur, IL 62522-2084
Telephone: 217-424-6210 or toll-free 800-373-7733 **Fax:** 217-425-4669
E-mail: admis@mail.millikin.edu

Academics

Millikin awards bachelor's **degrees**. Challenging opportunities include advanced placement, student-designed majors, an honors program, double majors, independent study, and a senior project. Special programs include internships, summer session for credit, off-campus study, and study-abroad. A complete listing of majors at Millikin appears in the Majors Index beginning on page 432.

The **faculty** at Millikin has 142 full-time members, 87% with terminal degrees. The student-faculty ratio is 13:1.

Students of Millikin

The student body is made up of 2,272 undergraduates. 58.9% are women and 41.1% are men. 0.7% are international students. 7.3% are African American, 0.2% American Indian, 1.3% Asian American, and 1.5% Hispanic American.

Facilities and Resources

Student rooms are linked to a campus network. 172 **computers** are available on campus that provide access to the Internet. The **library** has 142,048 books and 1,008 subscriptions.

Campus Life

There are 78 active organizations on campus, including a drama/theater group, newspaper, radio station, and choral group. 23% of eligible men and 24% of eligible women are members of national **fraternities** and national **sororities**.

Millikin is a member of the NCAA (Division III). **Intercollegiate sports** include baseball (m), basketball, cross-country running, football (m), golf, soccer, softball (w), swimming, tennis, track and field, volleyball (w), wrestling (m).

Campus Safety

Student safety services include late-night transport/escort service, 24-hour emergency telephone alarm devices, 24-hour patrols by trained security personnel, and electronically operated dormitory entrances.

Applying

Millikin requires SAT I or ACT, a high school transcript, 2 recommendations, and a minimum high school GPA of 2.0, and in some cases audition for school of music; portfolio review for art program. It recommends an interview. Application deadline: rolling admissions; 6/1 for financial aid, with a 4/1 priority date. Deferred admission is possible.

Getting in Last Year

2,461 applied
75% were accepted
595 enrolled (32%)
22% from top tenth of their h.s. class
38% had SAT verbal scores over 600
28% had SAT math scores over 600
47% had ACT scores over 24
5% had SAT verbal scores over 700
1% had SAT math scores over 700
6% had ACT scores over 30
19 valedictorians

Graduation and After

58% graduated in 4 years
4% graduated in 5 years
2% graduated in 6 years
19% pursued further study (11% arts and
   sciences, 2% education, 2% medicine)
98% had job offers within 6 months
91 organizations recruited on campus

Financial Matters

$16,008 tuition and fees (1999–2000)
$5593 room and board
89% average percent of need met
$14,497 average financial aid amount received
   per undergraduate (1999–2000)

 eApply

MILLSAPS COLLEGE

URBAN SETTING ■ PRIVATE ■ INDEPENDENT RELIGIOUS ■ COED
JACKSON, MISSISSIPPI

Web site: www.millsaps.edu
Contact: Mr. John Gaines, Director of Admissions, 1701 North State Street, Jackson, MS 39210-0001
Telephone: 601-974-1050 or toll-free 800-352-1050 **Fax:** 601-974-1059
E-mail: admissions@millsaps.edu

Millsaps College is a community founded on trust in disciplined learning as a key to a rewarding life. In keeping with its character as a liberal arts college and its historic role in the mission of the United Methodist Church, Millsaps seeks to provide a learning environment that increases knowledge, deepens understanding of faith, and inspires the development of mature citizens with the intellectual capacities, ethical principles, and sense of responsibility that are needed for leadership in all sectors of society.

Getting in Last Year
912 applied
87% were accepted
284 enrolled (36%)
44% from top tenth of their h.s. class
3.26 average high school GPA
55% had SAT verbal scores over 600
42% had SAT math scores over 600
74% had ACT scores over 24
11% had SAT verbal scores over 700
7% had SAT math scores over 700
16% had ACT scores over 30
7 National Merit Scholars
19 class presidents
19 valedictorians

Graduation and After
35% pursued further study
44% had job offers within 6 months
60 organizations recruited on campus

Financial Matters
$15,029 tuition and fees (1999–2000)
$6106 room and board
90% average percent of need met
$15,692 average financial aid amount received per undergraduate (1999–2000)

Academics
Millsaps awards bachelor's and master's **degrees**. Challenging opportunities include advanced placement, an honors program, double majors, a senior project, and Phi Beta Kappa. Special programs include internships, summer session for credit, off-campus study, study-abroad, and Army ROTC.

The most frequently chosen fields are business/marketing, social sciences and history, and English. A complete listing of majors at Millsaps appears in the Majors Index beginning on page 432.

The **faculty** at Millsaps has 89 full-time members, 94% with terminal degrees. The student-faculty ratio is 14:1.

Students of Millsaps
The student body totals 1,314, of whom 1,191 are undergraduates. 54.8% are women and 45.2% are men. Students come from 26 states and territories and 6 other countries. 57% are from Mississippi. 0.8% are international students. 8.9% are African American, 0.4% American Indian, 2.9% Asian American, and 0.7% Hispanic American. 85% returned for their sophomore year.

Facilities and Resources
Student rooms are linked to a campus network. 150 **computers** are available on campus that provide access to the Internet. The **library** has 117,705 books and 656 subscriptions.

Campus Life
There are 50 active organizations on campus, including a drama/theater group, newspaper, and choral group. 59% of eligible men and 56% of eligible women are members of national **fraternities** and national **sororities**.

Millsaps is a member of the NCAA (Division III). **Intercollegiate sports** include baseball (m), basketball, cross-country running, football (m), golf, soccer, softball (w), tennis, volleyball (w).

Campus Safety
Student safety services include self-defense education, lighted pathways and sidewalks, late-night transport/escort service, 24-hour emergency telephone alarm devices, 24-hour patrols by trained security personnel, student patrols, and electronically operated dormitory entrances.

Applying
Millsaps requires an essay, SAT I or ACT, a high school transcript, and a minimum high school GPA of 2.75. It recommends an interview and recommendations. Application deadline: 7/1. Deferred admission is possible.

MILLS COLLEGE

URBAN SETTING ■ PRIVATE ■ INDEPENDENT ■ WOMEN ONLY

OAKLAND, CALIFORNIA

Web site: www.mills.edu

Contact: Ms. Avis E. Hinkson, Dean of Admission, 5000 MacArthur
  Boulevard, Oakland, CA 94613-1000

Telephone: 510-430-2135 or toll-free 800-87-MILLS **Fax:** 510-430-3314

E-mail: admission@mills.edu

Academics

Mills awards bachelor's, master's, and doctoral **degrees**. Challenging opportunities
include advanced placement, student-designed majors, double majors, independent
study, a senior project, and Phi Beta Kappa. Special programs include internships, off-
campus study, and Army ROTC.

The most frequently chosen fields are interdisciplinary studies, social sciences and
history, and visual/performing arts. A complete listing of majors at Mills appears in the
Majors Index beginning on page 432.

The **faculty** at Mills has 81 full-time members. The student-faculty ratio is 11:1.

Students of Mills

The student body totals 1,122, of whom 727 are undergraduates. Students come from 39
states and territories and 10 other countries. 80% are from California. 0.4% are international students. 7.3% are African American, 1% American Indian, 8.1% Asian
American, and 7.3% Hispanic American. 77% returned for their sophomore year.

Facilities and Resources

Student rooms are linked to a campus network. 66 **computers** are available on campus
that provide access to the Internet. The 2 **libraries** have 189,814 books and 2,029
subscriptions.

Campus Life

There are 30 active organizations on campus, including a drama/theater group,
newspaper, and choral group. No national or local **sororities**.

Mills is a member of the NCAA (Division III). **Intercollegiate sports** include
basketball, crew, cross-country running, soccer, tennis, volleyball.

Campus Safety

Student safety services include late-night transport/escort service, 24-hour emergency
telephone alarm devices, 24-hour patrols by trained security personnel, and electronically operated dormitory entrances.

Applying

Mills requires SAT I or ACT, a high school transcript, 3 recommendations, and essay or
graded paper, statement of good standing from prior institution(s). It recommends SAT
II Subject Tests and an interview. Application deadline: 2/15; 2/15 priority date for
financial aid. Deferred admission is possible.

Why a women's college?
"I came to college to
study, and I wanted a
college that was very pro-women—
a college that would prepare me to
do well and succeed," says Mills
regional scholar Leah Hathaway.
And Mills does. Even in their first
year, bright students like Leah can
tackle original hands-on research
that most students don't experience
until graduate school. Since half the
professors at Mills are women (not
the case in coeducational
institutions), students have
successful role models in every field.
And all of Mills' undergraduate
resources are committed to women.
When women graduate from Mills,
they *know* they can succeed. That
confidence makes all the difference.

Getting in Last Year
461 applied
78% were accepted
116 enrolled (32%)
35% from top tenth of their h.s. class
3.52 average high school GPA
51% had SAT verbal scores over 600
24% had SAT math scores over 600
10% had SAT verbal scores over 700
3% had SAT math scores over 700

Graduation and After
17 organizations recruited on campus

Financial Matters
$17,852 tuition and fees (1999–2000)
$7296 room and board
87% average percent of need met
$18,246 average financial aid amount received
  per undergraduate (1999–2000 estimated)

---

eAPPLY

Getting in Last Year
1,837 applied
71% were accepted
511 enrolled (39%)
26% from top tenth of their h.s. class
3.4 average high school GPA
27% had SAT verbal scores over 600
56% had SAT math scores over 600
73% had ACT scores over 24
5% had SAT verbal scores over 700
18% had SAT math scores over 700
13% had ACT scores over 30

Graduation and After
29% graduated in 4 years
18% graduated in 5 years
1% graduated in 6 years
Graduates pursuing further study: 3% engineering, 2% business, 1% law
95% had job offers within 6 months
194 organizations recruited on campus

Financial Matters
$19,845 tuition and fees (2000–2001)
$4710 room and board
85% average percent of need met
$12,400 average financial aid amount received per undergraduate (1998–99)

MILWAUKEE SCHOOL OF ENGINEERING
URBAN SETTING ■ PRIVATE ■ INDEPENDENT ■ COED, PRIMARILY MEN
MILWAUKEE, WISCONSIN

Web site: www.msoe.edu
Contact: Mr. Tim A. Valley, Dean of Enrollment Management, 1025 North Broadway, Milwaukee, WI 53202-3109
Telephone: 414-277-6763 or toll-free 800-332-6763 **Fax:** 414-277-7475
E-mail: explore@msoe.edu

Academics
MSOE awards associate, bachelor's, and master's **degrees**. Challenging opportunities include advanced placement, accelerated degree programs, double majors, independent study, and a senior project. Special programs include internships, summer session for credit, study-abroad, and Army and Air Force ROTC.

The most frequently chosen fields are engineering/engineering technologies, business/marketing, and health professions and related sciences. A complete listing of majors at MSOE appears in the Majors Index beginning on page 432.

The **faculty** at MSOE has 117 full-time members, 49% with terminal degrees. The student-faculty ratio is 12:1.

Students of MSOE
The student body totals 2,711, of whom 2,343 are undergraduates. 17.3% are women and 82.7% are men. Students come from 34 states and territories and 27 other countries. 80% are from Wisconsin. 3.8% are international students. 3.5% are African American, 0.4% American Indian, 2.5% Asian American, and 1.9% Hispanic American. 76% returned for their sophomore year.

Facilities and Resources
Student rooms are linked to a campus network. 150 **computers** are available on campus that provide access to e-mail and the Internet. The **library** has 55,310 books and 565 subscriptions.

Campus Life
There are 62 active organizations on campus, including a drama/theater group, newspaper, and radio station. 11% of eligible men and 9% of eligible women are members of national **fraternities**, national **sororities**, local fraternities, and local sororities.

MSOE is a member of the NCAA (Division III). **Intercollegiate sports** include baseball (m), basketball, cross-country running, golf (m), ice hockey (m), soccer, softball (w), tennis, volleyball (w), wrestling (m).

Campus Safety
Student safety services include late-night transport/escort service, 24-hour emergency telephone alarm devices, 24-hour patrols by trained security personnel, and electronically operated dormitory entrances.

Applying
MSOE requires SAT I or ACT, a high school transcript, and a minimum high school GPA of 2.0, and in some cases an essay and an interview. Application deadline: rolling admissions; 3/15 priority date for financial aid. Deferred admission is possible.

MONMOUTH COLLEGE

SMALL-TOWN SETTING ■ PRIVATE ■ INDEPENDENT RELIGIOUS ■ COED
MONMOUTH, ILLINOIS

Web site: www.monm.edu
Contact: Mrs. Marybeth Kemp, Dean of Admission, 700 East Broadway,
  Monmouth, IL 61462-1998
Telephone: 309-457-2131 or toll-free 800-747-2687 **Fax:** 309-457-2141
E-mail: admit@monm.edu

eAPPLY

Academics

Monmouth awards bachelor's **degrees**. Challenging opportunities include advanced placement, student-designed majors, an honors program, double majors, independent study, and a senior project. Special programs include internships, off-campus study, study-abroad, and Army ROTC.

The most frequently chosen fields are business/marketing, education, and social sciences and history. A complete listing of majors at Monmouth appears in the Majors Index beginning on page 432.

The **faculty** at Monmouth has 65 full-time members. The student-faculty ratio is 14:1.

Students of Monmouth

The student body is made up of 1,057 undergraduates. 57.3% are women and 42.7% are men. Students come from 20 states and territories and 23 other countries. 93% are from Illinois. 4.2% are international students. 4.6% are African American, 0.2% American Indian, 1.2% Asian American, and 1.7% Hispanic American. 78% returned for their sophomore year.

Facilities and Resources

Student rooms are linked to a campus network. 300 **computers** are available on campus that provide access to the Internet. The **library** has 177,974 books and 1,709 subscriptions.

Campus Life

There are 50 active organizations on campus, including a drama/theater group, newspaper, radio station, television station, and choral group. 25% of eligible men and 30% of eligible women are members of national **fraternities** and national **sororities**.

Monmouth is a member of the NCAA (Division III). **Intercollegiate sports** include baseball (m), basketball, cross-country running, football (m), golf, soccer, softball (w), track and field, volleyball (w).

Campus Safety

Student safety services include night security, late-night transport/escort service, and 24-hour emergency telephone alarm devices.

Applying

Monmouth requires SAT I or ACT and a high school transcript, and in some cases an essay. It recommends an interview and 2 recommendations. Application deadline: 5/1; 4/15 priority date for financial aid. Deferred admission is possible.

Getting in Last Year
1,210 applied
77% were accepted
274 enrolled (29%)
14% from top tenth of their h.s. class
3.00 average high school GPA
36% had ACT scores over 24
6% had ACT scores over 30

Graduation and After
41% graduated in 4 years
9% graduated in 5 years
1% graduated in 6 years
20% pursued further study
90% had job offers within 6 months
21 organizations recruited on campus

Financial Matters
$15,720 tuition and fees (1999–2000)
$4410 room and board

MOREHOUSE COLLEGE

URBAN SETTING ■ PRIVATE ■ INDEPENDENT ■ MEN ONLY
ATLANTA, GEORGIA

Web site: www.morehouse.edu
Contact: Mr. André Pattillo, Director of Admissions, 830 Westview Drive, SW, Atlanta, GA 30314
Telephone: 404-215-2632 or toll-free 800-851-1254 **Fax:** 404-524-5635
E-mail: apattillo@morehouse.edu

Morehouse College seeks to develop leaders who will be qualified and committed to solving the problems of society with special attention given to those of African Americans. Inspired by the legacy of distinguished alumni, presidents, and professors—persons who have wrought significant social changes—the College supports and encourages programs that benefit all people and that seek to eradicate discrimination and injustice. Morehouse is firmly committed to attracting and enrolling students of high caliber from a wide variety of educational and economic backgrounds and providing them with learning and leadership development opportunities.

Getting in Last Year
2,785 applied
66% were accepted
748 enrolled (41%)
42% from top tenth of their h.s. class
3.01 average high school GPA
21% had SAT verbal scores over 600
20% had SAT math scores over 600
21% had ACT scores over 24
3% had SAT verbal scores over 700
4% had SAT math scores over 700
0% had ACT scores over 30

Graduation and After
30% graduated in 4 years
15% graduated in 5 years
6% graduated in 6 years
Graduates pursuing further study: 14% arts and sciences, 5% law, 4% medicine
30% had job offers within 6 months
55 organizations recruited on campus

Financial Matters
$11,738 tuition and fees (1999–2000)
$6970 room and board

Academics

Morehouse College awards bachelor's **degrees**. Challenging opportunities include advanced placement, an honors program, a senior project, and Phi Beta Kappa. Special programs include cooperative education, internships, summer session for credit, off-campus study, study-abroad, and Army, Navy and Air Force ROTC.

The most frequently chosen fields are business/marketing, social sciences and history, and psychology. A complete listing of majors at Morehouse College appears in the Majors Index beginning on page 432.

The **faculty** at Morehouse College has 184 full-time members, 76% with terminal degrees. The student-faculty ratio is 15:1.

Students of Morehouse College

The student body is made up of 3,012 undergraduates. Students come from 42 states and territories. 31% are from Georgia. 98.7% are African American, 0.2% Asian American, and 0.2% Hispanic American. 85% returned for their sophomore year.

Facilities and Resources

Student rooms are linked to a campus network. 325 **computers** are available on campus that provide access to the Internet. The **library** has 560,000 books and 1,000 subscriptions.

Campus Life

There are 34 active organizations on campus, including a drama/theater group, newspaper, choral group, and marching band. 7% of eligible undergraduates are members of national **fraternities**.

Morehouse College is a member of the NCAA (Division II). **Intercollegiate sports** (some offering scholarships) include basketball, cross-country running, football, tennis, track and field.

Campus Safety

Student safety services include late-night transport/escort service, 24-hour emergency telephone alarm devices, and 24-hour patrols by trained security personnel.

Applying

Morehouse College requires an essay, SAT I or ACT, a high school transcript, recommendations, and a minimum high school GPA of 2.8. It recommends an interview and a minimum high school GPA of 3.0. Application deadline: 2/15; 4/1 priority date for financial aid. Early and deferred admission are possible.

MOUNT HOLYOKE COLLEGE

SMALL-TOWN SETTING ■ PRIVATE ■ INDEPENDENT ■ WOMEN ONLY
SOUTH HADLEY, MASSACHUSETTS

Web site: www.mtholyoke.edu
Contact: Diane Anci, Director of Admission, 50 College Street, South Hadley, MA 01075
Telephone: 413-538-2023 **Fax:** 413-538-2409
E-mail: admissions@mtholyoke.edu

Academics

Mount Holyoke awards bachelor's **degrees**. Challenging opportunities include advanced placement, student-designed majors, an honors program, double majors, independent study, a senior project, Phi Beta Kappa, and Sigma Xi. Special programs include internships, off-campus study, study-abroad, and Army and Air Force ROTC.

The most frequently chosen fields are social sciences and history, biological/life sciences, and English. A complete listing of majors at Mount Holyoke appears in the Majors Index beginning on page 432.

The **faculty** at Mount Holyoke has 181 full-time members, 98% with terminal degrees. The student-faculty ratio is 10:1.

Students of Mount Holyoke

The student body totals 1,982, of whom 1,979 are undergraduates. Students come from 50 states and territories and 76 other countries. 34% are from Massachusetts. 11.9% are international students. 5.2% are African American, 0.7% American Indian, 8.8% Asian American, and 5% Hispanic American. 94% returned for their sophomore year.

Facilities and Resources

Student rooms are linked to a campus network. 245 **computers** are available on campus that provide access to the Internet. The 2 **libraries** have 2,696 subscriptions.

Campus Life

There are 125 active organizations on campus, including a drama/theater group, newspaper, radio station, and choral group. No national or local **sororities**.

Mount Holyoke is a member of the NCAA (Division III). **Intercollegiate sports** include basketball, crew, cross-country running, equestrian sports, field hockey, golf, ice hockey, lacrosse, soccer, squash, swimming, tennis, track and field, volleyball, water polo.

Campus Safety

Student safety services include late-night transport/escort service, 24-hour emergency telephone alarm devices, 24-hour patrols by trained security personnel, student patrols, and electronically operated dormitory entrances.

Applying

Mount Holyoke requires an essay, SAT I or ACT, a high school transcript, and 2 recommendations. It recommends an interview. Application deadline: 1/15; 2/15 for financial aid. Early and deferred admission are possible.

Located

in a small town in the Connecticut River Valley of Massachusetts, Mount Holyoke College is a liberal arts college for women, the oldest of its kind in the United States. Believing that the ability to make sound decisions is one of the chief benefits of a liberal education, the College gives its students primary responsibility for planning and achieving their educational goals. To this end, it offers a high degree of independence and a wide range of opportunities, including all that come with membership in the Five College Consortium with Amherst, Hampshire, and Smith Colleges and the University of Massachusetts.

Getting in Last Year

2,435 applied
60% were accepted
554 enrolled (38%)
48% from top tenth of their h.s. class
3.65 average high school GPA
70% had SAT verbal scores over 600
54% had SAT math scores over 600
86% had ACT scores over 24
20% had SAT verbal scores over 700
9% had SAT math scores over 700
17% had ACT scores over 30
20 National Merit Scholars
21 valedictorians

Graduation and After

73% graduated in 4 years
6% graduated in 5 years
1% graduated in 6 years
25% pursued further study
60 organizations recruited on campus
1 Marshall, 1 Fulbright scholar

Financial Matters

$24,354 tuition and fees (1999–2000)
$7110 room and board
100% average percent of need met
$20,966 average financial aid amount received per undergraduate (1999–2000 estimated)

MOUNT UNION COLLEGE

SUBURBAN SETTING ■ PRIVATE ■ INDEPENDENT RELIGIOUS ■ COED
ALLIANCE, OHIO

Web site: www.muc.edu
Contact: Mr. Greg King, Director of Admissions and Enrollment
Management, 1972 Clark Avenue, Alliance, OH 44601
Telephone: 330-823-2590 or toll-free 800-334-6682 (in-state), 800-992-6682
(out-of-state) **Fax:** 330-823-3457
E-mail: admissn@muc.edu

Mount Union College has established a reputation for producing successful graduates in a wide array of occupations. The College affirms the importance of reason, open inquiry, living faith, and individual worth. Mount Union's mission is to prepare students for meaningful work, fulfilling lives, and responsible citizenship. Mount Union strives to provide the best education possible for each of its students so that its graduates develop communication skills, critical thinking, a sensitivity to social responsibility, and a concern for human needs.

Getting in Last Year
1,901 applied
90% were accepted
661 enrolled (39%)
26% from top tenth of their h.s. class
38% had ACT scores over 24
4% had ACT scores over 30
15 valedictorians

Graduation and After
45% graduated in 4 years
12% graduated in 5 years
1% graduated in 6 years
25% pursued further study
94% had job offers within 6 months
40 organizations recruited on campus

Financial Matters
$14,880 tuition and fees (1999–2000)
$4370 room and board
87% average percent of need met
$12,720 average financial aid amount received
per undergraduate (1999–2000 estimated)

Academics

Mount Union awards bachelor's **degrees**. Challenging opportunities include advanced placement, accelerated degree programs, student-designed majors, an honors program, double majors, independent study, and a senior project. Special programs include cooperative education, internships, summer session for credit, off-campus study, study-abroad, and Army and Air Force ROTC.

The most frequently chosen fields are business/marketing, parks and recreation, and education. A complete listing of majors at Mount Union appears in the Majors Index beginning on page 432.

The **faculty** at Mount Union has 111 full-time members, 81% with terminal degrees. The student-faculty ratio is 18:1.

Students of Mount Union

The student body is made up of 2,277 undergraduates. 54.6% are women and 45.4% are men. Students come from 19 states and territories and 15 other countries. 88% are from Ohio. 2.2% are international students. 4% are African American, 0.3% American Indian, 0.5% Asian American, and 0.7% Hispanic American. 83% returned for their sophomore year.

Facilities and Resources

Student rooms are linked to a campus network. 150 **computers** are available on campus that provide access to the Internet. The 3 **libraries** have 223,980 books and 921 subscriptions.

Campus Life

There are 75 active organizations on campus, including a drama/theater group, newspaper, radio station, choral group, and marching band. 28% of eligible men and 32% of eligible women are members of national **fraternities**, national **sororities**, and local sororities.

Mount Union is a member of the NCAA (Division III). **Intercollegiate sports** include baseball (m), basketball, cross-country running, football (m), golf, soccer, softball (w), swimming, tennis, track and field, volleyball (w), wrestling (m).

Campus Safety

Student safety services include 24-hour locked residence hall entrances, outside phones, 24-hour emergency telephone alarm devices, 24-hour patrols by trained security personnel, and electronically operated dormitory entrances.

Applying

Mount Union requires an essay, SAT I or ACT, a high school transcript, 1 recommendation, and a minimum high school GPA of 2.0. It recommends an interview. Application deadline: rolling admissions. Early and deferred admission are possible.

MUHLENBERG COLLEGE

SUBURBAN SETTING ■ PRIVATE ■ INDEPENDENT RELIGIOUS ■ COED
ALLENTOWN, PENNSYLVANIA

Web site: www.muhlenberg.edu
Contact: Mr. Christopher Hooker-Haring, Dean of Admissions, 2400 Chew
 Street, Allentown, PA 18104-5586
Telephone: 484-664-3245 **Fax:** 484-664-3234
E-mail: adm@muhlenberg.edu

Academics

Muhlenberg awards bachelor's **degrees**. Challenging opportunities include advanced
placement, accelerated degree programs, student-designed majors, an honors program,
double majors, independent study, a senior project, and Phi Beta Kappa. Special
programs include internships, summer session for credit, off-campus study, study-abroad,
and Army ROTC.

The most frequently chosen fields are social sciences and history, biological/life sciences, and psychology. A complete listing of majors at Muhlenberg appears in the Majors
Index beginning on page 432.

The **faculty** at Muhlenberg has 131 full-time members, 88% with terminal degrees.
The student-faculty ratio is 13:1.

Students of Muhlenberg

The student body is made up of 2,443 undergraduates. 56.9% are women and 43.1% are
men. Students come from 37 states and territories and 5 other countries. 34% are from
Pennsylvania. 0.2% are international students. 1.9% are African American, 2.9% Asian
American, and 2.5% Hispanic American. 91% returned for their sophomore year.

Facilities and Resources

Student rooms are linked to a campus network. 150 **computers** are available on campus
that provide access to the Internet. The **library** has 270,700 books and 1,700 subscriptions.

Campus Life

There are 102 active organizations on campus, including a drama/theater group,
newspaper, radio station, television station, and choral group. 36% of eligible men and
37% of eligible women are members of national **fraternities** and national **sororities**.

Muhlenberg is a member of the NCAA (Division III). **Intercollegiate sports** include
baseball (m), basketball, cross-country running, field hockey (w), football (m), golf,
lacrosse (w), soccer, softball (w), tennis, track and field, volleyball (w), wrestling (m).

Campus Safety

Student safety services include late-night transport/escort service, 24-hour emergency
telephone alarm devices, 24-hour patrols by trained security personnel, and electronically operated dormitory entrances.

Applying

Muhlenberg requires an essay, a high school transcript, and 2 recommendations, and in
some cases SAT I or ACT and an interview. It recommends an interview. Application
deadline: 2/15; 2/15 for financial aid. Early and deferred admission are possible.

Getting in Last Year

3,274 applied
55% were accepted
552 enrolled (31%)
34% from top tenth of their h.s. class
3.56 average high school GPA
43% had SAT verbal scores over 600
44% had SAT math scores over 600
7% had SAT verbal scores over 700
7% had SAT math scores over 700
1 National Merit Scholar
24 class presidents
7 valedictorians

Graduation and After

Graduates pursuing further study: 12% arts
 and sciences, 7% medicine, 5% law
67% had job offers within 6 months
64 organizations recruited on campus

Financial Matters

$20,085 tuition and fees (1999–2000)
$5390 room and board
96% average percent of need met
$14,600 average financial aid amount received
 per undergraduate (1998–99)

NEBRASKA WESLEYAN UNIVERSITY

SUBURBAN SETTING ■ PRIVATE ■ INDEPENDENT RELIGIOUS ■ COED
LINCOLN, NEBRASKA

Web site: www.nebrwesleyan.edu
Contact: Mr. Kendal E. Sieg, Director of Admissions, 5000 Saint Paul
    Avenue, Lincoln, NE 68504-2796
Telephone: 402-465-2218 or toll-free 800-541-3818 **Fax:** 402-465-2179
E-mail: adm@nebrwesleyan.edu

> Nebraska Wesleyan is committed to providing an honors-quality experience for every student. Strong relationships with the faculty enable students to develop and refine interests, talents, and critical thinking and communication skills necessary to be competitive. Superior research facilities provide experience for students as early as their first year. The benefits of integrated advising, orientation, and career services are evident in Nebraska Wesleyan's high retention, graduation, and graduate/professional school placement rates. Development of leadership skills is well within reach of all students through more than 80 honoraries, clubs, and organizations, and through service learning and local, national, and international volunteer opportunities.

Getting in Last Year
1,105 applied
94% were accepted
359 enrolled (34%)
26% from top tenth of their h.s. class
54% had ACT scores over 24
6% had ACT scores over 30
22 valedictorians

Graduation and After
48% graduated in 4 years
13% graduated in 5 years
2% graduated in 6 years
77 organizations recruited on campus

Financial Matters
$12,826 tuition and fees (1999–2000)
$3974 room and board
73% average percent of need met
$9748 average financial aid amount received
    per undergraduate (1999–2000 estimated)

Academics

NWU awards bachelor's **degrees**. Challenging opportunities include advanced placement, accelerated degree programs, double majors, independent study, and a senior project. Special programs include internships, summer session for credit, off-campus study, study-abroad, and Army and Air Force ROTC.

The most frequently chosen fields are business/marketing, biological/life sciences, and psychology. A complete listing of majors at NWU appears in the Majors Index beginning on page 432.

The **faculty** at NWU has 92 full-time members, 80% with terminal degrees. The student-faculty ratio is 14:1.

Students of NWU

The student body is made up of 1,675 undergraduates. 57.6% are women and 42.4% are men. Students come from 24 states and territories. 94% are from Nebraska. 0.4% are international students. 1.5% are African American, 0.2% American Indian, 1% Asian American, and 1.2% Hispanic American. 79% returned for their sophomore year.

Facilities and Resources

Student rooms are linked to a campus network. 111 **computers** are available on campus that provide access to the Internet. The **library** has 132,758 books and 741 subscriptions.

Campus Life

There are 80 active organizations on campus, including a drama/theater group, newspaper, and choral group. 42% of eligible men and 34% of eligible women are members of national **fraternities**, national **sororities**, local fraternities, and local sororities.

NWU is a member of the NCAA (Division III) and NAIA. **Intercollegiate sports** include baseball (m), basketball, cross-country running, football (m), golf, soccer, softball (w), tennis, track and field, volleyball (w).

Campus Safety

Student safety services include late-night transport/escort service, 24-hour patrols by trained security personnel, and electronically operated dormitory entrances.

Applying

NWU requires SAT I or ACT, a high school transcript, and a minimum high school GPA of 2.0, and in some cases an essay and resume of activities. It recommends an interview and recommendations. Application deadline: 1/5; 3/1 for financial aid. Deferred admission is possible.

New College of the University of South Florida

Suburban setting ■ Public ■ State-supported ■ Coed
Sarasota, Florida

Web site: www.newcollege.usf.edu
Contact: Ms. Kathleen Killion, Director of Admissions, 5700 North Tamiami Trail, Sarasota, FL 34243-2197
Telephone: 941-359-4269 **Fax:** 941-359-4435
E-mail: ncadmissions@sar.usf.edu

eAPPLY

Academics
New College of USF awards bachelor's **degrees**. Challenging opportunities include accelerated degree programs, student-designed majors, double majors, independent study, and a senior project. Special programs include internships, off-campus study, study-abroad, and Army and Air Force ROTC.

The most frequently chosen field is liberal arts/general studies. A complete listing of majors at New College of USF appears in the Majors Index beginning on page 432.

The **faculty** at New College of USF has 55 full-time members, 98% with terminal degrees. The student-faculty ratio is 11:1.

Students of New College of USF
The student body is made up of 617 undergraduates. 63% are women and 37% are men. 62% are from Florida. 0.3% are international students. 2.3% are African American, 4.7% Asian American, and 7.1% Hispanic American. 88% returned for their sophomore year.

Facilities and Resources
Student rooms are linked to a campus network. The **library** has 254,889 books and 1,592 subscriptions.

Campus Life
There are 42 active organizations on campus, including a drama/theater group, newspaper, radio station, and choral group. No national or local **fraternities** or **sororities**.

This institution has no intercollegiate sports.

Campus Safety
Student safety services include late-night transport/escort service, 24-hour emergency telephone alarm devices, and 24-hour patrols by trained security personnel.

Applying
New College of USF requires an essay, SAT I or ACT, a high school transcript, 2 recommendations, and graded writing sample, and in some cases an interview. It recommends an interview and a minimum high school GPA of 3.0. Application deadline: 5/1; 3/1 priority date for financial aid. Early and deferred admission are possible.

Getting in Last Year
298 applied
75% were accepted
128 enrolled (57%)
53% from top tenth of their h.s. class
3.79 average high school GPA
91% had SAT verbal scores over 600
70% had SAT math scores over 600
93% had ACT scores over 24
41% had SAT verbal scores over 700
16% had SAT math scores over 700
20% had ACT scores over 30
12 National Merit Scholars

Graduation and After
50% graduated in 4 years
13% graduated in 5 years
3% graduated in 6 years
29% pursued further study (21% arts and sciences, 4% medicine, 3% law)
1 Marshall scholar

Financial Matters
$2492 resident tuition and fees (1999–2000)
$10,878 nonresident tuition and fees (1999–2000)
$4663 room and board
100% average percent of need met
$9962 average financial aid amount received per undergraduate (1999–2000)

NEW JERSEY INSTITUTE OF TECHNOLOGY

URBAN SETTING ■ PUBLIC ■ STATE-SUPPORTED ■ COED
NEWARK, NEW JERSEY

Web site: www.njit.edu
Contact: Ms. Kathy Kelly, Director of Admissions, University Heights,
   Newark, NJ 07102-1982
Telephone: 973-596-3300 or toll-free 800-925-NJIT **Fax:** 973-596-3461
E-mail: admissions@njit.edu

The Albert Dorman Honors College is one of the nation's leading technologically oriented honors programs. Admission is highly selective; successful applicants generally rank in the top 10% of their high schools, with SAT I scores above 1250. Honors College scholars receive at least a one-half tuition scholarship award. Exceptionally well prepared students may be eligible for additional scholarships and partial room grants. All degree programs are available through the Albert Dorman Honors College.

Getting in Last Year
2,369 applied
60% were accepted
681 enrolled (48%)
14% from top tenth of their h.s. class
21% had SAT verbal scores over 600
50% had SAT math scores over 600
3% had SAT verbal scores over 700
9% had SAT math scores over 700

Graduation and After
22% pursued further study
70% had job offers within 6 months
100 organizations recruited on campus

Financial Matters
$6480 resident tuition and fees (1999–2000)
$10,824 nonresident tuition and fees (1999–2000)
$7050 room and board
84% average percent of need met
$8817 average financial aid amount received per undergraduate (1998–99)

Academics

NJIT awards bachelor's, master's, and doctoral **degrees**. Challenging opportunities include advanced placement, accelerated degree programs, freshman honors college, an honors program, double majors, independent study, a senior project, and Sigma Xi. Special programs include cooperative education, internships, summer session for credit, off-campus study, study-abroad, and Air Force ROTC.

The most frequently chosen fields are engineering/engineering technologies, computer/information sciences, and architecture. A complete listing of majors at NJIT appears in the Majors Index beginning on page 432.

The **faculty** at NJIT has 399 full-time members, 100% with terminal degrees. The student-faculty ratio is 14:1.

Students of NJIT

The student body totals 8,261, of whom 5,270 are undergraduates. 21.8% are women and 78.2% are men. Students come from 33 states and territories and 42 other countries. 90% are from New Jersey. 6.2% are international students. 12.1% are African American, 0.2% American Indian, 21.2% Asian American, and 13.1% Hispanic American. 82% returned for their sophomore year.

Facilities and Resources

Student rooms are linked to a campus network. 4,015 **computers** are available on campus that provide access to the Internet. The 2 **libraries** have 140,575 books and 997 subscriptions.

Campus Life

There are 70 active organizations on campus, including a drama/theater group, newspaper, and radio station. 12% of eligible men and 9% of eligible women are members of national **fraternities**, national **sororities**, local fraternities, and local sororities.

NJIT is a member of the NCAA (Division II). **Intercollegiate sports** include baseball (m), basketball, cross-country running, fencing (m), golf (m), soccer (m), softball (w), swimming (w), tennis, track and field (w), volleyball.

Campus Safety

Student safety services include bicycle patrols, sexual assault response team, late-night transport/escort service, 24-hour emergency telephone alarm devices, 24-hour patrols by trained security personnel, and electronically operated dormitory entrances.

Applying

NJIT requires SAT I or ACT and a high school transcript, and in some cases an essay, SAT II Subject Tests, and an interview. It recommends 1 recommendation. Application deadline: 4/1; 4/15 priority date for financial aid. Early and deferred admission are possible.

New Mexico Institute of Mining and Technology

SMALL-TOWN SETTING ■ PUBLIC ■ STATE-SUPPORTED ■ COED
SOCORRO, NEW MEXICO

Web site: www.nmt.edu
Contact: Ms. Melissa Jaramillo-Fleming, Director of Admissions, 801 Leroy
Place, Socorro, NM 87801
Telephone: 505-835-5424 or toll-free 800-428-TECH **Fax:** 505-835-5989
E-mail: admission@admin.nmt.edu

Academics

New Mexico Tech awards associate, bachelor's, master's, and doctoral **degrees**. Challenging opportunities include advanced placement, accelerated degree programs, student-designed majors, double majors, independent study, a senior project, and Sigma Xi. Special programs include cooperative education, internships, summer session for credit, off-campus study, and study-abroad.

The most frequently chosen fields are engineering/engineering technologies, physical sciences, and biological/life sciences. A complete listing of majors at New Mexico Tech appears in the Majors Index beginning on page 432.

The **faculty** at New Mexico Tech has 99 full-time members, 100% with terminal degrees. The student-faculty ratio is 11:1.

Students of New Mexico Tech

The student body totals 1,513, of whom 1,218 are undergraduates. 36.5% are women and 63.5% are men. Students come from 52 states and territories and 14 other countries. 64% are from New Mexico. 2.3% are international students. 0.7% are African American, 3.9% American Indian, 2.6% Asian American, and 17.6% Hispanic American. 67% returned for their sophomore year.

Facilities and Resources

Student rooms are linked to a campus network. 225 **computers** are available on campus that provide access to the Internet. The 2 **libraries** have 89,725 books and 766 subscriptions.

Campus Life

There are 55 active organizations on campus, including a drama/theater group, newspaper, radio station, and choral group. No national or local **fraternities** or **sororities**.

This institution has no intercollegiate sports.

Campus Safety

Student safety services include late-night transport/escort service, 24-hour emergency telephone alarm devices, and 24-hour patrols by trained security personnel.

Applying

New Mexico Tech requires SAT I or ACT, a high school transcript, and a minimum high school GPA of 2.0, and in some cases 2 recommendations. It recommends SAT II Subject Tests and an interview. Application deadline: 8/1; 3/1 priority date for financial aid. Deferred admission is possible.

Getting in Last Year

1,168 applied
70% were accepted
249 enrolled (30%)
31% from top tenth of their h.s. class
3.5 average high school GPA
70% had ACT scores over 24
18% had ACT scores over 30

Graduation and After

15% graduated in 4 years
17% graduated in 5 years
5% graduated in 6 years
26% pursued further study (14% arts and sciences, 9% engineering, 2% education)
22 organizations recruited on campus

Financial Matters

$2328 resident tuition and fees (1999–2000)
$7328 nonresident tuition and fees (1999–2000)
$3584 room and board
90% average percent of need met
$7979 average financial aid amount received per undergraduate (1998–99)

eAPPLY

Getting in Last Year
28,794 applied
32% were accepted
3,642 enrolled (40%)
61% from top tenth of their h.s. class
3.53 average high school GPA
86% had SAT verbal scores over 600
83% had SAT math scores over 600
33% had SAT verbal scores over 700
31% had SAT math scores over 700
126 National Merit Scholars

Graduation and After
60% graduated in 4 years
9% graduated in 5 years
2% graduated in 6 years
400 organizations recruited on campus

Financial Matters
$23,456 tuition and fees (1999–2000)
$8860 room and board
73% average percent of need met
$15,999 average financial aid amount received
per undergraduate (1999–2000)

NEW YORK UNIVERSITY
URBAN SETTING ■ PRIVATE ■ INDEPENDENT ■ COED
NEW YORK, NEW YORK

Web site: www.nyu.edu
Contact: Mr. Richard Avitabile, Assistant Vice President for Enrollment
Services, 22 Washington Square North, New York, NY 10011
Telephone: 212-998-4500 **Fax:** 212-995-4902

Academics
NYU awards associate, bachelor's, master's, doctoral, and first-professional **degrees** and post-master's certificates. Challenging opportunities include advanced placement, student-designed majors, freshman honors college, an honors program, double majors, independent study, a senior project, Phi Beta Kappa, and Sigma Xi. Special programs include internships, summer session for credit, off-campus study, study-abroad, and Army and Air Force ROTC.

The most frequently chosen fields are visual/performing arts, business/marketing, and social sciences and history. A complete listing of majors at NYU appears in the Majors Index beginning on page 432.

The **faculty** at NYU has 1,465 full-time members, 99% with terminal degrees. The student-faculty ratio is 13:1.

Students of NYU
The student body totals 37,132, of whom 18,204 are undergraduates. 59% are women and 41% are men. Students come from 52 states and territories and 120 other countries. 53% are from New York. 4.8% are international students. 7.1% are African American, 0.1% American Indian, 15.9% Asian American, and 7.5% Hispanic American. 88% returned for their sophomore year.

Facilities and Resources
Student rooms are linked to a campus network. 859 **computers** are available on campus that provide access to the Internet. The 8 **libraries** have 4,056,642 books and 29,244 subscriptions.

Campus Life
There are 250 active organizations on campus, including a drama/theater group, newspaper, radio station, television station, choral group, and marching band. 7% of eligible men and 6% of eligible women are members of national **fraternities**, national **sororities**, and local sororities.

NYU is a member of the NCAA (Division III). **Intercollegiate sports** include badminton, baseball (m), basketball, crew, cross-country running, equestrian sports, fencing, golf (m), ice hockey (m), lacrosse, racquetball, soccer, softball (w), swimming, tennis, track and field, volleyball, water polo, wrestling.

Campus Safety
Student safety services include 24-hour security in residence halls, late-night transport/escort service, 24-hour emergency telephone alarm devices, 24-hour patrols by trained security personnel, student patrols, and electronically operated dormitory entrances.

Applying
NYU requires an essay, SAT I or ACT, a high school transcript, 2 recommendations, and a minimum high school GPA of 3.0, and in some cases SAT II Subject Tests, an interview, and audition, portfolio. It recommends SAT II Subject Tests and SAT II: Writing Test. Application deadline: 1/15; 2/15 priority date for financial aid. Early and deferred admission are possible.

NORTH CAROLINA STATE UNIVERSITY

SUBURBAN SETTING ■ PUBLIC ■ STATE-SUPPORTED ■ COED
RALEIGH, NORTH CAROLINA

Web site: www.ncsu.edu
Contact: Dr. George R. Dixon, Vice Provost and Director of Admissions, Box 7103, 112 Peele Hall, Raleigh, NC 27695
Telephone: 919-515-2434
E-mail: undergrad_admissions@ncsu.edu

eAPPLY

Academics

NC State awards associate, bachelor's, master's, doctoral, and first-professional **degrees** and first-professional certificates. Challenging opportunities include advanced placement, accelerated degree programs, student-designed majors, freshman honors college, an honors program, double majors, independent study, a senior project, Phi Beta Kappa, and Sigma Xi. Special programs include cooperative education, internships, summer session for credit, off-campus study, study-abroad, and Army, Navy and Air Force ROTC.

The most frequently chosen fields are engineering/engineering technologies, business/marketing, and agriculture. A complete listing of majors at NC State appears in the Majors Index beginning on page 432.

The student-faculty ratio is 13:1.

Students of NC State

The student body totals 28,011, of whom 21,684 are undergraduates. 41% are women and 59% are men. Students come from 51 states and territories and 65 other countries. 92% are from North Carolina. 0.9% are international students. 10.4% are African American, 0.7% American Indian, 4.7% Asian American, and 1.7% Hispanic American. 88% returned for their sophomore year.

Facilities and Resources

Student rooms are linked to a campus network. 4,600 **computers** are available on campus that provide access to the Internet. The 5 **libraries** have 35,194 subscriptions.

Campus Life

There are 300 active organizations on campus, including a drama/theater group, newspaper, radio station, television station, choral group, and marching band. NC State has national **fraternities** and national **sororities**.

NC State is a member of the NCAA (Division I). **Intercollegiate sports** (some offering scholarships) include baseball (m), basketball, cross-country running, fencing, football (m), golf, gymnastics, ice hockey (m), lacrosse (m), racquetball, riflery, rugby, sailing, skiing (downhill), soccer, swimming, tennis, track and field, volleyball, water polo, weight lifting, wrestling (m).

Campus Safety

Student safety services include late-night transport/escort service, 24-hour emergency telephone alarm devices, 24-hour patrols by trained security personnel, student patrols, and electronically operated dormitory entrances.

Applying

NC State requires SAT I or ACT and a high school transcript, and in some cases an interview and 1 recommendation. It recommends an essay and a minimum high school GPA of 3.0. Application deadline: 12/1; 3/1 priority date for financial aid. Deferred admission is possible.

Getting in Last Year

12,227 applied
62% were accepted
3,666 enrolled (49%)
36% from top tenth of their h.s. class
3.86 average high school GPA
37% had SAT verbal scores over 600
53% had SAT math scores over 600
63% had ACT scores over 24
7% had SAT verbal scores over 700
12% had SAT math scores over 700
12% had ACT scores over 30
41 National Merit Scholars
75 valedictorians

Graduation and After

25% graduated in 4 years
30% graduated in 5 years
7% graduated in 6 years
20% pursued further study
498 organizations recruited on campus
2 Fulbright scholars

Financial Matters

$2514 resident tuition and fees (1999–2000)
$12,566 nonresident tuition and fees (1999–2000)
$4560 room and board
84% average percent of need met
$5661 average financial aid amount received per undergraduate (1999–2000)

eAPPLY

NORTH CENTRAL COLLEGE

SUBURBAN SETTING ■ PRIVATE ■ INDEPENDENT RELIGIOUS ■ COED
NAPERVILLE, ILLINOIS

Web site: www.noctrl.edu
Contact: Mr. Stephen Potts, Coordinator of Freshman Admission, 30 North
    Brainard Street, PO Box 3063, Naperville, IL 60566-7063
Telephone: 630-637-5815 or toll-free 800-411-1861 **Fax:** 630-637-5819
E-mail: ncadm@noctrl.edu

North Central College is a community of learners dedicated to preparing informed, involved, principled, and productive citizens and leaders over a lifetime. This mission is grounded in the liberal arts, with a balanced curriculum emphasizing leadership, ethics, and values. North Central College is committed to undergraduate teaching and to sustaining its strong residential college tradition. The College offers more than 50 academic areas of concentration in business, science, education, communications, liberal arts, and preprofessional programs. Cocurricular opportunities include Division III intercollegiate athletics, a nationally recognized student radio station, a Model UN, forensics, community volunteering, and campus ministry. More than 90% of the freshman class receives financial assistance.

Getting in Last Year
1,453 applied
76% were accepted
402 enrolled (36%)
25% from top tenth of their h.s. class
3.50 average high school GPA
32% had SAT verbal scores over 600
35% had SAT math scores over 600
61% had ACT scores over 24
7% had SAT verbal scores over 700
5% had SAT math scores over 700
8% had ACT scores over 30
3 National Merit Scholars
13 valedictorians

Graduation and After
52% graduated in 4 years
5% graduated in 5 years
2% graduated in 6 years
10% pursued further study (6% arts and sciences, 2% business, 1% education)
77% had job offers within 6 months
60 organizations recruited on campus

Financial Matters
$15,216 tuition and fees (1999–2000)
$5250 room and board
88% average percent of need met
$13,316 average financial aid amount received per undergraduate (1999–2000 estimated)

Academics

North Central awards bachelor's and master's **degrees**. Challenging opportunities include advanced placement, accelerated degree programs, student-designed majors, an honors program, double majors, independent study, and a senior project. Special programs include cooperative education, internships, summer session for credit, off-campus study, study-abroad, and Army, Navy and Air Force ROTC.

The most frequently chosen fields are business/marketing, communications/communication technologies, and education. A complete listing of majors at North Central appears in the Majors Index beginning on page 432.

The **faculty** at North Central has 120 full-time members, 86% with terminal degrees. The student-faculty ratio is 13:1.

Students of North Central

The student body totals 2,545, of whom 2,179 are undergraduates. 57.9% are women and 42.1% are men. Students come from 25 states and territories and 23 other countries. 90% are from Illinois. 1.7% are international students. 4.2% are African American, 0.4% American Indian, 1.6% Asian American, and 3.1% Hispanic American. 80% returned for their sophomore year.

Facilities and Resources

Student rooms are linked to a campus network. 135 **computers** are available on campus that provide access to the Internet. The **library** has 126,057 books and 659 subscriptions.

Campus Life

There are 42 active organizations on campus, including a drama/theater group, newspaper, radio station, and choral group. No national or local **fraternities** or **sororities**.

North Central is a member of the NCAA (Division III). **Intercollegiate sports** include baseball (m), basketball, cross-country running, football (m), golf, soccer, softball (w), swimming, tennis, track and field, volleyball (w), wrestling (m).

Campus Safety

Student safety services include late-night transport/escort service.

Applying

North Central requires SAT I or ACT, a high school transcript, and a minimum high school GPA of 2.0, and in some cases an interview. It recommends an essay, ACT, and 1 recommendation. Application deadline: rolling admissions. Early and deferred admission are possible.

NORTHWESTERN COLLEGE

RURAL SETTING ■ PRIVATE ■ INDEPENDENT RELIGIOUS ■ COED
ORANGE CITY, IOWA

Web site: www.nwciowa.edu
Contact: Mr. Ronald K. DeJong, Director of Admissions, 101 College Lane, Orange City, IA 51041-1996
Telephone: 712-737-7130 or toll-free 800-747-4757 **Fax:** 712-737-7164
E-mail: markb@nwciowa.edu

Academics

Northwestern awards associate and bachelor's **degrees**. Challenging opportunities include advanced placement, accelerated degree programs, student-designed majors, freshman honors college, an honors program, double majors, independent study, and a senior project. Special programs include cooperative education, internships, summer session for credit, off-campus study, and study-abroad.

The most frequently chosen fields are education, business/marketing, and biological/life sciences. A complete listing of majors at Northwestern appears in the Majors Index beginning on page 432.

The **faculty** at Northwestern has 65 full-time members, 68% with terminal degrees. The student-faculty ratio is 16:1.

Students of Northwestern

The student body is made up of 1,219 undergraduates. 61% are women and 39% are men. Students come from 30 states and territories and 16 other countries. 64% are from Iowa. 2.8% are international students. 0.2% are African American, 0.5% American Indian, 0.5% Asian American, and 0.4% Hispanic American. 75% returned for their sophomore year.

Facilities and Resources

Student rooms are linked to a campus network. 250 **computers** are available on campus that provide access to the Internet. The 2 **libraries** have 107,567 books and 563 subscriptions.

Campus Life

There are 28 active organizations on campus, including a drama/theater group, newspaper, radio station, and choral group. No national or local **fraternities** or **sororities**.

Northwestern is a member of the NAIA. **Intercollegiate sports** (some offering scholarships) include baseball (m), basketball, cross-country running, football (m), golf, soccer, softball (w), tennis, track and field, volleyball (w), wrestling (m).

Campus Safety

Student safety services include 24-hour emergency telephone alarm devices and electronically operated dormitory entrances.

Applying

Northwestern requires an essay, SAT I or ACT, a high school transcript, 1 recommendation, and a minimum high school GPA of 2.0. It recommends an interview and a minimum high school GPA of 2.5. Application deadline: rolling admissions; 4/1 priority date for financial aid. Deferred admission is possible.

NORTHWESTERN UNIVERSITY

SUBURBAN SETTING ■ PRIVATE ■ INDEPENDENT ■ COED
EVANSTON, ILLINOIS

Web site: www.nwu.edu
Contact: Ms. Carol Lunkenheimer, Director of Admissions, 1801 Hinman
   Avenue, Evanston, IL 60208
Telephone: 847-491-7271
E-mail: ug-admission@nwu.edu

Getting in Last Year
15,460 applied
32% were accepted
1,952 enrolled (39%)
83% from top tenth of their h.s. class
87% had SAT verbal scores over 600
91% had SAT math scores over 600
97% had ACT scores over 24
42% had SAT verbal scores over 700
45% had SAT math scores over 700
63% had ACT scores over 30

Graduation and After
81% graduated in 4 years
9% graduated in 5 years
1% graduated in 6 years
522 organizations recruited on campus
2 Marshall scholars

Financial Matters
$23,562 tuition and fees (1999–2000)
$6970 room and board
100% average percent of need met
$19,985 average financial aid amount received
   per undergraduate (1999–2000 estimated)

Academics

Northwestern awards bachelor's, master's, doctoral, and first-professional **degrees**. Challenging opportunities include advanced placement, accelerated degree programs, student-designed majors, an honors program, double majors, independent study, a senior project, Phi Beta Kappa, and Sigma Xi. Special programs include cooperative education, internships, summer session for credit, off-campus study, study-abroad, and Army, Navy and Air Force ROTC.

The most frequently chosen fields are social sciences and history, engineering/engineering technologies, and English. A complete listing of majors at Northwestern appears in the Majors Index beginning on page 432.

The **faculty** at Northwestern has 2,134 full-time members. The student-faculty ratio is 8:1.

Students of Northwestern

The student body totals 15,406, of whom 7,842 are undergraduates. 52.5% are women and 47.5% are men. Students come from 50 states and territories and 80 other countries. 27% are from Illinois. 3.3% are international students. 6.1% are African American, 0.2% American Indian, 16.6% Asian American, and 4% Hispanic American. 95% returned for their sophomore year.

Facilities and Resources

Student rooms are linked to a campus network. 611 **computers** are available on campus that provide access to the Internet. The 11 **libraries** have 3,893,005 books and 40,124 subscriptions.

Campus Life

There are 250 active organizations on campus, including a drama/theater group, newspaper, radio station, television station, choral group, and marching band. 40% of eligible men and 39% of eligible women are members of national **fraternities** and national **sororities**.

Northwestern is a member of the NCAA (Division I). **Intercollegiate sports** (some offering scholarships) include baseball (m), basketball, cross-country running (w), fencing (w), field hockey (w), football (m), golf, soccer, softball (w), swimming, tennis, volleyball (w), wrestling (m).

Campus Safety

Student safety services include late-night transport/escort service, 24-hour emergency telephone alarm devices, 24-hour patrols by trained security personnel, and electronically operated dormitory entrances.

Applying

Northwestern requires an essay, SAT I or ACT, a high school transcript, and 1 recommendation, and in some cases SAT II Subject Tests and audition for music program. It recommends SAT II Subject Tests and an interview. Application deadline: 1/1; 2/1 priority date for financial aid. Early and deferred admission are possible.

OBERLIN COLLEGE

SMALL-TOWN SETTING ■ PRIVATE ■ INDEPENDENT ■ COED
OBERLIN, OHIO

Web site: www.oberlin.edu
Contact: Ms. Debra Chermonte, Director of College Admissions, Admissions Office, Carnegie Building, Oberlin, OH 44074-1090
Telephone: 440-775-8411 or toll-free 800-622-OBIE **Fax:** 440-775-6905
E-mail: college.admissions@oberlin.edu

 eAPPLY

Academics

Oberlin awards bachelor's and master's **degrees**. Challenging opportunities include advanced placement, accelerated degree programs, student-designed majors, an honors program, double majors, independent study, a senior project, Phi Beta Kappa, and Sigma Xi. Special programs include internships, off-campus study, and study-abroad.

The most frequently chosen fields are social sciences and history, English, and visual/performing arts. A complete listing of majors at Oberlin appears in the Majors Index beginning on page 432.

The **faculty** at Oberlin has 243 full-time members. The student-faculty ratio is 10:1.

Students of Oberlin

The student body totals 2,967, of whom 2,951 are undergraduates. 59.1% are women and 40.9% are men. Students come from 52 states and territories and 47 other countries. 9% are from Ohio. 5.8% are international students. 7.2% are African American, 0.7% American Indian, 7.1% Asian American, and 3.3% Hispanic American. 88% returned for their sophomore year.

Facilities and Resources

Student rooms are linked to a campus network. 275 **computers** are available on campus that provide access to the Internet. The 4 **libraries** have 1,541,260 books and 4,560 subscriptions.

Campus Life

There are 120 active organizations on campus, including a drama/theater group, newspaper, radio station, choral group, and marching band. No national or local **fraternities** or **sororities**.

Oberlin is a member of the NCAA (Division III). **Intercollegiate sports** include baseball (m), basketball, cross-country running, equestrian sports, fencing, field hockey (w), football (m), golf (m), ice hockey, lacrosse, racquetball, rugby, soccer, softball (w), squash, swimming, tennis, track and field, volleyball, water polo (m).

Campus Safety

Student safety services include crime prevention programs, late-night transport/escort service, 24-hour emergency telephone alarm devices, 24-hour patrols by trained security personnel, and electronically operated dormitory entrances.

Applying

Oberlin requires an essay, SAT I or ACT, a high school transcript, and 2 recommendations, and in some cases an interview. It recommends SAT II Subject Tests. Application deadline: 1/15; 2/15 priority date for financial aid. Early and deferred admission are possible.

As long as there has been an Oberlin, Oberlinians have been changing the world. Oberlin was the first coeducational school in the United States and a historic leader in educating African-American students. Among primarily undergraduate institutions, Oberlin ranks first for the number of students who go on to earn PhD degrees. Its alumni, who include 3 Nobel laureates, are leaders in law, scientific and scholarly research, medicine, the arts, theology, communication, business, and government. Oberlin also offers a 5-year double-degree program, combining studies at the Conservatory of Music and the College of Arts and Sciences.

Getting in Last Year
4,855 applied
50% were accepted
727 enrolled (30%)
56% from top tenth of their h.s. class
3.56 average high school GPA
87% had SAT verbal scores over 600
76% had SAT math scores over 600
91% had ACT scores over 24
43% had SAT verbal scores over 700
27% had SAT math scores over 700
40% had ACT scores over 30
37 National Merit Scholars
33 valedictorians

Graduation and After
61% graduated in 4 years
15% graduated in 5 years
2% graduated in 6 years
30% pursued further study
20 organizations recruited on campus

Financial Matters
$24,264 tuition and fees (1999–2000)
$6178 room and board
100% average percent of need met
$22,215 average financial aid amount received per undergraduate (1998–99)

eApply

Getting in Last Year
3,002 applied
60% were accepted
411 enrolled (23%)
44% from top tenth of their h.s. class
55% had SAT verbal scores over 600
55% had SAT math scores over 600
10% had SAT verbal scores over 700
13% had SAT math scores over 700
9 valedictorians

Graduation and After
73% graduated in 4 years
5% graduated in 5 years
1% graduated in 6 years
30% pursued further study (23% arts and sciences, 3% law, 3% medicine)
63% had job offers within 6 months
62 organizations recruited on campus

Financial Matters
$23,850 tuition and fees (2000–2001 estimated)
$6880 room and board
95% average percent of need met
$23,869 average financial aid amount received per undergraduate (1999–2000 estimated)

OCCIDENTAL COLLEGE
URBAN SETTING ■ PRIVATE ■ INDEPENDENT ■ COED
LOS ANGELES, CALIFORNIA

Web site: www.oxy.edu
Contact: Mr. Mark Hatch, Director of Admission, 1600 Campus Road, Los Angeles, CA 90041-3392
Telephone: 323-259-2700 or toll-free 800-825-5262 **Fax:** 323-341-4875
E-mail: admission@oxy.edu

Academics
OXY awards bachelor's and master's **degrees**. Challenging opportunities include advanced placement, accelerated degree programs, student-designed majors, an honors program, double majors, independent study, a senior project, and Phi Beta Kappa. Special programs include internships, summer session for credit, off-campus study, study-abroad, and Army, Navy and Air Force ROTC.

The most frequently chosen fields are social sciences and history, biological/life sciences, and visual/performing arts. A complete listing of majors at OXY appears in the Majors Index beginning on page 432.

The **faculty** at OXY has 138 full-time members, 93% with terminal degrees. The student-faculty ratio is 11:1.

Students of OXY
The student body totals 1,603, of whom 1,570 are undergraduates. 56.3% are women and 43.7% are men. Students come from 47 states and territories and 45 other countries. 60% are from California. 3.2% are international students. 5.6% are African American, 1.2% American Indian, 19.7% Asian American, and 13.6% Hispanic American. 87% returned for their sophomore year.

Facilities and Resources
Student rooms are linked to a campus network. 131 **computers** are available on campus that provide access to the Internet. The 3 **libraries** have 475,641 books and 2,100 subscriptions.

Campus Life
There are 90 active organizations on campus, including a drama/theater group, newspaper, radio station, and choral group. 11% of eligible men and 6% of eligible women are members of national **fraternities** and local **sororities**.

OXY is a member of the NCAA (Division III). **Intercollegiate sports** include badminton, baseball (m), basketball, cross-country running, fencing, field hockey (w), football (m), golf, lacrosse, rugby, skiing (downhill), soccer, softball (w), swimming, tennis, track and field, volleyball, water polo.

Campus Safety
Student safety services include community policing services, late-night transport/escort service, 24-hour emergency telephone alarm devices, 24-hour patrols by trained security personnel, student patrols, and electronically operated dormitory entrances.

Applying
OXY requires an essay, SAT I or ACT, a high school transcript, and 2 recommendations. It recommends SAT II Subject Tests, SAT II: Writing Test, and an interview. Application deadline: 1/15; 2/1 priority date for financial aid. Early and deferred admission are possible.

OGLETHORPE UNIVERSITY

Suburban setting ■ Private ■ Independent ■ Coed
Atlanta, Georgia

Web site: www.oglethorpe.edu
Contact: Mr. Dennis T. Matthews, Associate Dean for Enrollment
  Management, 4484 Peachtree Road, NE, Atlanta, GA 30319-2797
Telephone: 404-364-8307 or toll-free 800-428-4484 **Fax:** 404-364-8500
E-mail: admission@oglethorpe.edu

Academics

Oglethorpe awards bachelor's and master's **degrees**. Challenging opportunities include advanced placement, student-designed majors, an honors program, double majors, independent study, and a senior project. Special programs include cooperative education, internships, summer session for credit, off-campus study, and study-abroad.

The most frequently chosen fields are business/marketing, liberal arts/general studies, and psychology. A complete listing of majors at Oglethorpe appears in the Majors Index beginning on page 432.

The **faculty** at Oglethorpe has 138 members. The student-faculty ratio is 11:1.

Students of Oglethorpe

The student body totals 1,279, of whom 1,178 are undergraduates. 66% are women and 34% are men. 2.3% are international students. 14.5% are African American, 4.2% Asian American, and 2.3% Hispanic American. 81% returned for their sophomore year.

Facilities and Resources

Student rooms are linked to a campus network. 60 **computers** are available on campus that provide access to the Internet. The **library** has 131,375 books and 788 subscriptions.

Campus Life

There are 52 active organizations on campus, including a drama/theater group, newspaper, radio station, and choral group. 33% of eligible men and 28% of eligible women are members of national **fraternities** and national **sororities**.

Oglethorpe is a member of the NCAA (Division III). **Intercollegiate sports** include baseball (m), basketball, cross-country running, golf (m), soccer, tennis, track and field, volleyball (w).

Campus Safety

Student safety services include late-night transport/escort service, 24-hour emergency telephone alarm devices, 24-hour patrols by trained security personnel, student patrols, and electronically operated dormitory entrances.

Applying

Oglethorpe requires an essay, SAT I or ACT, a high school transcript, and 1 recommendation, and in some cases an interview. It recommends an interview and a minimum high school GPA of 2.5. Application deadline: 8/1. Deferred admission is possible.

It's not just the rigorous academic program, the small class discussions, and the motivating professors that make Oglethorpe different. It's the location—near the center of one of the country's most exciting, dynamic, international cities— Atlanta. A revamped honors program and a dynamic Urban Leadership Program are gaining much recognition from city leaders as Oglethorpe helps connect students to the rich resources of Atlanta. Internships are available in virtually every major and are very popular among the student body.

Getting in Last Year
751 applied
74% were accepted
198 enrolled (35%)
2.82 average high school GPA
59% had SAT verbal scores over 600
51% had SAT math scores over 600
83% had ACT scores over 24
14% had SAT verbal scores over 700
12% had SAT math scores over 700
18% had ACT scores over 30

Graduation and After
34% pursued further study (14% business, 11% arts and sciences, 4% medicine)
70% had job offers within 6 months

Financial Matters
$17,700 tuition and fees (1999–2000)
$5300 room and board
87% average percent of need met
$16,493 average financial aid amount received per undergraduate (1998–99)

OHIO NORTHERN UNIVERSITY

SMALL-TOWN SETTING ■ PRIVATE ■ INDEPENDENT RELIGIOUS ■ COED
ADA, OHIO

Web site: www.onu.edu
Contact: Ms. Karen Condeni, Vice President of Admissions and Financial Aid,
    525 South Main, Ada, OH 45810-1599
Telephone: 419-772-2260 **Fax:** 419-772-2313
E-mail: admissions-ug@onu.edu

National recognition, small classes, excellent facilities, strong faculty members who teach all classes, and a rich and diverse curriculum are just some of the features that set Ohio Northern apart from other colleges in the Midwest. But what truly makes ONU unique is its students. They reflect the value of service to others, which is the product of the individual attention they receive from the faculty, staff, and administration of ONU.

Getting in Last Year
2,357 applied
91% were accepted
622 enrolled (29%)
38% from top tenth of their h.s. class
3.48 average high school GPA
59% had ACT scores over 24
12% had ACT scores over 30
84 valedictorians

Graduation and After
30% graduated in 4 years
27% graduated in 5 years
6% graduated in 6 years
Graduates pursuing further study: 5% arts and sciences, 3% medicine, 2% engineering
88% had job offers within 6 months
232 organizations recruited on campus

Financial Matters
$21,435 tuition and fees (2000–2001)
$5265 room and board
89% average percent of need met
$17,640 average financial aid amount received per undergraduate (1999–2000)

Academics

Ohio Northern awards bachelor's and first-professional **degrees**. Challenging opportunities include advanced placement, double majors, a senior project, and Sigma Xi. Special programs include cooperative education, internships, summer session for credit, study-abroad, and Army and Air Force ROTC.

The most frequently chosen fields are health professions and related sciences, business/marketing, and engineering/engineering technologies. A complete listing of majors at Ohio Northern appears in the Majors Index beginning on page 432.

The **faculty** at Ohio Northern has 180 full-time members. The student-faculty ratio is 13:1.

Students of Ohio Northern

The student body totals 3,159, of whom 2,381 are undergraduates. 48.7% are women and 51.3% are men. Students come from 38 states and territories and 15 other countries. 86% are from Ohio. 1% are international students. 2.6% are African American, 0.3% American Indian, 1.1% Asian American, and 0.5% Hispanic American. 85% returned for their sophomore year.

Facilities and Resources

Student rooms are linked to a campus network. 412 **computers** are available on campus that provide access to the Internet. The 2 **libraries** have 246,103 books and 1,038 subscriptions.

Campus Life

There are 150 active organizations on campus, including a drama/theater group, newspaper, radio station, television station, choral group, and marching band. 25% of eligible men and 22% of eligible women are members of national **fraternities** and national **sororities**.

Ohio Northern is a member of the NCAA (Division III). **Intercollegiate sports** include baseball (m), basketball, cross-country running, football (m), golf, soccer, softball (w), swimming, tennis, track and field, volleyball (w), wrestling (m).

Campus Safety

Student safety services include late-night transport/escort service, 24-hour emergency telephone alarm devices, 24-hour patrols by trained security personnel, and electronically operated dormitory entrances.

Applying

Ohio Northern requires SAT I or ACT, a high school transcript, and a minimum high school GPA of 2.0. It recommends an essay and an interview. Application deadline: 8/15; 6/1 for financial aid, with a 4/15 priority date. Early and deferred admission are possible.

THE OHIO STATE UNIVERSITY

URBAN SETTING ■ PUBLIC ■ STATE-SUPPORTED ■ COED
COLUMBUS, OHIO

Web site: www.osu.edu
Contact: Dr. Robin Brown, Director of Undergraduate Admissions, 3rd Floor, Lincoln Tower, Columbus, OH 43210-1200
Telephone: 614-292-3980 **Fax:** 614-292-4818
E-mail: telecounseling@fa.adm.ohio-state.edu

Academics

Ohio State awards bachelor's, master's, doctoral, and first-professional **degrees** and post-master's certificates. Challenging opportunities include advanced placement, accelerated degree programs, student-designed majors, freshman honors college, an honors program, double majors, independent study, a senior project, Phi Beta Kappa, and Sigma Xi. Special programs include cooperative education, internships, summer session for credit, off-campus study, study-abroad, and Army, Navy and Air Force ROTC.

The most frequently chosen fields are business/marketing, social sciences and history, and home economics/vocational home economics. A complete listing of majors at Ohio State appears in the Majors Index beginning on page 432.

The **faculty** at Ohio State has 2,669 full-time members, 99% with terminal degrees. The student-faculty ratio is 14:1.

Students of Ohio State

The student body totals 48,003, of whom 36,092 are undergraduates. 48.2% are women and 51.8% are men. Students come from 53 states and territories and 87 other countries. 93% are from Ohio. 4.1% are international students. 7.8% are African American, 0.4% American Indian, 5.4% Asian American, and 1.8% Hispanic American. 83% returned for their sophomore year.

Facilities and Resources

Student rooms are linked to a campus network. 1,000 **computers** are available on campus that provide access to the Internet. The 13 **libraries** have 5,177,386 books and 36,020 subscriptions.

Campus Life

There are 550 active organizations on campus, including a drama/theater group, newspaper, radio station, television station, choral group, and marching band. 6% of eligible men and 7% of eligible women are members of national **fraternities** and national **sororities**.

Ohio State is a member of the NCAA (Division I). **Intercollegiate sports** (some offering scholarships) include baseball (m), basketball, crew (w), cross-country running, fencing, field hockey (w), football (m), golf, gymnastics, ice hockey, lacrosse, riflery, soccer, softball (w), swimming, tennis, track and field, volleyball, wrestling (m).

Campus Safety

Student safety services include dormitory entrances locked after 9 p.m, late-night transport/escort service, 24-hour emergency telephone alarm devices, 24-hour patrols by trained security personnel, student patrols, and electronically operated dormitory entrances.

Applying

Ohio State requires SAT I or ACT and a high school transcript. Application deadline: 2/15; 2/15 priority date for financial aid.

Getting in Last Year

19,805 applied
74% were accepted
6,119 enrolled (42%)
29% from top tenth of their h.s. class
36% had SAT verbal scores over 600
44% had SAT math scores over 600
59% had ACT scores over 24
8% had SAT verbal scores over 700
11% had SAT math scores over 700
12% had ACT scores over 30
104 National Merit Scholars
231 valedictorians

Graduation and After

19% graduated in 4 years
30% graduated in 5 years
7% graduated in 6 years
10% pursued further study
83% had job offers within 6 months
3 Fulbright scholars

Financial Matters

$4137 resident tuition and fees (1999–2000)
$12,087 nonresident tuition and fees (1999–2000)
$5328 room and board
74% average percent of need met
$7043 average financial aid amount received per undergraduate (1999–2000 estimated)

OHIO UNIVERSITY

SMALL-TOWN SETTING ■ PUBLIC ■ STATE-SUPPORTED ■ COED
ATHENS, OHIO

Web site: www.ohio.edu
Contact: Shirley Kasler-Thimmes, Director of Admissions, Athens, OH
45701-2979
Telephone: 740-593-4100
E-mail: uadmiss1@ohiou.edu

Getting in Last Year
11,785 applied
80% were accepted
3,448 enrolled (37%)
18% from top tenth of their h.s. class
3.42 average high school GPA
26% had SAT verbal scores over 600
27% had SAT math scores over 600
49% had ACT scores over 24
4% had SAT verbal scores over 700
3% had SAT math scores over 700
5% had ACT scores over 30
6 National Merit Scholars
62 valedictorians

Graduation and After
43% graduated in 4 years
23% graduated in 5 years
4% graduated in 6 years
28% pursued further study (7% arts and sciences, 5% education, 3% business)
79% had job offers within 6 months
450 organizations recruited on campus

Financial Matters
$4800 resident tuition and fees (1999–2000)
$10,101 nonresident tuition and fees (1999–2000)
$5484 room and board
80% average percent of need met
$6528 average financial aid amount received per undergraduate (1999–2000 estimated)

Academics

Ohio awards associate, bachelor's, master's, doctoral, and first-professional **degrees**. Challenging opportunities include advanced placement, accelerated degree programs, student-designed majors, an honors program, double majors, independent study, a senior project, Phi Beta Kappa, and Sigma Xi. Special programs include cooperative education, internships, summer session for credit, off-campus study, study-abroad, and Army and Air Force ROTC.

The most frequently chosen fields are liberal arts/general studies, business/marketing, and English. A complete listing of majors at Ohio appears in the Majors Index beginning on page 432.

The **faculty** at Ohio has 837 full-time members, 91% with terminal degrees. The student-faculty ratio is 21:1.

Students of Ohio

The student body totals 19,638, of whom 16,554 are undergraduates. 54.9% are women and 45.1% are men. Students come from 52 states and territories and 17 other countries. 89% are from Ohio. 2.2% are international students. 3.5% are African American, 0.3% American Indian, 0.8% Asian American, and 1% Hispanic American. 84% returned for their sophomore year.

Facilities and Resources

Student rooms are linked to a campus network. 1,500 **computers** are available on campus that provide access to the Internet. The **library** has 2,110,594 books and 40,417 subscriptions.

Campus Life

There are 360 active organizations on campus, including a drama/theater group, newspaper, radio station, television station, choral group, and marching band. 12% of eligible men and 16% of eligible women are members of national **fraternities** and national **sororities**.

Ohio is a member of the NCAA (Division I). **Intercollegiate sports** (some offering scholarships) include baseball (m), basketball, cross-country running, equestrian sports, field hockey (w), football (m), golf, ice hockey (m), lacrosse, rugby, soccer, softball (w), swimming, track and field, volleyball, water polo, weight lifting (m), wrestling (m).

Campus Safety

Student safety services include security lighting, late-night transport/escort service, 24-hour emergency telephone alarm devices, 24-hour patrols by trained security personnel, and electronically operated dormitory entrances.

Applying

Ohio requires SAT I or ACT and a high school transcript, and in some cases an essay and an interview. It recommends 2 recommendations. Application deadline: 2/15; 3/15 priority date for financial aid. Early and deferred admission are possible.

OHIO WESLEYAN UNIVERSITY

SMALL-TOWN SETTING ■ PRIVATE ■ INDEPENDENT RELIGIOUS ■ COED
DELAWARE, OHIO

Web site: www.owu.edu
Contact: Ms. Margaret L. Drugovich, Vice President of Admission and
    Financial Aid, 61 South Sandusky Street, Delaware, OH 43015
Telephone: 740-368-3020 or toll-free 800-922-8953 **Fax:** 740-368-3314
E-mail: owuadmit@cc.owu.edu

Academics

Ohio Wesleyan awards bachelor's **degrees**. Challenging opportunities include advanced placement, accelerated degree programs, student-designed majors, freshman honors college, an honors program, double majors, independent study, a senior project, Phi Beta Kappa, and Sigma Xi. Special programs include internships, summer session for credit, off-campus study, study-abroad, and Army ROTC.

The most frequently chosen fields are social sciences and history, business/marketing, and psychology. A complete listing of majors at Ohio Wesleyan appears in the Majors Index beginning on page 432.

The **faculty** at Ohio Wesleyan has 126 full-time members, 99% with terminal degrees. The student-faculty ratio is 13:1.

Students of Ohio Wesleyan

The student body is made up of 1,930 undergraduates. 51.2% are women and 48.8% are men. Students come from 40 states and territories and 56 other countries. 50% are from Ohio. 11.3% are international students. 3.9% are African American, 0.2% American Indian, 1.8% Asian American, and 1.6% Hispanic American. 77% returned for their sophomore year.

Facilities and Resources

Student rooms are linked to a campus network. 170 **computers** are available on campus that provide access to the Internet. The 4 **libraries** have 473,193 books and 1,060 subscriptions.

Campus Life

There are 100 active organizations on campus, including a drama/theater group, newspaper, radio station, television station, and choral group. 44% of eligible men and 37% of eligible women are members of national **fraternities** and national **sororities**.

Ohio Wesleyan is a member of the NCAA (Division III). **Intercollegiate sports** include baseball (m), basketball, cross-country running, equestrian sports, field hockey (w), football (m), golf (m), ice hockey (m), lacrosse, rugby, sailing, soccer, softball (w), swimming, tennis, track and field, volleyball.

Campus Safety

Student safety services include late-night transport/escort service, 24-hour emergency telephone alarm devices, 24-hour patrols by trained security personnel, and electronically operated dormitory entrances.

Applying

Ohio Wesleyan requires an essay, SAT I or ACT, a high school transcript, and 2 recommendations. It recommends SAT II Subject Tests and an interview. Application deadline: 3/1; 3/15 priority date for financial aid. Early and deferred admission are possible.

O hio Wesleyan is one of the nation's most balanced selective liberal arts colleges. Students praise the faculty for its dedication to teaching and active encouragement in the classroom. Students balance their academic experience with strong participation in community service, athletics, and student government. Each year the University offers a speaker series and seminar classes that focus on a major public issue of concern (National Colloquium). Loren Pope, author of *Beyond the Ivy League,* says "Ohio Wesleyan has a much more diverse, cosmopolitan, and friendly student body than a lot of the selective east and west coast schools."

Getting in Last Year

2,057 applied
83% were accepted
524 enrolled (31%)
30% from top tenth of their h.s. class
3.30 average high school GPA
56% had SAT verbal scores over 600
62% had SAT math scores over 600
76% had ACT scores over 24
13% had SAT verbal scores over 700
15% had SAT math scores over 700
16% had ACT scores over 30
6 National Merit Scholars
21 valedictorians

Graduation and After

64% graduated in 4 years
4% graduated in 5 years
2% graduated in 6 years
Graduates pursuing further study: 10% arts and sciences, 7% law, 7% medicine
28 organizations recruited on campus

Financial Matters

$20,940 tuition and fees (1999–2000)
$6560 room and board
98% average percent of need met
$19,785 average financial aid amount received per undergraduate (1999–2000)

Getting in Last Year

5,513 applied
86% were accepted
2,639 enrolled (55%)
30% from top tenth of their h.s. class
3.51 average high school GPA
39% had SAT verbal scores over 600
43% had SAT math scores over 600
55% had ACT scores over 24
7% had SAT verbal scores over 700
8% had SAT math scores over 700
11% had ACT scores over 30
22 National Merit Scholars
296 valedictorians

Graduation and After

20% graduated in 4 years
24% graduated in 5 years
7% graduated in 6 years
70% had job offers within 6 months
363 organizations recruited on campus
1 Fulbright scholar

Financial Matters

$2458 resident tuition and fees (1999–2000)
$6538 nonresident tuition and fees (1999–2000)
$4536 room and board
80% average percent of need met
$7292 average financial aid amount received per undergraduate (1998–99)

OKLAHOMA STATE UNIVERSITY

SMALL-TOWN SETTING ■ PUBLIC ■ STATE-SUPPORTED ■ COED
STILLWATER, OKLAHOMA

Web site: www.okstate.edu
Contact: Ms. Paulette Cundiff, Coordinator of Admissions Processing, Undergraduate Admissions, 324 Student Union, Stillwater, OK 74078
Telephone: 405-744-6858 or toll-free 800-233-5019 (in-state), 800-852-1255 (out-of-state) **Fax:** 405-744-5285
E-mail: admit@okstate.edu

Academics

OSU awards bachelor's, master's, doctoral, and first-professional **degrees**. Challenging opportunities include advanced placement, accelerated degree programs, student-designed majors, an honors program, double majors, independent study, a senior project, and Sigma Xi. Special programs include cooperative education, internships, summer session for credit, off-campus study, study-abroad, and Army and Air Force ROTC.

The most frequently chosen fields are business/marketing, engineering/engineering technologies, and education. A complete listing of majors at OSU appears in the Majors Index beginning on page 432.

The **faculty** at OSU has 891 full-time members, 91% with terminal degrees. The student-faculty ratio is 18:1.

Students of OSU

The student body totals 20,466, of whom 15,508 are undergraduates. 46.6% are women and 53.4% are men. Students come from 50 states and territories and 119 other countries. 88% are from Oklahoma. 6.4% are international students. 2.6% are African American, 7.7% American Indian, 1.6% Asian American, and 1.6% Hispanic American. 82% returned for their sophomore year.

Facilities and Resources

Student rooms are linked to a campus network. 2,000 **computers** are available on campus that provide access to the Internet. The **library** has 1,961,478 books and 16,249 subscriptions.

Campus Life

There are 358 active organizations on campus, including a drama/theater group, newspaper, radio station, television station, choral group, and marching band. 13% of eligible men and 16% of eligible women are members of national **fraternities** and national **sororities**.

OSU is a member of the NCAA (Division I). **Intercollegiate sports** (some offering scholarships) include baseball (m), basketball, cross-country running, equestrian sports (w), football (m), golf, soccer (w), softball (w), tennis, track and field, wrestling (m).

Campus Safety

Student safety services include 24-hour emergency telephone alarm devices, 24-hour patrols by trained security personnel, student patrols, and electronically operated dormitory entrances.

Applying

OSU requires SAT I or ACT, a high school transcript, class rank, and a minimum high school GPA of 3.0, and in some cases an interview. Application deadline: rolling admissions. Early admission is possible.

OUACHITA BAPTIST UNIVERSITY

SMALL-TOWN SETTING ■ PRIVATE ■ INDEPENDENT RELIGIOUS ■ COED
ARKADELPHIA, ARKANSAS

Web site: www.obu.edu
Contact: Mrs. Rebecca Jones, Director of Admissions Counseling, 410
Ouachita Street, Arkadelphia, AR 71998-0001
Telephone: 870-245-5110 or toll-free 800-342-5628 (in-state) **Fax:**
870-245-5500
E-mail: jonesj@sigma.obu.edu

Academics

Ouachita awards associate and bachelor's **degrees**. Challenging opportunities include advanced placement, accelerated degree programs, an honors program, double majors, and a senior project. Special programs include cooperative education, internships, summer session for credit, off-campus study, study-abroad, and Army ROTC.

The most frequently chosen fields are education, philosophy, and business/marketing. A complete listing of majors at Ouachita appears in the Majors Index beginning on page 432.

The **faculty** at Ouachita has 103 full-time members, 71% with terminal degrees. The student-faculty ratio is 13:1.

Students of Ouachita

The student body is made up of 1,638 undergraduates. 54.8% are women and 45.2% are men. Students come from 36 states and territories and 58 other countries. 56% are from Arkansas. 4.3% are international students. 3.8% are African American, 0.4% American Indian, 0.4% Asian American, and 0.9% Hispanic American. 75% returned for their sophomore year.

Facilities and Resources

Student rooms are linked to a campus network. 146 **computers** are available on campus that provide access to the Internet. The 2 **libraries** have 119,437 books and 1,862 subscriptions.

Campus Life

There are 60 active organizations on campus, including a drama/theater group, newspaper, television station, choral group, and marching band. 20% of eligible men and 25% of eligible women are members of local **fraternities** and local **sororities**.

Ouachita is a member of the NCAA (Division II). **Intercollegiate sports** (some offering scholarships) include baseball (m), basketball, cross-country running, football (m), golf (m), soccer (m), swimming, tennis, volleyball (w).

Campus Safety

Student safety services include 24-hour emergency telephone alarm devices, 24-hour patrols by trained security personnel, and electronically operated dormitory entrances.

Applying

Ouachita requires SAT I or ACT, a high school transcript, and a minimum high school GPA of 2.5. It recommends an interview. Application deadline: 8/15; 6/1 for financial aid, with a 2/15 priority date. Early and deferred admission are possible.

Getting in Last Year

931 applied
71% were accepted
448 enrolled (67%)
31% from top tenth of their h.s. class
3.47 average high school GPA
30% had SAT verbal scores over 600
28% had SAT math scores over 600
53% had ACT scores over 24
7% had SAT verbal scores over 700
7% had SAT math scores over 700
9% had ACT scores over 30
3 National Merit Scholars
15 valedictorians

Graduation and After

41% graduated in 4 years
9% graduated in 5 years
2% graduated in 6 years
10% pursued further study
60% had job offers within 6 months
20 organizations recruited on campus

Financial Matters

$9010 tuition and fees (1999–2000)
$3450 room and board
75% average percent of need met
$10,614 average financial aid amount received
per undergraduate (1999–2000 estimated)

 eAPPLY

PACIFIC LUTHERAN UNIVERSITY

SUBURBAN SETTING ■ PRIVATE ■ INDEPENDENT RELIGIOUS ■ COED
TACOMA, WASHINGTON

Web site: www.plu.edu
Contact: Office of Admissions, Tacoma, WA 98447
Telephone: 253-535-7151 or toll-free 800-274-6758 **Fax:** 253-536-5136
E-mail: admissions@plu.edu

When Russia's international airline, Aeroflot, wanted to learn Western accounting systems, it sent 80 of its executives to Pacific Lutheran; when Israel needed a world authority on the Holocaust, a PLU history professor was chosen; when Chinese officials needed to know how to deal with social changes brought about by free enterprise, a PLU anthropology professor was consulted; and when Russia's universities wanted an economics text on market economics, they chose a text by a PLU economics professor. These and many other top-flight scholars teach undergraduates at PLU because teaching is their first love.

Getting in Last Year
1,685 applied
84% were accepted
568 enrolled (40%)
35% from top tenth of their h.s. class
3.61 average high school GPA
32% had SAT verbal scores over 600
28% had SAT math scores over 600
55% had ACT scores over 24
7% had SAT verbal scores over 700
3% had SAT math scores over 700
10% had ACT scores over 30
5 National Merit Scholars
32 valedictorians

Graduation and After
44% graduated in 4 years
21% graduated in 5 years
4% graduated in 6 years
9% pursued further study
69% had job offers within 6 months
69 organizations recruited on campus
3 Fulbright scholars

Financial Matters
$16,224 tuition and fees (1999–2000)
$5038 room and board
90% average percent of need met
$14,990 average financial aid amount received per undergraduate (1999–2000 estimated)

Academics
PLU awards bachelor's and master's **degrees**. Challenging opportunities include advanced placement, accelerated degree programs, student-designed majors, freshman honors college, an honors program, double majors, independent study, and a senior project. Special programs include cooperative education, internships, summer session for credit, study-abroad, and Army ROTC.

The most frequently chosen fields are business/marketing, education, and health professions and related sciences. A complete listing of majors at PLU appears in the Majors Index beginning on page 432.

The **faculty** at PLU has 237 full-time members, 82% with terminal degrees. The student-faculty ratio is 15:1.

Students of PLU
The student body totals 3,602, of whom 3,302 are undergraduates. 60.2% are women and 39.8% are men. Students come from 44 states and territories and 26 other countries. 72% are from Washington. 7.4% are international students. 2.4% are African American, 0.7% American Indian, 5.3% Asian American, and 2% Hispanic American. 81% returned for their sophomore year.

Facilities and Resources
Student rooms are linked to a campus network. 200 **computers** are available on campus that provide access to the Internet. The **library** has 353,766 books and 2,255 subscriptions.

Campus Life
There are 45 active organizations on campus, including a drama/theater group, newspaper, radio station, television station, and choral group. No national or local **fraternities** or **sororities**.

PLU is a member of the NCAA (Division III). **Intercollegiate sports** include baseball (m), basketball, crew, cross-country running, football (m), golf, lacrosse, rugby (m), skiing (cross-country), skiing (downhill), soccer, softball (w), swimming, tennis, track and field, volleyball, wrestling (m).

Campus Safety
Student safety services include late-night transport/escort service, 24-hour emergency telephone alarm devices, 24-hour patrols by trained security personnel, and student patrols.

Applying
PLU requires an essay, SAT I or ACT, a high school transcript, 1 recommendation, and a minimum high school GPA of 2.5, and in some cases an interview. Application deadline: rolling admissions; 3/1 priority date for financial aid. Early and deferred admission are possible.

PENNSYLVANIA STATE UNIVERSITY UNIVERSITY PARK CAMPUS

SMALL-TOWN SETTING ■ PUBLIC ■ STATE-RELATED ■ COED
UNIVERSITY PARK, PENNSYLVANIA

Web site: www.psu.edu
Contact: Mr. Geoffrey Harford, Director-Admissions Services and Evaluation, 201 Old Main, University Park, PA 16802-1503
Telephone: 814-863-0233 **Fax:** 814-863-7590
E-mail: admissions@psu.edu

Academics

Penn State awards associate, bachelor's, master's, and doctoral **degrees**. Challenging opportunities include advanced placement, student-designed majors, freshman honors college, an honors program, independent study, a senior project, Phi Beta Kappa, and Sigma Xi. Special programs include cooperative education, internships, summer session for credit, study-abroad, and Army, Navy and Air Force ROTC.

The most frequently chosen fields are business/marketing, engineering/engineering technologies, and health professions and related sciences. A complete listing of majors at Penn State appears in the Majors Index beginning on page 432.

The **faculty** at Penn State has 1,994 full-time members, 77% with terminal degrees. The student-faculty ratio is 18:1.

Students of Penn State

The student body totals 40,658, of whom 34,505 are undergraduates. 46.2% are women and 53.8% are men. Students come from 54 states and territories. 81% are from Pennsylvania. 1.1% are international students. 4.1% are African American, 0.1% American Indian, 5.1% Asian American, and 2.9% Hispanic American. 93% returned for their sophomore year.

Facilities and Resources

Student rooms are linked to a campus network. 3,589 **computers** are available on campus that provide access to the Internet. The 8 **libraries** have 2,800,000 books and 22,879 subscriptions.

Campus Life

There are 400 active organizations on campus, including a drama/theater group, newspaper, radio station, choral group, and marching band. 14% of eligible men and 11% of eligible women are members of national **fraternities** and national **sororities**.

Penn State is a member of the NCAA (Division I). **Intercollegiate sports** (some offering scholarships) include baseball (m), basketball, bowling (m), cross-country running, equestrian sports, fencing, field hockey (w), football (m), golf, gymnastics, ice hockey, lacrosse, rugby, skiing (downhill), soccer, softball (w), swimming, table tennis (m), tennis, track and field, volleyball, water polo, weight lifting, wrestling (m).

Campus Safety

Student safety services include late-night transport/escort service, 24-hour emergency telephone alarm devices, 24-hour patrols by trained security personnel, student patrols, and electronically operated dormitory entrances.

Applying

Penn State requires SAT I or ACT, a high school transcript, and a minimum high school GPA of 2.0, and in some cases an interview and 1 recommendation. It recommends an essay. Application deadline: rolling admissions. Deferred admission is possible.

Getting in Last Year

26,079 applied
49% were accepted
5,069 enrolled (39%)
49% from top tenth of their h.s. class
3.78 average high school GPA
46% had SAT verbal scores over 600
62% had SAT math scores over 600
10% had SAT verbal scores over 700
16% had SAT math scores over 700

Graduation and After

60% graduated in 4 years
18% graduated in 5 years
2% graduated in 6 years
70% had job offers within 6 months
970 organizations recruited on campus
11 Fulbright scholars

Financial Matters

$6436 resident tuition and fees (1999–2000)
$13,552 nonresident tuition and fees (1999–2000)
$4690 room and board

PEPPERDINE UNIVERSITY
SMALL-TOWN SETTING ■ PRIVATE ■ INDEPENDENT RELIGIOUS ■ COED
MALIBU, CALIFORNIA

Getting in Last Year
4,652 applied
32% were accepted
3.79 average high school GPA
64% had SAT verbal scores over 600
68% had SAT math scores over 600
87% had ACT scores over 24
15% had SAT verbal scores over 700
18% had SAT math scores over 700
35% had ACT scores over 30

Graduation and After
63% pursued further study
40% had job offers within 6 months
78 organizations recruited on campus

Financial Matters
$23,070 tuition and fees (1999–2000)
$7010 room and board

Web site: www.pepperdine.edu
Contact: Mr. Paul A. Long, Dean of Admission, 24255 Pacific Coast
   Highway, Malibu, CA 90263-0002
Telephone: 310-456-4392 **Fax:** 310-456-4861
E-mail: admission-seaver@pepperdine.edu

Academics
Pepperdine awards bachelor's, master's, doctoral, and first-professional **degrees** (the university is organized into five colleges: Seaver, the School of Law, the School of Business and Management, the School of Public Policy, and the Graduate School of Education and Psychology. Seaver College is the undergraduate, residential, liberal arts school of the University and is committed to providing education of outstanding academic quality with particular attention to Christian values). Challenging opportunities include advanced placement, accelerated degree programs, student-designed majors, an honors program, and a senior project. Special programs include internships, summer session for credit, study-abroad, and Army, Navy and Air Force ROTC.

The most frequently chosen fields are business/marketing, communications/communication technologies, and liberal arts/general studies. A complete listing of majors at Pepperdine appears in the Majors Index beginning on page 432.

The **faculty** at Pepperdine has 167 full-time members, 100% with terminal degrees. The student-faculty ratio is 13:1.

Students of Pepperdine
The student body totals 7,885, of whom 3,230 are undergraduates. 59.8% are women and 40.2% are men. Students come from 51 states and territories and 70 other countries. 8.1% are international students. 4.6% are African American, 1% American Indian, 6.1% Asian American, and 8.3% Hispanic American. 88% returned for their sophomore year.

Facilities and Resources
Student rooms are linked to a campus network. 292 **computers** are available on campus that provide access to the Internet. The 3 **libraries** have 515,238 books and 3,882 subscriptions.

Campus Life
There are 50 active organizations on campus, including a drama/theater group, newspaper, radio station, television station, and choral group. 25% of eligible men and 25% of eligible women are members of national **fraternities** and national **sororities**.

Pepperdine is a member of the NCAA (Division I). **Intercollegiate sports** (some offering scholarships) include baseball (m), basketball, cross-country running, golf, lacrosse (m), rugby (m), soccer, swimming (w), tennis, volleyball, water polo (m).

Campus Safety
Student safety services include front gate security, 24-hour security in residence halls, controlled access, crime prevention programs, late-night transport/escort service, 24-hour emergency telephone alarm devices, 24-hour patrols by trained security personnel, and student patrols.

Applying
Pepperdine requires an essay, SAT I or ACT, a high school transcript, and 2 recommendations. It recommends an interview. Application deadline: 1/15; 4/1 for financial aid, with a 1/15 priority date.

PITZER COLLEGE

SUBURBAN SETTING ■ PRIVATE ■ INDEPENDENT ■ COED
CLAREMONT, CALIFORNIA

Web site: www.pitzer.edu
Contact: Dr. Arnaldo Rodriguez, Vice President for Admission and Financial
Aid, 1050 North Mills Avenue, Claremont, CA 91711-6101
Telephone: 909-621-8129 or toll-free 800-748-9371 **Fax:** 909-621-8770
E-mail: admission@pitzer.edu

Academics

Pitzer awards bachelor's **degrees**. Challenging opportunities include advanced placement, student-designed majors, an honors program, double majors, independent study, a
senior project, and Sigma Xi. Special programs include cooperative education, internships, off-campus study, and study-abroad.

The most frequently chosen fields are social sciences and history, psychology, and
visual/performing arts. A complete listing of majors at Pitzer appears in the Majors Index
beginning on page 432.

The **faculty** at Pitzer has 58 full-time members. The student-faculty ratio is 12:1.

Students of Pitzer

The student body is made up of 930 undergraduates. 63.7% are women and 36.3% are
men. Students come from 29 states and territories and 6 other countries. 59% are from
California. 5% are international students. 4.7% are African American, 0.6% American
Indian, 11.1% Asian American, and 14.5% Hispanic American. 79% returned for their
sophomore year.

Facilities and Resources

Student rooms are linked to a campus network. The 2 **libraries** have 1,381,108 books
and 4,321 subscriptions.

Campus Life

There are 75 active organizations on campus, including a drama/theater group,
newspaper, radio station, and choral group. No national or local **fraternities** or **sororities.**

Pitzer is a member of the NCAA (Division III). **Intercollegiate sports** include
baseball (m), basketball, cross-country running, football (m), golf (m), soccer, softball (w),
swimming, tennis, track and field, volleyball (w), water polo, wrestling (m).

Campus Safety

Student safety services include late-night transport/escort service, 24-hour emergency
telephone alarm devices, 24-hour patrols by trained security personnel, and electronically operated dormitory entrances.

Applying

Pitzer requires an essay, SAT I or ACT, a high school transcript, and 2 recommendations. It recommends SAT II Subject Tests, SAT II: Writing Test, and an interview. Application deadline: 2/1; 2/1 for financial aid. Early and deferred admission are possible.

Pitzer, a liberal arts and
sciences college, offers
students membership in a
closely knit academic community and
access to the resources of a
midsized university through its
partnership with the Claremont
Colleges. Pitzer's distinctive
curriculum encourages students to
discover the relationship among
different academic subjects
(interdisciplinary learning), gives
students a chance to see issues and
events from different cultural
perspectives (intercultural
understanding), and shows students
how to take responsibility for
making the world a better place
(social responsibility). Pitzer believes
that students should have the
freedom and responsibility for
selecting what courses to take;
therefore, required general education
courses are few.

Getting in Last Year
1,716 applied
72% were accepted
246 enrolled (20%)
34% from top tenth of their h.s. class
3.55 average high school GPA
49% had SAT verbal scores over 600
42% had SAT math scores over 600
67% had ACT scores over 24
13% had SAT verbal scores over 700
6% had SAT math scores over 700
10% had ACT scores over 30

Graduation and After
59% graduated in 4 years
6% graduated in 5 years
3% graduated in 6 years
75% had job offers within 6 months
50 organizations recruited on campus
2 Fulbright scholars

Financial Matters
$24,096 tuition and fees (1999–2000)
$6290 room and board
100% average percent of need met
$22,648 average financial aid amount received
per undergraduate (1999–2000 estimated)

POLYTECHNIC UNIVERSITY, BROOKLYN CAMPUS

URBAN SETTING ■ PRIVATE ■ INDEPENDENT ■ COED
BROOKLYN, NEW YORK

Web site: www.poly.edu
Contact: Mr. John S. Kerge, Dean of Admissions, Six Metrotech Center, Brooklyn, NY 11201-2990
Telephone: 718-260-3100 or toll-free 800-POLYTECH **Fax:** 718-260-3446
E-mail: admitme@poly.edu

Polytechnic University is the second-oldest engineering, science, and technology university in the country and is rated consistently high by the Gourman Report for all undergraduate programs. The location of Polytechnic's campuses puts students at the center of the world's greatest laboratory—the New York metro area—where access to cooperative education and internship opportunities in engineering, the sciences, communications, computer science, medicine, law, business, finance, and education abounds. Poly students have access to co-op or internship opportunities at more than 250 companies in the metropolitan area. Polytechnic's 36,000 alumni include patent holders, Nobel Prize winners, and hundreds of chief executive officers at major U.S. firms in the metropolitan New York area and around the country.

Getting in Last Year
1,389 applied
70% were accepted
468 enrolled (48%)
3.30 average high school GPA
31% had SAT verbal scores over 600
72% had SAT math scores over 600
4% had SAT verbal scores over 700
16% had SAT math scores over 700

Graduation and After
34% graduated in 4 years
14% graduated in 5 years
4% graduated in 6 years
8% pursued further study

Financial Matters
$20,810 tuition and fees (1999–2000)
$5470 room and board
81% average percent of need met
$17,554 average financial aid amount received per undergraduate (1998–99)

Academics

Polytechnic awards bachelor's, master's, and doctoral **degrees** (most information given is for both Brooklyn and Farmingdale campuses). Challenging opportunities include advanced placement, accelerated degree programs, an honors program, double majors, a senior project, and Sigma Xi. Special programs include cooperative education, summer session for credit, and Air Force ROTC.

The most frequently chosen fields are engineering/engineering technologies, computer/information sciences, and physical sciences. A complete listing of majors at Polytechnic appears in the Majors Index beginning on page 432.

The **faculty** at Polytechnic has 162 full-time members, 91% with terminal degrees. The student-faculty ratio is 12:1.

Students of Polytechnic

The student body totals 3,420, of whom 1,807 are undergraduates. 18% are women and 82% are men. Students come from 6 states and territories and 19 other countries. 97% are from New York. 3% are international students. 11.1% are African American, 0.4% American Indian, 36.6% Asian American, and 5.7% Hispanic American. 79% returned for their sophomore year.

Facilities and Resources

350 **computers** are available on campus that provide access to the Internet. The **library** has 148,000 books and 613 subscriptions.

Campus Life

There are 47 active organizations on campus, including a newspaper and radio station. 6% of eligible men and 3% of eligible women are members of national **fraternities**, local fraternities, and coed fraternity.

Polytechnic is a member of the NCAA (Division III). **Intercollegiate sports** include baseball (m), basketball (m), cross-country running, soccer, softball (w), tennis, track and field, volleyball.

Campus Safety

Student safety services include 24-hour patrols by trained security personnel.

Applying

Polytechnic requires an essay, SAT I or ACT, a high school transcript, and 2 recommendations. It recommends SAT II Subject Tests, SAT II: Writing Test, and an interview. Application deadline: rolling admissions. Deferred admission is possible.

POLYTECHNIC UNIVERSITY, FARMINGDALE CAMPUS

SUBURBAN SETTING ■ PRIVATE ■ INDEPENDENT ■ COED
FARMINGDALE, NEW YORK

Web site: rama.poly.edu
Contact: Mr. John Steven Kerge, Dean of Admissions, Long Island Center,
    Route 110, Farmingdale, NY 11735-3995
Telephone: 516-755-4200 or toll-free 800-POLYTECH **Fax:** 516-755-4404
E-mail: admitme@poly.edu

Academics

Polytechnic awards bachelor's, master's, and doctoral **degrees** (most information given
is for both Brooklyn and Farmingdale campuses). Challenging opportunities include
advanced placement, accelerated degree programs, an honors program, double majors,
and a senior project. Special programs include cooperative education, summer session for
credit, and Air Force ROTC.

The most frequently chosen fields are engineering/engineering technologies,
computer/information sciences, and physical sciences. A complete listing of majors at
Polytechnic appears in the Majors Index beginning on page 432.

The **faculty** at Polytechnic has 162 full-time members, 91% with terminal degrees.
The student-faculty ratio is 12:1.

Students of Polytechnic

The student body totals 3,420, of whom 1,807 are undergraduates. 18% are women and
82% are men. Students come from 6 states and territories and 19 other countries. 97%
are from New York. 3% are international students. 11.1% are African American, 0.4%
American Indian, 36.6% Asian American, and 5.7% Hispanic American. 79% returned
for their sophomore year.

Facilities and Resources

Student rooms are linked to a campus network. 86 **computers** are available on campus
that provide access to the Internet. The **library** has 48,100 books and 110 subscriptions.

Campus Life

There are 24 active organizations on campus, including a drama/theater group and
newspaper. 15% of eligible men and 15% of eligible women are members of national
fraternities, local fraternities, local **sororities**, and coed fraternity.

Polytechnic is a member of the NCAA (Division III). **Intercollegiate sports** include
baseball (m), basketball (m), cross-country running, lacrosse (m), soccer (m), softball (w),
tennis, track and field, volleyball.

Campus Safety

Student safety services include patrols by trained security personnel and electronically
operated dormitory entrances.

Applying

Polytechnic requires an essay, SAT I or ACT, a high school transcript, and 2 recommendations. It recommends SAT II Subject Tests, SAT II: Writing Test, and an
interview. Application deadline: rolling admissions. Deferred admission is possible.

Getting in Last Year
1,389 applied
70% were accepted
468 enrolled (48%)
3.30 average high school GPA
31% had SAT verbal scores over 600
72% had SAT math scores over 600
4% had SAT verbal scores over 700
16% had SAT math scores over 700

Graduation and After
34% graduated in 4 years
14% graduated in 5 years
4% graduated in 6 years
8% pursued further study

Financial Matters
$20,810 tuition and fees (1999–2000)
$5470 room and board

POMONA COLLEGE

SUBURBAN SETTING ■ PRIVATE ■ INDEPENDENT ■ COED
CLAREMONT, CALIFORNIA

Web site: www.pomona.edu
Contact: Mr. Bruce Poch, Vice President and Dean of Admissions, 333 North College Way, Claremont, CA 91711
Telephone: 909-621-8134 **Fax:** 909-621-8403
E-mail: admissions@pomona.edu

Pomona College is located in Claremont, California, 35 miles east of Los Angeles, and is the founding member of the Claremont Colleges. Recognized as one of the nation's premier liberal arts colleges, Pomona offers a comprehensive undergraduate curriculum and enrolls students from around the nation and across class and ethnicity. With financial resources among the strongest of any national liberal arts college, Pomona offers a broad range of resources and opportunities, including an extensive study-abroad program. The community enjoys academic, cultural, and extracurricular activities usually found only at large universities, with all of the benefits and advantages of a small college.

Getting in Last Year
3,612 applied
32% were accepted
390 enrolled (34%)
80% from top tenth of their h.s. class
94% had SAT verbal scores over 600
96% had SAT math scores over 600
99% had ACT scores over 24
65% had SAT verbal scores over 700
59% had SAT math scores over 700
76% had ACT scores over 30
41 National Merit Scholars
6 class presidents
32 valedictorians

Graduation and After
83% graduated in 4 years
5% graduated in 5 years
1% graduated in 6 years
33% pursued further study (17% arts and sciences, 9% law, 9% medicine)
60% had job offers within 6 months
165 organizations recruited on campus
5 Fulbright scholars

Financial Matters
$23,170 tuition and fees (1999–2000)
$7750 room and board
100% average percent of need met
$22,032 average financial aid amount received per undergraduate (1999–2000)

Academics
Pomona awards bachelor's **degrees**. Challenging opportunities include advanced placement, student-designed majors, double majors, independent study, a senior project, Phi Beta Kappa, and Sigma Xi. Special programs include internships, off-campus study, and study-abroad.

The most frequently chosen fields are social sciences and history, biological/life sciences, and physical sciences. A complete listing of majors at Pomona appears in the Majors Index beginning on page 432.

The **faculty** at Pomona has 155 full-time members, 100% with terminal degrees. The student-faculty ratio is 9:1.

Students of Pomona
The student body is made up of 1,549 undergraduates. 46.8% are women and 53.2% are men. Students come from 49 states and territories. 39% are from California. 1.8% are international students. 4.4% are African American, 1.1% American Indian, 18.4% Asian American, and 9.7% Hispanic American. 98% returned for their sophomore year.

Facilities and Resources
Student rooms are linked to a campus network. 180 **computers** are available on campus that provide access to the Internet. The 4 **libraries** have 1,900,000 books and 5,967 subscriptions.

Campus Life
There are 280 active organizations on campus, including a drama/theater group, newspaper, radio station, and choral group. 6% of eligible men are members of local **fraternities** and local coed fraternities.

Pomona is a member of the NCAA (Division III). **Intercollegiate sports** include baseball (m), basketball, cross-country running, football (m), golf, soccer, softball (w), swimming, tennis, track and field, volleyball (w), water polo.

Campus Safety
Student safety services include late-night transport/escort service, 24-hour emergency telephone alarm devices, 24-hour patrols by trained security personnel, and electronically operated dormitory entrances.

Applying
Pomona requires an essay, SAT I and SAT II or ACT, 3 SAT II Subject Tests (including SAT II Writing Test), a high school transcript, and 2 recommendations. It recommends an interview, portfolio or tapes for art and performing arts programs, and a minimum high school GPA of 3.0. Application deadline: 1/1; 2/1 for financial aid. Early and deferred admission are possible.

PRESBYTERIAN COLLEGE

SMALL-TOWN SETTING ■ PRIVATE ■ INDEPENDENT RELIGIOUS ■ COED
CLINTON, SOUTH CAROLINA

Web site: www.presby.edu
Contact: Mr. Richard Dana Paul, Vice President of Enrollment and Dean of
Admissions, South Broad Street, Clinton, SC 29325
Telephone: 864-833-8229 or toll-free 800-476-7272 **Fax:** 864-833-8481
E-mail: rdpaul@admin.presby.edu

 eAPPLY

Academics
Presbyterian College awards bachelor's **degrees**. Challenging opportunities include
advanced placement, freshman honors college, an honors program, double majors,
independent study, and a senior project. Special programs include internships, summer
session for credit, off-campus study, study-abroad, and Army ROTC.

The most frequently chosen fields are business/marketing, social sciences and history,
and biological/life sciences. A complete listing of majors at Presbyterian College appears
in the Majors Index beginning on page 432.

The **faculty** at Presbyterian College has 77 full-time members, 90% with terminal
degrees. The student-faculty ratio is 12:1.

Students of Presbyterian College
The student body is made up of 1,119 undergraduates. 52.1% are women and 47.9% are
men. Students come from 26 states and territories. 57% are from South Carolina. 4.7%
are African American, 0.1% American Indian, 0.3% Asian American, and 0.4% Hispanic
American. 87% returned for their sophomore year.

Facilities and Resources
Student rooms are linked to a campus network. 130 **computers** are available on campus
that provide access to the Internet. The **library** has 165,159 books and 787 subscriptions.

Campus Life
There are 60 active organizations on campus, including a drama/theater group,
newspaper, radio station, and choral group. 44% of eligible men and 41% of eligible
women are members of national **fraternities**, national **sororities**, and minority social
club.

Presbyterian College is a member of the NCAA (Division II). **Intercollegiate sports**
(some offering scholarships) include baseball (m), basketball, cross-country running,
football (m), golf (m), riflery, soccer, softball (w), tennis, volleyball (w).

Campus Safety
Student safety services include late-night transport/escort service, 24-hour emergency
telephone alarm devices, 24-hour patrols by trained security personnel, and electronically operated dormitory entrances.

Applying
Presbyterian College requires an essay, SAT I or ACT, a high school transcript, and 1
recommendation. It recommends an interview. Application deadline: 4/1; 3/1 priority
date for financial aid. Deferred admission is possible.

> **P**resbyterian College—with
> 43 national and
> international scholarship
> recipients in recent years—provides
> an environment that nurtures the
> best and brightest. Students respect
> and live by a strong Honor Code,
> and well over half volunteer for
> community service. Students also
> may study under PC's Service
> Learning Program, participate in a
> comprehensive Honors Program, or
> study abroad in locations around the
> world. To prepare for graduate
> school and the job market, students
> may intern or conduct research
> alongside professors. A scholarship
> program for outstanding students is
> supported by one of the largest
> per-student endowments in the
> region.

Getting in Last Year
994 applied
81% were accepted
333 enrolled (41%)
36% from top tenth of their h.s. class
3.3 average high school GPA
38% had SAT verbal scores over 600
35% had SAT math scores over 600
56% had ACT scores over 24
6% had SAT verbal scores over 700
4% had SAT math scores over 700
8% had ACT scores over 30
19 class presidents
5 valedictorians

Graduation and After
71% graduated in 4 years
7% graduated in 5 years
Graduates pursuing further study: 4% arts and
sciences, 3% law, 2% education
76% had job offers within 6 months
45 organizations recruited on campus

Financial Matters
$16,524 tuition and fees (1999–2000)
$4650 room and board
$15,331 average financial aid amount received
per undergraduate (1999–2000 estimated)

PRINCETON UNIVERSITY

SUBURBAN SETTING ■ PRIVATE ■ INDEPENDENT ■ COED
PRINCETON, NEW JERSEY

Web site: www.princeton.edu
Contact: Mr. Fred A. Hargadon, Dean of Admission, PO Box 430, Princeton, NJ 08544
Telephone: 609-258-3062 **Fax:** 609-258-6743

The fourth-oldest college in the country, Princeton was chartered in 1746. Any list of the most frequently cited strengths of Princeton would doubtless include the following: the quality of its academic programs, its relatively small size combined with the resources of one of the world's major research universities, and the emphasis it has always placed on undergraduate education. Students at Princeton are asked to make a significant commitment of their own time and energy, and, in return, the University provides them with an abundance of opportunities to grow and learn, both in and out of the classroom.

Getting in Last Year
14,875 applied
11% were accepted
1,148 enrolled (68%)
92% from top tenth of their h.s. class
3.82 average high school GPA
95% had SAT verbal scores over 600
96% had SAT math scores over 600
67% had SAT verbal scores over 700
69% had SAT math scores over 700

Graduation and After
91% graduated in 4 years
4% graduated in 5 years
1% graduated in 6 years
24% pursued further study (8% arts and sciences, 5% medicine, 5% law)
47.1% had job offers within 6 months
300 organizations recruited on campus
1 Marshall, 18 Fulbright scholars

Financial Matters
$24,630 tuition and fees (1999–2000)
$6969 room and board
100% average percent of need met
$21,800 average financial aid amount received per undergraduate (1999–2000 estimated)

Academics

Princeton awards bachelor's, master's, and doctoral **degrees**. Challenging opportunities include advanced placement, accelerated degree programs, student-designed majors, an honors program, independent study, a senior project, Phi Beta Kappa, and Sigma Xi. Special programs include cooperative education, internships, off-campus study, study-abroad, and Army and Air Force ROTC.

The most frequently chosen fields are social sciences and history, engineering/engineering technologies, and biological/life sciences. A complete listing of majors at Princeton appears in the Majors Index beginning on page 432.

The **faculty** at Princeton has 726 full-time members, 94% with terminal degrees.

Students of Princeton

The student body totals 6,440, of whom 4,672 are undergraduates. 47% are women and 53% are men. Students come from 53 states and territories and 55 other countries. 15% are from New Jersey. 5.1% are international students. 7.2% are African American, 0.6% American Indian, 12.3% Asian American, and 6.3% Hispanic American. 99% returned for their sophomore year.

Facilities and Resources

Student rooms are linked to a campus network. 500 **computers** are available on campus that provide access to the Internet. The 23 **libraries** have 5,095,379 books and 34,348 subscriptions.

Campus Life

There are 174 active organizations on campus, including a drama/theater group, newspaper, radio station, choral group, and marching band. 70% of eligible men and 70% of eligible women are members of eating clubs.

Princeton is a member of the NCAA (Division I). **Intercollegiate sports** include baseball (m), basketball, crew, cross-country running, fencing, field hockey (w), football (m), golf, ice hockey, lacrosse, soccer, softball (w), squash, swimming, tennis, track and field, volleyball, water polo, wrestling (m).

Campus Safety

Student safety services include late-night transport/escort service, 24-hour emergency telephone alarm devices, 24-hour patrols by trained security personnel, student patrols, and electronically operated dormitory entrances.

Applying

Princeton requires an essay, SAT I, SAT II Subject Tests, a high school transcript, and 3 recommendations. It recommends an interview. Application deadline: 1/1; 2/1 priority date for financial aid. Early and deferred admission are possible.

PROVIDENCE COLLEGE
SUBURBAN SETTING ■ PRIVATE ■ INDEPENDENT RELIGIOUS ■ COED
PROVIDENCE, RHODE ISLAND

Web site: www.providence.edu
Contact: Mr. Christopher Lydon, Dean of Enrollment Management, River
  Avenue and Eaton Street, Providence, RI 02918
Telephone: 401-865-2535 or toll-free 800-721-6444 **Fax:** 401-865-2826
E-mail: pcadmiss@providence.edu

Academics
PC awards associate, bachelor's, and master's **degrees**. Challenging opportunities
include advanced placement, student-designed majors, an honors program, double
majors, independent study, and a senior project. Special programs include cooperative
education, internships, summer session for credit, study-abroad, and Army ROTC.

The most frequently chosen fields are business/marketing, social sciences and history,
and education. A complete listing of majors at PC appears in the Majors Index beginning
on page 432.

The **faculty** at PC has 256 full-time members, 88% with terminal degrees. The student-faculty ratio is 13:1.

Students of PC
The student body totals 5,442, of whom 4,505 are undergraduates. 58.9% are women
and 41.1% are men. Students come from 38 states and territories and 12 other countries.
20% are from Rhode Island. 0.8% are international students. 1.9% are African
American, 0.1% American Indian, 1.2% Asian American, and 3.5% Hispanic American.
90% returned for their sophomore year.

Facilities and Resources
Student rooms are linked to a campus network. 130 **computers** are available on campus
that provide access to the Internet. The **library** has 229,154 books and 1,656 subscriptions.

Campus Life
There are 85 active organizations on campus, including a drama/theater group,
newspaper, radio station, television station, and choral group. No national or local
fraternities or **sororities**.

PC is a member of the NCAA (Division I). **Intercollegiate sports** (some offering
scholarships) include basketball, cross-country running, field hockey (w), ice hockey,
lacrosse (m), racquetball, rugby, soccer, softball (w), swimming, tennis (w), track and
field, volleyball (w).

Campus Safety
Student safety services include late-night transport/escort service, 24-hour emergency
telephone alarm devices, 24-hour patrols by trained security personnel, student patrols,
and electronically operated dormitory entrances.

Applying
PC requires an essay, SAT I or ACT, a high school transcript, and 2 recommendations. It
recommends SAT II Subject Tests, SAT II: Writing Test, an interview, and a minimum
high school GPA of 3.25. Application deadline: 1/15; 2/1 for financial aid. Early and
deferred admission are possible.

Getting in Last Year
5,331 applied
60% were accepted
978 enrolled (31%)
37% from top tenth of their h.s. class
3.34 average high school GPA
45% had SAT verbal scores over 600
45% had SAT math scores over 600
61% had ACT scores over 24
7% had SAT verbal scores over 700
6% had SAT math scores over 700
7% had ACT scores over 30
41 National Merit Scholars
18 class presidents
15 valedictorians

Graduation and After
79% graduated in 4 years
2% graduated in 5 years
25% pursued further study (13% arts and
  sciences, 5% law, 3% education)
96% had job offers within 6 months
110 organizations recruited on campus

Financial Matters
$17,945 tuition and fees (1999–2000)
$7355 room and board
85% average percent of need met
$14,350 average financial aid amount received
  per undergraduate (1999–2000 estimated)

PURDUE UNIVERSITY

SUBURBAN SETTING ■ PUBLIC ■ STATE-SUPPORTED ■ COED
WEST LAFAYETTE, INDIANA

Web site: www.purdue.edu
Contact: Director of Admissions, Schleman Hall, West Lafayette, IN 47907-1080
Telephone: 765-494-4600
E-mail: admissions@purdue.edu

Academics

Purdue awards associate, bachelor's, master's, doctoral, and first-professional **degrees**. Challenging opportunities include advanced placement, accelerated degree programs, student-designed majors, freshman honors college, an honors program, double majors, independent study, a senior project, Phi Beta Kappa, and Sigma Xi. Special programs include cooperative education, internships, summer session for credit, study-abroad, and Army, Navy and Air Force ROTC.

The most frequently chosen fields are engineering/engineering technologies, business/marketing, and education. A complete listing of majors at Purdue appears in the Majors Index beginning on page 432.

The **faculty** at Purdue has 2,023 full-time members, 85% with terminal degrees.

Students of Purdue

The student body totals 37,762, of whom 30,835 are undergraduates. 43.3% are women and 56.7% are men. Students come from 53 states and territories and 101 other countries. 80% are from Indiana. 5.6% are international students. 3.4% are African American, 0.5% American Indian, 3.3% Asian American, and 2% Hispanic American. 86% returned for their sophomore year.

Facilities and Resources

Student rooms are linked to a campus network. 2,100 **computers** are available on campus that provide access to the Internet. The 15 **libraries** have 2,280,681 books and 19,025 subscriptions.

Campus Life

There are 635 active organizations on campus, including a drama/theater group, newspaper, radio station, choral group, and marching band. 18% of eligible men and 17% of eligible women are members of national **fraternities** and national **sororities**.

Purdue is a member of the NCAA (Division I). **Intercollegiate sports** (some offering scholarships) include archery, badminton, baseball (m), basketball, crew, cross-country running, equestrian sports, fencing, football (m), golf, gymnastics, ice hockey (m), lacrosse, racquetball, riflery, rugby, sailing, skiing (downhill), soccer, softball (w), squash, swimming, table tennis, tennis, track and field, volleyball, water polo, weight lifting, wrestling (m).

Campus Safety

Student safety services include late-night transport/escort service, 24-hour emergency telephone alarm devices, 24-hour patrols by trained security personnel, student patrols, and electronically operated dormitory entrances.

Applying

Purdue requires SAT I or ACT and a high school transcript. Application deadline: rolling admissions; 3/1 priority date for financial aid. Early admission is possible.

QUINCY UNIVERSITY

SMALL-TOWN SETTING ■ PRIVATE ■ INDEPENDENT RELIGIOUS ■ COED
QUINCY, ILLINOIS

Web site: www.quincy.edu
Contact: Mr. Jeff Van Camp, Director of Admissions, 1800 College Avenue,
Quincy, IL 62301-2699
Telephone: 217-222-8020 ext. 5215 or toll-free 800-688-4295
E-mail: admissions@quincy.edu

Academics

Quincy University awards associate, bachelor's, and master's **degrees**. Challenging
opportunities include advanced placement, accelerated degree programs, student-
designed majors, an honors program, double majors, independent study, and a senior
project. Special programs include internships, summer session for credit, and study-
abroad.

The most frequently chosen fields are business/marketing, education, and social sciences and history. A complete listing of majors at Quincy University appears in the
Majors Index beginning on page 432.

The **faculty** at Quincy University has 62 full-time members, 84% with terminal
degrees. The student-faculty ratio is 13:1.

Students of Quincy University

The student body totals 1,186, of whom 1,051 are undergraduates. 54.6% are women
and 45.4% are men. Students come from 35 states and territories and 16 other countries.
69% are from Illinois. 1.7% are international students. 6.2% are African American, 0.4%
American Indian, 0.7% Asian American, and 2.6% Hispanic American. 73% returned for
their sophomore year.

Facilities and Resources

Student rooms are linked to a campus network. 196 **computers** are available on campus
that provide access to the Internet. The **library** has 236,769 books and 669 subscriptions.

Campus Life

There are 41 active organizations on campus, including a drama/theater group,
newspaper, radio station, and choral group. 11% of eligible men and 4% of eligible
women are members of national **fraternities** and national **sororities**.

Quincy University is a member of the NCAA (Division II). **Intercollegiate sports**
(some offering scholarships) include baseball (m), basketball, cross-country running,
football (m), golf, soccer, softball (w), tennis, track and field, volleyball.

Campus Safety

Student safety services include late-night transport/escort service, 24-hour emergency
telephone alarm devices, 24-hour patrols by trained security personnel, student patrols,
and electronically operated dormitory entrances.

Applying

Quincy University requires SAT I or ACT and a high school transcript. It recommends
an interview and a minimum high school GPA of 2.0. Application deadline: rolling
admissions; 4/15 priority date for financial aid. Early and deferred admission are possible.

Quincy University is a
dynamic community
located in the heart of
Quincy, Illinois. The liberal arts–
based curriculum and extensive
internship program prepare students
for their chosen fields; the numerous
opportunities for leadership outside
the classroom help prepare students
to take an active role in society.
Strong scholarship opportunities
enable students from all walks of
life to experience the Quincy
advantage. While many things make
Quincy unique, most important are
the people that make up the
University community. QU's
Franciscan heritage of complete
respect for all individuals and their
unique gifts is at the heart of
university life.

Getting in Last Year
1,451 applied
81% were accepted
274 enrolled (23%)
15% from top tenth of their h.s. class
3.13 average high school GPA
22% had SAT verbal scores over 600
28% had SAT math scores over 600
33% had ACT scores over 24
11% had SAT verbal scores over 700
11% had SAT math scores over 700
3% had ACT scores over 30
1 National Merit Scholar

Graduation and After
18% pursued further study (9% arts and sciences, 3% law, 2% business)
80% had job offers within 6 months
26 organizations recruited on campus

Financial Matters
$14,700 tuition and fees (2000–2001)
$4780 room and board
$13,455 average financial aid amount received
per undergraduate (1999–2000 estimated)

RANDOLPH-MACON WOMAN'S COLLEGE

SUBURBAN SETTING ■ PRIVATE ■ INDEPENDENT RELIGIOUS ■ WOMEN ONLY
LYNCHBURG, VIRGINIA

Web site: www.rmwc.edu
Contact: Pat LeDonne, Director of Admissions, 2500 Rivermont Avenue,
   Lynchburg, VA 24503-1526
Telephone: 804-947-8100 or toll-free 800-745-7692 **Fax:** 804-947-8996
E-mail: admissions@rmwc.edu

Academics

R-MWC awards bachelor's **degrees**. Challenging opportunities include advanced placement, accelerated degree programs, student-designed majors, an honors program, double majors, independent study, a senior project, and Phi Beta Kappa. Special programs include internships, off-campus study, and study-abroad.

The most frequently chosen fields are social sciences and history, psychology, and biological/life sciences. A complete listing of majors at R-MWC appears in the Majors Index beginning on page 432.

The **faculty** at R-MWC has 73 full-time members, 93% with terminal degrees. The student-faculty ratio is 9:1.

Students of R-MWC

The student body is made up of 710 undergraduates. Students come from 48 states and territories and 34 other countries. 40% are from Virginia. 8.9% are international students. 7.5% are African American, 0.4% American Indian, 2.8% Asian American, and 3.1% Hispanic American. 73% returned for their sophomore year.

Facilities and Resources

Student rooms are linked to a campus network. 110 **computers** are available on campus that provide access to the Internet. The **library** has 115,222 books and 1,680 subscriptions.

Campus Life

There are 30 active organizations on campus, including a drama/theater group, newspaper, radio station, and choral group. No national or local **sororities**.

R-MWC is a member of the NCAA (Division III). **Intercollegiate sports** include basketball, equestrian sports, field hockey, lacrosse, soccer, softball, swimming, tennis, volleyball.

Campus Safety

Student safety services include late-night transport/escort service, 24-hour emergency telephone alarm devices, and 24-hour patrols by trained security personnel.

Applying

R-MWC requires an essay, SAT I or ACT, a high school transcript, and 2 recommendations. It recommends an interview. Application deadline: 2/15; 3/1 for financial aid, with a 2/1 priority date. Early and deferred admission are possible.

Education in the singular, self-awareness, and involvement—these are priorities at Randolph-Macon Woman's College. Students seize opportunities to study abroad, participate in internships, conduct original research with faculty members, coordinate programs and hold leadership positions in campus organizations, and volunteer in the community. The exciting and engaging atmosphere fosters academic excellence and helps develop leadership potential. Since class size is small (70% of all classes have 15 or fewer students), students have easy access to their professors. Contemporary facilities and advanced technology afford women a competitive edge for career prospects or advanced study. The College provides a setting for learning and living that prepares women for meaningful personal and professional lives.

Getting in Last Year
719 applied
84% were accepted
201 enrolled (33%)
39% from top tenth of their h.s. class
3.4 average high school GPA
53% had SAT verbal scores over 600
34% had SAT math scores over 600
83% had ACT scores over 24
19% had SAT verbal scores over 700
4% had SAT math scores over 700
21% had ACT scores over 30
1 National Merit Scholar
2 valedictorians

Graduation and After
60% graduated in 4 years
3% graduated in 5 years
1% graduated in 6 years
Graduates pursuing further study: 21% arts
   and sciences, 2% education, 2% law
60% had job offers within 6 months
15 organizations recruited on campus

Financial Matters
$17,080 tuition and fees (1999–2000)
$7010 room and board
92% average percent of need met
$15,515 average financial aid amount received
   per undergraduate (1999–2000 estimated)

REED COLLEGE

SUBURBAN SETTING ■ PRIVATE ■ INDEPENDENT ■ COED
PORTLAND, OREGON

Web site: www.reed.edu
Contact: Dr. Nancy Donehower, Dean of Admission, 3203 Southeast
  Woodstock Boulevard, Portland, OR 97202-8199
Telephone: 503-777-7511 or toll-free 800-547-4750 (out-of-state) **Fax:**
  503-777-7553
E-mail: admission@reed.edu

Academics

Reed awards bachelor's and master's **degrees**. Challenging opportunities include advanced placement, accelerated degree programs, student-designed majors, double majors, independent study, a senior project, and Phi Beta Kappa. Special programs include off-campus study, study-abroad, and Army ROTC.

The most frequently chosen fields are biological/life sciences, English, and psychology. A complete listing of majors at Reed appears in the Majors Index beginning on page 432.

The **faculty** at Reed has 112 full-time members, 88% with terminal degrees. The student-faculty ratio is 10:1.

Students of Reed

The student body totals 1,373, of whom 1,353 are undergraduates. 53.7% are women and 46.3% are men. Students come from 57 states and territories and 29 other countries. 15% are from Oregon. 2.6% are international students. 0.4% are African American, 0.9% American Indian, 4.7% Asian American, and 3.6% Hispanic American. 88% returned for their sophomore year.

Facilities and Resources

Student rooms are linked to a campus network. 203 **computers** are available on campus that provide access to the Internet. The 2 **libraries** have 438,119 books and 2,088 subscriptions.

Campus Life

There are 59 active organizations on campus, including a drama/theater group, newspaper, radio station, and choral group. No national or local **fraternities** or **sororities**.

Intercollegiate sports include basketball (m), crew, fencing, rugby, sailing, soccer, squash.

Campus Safety

Student safety services include 24-hour emergency dispatch, late-night transport/escort service, 24-hour emergency telephone alarm devices, 24-hour patrols by trained security personnel, student patrols, and electronically operated dormitory entrances.

Applying

Reed requires an essay, SAT I or ACT, a high school transcript, and 2 recommendations. It recommends SAT II Subject Tests, SAT II: Writing Test, an interview, and a minimum high school GPA of 3.0. Application deadline: 1/15; 1/15 for financial aid. Early and deferred admission are possible.

Getting in Last Year

2,018 applied
68% were accepted
334 enrolled (24%)
52% from top tenth of their h.s. class
3.7 average high school GPA
92% had SAT verbal scores over 600
80% had SAT math scores over 600
98% had ACT scores over 24
49% had SAT verbal scores over 700
28% had SAT math scores over 700
45% had ACT scores over 30
11 National Merit Scholars
19 valedictorians

Graduation and After

48% graduated in 4 years
17% graduated in 5 years
3% graduated in 6 years
Graduates pursuing further study: 36% arts and sciences, 7% law, 5% business
24 organizations recruited on campus
1 Rhodes scholar

Financial Matters

$24,050 tuition and fees (1999–2000)
$6650 room and board
100% average percent of need met
$21,116 average financial aid amount received per undergraduate (1999–2000 estimated)

RENSSELAER POLYTECHNIC INSTITUTE

SUBURBAN SETTING ■ PRIVATE ■ INDEPENDENT ■ COED
TROY, NEW YORK

Web site: www.rpi.edu
Contact: Ms. Teresa Duffy, Dean of Admissions, 110 8th Street, Troy, NY 12180-3590
Telephone: 518-276-6216 or toll-free 800-448-6562 **Fax:** 518-276-4072
E-mail: admissions@rpi.edu

Rensselaer celebrates discovery and prepares leaders for the technologically based marketplace. The students are challenged by a rigorous curriculum and taught through new interactive learning methods pioneered at Rensselaer. The unique methods of learning have earned Rensselaer 3 prestigious awards: the Hesburgh Award, the Boeing Excellence in Education Award, and the Pew Charitable Trust Award for innovation in undergraduate education. Rensselaer undergraduates have numerous opportunities to conduct research through the university-funded Undergraduate Research Program and to gain valuable job experience by participation in the Cooperative Education Program. Among successful Rensselaer graduates are Washington Roebling, chief engineer of the Brooklyn Bridge; Nancy Fitzroy, the first woman president of the American Society of Mechanical Engineers; and William Mow, founder of Bugle Boy Industries.

Getting in Last Year
5,264 applied
78% were accepted
1,323 enrolled (32%)
54% from top tenth of their h.s. class
60% had SAT verbal scores over 600
85% had SAT math scores over 600
82% had ACT scores over 24
14% had SAT verbal scores over 700
34% had SAT math scores over 700
14% had ACT scores over 30
26 National Merit Scholars
101 valedictorians

Graduation and After
44% graduated in 4 years
25% graduated in 5 years
4% graduated in 6 years
21% pursued further study
77% had job offers within 6 months
377 organizations recruited on campus

Financial Matters
$22,955 tuition and fees (1999–2000)
$7692 room and board
84% average percent of need met
$17,537 average financial aid amount received per undergraduate (1999–2000 estimated)

Academics

Rensselaer awards bachelor's, master's, and doctoral **degrees**. Challenging opportunities include advanced placement, accelerated degree programs, student-designed majors, an honors program, double majors, independent study, a senior project, and Sigma Xi. Special programs include cooperative education, internships, summer session for credit, off-campus study, study-abroad, and Army, Navy and Air Force ROTC.

The most frequently chosen fields are engineering/engineering technologies, business/marketing, and architecture. A complete listing of majors at Rensselaer appears in the Majors Index beginning on page 432.

The **faculty** at Rensselaer has 343 full-time members, 100% with terminal degrees. The student-faculty ratio is 18:1.

Students of Rensselaer

The student body totals 7,650, of whom 4,926 are undergraduates. 24% are women and 76% are men. Students come from 53 states and territories and 78 other countries. 51% are from New York. 4.3% are international students. 3.6% are African American, 0.3% American Indian, 11.1% Asian American, and 4.2% Hispanic American. 90% returned for their sophomore year.

Facilities and Resources

Student rooms are linked to a campus network. 720 **computers** are available on campus that provide access to the Internet. The 2 **libraries** have 309,171 books and 10,210 subscriptions.

Campus Life

There are 130 active organizations on campus, including a drama/theater group, newspaper, radio station, and choral group. 30% of eligible men and 20% of eligible women are members of national **fraternities**, national **sororities**, local fraternities, and local sororities.

Rensselaer is a member of the NCAA (Division III). **Intercollegiate sports** include archery, badminton, baseball (m), basketball, crew, cross-country running, equestrian sports, fencing, field hockey (w), football (m), golf (m), gymnastics, ice hockey, lacrosse, racquetball, riflery, rugby (m), sailing, skiing (cross-country), skiing (downhill), soccer, softball (w), squash, swimming, table tennis, tennis, track and field, volleyball, water polo, weight lifting.

Campus Safety

Student safety services include campus foot patrols at night, late-night transport/escort service, 24-hour emergency telephone alarm devices, 24-hour patrols by trained security personnel, and electronically operated dormitory entrances.

Applying

Rensselaer requires an essay, SAT I or ACT, a high school transcript, and 1 recommendation, and in some cases SAT II Subject Tests and portfolio for architecture program. Application deadline: 1/1; 2/15 priority date for financial aid. Early and deferred admission are possible.

RHODES COLLEGE

SUBURBAN SETTING ■ PRIVATE ■ INDEPENDENT RELIGIOUS ■ COED
MEMPHIS, TENNESSEE

Web site: www.rhodes.edu
Contact: Mr. David J. Wottle, Dean of Admissions and Financial Aid, 2000 North Parkway, Memphis, TN 38112-1690
Telephone: 901-843-3700 or toll-free 800-844-5969 (out-of-state) **Fax:** 901-843-3719
E-mail: adminfo@rhodes.edu

eAPPLY

Academics

Rhodes awards bachelor's and master's **degrees** (master's degree in accounting only). Challenging opportunities include advanced placement, accelerated degree programs, student-designed majors, double majors, independent study, a senior project, and Phi Beta Kappa. Special programs include internships, summer session for credit, off-campus study, study-abroad, and Army and Air Force ROTC.

The most frequently chosen fields are social sciences and history, business/marketing, and biological/life sciences. A complete listing of majors at Rhodes appears in the Majors Index beginning on page 432.

The **faculty** at Rhodes has 121 full-time members. The student-faculty ratio is 12:1.

Students of Rhodes

The student body totals 1,510, of whom 1,499 are undergraduates. 54.5% are women and 45.5% are men. Students come from 45 states and territories and 17 other countries. 28% are from Tennessee. 1.5% are international students. 3.8% are African American, 0.1% American Indian, 2.6% Asian American, and 1.4% Hispanic American. 90% returned for their sophomore year.

Facilities and Resources

Student rooms are linked to a campus network. 125 **computers** are available on campus that provide access to the Internet. The 4 **libraries** have 250,000 books and 1,200 subscriptions.

Campus Life

There are 44 active organizations on campus, including a drama/theater group, newspaper, and choral group. 57% of eligible men and 55% of eligible women are members of national **fraternities** and national **sororities**.

Rhodes is a member of the NCAA (Division III). **Intercollegiate sports** include baseball (m), basketball, cross-country running, equestrian sports, field hockey (w), football (m), golf, lacrosse (m), rugby (m), soccer, softball (w), swimming, tennis, track and field, volleyball (w).

Campus Safety

Student safety services include 24-hour monitored security cameras in parking areas, fenced campus with monitored access at night, late-night transport/escort service, 24-hour emergency telephone alarm devices, 24-hour patrols by trained security personnel, and student patrols.

Applying

Rhodes requires an essay, SAT I or ACT, a high school transcript, and 2 recommendations. It recommends an interview. Application deadline: 2/1; 3/1 priority date for financial aid. Early and deferred admission are possible.

Getting in Last Year

2,247 applied
78% were accepted
439 enrolled (25%)
56% from top tenth of their h.s. class
3.51 average high school GPA
74% had SAT verbal scores over 600
77% had SAT math scores over 600
95% had ACT scores over 24
29% had SAT verbal scores over 700
24% had SAT math scores over 700
33% had ACT scores over 30
25 National Merit Scholars
29 class presidents
34 valedictorians

Graduation and After

33% pursued further study (15% arts and sciences, 6% law, 5% medicine)
55 organizations recruited on campus
2 Fulbright scholars

Financial Matters

$19,303 tuition and fees (2000–2001)
$5353 room and board
93% average percent of need met
$18,024 average financial aid amount received per undergraduate (1999–2000 estimated)

RICE UNIVERSITY

URBAN SETTING ■ PRIVATE ■ INDEPENDENT ■ COED
HOUSTON, TEXAS

Web site: www.rice.edu
Contact: Ms. Julie M. Browning, Dean for Undergraduate Admission, PO Box 1892, MS 17, Houston, TX 77251-1892
Telephone: 713-348-RICE or toll-free 800-527-OWLS
E-mail: admission@rice.edu

Academics

Rice awards bachelor's, master's, and doctoral **degrees**. Challenging opportunities include advanced placement, accelerated degree programs, student-designed majors, an honors program, a senior project, Phi Beta Kappa, and Sigma Xi. Special programs include internships, summer session for credit, off-campus study, study-abroad, and Army and Navy ROTC. A complete listing of majors at Rice appears in the Majors Index beginning on page 432.

Students of Rice

The student body totals 4,310, of whom 2,769 are undergraduates. 46.8% are women and 53.2% are men. Students come from 50 states and territories and 28 other countries. 50% are from Texas. 2.9% are international students. 6.9% are African American, 0.7% American Indian, 15.3% Asian American, and 10.2% Hispanic American. 95% returned for their sophomore year.

Facilities and Resources

Student rooms are linked to a campus network. 185 **computers** are available on campus that provide access to the Internet. The **library** has 1,900,000 books and 14,000 subscriptions.

Campus Life

There are 125 active organizations on campus, including a drama/theater group, newspaper, radio station, television station, choral group, and marching band. No national or local **fraternities** or **sororities**.

Rice is a member of the NCAA (Division I). **Intercollegiate sports** (some offering scholarships) include baseball (m), basketball, crew, cross-country running, football (m), golf (m), lacrosse, riflery, rugby, sailing, soccer, swimming (w), tennis, track and field, volleyball (w).

Campus Safety

Student safety services include late-night transport/escort service, 24-hour emergency telephone alarm devices, 24-hour patrols by trained security personnel, and electronically operated dormitory entrances.

Applying

Rice requires an essay, SAT II Subject Tests, SAT II: Writing Test, SAT I or ACT, a high school transcript, and 2 recommendations. It recommends an interview. Application deadline: 1/2. Early and deferred admission are possible.

Nobel Prize-winning scholars who teach freshmen, the lowest student indebtedness in the country, easy access to the world's largest medical center, the cultural richness of the nation's fourth-largest city, and a student-faculty ratio of 5:1—most universities would be proud to have any one of these features; Rice University has them all. Along with top students, faculty members devoted to undergraduate teaching, and world-class facilities, Rice's distinctive character is derived from its residential colleges, which underlie its strong sense of community. Even the price is right. Rice has long been recognized as one of the best educational values in the country.

Getting in Last Year
5,740 applied
28% were accepted
93% from top tenth of their h.s. class
89% had SAT verbal scores over 600
91% had SAT math scores over 600
99% had ACT scores over 24
56% had SAT verbal scores over 700
64% had SAT math scores over 700
70% had ACT scores over 30
244 National Merit Scholars
132 valedictorians

Graduation and After
Graduates pursuing further study: 18% arts and sciences, 11% medicine, 6% law
2 Fulbright scholars

Financial Matters
$15,796 tuition and fees (1999–2000)
$6600 room and board

RIPON COLLEGE
SMALL-TOWN SETTING ■ PRIVATE ■ INDEPENDENT ■ COED
RIPON, WISCONSIN

Web site: www.ripon.edu
Contact: Mr. Scott J. Goplin, Vice President and Dean of Admission and
  Financial Aid, 300 Seward Street, PO Box 248, Ripon, WI 54971
Telephone: 920-748-8185 or toll-free 800-947-4766 **Fax:** 920-748-8335
E-mail: adminfo@ripon.edu

Academics
Ripon awards bachelor's **degrees**. Challenging opportunities include advanced placement, accelerated degree programs, student-designed majors, double majors, a senior
project, and Phi Beta Kappa. Special programs include internships, off-campus study,
study-abroad, and Army ROTC.

The most frequently chosen fields are social sciences and history, biological/life sciences, and English. A complete listing of majors at Ripon appears in the Majors Index
beginning on page 432.

The **faculty** at Ripon has 61 full-time members. The student-faculty ratio is 10:1.

Students of Ripon
The student body is made up of 746 undergraduates. 52% are women and 48% are men.
Students come from 35 states and territories and 11 other countries. 71% are from
Wisconsin. 1.5% are international students. 1.4% are African American, 0.8% American
Indian, 1.8% Asian American, and 2.7% Hispanic American. 85% returned for their
sophomore year.

Facilities and Resources
Student rooms are linked to a campus network. 150 **computers** are available on campus
that provide access to the Internet. The **library** has 161,396 books and 710 subscriptions.

Campus Life
There are 45 active organizations on campus, including a drama/theater group,
newspaper, radio station, and choral group. 59% of eligible men and 33% of eligible
women are members of national **fraternities**, national **sororities**, local fraternities, and
local sororities.

Ripon is a member of the NCAA (Division III). **Intercollegiate sports** include
baseball (m), basketball, cross-country running, football (m), golf, ice hockey, rugby (m),
soccer, softball (w), swimming, tennis, track and field, volleyball (w), wrestling.

Campus Safety
Student safety services include late-night transport/escort service, 24-hour emergency
telephone alarm devices, 24-hour patrols by trained security personnel, student patrols,
and electronically operated dormitory entrances.

Applying
Ripon requires SAT I or ACT, a high school transcript, 1 recommendation, and a
minimum high school GPA of 2.0. It recommends an essay and an interview. Application
deadline: 3/15.

With an enduring focus on thinking critically, speaking convincingly, writing clearly, and using modern technology, Ripon graduates are prepared for the professional world—and the twenty-first century. Founded in 1851, Ripon continues in its steadfast belief that the liberal arts are the key for a life of both personal and professional success. Embedded in the liberal arts and fundamental to the world of work is the ability to communicate and think critically. Ripon provides an intensely personal undergraduate education that facilitates what employers want most—solid communication and problem-solving skills.

Getting in Last Year
824 applied
87% were accepted
283 enrolled (39%)
28% from top tenth of their h.s. class
3.40 average high school GPA
62% had SAT verbal scores over 600
58% had SAT math scores over 600
60% had ACT scores over 24
18% had SAT verbal scores over 700
9% had SAT math scores over 700
8% had ACT scores over 30
15 valedictorians

Graduation and After
49% graduated in 4 years
6% graduated in 5 years
2% graduated in 6 years
Graduates pursuing further study: 17% arts
  and sciences, 5% law, 4% education
74% had job offers within 6 months
20 organizations recruited on campus

Financial Matters
$18,240 tuition and fees (1999–2000)
$4400 room and board
99% average percent of need met
$16,798 average financial aid amount received
  per undergraduate (1999–2000)

ROCHESTER INSTITUTE OF TECHNOLOGY

SUBURBAN SETTING ■ PRIVATE ■ INDEPENDENT ■ COED
ROCHESTER, NEW YORK

Web site: www.rit.edu
Contact: Mr. Daniel Shelley, Director of Admissions, 60 Lomb Memorial
   Drive, Rochester, NY 14623-5604
Telephone: 716-475-6631 **Fax:** 716-475-7424
E-mail: admissons@rit.edu

Getting in Last Year
7,497 applied
77% were accepted
2,186 enrolled (38%)
25% from top tenth of their h.s. class
3.7 average high school GPA
40% had SAT verbal scores over 600
54% had SAT math scores over 600
66% had ACT scores over 24
7% had SAT verbal scores over 700
12% had SAT math scores over 700
14% had ACT scores over 30
16 National Merit Scholars
40 valedictorians

Graduation and After
10% pursued further study
92% had job offers within 6 months
600 organizations recruited on campus

Financial Matters
$17,637 tuition and fees (1999–2000)
$6852 room and board
90% average percent of need met
$14,700 average financial aid amount received
   per undergraduate (1998–99)

Academics
RIT awards associate, bachelor's, master's, and doctoral **degrees** and post-bachelor's certificates. Challenging opportunities include advanced placement, accelerated degree programs, student-designed majors, independent study, and a senior project. Special programs include cooperative education, internships, summer session for credit, off-campus study, study-abroad, and Army, Navy and Air Force ROTC.

The most frequently chosen fields are engineering/engineering technologies, visual/performing arts, and business/marketing. A complete listing of majors at RIT appears in the Majors Index beginning on page 432.

The **faculty** at RIT has 605 full-time members, 80% with terminal degrees. The student-faculty ratio is 13:1.

Students of RIT
The student body totals 12,775, of whom 10,746 are undergraduates. 34.2% are women and 65.8% are men. Students come from 50 states and territories and 85 other countries. 60% are from New York. 4.8% are international students. 4.9% are African American, 0.4% American Indian, 5.3% Asian American, and 3.2% Hispanic American. 84% returned for their sophomore year.

Facilities and Resources
Student rooms are linked to a campus network. 1,000 **computers** are available on campus that provide access to student account information and the Internet. The **library** has 350,000 books and 4,305 subscriptions.

Campus Life
There are 170 active organizations on campus, including a drama/theater group, newspaper, radio station, and choral group. 8% of eligible men and 8% of eligible women are members of national **fraternities**, national **sororities**, local fraternities, and local sororities.

RIT is a member of the NCAA (Division III). **Intercollegiate sports** include baseball (m), basketball, bowling, crew, cross-country running (m), equestrian sports (w), field hockey (w), ice hockey, lacrosse, rugby, skiing (downhill), soccer, softball (w), swimming, tennis, track and field, volleyball, water polo (m), wrestling (m).

Campus Safety
Student safety services include late-night transport/escort service, 24-hour emergency telephone alarm devices, 24-hour patrols by trained security personnel, and student patrols.

Applying
RIT requires an essay, SAT I or ACT, and a high school transcript, and in some cases portfolio for art program. It recommends an interview, 1 recommendation, and a minimum high school GPA of 3.0. Application deadline: 7/1; 3/15 priority date for financial aid. Early and deferred admission are possible.

ROCKHURST UNIVERSITY

URBAN SETTING ■ PRIVATE ■ INDEPENDENT RELIGIOUS ■ COED
KANSAS CITY, MISSOURI

Web site: www.rockhurst.edu
Contact: Mr. Mark Kopenski, Vice President of Enrollment Management
Services, 1100 Rockhurst Road, Kansas City, MO 64110-2561
Telephone: 816-501-4100 or toll-free 800-842-6776 **Fax:** 816-501-4241
E-mail: admission@rockhurst.edu

Academics

Rockhurst awards bachelor's and master's **degrees** and post-bachelor's certificates. Challenging opportunities include advanced placement, accelerated degree programs, freshman honors college, an honors program, double majors, independent study, and a senior project. Special programs include cooperative education, internships, summer session for credit, off-campus study, study-abroad, and Army ROTC.

The most frequently chosen fields are (pre)law, business/marketing, and health professions and related sciences. A complete listing of majors at Rockhurst appears in the Majors Index beginning on page 432.

The **faculty** at Rockhurst has 115 full-time members, 84% with terminal degrees. The student-faculty ratio is 9:1.

Students of Rockhurst

The student body totals 2,955, of whom 2,097 are undergraduates. 57.5% are women and 42.5% are men. Students come from 25 states and territories and 9 other countries. 69% are from Missouri. 1.4% are international students. 6.8% are African American, 0.7% American Indian, 2.7% Asian American, and 4.3% Hispanic American. 83% returned for their sophomore year.

Facilities and Resources

400 **computers** are available on campus that provide access to the Internet. The **library** has 53,720 books and 100 subscriptions.

Campus Life

There are 54 active organizations on campus, including a drama/theater group, newspaper, radio station, and choral group. 50% of eligible men and 50% of eligible women are members of national **fraternities** and national **sororities**.

Rockhurst is a member of the NCAA (Division II). **Intercollegiate sports** (some offering scholarships) include baseball (m), basketball, cross-country running, golf, soccer, tennis, volleyball (w).

Campus Safety

Student safety services include closed circuit TV monitors, late-night transport/escort service, 24-hour emergency telephone alarm devices, 24-hour patrols by trained security personnel, student patrols, and electronically operated dormitory entrances.

Applying

Rockhurst requires SAT I or ACT, a high school transcript, 1 recommendation, and a minimum high school GPA of 2.0, and in some cases an essay and an interview. Application deadline: 6/30; 2/15 priority date for financial aid. Early and deferred admission are possible.

Rockhurst defines itself by those points that are unique to Rockhurst: the ideal campus location, the Jesuit tradition of academic excellence, talented and involved students, and successful graduates. Rockhurst prides itself on teaching students not what to think but how to think, using the method of critical questioning based on the 450-year-old Jesuit tradition. In addition, Rockhurst prepares students for success after graduation; "Famous Rocks," as its distinguished alumni are known, serve in leadership roles throughout the nation in many fields. Rockhurst is open year-round for visits from prospective students.

Getting in Last Year

1,186 applied
90% were accepted
309 enrolled (29%)
22% from top tenth of their h.s. class
3.10 average high school GPA
32% had SAT verbal scores over 600
35% had SAT math scores over 600
45% had ACT scores over 24
3% had SAT verbal scores over 700
7% had SAT math scores over 700
8% had ACT scores over 30
5 valedictorians

Graduation and After

49% graduated in 4 years
13% graduated in 5 years
3% graduated in 6 years
27% pursued further study (20% arts and sciences, 3% business, 2% law)
63% had job offers within 6 months
55 organizations recruited on campus

Financial Matters

$13,845 tuition and fees (2000–2001 estimated)
$5020 room and board
$12,785 average financial aid amount received per undergraduate (1999–2000 estimated)

eAPPLY

Getting in Last Year
1,748 applied
73% were accepted
448 enrolled (35%)
37% from top tenth of their h.s. class
40% had SAT verbal scores over 600
40% had SAT math scores over 600
55% had ACT scores over 24
5% had SAT verbal scores over 700
5% had SAT math scores over 700
15% had ACT scores over 30

Graduation and After
49% graduated in 4 years
7% graduated in 5 years
2% graduated in 6 years
29% pursued further study (17% arts and sciences, 6% law, 2% business)
65% had job offers within 6 months
25 organizations recruited on campus
1 Fulbright scholar

Financial Matters
$21,852 tuition and fees (1999–2000)
$6700 room and board
90% average percent of need met
$23,356 average financial aid amount received per undergraduate (1999–2000 estimated)

ROLLINS COLLEGE
SUBURBAN SETTING ■ PRIVATE ■ INDEPENDENT ■ COED
WINTER PARK, FLORIDA

Web site: www.rollins.edu
Contact: Mr. David Erdmann, Dean of Admissions and Student Financial Planning, 1000 Holt Avenue, Winter Park, FL 32789-4499
Telephone: 407-646-2161 **Fax:** 407-646-1502
E-mail: admission@rollins.edu

Academics
Rollins awards bachelor's and master's **degrees**. Challenging opportunities include advanced placement, accelerated degree programs, student-designed majors, an honors program, double majors, independent study, a senior project, and Sigma Xi. Special programs include internships, off-campus study, and study-abroad.

The most frequently chosen fields are social sciences and history, psychology, and visual/performing arts. A complete listing of majors at Rollins appears in the Majors Index beginning on page 432.

The **faculty** at Rollins has 154 full-time members, 89% with terminal degrees. The student-faculty ratio is 12:1.

Students of Rollins
The student body totals 2,256, of whom 1,519 are undergraduates. 60% are women and 40% are men. Students come from 44 states and territories and 37 other countries. 50% are from Florida. 5.1% are international students. 2.3% are African American, 0.6% American Indian, 2.7% Asian American, and 7.8% Hispanic American. 82% returned for their sophomore year.

Facilities and Resources
Student rooms are linked to a campus network. 150 **computers** are available on campus that provide access to the Internet. The **library** has 276,144 books.

Campus Life
There are 54 active organizations on campus, including a drama/theater group, newspaper, radio station, and choral group. 27% of eligible men and 27% of eligible women are members of national **fraternities**, national **sororities**, local fraternities, and local sororities.

Rollins is a member of the NCAA (Division II). **Intercollegiate sports** (some offering scholarships) include baseball (m), basketball, crew, cross-country running, golf, sailing, soccer, softball (w), tennis, volleyball (w).

Campus Safety
Student safety services include late-night transport/escort service, 24-hour emergency telephone alarm devices, 24-hour patrols by trained security personnel, and electronically operated dormitory entrances.

Applying
Rollins requires an essay, SAT I or ACT, a high school transcript, and 1 recommendation. It recommends SAT II Subject Tests and an interview. Application deadline: 2/15; 3/1 for financial aid. Early and deferred admission are possible.

ROSE-HULMAN INSTITUTE OF TECHNOLOGY

RURAL SETTING ■ PRIVATE ■ INDEPENDENT ■ COED, PRIMARILY MEN
TERRE HAUTE, INDIANA

Web site: www.rose-hulman.edu
Contact: Mr. Charles G. Howard, Dean of Admissions/Vice President, 5500 Wabash Avenue, Terre Haute, IN 47803-3920
Telephone: 812-877-8213 or toll-free 800-552-0725 (in-state), 800-248-7448 (out-of-state) **Fax:** 812-877-8941
E-mail: admis.ofc@rose-hulman.edu

Academics

Rose-Hulman awards bachelor's and master's **degrees**. Challenging opportunities include advanced placement, an honors program, double majors, independent study, and a senior project. Special programs include cooperative education, internships, summer session for credit, off-campus study, study-abroad, and Army and Air Force ROTC.

The most frequently chosen fields are engineering/engineering technologies, computer/information sciences, and physical sciences. A complete listing of majors at Rose-Hulman appears in the Majors Index beginning on page 432.

The **faculty** at Rose-Hulman has 119 full-time members, 98% with terminal degrees. The student-faculty ratio is 14:1.

Students of Rose-Hulman

The student body totals 1,678, of whom 1,545 are undergraduates. 17% are women and 83% are men. Students come from 45 states and territories and 12 other countries. 48% are from Indiana. 1% are international students. 1.3% are African American, 0.2% American Indian, 2.8% Asian American, and 0.8% Hispanic American. 96% returned for their sophomore year.

Facilities and Resources

Student rooms are linked to a campus network. 200 **computers** are available on campus that provide access to the Internet. The **library** has 55,000 books and 170 subscriptions.

Campus Life

There are 60 active organizations on campus, including a drama/theater group, newspaper, radio station, and choral group. 40% of eligible men and 50% of eligible women are members of national **fraternities** and national **sororities**.

Rose-Hulman is a member of the NCAA (Division III). **Intercollegiate sports** include baseball (m), basketball, cross-country running, football (m), golf (m), riflery, soccer, softball (w), swimming, tennis, track and field, volleyball (w), wrestling (m).

Campus Safety

Student safety services include late-night transport/escort service, 24-hour emergency telephone alarm devices, 24-hour patrols by trained security personnel, and electronically operated dormitory entrances.

Applying

Rose-Hulman requires SAT I or ACT, a high school transcript, 1 recommendation, and a minimum high school GPA of 3.5. It recommends an essay and an interview. Application deadline: 3/1; 3/1 priority date for financial aid. Deferred admission is possible.

Getting in Last Year
3,295 applied
67% were accepted
395 enrolled (18%)
51% from top tenth of their h.s. class
70% had SAT verbal scores over 600
95% had SAT math scores over 600
100% had ACT scores over 24
28% had SAT verbal scores over 700
56% had SAT math scores over 700
40% had ACT scores over 30
19 National Merit Scholars
12 class presidents
42 valedictorians

Graduation and After
59% graduated in 4 years
11% graduated in 5 years
2% graduated in 6 years
15% pursued further study (58% engineering, 5% business, 1% law)
99% had job offers within 6 months
280 organizations recruited on campus
1 Fulbright scholar

Financial Matters
$19,545 tuition and fees (1999–2000)
$5475 room and board
78% average percent of need met
$12,274 average financial aid amount received per undergraduate (1999–2000 estimated)

RUTGERS, THE STATE UNIVERSITY OF NEW JERSEY, SCHOOL OF ENGINEERING

SMALL-TOWN SETTING ■ PUBLIC ■ STATE-SUPPORTED ■ COED
PISCATAWAY, NEW JERSEY

Web site: www.rutgers.edu
Contact: Ms. Diane Wms. Harris, Associate Director of University
Undergraduate Admissions, 65 Davidson Road, Room 202, Piscataway, NJ
08854-8097
Telephone: 732-932-4636 **Fax:** 732-445-0237
E-mail: admissions@asb-ugadm.rutgers.edu

Getting in Last Year
3,806 applied
68% were accepted
550 enrolled (21%)
35% from top tenth of their h.s. class
42% had SAT verbal scores over 600
80% had SAT math scores over 600
7% had SAT verbal scores over 700
30% had SAT math scores over 700
7 valedictorians

Graduation and After
30% graduated in 4 years
30% graduated in 5 years
8% graduated in 6 years
80% had job offers within 6 months
500 organizations recruited on campus

Financial Matters
$6576 resident tuition and fees (1999–2000)
$12,044 nonresident tuition and fees (1999–2000)
$6098 room and board
83% average percent of need met
$8988 average financial aid amount received per undergraduate (1999–2000)

Academics

Rutgers, The State University of New Jersey, School of Engineering awards bachelor's **degrees** (master of science, master of philosophy, and doctor of philosophy degrees are offered through the Graduate School, New Brunswick). Challenging opportunities include advanced placement, student-designed majors, an honors program, double majors, and a senior project. Special programs include cooperative education, internships, summer session for credit, off-campus study, study-abroad, and Army and Air Force ROTC.

The most frequently chosen field is engineering/engineering technologies. A complete listing of majors at Rutgers, The State University of New Jersey, School of Engineering appears in the Majors Index beginning on page 432.

The **faculty** at Rutgers, The State University of New Jersey, School of Engineering has 139 full-time members. The student-faculty ratio is 15:1.

Students of Rutgers

The student body is made up of 2,190 undergraduates. 22.1% are women and 77.9% are men. Students come from 19 states and territories and 39 other countries. 91% are from New Jersey. 6.1% are international students. 6.6% are African American, 27.1% Asian American, and 6.2% Hispanic American. 88% returned for their sophomore year.

Facilities and Resources

Student rooms are linked to a campus network. 1,450 **computers** are available on campus that provide access to online grade reports and the Internet. The 15 **libraries** have 6,362,037 books and 28,934 subscriptions.

Campus Life

There are 400 active organizations on campus, including a drama/theater group, newspaper, radio station, television station, choral group, and marching band. 8% of eligible men and 5% of eligible women are members of national **fraternities** and national **sororities**.

Rutgers, The State University of New Jersey, School of Engineering is a member of the NCAA (Division I). **Intercollegiate sports** (some offering scholarships) include baseball (m), basketball, crew, cross-country running, fencing, field hockey (w), football (m), golf, gymnastics (w), lacrosse, soccer, softball (w), swimming, tennis, track and field, volleyball (w), wrestling (m).

Campus Safety

Student safety services include late-night transport/escort service, 24-hour emergency telephone alarm devices, 24-hour patrols by trained security personnel, student patrols, and electronically operated dormitory entrances.

Applying

Rutgers, The State University of New Jersey, School of Engineering requires SAT I or ACT and a high school transcript, and in some cases SAT II Subject Tests. Application deadline: 12/15; 3/15 priority date for financial aid. Early and deferred admission are possible.

RUTGERS, THE STATE UNIVERSITY OF NEW JERSEY, COLLEGE OF PHARMACY

SMALL-TOWN SETTING ■ PUBLIC ■ STATE-SUPPORTED ■ COED
PISCATAWAY, NEW JERSEY

Web site: www.rutgers.edu
Contact: Ms. Diane Wms. Harris, Associate Director of University
  Undergraduate Admissions, 65 Davidson Road, Room 202, Piscataway, NJ
  08854-8097
Telephone: 732-932-4636 **Fax:** 732-445-0237
E-mail: admissions@asb-ugadm.rutgers.edu

Academics

Rutgers, The State University of New Jersey, College of Pharmacy awards bachelor's, doctoral, and first-professional **degrees** (6-year doctor of pharmacy [PharmD] degree program is offered to students applying directly from high school). Challenging opportunities include advanced placement, an honors program, independent study, and a senior project. Special programs include internships, summer session for credit, off-campus study, study-abroad, and Army and Air Force ROTC.

The most frequently chosen field is health professions and related sciences. A complete listing of majors at Rutgers, The State University of New Jersey, College of Pharmacy appears in the Majors Index beginning on page 432.

The **faculty** at Rutgers, The State University of New Jersey, College of Pharmacy has 63 full-time members, 98% with terminal degrees. The student-faculty ratio is 11:1.

Students of Rutgers

The student body totals 1,016, of whom 825 are undergraduates. 63.6% are women and 36.4% are men. Students come from 18 states and territories and 9 other countries. 85% are from New Jersey. 1.7% are international students. 5.9% are African American, 47.4% Asian American, and 6.8% Hispanic American. 92% returned for their sophomore year.

Facilities and Resources

Student rooms are linked to a campus network. 1,450 **computers** are available on campus that provide access to online grade reports and the Internet. The 15 **libraries** have 6,362,037 books and 28,934 subscriptions.

Campus Life

There are 400 active organizations on campus, including a drama/theater group, newspaper, radio station, television station, choral group, and marching band. 8% of eligible men and 5% of eligible women are members of national **fraternities** and national **sororities**.

Rutgers, The State University of New Jersey, College of Pharmacy is a member of the NCAA (Division I). **Intercollegiate sports** (some offering scholarships) include baseball (m), basketball, crew, cross-country running, fencing, field hockey (w), football (m), golf, gymnastics (w), lacrosse, soccer, softball (w), swimming, tennis, track and field, volleyball (w), wrestling (m).

Campus Safety

Student safety services include late-night transport/escort service, 24-hour emergency telephone alarm devices, 24-hour patrols by trained security personnel, student patrols, and electronically operated dormitory entrances.

Applying

Rutgers, The State University of New Jersey, College of Pharmacy requires SAT I or ACT and a high school transcript, and in some cases SAT II Subject Tests. Application deadline: 12/15; 3/15 priority date for financial aid. Early and deferred admission are possible.

Getting in Last Year

1,401 applied
45% were accepted
184 enrolled (29%)
68% from top tenth of their h.s. class
68% had SAT verbal scores over 600
84% had SAT math scores over 600
10% had SAT verbal scores over 700
32% had SAT math scores over 700
14 valedictorians

Graduation and After

53% graduated in 5 years
23% graduated in 6 years
80% had job offers within 6 months
500 organizations recruited on campus

Financial Matters

$6576 resident tuition and fees (1999–2000)
$12,044 nonresident tuition and fees (1999–2000)
$6098 room and board
82% average percent of need met
$8611 average financial aid amount received per undergraduate (1999–2000)

RUTGERS, THE STATE UNIVERSITY OF NEW JERSEY, COOK COLLEGE

SMALL-TOWN SETTING ■ PUBLIC ■ STATE-SUPPORTED ■ COED
NEW BRUNSWICK, NEW JERSEY

Web site: www.rutgers.edu
Contact: Ms. Diane Wms. Harris, Associate Director of University
Undergraduate Admissions, 65 Davidson Road, Room 202, Piscataway, NJ
08854-8097
Telephone: 732-932-4636 **Fax:** 732-445-0237
E-mail: admissions@asb-ugadm.rutgers.edu

Getting in Last Year
6,673 applied
64% were accepted
627 enrolled (15%)
28% from top tenth of their h.s. class
31% had SAT verbal scores over 600
43% had SAT math scores over 600
3% had SAT verbal scores over 700
6% had SAT math scores over 700
5 National Merit Scholars
6 valedictorians

Graduation and After
42% graduated in 4 years
26% graduated in 5 years
5% graduated in 6 years
80% had job offers within 6 months
500 organizations recruited on campus

Financial Matters
$6544 resident tuition and fees (1999–2000)
$12,012 nonresident tuition and fees (1999–2000)
$6098 room and board
82% average percent of need met
$8198 average financial aid amount received per undergraduate (1999–2000)

Academics

Rutgers, The State University of New Jersey, Cook College awards bachelor's **degrees**. Challenging opportunities include advanced placement, student-designed majors, an honors program, double majors, independent study, and a senior project. Special programs include cooperative education, internships, summer session for credit, off-campus study, study-abroad, and Army and Air Force ROTC.

The most frequently chosen fields are biological/life sciences, natural resources/environmental science, and agriculture. A complete listing of majors at Rutgers, The State University of New Jersey, Cook College appears in the Majors Index beginning on page 432.

The **faculty** at Rutgers, The State University of New Jersey, Cook College has 256 full-time members, 98% with terminal degrees. The student-faculty ratio is 11:1.

Students of Rutgers

The student body is made up of 3,231 undergraduates. 49.8% are women and 50.2% are men. Students come from 27 states and territories and 23 other countries. 91% are from New Jersey. 1.8% are international students. 5.8% are African American, 0.3% American Indian, 12.9% Asian American, and 6.3% Hispanic American. 91% returned for their sophomore year.

Facilities and Resources

Student rooms are linked to a campus network. 1,450 **computers** are available on campus that provide access to the Internet. The 15 **libraries** have 6,362,037 books and 28,934 subscriptions.

Campus Life

There are 400 active organizations on campus, including a drama/theater group, newspaper, radio station, television station, choral group, and marching band. 5% of eligible men and 4% of eligible women are members of national **fraternities** and national **sororities**.

Rutgers, The State University of New Jersey, Cook College is a member of the NCAA (Division I). **Intercollegiate sports** (some offering scholarships) include baseball (m), basketball, crew, cross-country running, fencing, field hockey (w), football (m), golf, gymnastics (w), lacrosse, soccer, softball (w), swimming, tennis, track and field, volleyball (w), wrestling (m).

Campus Safety

Student safety services include late-night transport/escort service, 24-hour emergency telephone alarm devices, 24-hour patrols by trained security personnel, student patrols, and electronically operated dormitory entrances.

Applying

Rutgers, The State University of New Jersey, Cook College requires SAT I or ACT and a high school transcript, and in some cases SAT II Subject Tests. Application deadline: 12/15; 3/15 priority date for financial aid. Early and deferred admission are possible.

RUTGERS, THE STATE UNIVERSITY OF NEW JERSEY, DOUGLASS COLLEGE

SMALL-TOWN SETTING ■ PUBLIC ■ STATE-SUPPORTED ■ WOMEN ONLY
NEW BRUNSWICK, NEW JERSEY

Web site: www.rutgers.edu
Contact: Ms. Diane Wms. Harris, Associate Director of University
Undergraduate Admissions, 65 Davidson Road, Room 202, Piscataway, NJ
08854-8097
Telephone: 732-932-4636 **Fax:** 732-445-0237
E-mail: admissions@asb-ugadm.rutgers.edu

Academics

Rutgers, The State University of New Jersey, Douglass College awards bachelor's
degrees. Challenging opportunities include advanced placement, student-designed
majors, an honors program, double majors, independent study, a senior project, and Phi
Beta Kappa. Special programs include internships, summer session for credit, off-campus
study, study-abroad, and Army and Air Force ROTC.

The most frequently chosen fields are psychology, social sciences and history, and
communications/communication technologies. A complete listing of majors at Rutgers,
The State University of New Jersey, Douglass College appears in the Majors Index
beginning on page 432.

The **faculty** at Rutgers, The State University of New Jersey, Douglass College has
1,051 full-time members, 98% with terminal degrees. The student-faculty ratio is 15:1.

Students of Rutgers

The student body is made up of 3,099 undergraduates. Students come from 29 states and
territories and 25 other countries. 94% are from New Jersey. 2% are international
students. 12.2% are African American, 0.2% American Indian, 14% Asian American, and
7.7% Hispanic American. 88% returned for their sophomore year.

Facilities and Resources

Student rooms are linked to a campus network. 1,450 **computers** are available on
campus that provide access to online grade reports and the Internet. The 15 **libraries**
have 6,362,037 books and 28,934 subscriptions.

Campus Life

There are 400 active organizations on campus, including a drama/theater group,
newspaper, radio station, television station, choral group, and marching band. 5% of
eligible undergraduates are members of national **sororities**.

Rutgers, The State University of New Jersey, Douglass College is a member of the
NCAA (Division I). **Intercollegiate sports** (some offering scholarships) include
basketball, crew, cross-country running, fencing, field hockey, golf, gymnastics, lacrosse,
soccer, softball, swimming, tennis, track and field, volleyball.

Campus Safety

Student safety services include late-night transport/escort service, 24-hour emergency
telephone alarm devices, 24-hour patrols by trained security personnel, student patrols,
and electronically operated dormitory entrances.

Applying

Rutgers, The State University of New Jersey, Douglass College requires SAT I or ACT
and a high school transcript, and in some cases SAT II Subject Tests. Application
deadline: 12/15; 3/15 priority date for financial aid. Early and deferred admission are
possible.

Getting in Last Year

6,453 applied
68% were accepted
648 enrolled (15%)
19% from top tenth of their h.s. class
22% had SAT verbal scores over 600
21% had SAT math scores over 600
3% had SAT verbal scores over 700
2% had SAT math scores over 700
3 valedictorians

Graduation and After

52% graduated in 4 years
22% graduated in 5 years
3% graduated in 6 years
80% had job offers within 6 months
500 organizations recruited on campus

Financial Matters

$6017 resident tuition and fees (1999–2000)
$10,947 nonresident tuition and fees (1999–2000)
$6098 room and board
86% average percent of need met
$8541 average financial aid amount received per undergraduate (1999–2000)

RUTGERS, THE STATE UNIVERSITY OF NEW JERSEY, RUTGERS COLLEGE

SMALL-TOWN SETTING ■ PUBLIC ■ STATE-SUPPORTED ■ COED
NEW BRUNSWICK, NEW JERSEY

Web site: www.rutgers.edu
Contact: Ms. Diane Wms. Harris, Associate Director of University
Undergraduate Admissions, 65 Davidson Road, Piscataway, NJ 08854-8097
Telephone: 732-932-4636 **Fax:** 732-445-0237
E-mail: admissions@asb-ugadm.rutgers.edu

Getting in Last Year
20,441 applied
48% were accepted
2,437 enrolled (25%)
43% from top tenth of their h.s. class
48% had SAT verbal scores over 600
59% had SAT math scores over 600
11% had SAT verbal scores over 700
16% had SAT math scores over 700
24 valedictorians

Graduation and After
53% graduated in 4 years
20% graduated in 5 years
3% graduated in 6 years
80% had job offers within 6 months
500 organizations recruited on campus
10 Fulbright scholars

Financial Matters
$6052 resident tuition and fees (1999–2000)
$10,982 nonresident tuition and fees (1999–2000)
$6098 room and board
84% average percent of need met
$8586 average financial aid amount received per undergraduate (1999–2000)

Academics
Rutgers, The State University of New Jersey, Rutgers College awards bachelor's **degrees**. Challenging opportunities include advanced placement, student-designed majors, an honors program, double majors, independent study, a senior project, Phi Beta Kappa, and Sigma Xi. Special programs include internships, summer session for credit, off-campus study, study-abroad, and Army and Air Force ROTC.

The most frequently chosen fields are social sciences and history, psychology, and biological/life sciences. A complete listing of majors at Rutgers, The State University of New Jersey, Rutgers College appears in the Majors Index beginning on page 432.

The **faculty** at Rutgers, The State University of New Jersey, Rutgers College has 1,051 full-time members, 98% with terminal degrees. The student-faculty ratio is 15:1.

Students of Rutgers
The student body is made up of 10,993 undergraduates. 51.4% are women and 48.6% are men. Students come from 43 states and territories and 69 other countries. 90% are from New Jersey. 2.7% are international students. 7% are African American, 0.1% American Indian, 19.7% Asian American, and 9% Hispanic American. 90% returned for their sophomore year.

Facilities and Resources
Student rooms are linked to a campus network. 1,450 **computers** are available on campus that provide access to online grade reports and the Internet. The 15 **libraries** have 6,362,037 books and 28,934 subscriptions.

Campus Life
There are 400 active organizations on campus, including a drama/theater group, newspaper, radio station, television station, choral group, and marching band. 8% of eligible men and 5% of eligible women are members of national **fraternities** and national **sororities**.

Rutgers, The State University of New Jersey, Rutgers College is a member of the NCAA (Division I). **Intercollegiate sports** (some offering scholarships) include baseball (m), basketball, crew, cross-country running, fencing, field hockey (w), football (m), golf, gymnastics (w), lacrosse, soccer, softball (w), swimming, tennis, track and field, volleyball (w), wrestling (m).

Campus Safety
Student safety services include late-night transport/escort service, 24-hour emergency telephone alarm devices, 24-hour patrols by trained security personnel, student patrols, and electronically operated dormitory entrances.

Applying
Rutgers, The State University of New Jersey, Rutgers College requires SAT I or ACT and a high school transcript, and in some cases SAT II Subject Tests. Application deadline: 12/15; 3/15 priority date for financial aid. Early and deferred admission are possible.

St. John's College

SMALL-TOWN SETTING ■ PRIVATE ■ INDEPENDENT ■ COED
ANNAPOLIS, MARYLAND

Web site: www.sjca.edu
Contact: Mr. John Christensen, Director of Admissions, PO Box 2800, 60 College Avenue, Annapolis, MD 21404
Telephone: 410-626-2522 or toll-free 800-727-9238 **Fax:** 410-269-7916
E-mail: admissions@sjca.edu

Academics

St. John's awards bachelor's and master's **degrees**. A senior project is a challenging opportunity. Off-campus study is a special program.

The most frequently chosen field is liberal arts/general studies. A complete listing of majors at St. John's appears in the Majors Index beginning on page 432.

The **faculty** at St. John's has 64 full-time members, 69% with terminal degrees. The student-faculty ratio is 8:1.

Students of St. John's

The student body totals 516, of whom 452 are undergraduates. 45.1% are women and 54.9% are men. Students come from 44 states and territories and 13 other countries. 18% are from Maryland. 3.8% are international students. 0.7% are African American, 2% Asian American, and 2% Hispanic American. 81% returned for their sophomore year.

Facilities and Resources

16 **computers** are available on campus that provide access to the Internet. The 2 **libraries** have 102,133 books and 114 subscriptions.

Campus Life

There are 35 active organizations on campus, including a drama/theater group, newspaper, and choral group. No national or local **fraternities** or **sororities**.

Intercollegiate sports include crew, fencing.

Campus Safety

Student safety services include late-night transport/escort service, 24-hour emergency telephone alarm devices, 24-hour patrols by trained security personnel, and electronically operated dormitory entrances.

Applying

St. John's requires an essay, a high school transcript, and 2 recommendations, and in some cases SAT I or ACT. It recommends SAT I or ACT and an interview. Application deadline: rolling admissions; 2/15 priority date for financial aid. Early and deferred admission are possible.

> **G**reat Books Program: St. John's offers an integrated liberal arts and sciences curriculum structured around seminar discussions of major works of Western civilization. These discussions are supported by tutorials in mathematics, music, language, and the physical sciences. Only original sources are read, and all classes are small discussion groups.

Getting in Last Year

446 applied
78% were accepted
133 enrolled (38%)
36% from top tenth of their h.s. class
93% had SAT verbal scores over 600
68% had SAT math scores over 600
54% had SAT verbal scores over 700
19% had SAT math scores over 700
6 National Merit Scholars

Graduation and After

58% graduated in 4 years
8% graduated in 5 years
3% graduated in 6 years
Graduates pursuing further study: 37% arts and sciences, 10% law, 7% business
50% had job offers within 6 months
7 organizations recruited on campus
2 Fulbright scholars

Financial Matters

$23,490 tuition and fees (1999–2000)
$6360 room and board
95% average percent of need met
$20,763 average financial aid amount received per undergraduate (1999–2000)

ST. JOHN'S COLLEGE

SMALL-TOWN SETTING ■ PRIVATE ■ INDEPENDENT ■ COED
SANTA FE, NEW MEXICO

Web site: www.sjcsf.edu
Contact: Mr. Larry Clendenin, Director of Admissions, 1160 Camino Cruz
  Blanca, Santa Fe, NM 87501
Telephone: 505-984-6060 or toll-free 800-331-5232 **Fax:** 505-984-6003
E-mail: admissions@mail.sjcsf.edu

Academics

St. John's awards bachelor's and master's **degrees**. A senior project is a challenging opportunity. Off-campus study is a special program.

The most frequently chosen field is liberal arts/general studies. A complete listing of majors at St. John's appears in the Majors Index beginning on page 432.

The **faculty** at St. John's has 54 full-time members, 83% with terminal degrees. The student-faculty ratio is 8:1.

Students of St. John's

The student body totals 556, of whom 431 are undergraduates. 43.4% are women and 56.6% are men. Students come from 48 states and territories and 1 other country. 11% are from New Mexico. 0.2% are international students. 0.2% are African American, 2.3% American Indian, 2.3% Asian American, and 7% Hispanic American. 73% returned for their sophomore year.

Facilities and Resources

14 **computers** are available on campus that provide access to the Internet. The **library** has 40,103 books and 135 subscriptions.

Campus Life

Active organizations on campus include a drama/theater group, newspaper, and choral group. No national or local **fraternities** or **sororities**.

This institution has no intercollegiate sports.

Campus Safety

Student safety services include late-night transport/escort service, 24-hour emergency telephone alarm devices, 24-hour patrols by trained security personnel, and student patrols.

Applying

St. John's requires an essay, a high school transcript, and 3 recommendations, and in some cases SAT I or ACT and an interview. It recommends an interview. Application deadline: rolling admissions; 2/15 for financial aid, with a 12/1 priority date. Early and deferred admission are possible.

St. John's appeals to students who value good books, love to read, and are passionate about discourse and debate. There are no lectures and virtually no tests or electives. Instead, there are discussion-based classes of 17–21 students where professors are as likely as students to be asked to defend their points of view. Great Books provide the direction, context, and stimulus for conversation. The entire student body adheres to the same all-required arts and sciences curriculum. Seventy-five percent of the College's alumni obtain graduate and professional degrees in law, medicine, humanities, natural sciences, business, journalism, fine and performing arts, or architecture.

Getting in Last Year
355 applied
84% were accepted
109 enrolled (37%)
29% from top tenth of their h.s. class
91% had SAT verbal scores over 600
65% had SAT math scores over 600
88% had ACT scores over 24
45% had SAT verbal scores over 700
17% had SAT math scores over 700
36% had ACT scores over 30
1 National Merit Scholar
4 class presidents
4 valedictorians

Graduation and After
39% graduated in 4 years
13% graduated in 5 years
3% graduated in 6 years
75% pursued further study (37% arts and sciences, 10% law, 7% business)
20 organizations recruited on campus

Financial Matters
$22,200 tuition and fees (1999–2000)
$6386 room and board
99% average percent of need met
$20,220 average financial aid amount received per undergraduate (1999–2000)

Saint John's University
COORDINATE WITH COLLEGE OF SAINT BENEDICT

RURAL SETTING ■ PRIVATE ■ INDEPENDENT RELIGIOUS ■ MEN ONLY
COLLEGEVILLE, MINNESOTA

Web site: www.csbsju.edu
Contact: Ms. Mary Milbert, Dean of Admissions, PO Box 7155, Collegeville, MN 56321-7155
Telephone: 320-363-2196 or toll-free 800-24JOHNS **Fax:** 320-363-3206
E-mail: admissions@csbsju.edu

eAPPLY

Academics

St. John's awards bachelor's, master's, and first-professional **degrees**. Challenging opportunities include advanced placement, accelerated degree programs, student-designed majors, an honors program, double majors, independent study, and a senior project. Special programs include internships, off-campus study, study-abroad, and Army ROTC.

The most frequently chosen fields are business/marketing, social sciences and history, and biological/life sciences. A complete listing of majors at St. John's appears in the Majors Index beginning on page 432.

The **faculty** at St. John's has 156 full-time members, 88% with terminal degrees. The student-faculty ratio is 13:1.

Students of St. John's

The student body totals 1,932, of whom 1,803 are undergraduates. Students come from 29 states and territories and 24 other countries. 85% are from Minnesota. 2.2% are international students. 0.3% are African American, 0.3% American Indian, 1.4% Asian American, and 0.8% Hispanic American. 92% returned for their sophomore year.

Facilities and Resources

Student rooms are linked to a campus network. 350 **computers** are available on campus that provide access to the Internet. The 3 **libraries** have 726,844 books and 8,564 subscriptions.

Campus Life

There are 80 active organizations on campus, including a drama/theater group, newspaper, radio station, and choral group. No national or local **fraternities**.

St. John's is a member of the NCAA (Division III). **Intercollegiate sports** include baseball, basketball, crew, cross-country running, football, golf, ice hockey, lacrosse, riflery, rugby, skiing (cross-country), soccer, swimming, tennis, track and field, volleyball, water polo, wrestling.

Campus Safety

Student safety services include well-lit pathways, 911 center on campus, closed circuit TV monitors, late-night transport/escort service, 24-hour emergency telephone alarm devices, and 24-hour patrols by trained security personnel.

Applying

St. John's requires an essay, SAT I or ACT, and a high school transcript, and in some cases 3 recommendations. It recommends an interview and a minimum high school GPA of 2.8. Application deadline: rolling admissions; 3/1 priority date for financial aid. Early and deferred admission are possible.

Getting in Last Year

1,119 applied
85% were accepted
475 enrolled (50%)
21% from top tenth of their h.s. class
3.5 average high school GPA
39% had SAT verbal scores over 600
49% had SAT math scores over 600
66% had ACT scores over 24
11% had SAT verbal scores over 700
11% had SAT math scores over 700
10% had ACT scores over 30

Graduation and After

60% graduated in 4 years
7% graduated in 5 years
1% graduated in 6 years
19% pursued further study (7% arts and sciences, 5% law, 4% business)
79% had job offers within 6 months
85 organizations recruited on campus

Financial Matters

$16,441 tuition and fees (1999–2000)
$4930 room and board
96% average percent of need met
$13,677 average financial aid amount received per undergraduate (1999–2000 estimated)

SAINT JOSEPH'S UNIVERSITY

SUBURBAN SETTING ■ PRIVATE ■ INDEPENDENT RELIGIOUS ■ COED
PHILADELPHIA, PENNSYLVANIA

Web site: www.sju.edu
Contact: Mr. David Conway, Assistant Vice President of Enrollment
  Management, 5600 City Avenue, Philadelphia, PA 19131-1395
Telephone: 610-660-1300 or toll-free 888-BEAHAWK (in-state) **Fax:**
  610-660-1314
E-mail: admi@sju.edu

Academics

St. Joseph's awards associate, bachelor's, master's, and doctoral **degrees** and post-master's certificates. Challenging opportunities include advanced placement, accelerated degree programs, student-designed majors, an honors program, double majors, independent study, a senior project, and Sigma Xi. Special programs include cooperative education, internships, summer session for credit, off-campus study, study-abroad, and Army, Navy and Air Force ROTC. A complete listing of majors at St. Joseph's appears in the Majors Index beginning on page 432.

Students of St. Joseph's

The student body totals 6,978, of whom 4,407 are undergraduates. 55.4% are women and 44.6% are men. Students come from 38 states and territories and 24 other countries. 50% are from Pennsylvania. 2.2% are international students. 7.5% are African American, 0.1% American Indian, 2.3% Asian American, and 2.5% Hispanic American. 89% returned for their sophomore year.

Facilities and Resources

Student rooms are linked to a campus network. 180 **computers** are available on campus that provide access to the Internet. The 2 **libraries** have 344,801 books and 1,800 subscriptions.

Campus Life

There are 73 active organizations on campus, including a drama/theater group, newspaper, radio station, and choral group. 9% of eligible men and 12% of eligible women are members of national **fraternities** and national **sororities**.

St. Joseph's is a member of the NCAA (Division I). **Intercollegiate sports** (some offering scholarships) include baseball (m), basketball, crew, cross-country running, field hockey (w), golf (m), lacrosse, soccer, softball (w), tennis, track and field.

Campus Safety

Student safety services include 24-hour shuttle/escort service, bicycle patrols, late-night transport/escort service, 24-hour emergency telephone alarm devices, 24-hour patrols by trained security personnel, and electronically operated dormitory entrances.

Applying

St. Joseph's requires an essay, SAT I or ACT, a high school transcript, and 1 recommendation, and in some cases an interview. It recommends SAT II Subject Tests, an interview, and a minimum high school GPA of 3.0. Application deadline: rolling admissions; 2/15 priority date for financial aid. Early and deferred admission are possible.

Saint Joseph's, Philadelphia's Jesuit university, is located on a beautiful 65-acre suburban campus on the western edge of the city and offers its students a vital relationship with the educational opportunities and rich cultural resources of both the suburban and metropolitan Philadelphia areas. Distinguished by its comprehensive academic opportunities, respected teaching faculty, personal size, and highly successful students and alumni, Saint Joseph's draws top students from across the country and around the world while remaining dedicated to its tradition of service to others. New to Saint Joseph's list of offerings are four 5-year programs (student earns both a BS and MS) in criminal justice, elementary education, international marketing, and psychology.

Getting in Last Year
5,358 applied
74% were accepted
971 enrolled (24%)
44% from top tenth of their h.s. class
3.38 average high school GPA
42% had SAT verbal scores over 600
55% had SAT math scores over 600
9% had SAT verbal scores over 700
9% had SAT math scores over 700
15 valedictorians

Graduation and After
56% graduated in 4 years
10% graduated in 5 years
2% graduated in 6 years
24% pursued further study
65% had job offers within 6 months
120 organizations recruited on campus
1 Fulbright scholar

Financial Matters
$18,430 tuition and fees (1999–2000)
$7514 room and board
$11,150 average financial aid amount received per undergraduate (1999–2000 estimated)

eAPPLY

ST. LAWRENCE UNIVERSITY

SMALL-TOWN SETTING ■ PRIVATE ■ INDEPENDENT ■ COED
CANTON, NEW YORK

Web site: www.stlawu.edu
Contact: Ms. Terry Cowdrey, Dean of Admissions and Financial Aid, Canton, NY 13617-1455
Telephone: 315-229-5261 or toll-free 800-285-1856 **Fax:** 315-229-5818
E-mail: admissions@stlawu.edu

Academics

St. Lawrence awards bachelor's and master's **degrees** and post-master's certificates. Challenging opportunities include advanced placement, accelerated degree programs, student-designed majors, double majors, independent study, a senior project, and Phi Beta Kappa. Special programs include internships, summer session for credit, off-campus study, study-abroad, and Army and Air Force ROTC.

The most frequently chosen fields are social sciences and history, biological/life sciences, and psychology. A complete listing of majors at St. Lawrence appears in the Majors Index beginning on page 432.

The **faculty** at St. Lawrence has 156 full-time members. The student-faculty ratio is 11:1.

Students of St. Lawrence

The student body totals 1,978, of whom 1,875 are undergraduates. 51.2% are women and 48.8% are men. Students come from 38 states and territories and 18 other countries. 3% are international students. 1.9% are African American, 0.5% American Indian, 1% Asian American, and 1.8% Hispanic American. 83% returned for their sophomore year.

Facilities and Resources

Student rooms are linked to a campus network. 600 **computers** are available on campus that provide access to the Internet. The 2 **libraries** have 484,460 books and 1,972 subscriptions.

Campus Life

There are 100 active organizations on campus, including a drama/theater group, newspaper, radio station, television station, and choral group. 19% of eligible men and 28% of eligible women are members of national **fraternities**, national **sororities**, and local sororities.

St. Lawrence is a member of the NCAA (Division III). **Intercollegiate sports** (some offering scholarships) include baseball (m), basketball, crew, cross-country running, equestrian sports, field hockey (w), football (m), golf, ice hockey, lacrosse, rugby, skiing (cross-country), skiing (downhill), soccer, softball (w), squash, swimming, tennis, track and field, volleyball (w).

Campus Safety

Student safety services include late-night transport/escort service, 24-hour emergency telephone alarm devices, 24-hour patrols by trained security personnel, student patrols, and electronically operated dormitory entrances.

Applying

St. Lawrence requires an essay, SAT I or ACT, a high school transcript, and 2 recommendations. It recommends SAT II Subject Tests, an interview, and a minimum high school GPA of 2.0. Application deadline: 2/15; 2/15 priority date for financial aid. Deferred admission is possible.

With more than 30 majors and minors from which to choose, St. Lawrence students can sample from a variety of disciplines and specialize in those areas that are most intriguing to them. The diverse options for cocurricular activities, including 32 varsity sports, encourage students to further develop their abilities and interests outside of the classroom. The University's location provides students with a residential community while providing access to the Adirondack Mountains as well as to Ottawa and Montreal. St. Lawrence alumni successfully pursue careers and graduate study, consistently achieving placement rates higher than 95% within one year of graduation.

Getting in Last Year
2,235 applied
74% were accepted
575 enrolled (35%)
30% from top tenth of their h.s. class
3.28 average high school GPA
31% had SAT verbal scores over 600
35% had SAT math scores over 600
62% had ACT scores over 24
5% had SAT verbal scores over 700
4% had SAT math scores over 700
6% had ACT scores over 30
16 valedictorians

Graduation and After
23% pursued further study
73% had job offers within 6 months

Financial Matters
$23,165 tuition and fees (1999–2000)
$7205 room and board
91% average percent of need met
$22,736 average financial aid amount received per undergraduate (1999–2000)

St. Louis College of Pharmacy

Urban setting ■ Private ■ Independent ■ Coed
St. Louis, Missouri

Web site: www.stlcop.edu
Contact: Ms. Penny Bryant, Director of Admissions, 4588 Parkview Place, St. Louis, MO 63110-1088
Telephone: 314-367-8700 ext. 1067 or toll-free 800-278-5267 (in-state) **Fax:** 314-367-2784
E-mail: pbryant@stlcop.edu

Getting in Last Year
268 applied
62% were accepted
132 enrolled (80%)
40% from top tenth of their h.s. class
3.64 average high school GPA
58% had ACT scores over 24
6% had ACT scores over 30
10 valedictorians

Graduation and After
6% pursued further study (2% arts and sciences, 2% business, 1% law)

Financial Matters
$13,370 tuition and fees (2000–2001 estimated)
$5375 room and board
36% average percent of need met
$8469 average financial aid amount received per undergraduate (1999–2000)

Academics
St. Louis College of Pharmacy awards bachelor's, master's, and first-professional **degrees**. Challenging opportunities include advanced placement and a senior project. Special programs include internships and summer session for credit. A complete listing of majors at St. Louis College of Pharmacy appears in the Majors Index beginning on page 432.

The **faculty** at St. Louis College of Pharmacy has 63 full-time members, 90% with terminal degrees.

Students of St. Louis College of Pharmacy
The student body totals 875, of whom 815 are undergraduates. 65.5% are women and 34.5% are men. Students come from 15 states and territories. 5% are African American, 11.3% Asian American, and 1.5% Hispanic American. 89% returned for their sophomore year.

Facilities and Resources
Student rooms are linked to a campus network. 60 **computers** are available on campus that provide access to the Internet. The **library** has 27,391 books and 308 subscriptions.

Campus Life
There are 15 active organizations on campus, including a drama/theater group, newspaper, and choral group. 70% of eligible men and 65% of eligible women are members of national **fraternities** and national **sororities**.

St. Louis College of Pharmacy is a member of the NAIA. **Intercollegiate sports** include basketball (m), volleyball (w).

Campus Safety
Student safety services include late-night transport/escort service, 24-hour emergency telephone alarm devices, 24-hour patrols by trained security personnel, and electronically operated dormitory entrances.

Applying
St. Louis College of Pharmacy requires an essay, SAT I or ACT, a high school transcript, recommendations, and a minimum high school GPA of 2.5. It recommends a minimum high school GPA of 3.0. Application deadline: rolling admissions; 11/15 for financial aid, with a 4/1 priority date.

SAINT LOUIS UNIVERSITY

URBAN SETTING ■ PRIVATE ■ INDEPENDENT RELIGIOUS ■ COED
ST. LOUIS, MISSOURI

 eAPPLY

Web site: www.slu.edu
Contact: Ms. Patsy Brooks, Credential Evaluator for Undergraduate
Admissions, 221 North Grand Boulevard, St. Louis, MO 63103-2097
Telephone: 314-977-2500 or toll-free 800-758-3678 (out-of-state) **Fax:**
314-977-7136
E-mail: admitme@slu.edu

Academics

SLU awards associate, bachelor's, master's, doctoral, and first-professional **degrees** and
post-bachelor's and post-master's certificates. Challenging opportunities include
advanced placement, accelerated degree programs, student-designed majors, freshman
honors college, an honors program, double majors, independent study, a senior project,
Phi Beta Kappa, and Sigma Xi. Special programs include cooperative education, internships, summer session for credit, off-campus study, study-abroad, and Army and Air
Force ROTC.

The most frequently chosen fields are business/marketing, health professions and
related sciences, and psychology. A complete listing of majors at SLU appears in the
Majors Index beginning on page 432.

The **faculty** at SLU has 1,150 full-time members, 95% with terminal degrees. The
student-faculty ratio is 14:1.

Students of SLU

The student body totals 14,062, of whom 9,882 are undergraduates. 56.6% are women
and 43.4% are men. Students come from 50 states and territories and 83 other countries.
62% are from Missouri. 5.8% are international students. 9.4% are African American,
0.3% American Indian, 4.5% Asian American, and 1.9% Hispanic American. 87%
returned for their sophomore year.

Facilities and Resources

Student rooms are linked to a campus network. 500 **computers** are available on campus
that provide access to the Internet. The 4 **libraries** have 1,241,799 books and 13,941
subscriptions.

Campus Life

There are 100 active organizations on campus, including a drama/theater group,
newspaper, radio station, television station, and choral group. 17% of eligible men and
13% of eligible women are members of national **fraternities** and national **sororities**.

SLU is a member of the NCAA (Division I). **Intercollegiate sports** (some offering
scholarships) include baseball (m), basketball, cross-country running, field hockey (w),
golf (m), ice hockey (m), riflery, rugby (m), soccer, softball (w), swimming, tennis, volleyball (w).

Campus Safety

Student safety services include crime prevention program, bicycle patrols, late-night
transport/escort service, 24-hour emergency telephone alarm devices, 24-hour patrols by
trained security personnel, student patrols, and electronically operated dormitory
entrances.

Applying

SLU requires an essay, ACT, a high school transcript, and secondary school report form.
It recommends an interview and 2 recommendations. Application deadline: rolling
admissions; 3/1 priority date for financial aid. Early and deferred admission are possible.

For almost 180 years, Saint
Louis University has had a
reputation for excellence in
education. In its history, Saint Louis
has accomplished a list of firsts that
makes it a true center of higher
learning: first university west of the
Mississippi; first Catholic college in
the United States to have faculty in
schools of philosophy, theology,
medicine, law, and business; first
federally certified air college (Parks
College of Engineering and Aviation);
and first free-standing European
campus (Madrid, Spain) operated by
an American university. Saint Louis's
academic reputation is the
foundation of its success today.

Getting in Last Year
4,990 applied
69% were accepted
1,274 enrolled (37%)
36% from top tenth of their h.s. class
3.46 average high school GPA
69% had ACT scores over 24
17% had ACT scores over 30
23 National Merit Scholars

Graduation and After
46% graduated in 4 years
15% graduated in 5 years
3% graduated in 6 years
25% pursued further study
75% had job offers within 6 months
142 organizations recruited on campus
2 Fulbright scholars

Financial Matters
$17,268 tuition and fees (1999–2000)
$5900 room and board
78% average percent of need met

eApply

Saint Mary's College

Suburban setting ■ Private ■ Independent Religious ■ Women Only
Notre Dame, Indiana

Web site: www.saintmarys.edu
Contact: Ms. Mary Pat Nolan, Director of Admissions, Notre Dame, IN
46556
Telephone: 219-284-4587 or toll-free 800-551-7621 (in-state), 219-284-4716
(out-of-state)
E-mail: admission@saintmarys.edu

Getting in Last Year

1,041 applied
83% were accepted
424 enrolled (49%)
31% from top tenth of their h.s. class
3.58 average high school GPA
35% had SAT verbal scores over 600
33% had SAT math scores over 600
68% had ACT scores over 24
4% had SAT verbal scores over 700
3% had SAT math scores over 700
9% had ACT scores over 30
6 National Merit Scholars
15 class presidents
18 valedictorians

Graduation and After

72% graduated in 4 years
4% graduated in 5 years
15% pursued further study (4% arts and sciences, 3% education, 2% business)
72% had job offers within 6 months
47 organizations recruited on campus

Financial Matters

$16,994 tuition and fees (1999–2000)
$5962 room and board
86% average percent of need met
$14,440 average financial aid amount received per undergraduate (1999–2000 estimated)

Academics

Saint Mary's awards bachelor's **degrees**. Challenging opportunities include advanced placement, accelerated degree programs, student-designed majors, double majors, independent study, and a senior project. Special programs include internships, off-campus study, study-abroad, and Army, Navy and Air Force ROTC.

The most frequently chosen fields are education, business/marketing, and social sciences and history. A complete listing of majors at Saint Mary's appears in the Majors Index beginning on page 432.

The **faculty** at Saint Mary's has 107 full-time members, 97% with terminal degrees. The student-faculty ratio is 12:1.

Students of Saint Mary's

The student body totals 1,417, of whom 1,409 are undergraduates. Students come from 51 states and territories and 13 other countries. 25% are from Indiana. 1% are international students. 0.7% are African American, 0.3% American Indian, 1.2% Asian American, and 4.8% Hispanic American. 82% returned for their sophomore year.

Facilities and Resources

Student rooms are linked to a campus network. 137 **computers** are available on campus that provide access to the Internet. The **library** has 201,253 books and 758 subscriptions.

Campus Life

There are 116 active organizations on campus, including a drama/theater group, newspaper, radio station, choral group, and marching band. No national or local **sororities**.

Saint Mary's is a member of the NCAA (Division III). **Intercollegiate sports** include basketball, crew, cross-country running, equestrian sports, gymnastics, sailing, skiing (downhill), soccer, softball, swimming, tennis, track and field, volleyball.

Campus Safety

Student safety services include late-night transport/escort service, 24-hour emergency telephone alarm devices, 24-hour patrols by trained security personnel, and electronically operated dormitory entrances.

Applying

Saint Mary's requires an essay, SAT I and SAT II or ACT, a high school transcript, and 1 recommendation. It recommends an interview. Application deadline: 3/1; 3/1 priority date for financial aid. Early and deferred admission are possible.

SAINT MARY'S COLLEGE OF CALIFORNIA

SUBURBAN SETTING ■ PRIVATE ■ INDEPENDENT RELIGIOUS ■ COED
MORAGA, CALIFORNIA

Web site: www.stmarys-ca.edu
Contact: Ms. Dorothy Benjamin, Director of Admissions, PO Box 4800, Moraga, CA 94556-4800
Telephone: 925-631-4224 or toll-free 800-800-4SMC **Fax:** 925-376-7193
E-mail: smcadmit@stmarys-ca.edu

eAPPLY

Academics

Saint Mary's awards bachelor's, master's, and doctoral **degrees**. Challenging opportunities include advanced placement, accelerated degree programs, student-designed majors, an honors program, double majors, independent study, a senior project, and Sigma Xi. Special programs include internships, off-campus study, study-abroad, and Army, Navy and Air Force ROTC.

The most frequently chosen fields are business/marketing, social sciences and history, and health professions and related sciences. A complete listing of majors at Saint Mary's appears in the Majors Index beginning on page 432.

The **faculty** at Saint Mary's has 175 full-time members, 53% with terminal degrees. The student-faculty ratio is 13:1.

Students of Saint Mary's

The student body totals 4,063, of whom 2,863 are undergraduates. 61.1% are women and 38.9% are men. Students come from 31 states and territories and 14 other countries. 89% are from California. 2.7% are international students. 5.5% are African American, 1% American Indian, 8.3% Asian American, and 12.7% Hispanic American. 82% returned for their sophomore year.

Facilities and Resources

Student rooms are linked to a campus network. 255 **computers** are available on campus that provide access to the Internet. The 2 **libraries** have 149,200 books and 1,069 subscriptions.

Campus Life

There are 45 active organizations on campus, including a drama/theater group, newspaper, radio station, television station, and choral group. No national or local **fraternities** or **sororities**.

Saint Mary's is a member of the NCAA (Division I). **Intercollegiate sports** (some offering scholarships) include baseball (m), basketball, crew (w), cross-country running, football (m), golf (m), lacrosse, rugby (m), soccer, softball (w), tennis, volleyball.

Campus Safety

Student safety services include late-night transport/escort service, 24-hour emergency telephone alarm devices, and 24-hour patrols by trained security personnel.

Applying

Saint Mary's requires an essay, SAT I or ACT, a high school transcript, 1 recommendation, and a minimum high school GPA of 2.0, and in some cases an interview and a minimum high school GPA of 3.0. It recommends a minimum high school GPA of 3.0. Application deadline: 2/1; 3/2 priority date for financial aid. Deferred admission is possible.

It has been said that Saint Mary's College is "a classic example of a school committed to teaching students *how* to think rather than *what* to think." It is home to some of the "happiest students in the nation," has a safe and beautiful campus, and is a "good buy." Saint Mary's intimate academic community of 2,900 undergraduates is located 20 miles east of San Francisco. Operated and owned by the Christian Brothers, the College is committed to providing students with a comprehensive liberal arts education that includes reading and discussing the Great Books.

Getting in Last Year
2,830 applied
85% were accepted
706 enrolled (29%)
3.38 average high school GPA
23% had SAT verbal scores over 600
25% had SAT math scores over 600
2% had SAT verbal scores over 700
2% had SAT math scores over 700

Graduation and After
61% graduated in 4 years
5% graduated in 5 years
28% pursued further study
132 organizations recruited on campus

Financial Matters
$17,475 tuition and fees (1999–2000)
$7370 room and board
76% average percent of need met
$18,886 average financial aid amount received per undergraduate (1999–2000 estimated)

ST. MARY'S COLLEGE OF MARYLAND

RURAL SETTING ■ PUBLIC ■ STATE-SUPPORTED ■ COED
ST. MARY'S CITY, MARYLAND

Web site: www.smcm.edu
Contact: Mr. Richard J. Edgar, Director of Admissions, 18952 East Fisher Road, St. Mary's City, MD 20686-3001
Telephone: 301-862-0292 or toll-free 800-492-7181 **Fax:** 301-862-0906
E-mail: admissions@honors.smcm.edu

St. Mary's College of Maryland, with its distinctive identity as Maryland's "Public Honors College," has emerged as one of the finest liberal arts colleges in the country. A lively academic atmosphere combines with the serene yet stunning natural beauty of a riverfront campus to create a challenging and memorable college experience. Construction over the past several years includes a state-of-the-art science building, 40 town-house residences, the history and social science complex, and, opening in fall 2000, the new campus center.

Getting in Last Year

1,285 applied
65% were accepted
276 enrolled (33%)
50% from top tenth of their h.s. class
3.40 average high school GPA
73% had SAT verbal scores over 600
59% had SAT math scores over 600
20% had SAT verbal scores over 700
9% had SAT math scores over 700
11 National Merit Scholars
13 valedictorians

Graduation and After

58% graduated in 4 years
13% graduated in 5 years
37% pursued further study (28% arts and sciences, 4% law, 3% business)
9 organizations recruited on campus

Financial Matters

$7360 resident tuition and fees (2000–2001)
$12,200 nonresident tuition and fees (2000–2001)
$6325 room and board

Academics

St. Mary's awards bachelor's **degrees**. Challenging opportunities include advanced placement, student-designed majors, freshman honors college, an honors program, double majors, independent study, a senior project, and Phi Beta Kappa. Special programs include internships, summer session for credit, off-campus study, and study-abroad.

The most frequently chosen fields are social sciences and history, psychology, and biological/life sciences. A complete listing of majors at St. Mary's appears in the Majors Index beginning on page 432.

The **faculty** at St. Mary's has 117 full-time members, 95% with terminal degrees. The student-faculty ratio is 12:1.

Students of St. Mary's

The student body is made up of 1,613 undergraduates. 58% are women and 42% are men. Students come from 36 states and territories. 84% are from Maryland. 0.9% are international students. 9.6% are African American, 0.4% American Indian, 4.1% Asian American, and 2.2% Hispanic American. 85% returned for their sophomore year.

Facilities and Resources

Student rooms are linked to a campus network. 155 **computers** are available on campus that provide access to the Internet. The **library** has 110,642 books.

Campus Life

There are 68 active organizations on campus, including a drama/theater group, newspaper, radio station, television station, and choral group. No national or local **fraternities** or **sororities**.

St. Mary's is a member of the NCAA (Division III). **Intercollegiate sports** include baseball (m), basketball, crew, fencing, field hockey (w), golf, lacrosse, rugby, sailing, soccer, softball (w), swimming, tennis, volleyball, wrestling (m).

Campus Safety

Student safety services include late-night transport/escort service, 24-hour emergency telephone alarm devices, 24-hour patrols by trained security personnel, student patrols, and electronically operated dormitory entrances.

Applying

St. Mary's requires an essay, SAT I or ACT, a high school transcript, and a minimum high school GPA of 2.0. It recommends an interview and 3 recommendations. Application deadline: 1/15; 3/1 for financial aid. Early admission is possible.

St. Norbert College

Suburban setting ■ Private ■ Independent Religious ■ Coed
De Pere, Wisconsin

Web site: www.snc.edu
Contact: Mr. Daniel L. Meyer, Dean of Admission and Enrollment
Management, 100 Grant Street, Office of Admission, De Pere, WI
54115-2099
Telephone: 920-403-3005 or toll-free 800-236-4878 **Fax:** 920-403-4072
E-mail: admit@mail.snc.edu

Academics
St. Norbert awards bachelor's and master's **degrees**. Challenging opportunities include advanced placement, accelerated degree programs, student-designed majors, an honors program, double majors, independent study, and a senior project. Special programs include internships, summer session for credit, off-campus study, study-abroad, and Army ROTC.

The most frequently chosen fields are business/marketing, education, and social sciences and history. A complete listing of majors at St. Norbert appears in the Majors Index beginning on page 432.

The **faculty** at St. Norbert has 115 full-time members, 90% with terminal degrees. The student-faculty ratio is 15:1.

Students of St. Norbert
The student body totals 1,959, of whom 1,950 are undergraduates. 58.5% are women and 41.5% are men. Students come from 27 states and territories and 28 other countries. 72% are from Wisconsin. 3.7% are international students. 0.8% are African American, 1.2% American Indian, 1.1% Asian American, and 1.2% Hispanic American. 83% returned for their sophomore year.

Facilities and Resources
Student rooms are linked to a campus network. 174 **computers** are available on campus that provide access to the Internet. The **library** has 134,203 books and 698 subscriptions.

Campus Life
There are 71 active organizations on campus, including a drama/theater group, newspaper, radio station, television station, and choral group. 20% of eligible men and 20% of eligible women are members of national **fraternities**, national **sororities**, local fraternities, and local sororities.

St. Norbert is a member of the NCAA (Division III). **Intercollegiate sports** include baseball (m), basketball, cross-country running, football (m), golf, ice hockey (m), soccer, softball (w), swimming (w), tennis, track and field, volleyball (w).

Campus Safety
Student safety services include crime prevention programs, late-night transport/escort service, 24-hour emergency telephone alarm devices, 24-hour patrols by trained security personnel, and student patrols.

Applying
St. Norbert requires an essay, SAT I or ACT, a high school transcript, and 1 recommendation. It recommends an interview. Application deadline: rolling admissions; 3/1 priority date for financial aid. Deferred admission is possible.

 eApply

R ecognized nationally for its academic program, St. Norbert College provides students with the resources necessary to compete with the nation's best. With a faculty determined to provide the best possible instruction and advising, the College is committed to helping students achieve their education goals. The College community, steeped in the values of the Norbertine tradition, encourages students to discover ways in which they can enrich their lives, society, and the world. Students considering St. Norbert are welcome to visit the campus, sit in on classes, and meet with faculty members.

Getting in Last Year
1,396 applied
90% were accepted
519 enrolled (41%)
31% from top tenth of their h.s. class
3.40 average high school GPA
51% had ACT scores over 24
7% had ACT scores over 30
3 National Merit Scholars
15 class presidents
19 valedictorians

Graduation and After
66% graduated in 4 years
8% graduated in 5 years
76% had job offers within 6 months
38 organizations recruited on campus

Financial Matters
$15,800 tuition and fees (1999–2000)
$5762 room and board
91% average percent of need met
$13,045 average financial aid amount received
per undergraduate (1999–2000 estimated)

eAPPLY

ST. OLAF COLLEGE

SMALL-TOWN SETTING ■ PRIVATE ■ INDEPENDENT RELIGIOUS ■ COED
NORTHFIELD, MINNESOTA

Web site: www.stolaf.edu
Contact: Ms. Sara Kyle, Interim Director of Admissions, 1520 St. Olaf Avenue, Northfield, MN 55057-1098
Telephone: 507-646-3025 or toll-free 800-800-3025 (in-state) **Fax:** 507-646-3832
E-mail: admiss@stolaf.edu

Academics

St. Olaf awards bachelor's **degrees**. Challenging opportunities include advanced placement, accelerated degree programs, student-designed majors, double majors, independent study, a senior project, and Phi Beta Kappa. Special programs include internships, summer session for credit, off-campus study, and study-abroad.

The most frequently chosen fields are social sciences and history, visual/performing arts, and English. A complete listing of majors at St. Olaf appears in the Majors Index beginning on page 432.

The **faculty** at St. Olaf has 217 full-time members, 85% with terminal degrees. The student-faculty ratio is 12:1.

Students of St. Olaf

The student body is made up of 2,998 undergraduates. 57.4% are women and 42.6% are men. Students come from 46 states and territories and 27 other countries. 53% are from Minnesota. 1.5% are international students. 1.2% are African American, 0.2% American Indian, 2.6% Asian American, and 1.4% Hispanic American. 92% returned for their sophomore year.

Facilities and Resources

Student rooms are linked to a campus network. 450 **computers** are available on campus that provide access to the Internet. The 4 **libraries** have 488,299 books and 1,703 subscriptions.

Campus Life

There are 96 active organizations on campus, including a drama/theater group, newspaper, radio station, and choral group. No national or local **fraternities** or **sororities**.

St. Olaf is a member of the NCAA (Division III). **Intercollegiate sports** include baseball (m), basketball, cross-country running, football (m), golf (w), ice hockey (m), skiing (cross-country), skiing (downhill), soccer, softball (w), swimming, tennis, track and field, volleyball (w), wrestling (m).

Campus Safety

Student safety services include late-night transport/escort service, 24-hour emergency telephone alarm devices, 24-hour patrols by trained security personnel, and electronically operated dormitory entrances.

Applying

St. Olaf requires an essay, SAT I or ACT, a high school transcript, 2 recommendations, and a minimum high school GPA of 3.0. It recommends an interview. Application deadline: rolling admissions; 3/1 priority date for financial aid. Early and deferred admission are possible.

SAMFORD UNIVERSITY

SUBURBAN SETTING ■ PRIVATE ■ INDEPENDENT RELIGIOUS ■ COED
BIRMINGHAM, ALABAMA

Web site: www.samford.edu
Contact: Mr. Phil Kimrey, Dean of Admissions and Financial Aid, 800
    Lakeshore Drive, Samford Hall, Birmingham, AL 35229-0002
Telephone: 205-726-3673 or toll-free 800-888-7218 **Fax:** 205-870-2171
E-mail: seberry@samford.edu

Academics

Samford awards associate, bachelor's, master's, doctoral, and first-professional **degrees**
and post-bachelor's and post-master's certificates. Challenging opportunities include
advanced placement, accelerated degree programs, student-designed majors, an honors
program, double majors, and a senior project. Special programs include cooperative
education, internships, summer session for credit, off-campus study, study-abroad, and
Army and Air Force ROTC.

    The most frequently chosen fields are business/marketing, education, and health
professions and related sciences. A complete listing of majors at Samford appears in the
Majors Index beginning on page 432.

    The **faculty** at Samford has 243 full-time members, 81% with terminal degrees. The
student-faculty ratio is 14:1.

Students of Samford

The student body totals 4,494, of whom 2,855 are undergraduates. 61.6% are women
and 38.4% are men. Students come from 39 states and territories and 25 other countries.
44% are from Alabama. 0.7% are international students. 5.2% are African American,
0.4% American Indian, 0.5% Asian American, and 0.6% Hispanic American. 80%
returned for their sophomore year.

Facilities and Resources

Student rooms are linked to a campus network. 315 **computers** are available on campus
that provide access to the Internet. The 4 **libraries** have 844,250 books and 5,387
subscriptions.

Campus Life

There are 134 active organizations on campus, including a drama/theater group,
newspaper, radio station, television station, choral group, and marching band. 42% of
eligible men and 48% of eligible women are members of national **fraternities** and
national **sororities**.

    Samford is a member of the NCAA (Division I). **Intercollegiate sports** (some offer-
ing scholarships) include baseball (m), basketball, cross-country running, football (m),
golf, soccer (w), softball (w), tennis, track and field, volleyball (w).

Campus Safety

Student safety services include late-night transport/escort service, 24-hour emergency
telephone alarm devices, 24-hour patrols by trained security personnel, student patrols,
and electronically operated dormitory entrances.

Applying

Samford requires an essay, SAT I or ACT, a high school transcript, and 2 recommendations. It recommends an interview. Application deadline: 3/1 priority date for financial
aid. Early and deferred admission are possible.

Samford University is the
largest private accredited
university in Alabama, yet
with 4,500 students, it is an ideal
size. More than half the
undergraduates reside on campus.
Students from 39 states and
territories and 25 other countries
enjoy a beautiful setting
characterized by Georgian-Colonial
architecture. The institution takes
seriously its Christian heritage and
is consistently listed in rankings of
Southeastern institutions. Faculty
members have earned degrees from
more than 160 colleges and
universities, with over 80% holding
the terminal degree in their field.
Excellent opportunity to "stretch"
academically, socially, physically, and
spiritually is provided, along with
special opportunities in computer
competency, in international
experiences, and in externships.

Getting in Last Year
1,974 applied
88% were accepted
675 enrolled (39%)
38% from top tenth of their h.s. class
3.60 average high school GPA
41% had SAT verbal scores over 600
34% had SAT math scores over 600
61% had ACT scores over 24
8% had SAT verbal scores over 700
3% had SAT math scores over 700
10% had ACT scores over 30
5 National Merit Scholars
31 class presidents
35 valedictorians

Graduation and After
45% graduated in 4 years
17% graduated in 5 years
4% graduated in 6 years
65 organizations recruited on campus

Financial Matters
$10,300 tuition and fees (1999–2000)
$4560 room and board
80% average percent of need met
$8748 average financial aid amount received
   per undergraduate (1999–2000)

eAPPLY

Santa Clara University
Suburban setting ■ Private ■ Independent Religious ■ Coed
Santa Clara, California

Web site: www.scu.edu
Contact: Sr. Annette Schmeling, Dean of Undergraduate Admissions, 500 El
    Camino Real, Santa Clara, CA 95053
Telephone: 408-554-4700 **Fax:** 408-554-5255
E-mail: ugadmissions@scu.edu

Getting in Last Year
5,562 applied
70% were accepted
1,103 enrolled (29%)
37% from top tenth of their h.s. class
3.51 average high school GPA
45% had SAT verbal scores over 600
57% had SAT math scores over 600
7% had SAT verbal scores over 700
12% had SAT math scores over 700
1 National Merit Scholar
42 valedictorians

Graduation and After
73% graduated in 4 years
7% graduated in 5 years
1% graduated in 6 years
28% pursued further study (4% arts and sciences, 4% medicine, 3% education)
63% had job offers within 6 months
300 organizations recruited on campus

Financial Matters
$19,311 tuition and fees (1999–2000)
$7644 room and board

Academics
Santa Clara awards bachelor's, master's, doctoral, and first-professional **degrees** and post-bachelor's and post-master's certificates. Challenging opportunities include advanced placement, student-designed majors, an honors program, double majors, independent study, a senior project, Phi Beta Kappa, and Sigma Xi. Special programs include cooperative education, internships, summer session for credit, study-abroad, and Army and Air Force ROTC.

The most frequently chosen fields are business/marketing, social sciences and history, and engineering/engineering technologies. A complete listing of majors at Santa Clara appears in the Majors Index beginning on page 432.

The **faculty** at Santa Clara has 348 full-time members. The student-faculty ratio is 15:1.

Students of Santa Clara
The student body totals 7,670, of whom 4,477 are undergraduates. 54.3% are women and 45.7% are men. 3.1% are international students. 2.4% are African American, 0.5% American Indian, 18.9% Asian American, and 13.3% Hispanic American. 90% returned for their sophomore year.

Facilities and Resources
Student rooms are linked to a campus network. 350 **computers** are available on campus that provide access to the Internet. The 2 **libraries** have 454,470 books and 8,611 subscriptions.

Campus Life
There are 55 active organizations on campus, including a drama/theater group, newspaper, radio station, television station, and choral group. 13% of eligible men and 14% of eligible women are members of national **fraternities**, national **sororities**, local fraternities, and local sororities.

Santa Clara is a member of the NCAA (Division I). **Intercollegiate sports** (some offering scholarships) include baseball (m), basketball, crew, cross-country running, field hockey (w), golf, lacrosse, rugby, soccer, softball (w), tennis, volleyball, water polo (m).

Campus Safety
Student safety services include late-night transport/escort service, 24-hour emergency telephone alarm devices, 24-hour patrols by trained security personnel, and electronically operated dormitory entrances.

Applying
Santa Clara requires an essay, SAT I or ACT, a high school transcript, and 1 recommendation. It recommends an interview. Application deadline: 1/15; 2/1 priority date for financial aid. Deferred admission is possible.

SARAH LAWRENCE COLLEGE

SUBURBAN SETTING ■ PRIVATE ■ INDEPENDENT ■ COED
BRONXVILLE, NEW YORK

Web site: www.slc.edu
Contact: Ms. Thyra L. Briggs, Dean of Admissions, 1 Mead Way, Bronxville, NY 10708-5999
Telephone: 914-395-2510 or toll-free 800-888-2858 **Fax:** 914-395-2676
E-mail: slcadmit@slc.edu

 eAPPLY

Academics

Sarah Lawrence awards bachelor's and master's **degrees**. Challenging opportunities include advanced placement, student-designed majors, double majors, and independent study. Special programs include internships, off-campus study, and study-abroad.

The most frequently chosen field is liberal arts/general studies. A complete listing of majors at Sarah Lawrence appears in the Majors Index beginning on page 432.

The **faculty** at Sarah Lawrence has 178 full-time members. The student-faculty ratio is 6:1.

Students of Sarah Lawrence

The student body totals 1,495, of whom 1,178 are undergraduates. 73.4% are women and 26.6% are men. Students come from 51 states and territories and 27 other countries. 21% are from New York. 1.5% are international students. 5.7% are African American, 0.4% American Indian, 5% Asian American, and 5.2% Hispanic American. 92% returned for their sophomore year.

Facilities and Resources

Student rooms are linked to a campus network. 46 **computers** are available on campus that provide access to the Internet. The 3 **libraries** have 292,839 books and 1,068 subscriptions.

Campus Life

There are 20 active organizations on campus, including a drama/theater group, newspaper, radio station, and choral group. No national or local **fraternities** or **sororities**.

Intercollegiate sports include crew, cross-country running, equestrian sports, tennis, volleyball (w).

Campus Safety

Student safety services include late-night transport/escort service, 24-hour emergency telephone alarm devices, 24-hour patrols by trained security personnel, student patrols, and electronically operated dormitory entrances.

Applying

Sarah Lawrence requires an essay, SAT I or ACT or any 3 SAT II Subject Tests, a high school transcript, and 3 recommendations. It recommends an interview and a minimum high school GPA of 3.0. Application deadline: 2/1; 2/1 for financial aid. Early and deferred admission are possible.

Sarah Lawrence, a private, coeducational liberal arts college founded in 1926, is a lively community of students, scholars, and artists just 30 minutes from midtown Manhattan. In its distinctive seminar/conference system, each course consists of two parts: the seminar, limited to 15 students, and the conference, a private biweekly meeting with the seminar professor. In conference, student and teacher create a project that extends the seminar material and connects it to the student's academic goals. To prepare for this rigorous work, all first-year students enroll in a First-Year Studies Seminar. This seminar teacher will be the student's don, or adviser, throughout his or her Sarah Lawrence years.

Getting in Last Year
2,070 applied
43% were accepted
277 enrolled (31%)
38% from top tenth of their h.s. class
3.30 average high school GPA
70% had SAT verbal scores over 600
36% had SAT math scores over 600
71% had ACT scores over 24
25% had SAT verbal scores over 700
2% had SAT math scores over 700
8% had ACT scores over 30
5 National Merit Scholars
4 valedictorians

Graduation and After
57% graduated in 4 years
8% graduated in 5 years
30% pursued further study (10% arts and sciences, 10% law, 5% education)
65% had job offers within 6 months
58 organizations recruited on campus
1 Fulbright scholar

Financial Matters
$25,406 tuition and fees (1999–2000)
$8648 room and board
92% average percent of need met
$17,957 average financial aid amount received per undergraduate (1998–99)

eAPPLY

Getting in Last Year
1,063 applied
70% were accepted
212 enrolled (28%)
48% from top tenth of their h.s. class
3.67 average high school GPA
74% had SAT verbal scores over 600
60% had SAT math scores over 600
85% had ACT scores over 24
22% had SAT verbal scores over 700
11% had SAT math scores over 700
25% had ACT scores over 30
1 National Merit Scholar
10 valedictorians

Graduation and After
67% graduated in 4 years
2% graduated in 5 years
30% pursued further study
69% had job offers within 6 months
200 organizations recruited on campus

Financial Matters
$21,130 tuition and fees (1999–2000)
$7870 room and board
97% average percent of need met
$19,799 average financial aid amount received
  per undergraduate (1999–2000)

SCRIPPS COLLEGE
SUBURBAN SETTING ■ PRIVATE ■ INDEPENDENT ■ WOMEN ONLY
CLAREMONT, CALIFORNIA

Web site: www.ScrippsCol.edu
Contact: Ms. Patricia F. Goldsmith, Dean of Admission and Financial Aid,
  1030 Columbia Avenue, Claremont, CA 91711-3948
Telephone: 909-621-8149 or toll-free 800-770-1333 **Fax:** 909-607-7508
E-mail: admofc@ad.scrippscol.edu

Academics
Scripps awards bachelor's **degrees** and post-bachelor's certificates. Challenging opportunities include advanced placement, accelerated degree programs, student-designed majors, an honors program, double majors, independent study, a senior project, and Phi Beta Kappa. Special programs include internships, off-campus study, study-abroad, and Army and Air Force ROTC.

The most frequently chosen fields are social sciences and history, visual/performing arts, and interdisciplinary studies. A complete listing of majors at Scripps appears in the Majors Index beginning on page 432.

The **faculty** at Scripps has 57 full-time members, 96% with terminal degrees. The student-faculty ratio is 12:1.

Students of Scripps
The student body totals 790, of whom 773 are undergraduates. Students come from 41 states and territories and 19 other countries. 50% are from California. 2.5% are international students. 2.9% are African American, 0.5% American Indian, 15.1% Asian American, and 6.2% Hispanic American. 88% returned for their sophomore year.

Facilities and Resources
Student rooms are linked to a campus network. 72 **computers** are available on campus that provide access to the Internet. The 5 **libraries** have 2,028,793 books and 4,113 subscriptions.

Campus Life
There are 200 active organizations on campus, including a drama/theater group, newspaper, radio station, and choral group. No national or local **sororities**.

Scripps is a member of the NCAA (Division III). **Intercollegiate sports** include basketball, cross-country running, fencing, golf, lacrosse, rugby, skiing (downhill), soccer, softball, swimming, tennis, track and field, volleyball, water polo.

Campus Safety
Student safety services include late-night transport/escort service, 24-hour emergency telephone alarm devices, 24-hour patrols by trained security personnel, and electronically operated dormitory entrances.

Applying
Scripps requires an essay, SAT I or ACT, a high school transcript, 3 recommendations, and graded writing sample. It recommends an interview and a minimum high school GPA of 3.0. Application deadline: 2/1; 11/15 priority date for financial aid. Early and deferred admission are possible.

SHEPHERD COLLEGE

SMALL-TOWN SETTING ■ PUBLIC ■ STATE-SUPPORTED ■ COED
SHEPHERDSTOWN, WEST VIRGINIA

Web site: www.shepherd.edu
Contact: Mr. Karl L. Wolf, Director of Admissions, King Street,
   Shepherdstown, WV 25443-3210
Telephone: 304-876-5212 or toll-free 800-344-5231 **Fax:** 304-876-5165
E-mail: admoff@shepherd.edu

Academics

Shepherd awards associate and bachelor's **degrees**. Challenging opportunities include advanced placement, accelerated degree programs, an honors program, double majors, and a senior project. Special programs include cooperative education, internships, summer session for credit, and Army and Air Force ROTC.

The most frequently chosen fields are engineering/engineering technologies, interdisciplinary studies, and (pre)law. A complete listing of majors at Shepherd appears in the Majors Index beginning on page 432.

The **faculty** at Shepherd has 104 full-time members, 73% with terminal degrees. The student-faculty ratio is 19:1.

Students of Shepherd

The student body is made up of 4,597 undergraduates. 58.4% are women and 41.6% are men. Students come from 50 states and territories. 66% are from West Virginia. 4.8% are African American, 0.5% American Indian, 1.3% Asian American, and 1.2% Hispanic American. 66% returned for their sophomore year.

Facilities and Resources

300 **computers** are available on campus that provide access to personal web pages and the Internet. The **library** has 176,061 books and 2,408 subscriptions.

Campus Life

There are 42 active organizations on campus, including a drama/theater group, newspaper, radio station, choral group, and marching band. 10% of eligible men and 10% of eligible women are members of national **fraternities** and national **sororities**.

Shepherd is a member of the NCAA (Division II). **Intercollegiate sports** (some offering scholarships) include baseball (m), basketball, cross-country running, football (m), golf (m), soccer, softball (w), tennis, volleyball (w).

Campus Safety

Student safety services include late-night transport/escort service, 24-hour emergency telephone alarm devices, 24-hour patrols by trained security personnel, and electronically operated dormitory entrances.

Applying

Shepherd requires SAT I or ACT, a high school transcript, and a minimum high school GPA of 2.5. It recommends an essay, an interview, 3 recommendations, and a minimum high school GPA of 3.0. Application deadline: 2/1; 3/1 priority date for financial aid. Early and deferred admission are possible.

Since Shepherd College is located only 1 hour's drive from the Baltimore and Washington Beltways, it offers its 4,600 students numerous internships and co-op programs with government agencies, scientific research centers, and corporations in the area. It is also the home of the George Tyler Moore Center for the Study of the Civil War and the professional equity Contemporary American Theater Festival. The Honors Program offers a stimulating curriculum for students.

Getting in Last Year
1,668 applied
84% were accepted
714 enrolled (51%)
3.13 average high school GPA
12% had SAT verbal scores over 600
12% had SAT math scores over 600
16% had ACT scores over 24
1% had SAT verbal scores over 700
1% had SAT math scores over 700
1% had ACT scores over 30

Graduation and After
1% graduated in 4 years
17% graduated in 5 years
22% graduated in 6 years
15% pursued further study
72% had job offers within 6 months
250 organizations recruited on campus

Financial Matters
$2430 resident tuition and fees (1999–2000)
$5754 nonresident tuition and fees (1999–2000)
$4432 room and board
78% average percent of need met
$6609 average financial aid amount received per undergraduate (1999–2000 estimated)

SIENA COLLEGE

SUBURBAN SETTING ■ PRIVATE ■ INDEPENDENT RELIGIOUS ■ COED
LOUDONVILLE, NEW YORK

Web site: www.siena.edu
Contact: Mr. Edward Jones, Director of Admissions, 515 Loudon Road,
   Loudonville, NY 12211-1462
Telephone: 518-783-2423 or toll-free 800-45SIENA **Fax:** 518-783-2436
E-mail: admit@siena.edu

Academics

Siena awards bachelor's and master's **degrees**. Challenging opportunities include advanced placement, an honors program, double majors, independent study, and a senior project. Special programs include internships, summer session for credit, off-campus study, study-abroad, and Army and Air Force ROTC.

The most frequently chosen fields are business/marketing, social sciences and history, and English. A complete listing of majors at Siena appears in the Majors Index beginning on page 432.

The **faculty** at Siena has 153 full-time members, 83% with terminal degrees. The student-faculty ratio is 14:1.

Students of Siena

The student body totals 3,024, of whom 3,002 are undergraduates. 53.5% are women and 46.5% are men. Students come from 28 states and territories and 6 other countries. 84% are from New York. 0.3% are international students. 1.8% are African American, 0.2% American Indian, 2.5% Asian American, and 2.6% Hispanic American. 89% returned for their sophomore year.

Facilities and Resources

Student rooms are linked to a campus network. 475 **computers** are available on campus that provide access to the Internet. The **library** has 206,559 books and 1,606 subscriptions.

Campus Life

There are 78 active organizations on campus, including a drama/theater group, newspaper, radio station, television station, and choral group. No national or local **fraternities** or **sororities**.

Siena is a member of the NCAA (Division I). **Intercollegiate sports** (some offering scholarships) include baseball (m), basketball, cross-country running, equestrian sports, field hockey (w), football (m), golf, ice hockey (m), lacrosse, rugby (m), soccer, softball (w), swimming (w), tennis, track and field, volleyball (w).

Campus Safety

Student safety services include call boxes in parking lots and on roadways, late-night transport/escort service, 24-hour emergency telephone alarm devices, 24-hour patrols by trained security personnel, and electronically operated dormitory entrances.

Applying

Siena requires an essay, SAT I or ACT, a high school transcript, and 1 recommendation, and in some cases an interview. Application deadline: 3/1; 2/1 priority date for financial aid. Early and deferred admission are possible.

Getting in Last Year
3,121 applied
73% were accepted
680 enrolled (30%)
20% from top tenth of their h.s. class
22% had SAT verbal scores over 600
26% had SAT math scores over 600
58% had ACT scores over 24
2% had SAT verbal scores over 700
4% had SAT math scores over 700
5% had ACT scores over 30

Graduation and After
68% graduated in 4 years
7% graduated in 5 years
1% graduated in 6 years
Graduates pursuing further study: 4% education, 4% medicine, 3% law
74% had job offers within 6 months
180 organizations recruited on campus

Financial Matters
$14,130 tuition and fees (1999–2000)
$6215 room and board

Simon's Rock College of Bard

RURAL SETTING ■ PRIVATE ■ INDEPENDENT ■ COED
GREAT BARRINGTON, MASSACHUSETTS

Web site: www.simons-rock.edu
Contact: Ms. Mary King Austin, Director of Admissions, 84 Alford Road,
 Great Barrington, MA 01230-9702
Telephone: 413-528-7317 or toll-free 800-235-7186 **Fax:** 413-528-7334
E-mail: admit@simons-rock.edu

Academics

Simon's Rock awards associate and bachelor's **degrees**. Challenging opportunities include student-designed majors, double majors, independent study, and a senior project. Special programs include internships, off-campus study, and study-abroad.

 The most frequently chosen fields are liberal arts/general studies, visual/performing arts, and social sciences and history. A complete listing of majors at Simon's Rock appears in the Majors Index beginning on page 432.

 The **faculty** at Simon's Rock has 35 full-time members, 94% with terminal degrees. The student-faculty ratio is 8:1.

Students of Simon's Rock

The student body is made up of 372 undergraduates. 56.5% are women and 43.5% are men. Students come from 39 states and territories and 4 other countries. 19% are from Massachusetts. 0.5% are international students. 3% are African American, 0.5% American Indian, 4% Asian American, and 1.6% Hispanic American. 76% returned for their sophomore year.

Facilities and Resources

Student rooms are linked to a campus network. 25 **computers** are available on campus that provide access to the Internet. The **library** has 70,000 books and 350 subscriptions.

Campus Life

There are 21 active organizations on campus, including a drama/theater group, newspaper, radio station, and choral group. No national or local **fraternities** or **sororities**.

 Intercollegiate sports include basketball, soccer, tennis.

Campus Safety

Student safety services include 24-hour weekend patrols by trained security personnel, late-night transport/escort service, 24-hour emergency telephone alarm devices, and electronically operated dormitory entrances.

Applying

Simon's Rock requires an essay, SAT I, PSAT, a high school transcript, an interview, 2 recommendations, parent application, and a minimum high school GPA of 2.0. It recommends ACT and a minimum high school GPA of 3.0. Application deadline: 6/15; 6/30 priority date for financial aid. Early and deferred admission are possible.

Simon's Rock College of Bard is a selective, private, coeducational college specifically designed to offer highly motivated students the opportunity to begin college after the tenth or eleventh grade. The academic and social programs are designed to meet the needs of younger scholars. The AA program combines a substantial core curriculum in the liberal arts and sciences, with opportunities to pursue individual interests. The BA program includes advanced course work, tutorials, independent study, and a yearlong thesis project in one of 34 areas of concentration. The Acceleration to Excellence Program, a scholarship competition for high school sophomores, covers the full cost of attending the College for 2 years.

Getting in Last Year
246 applied
85% were accepted
143 enrolled (69%)
70% had SAT verbal scores over 600
50% had SAT math scores over 600
90% had ACT scores over 24
28% had SAT verbal scores over 700
12% had SAT math scores over 700
40% had ACT scores over 30

Graduation and After
Graduates pursuing further study: 16% arts
 and sciences, 8% medicine, 4% education
56% had job offers within 6 months

Financial Matters
$23,300 tuition and fees (1999–2000)
$6410 room and board
76% average percent of need met
$15,908 average financial aid amount received
 per undergraduate (1998–99)

SIMPSON COLLEGE

SMALL-TOWN SETTING ■ PRIVATE ■ INDEPENDENT RELIGIOUS ■ COED
INDIANOLA, IOWA

Web site: www.simpson.edu
Contact: Mr. John Kellogg, Vice President of Enrollment, 701 North C
   Street, Indianola, IA 50125-1297
Telephone: 515-961-1624 or toll-free 800-362-2454 **Fax:** 515-961-1870
E-mail: admiss@simpson.edu

S impson College combines the best of a liberal arts education with outstanding career preparation and extracurricular programs. Activities range from an award-winning music program to nationally recognized NCAA Division III teams. Located 12 miles from Des Moines, Simpson offers the friendliness of a small town and the advantages of a metropolitan area. Outstanding facilities have been enhanced with recent multimillion-dollar expansions and renovations, including the state-of-the-art Carver Science Center, named after Simpson's most distinguished alumnus, George Washington Carver. The 4-4-1 academic calendar includes a May Term that provides students with unique learning opportunities. Simpson's beautiful 73-acre tree-lined campus provides a setting that nurtures creativity, energy, and productivity.

Academics

Simpson awards bachelor's **degrees**. Challenging opportunities include advanced placement, accelerated degree programs, student-designed majors, freshman honors college, an honors program, double majors, independent study, and a senior project. Special programs include cooperative education, internships, summer session for credit, off-campus study, and study-abroad.

The most frequently chosen fields are business/marketing, education, and communications/communication technologies. A complete listing of majors at Simpson appears in the Majors Index beginning on page 432.

The **faculty** at Simpson has 80 full-time members, 81% with terminal degrees. The student-faculty ratio is 17:1.

Students of Simpson

The student body is made up of 1,897 undergraduates. 56.6% are women and 43.4% are men. Students come from 26 states and territories and 10 other countries. 89% are from Iowa. 0.7% are international students. 0.8% are African American, 0.6% American Indian, 0.9% Asian American, and 1% Hispanic American. 82% returned for their sophomore year.

Facilities and Resources

Student rooms are linked to a campus network. 180 **computers** are available on campus that provide access to the Internet. The 2 **libraries** have 159,949 books and 623 subscriptions.

Campus Life

There are 81 active organizations on campus, including a drama/theater group, newspaper, radio station, and choral group. 23% of eligible men and 31% of eligible women are members of national **fraternities**, national **sororities**, and local fraternities.

Simpson is a member of the NCAA (Division III). **Intercollegiate sports** include baseball (m), basketball, cross-country running, football (m), golf, rugby, soccer, softball (w), swimming, tennis, track and field, volleyball (w), wrestling (m).

Campus Safety

Student safety services include late-night transport/escort service, 24-hour emergency telephone alarm devices, 24-hour patrols by trained security personnel, student patrols, and electronically operated dormitory entrances.

Applying

Simpson requires SAT I or ACT, a high school transcript, and 1 recommendation. It recommends an interview and rank in upper 50% of high school class. Application deadline: 4/1 priority date for financial aid. Early and deferred admission are possible.

Getting in Last Year
1,164 applied
84% were accepted
352 enrolled (36%)
24% from top tenth of their h.s. class
33% had SAT verbal scores over 600
37% had SAT math scores over 600
57% had ACT scores over 24
6% had SAT verbal scores over 700
6% had SAT math scores over 700
10% had ACT scores over 30
19 valedictorians

Graduation and After
54% graduated in 4 years
7% graduated in 5 years
1% graduated in 6 years
16% pursued further study (6% arts and sciences, 3% law, 3% medicine)
83% had job offers within 6 months
89 organizations recruited on campus

Financial Matters
$14,430 tuition and fees (1999–2000)
$4800 room and board
91% average percent of need met
$15,174 average financial aid amount received per undergraduate (1999–2000)

SKIDMORE COLLEGE

SMALL-TOWN SETTING ■ PRIVATE ■ INDEPENDENT ■ COED
SARATOGA SPRINGS, NEW YORK

Web site: www.skidmore.edu
Contact: Ms. Mary Lou W. Bates, Director of Admissions, 815 North
Broadway, Saratoga Springs, NY 12866-1632
Telephone: 518-580-5570 or toll-free 800-867-6007 **Fax:** 518-580-5584
E-mail: admissions@skidmore.edu

 eAPPLY

Academics

Skidmore awards bachelor's and master's **degrees**. Challenging opportunities include advanced placement, accelerated degree programs, student-designed majors, an honors program, double majors, independent study, a senior project, and Phi Beta Kappa. Special programs include internships, summer session for credit, off-campus study, study-abroad, and Army and Air Force ROTC.

The most frequently chosen fields are visual/performing arts, business/marketing, and social sciences and history. A complete listing of majors at Skidmore appears in the Majors Index beginning on page 432.

The **faculty** at Skidmore has 189 full-time members, 84% with terminal degrees. The student-faculty ratio is 11:1.

Students of Skidmore

The student body totals 2,592, of whom 2,540 are undergraduates. 59.8% are women and 40.2% are men. Students come from 43 states and territories and 25 other countries. 27% are from New York. 0.9% are international students. 2.2% are African American, 0.3% American Indian, 3.4% Asian American, and 4.8% Hispanic American. 91% returned for their sophomore year.

Facilities and Resources

Student rooms are linked to a campus network. 276 **computers** are available on campus that provide access to the Internet. The **library** has 673,877 books and 1,843 subscriptions.

Campus Life

There are 80 active organizations on campus, including a drama/theater group, newspaper, radio station, television station, and choral group. No national or local **fraternities** or **sororities**.

Skidmore is a member of the NCAA (Division III). **Intercollegiate sports** include baseball (m), basketball, crew, equestrian sports, field hockey (w), golf (m), ice hockey, lacrosse, skiing (downhill), soccer, softball (w), swimming, tennis, volleyball (w).

Campus Safety

Student safety services include well-lit campus, late-night transport/escort service, 24-hour emergency telephone alarm devices, 24-hour patrols by trained security personnel, and electronically operated dormitory entrances.

Applying

Skidmore requires an essay, SAT I or ACT, a high school transcript, and 2 recommendations. It recommends SAT II Subject Tests, SAT II: Writing Test, and an interview. Application deadline: 1/15; 2/1 for financial aid. Early and deferred admission are possible.

Skidmore College, located on a beautiful 850-acre campus, is a liberal arts college with a history of innovation and imagination. An interdisciplinary liberal studies curriculum challenges students to explore broadly. A rich cocurricular program provides further opportunities for personal growth and leadership. Among the largest majors are business, studio art, English, psychology, government, and biology/chemistry. A total of 2,592 students from 43 states and territories and 25 countries live and learn in Skidmore's lively intellectual climate and beautiful campus surroundings.

Getting in Last Year
5,414 applied
49% were accepted
648 enrolled (24%)
27% from top tenth of their h.s. class
56% had SAT verbal scores over 600
55% had SAT math scores over 600
91% had ACT scores over 24
8% had SAT verbal scores over 700
8% had SAT math scores over 700
23% had ACT scores over 30

Graduation and After
15% pursued further study (7% arts and sciences, 3% law, 1% business)
76% had job offers within 6 months
206 organizations recruited on campus

Financial Matters
$31,200 comprehensive fee (1999–2000)
96% average percent of need met
$18,355 average financial aid amount received per undergraduate (1999–2000 estimated)

SMITH COLLEGE

URBAN SETTING ■ PRIVATE ■ INDEPENDENT ■ WOMEN ONLY
NORTHAMPTON, MASSACHUSETTS

Web site: www.smith.edu
Contact: Ms. Nanci Tessier, Director of Admissions, 7 College Lane,
Northampton, MA 01063
Telephone: 413-585-2500 **Fax:** 413-585-2527
E-mail: admission@smith.edu

S tudents choose Smith because of its outstanding academic reputation. From its founding in 1871, the College has been committed to providing women with countless opportunities for personal and intellectual growth. The open curriculum allows each student, with the assistance of a faculty adviser, to plan an individualized course of study outside the major. Superb facilities, a beautiful New England campus, and a diverse student body complement the rigorous academic program. New initiatives include the first engineering major at a women's college and the guarantee that all students will receive funding for an internship related to their career and academic goals.

Academics

Smith awards bachelor's, master's, and doctoral **degrees** and post-bachelor's and post-master's certificates. Challenging opportunities include advanced placement, accelerated degree programs, student-designed majors, an honors program, double majors, independent study, a senior project, Phi Beta Kappa, and Sigma Xi. Special programs include internships, off-campus study, study-abroad, and Army and Air Force ROTC.

The most frequently chosen fields are social sciences and history, visual/performing arts, and biological/life sciences. A complete listing of majors at Smith appears in the Majors Index beginning on page 432.

The **faculty** at Smith has 257 full-time members, 97% with terminal degrees. The student-faculty ratio is 10:1.

Students of Smith

The student body totals 3,168, of whom 2,665 are undergraduates. Students come from 53 states and territories and 48 other countries. 22% are from Massachusetts. 6.1% are international students. 4.1% are African American, 0.6% American Indian, 9.4% Asian American, and 4.1% Hispanic American. 89% returned for their sophomore year.

Facilities and Resources

Student rooms are linked to a campus network. 550 **computers** are available on campus that provide access to e-mail and the Internet. The 4 **libraries** have 1,225,078 books and 4,957 subscriptions.

Campus Life

There are 112 active organizations on campus, including a drama/theater group, newspaper, radio station, and choral group. No national or local **sororities**.

Smith is a member of the NCAA (Division III). **Intercollegiate sports** include basketball, crew, cross-country running, equestrian sports, field hockey, lacrosse, skiing (downhill), soccer, softball, squash, swimming, tennis, track and field, volleyball.

Campus Safety

Student safety services include self-defense workshops, emergency telephones, programs in crime and sexual assault prevention, late-night transport/escort service, 24-hour emergency telephone alarm devices, and 24-hour patrols by trained security personnel.

Applying

Smith requires an essay, SAT I or ACT, a high school transcript, and 2 recommendations. It recommends SAT II Subject Tests, SAT II: Writing Test, and an interview. Application deadline: 1/15; 2/1 for financial aid. Early and deferred admission are possible.

Getting in Last Year
2,998 applied
56% were accepted
667 enrolled (40%)
52% from top tenth of their h.s. class
3.74 average high school GPA
81% had SAT verbal scores over 600
66% had SAT math scores over 600
89% had ACT scores over 24
31% had SAT verbal scores over 700
16% had SAT math scores over 700
24% had ACT scores over 30

Graduation and After
77% graduated in 4 years
5% graduated in 5 years
1% graduated in 6 years
15% pursued further study (7% arts and sciences, 3% law, 1% education)
550 organizations recruited on campus

Financial Matters
$22,622 tuition and fees (1999–2000)
$7820 room and board
100% average percent of need met
$21,548 average financial aid amount received per undergraduate (1999–2000)

SOUTH DAKOTA SCHOOL OF MINES AND TECHNOLOGY

SUBURBAN SETTING ■ PUBLIC ■ STATE-SUPPORTED ■ COED
RAPID CITY, SOUTH DAKOTA

Web site: www.sdsmt.edu
Contact: Mr. Donald Hapward, Director of Admissions, 501 East Saint
Joseph, Rapid City, SD 57701-3995
Telephone: 605-394-2414 ext. 1266 or toll-free 800-544-8162 ext. 2414 **Fax:**
605-394-1268
E-mail: undergraduate_admissions@silver.sdsmt.edu

Academics

SDSM&T awards bachelor's, master's, and doctoral **degrees**. Challenging opportunities include advanced placement, double majors, independent study, a senior project, and Sigma Xi. Special programs include cooperative education, internships, summer session for credit, study-abroad, and Army ROTC.

The most frequently chosen fields are engineering/engineering technologies, computer/information sciences, and mathematics. A complete listing of majors at SDSM&T appears in the Majors Index beginning on page 432.

The **faculty** at SDSM&T has 114 full-time members, 82% with terminal degrees. The student-faculty ratio is 15:1.

Students of SDSM&T

The student body totals 2,272, of whom 2,020 are undergraduates. 30.8% are women and 69.2% are men. Students come from 38 states and territories and 23 other countries. 67% are from South Dakota. 3.2% are international students. 0.4% are African American, 1.6% American Indian, 0.8% Asian American, and 0.9% Hispanic American. 68% returned for their sophomore year.

Facilities and Resources

Student rooms are linked to a campus network. 130 **computers** are available on campus that provide access to the Internet. The **library** has 137,864 books and 461 subscriptions.

Campus Life

Active organizations on campus include a drama/theater group, newspaper, radio station, and choral group. 11% of eligible men and 10% of eligible women are members of national **fraternities** and national **sororities**.

SDSM&T is a member of the NAIA. **Intercollegiate sports** (some offering scholarships) include basketball, cross-country running, football (m), tennis (m), track and field, volleyball (w).

Campus Safety

Student safety services include late-night transport/escort service, 24-hour emergency telephone alarm devices, 24-hour patrols by trained security personnel, student patrols, and electronically operated dormitory entrances.

Applying

SDSM&T requires SAT I or ACT and a high school transcript, and in some cases a minimum high school GPA of 2.6. Application deadline: rolling admissions; 4/15 priority date for financial aid.

Getting in Last Year

664 applied
97% were accepted
423 enrolled (66%)
21% from top tenth of their h.s. class
3.44 average high school GPA
26% had SAT verbal scores over 600
63% had SAT math scores over 600
55% had ACT scores over 24
5% had SAT math scores over 700
14% had ACT scores over 30
2 National Merit Scholars
17 class presidents
11 valedictorians

Graduation and After

4% graduated in 4 years
22% graduated in 5 years
7% graduated in 6 years
Graduates pursuing further study: 3% business, 1% law, 1% medicine
80% had job offers within 6 months
98 organizations recruited on campus

Financial Matters

$3850 resident tuition and fees (1999–2000)
$7924 nonresident tuition and fees (1999–2000)
$3122 room and board
97% average percent of need met
$4058 average financial aid amount received per undergraduate (1998–99)

SOUTHERN METHODIST UNIVERSITY

SUBURBAN SETTING ■ PRIVATE ■ INDEPENDENT RELIGIOUS ■ COED
DALLAS, TEXAS

Web site: www.smu.edu
Contact: Mr. Ron W. Moss, Director of Admission and Enrollment
 Management, 6425 Boaz, Dallas, TX 75275
Telephone: 214-768-2058 or toll-free 800-323-0672 **Fax:** 214-768-2507
E-mail: ugadmission@smu.edu

SMU offers an education as individual as each of its students, with nearly 70 undergraduate majors in the humanities, sciences, business, engineering, and the arts. Classes are small enough to provide opportunities for faculty-student interaction and mentoring relationships. SMU offers more than 10 study-abroad programs and a summer campus near Taos, New Mexico. SMU's diverse student body represents 48 states and territories, many countries, and numerous faiths; 21% of the total student population are members of minority groups. Seventy-two percent of undergraduates receive some form of financial assistance. SMU's parklike campus is just 5 miles north of downtown Dallas, a dynamic center of commerce and culture.

Academics

SMU awards bachelor's, master's, doctoral, and first-professional **degrees** and post-bachelor's certificates. Challenging opportunities include advanced placement, accelerated degree programs, student-designed majors, an honors program, double majors, independent study, Phi Beta Kappa, and Sigma Xi. Special programs include cooperative education, internships, summer session for credit, study-abroad, and Army and Air Force ROTC.

The most frequently chosen fields are business/marketing, communications/communication technologies, and social sciences and history. A complete listing of majors at SMU appears in the Majors Index beginning on page 432.

The **faculty** at SMU has 519 full-time members, 87% with terminal degrees. The student-faculty ratio is 11:1.

Students of SMU

The student body totals 10,361, of whom 5,552 are undergraduates. 53.6% are women and 46.4% are men. Students come from 48 states and territories and 54 other countries. 65% are from Texas. 2.5% are international students. 6.6% are African American, 0.5% American Indian, 5.7% Asian American, and 8.9% Hispanic American. 84% returned for their sophomore year.

Facilities and Resources

Student rooms are linked to a campus network. 409 **computers** are available on campus that provide access to the Internet. The 8 **libraries** have 3,130,179 books and 11,216 subscriptions.

Campus Life

There are 152 active organizations on campus, including a drama/theater group, newspaper, radio station, choral group, and marching band. 36% of eligible men and 37% of eligible women are members of national **fraternities** and national **sororities**.

SMU is a member of the NCAA (Division I). **Intercollegiate sports** (some offering scholarships) include baseball (m), basketball, crew, cross-country running, fencing, football (m), golf, ice hockey (m), lacrosse, rugby (m), sailing, soccer, swimming, tennis, track and field, volleyball, wrestling (m).

Campus Safety

Student safety services include late-night transport/escort service, 24-hour emergency telephone alarm devices, 24-hour patrols by trained security personnel, and electronically operated dormitory entrances.

Applying

SMU requires an essay, SAT I or ACT, a high school transcript, and 1 recommendation, and in some cases SAT II Subject Tests. Application deadline: 4/1; 2/1 priority date for financial aid. Early and deferred admission are possible.

Getting in Last Year
4,280 applied
89% were accepted
1,331 enrolled (35%)
31% from top tenth of their h.s. class
3.19 average high school GPA
36% had SAT verbal scores over 600
42% had SAT math scores over 600
61% had ACT scores over 24
6% had SAT verbal scores over 700
7% had SAT math scores over 700
9% had ACT scores over 30
16 National Merit Scholars

Graduation and After
54% graduated in 4 years
14% graduated in 5 years
2% graduated in 6 years
16% pursued further study (5% arts and sciences, 4% engineering, 3% law)
80% had job offers within 6 months
210 organizations recruited on campus
4 Fulbright scholars

Financial Matters
$18,510 tuition and fees (1999–2000)
$6901 room and board
91% average percent of need met
$19,298 average financial aid amount received per undergraduate (1999–2000)

SOUTHWESTERN UNIVERSITY

SUBURBAN SETTING ■ PRIVATE ■ INDEPENDENT RELIGIOUS ■ COED
GEORGETOWN, TEXAS

Web site: www.southwestern.edu
Contact: Mr. John W. Lind, Vice President for Enrollment Management,
1001 East University Avenue, Georgetown, TX 78626
Telephone: 512-863-1200 or toll-free 800-252-3166 **Fax:** 512-863-9601
E-mail: admission@southwestern.edu

eAPPLY

Academics

SU awards bachelor's **degrees**. Challenging opportunities include advanced placement, accelerated degree programs, student-designed majors, freshman honors college, an honors program, double majors, independent study, a senior project, and Phi Beta Kappa. Special programs include internships, summer session for credit, and study-abroad.

The most frequently chosen fields are social sciences and history, biological/life sciences, and business/marketing. A complete listing of majors at SU appears in the Majors Index beginning on page 432.

The **faculty** at SU has 100 full-time members, 94% with terminal degrees. The student-faculty ratio is 11:1.

Students of SU

The student body is made up of 1,256 undergraduates. 58.1% are women and 41.9% are men. Students come from 35 states and territories. 90% are from Texas. 0.6% are international students. 2.7% are African American, 0.2% American Indian, 3.3% Asian American, and 9.4% Hispanic American. 88% returned for their sophomore year.

Facilities and Resources

Student rooms are linked to a campus network. 223 **computers** are available on campus that provide access to the Internet. The **library** has 288,010 books and 1,404 subscriptions.

Campus Life

There are 81 active organizations on campus, including a drama/theater group, newspaper, and choral group. 31% of eligible men and 32% of eligible women are members of national **fraternities** and national **sororities**.

SU is a member of the NCAA (Division III). **Intercollegiate sports** include baseball (m), basketball, cross-country running, golf, soccer, swimming, tennis, volleyball (w).

Campus Safety

Student safety services include late-night transport/escort service, 24-hour emergency telephone alarm devices, 24-hour patrols by trained security personnel, student patrols, and electronically operated dormitory entrances.

Applying

SU requires an essay, SAT I or ACT, a high school transcript, and 1 recommendation, and in some cases an interview. It recommends an interview. Application deadline: 2/15; 3/1 priority date for financial aid. Early and deferred admission are possible.

Southwestern University (SU) is a national liberal arts college recognized for a high-quality undergraduate academic program, professor-scholars who are committed to teaching, superior facilities, and a price that is lower than comparable institutions. Located just north of eclectic Austin, Texas, SU offers its 1,250 students a values-centered experience through a broad-based curriculum, preprofessional programs, and extensive extracurricular opportunities, such as internships, study abroad, and NCAA Division III competition. SU's facilities are outstanding among schools of its type. In the past 5 years, SU has built an $11.3-million campus center, a $6.8-million recreational activities center, a $6.8-million electronic academic building, a $4-million science hall addition, residence halls, on-campus apartments, and a $3.5-million fine arts addition.

Getting in Last Year
1,495 applied
67% were accepted
354 enrolled (36%)
58% from top tenth of their h.s. class
3.5 average high school GPA
61% had SAT verbal scores over 600
64% had SAT math scores over 600
84% had ACT scores over 24
19% had SAT verbal scores over 700
16% had SAT math scores over 700
24% had ACT scores over 30
10 National Merit Scholars
73 class presidents
21 valedictorians

Graduation and After
55% graduated in 4 years
13% graduated in 5 years
2% graduated in 6 years
31% pursued further study (8% medicine, 7% arts and sciences, 7% law)
63% had job offers within 6 months
23 organizations recruited on campus

Financial Matters
$15,750 tuition and fees (2000–2001)
$6320 room and board
98% average percent of need met
$14,024 average financial aid amount received per undergraduate (1999–2000 estimated)

eApply

Getting in Last Year
3,275 applied
53% were accepted
47% from top tenth of their h.s. class
3.2 average high school GPA
27% had SAT verbal scores over 600
14% had SAT math scores over 600
47% had ACT scores over 24
24% had ACT scores over 30
10 National Merit Scholars
52 class presidents

Graduation and After
38% pursued further study
1 Fulbright scholar

Financial Matters
$10,985 tuition and fees (1999–2000)
$6730 room and board

SPELMAN COLLEGE
URBAN SETTING ■ PRIVATE ■ INDEPENDENT ■ WOMEN ONLY
ATLANTA, GEORGIA

Web site: www.spelman.edu
Contact: Roxie M. Shabazz, Interim Director of Admissions and Orientation Services, 350 Spelman Lane, SW, Atlanta, GA 30314-4399
Telephone: 404-681-3643 ext. 2188 or toll-free 800-982-2411 (out-of-state)
Fax: 404-215-7788
E-mail: admiss@spelman.edu

Academics
Spelman awards bachelor's **degrees**. Challenging opportunities include advanced placement, accelerated degree programs, student-designed majors, an honors program, a senior project, and Phi Beta Kappa. Special programs include internships, off-campus study, study-abroad, and Army, Navy and Air Force ROTC. A complete listing of majors at Spelman appears in the Majors Index beginning on page 432.

The **faculty** at Spelman has 147 full-time members, 86% with terminal degrees. The student-faculty ratio is 14:1.

Students of Spelman
The student body is made up of 1,952 undergraduates. Students come from 45 states and territories and 21 other countries. 90% returned for their sophomore year.

Facilities and Resources
105 **computers** are available on campus that provide access to the Internet. The **library** has 404,991 books and 2,693 subscriptions.

Campus Life
Active organizations on campus include a drama/theater group, newspaper, and choral group. 15% of eligible undergraduates are members of national **sororities**.

Intercollegiate sports include basketball, tennis, track and field, volleyball.

Campus Safety
Student safety services include late-night transport/escort service, 24-hour emergency telephone alarm devices, 24-hour patrols by trained security personnel, and electronically operated dormitory entrances.

Applying
Spelman requires an essay, SAT I or ACT, a high school transcript, 2 recommendations, and a minimum high school GPA of 2.0, and in some cases an interview. Application deadline: 2/1. Early admission is possible.

STANFORD UNIVERSITY
SUBURBAN SETTING ■ PRIVATE ■ INDEPENDENT ■ COED
STANFORD, CALIFORNIA

Web site: www.stanford.edu
Contact: Mr. Robert M. Kinnally, Dean of Undergraduate Admissions and Financial Aid, Stanford, CA 94305-9991
Telephone: 650-723-2091 **Fax:** 650-725-2846
E-mail: undergrad.admissions@forsythe.stanford.edu

Academics
Stanford awards bachelor's, master's, doctoral, and first-professional **degrees**. Challenging opportunities include advanced placement, accelerated degree programs, student-designed majors, an honors program, a senior project, Phi Beta Kappa, and Sigma Xi. Special programs include internships, summer session for credit, off-campus study, study-abroad, and Army, Navy and Air Force ROTC.

The most frequently chosen fields are social sciences and history, engineering/engineering technologies, and interdisciplinary studies. A complete listing of majors at Stanford appears in the Majors Index beginning on page 432.

The **faculty** at Stanford has 1,608 full-time members, 98% with terminal degrees. The student-faculty ratio is 8:1.

Students of Stanford
The student body totals 18,083, of whom 7,784 are undergraduates. 51.2% are women and 48.8% are men. Students come from 52 states and territories and 55 other countries. 44% are from California. 4.7% are international students. 8.5% are African American, 1.2% American Indian, 24% Asian American, and 10.7% Hispanic American. 99% returned for their sophomore year.

Facilities and Resources
7,100 **computers** are available on campus that provide access to the Internet. The 18 **libraries** have 44,504 subscriptions.

Campus Life
There are 500 active organizations on campus, including a drama/theater group, newspaper, radio station, television station, choral group, and marching band. Stanford has national **fraternities**, national **sororities**, and eating clubs.

Stanford is a member of the NCAA (Division I) and NAIA. **Intercollegiate sports** (some offering scholarships) include baseball (m), basketball, crew, cross-country running, equestrian sports, fencing, field hockey, football (m), golf, gymnastics, ice hockey (m), lacrosse, racquetball, rugby, sailing, skiing (cross-country), skiing (downhill), soccer, softball (w), squash, swimming, tennis, track and field, volleyball, water polo, wrestling (m).

Campus Safety
Student safety services include late-night transport/escort service, 24-hour emergency telephone alarm devices, 24-hour patrols by trained security personnel, and electronically operated dormitory entrances.

Applying
Stanford requires an essay, SAT I or ACT, a high school transcript, and 2 recommendations. It recommends SAT II Subject Tests and SAT II: Writing Test. Application deadline: 12/15; 2/1 priority date for financial aid. Early and deferred admission are possible.

Getting in Last Year
17,919 applied
15% were accepted
1,749 enrolled (65%)
88% from top tenth of their h.s. class
3.90 average high school GPA
94% had SAT verbal scores over 600
96% had SAT math scores over 600
89% had ACT scores over 24
67% had SAT verbal scores over 700
71% had SAT math scores over 700
60% had ACT scores over 30

Graduation and After
450 organizations recruited on campus
2 Marshall, 8 Fulbright scholars

Financial Matters
$23,058 tuition and fees (1999–2000)
$7881 room and board
99% average percent of need met
$20,926 average financial aid amount received per undergraduate (1998–99)

STATE UNIVERSITY OF NEW YORK AT ALBANY

SUBURBAN SETTING ■ PUBLIC ■ STATE-SUPPORTED ■ COED
ALBANY, NEW YORK

Web site: www.albany.edu
Contact: Mr. Harry Wood, Director of Undergraduate Admissions, 1400
  Washington Avenue, Albany, NY 12222-0001
Telephone: 518-442-5435
E-mail: ugadmit@safnet.albany.edu

Getting in Last Year
15,312 applied
61% were accepted
2,282 enrolled (24%)
12% from top tenth of their h.s. class
25% had SAT verbal scores over 600
32% had SAT math scores over 600
3% had SAT verbal scores over 700
4% had SAT math scores over 700
3 valedictorians

Graduation and After
52% graduated in 4 years
13% graduated in 5 years
1% graduated in 6 years
45% pursued further study (21% arts and
  sciences, 9% law, 6% business)
120 organizations recruited on campus
1 Fulbright scholar

Financial Matters
$4338 resident tuition and fees (1999–2000)
$9238 nonresident tuition and fees (1999–
  2000)
$5828 room and board
74% average percent of need met
$6962 average financial aid amount received
  per undergraduate (1999–2000)

Academics

University at Albany awards bachelor's, master's, and doctoral **degrees** and post-master's certificates. Challenging opportunities include advanced placement, student-designed majors, freshman honors college, an honors program, double majors, independent study, a senior project, Phi Beta Kappa, and Sigma Xi. Special programs include internships, summer session for credit, off-campus study, study-abroad, and Army and Air Force ROTC.

The most frequently chosen fields are social sciences and history, business/marketing, and psychology. A complete listing of majors at University at Albany appears in the Majors Index beginning on page 432.

The **faculty** at University at Albany has 590 full-time members. The student-faculty ratio is 18:1.

Students of University at Albany

The student body totals 16,901, of whom 11,737 are undergraduates. 49% are women and 51% are men. Students come from 38 states and territories and 36 other countries. 67% are from New York. 1.2% are international students. 9.2% are African American, 0.3% American Indian, 7.6% Asian American, and 6.4% Hispanic American. 83% returned for their sophomore year.

Facilities and Resources

Student rooms are linked to a campus network. 500 **computers** are available on campus that provide access to the Internet. The 2 **libraries** have 1,106,578 books and 16,103 subscriptions.

Campus Life

There are 160 active organizations on campus, including a drama/theater group, newspaper, radio station, and choral group. 15% of eligible men and 15% of eligible women are members of national **fraternities**, national **sororities**, local fraternities, and local sororities.

University at Albany is a member of the NCAA (Division I). **Intercollegiate sports** (some offering scholarships) include baseball (m), basketball, crew, cross-country running, field hockey (w), football (m), golf (w), lacrosse, rugby, soccer, softball (w), tennis (w), track and field, volleyball (w).

Campus Safety

Student safety services include late-night transport/escort service, 24-hour emergency telephone alarm devices, 24-hour patrols by trained security personnel, and electronically operated dormitory entrances.

Applying

University at Albany requires SAT I or ACT and a high school transcript, and in some cases portfolio, audition. It recommends an essay. Application deadline: 3/1; 3/15 priority date for financial aid. Early and deferred admission are possible.

STATE UNIVERSITY OF NEW YORK AT BINGHAMTON

SUBURBAN SETTING ■ PUBLIC ■ STATE-SUPPORTED ■ COED
BINGHAMTON, NEW YORK

Web site: www.binghamton.edu
Contact: Mr. Geoffrey D. Gould, Director of Admissions, PO Box 6001,
    Binghamton, NY 13902-6001
Telephone: 607-777-2171 **Fax:** 607-777-4445
E-mail: admit@binghamton.edu

Academics

Binghamton University awards bachelor's, master's, and doctoral **degrees** and post-master's certificates. Challenging opportunities include advanced placement, accelerated degree programs, student-designed majors, an honors program, double majors, independent study, a senior project, and Phi Beta Kappa. Special programs include internships, summer session for credit, off-campus study, study-abroad, and Air Force ROTC.

The most frequently chosen fields are social sciences and history, business/marketing, and psychology. A complete listing of majors at Binghamton University appears in the Majors Index beginning on page 432.

The **faculty** at Binghamton University has 510 full-time members, 95% with terminal degrees. The student-faculty ratio is 18:1.

Students of Binghamton University

The student body totals 12,564, of whom 9,872 are undergraduates. 53.2% are women and 46.8% are men. Students come from 33 states and territories and 43 other countries. 96% are from New York. 1.7% are international students. 5.5% are African American, 0.2% American Indian, 17.1% Asian American, and 5.6% Hispanic American. 91% returned for their sophomore year.

Facilities and Resources

Student rooms are linked to a campus network. 4,000 **computers** are available on campus that provide access to the Internet. The 2 **libraries** have 1,632,194 books and 7,265 subscriptions.

Campus Life

There are 156 active organizations on campus, including a drama/theater group, newspaper, radio station, television station, and choral group. 18% of eligible men and 14% of eligible women are members of national **fraternities**, national **sororities**, local fraternities, and local sororities.

Binghamton University is a member of the NCAA (Division II). **Intercollegiate sports** (some offering scholarships) include badminton, baseball (m), basketball, bowling, crew, cross-country running, equestrian sports, fencing, golf (m), ice hockey (m), lacrosse, racquetball, rugby, skiing (downhill), soccer, softball (w), swimming, table tennis, tennis, track and field, volleyball, wrestling (m).

Campus Safety

Student safety services include safety awareness programs, well-lit campus, self-defense education, secured campus entrance 12 a.m.-5 a.m., emergency telephones, late-night transport/escort service, 24-hour emergency telephone alarm devices, 24-hour patrols by trained security personnel, student patrols, and electronically operated dormitory entrances.

Applying

Binghamton University requires an essay, SAT I or ACT, and a high school transcript, and in some cases 1 recommendation and portfolio, audition. Application deadline: rolling admissions; 3/1 priority date for financial aid. Early and deferred admission are possible.

Binghamton University, the "Crown Jewel" of the SUNY system, combines academic excellence with affordability. Binghamton's 80 challenging majors and innovative interdisciplinary programs attract high-achieving students. Its accessible faculty members are dedicated teachers who are engaged in research and development. Professors strongly encourage their students to go beyond the textbook and participate in hands-on, experiential learning. Students are offered a vast array of opportunities for personal growth, including internships, honors programs, study-abroad options, more than 150 clubs and organizations, residential communities with special-interest housing, and Division II athletics. Binghamton University offers students affordable excellence and the foundation to develop what they need to succeed in today's global society.

Getting in Last Year
16,386 applied
42% were accepted
2,050 enrolled (30%)
50% from top tenth of their h.s. class
3.6 average high school GPA
47% had SAT verbal scores over 600
62% had SAT math scores over 600
7% had SAT verbal scores over 700
14% had SAT math scores over 700
18 valedictorians

Graduation and After
72% graduated in 4 years
10% graduated in 5 years
1% graduated in 6 years
38% pursued further study (15% arts and sciences, 6% law, 4% medicine)
200 organizations recruited on campus
2 Fulbright scholars

Financial Matters
$4416 resident tuition and fees (1999–2000)
$9316 nonresident tuition and fees (1999–2000)
$5516 room and board
100% average percent of need met
$9573 average financial aid amount received per undergraduate (1999–2000)

STATE UNIVERSITY OF NEW YORK AT BUFFALO

SUBURBAN SETTING ■ PUBLIC ■ STATE-SUPPORTED ■ COED
BUFFALO, NEW YORK

Web site: www.buffalo.edu
Contact: Ms. Regina Toomey, Director of Admissions, Capen Hall, Room 17,
North Campus, Buffalo, NY 14260-1660
Telephone: 716-645-6900 **Fax:** 716-645-6411
E-mail: ubadmissions@admissions.buffalo.edu

S tudents are invited to learn more about the University at Buffalo, New York's premier public research university—an academic community in which undergraduates can explore an exceptional range of possible futures with faculty members working on the cutting edge in their fields. UB offers the most comprehensive selection of undergraduate and graduate programs in the State University of New York System. In a community of student and faculty scholars, students are encouraged to explore the possibilities among extensive programs in architecture, arts and letters, engineering, health sciences, management, medicine and biomedical sciences, natural sciences and mathematics, nursing, and pharmacy.

Getting in Last Year
14,836 applied
74% were accepted
3,223 enrolled (29%)
18% from top tenth of their h.s. class
3.10 average high school GPA
26% had SAT verbal scores over 600
37% had SAT math scores over 600
54% had ACT scores over 24
4% had SAT verbal scores over 700
7% had SAT math scores over 700
8% had ACT scores over 30

Graduation and After
32% graduated in 4 years
23% graduated in 5 years
4% graduated in 6 years
4 Fulbright scholars

Financial Matters
$4655 resident tuition and fees (1999–2000)
$9555 nonresident tuition and fees (1999–2000)
$5904 room and board
70% average percent of need met
$5940 average financial aid amount received per undergraduate (1999–2000 estimated)

Academics

UB awards bachelor's, master's, doctoral, and first-professional **degrees** and post-master's certificates. Challenging opportunities include advanced placement, student-designed majors, freshman honors college, an honors program, double majors, independent study, a senior project, Phi Beta Kappa, and Sigma Xi. Special programs include internships, summer session for credit, off-campus study, study-abroad, and Army ROTC.

The most frequently chosen fields are business/marketing, health professions and related sciences, and social sciences and history. A complete listing of majors at UB appears in the Majors Index beginning on page 432.

The **faculty** at UB has 1,211 full-time members, 98% with terminal degrees. The student-faculty ratio is 13:1.

Students of UB

The student body totals 24,257, of whom 16,259 are undergraduates. 46.9% are women and 53.1% are men. Students come from 36 states and territories and 66 other countries. 98% are from New York. 3.5% are international students. 8.5% are African American, 0.6% American Indian, 10.7% Asian American, and 3.6% Hispanic American. 84% returned for their sophomore year.

Facilities and Resources

Student rooms are linked to a campus network. 1,800 **computers** are available on campus that provide access to the Internet. The 8 **libraries** have 3,106,748 books and 21,262 subscriptions.

Campus Life

There are 150 active organizations on campus, including a drama/theater group, newspaper, radio station, television station, choral group, and marching band. 1% of eligible men and 1% of eligible women are members of national **fraternities**, national **sororities**, local fraternities, and local sororities.

UB is a member of the NCAA (Division I). **Intercollegiate sports** (some offering scholarships) include baseball (m), basketball, crew (w), cross-country running, football (m), soccer, softball (w), swimming, tennis, track and field, volleyball (w), wrestling (m).

Campus Safety

Student safety services include self-defense programs, awareness programs, late-night transport/escort service, 24-hour emergency telephone alarm devices, 24-hour patrols by trained security personnel, student patrols, and electronically operated dormitory entrances.

Applying

UB requires SAT I or ACT and a high school transcript, and in some cases recommendations and portfolio, audition. Application deadline: rolling admissions; 3/1 priority date for financial aid. Early admission is possible.

STATE UNIVERSITY OF NEW YORK COLLEGE AT GENESEO

SMALL-TOWN SETTING ■ PUBLIC ■ STATE-SUPPORTED ■ COED
GENESEO, NEW YORK

Web site: www.geneseo.edu
Contact: Mr. Scott Hooker, Director of Admissions, 1 College Circle, Geneseo, NY 14454-1401
Telephone: 716-245-5571 **Fax:** 716-245-5550
E-mail: admissions@geneseo.edu

Academics

Geneseo College awards bachelor's and master's **degrees**. Challenging opportunities include advanced placement, an honors program, double majors, independent study, and a senior project. Special programs include internships, summer session for credit, off-campus study, study-abroad, and Army and Air Force ROTC.

The most frequently chosen fields are education, social sciences and history, and business/marketing. A complete listing of majors at Geneseo College appears in the Majors Index beginning on page 432.

The **faculty** at Geneseo College has 255 full-time members, 86% with terminal degrees. The student-faculty ratio is 19:1.

Students of Geneseo College

The student body totals 5,604, of whom 5,322 are undergraduates. 66% are women and 34% are men. Students come from 18 states and territories and 9 other countries. 98% are from New York. 0.2% are international students. 1.8% are African American, 0.3% American Indian, 4% Asian American, and 3% Hispanic American. 92% returned for their sophomore year.

Facilities and Resources

Student rooms are linked to a campus network. 700 **computers** are available on campus that provide access to the Internet. The 2 **libraries** have 493,299 books and 3,117 subscriptions.

Campus Life

There are 157 active organizations on campus, including a drama/theater group, newspaper, radio station, television station, and choral group. 10% of eligible men and 10% of eligible women are members of national **fraternities**, national **sororities**, local fraternities, and local sororities.

Geneseo College is a member of the NCAA (Division III). **Intercollegiate sports** include basketball, crew, cross-country running, equestrian sports, field hockey (w), ice hockey (m), lacrosse, racquetball, rugby, sailing, soccer, softball (w), squash, swimming, tennis (w), track and field, volleyball.

Campus Safety

Student safety services include late-night transport/escort service, 24-hour emergency telephone alarm devices, 24-hour patrols by trained security personnel, student patrols, and electronically operated dormitory entrances.

Applying

Geneseo College requires an essay, SAT I or ACT, and a high school transcript. It recommends an interview and recommendations. Application deadline: 2/15; 2/15 priority date for financial aid. Early and deferred admission are possible.

The *New York Times* cited Geneseo as "one of the nation's most selective, highly regarded colleges." This reputation is derived not only from the extraordinarily able students who enroll but also from the College's total dedication to a single mission: teaching undergraduates. Geneseo offers a personal atmosphere in which students, faculty, and staff are concerned about each other. Students have the opportunity to study with others who have demonstrated a seriousness of purpose and a high level of academic achievement. The Geneseo experience is created by a collegiate environment, small size, excellent curricular offerings, and idyllic location.

Getting in Last Year

7,974 applied
52% were accepted
1,169 enrolled (28%)
44% from top tenth of their h.s. class
3.62 average high school GPA
50% had SAT verbal scores over 600
54% had SAT math scores over 600
96% had ACT scores over 24
7% had SAT verbal scores over 700
5% had SAT math scores over 700
10% had ACT scores over 30

Graduation and After

64% graduated in 4 years
12% graduated in 5 years
1% graduated in 6 years
Graduates pursuing further study: 17% arts and sciences, 3% education, 2% law
54% had job offers within 6 months
40 organizations recruited on campus
2 Fulbright scholars

Financial Matters

$4221 resident tuition and fees (1999–2000)
$9121 nonresident tuition and fees (1999–2000)
$4940 room and board
85% average percent of need met
$6730 average financial aid amount received per undergraduate (1999–2000 estimated)

Getting in Last Year
587 applied
50% were accepted
142 enrolled (48%)
31% from top tenth of their h.s. class
3.64 average high school GPA
41% had SAT verbal scores over 600
43% had SAT math scores over 600
73% had ACT scores over 24
6% had SAT verbal scores over 700
5% had SAT math scores over 700
14% had ACT scores over 30
3 class presidents
4 valedictorians

Graduation and After
21% pursued further study (13% arts and sciences, 2% education, 2% engineering)
73% had job offers within 6 months
25 organizations recruited on campus

Financial Matters
$3762 resident tuition and fees (1999–2000)
$8662 nonresident tuition and fees (1999–2000)
$7370 room and board
85% average percent of need met
$8456 average financial aid amount received per undergraduate (1998–99)

STATE UNIVERSITY OF NEW YORK COLLEGE OF ENVIRONMENTAL SCIENCE AND FORESTRY

URBAN SETTING ■ PUBLIC ■ STATE-SUPPORTED ■ COED
SYRACUSE, NEW YORK

Web site: www.esf.edu
Contact: Ms. Susan Sanford, Director of Admissions, 1 Forestry Drive, Syracuse, NY 13210-2779
Telephone: 315-470-6600 or toll-free 800-777-7373 **Fax:** 315-470-6933
E-mail: esfinfo@1mailbox.syr.edu

Academics
ESF awards bachelor's, master's, and doctoral **degrees**. Challenging opportunities include advanced placement, an honors program, and a senior project. Special programs include internships, off-campus study, and Army and Air Force ROTC. A complete listing of majors at ESF appears in the Majors Index beginning on page 432.

The **faculty** at ESF has 114 full-time members.

Students of ESF
The student body totals 1,729, of whom 1,171 are undergraduates. 37% are women and 63% are men. Students come from 18 states and territories and 7 other countries. 93% are from New York. 0.7% are international students. 3% are African American, 0.3% American Indian, 1.3% Asian American, and 1.7% Hispanic American. 91% returned for their sophomore year.

Facilities and Resources
Student rooms are linked to a campus network. 150 **computers** are available on campus that provide access to the Internet. The 2 **libraries** have 122,377 books.

Campus Life
There are 300 active organizations on campus, including a drama/theater group, newspaper, radio station, choral group, and marching band. 10% of eligible men and 10% of eligible women are members of national **fraternities** and national **sororities**.

This institution has no intercollegiate sports.

Campus Safety
Student safety services include late-night transport/escort service, 24-hour emergency telephone alarm devices, and 24-hour patrols by trained security personnel.

Applying
ESF requires an essay, SAT I or ACT, a high school transcript, inventory of courses-in-progress form, and a minimum high school GPA of 3.3. It recommends an interview and 3 recommendations. Application deadline: rolling admissions; 3/1 priority date for financial aid. Early and deferred admission are possible.

STATE UNIVERSITY OF NEW YORK MARITIME COLLEGE

SUBURBAN SETTING ■ PUBLIC ■ STATE-SUPPORTED ■ COED
THROGGS NECK, NEW YORK

Web site: www.sunymaritime.edu
Contact: Ms. Deidre Whitman, Vice President of Enrollment and Campus Life, 6 Pennyfield Avenue, Fort Schuyler, Throggs Neck, NY 10465-4198
Telephone: 718-409-7220 ext. 7222 or toll-free 800-654-1874 (in-state), 800-642-1874 (out-of-state) **Fax:** 718-409-7465
E-mail: admissions@sunymaritime.edu

Academics
Maritime College awards associate, bachelor's, and master's **degrees**. Challenging opportunities include advanced placement, student-designed majors, independent study, and a senior project. Special programs include cooperative education, internships, summer session for credit, and Navy and Air Force ROTC. A complete listing of majors at Maritime College appears in the Majors Index beginning on page 432.

Students of Maritime College
The student body totals 829, of whom 666 are undergraduates. Students come from 23 states and territories and 15 other countries. 76% are from New York. 5% are international students. 7.1% are African American, 0.2% American Indian, 4.4% Asian American, and 7.4% Hispanic American. 84% returned for their sophomore year.

Facilities and Resources
Student rooms are linked to a campus network. 85 **computers** are available on campus that provide access to the Internet. The **library** has 69,593 books and 2,043 subscriptions.

Campus Life
There are 35 active organizations on campus, including a newspaper and marching band. 4% of eligible men are members of local **fraternities**.
Maritime College is a member of the NCAA (Division III). **Intercollegiate sports** include baseball (m), basketball, crew, cross-country running, ice hockey (m), lacrosse (m), riflery, sailing, soccer (m), softball (w), swimming, tennis, volleyball (w), wrestling (m).

Campus Safety
Student safety services include late-night transport/escort service, 24-hour emergency telephone alarm devices, 24-hour patrols by trained security personnel, and student patrols.

Applying
Maritime College requires SAT I or ACT, a high school transcript, 1 recommendation, medical history, and a minimum high school GPA of 2.5. It recommends an essay, SAT II Subject Tests, and an interview. Application deadline: rolling admissions; 2/15 priority date for financial aid. Early and deferred admission are possible.

M aritime graduates may pursue on-shore careers in industry, government service, or the professions; careers at sea as civilian officers in the Merchant Marine; or careers in the Navy, Marine Corps, Coast Guard, Air Force, or NOAA. The College offers BS or BE degrees in engineering, business administration/marine transportation, naval architecture, marine environmental science, and a humanities concentration. The annual 2-month Summer Sea Term aboard the training ship *Empire State* provides hands-on training to cadets who, under supervision, assume responsibility for the ship's operation in preparation for the U.S. Merchant Marine Officer's license. Graduates have a 100% job placement rate within 3 months of graduation in maritime and related industries.

Getting in Last Year
663 applied
31% were accepted
156 enrolled (75%)
3% from top tenth of their h.s. class
2.90 average high school GPA
12% had SAT verbal scores over 600
19% had SAT math scores over 600
1% had SAT verbal scores over 700
1% had SAT math scores over 700

Graduation and After
55% graduated in 4 years
45% graduated in 5 years
4% pursued further study (2% business, 2% engineering)
100% had job offers within 6 months
30 organizations recruited on campus

Financial Matters
$4195 resident tuition and fees (1999–2000)
$9095 nonresident tuition and fees (1999–2000)
$5600 room and board
85% average percent of need met
$10,000 average financial aid amount received per undergraduate (1998–99)

Getting in Last Year
1,913 applied
80% were accepted
550 enrolled (36%)
30% from top tenth of their h.s. class
3.54 average high school GPA
32% had SAT verbal scores over 600
32% had SAT math scores over 600
7% had SAT verbal scores over 700
5% had SAT math scores over 700
8 valedictorians

Graduation and After
46% graduated in 4 years
11% graduated in 5 years
2% graduated in 6 years
Graduates pursuing further study: **19%** arts and sciences, **11%** business, **6%** law
50 organizations recruited on campus

Financial Matters
$18,385 tuition and fees (2000–2001 estimated)
$6070 room and board
86% average percent of need met
$17,540 average financial aid amount received per undergraduate (1999–2000)

STETSON UNIVERSITY
SMALL-TOWN SETTING ■ PRIVATE ■ INDEPENDENT ■ COED
DeLAND, FLORIDA

Web site: www.stetson.edu
Contact: Ms. Mary Napier, Dean of Admissions, 421 North Woodland Boulevard, DeLand, FL 32720-3781
Telephone: 904-822-7100 or toll-free 800-688-0101 **Fax:** 904-822-8832
E-mail: admissions@stetson.edu

Academics
Stetson awards bachelor's, master's, and first-professional **degrees** and post-master's certificates. Challenging opportunities include advanced placement, accelerated degree programs, student-designed majors, an honors program, double majors, independent study, a senior project, and Phi Beta Kappa. Special programs include internships, summer session for credit, off-campus study, study-abroad, and Army ROTC.

The most frequently chosen fields are business/marketing, education, and social sciences and history. A complete listing of majors at Stetson appears in the Majors Index beginning on page 432.

The **faculty** at Stetson has 181 full-time members. The student-faculty ratio is 10:1.

Students of Stetson
The student body totals 3,053, of whom 2,062 are undergraduates. 58.1% are women and 41.9% are men. Students come from 42 states and territories and 55 other countries. 80% are from Florida. 7.1% are international students. 3.5% are African American, 0.4% American Indian, 1.5% Asian American, and 4.8% Hispanic American. 81% returned for their sophomore year.

Facilities and Resources
Student rooms are linked to a campus network. 143 **computers** are available on campus that provide access to the Internet. The 3 **libraries** have 324,000 books and 1,392 subscriptions.

Campus Life
There are 90 active organizations on campus, including a drama/theater group, newspaper, radio station, and choral group. 33% of eligible men and 29% of eligible women are members of national **fraternities** and national **sororities**.

Stetson is a member of the NCAA (Division I). **Intercollegiate sports** (some offering scholarships) include baseball (m), basketball, crew, cross-country running, golf, soccer, softball (w), tennis, volleyball (w).

Campus Safety
Student safety services include late-night transport/escort service, 24-hour emergency telephone alarm devices, and 24-hour patrols by trained security personnel.

Applying
Stetson requires an essay, SAT I or ACT, a high school transcript, and recommendations. It recommends SAT II Subject Tests and an interview. Application deadline: 3/15; 4/15 priority date for financial aid. Early admission is possible.

Stevens Institute of Technology

Urban setting ■ Private ■ Independent ■ Coed
Hoboken, New Jersey

Web site: www.stevens-tech.edu
Contact: Mr. Daniel Gallagher, Director of Undergraduate Admissions, Castle Point on Hudson, Hoboken, NJ 07030
Telephone: 201-216-5197 or toll-free 800-458-5323 **Fax:** 201-216-8348
E-mail: admissions@stevens-tech.edu

eApply

Academics
Stevens awards bachelor's, master's, and doctoral **degrees** and post-bachelor's certificates. Challenging opportunities include advanced placement, accelerated degree programs, an honors program, double majors, independent study, a senior project, and Sigma Xi. Special programs include cooperative education, internships, summer session for credit, off-campus study, study-abroad, and Army and Air Force ROTC.

The most frequently chosen fields are engineering/engineering technologies, computer/information sciences, and biological/life sciences. A complete listing of majors at Stevens appears in the Majors Index beginning on page 432.

The **faculty** at Stevens has 102 full-time members, 100% with terminal degrees. The student-faculty ratio is 9:1.

Students of Stevens
The student body totals 3,467, of whom 1,564 are undergraduates. 22.6% are women and 77.4% are men. Students come from 34 states and territories and 50 other countries. 70% are from New Jersey. 7.9% are international students. 4.6% are African American, 0.3% American Indian, 21.7% Asian American, and 12.1% Hispanic American. 87% returned for their sophomore year.

Facilities and Resources
Student rooms are linked to a campus network. 1,700 **computers** are available on campus that provide access to the Internet. The **library** has 57,671 books and 145 subscriptions.

Campus Life
There are 70 active organizations on campus, including a drama/theater group, newspaper, radio station, television station, and choral group. 30% of eligible men and 33% of eligible women are members of national **fraternities**, national **sororities**, and local sororities.

Stevens is a member of the NCAA (Division III). **Intercollegiate sports** include baseball (m), basketball, cross-country running, fencing, golf, lacrosse, sailing, skiing (downhill), soccer, swimming (w), tennis, track and field, volleyball.

Campus Safety
Student safety services include late-night transport/escort service, 24-hour emergency telephone alarm devices, 24-hour patrols by trained security personnel, and electronically operated dormitory entrances.

Applying
Stevens requires SAT I or ACT, a high school transcript, and an interview, and in some cases SAT II Subject Tests, SAT II: Writing Test, and SAT I and SAT II or ACT. It recommends an essay, SAT II Subject Tests, SAT II: Writing Test, and recommendations. Application deadline: 3/1; 2/15 priority date for financial aid. Early and deferred admission are possible.

Stevens ranks in the top 5% among the nation's technological universities as it continues to educate future leaders and innovators. Each undergraduate program—business, engineering, science, computer science, and the humanities—follows a broad-based course curriculum taught by distinguished faculty members. The 9:1 student-faculty ratio enables personal attention and growth. Students can combine their classroom and laboratory experience with cooperative education, internships, or research opportunities to enhance their prestigious Stevens education. Located in one of America's most desirable towns, Hoboken, New Jersey, Stevens is just minutes from New York City.

Getting in Last Year
1,894 applied
59% were accepted
372 enrolled (33%)
53% from top tenth of their h.s. class
3.7 average high school GPA
49% had SAT verbal scores over 600
82% had SAT math scores over 600
11% had SAT verbal scores over 700
29% had SAT math scores over 700

Graduation and After
21% pursued further study
90% had job offers within 6 months
350 organizations recruited on campus

Financial Matters
$21,140 tuition and fees (1999–2000)
$7280 room and board
97% average percent of need met
$19,815 average financial aid amount received per undergraduate (1999–2000 estimated)

SUSQUEHANNA UNIVERSITY
SMALL-TOWN SETTING ■ PRIVATE ■ INDEPENDENT RELIGIOUS ■ COED
SELINSGROVE, PENNSYLVANIA

Web site: www.susqu.edu
Contact: Mr. Chris Markle, Director of Admissions, 514 University Avenue, Selinsgrove, PA 17870-1040
Telephone: 570-372-4260 or toll-free 800-326-9672 **Fax:** 570-372-2722
E-mail: suadmiss@susqu.edu

With the qualities of both a residential college and a challenging university, Susquehanna University offers a liberal arts curriculum that builds a broad base of knowledge to help students become educated citizens of the world. It also offers the in-depth preparation students need to succeed in graduate and professional schools and jobs. Faculty members are credentialed and accessible to students. Advising helps students discover their interests and strengths, and the academic program develops students' intellectual skills, self-confidence, and desire for learning. Students benefit from professional experiences in joint research programs with faculty members, extensive internship opportunities, study abroad, award-winning community service programs, and leadership opportunities in all areas of the University. The campus is wired, with Internet access from every residence hall room.

Getting in Last Year
2,143 applied
75% were accepted
464 enrolled (29%)
27% from top tenth of their h.s. class
36% had SAT verbal scores over 600
37% had SAT math scores over 600
5% had SAT verbal scores over 700
6% had SAT math scores over 700
1 National Merit Scholar
15 class presidents
4 valedictorians

Graduation and After
67% graduated in 4 years
4% graduated in 5 years
24% pursued further study (13% arts and sciences, 3% law, 2% business)
76% had job offers within 6 months
38 organizations recruited on campus

Financial Matters
$19,670 tuition and fees (1999–2000)
$5550 room and board
91% average percent of need met
$16,518 average financial aid amount received per undergraduate (1999–2000)

Academics
Susquehanna awards bachelor's **degrees** (also offers associate degree through evening program to local students). Challenging opportunities include advanced placement, accelerated degree programs, student-designed majors, an honors program, double majors, independent study, and a senior project. Special programs include internships, summer session for credit, off-campus study, study-abroad, and Army ROTC.

The most frequently chosen fields are business/marketing, communications/communication technologies, and social sciences and history. A complete listing of majors at Susquehanna appears in the Majors Index beginning on page 432.

The **faculty** at Susquehanna has 97 full-time members, 89% with terminal degrees. The student-faculty ratio is 14:1.

Students of Susquehanna
The student body is made up of 1,772 undergraduates. 57.6% are women and 42.4% are men. Students come from 28 states and territories. 60% are from Pennsylvania. 0.7% are international students. 2.4% are African American, 0.3% American Indian, 1.7% Asian American, and 2.4% Hispanic American. 86% returned for their sophomore year.

Facilities and Resources
Student rooms are linked to a campus network. 125 **computers** are available on campus that provide access to the Internet. The 2 **libraries** have 252,000 books and 2,176 subscriptions.

Campus Life
There are 100 active organizations on campus, including a drama/theater group, newspaper, radio station, and choral group. 25% of eligible men and 25% of eligible women are members of national **fraternities** and national **sororities**.

Susquehanna is a member of the NCAA (Division III). **Intercollegiate sports** include baseball (m), basketball, crew, cross-country running, field hockey (w), football (m), golf (m), lacrosse, rugby, soccer, softball (w), swimming, tennis, track and field, volleyball.

Campus Safety
Student safety services include late-night transport/escort service, 24-hour patrols by trained security personnel, and electronically operated dormitory entrances.

Applying
Susquehanna requires an essay, a high school transcript, 1 recommendation, and a minimum high school GPA of 2.5, and in some cases SAT I or ACT and writing portfolio. It recommends SAT II Subject Tests, SAT II: Writing Test, an interview, and a minimum high school GPA of 3.0. Application deadline: 3/1; 3/1 priority date for financial aid. Early and deferred admission are possible.

Swarthmore College

SUBURBAN SETTING ■ PRIVATE ■ INDEPENDENT ■ COED
SWARTHMORE, PENNSYLVANIA

Web site: www.swarthmore.edu
Contact: Office of Admissions, 500 College Avenue, Swarthmore, PA
 19081-1397
Telephone: 610-328-8300 or toll-free 800-667-3110 **Fax:** 610-328-8582
E-mail: admissions@swarthmore.edu

  eAPPLY

Academics

Swarthmore awards bachelor's **degrees**. Challenging opportunities include advanced placement, student-designed majors, an honors program, double majors, independent study, a senior project, Phi Beta Kappa, and Sigma Xi. Special programs include internships, off-campus study, study-abroad, and Army, Navy and Air Force ROTC.

The most frequently chosen fields are social sciences and history, biological/life sciences, and English. A complete listing of majors at Swarthmore appears in the Majors Index beginning on page 432.

The **faculty** at Swarthmore has 166 full-time members, 96% with terminal degrees. The student-faculty ratio is 8:1.

Students of Swarthmore

The student body is made up of 1,467 undergraduates. 52.6% are women and 47.4% are men. Students come from 50 states and territories and 43 other countries. 18% are from Pennsylvania. 7.1% are international students. 8.9% are African American, 0.6% American Indian, 13.5% Asian American, and 9.3% Hispanic American. 95% returned for their sophomore year.

Facilities and Resources

Student rooms are linked to a campus network. 160 **computers** are available on campus that provide access to the Internet. The 5 **libraries** have 1,000,000 books and 6,407 subscriptions.

Campus Life

There are 100 active organizations on campus, including a drama/theater group, newspaper, radio station, and choral group. 4% of eligible men are members of national **fraternities** and local fraternities.

Swarthmore is a member of the NCAA (Division III). **Intercollegiate sports** include badminton, baseball (m), basketball, cross-country running, field hockey (w), football (m), golf (m), lacrosse, rugby, soccer, softball (w), swimming, tennis, track and field, volleyball (w), wrestling (m).

Campus Safety

Student safety services include late-night transport/escort service, 24-hour emergency telephone alarm devices, 24-hour patrols by trained security personnel, and student patrols.

Applying

Swarthmore requires an essay, SAT II Subject Tests, SAT II: Writing Test, SAT I or ACT, a high school transcript, and 2 recommendations, and in some cases SAT II subject test in math. It recommends an interview. Application deadline: 1/1; 2/15 priority date for financial aid. Early and deferred admission are possible.

Swarthmore is a selective college of liberal arts and engineering, located 11 miles southwest of Philadelphia. Founded as a coeducational institution in 1864, it is nonsectarian but reflects many traditions and values of its Quaker founders. Swarthmore's Honors Program provides an option to study in small seminars during the junior and senior years. The campus occupies more than 330 acres of woodland and is officially designated an arboretum. A small school by deliberate policy, its enrollment is about 1,400, with a student-faculty ratio of about 8:1. It attracts students from 50 states and 43 other countries.

Getting in Last Year
4,163 applied
22% were accepted
368 enrolled (41%)
82% from top tenth of their h.s. class
92% had SAT verbal scores over 600
91% had SAT math scores over 600
60% had SAT verbal scores over 700
56% had SAT math scores over 700
32 National Merit Scholars
56 valedictorians

Graduation and After
81% graduated in 4 years
10% graduated in 5 years
1% graduated in 6 years
19% pursued further study (11% arts and
 sciences, 5% law, 2% medicine)
99 organizations recruited on campus
1 Rhodes, 7 Fulbright scholars

Financial Matters
$24,190 tuition and fees (1999–2000)
$7500 room and board
100% average percent of need met
$23,515 average financial aid amount received
 per undergraduate (1999–2000 estimated)

SWEET BRIAR COLLEGE

RURAL SETTING ■ PRIVATE ■ INDEPENDENT ■ WOMEN ONLY
SWEET BRIAR, VIRGINIA

Web site: www.sbc.edu
Contact: Ms. Nancy E. Church, Dean of Admissions, PO Box B, Sweet Briar, VA 24595
Telephone: 804-381-6142 or toll-free 800-381-6142 **Fax:** 804-381-6152
E-mail: admissions@sbc.edu

Sweet Briar women take charge and revel in their accomplishments. This attitude helps graduates compete confidently in graduate school and in the corporate world as scientists and writers, lawyers and judges, and dancers and art historians. Sweet Briar attracts women who enjoy being involved not only in a first-rate academic program but also in meaningful activities outside the classroom. A hands-on, one-on-one approach to the sciences, a 4-year honors program, and superior study-abroad programs encourage bright students to excel. Sweet Briar students are taken seriously, and professors take an interest in their intellectual development and personal growth.

Getting in Last Year
499 applied
89% were accepted
188 enrolled (42%)
26% from top tenth of their h.s. class
3.36 average high school GPA
40% had SAT verbal scores over 600
19% had SAT math scores over 600
57% had ACT scores over 24
8% had SAT verbal scores over 700
3% had SAT math scores over 700
11% had ACT scores over 30
1 class president
5 valedictorians

Graduation and After
Graduates pursuing further study: 14% arts
  and sciences, 2% law, 2% medicine
67% had job offers within 6 months
13 organizations recruited on campus

Financial Matters
$17,150 tuition and fees (2000–2001
  estimated)
$7000 room and board
86% average percent of need met
$14,621 average financial aid amount received
  per undergraduate (1999–2000)

Academics
Sweet Briar awards bachelor's **degrees**. Challenging opportunities include advanced placement, accelerated degree programs, student-designed majors, an honors program, double majors, independent study, a senior project, and Phi Beta Kappa. Special programs include internships, off-campus study, and study-abroad.

The most frequently chosen fields are social sciences and history, psychology, and English. A complete listing of majors at Sweet Briar appears in the Majors Index beginning on page 432.

The **faculty** at Sweet Briar has 69 full-time members, 97% with terminal degrees. The student-faculty ratio is 7:1.

Students of Sweet Briar
The student body is made up of 710 undergraduates. Students come from 43 states and territories and 12 other countries. 37% are from Virginia. 2.2% are international students. 4.8% are African American, 0.9% American Indian, 2.1% Asian American, and 3.8% Hispanic American. 80% returned for their sophomore year.

Facilities and Resources
Student rooms are linked to a campus network. 117 **computers** are available on campus that provide access to the Internet. The 4 **libraries** have 474,818 books and 9,792 subscriptions.

Campus Life
There are 45 active organizations on campus, including a drama/theater group, newspaper, radio station, and choral group. No national or local **sororities**.

Sweet Briar is a member of the NCAA (Division III). **Intercollegiate sports** include basketball, equestrian sports, fencing, field hockey, lacrosse, soccer, softball, swimming, tennis, volleyball.

Campus Safety
Student safety services include front gate security, late-night transport/escort service, 24-hour emergency telephone alarm devices, 24-hour patrols by trained security personnel, and electronically operated dormitory entrances.

Applying
Sweet Briar requires an essay, SAT I or ACT, a high school transcript, and 2 recommendations. It recommends SAT II Subject Tests and an interview. Application deadline: 2/15; 3/1 priority date for financial aid. Early and deferred admission are possible.

Syracuse University

Urban setting ■ Private ■ Independent ■ Coed
Syracuse, New York

Web site: www.syracuse.edu
Contact: Office of Admissions, 201 Tolley Administration Building, Syracuse, NY 13244-1100
Telephone: 315-443-3611
E-mail: orange@syr.edu

Academics

SU awards bachelor's, master's, doctoral, and first-professional **degrees** and post-master's certificates. Challenging opportunities include advanced placement, accelerated degree programs, student-designed majors, an honors program, double majors, independent study, a senior project, Phi Beta Kappa, and Sigma Xi. Special programs include cooperative education, internships, summer session for credit, off-campus study, study-abroad, and Army and Air Force ROTC.

The most frequently chosen fields are communications/communication technologies, business/marketing, and social sciences and history. A complete listing of majors at SU appears in the Majors Index beginning on page 432.

The **faculty** at SU has 822 full-time members, 86% with terminal degrees. The student-faculty ratio is 12:1.

Students of SU

The student body totals 14,668, of whom 10,685 are undergraduates. 53.7% are women and 46.3% are men. Students come from 53 states and territories and 62 other countries. 47% are from New York. 3.7% are international students. 7.2% are African American, 0.3% American Indian, 4.5% Asian American, and 4.1% Hispanic American.

Facilities and Resources

Student rooms are linked to a campus network. 850 **computers** are available on campus that provide access to online services, networked client and server computing and the Internet. The 7 **libraries** have 2,700,000 books and 16,700 subscriptions.

Campus Life

There are 250 active organizations on campus, including a drama/theater group, newspaper, radio station, television station, choral group, and marching band. 20% of eligible men and 30% of eligible women are members of national **fraternities**, national **sororities**, and local fraternities.

SU is a member of the NCAA (Division I). **Intercollegiate sports** (some offering scholarships) include archery, badminton, baseball (m), basketball, bowling, crew, cross-country running, equestrian sports, fencing, field hockey (w), football (m), gymnastics, ice hockey, lacrosse, racquetball, riflery, rugby, sailing, skiing (downhill), soccer, softball, squash, swimming, table tennis, tennis, track and field, volleyball, water polo, weight lifting, wrestling.

Campus Safety

Student safety services include crime prevention programs, late-night transport/escort service, 24-hour emergency telephone alarm devices, 24-hour patrols by trained security personnel, and electronically operated dormitory entrances.

Applying

SU requires an essay, SAT I or ACT, a high school transcript, and 2 recommendations, and in some cases audition for drama and music programs, portfolio for art and architecture programs. It recommends an interview. Application deadline: 1/15; 2/15 priority date for financial aid. Early and deferred admission are possible.

Getting in Last Year
12,663 applied
59% were accepted
2,752 enrolled (37%)
38% from top tenth of their h.s. class
3.46 average high school GPA
48% had SAT verbal scores over 600
59% had SAT math scores over 600
9% had SAT verbal scores over 700
12% had SAT math scores over 700
39 valedictorians

Graduation and After
57% graduated in 4 years
12% graduated in 5 years
2% graduated in 6 years
20% pursued further study (6% business, 4% law, 4% medicine)
80% had job offers within 6 months
230 organizations recruited on campus

Financial Matters
$19,784 tuition and fees (1999–2000)
$8400 room and board
$15,700 average financial aid amount received per undergraduate (1999–2000)

TAYLOR UNIVERSITY

RURAL SETTING ■ PRIVATE ■ INDEPENDENT RELIGIOUS ■ COED
UPLAND, INDIANA

Web site: www.tayloru.edu
Contact: Mr. Stephen R. Mortland, Director of Admissions, 236 West Reade
Avenue, Upland, IN 46989-1001
Telephone: 765-998-5134 or toll-free 800-882-3456 **Fax:** 765-998-4925
E-mail: admissions_u@tayloru.edu

Getting in Last Year

1,624 applied
78% were accepted
475 enrolled (37%)
42% from top tenth of their h.s. class
3.6 average high school GPA
48% had SAT verbal scores over 600
45% had SAT math scores over 600
75% had ACT scores over 24
13% had SAT verbal scores over 700
9% had SAT math scores over 700
18% had ACT scores over 30
8 National Merit Scholars
37 valedictorians

Graduation and After

71% graduated in 4 years
3% graduated in 5 years
1% graduated in 6 years
Graduates pursuing further study: 6% arts and
sciences, 3% theology, 1% business
48% had job offers within 6 months
125 organizations recruited on campus

Financial Matters

$15,118 tuition and fees (1999–2000)
$4630 room and board
82% average percent of need met
$11,273 average financial aid amount received
per undergraduate (1999–2000 estimated)

Academics

Taylor awards associate and bachelor's **degrees**. Challenging opportunities include advanced placement, accelerated degree programs, student-designed majors, an honors program, double majors, independent study, and a senior project. Special programs include internships, summer session for credit, off-campus study, and study-abroad.

The most frequently chosen fields are liberal arts/general studies, education, and business/marketing. A complete listing of majors at Taylor appears in the Majors Index beginning on page 432.

The **faculty** at Taylor has 113 full-time members, 72% with terminal degrees. The student-faculty ratio is 16:1.

Students of Taylor

The student body is made up of 1,897 undergraduates. 52.8% are women and 47.2% are men. Students come from 48 states and territories and 19 other countries. 27% are from Indiana. 2% are international students. 1.2% are African American, 0.5% American Indian, 1.2% Asian American, and 1.6% Hispanic American. 89% returned for their sophomore year.

Facilities and Resources

Student rooms are linked to a campus network. 235 **computers** are available on campus that provide access to the Internet. The **library** has 188,000 books and 737 subscriptions.

Campus Life

There are 30 active organizations on campus, including a drama/theater group, newspaper, radio station, and choral group. No national or local **fraternities** or **sororities**.

Taylor is a member of the NAIA and NCCAA. **Intercollegiate sports** (some offering scholarships) include baseball (m), basketball, cross-country running, equestrian sports, football (m), golf (m), lacrosse (m), soccer, softball (w), tennis, track and field, volleyball.

Campus Safety

Student safety services include late-night transport/escort service, 24-hour patrols by trained security personnel, and student patrols.

Applying

Taylor requires an essay, SAT I or ACT, a high school transcript, an interview, and 2 recommendations. It recommends a minimum high school GPA of 2.8. Application deadline: rolling admissions; 3/1 for financial aid. Deferred admission is possible.

TEXAS A&M UNIVERSITY

SUBURBAN SETTING ■ PUBLIC ■ STATE-SUPPORTED ■ COED
COLLEGE STATION, TEXAS

Web site: www.tamu.edu
Contact: Ms. Stephanie D. Hays, Associate Director of Admissions, 217 John
   J. Koldus Building, College Station, TX 77843-1265
Telephone: 409-845-3741 **Fax:** 409-847-8737
E-mail: admissions@tamu.edu

Academics

Texas A&M awards bachelor's, master's, doctoral, and first-professional **degrees** and
post-bachelor's certificates. Challenging opportunities include advanced placement, an
honors program, double majors, independent study, a senior project, and Sigma Xi.
Special programs include cooperative education, internships, summer session for credit,
off-campus study, study-abroad, and Army, Navy and Air Force ROTC.

The most frequently chosen fields are business/marketing, education, and home
economics/vocational home economics. A complete listing of majors at Texas A&M appears in the Majors Index beginning on page 432.

The **faculty** at Texas A&M has 1,879 full-time members, 91% with terminal degrees.
The student-faculty ratio is 21:1.

Students of Texas A&M

The student body totals 43,442, of whom 36,082 are undergraduates. 47.7% are women
and 52.3% are men. Students come from 52 states and territories and 110 other
countries. 94% are from Texas. 1.4% are international students. 2.7% are African
American, 0.5% American Indian, 3.3% Asian American, and 9.4% Hispanic American.
88% returned for their sophomore year.

Facilities and Resources

Student rooms are linked to a campus network. 1,500 **computers** are available on
campus that provide access to the Internet. The 5 **libraries** have 2,375,488 books and
26,625 subscriptions.

Campus Life

There are 700 active organizations on campus, including a drama/theater group,
newspaper, radio station, television station, choral group, and marching band. 6% of
eligible men and 14% of eligible women are members of national **fraternities**, national
sororities, local fraternities, and local sororities.

Texas A&M is a member of the NCAA (Division I). **Intercollegiate sports** (some
offering scholarships) include archery (w), baseball (m), basketball, cross-country running, equestrian sports (w), football (m), golf, soccer (w), softball (w), swimming, tennis,
track and field, volleyball (w).

Campus Safety

Student safety services include student escorts, late-night transport/escort service, 24-
hour emergency telephone alarm devices, 24-hour patrols by trained security personnel,
and electronically operated dormitory entrances.

Applying

Texas A&M requires SAT I or ACT and a high school transcript. Application deadline:
2/15; 4/1 priority date for financial aid.

Texas A&M University, one of a select few universities in the nation to hold land-, sea-, and space-grant designations, is widely recognized for its undergraduate curricular and extracurricular programs. An outstanding student body is attracted from 50 states and 110 countries to pursue degrees in more than 150 fields of study. New attractions and facilities include the George Bush Library and Museum and the George Bush School of Government and Public Service. More than 700 student organizations provide unparalleled opportunities for leadership development.

Getting in Last Year

14,453 applied
74% were accepted
6,695 enrolled (62%)
49% from top tenth of their h.s. class
38% had SAT verbal scores over 600
53% had SAT math scores over 600
69% had ACT scores over 24
7% had SAT verbal scores over 700
13% had SAT math scores over 700
11% had ACT scores over 30
149 National Merit Scholars

Graduation and After

42% graduated in 4 years
25% graduated in 5 years
4% graduated in 6 years
17% pursued further study
52% had job offers within 6 months
1501 organizations recruited on campus
1 Marshall, 1 Fulbright scholar

Financial Matters

$2639 resident tuition and fees (1999–2000)
$7823 nonresident tuition and fees (1999–2000)
$4898 room and board
77% average percent of need met
$6959 average financial aid amount received
   per undergraduate (1998–99)

THOMAS AQUINAS COLLEGE

RURAL SETTING ■ PRIVATE ■ INDEPENDENT RELIGIOUS ■ COED
SANTA PAULA, CALIFORNIA

Web site: www.thomasaquinas.edu
Contact: Mr. Thomas J. Susanka Jr., Director of Admissions, 10000 North
    Ojai Road, Santa Paula, CA 93060-9980
Telephone: 805-525-4417 ext. 361 or toll-free 800-634-9797 **Fax:**
    805-525-9342
E-mail: admissions@thomasaquinas.edu

Academics

TAC awards bachelor's **degrees**. A senior project is a challenging opportunity.
    The most frequently chosen field is liberal arts/general studies. A complete listing of majors at TAC appears in the Majors Index beginning on page 432.
    The **faculty** at TAC has 24 full-time members, 79% with terminal degrees. The student-faculty ratio is 11:1.

Students of TAC

The student body is made up of 267 undergraduates. Students come from 35 states and territories and 5 other countries. 37% are from California. 8.6% are international students. 0.4% are African American, 1.9% Asian American, and 8.6% Hispanic American. 74% returned for their sophomore year.

Facilities and Resources

10 **computers** are available on campus that provide access to the Internet. The **library** has 45,000 books and 48 subscriptions.

Campus Life

There are 5 active organizations on campus, including a drama/theater group and choral group. No national or local **fraternities** or **sororities**.
    This institution has no intercollegiate sports.

Campus Safety

Student safety services include weekend security patrol, 24-hour emergency telephone alarm devices, and student patrols.

Applying

TAC requires an essay, SAT I or ACT, a high school transcript, and 3 recommendations, and in some cases an interview. It recommends a minimum high school GPA of 2.0. Application deadline: rolling admissions. Early and deferred admission are possible.

TRANSYLVANIA UNIVERSITY
URBAN SETTING ■ PRIVATE ■ INDEPENDENT RELIGIOUS ■ COED
LEXINGTON, KENTUCKY

Web site: www.transy.edu
Contact: Ms. Sarah Coen, Director of Admissions, 300 North Broadway, Lexington, KY 40508-1797
Telephone: 606-233-8242 or toll-free 800-872-6798 **Fax:** 606-233-8797
E-mail: admissions@transy.edu

Academics
Transylvania awards bachelor's **degrees**. Challenging opportunities include advanced placement, student-designed majors, and double majors. Special programs include internships, summer session for credit, off-campus study, study-abroad, and Army and Air Force ROTC.

The most frequently chosen fields are business/marketing, biological/life sciences, and social sciences and history. A complete listing of majors at Transylvania appears in the Majors Index beginning on page 432.

The **faculty** at Transylvania has 70 full-time members, 96% with terminal degrees. The student-faculty ratio is 13:1.

Students of Transylvania
The student body is made up of 1,070 undergraduates. 58.5% are women and 41.5% are men. Students come from 28 states and territories and 3 other countries. 82% are from Kentucky. 0.7% are international students. 2.3% are African American, 0.4% American Indian, 2.6% Asian American, and 0.5% Hispanic American. 81% returned for their sophomore year.

Facilities and Resources
Student rooms are linked to a campus network. 125 **computers** are available on campus that provide access to the Internet. The **library** has 94,926 books.

Campus Life
There are 51 active organizations on campus, including a drama/theater group, newspaper, radio station, and choral group. 60% of eligible men and 60% of eligible women are members of national **fraternities** and national **sororities**.

Transylvania is a member of the NAIA. **Intercollegiate sports** include baseball (m), basketball, cross-country running, field hockey (w), golf, soccer, softball (w), swimming, tennis.

Campus Safety
Student safety services include late-night transport/escort service, 24-hour emergency telephone alarm devices, and 24-hour patrols by trained security personnel.

Applying
Transylvania requires an essay, SAT I or ACT, a high school transcript, 2 recommendations, and a minimum high school GPA of 2.75, and in some cases an interview. It recommends an interview. Application deadline: 2/1; 3/1 priority date for financial aid. Early and deferred admission are possible.

Founded in 1780 as the nation's 16th college, Transylvania is known for its ongoing legacy of academic excellence. It is consistently ranked among the nation's best liberal arts colleges and is considered an exceptional value in education. Students benefit from an innovative teacher-recognition program, the first in the nation to attract and reward outstanding teaching on a substantial scale. Small classes and individual attention from faculty members prepare students well for highly selective graduate and professional schools, especially in law and medicine. Transylvania's location in a historic district near downtown Lexington, Kentucky, provides opportunities for internships, jobs, and cultural activities.

Getting in Last Year
1,011 applied
89% were accepted
308 enrolled (34%)
54% from top tenth of their h.s. class
3.49 average high school GPA
49% had SAT verbal scores over 600
51% had SAT math scores over 600
73% had ACT scores over 24
15% had SAT verbal scores over 700
11% had SAT math scores over 700
18% had ACT scores over 30
16 National Merit Scholars
31 valedictorians

Graduation and After
61% graduated in 4 years
5% graduated in 5 years
1% graduated in 6 years
44% pursued further study (22% arts and sciences, 11% medicine, 6% law)
45% had job offers within 6 months
66 organizations recruited on campus

Financial Matters
$14,600 tuition and fees (1999–2000)
$5350 room and board
90% average percent of need met
$13,021 average financial aid amount received per undergraduate (1999–2000 estimated)

eApply

TRINITY COLLEGE
URBAN SETTING ■ PRIVATE ■ INDEPENDENT ■ COED
HARTFORD, CONNECTICUT

Web site: www.trincoll.edu
Contact: Mr. Larry Dow, Dean of Admissions and Financial Aid, 300 Summit Street, Hartford, CT 06106-3100
Telephone: 860-297-2180 **Fax:** 860-297-2287
E-mail: admissions.office@trincoll.edu

Founded in 1823, Trinity College in Hartford is an independent, nonsectarian liberal arts college of the highest quality. Its rigorous curriculum is firmly grounded in the traditional liberal arts disciplines and marked by an array of interdisciplinary studies, exceptional offerings in science and engineering, and distinctive educational connections with Connecticut's capital city and cities around the world. A highly active community outreach program and an exceptionally strong internship program provide Trinity students with uncommonly rich opportunities to extend classroom learning, explore potential careers, and make a difference on campus and in the community.

Getting in Last Year
4,648 applied
40% were accepted
566 enrolled (31%)
51% from top tenth of their h.s. class
70% had SAT verbal scores over 600
72% had SAT math scores over 600
90% had ACT scores over 24
18% had SAT verbal scores over 700
17% had SAT math scores over 700
20% had ACT scores over 30

Graduation and After
75% graduated in 4 years
6% graduated in 5 years
1% graduated in 6 years
14% pursued further study
75% had job offers within 6 months
261 organizations recruited on campus

Financial Matters
$24,490 tuition and fees (1999–2000)
$6890 room and board
100% average percent of need met
$22,495 average financial aid amount received per undergraduate (1999–2000)

Academics
Trinity College awards bachelor's and master's **degrees**. Challenging opportunities include advanced placement, accelerated degree programs, student-designed majors, an honors program, double majors, independent study, a senior project, and Phi Beta Kappa. Special programs include internships, summer session for credit, off-campus study, study-abroad, and Army ROTC.

The most frequently chosen fields are social sciences and history, biological/life sciences, and English. A complete listing of majors at Trinity College appears in the Majors Index beginning on page 432.

The **faculty** at Trinity College has 166 full-time members, 93% with terminal degrees. The student-faculty ratio is 10:1.

Students of Trinity College
The student body totals 2,371, of whom 2,169 are undergraduates. 48.7% are women and 51.3% are men. Students come from 44 states and territories and 29 other countries. 24% are from Connecticut. 2.3% are international students. 5.8% are African American, 0.1% American Indian, 5.1% Asian American, and 4.6% Hispanic American. 92% returned for their sophomore year.

Facilities and Resources
Student rooms are linked to a campus network. 200 **computers** are available on campus that provide access to the Internet. The 3 **libraries** have 941,010 books and 3,126 subscriptions.

Campus Life
There are 112 active organizations on campus, including a drama/theater group, newspaper, radio station, television station, and choral group. 19% of eligible men and 19% of eligible women are members of coed fraternities.

Trinity College is a member of the NCAA (Division III). **Intercollegiate sports** include baseball (m), basketball, crew, cross-country running, equestrian sports, fencing, field hockey (w), football (m), golf (m), ice hockey, lacrosse, riflery, rugby, sailing, skiing (downhill), soccer, softball (w), squash, swimming, tennis, track and field, volleyball, water polo, wrestling (m).

Campus Safety
Student safety services include late-night transport/escort service, 24-hour emergency telephone alarm devices, 24-hour patrols by trained security personnel, and electronically operated dormitory entrances.

Applying
Trinity College requires an essay, SAT II: Writing Test, SAT I and SAT II or ACT, a high school transcript, and 3 recommendations. It recommends an interview. Application deadline: 1/15; 3/1 for financial aid, with a 2/1 priority date. Early and deferred admission are possible.

TRINITY UNIVERSITY

URBAN SETTING ■ PRIVATE ■ INDEPENDENT RELIGIOUS ■ COED
SAN ANTONIO, TEXAS

Web site: www.trinity.edu
Contact: Dr. George Boyd, Director of Admissions, 715 Stadium Drive, San Antonio, TX 78212-7200
Telephone: 210-999-7207 or toll-free 800-TRINITY **Fax:** 210-999-8164
E-mail: admissions@trinity.edu

  eAPPLY

Academics

Trinity awards bachelor's and master's **degrees**. Challenging opportunities include advanced placement, accelerated degree programs, an honors program, double majors, independent study, a senior project, and Phi Beta Kappa. Special programs include internships, summer session for credit, study-abroad, and Air Force ROTC.

The most frequently chosen fields are business/marketing, social sciences and history, and biological/life sciences. A complete listing of majors at Trinity appears in the Majors Index beginning on page 432.

The **faculty** at Trinity has 210 full-time members, 99% with terminal degrees. The student-faculty ratio is 11:1.

Students of Trinity

The student body totals 2,515, of whom 2,278 are undergraduates. 51.2% are women and 48.8% are men. Students come from 49 states and territories and 21 other countries. 73% are from Texas. 1.3% are international students. 2.3% are African American, 0.5% American Indian, 7.6% Asian American, and 10.2% Hispanic American. 86% returned for their sophomore year.

Facilities and Resources

Student rooms are linked to a campus network. 100 **computers** are available on campus that provide access to the Internet. The **library** has 838,262 books and 3,476 subscriptions.

Campus Life

Active organizations on campus include a drama/theater group, newspaper, radio station, television station, and choral group. 26% of eligible men and 28% of eligible women are members of local **fraternities** and local **sororities**.

Trinity is a member of the NCAA (Division III). **Intercollegiate sports** include baseball (m), basketball, cross-country running, football (m), golf, lacrosse, riflery, soccer, softball (w), swimming, tennis, track and field, volleyball.

Campus Safety

Student safety services include late-night transport/escort service, 24-hour emergency telephone alarm devices, 24-hour patrols by trained security personnel, and student patrols.

Applying

Trinity requires an essay, SAT I or ACT, a high school transcript, and 2 recommendations. It recommends an interview. Application deadline: 2/1; 2/1 priority date for financial aid. Deferred admission is possible.

Trinity University is a highly selective liberal arts and sciences institution that also offers several professional programs that are nationally cited as models in their fields. Trinity offers its students a unique undergraduate experience. Class sizes are small, research labs and other facilities equal to those of moderate-sized Ph.D.-granting institutions are devoted exclusively to undergraduates, and contact with professors is frequent and personal. (Trinity employs no graduate assistants and few part-time faculty members.) The 117-acre campus is known for its beauty and for its skyline view of downtown San Antonio, one of America's most interesting multicultural cities.

Getting in Last Year
2,743 applied
76% were accepted
637 enrolled (31%)
53% from top tenth of their h.s. class
3.7 average high school GPA
69% had SAT verbal scores over 600
74% had SAT math scores over 600
87% had ACT scores over 24
22% had SAT verbal scores over 700
18% had SAT math scores over 700
24% had ACT scores over 30
22 National Merit Scholars

Graduation and After
62% graduated in 4 years
9% graduated in 5 years
Graduates pursuing further study: 8% arts and sciences, 5% education, 4% dentistry
39% had job offers within 6 months
82 organizations recruited on campus
1 Fulbright scholar

Financial Matters
$15,804 tuition and fees (2000–2001 estimated)
$6330 room and board
100% average percent of need met
$15,745 average financial aid amount received per undergraduate (1999–2000 estimated)

TRUMAN STATE UNIVERSITY
SMALL-TOWN SETTING ■ PUBLIC ■ STATE-SUPPORTED ■ COED
KIRKSVILLE, MISSOURI

Web site: www.truman.edu
Contact: Mr. Brad Chambers, Co-Director of Admissions, 205 McClain Hall, Kirksville, MO 63501-4221
Telephone: 660-785-4114 or toll-free 800-892-7792 (in-state) **Fax:** 660-785-7456
E-mail: admissions@truman.edu

Getting in Last Year
5,159 applied
81% were accepted
1,457 enrolled (35%)
45% from top tenth of their h.s. class
3.72 average high school GPA
60% had SAT verbal scores over 600
61% had SAT math scores over 600
87% had ACT scores over 24
18% had SAT verbal scores over 700
13% had SAT math scores over 700
26% had ACT scores over 30
18 National Merit Scholars
115 class presidents
137 valedictorians

Graduation and After
39% graduated in 4 years
23% graduated in 5 years
2% graduated in 6 years
Graduates pursuing further study: 11% arts and sciences, 9% education, 5% medicine
58% had job offers within 6 months
220 organizations recruited on campus

Financial Matters
$3562 resident tuition and fees (1999–2000)
$6362 nonresident tuition and fees (1999–2000)
$4400 room and board
82% average percent of need met
$5200 average financial aid amount received per undergraduate (1999–2000)

Academics
Truman awards bachelor's and master's **degrees**. Challenging opportunities include advanced placement, accelerated degree programs, an honors program, double majors, and a senior project. Special programs include internships, summer session for credit, off-campus study, study-abroad, and Army ROTC.

The most frequently chosen fields are business/marketing, biological/life sciences, and English. A complete listing of majors at Truman appears in the Majors Index beginning on page 432.

The **faculty** at Truman has 364 full-time members. The student-faculty ratio is 16:1.

Students of Truman
The student body totals 6,236, of whom 5,963 are undergraduates. 58.1% are women and 41.9% are men. Students come from 43 states and territories and 51 other countries. 72% are from Missouri. 2.7% are international students. 3.2% are African American, 0.2% American Indian, 2.2% Asian American, and 1.6% Hispanic American. 84% returned for their sophomore year.

Facilities and Resources
Student rooms are linked to a campus network. 519 **computers** are available on campus that provide access to the Internet. The 2 **libraries** have 398,749 books and 3,541 subscriptions.

Campus Life
There are 193 active organizations on campus, including a drama/theater group, newspaper, radio station, television station, choral group, and marching band. 30% of eligible men and 21% of eligible women are members of national **fraternities**, national **sororities**, and local sororities.

Truman is a member of the NCAA (Division II). **Intercollegiate sports** (some offering scholarships) include baseball (m), basketball, cross-country running, equestrian sports, football (m), golf, lacrosse (w), rugby, soccer, softball (w), swimming, tennis, track and field, volleyball, wrestling (m).

Campus Safety
Student safety services include patrols by commissioned officers, late-night transport/escort service, 24-hour emergency telephone alarm devices, 24-hour patrols by trained security personnel, and student patrols.

Applying
Truman requires an essay, SAT I or ACT, and a high school transcript. It recommends ACT, an interview, and a minimum high school GPA of 3.0. Application deadline: 3/1; 4/1 priority date for financial aid. Early and deferred admission are possible.

TUFTS UNIVERSITY

SUBURBAN SETTING ■ PRIVATE ■ INDEPENDENT ■ COED
MEDFORD, MASSACHUSETTS

Web site: www.tufts.edu
Contact: Mr. David D. Cuttino, Dean of Undergraduate Admissions,
Bendetson Hall, Tufts University, Medford, MA 02155
Telephone: 617-627-3170 **Fax:** 617-627-3860
E-mail: uadmiss_inquiry@infonet.tufts.edu

eAPPLY

Academics

Tufts awards bachelor's, master's, doctoral, and first-professional **degrees** and post-master's certificates. Challenging opportunities include advanced placement, student-designed majors, an honors program, double majors, independent study, a senior project, Phi Beta Kappa, and Sigma Xi. Special programs include internships, summer session for credit, off-campus study, study-abroad, and Army, Navy and Air Force ROTC.

The most frequently chosen fields are social sciences and history, engineering/engineering technologies, and biological/life sciences. A complete listing of majors at Tufts appears in the Majors Index beginning on page 432.

The **faculty** at Tufts has 641 full-time members. The student-faculty ratio is 10:1.

Students of Tufts

The student body totals 9,269, of whom 4,977 are undergraduates. 52.6% are women and 47.4% are men. Students come from 52 states and territories and 69 other countries. 25% are from Massachusetts. 7.6% are international students. 5.6% are African American, 0.2% American Indian, 13.4% Asian American, and 6.2% Hispanic American. 99% returned for their sophomore year.

Facilities and Resources

Student rooms are linked to a campus network. 254 **computers** are available on campus that provide access to the Internet. The 2 **libraries** have 957,500 books and 5,282 subscriptions.

Campus Life

There are 160 active organizations on campus, including a drama/theater group, newspaper, radio station, television station, choral group, and marching band. 15% of eligible men and 4% of eligible women are members of national **fraternities** and national **sororities**.

Tufts is a member of the NCAA (Division III). **Intercollegiate sports** include baseball (m), basketball, crew, cross-country running, fencing (w), field hockey (w), football (m), golf (m), ice hockey (m), lacrosse, sailing, soccer, softball (w), squash, swimming, tennis, track and field, volleyball (w).

Campus Safety

Student safety services include security lighting, call boxes to campus police, late-night transport/escort service, 24-hour emergency telephone alarm devices, 24-hour patrols by trained security personnel, and electronically operated dormitory entrances.

Applying

Tufts requires an essay, SAT II: Writing Test, SAT I and SAT II or ACT, a high school transcript, and 1 recommendation. It recommends an interview. Application deadline: 1/1; 2/15 for financial aid, with a 2/1 priority date. Early and deferred admission are possible.

Getting in Last Year
13,471 applied
32% were accepted
1,351 enrolled (31%)
70% from top tenth of their h.s. class
81% had SAT verbal scores over 600
88% had SAT math scores over 600
93% had ACT scores over 24
31% had SAT verbal scores over 700
41% had SAT math scores over 700
39% had ACT scores over 30
35 National Merit Scholars

Graduation and After
77% graduated in 4 years
7% graduated in 5 years
2% graduated in 6 years
30% pursued further study (11% law, 9% medicine, 8% business)
214 organizations recruited on campus
10 Fulbright scholars

Financial Matters
$24,751 tuition and fees (1999–2000)
$7375 room and board
100% average percent of need met
$19,785 average financial aid amount received per undergraduate (1999–2000 estimated)

TULANE UNIVERSITY

URBAN SETTING ■ PRIVATE ■ INDEPENDENT ■ COED
NEW ORLEANS, LOUISIANA

Web site: www.tulane.edu
Contact: Mr. Richard Whiteside, Vice President of Enrollment Management and Institutional Research, 6823 St Charles Avenue, New Orleans, LA 70118-5669
Telephone: 504-865-5731 or toll-free 800-873-9283 **Fax:** 504-862-8715
E-mail: undergrad.admission@tulane.edu

mong national universities, Tulane is known for its emphasis on undergraduate teaching and its accomplishments in research. The same senior faculty members who do research regularly teach freshmen and sophomores. With 7,100 students in 5 divisions, Tulane gives each student the personal attention and teaching excellence typically associated with smaller colleges while providing the state-of-the-art facilities and interdisciplinary resources usually found only at major universities. Tulane students play active roles in more than 200 campus organizations and have numerous internship opportunities in the exciting city of New Orleans. Close student-teacher relationships pay off—graduates frequently win prestigious fellowships, and many go on to earn advanced degrees in their chosen field of study.

Getting in Last Year
8,388 applied
78% were accepted
2,445 enrolled (37%)
52% from top tenth of their h.s. class
75% had SAT verbal scores over 600
71% had SAT math scores over 600
29% had SAT verbal scores over 700
20% had SAT math scores over 700

Graduation and After
60% graduated in 4 years
10% graduated in 5 years
3% graduated in 6 years
Graduates pursuing further study: 9% business, 8% law, 7% medicine
557 organizations recruited on campus
1 Marshall scholar

Financial Matters
$24,214 tuition and fees (1999–2000)
$7042 room and board
94% average percent of need met
$22,948 average financial aid amount received per undergraduate (1999–2000)

Academics

Tulane awards associate, bachelor's, master's, doctoral, and first-professional **degrees**. Challenging opportunities include advanced placement, accelerated degree programs, student-designed majors, freshman honors college, an honors program, double majors, independent study, a senior project, Phi Beta Kappa, and Sigma Xi. Special programs include cooperative education, internships, summer session for credit, off-campus study, study-abroad, and Army, Navy and Air Force ROTC.

The most frequently chosen fields are business/marketing, social sciences and history, and engineering/engineering technologies. A complete listing of majors at Tulane appears in the Majors Index beginning on page 432.

The **faculty** at Tulane has 655 full-time members, 82% with terminal degrees. The student-faculty ratio is 9:1.

Students of Tulane

The student body totals 11,438, of whom 7,163 are undergraduates. 52.6% are women and 47.4% are men. Students come from 52 states and territories and 64 other countries. 34% are from Louisiana. 3.8% are international students. 5% are African American, 0.4% American Indian, 6.6% Asian American, and 4.3% Hispanic American. 86% returned for their sophomore year.

Facilities and Resources

Student rooms are linked to a campus network. The 9 **libraries** have 2,148,660 books and 14,986 subscriptions.

Campus Life

There are 200 active organizations on campus, including a drama/theater group, newspaper, radio station, television station, and choral group. 16% of eligible men and 19% of eligible women are members of national **fraternities** and national **sororities**.

Tulane is a member of the NCAA (Division I). **Intercollegiate sports** (some offering scholarships) include baseball (m), basketball, crew, cross-country running, equestrian sports, fencing, field hockey, football (m), golf, gymnastics, ice hockey, lacrosse, riflery, rugby (m), sailing, soccer, softball (w), swimming, tennis, track and field, volleyball, water polo.

Campus Safety

Student safety services include on and off-campus shuttle service, crime prevention programs, late-night transport/escort service, 24-hour emergency telephone alarm devices, 24-hour patrols by trained security personnel, student patrols, and electronically operated dormitory entrances.

Applying

Tulane requires an essay, SAT I or ACT, a high school transcript, and 1 recommendation, and in some cases SAT II Subject Tests. It recommends SAT II Subject Tests. Application deadline: 1/15; 2/1 for financial aid, with a 1/15 priority date. Early and deferred admission are possible.

UNION COLLEGE

SUBURBAN SETTING ■ PRIVATE ■ INDEPENDENT ■ COED
SCHENECTADY, NEW YORK

Web site: www.union.edu
Contact: Mr. Daniel Lundquist, Vice President for Admissions and Financial
Aid, Schenectady, NY 12308-2311
Telephone: 518-388-6112 or toll-free 888-843-6688 (in-state) **Fax:**
518-388-6986
E-mail: admissions@union.edu

Academics

Union College awards bachelor's and master's **degrees**. Challenging opportunities
include advanced placement, accelerated degree programs, student-designed majors, an
honors program, double majors, independent study, a senior project, Phi Beta Kappa,
and Sigma Xi. Special programs include cooperative education, internships, summer session for credit, off-campus study, study-abroad, and Army, Navy and Air Force ROTC.

The most frequently chosen fields are social sciences and history, biological/life sciences, and psychology. A complete listing of majors at Union College appears in the
Majors Index beginning on page 432.

The **faculty** at Union College has 189 full-time members, 96% with terminal
degrees. The student-faculty ratio is 11:1.

Students of Union College

The student body totals 2,432, of whom 2,150 are undergraduates. 47.5% are women
and 52.5% are men. Students come from 37 states and territories and 22 other countries.
52% are from New York. 2.5% are international students. 4.2% are African American,
0.2% American Indian, 4.8% Asian American, and 4.1% Hispanic American. 94%
returned for their sophomore year.

Facilities and Resources

Student rooms are linked to a campus network. 320 **computers** are available on campus
that provide access to the Internet. The **library** has 275,064 books and 2,766 subscriptions.

Campus Life

There are 95 active organizations on campus, including a drama/theater group,
newspaper, radio station, and choral group. 31% of eligible men and 26% of eligible
women are members of national **fraternities**, national **sororities**, local fraternities, local
sororities, and theme houses.

Union College is a member of the NCAA (Division III). **Intercollegiate sports**
include baseball (m), basketball, crew, cross-country running, fencing, field hockey (w),
football (m), ice hockey, lacrosse, rugby, skiing (cross-country), skiing (downhill), soccer,
softball (w), swimming, tennis, track and field, volleyball (w), water polo.

Campus Safety

Student safety services include awareness programs, bicycle patrol, shuttle service, late-
night transport/escort service, 24-hour emergency telephone alarm devices, 24-hour
patrols by trained security personnel, student patrols, and electronically operated dormitory entrances.

Applying

Union College requires an essay, SAT I or ACT or 3 SAT II Subject Tests (including
SAT II: Writing Test), a high school transcript, and 2 recommendations. It recommends
an interview. Application deadline: 2/1; 2/1 priority date for financial aid. Early and
deferred admission are possible.

Union College, one of the
oldest nondenominational
colleges in America, is
located in the small city of
Schenectady, about 3 hours north of
New York City. Its distinctive
curriculum combines the traditional
liberal arts with engineering study.
Three basic tenets undergird a Union
education: commitments to lifelong
learning, the liberal arts, and a close
working relationship between
students and faculty. People from
many different backgrounds come to
Union, attracted by these values and
the opportunities they imply: small
classes, excellent access to superb
facilities, a caring and committed
faculty, and an academic program of
depth and diversity.

Getting in Last Year
3,761 applied
46% were accepted
535 enrolled (31%)
50% from top tenth of their h.s. class
3.45 average high school GPA
55% had SAT verbal scores over 600
68% had SAT math scores over 600
7% had SAT verbal scores over 700
14% had SAT math scores over 700

Graduation and After
78% graduated in 4 years
5% graduated in 5 years
1% graduated in 6 years
30% pursued further study (9% arts and sciences, 7% medicine, 5% education)
54 organizations recruited on campus

Financial Matters
$24,099 tuition and fees (1999–2000)
$6474 room and board
97% average percent of need met
$21,084 average financial aid amount received
per undergraduate (1998–99)

UNION UNIVERSITY

SMALL-TOWN SETTING ■ PRIVATE ■ INDEPENDENT RELIGIOUS ■ COED
JACKSON, TENNESSEE

Web site: www.uu.edu
Contact: Ms. Robbie Graves, Director of Enrollment Services, 1050 Union
University Drive, Jackson, TN 38305-3697
Telephone: 901-661-5008 or toll-free 800-33-UNION **Fax:** 901-661-5017
E-mail: info@uu.edu

Getting in Last Year
913 applied
85% were accepted
424 enrolled (55%)
36% from top tenth of their h.s. class
3.48 average high school GPA
55% had ACT scores over 24
16% had ACT scores over 30
4 National Merit Scholars
44 valedictorians

Graduation and After
46% graduated in 4 years
12% graduated in 5 years
2% graduated in 6 years
40% pursued further study
85 organizations recruited on campus

Financial Matters
$11,900 tuition and fees (2000–2001)
$3850 room and board
80% average percent of need met
$7800 average financial aid amount received
per undergraduate (1999–2000 estimated)

Academics

Union awards associate, bachelor's, and master's **degrees**. Challenging opportunities include advanced placement, accelerated degree programs, an honors program, double majors, independent study, and a senior project. Special programs include internships, summer session for credit, off-campus study, and study-abroad.

The most frequently chosen fields are health professions and related sciences, education, and business/marketing. A complete listing of majors at Union appears in the Majors Index beginning on page 432.

The **faculty** at Union has 126 full-time members, 63% with terminal degrees. The student-faculty ratio is 13:1.

Students of Union

The student body totals 2,297, of whom 1,931 are undergraduates. 59.3% are women and 40.7% are men. Students come from 40 states and territories and 26 other countries. 74% are from Tennessee. 1.9% are international students. 6.5% are African American, 0.2% American Indian, 0.7% Asian American, and 0.6% Hispanic American. 93% returned for their sophomore year.

Facilities and Resources

175 **computers** are available on campus that provide access to the Internet. The **library** has 129,678 books and 2,653 subscriptions.

Campus Life

There are 73 active organizations on campus, including a drama/theater group, newspaper, and choral group. 26% of eligible men and 23% of eligible women are members of national **fraternities** and national **sororities**.

Union is a member of the NAIA and NCCAA. **Intercollegiate sports** (some offering scholarships) include baseball (m), basketball, cross-country running (w), golf (m), soccer (m), softball (w), tennis, volleyball (w).

Campus Safety

Student safety services include late-night transport/escort service, 24-hour emergency telephone alarm devices, 24-hour patrols by trained security personnel, and student patrols.

Applying

Union requires SAT I or ACT, a high school transcript, and a minimum high school GPA of 2.5, and in some cases recommendations. It recommends an essay and an interview. Application deadline: rolling admissions; 2/15 priority date for financial aid. Early admission is possible.

UNITED STATES AIR FORCE ACADEMY

SUBURBAN SETTING ■ PUBLIC ■ FEDERALLY SUPPORTED ■ COED
USAF ACADEMY, COLORADO

Web site: www.usafa.af.mil
Contact: Mr. Rolland Stoneman, Associate Director of Admissions/Selections, HQ USAFA/RR 2304 Cadet Drive, Suite 200, USAF Academy, CO 80840-5025
Telephone: 719-333-2520 or toll-free 800-443-9266 **Fax:** 719-333-3012
E-mail: rrmail.rr@usafa.af.mil

Academics

USAFA awards bachelor's **degrees**. Challenging opportunities include advanced placement, student-designed majors, double majors, independent study, and a senior project. Special programs include internships, summer session for credit, off-campus study, and study-abroad.

The most frequently chosen fields are engineering/engineering technologies, social sciences and history, and business/marketing. A complete listing of majors at USAFA appears in the Majors Index beginning on page 432.

The **faculty** at USAFA has 531 full-time members, 50% with terminal degrees. The student-faculty ratio is 7:1.

Students of USAFA

The student body is made up of 4,161 undergraduates. 16.3% are women and 83.7% are men. Students come from 54 states and territories and 22 other countries. 5% are from Colorado. 0.9% are international students. 5.1% are African American, 1.3% American Indian, 3.8% Asian American, and 7.3% Hispanic American. 89% returned for their sophomore year.

Facilities and Resources

Student rooms are linked to a campus network. The 3 **libraries** have 445,379 books and 1,693 subscriptions.

Campus Life

There are 85 active organizations on campus, including a drama/theater group, newspaper, radio station, choral group, and marching band. No national or local **fraternities** or **sororities**.

USAFA is a member of the NCAA (Division I). **Intercollegiate sports** include baseball (m), basketball, cross-country running, fencing, football (m), golf (m), gymnastics, ice hockey (m), lacrosse (m), riflery, rugby (w), skiing (cross-country), skiing (downhill), soccer, softball (w), swimming, tennis, track and field, volleyball (w), water polo (m), weight lifting, wrestling (m).

Campus Safety

Student safety services include self-defense education, well-lit campus, late-night transport/escort service, 24-hour emergency telephone alarm devices, and 24-hour patrols by trained security personnel.

Applying

USAFA requires an essay, SAT I or ACT, a high school transcript, an interview, and authorized nomination. Application deadline: 1/31.

The Air Force Academy challenge requires a well-rounded academic, physical, and leadership background. Cadets must accept discipline, be competitive, and have a desire to serve others with a sense of duty and integrity. Applicants should prepare early to meet the admissions requirements, competition, and demands they will face at the Academy.

Getting in Last Year
8,828 applied
20% were accepted
1,282 enrolled (73%)
52% from top tenth of their h.s. class
3.8 average high school GPA
71% had SAT verbal scores over 600
87% had SAT math scores over 600
16% had SAT verbal scores over 700
27% had SAT math scores over 700
175 National Merit Scholars
159 class presidents
106 valedictorians

Graduation and After
77% graduated in 4 years
1% graduated in 5 years
2% graduated in 6 years
Graduates pursuing further study: 4% arts and sciences, 2% medicine, 2% engineering
100% had job offers within 6 months
1 organization recruited on campus
1 Marshall scholar

Financial Matters
$0 comprehensive fee (2000–2001)

UNITED STATES COAST GUARD ACADEMY
SUBURBAN SETTING ■ PUBLIC ■ FEDERALLY SUPPORTED ■ COED
NEW LONDON, CONNECTICUT

Web site: www.cga.edu
Contact: Capt. R. W. Thorne, Director of Admissions, 31 Mohegan Avenue, New London, CT 06320-4195
Telephone: 860-444-8500 or toll-free 800-883-8724 **Fax:** 860-701-6700
E-mail: admissions@cga.uscg.mil

The United States Coast Guard Academy, located halfway between New York City and Boston on Connecticut's shoreline, is committed to the development of professional career Coast Guard officers. Not only as a highly selective academic institution, but also as a multimissioned training facility for today's officer, the Academy provides solid academic studies, hands-on leadership experiences, and military training necessary to be successful in the world's premier maritime service. Whether it is rescuing a stranded mariner or enforcing maritime laws, the U.S. Coast Guard can be found in all corners of the world, supporting and shaping national policy every day.

Academics
USCGA awards bachelor's **degrees**. Challenging opportunities include an honors program, double majors, independent study, and a senior project. Special programs include internships, summer session for credit, and off-campus study.

The most frequently chosen fields are engineering/engineering technologies, (pre)law, and business/marketing. A complete listing of majors at USCGA appears in the Majors Index beginning on page 432.

The **faculty** at USCGA has 112 full-time members, 40% with terminal degrees. The student-faculty ratio is 7:1.

Students of USCGA
The student body is made up of 838 undergraduates. 28.5% are women and 71.5% are men. Students come from 50 states and territories and 6 other countries. 9% are from Connecticut. 2% are international students. 5.1% are African American, 1.1% American Indian, 5.1% Asian American, and 5.6% Hispanic American. 83% returned for their sophomore year.

Facilities and Resources
Student rooms are linked to a campus network. 120 **computers** are available on campus that provide access to the Internet. The **library** has 150,000 books and 1,690 subscriptions.

Campus Life
Active organizations on campus include a drama/theater group, choral group, and marching band. No national or local **fraternities** or **sororities**.

USCGA is a member of the NCAA (Division III). **Intercollegiate sports** include baseball (m), basketball, bowling, crew, cross-country running, football (m), golf, ice hockey (m), lacrosse, riflery, rugby, sailing, soccer, softball (w), swimming, tennis, track and field, volleyball (w), water polo (m), wrestling (m).

Campus Safety
Student safety services include 24-hour patrols by trained security personnel and student patrols.

Applying
USCGA requires an essay, SAT I or ACT, a high school transcript, and 3 recommendations, and in some cases an interview. Application deadline: 12/15.

Getting in Last Year
5,457 applied
6% were accepted
264 enrolled (81%)
44% from top tenth of their h.s. class
3.67 average high school GPA
67% had SAT verbal scores over 600
86% had SAT math scores over 600
89% had ACT scores over 24
10% had SAT verbal scores over 700
17% had SAT math scores over 700
11% had ACT scores over 30
27 class presidents
9 valedictorians

Graduation and After
75% graduated in 4 years

Financial Matters
$0 comprehensive fee (1999–2000)

UNITED STATES MERCHANT MARINE ACADEMY

SUBURBAN SETTING ■ PUBLIC ■ FEDERALLY SUPPORTED ■ COED
KINGS POINT, NEW YORK

Web site: www.usmma.edu
Contact: Capt. James M. Skinner, Director of Admissions, Kings Point, NY
11024-1699
Telephone: 516-773-5391 or toll-free 800-732-6267 (out-of-state) **Fax:**
516-773-5390
E-mail: admissions@usmma.edu

Academics

United States Merchant Marine Academy awards bachelor's **degrees**. Challenging opportunities include an honors program and a senior project. Special programs include cooperative education and internships.

The most frequently chosen fields are engineering/engineering technologies and military science/technologies. A complete listing of majors at United States Merchant Marine Academy appears in the Majors Index beginning on page 432.

The **faculty** at United States Merchant Marine Academy has 80 full-time members.

Students of United States Merchant Marine Academy

The student body is made up of 921 undergraduates. Students come from 53 states and territories and 3 other countries. 87% returned for their sophomore year.

Facilities and Resources

Student rooms are linked to a campus network. 1,200 **computers** are available on campus that provide access to engineering and economics software and the Internet. The **library** has 232,576 books and 985 subscriptions.

Campus Life

There are 45 active organizations on campus, including a drama/theater group, newspaper, choral group, and marching band. No national or local **fraternities** or **sororities**.

United States Merchant Marine Academy is a member of the NCAA (Division III). **Intercollegiate sports** include baseball (m), basketball, crew, cross-country running, football (m), golf, ice hockey (m), lacrosse (m), riflery, rugby (m), sailing, soccer (m), softball (w), swimming, tennis, track and field, volleyball, water polo (m), wrestling (m).

Campus Safety

Student safety services include 24-hour patrols by trained security personnel.

Applying

United States Merchant Marine Academy requires an essay, SAT I or ACT, a high school transcript, and 3 recommendations, and in some cases SAT II Subject Tests. It recommends an interview. Application deadline: 3/1.

The United States Merchant Marine Academy is a 4-year federal service academy dedicated to educating and training young men and women as officers in America's merchant marine and U.S. Naval Reserve and as future leaders of the maritime and transportation industries. The Academy, in Kings Point, Long Island, offers accredited programs in marine transportation and engineering leading to a BS degree, a U.S. merchant marine officer's license, and a Naval Reserve commission. Students spend two 6-month periods at sea aboard U.S. cargo ships as part of their training.

Getting in Last Year
910 applied
40% were accepted
34% from top tenth of their h.s. class
3.50 average high school GPA
41% had SAT verbal scores over 600
57% had SAT math scores over 600
10% had SAT verbal scores over 700
7% had SAT math scores over 700

Graduation and After
2% pursued further study (1% business, 1% engineering)
96% had job offers within 6 months
34 organizations recruited on campus

Financial Matters
$0 comprehensive fee (1999–2000)

UNITED STATES MILITARY ACADEMY

SMALL-TOWN SETTING ■ PUBLIC ■ FEDERALLY SUPPORTED ■ COED, PRIMARILY MEN
WEST POINT, NEW YORK

Web site: www.usma.edu
Contact: Col. Michael C. Jones, Director of Admissions, United States
   Military Academy, West Point, NY 10996
Telephone: 914-938-4041
E-mail: 8dad@sunams.usma.army.mil

Getting in Last Year
11,490 applied
13% were accepted
1,100 enrolled (74%)
50% from top tenth of their h.s. class
67% had SAT verbal scores over 600
55% had SAT math scores over 600
92% had ACT scores over 24
18% had SAT verbal scores over 700
22% had SAT math scores over 700
36% had ACT scores over 30
227 National Merit Scholars
208 class presidents
82 valedictorians

Graduation and After
80% graduated in 4 years
2% graduated in 5 years
1% graduated in 6 years
2% pursued further study (2% medicine)
3 Rhodes scholars

Financial Matters
$0 comprehensive fee (1999–2000)

Academics
West Point awards bachelor's **degrees**. Challenging opportunities include advanced placement and double majors. Special programs include summer session for credit and off-campus study.

The most frequently chosen fields are engineering/engineering technologies, social sciences and history, and physical sciences. A complete listing of majors at West Point appears in the Majors Index beginning on page 432.

The **faculty** at West Point has 575 full-time members, 39% with terminal degrees. The student-faculty ratio is 7:1.

Students of West Point
The student body is made up of 4,154 undergraduates. Students come from 53 states and territories and 18 other countries. 8% are from New York. 0.9% are international students. 7.6% are African American, 0.6% American Indian, 5.3% Asian American, and 5.7% Hispanic American. 92% returned for their sophomore year.

Facilities and Resources
Student rooms are linked to a campus network. 5,500 **computers** are available on campus that provide access to the Internet. The 2 **libraries** have 457,340 books and 2,220 subscriptions.

Campus Life
There are 114 active organizations on campus, including a drama/theater group, radio station, and choral group. No national or local **fraternities** or **sororities**.

West Point is a member of the NCAA (Division I). **Intercollegiate sports** include baseball (m), basketball, bowling, crew, cross-country running, equestrian sports, fencing, football (m), golf (m), gymnastics (m), ice hockey (m), lacrosse, racquetball, riflery, rugby (m), sailing, skiing (cross-country), skiing (downhill), soccer, softball (w), squash, swimming, tennis, track and field, volleyball, water polo (m), weight lifting, wrestling (m).

Campus Safety
Student safety services include late-night transport/escort service, 24-hour emergency telephone alarm devices, 24-hour patrols by trained security personnel, and student patrols.

Applying
West Point requires an essay, SAT I or ACT, a high school transcript, 4 recommendations, and medical examination, authorized nomination. It recommends an interview. Application deadline: 3/21.

United States Naval Academy

Small-town setting ■ Public ■ Federally supported ■ Coed, Primarily Men
Annapolis, Maryland

Web site: www.usna.edu
Contact: Col. David A. Vetter, Dean of Admissions, 117 Decatur Road,
    Annapolis, MD 21402-5000
Telephone: 410-293-4361 **Fax:** 410-293-4348

Academics

Naval Academy awards bachelor's **degrees**. Challenging opportunities include advanced placement, an honors program, double majors, independent study, and Sigma Xi. Summer session for credit is a special program.

The most frequently chosen fields are engineering/engineering technologies, social sciences and history, and physical sciences. A complete listing of majors at Naval Academy appears in the Majors Index beginning on page 432.

The **faculty** at Naval Academy has 553 full-time members, 46% with terminal degrees. The student-faculty ratio is 9:1.

Students of Naval Academy

The student body is made up of 4,123 undergraduates. Students come from 54 states and territories and 20 other countries. 4% are from Maryland. 0.8% are international students. 6% are African American, 0.8% American Indian, 4.3% Asian American, and 7.5% Hispanic American. 94% returned for their sophomore year.

Facilities and Resources

Student rooms are linked to a campus network. 6,100 **computers** are available on campus that provide access to the Internet. The 2 **libraries** have 800,000 books and 1,892 subscriptions.

Campus Life

There are 75 active organizations on campus, including a drama/theater group, radio station, choral group, and marching band. No national or local **fraternities** or **sororities**.

Naval Academy is a member of the NCAA (Division I). **Intercollegiate sports** include baseball (m), basketball, crew, cross-country running, football (m), golf (m), gymnastics, ice hockey (m), lacrosse, riflery, rugby, sailing, skiing (downhill), soccer, softball (w), squash (m), swimming, tennis, track and field, volleyball, water polo (m), weight lifting, wrestling (m).

Campus Safety

Student safety services include front gate security, 24-hour emergency telephone alarm devices, 24-hour patrols by trained security personnel, and student patrols.

Applying

Naval Academy requires an essay, SAT I or ACT, a high school transcript, an interview, 2 recommendations, authorized nomination, and a minimum high school GPA of 2.0. Application deadline: 2/28.

Getting in Last Year
10,145 applied
15% were accepted
1,144 enrolled (76%)
61% from top tenth of their h.s. class
74% had SAT verbal scores over 600
86% had SAT math scores over 600
20% had SAT verbal scores over 700
34% had SAT math scores over 700
148 class presidents

Graduation and After
76% graduated in 4 years
1% graduated in 5 years
2% pursued further study (1% medicine)
100% had job offers within 6 months
1 Marshall scholar

Financial Matters
$0 comprehensive fee (1999–2000)

THE UNIVERSITY OF ALABAMA IN HUNTSVILLE

SUBURBAN SETTING ■ PUBLIC ■ STATE-SUPPORTED ■ COED
HUNTSVILLE, ALABAMA

Web site: www.uah.edu
Contact: Ms. Sabrina Williams, Associate Director of Admissions, 301 Sparkman Drive, Huntsville, AL 35899
Telephone: 256-890-6070 or toll-free 800-UAH-CALL **Fax:** 256-890-6073
E-mail: admitme@email.uah.edu

The University of Alabama in Huntsville is strategically located in the second-largest research park in America. UAH is a partner with more than 100 high-tech industries as well as major federal laboratories such as NASA's Marshall Space Flight Center and the U.S. Army. Its unique location makes possible many co-op opportunities for students to earn much of their college costs and to maximize their employment potential. Huntsville is an international university: 7,000 students hail from 66 countries. Students have many opportunities to work with some of the top scientists in the country. Some of their research has flown aboard the space shuttle while others have helped solve human problems and improve business management.

Getting in Last Year
1,100 applied
92% were accepted
574 enrolled (57%)
32% from top tenth of their h.s. class
3.30 average high school GPA
42% had SAT verbal scores over 600
42% had SAT math scores over 600
63% had ACT scores over 24
10% had SAT verbal scores over 700
9% had SAT math scores over 700
11% had ACT scores over 30
2 National Merit Scholars
1 valedictorian

Graduation and After
8% graduated in 4 years
17% graduated in 5 years
10% graduated in 6 years
15% pursued further study (9% arts and sciences, 3% engineering, 2% business)
310 organizations recruited on campus

Financial Matters
$3112 resident tuition and fees (1999–2000)
$6516 nonresident tuition and fees (1999–2000)
$3780 room and board
67% average percent of need met
$6145 average financial aid amount received per undergraduate (1999–2000)

Academics

UAH awards bachelor's, master's, and doctoral **degrees** and post-bachelor's and post-master's certificates. Challenging opportunities include advanced placement, accelerated degree programs, an honors program, double majors, independent study, a senior project, and Sigma Xi. Special programs include cooperative education, internships, summer session for credit, off-campus study, and Army and Air Force ROTC.

The most frequently chosen fields are engineering/engineering technologies, health professions and related sciences, and business/marketing. A complete listing of majors at UAH appears in the Majors Index beginning on page 432.

The **faculty** at UAH has 277 full-time members, 92% with terminal degrees. The student-faculty ratio is 14:1.

Students of UAH

The student body totals 6,874, of whom 5,513 are undergraduates. 50.4% are women and 49.6% are men. Students come from 49 states and territories and 66 other countries. 90% are from Alabama. 4.2% are international students. 14.9% are African American, 2.2% American Indian, 4.1% Asian American, and 1.6% Hispanic American. 77% returned for their sophomore year.

Facilities and Resources

Student rooms are linked to a campus network. 300 **computers** are available on campus that provide access to the Internet. The **library** has 2,687 subscriptions.

Campus Life

There are 111 active organizations on campus, including a drama/theater group, newspaper, and choral group. 6% of eligible men and 5% of eligible women are members of national **fraternities** and national **sororities**.

UAH is a member of the NCAA (Division II). **Intercollegiate sports** (some offering scholarships) include baseball (m), basketball, cross-country running, ice hockey (m), soccer, softball (w), tennis, volleyball (w).

Campus Safety

Student safety services include late-night transport/escort service, 24-hour emergency telephone alarm devices, 24-hour patrols by trained security personnel, and electronically operated dormitory entrances.

Applying

UAH requires SAT I or ACT and a high school transcript. Application deadline: 8/15; 4/1 priority date for financial aid. Early and deferred admission are possible.

THE UNIVERSITY OF ARIZONA

URBAN SETTING ■ PUBLIC ■ STATE-SUPPORTED ■ COED
TUCSON, ARIZONA

Web site: www.arizona.edu
Contact: Ms. Lori Goldman, Director of Admissions, PO Box 210040,
Tucson, AZ 85721-0040
Telephone: 520-621-3237 **Fax:** 520-621-9799
E-mail: appinfo@arizona.edu

Academics

UA awards bachelor's, master's, doctoral, and first-professional **degrees**. Challenging opportunities include advanced placement, student-designed majors, freshman honors college, an honors program, a senior project, Phi Beta Kappa, and Sigma Xi. Special programs include cooperative education, internships, summer session for credit, study-abroad, and Army, Navy and Air Force ROTC.

The most frequently chosen fields are business/marketing, social sciences and history, and biological/life sciences. A complete listing of majors at UA appears in the Majors Index beginning on page 432.

The **faculty** at UA has 1,348 full-time members, 97% with terminal degrees. The student-faculty ratio is 18:1.

Students of UA

The student body totals 34,326, of whom 26,258 are undergraduates. 52.8% are women and 47.2% are men. Students come from 55 states and territories and 126 other countries. 71% are from Arizona. 4.1% are international students. 2.9% are African American, 2.3% American Indian, 5.5% Asian American, and 14.4% Hispanic American. 77% returned for their sophomore year.

Facilities and Resources

Student rooms are linked to a campus network. 1,750 **computers** are available on campus that provide access to the Internet. The 6 **libraries** have 4,000,000 books and 18,961 subscriptions.

Campus Life

There are 280 active organizations on campus, including a drama/theater group, newspaper, radio station, choral group, and marching band. 15% of eligible men and 15% of eligible women are members of national **fraternities**, national **sororities**, local fraternities, and local sororities.

UA is a member of the NCAA (Division I). **Intercollegiate sports** (some offering scholarships) include baseball (m), basketball, cross-country running, football (m), golf, gymnastics (w), ice hockey (m), lacrosse, rugby, soccer, softball (w), swimming, tennis, track and field, volleyball, wrestling (m).

Campus Safety

Student safety services include emergency telephones, late-night transport/escort service, 24-hour patrols by trained security personnel, and student patrols.

Applying

UA requires SAT I or ACT and a high school transcript, and in some cases an interview, recommendations, and a minimum high school GPA of 3.0. Application deadline: 4/1; 3/1 priority date for financial aid. Early and deferred admission are possible.

The University of Arizona offers a top-drawer education in a resort-like setting. Some of the nation's highest-ranked departments make their homes here. Tucson's clear skies provide an ideal setting for one of the country's best astronomy programs. Anthropology, nursing, management information systems, and optical sciences are also nationally ranked. The University balances a strong research component with an emphasis on teaching, including the current construction of a learning/advising/computing center for freshmen.

Getting in Last Year
17,700 applied
84% were accepted
5,365 enrolled (36%)
32% from top tenth of their h.s. class
3.33 average high school GPA
28% had SAT verbal scores over 600
32% had SAT math scores over 600
48% had ACT scores over 24
5% had SAT verbal scores over 700
6% had SAT math scores over 700
7% had ACT scores over 30
54 National Merit Scholars
105 valedictorians

Graduation and After
21% graduated in 4 years
25% graduated in 5 years
7% graduated in 6 years

Financial Matters
$2264 resident tuition and fees (1999–2000)
$9416 nonresident tuition and fees (1999–2000)
$5548 room and board
$8808 average financial aid amount received per undergraduate (1998–99)

UNIVERSITY OF CALIFORNIA, BERKELEY

URBAN SETTING ■ PUBLIC ■ STATE-SUPPORTED ■ COED
BERKELEY, CALIFORNIA

Web site: www.berkeley.edu
Contact: Pre-Admission Advising, Office of Undergraduate Admission and Relations With Schools, Berkeley, CA 94720-1500
Telephone: 510-642-3175 **Fax:** 510-642-7333
E-mail: ouars@uclink.berkeley.edu

Getting in Last Year

31,108 applied
27% were accepted
3,727 enrolled (44%)
96% from top tenth of their h.s. class
3.90 average high school GPA
71% had SAT verbal scores over 600
81% had SAT math scores over 600
30% had SAT verbal scores over 700
44% had SAT math scores over 700
184 National Merit Scholars

Graduation and After

48% graduated in 4 years
30% graduated in 5 years
5% graduated in 6 years
600 organizations recruited on campus
28 Fulbright scholars

Financial Matters

$4046 resident tuition and fees (1999–2000)
$13,850 nonresident tuition and fees (1999–2000)
$8266 room and board
94% average percent of need met
$10,456 average financial aid amount received per undergraduate (1998–99)

Academics

Cal awards bachelor's, master's, doctoral, and first-professional **degrees**. Challenging opportunities include advanced placement, accelerated degree programs, student-designed majors, an honors program, double majors, a senior project, Phi Beta Kappa, and Sigma Xi. Special programs include cooperative education, internships, summer session for credit, off-campus study, study-abroad, and Army, Navy and Air Force ROTC. A complete listing of majors at Cal appears in the Majors Index beginning on page 432.

The **faculty** at Cal has 1,438 members, 93% with terminal degrees. The student-faculty ratio is 17:1.

Students of Cal

The student body totals 31,011, of whom 22,261 are undergraduates. 50.3% are women and 49.7% are men. Students come from 53 states and territories and 100 other countries. 90% are from California. 3.9% are international students. 4.9% are African American, 0.8% American Indian, 41.1% Asian American, and 10.8% Hispanic American. 94% returned for their sophomore year.

Facilities and Resources

Student rooms are linked to a campus network. 600 **computers** are available on campus that provide access to the Internet. The 31 **libraries** have 8,450,000 books and 83,000 subscriptions.

Campus Life

There are 400 active organizations on campus, including a drama/theater group, newspaper, radio station, choral group, and marching band. 10% of eligible men and 10% of eligible women are members of national **fraternities**, national **sororities**, local fraternities, and local sororities.

Cal is a member of the NCAA (Division I). **Intercollegiate sports** (some offering scholarships) include baseball (m), basketball, crew, cross-country running, field hockey (w), football (m), golf, gymnastics, lacrosse (w), rugby (m), soccer, softball (w), swimming, tennis, track and field, volleyball (w), water polo.

Campus Safety

Student safety services include Office of Emergency Preparedness, late-night transport/escort service, 24-hour emergency telephone alarm devices, 24-hour patrols by trained security personnel, and electronically operated dormitory entrances.

Applying

Cal requires an essay, SAT II Subject Tests, SAT II: Writing Test, a high school transcript, and minimum 3.3 GPA for California residents; 3.4 for all others. Application deadline: 11/30; 3/2 priority date for financial aid.

UNIVERSITY OF CALIFORNIA, DAVIS

SUBURBAN SETTING ■ PUBLIC ■ STATE-SUPPORTED ■ COED
DAVIS, CALIFORNIA

Web site: www.ucdavis.edu
Contact: Dr. Gary Tudor, Director of Undergraduate Admissions,
    Undergraduate Admission and Outreach Services, 175 Mrak Hall, Davis,
    CA 95616
Telephone: 530-752-2971 **Fax:** 530-752-1280
E-mail: thinkucd@ucdavis.edu

Academics

UC Davis awards bachelor's, master's, doctoral, and first-professional **degrees** and post-bachelor's certificates. Challenging opportunities include advanced placement, student-designed majors, freshman honors college, an honors program, double majors, independent study, a senior project, Phi Beta Kappa, and Sigma Xi. Special programs include internships, summer session for credit, study-abroad, and Army and Air Force ROTC.

The most frequently chosen fields are biological/life sciences, social sciences and history, and psychology. A complete listing of majors at UC Davis appears in the Majors Index beginning on page 432.

The **faculty** at UC Davis has 1,371 full-time members.

Students of UC Davis

The student body totals 25,092, of whom 19,517 are undergraduates. 56.3% are women and 43.7% are men. Students come from 48 states and territories and 117 other countries. 97% are from California. 1.4% are international students. 2.8% are African American, 1% American Indian, 34.9% Asian American, and 9.8% Hispanic American. 89% returned for their sophomore year.

Facilities and Resources

Student rooms are linked to a campus network. 600 **computers** are available on campus that provide access to software packages and the Internet. The 6 **libraries** have 2,879,533 books and 45,665 subscriptions.

Campus Life

There are 316 active organizations on campus, including a drama/theater group, newspaper, radio station, choral group, and marching band. 6% of eligible men and 7% of eligible women are members of national **fraternities**, national **sororities**, and state fraternities and sororities.

UC Davis is a member of the NCAA (Division II). **Intercollegiate sports** include baseball (m), basketball, cross-country running, football (m), golf (m), gymnastics (w), soccer, softball (w), swimming, tennis, track and field, volleyball (w), water polo (m), wrestling (m).

Campus Safety

Student safety services include rape prevention programs, late-night transport/escort service, 24-hour emergency telephone alarm devices, 24-hour patrols by trained security personnel, student patrols, and electronically operated dormitory entrances.

Applying

UC Davis requires an essay, SAT II: Writing Test, SAT I and SAT II or ACT, and a high school transcript. Application deadline: 11/30; 3/2 priority date for financial aid. Deferred admission is possible.

Getting in Last Year

23,126 applied
62% were accepted
3,819 enrolled (27%)
3.73 average high school GPA
39% had SAT verbal scores over 600
54% had SAT math scores over 600
51% had ACT scores over 24
9% had SAT verbal scores over 700
13% had SAT math scores over 700
6% had ACT scores over 30
16 National Merit Scholars

Graduation and After

41% pursued further study (17% arts and
    sciences, 7% medicine, 6% education)
91% had job offers within 6 months
3 Fulbright scholars

Financial Matters

$4214 resident tuition and fees (1999–2000)
$14,536 nonresident tuition and fees (1999–
    2000)
$7012 room and board
78% average percent of need met
$8632 average financial aid amount received
    per undergraduate (1998–99)

UNIVERSITY OF CALIFORNIA, LOS ANGELES

URBAN SETTING ■ PUBLIC ■ STATE-SUPPORTED ■ COED
LOS ANGELES, CALIFORNIA

Web site: www.ucla.edu
Contact: Dr. Rae Lee Siporin, Director of Undergraduate Admissions, 405 Hilgard Avenue, Los Angeles, CA 90095
Telephone: 310-825-3101
E-mail: ugadm@saonet.ucla.edu

Getting in Last Year
35,681 applied
29% were accepted
3,751 enrolled (36%)
97% from top tenth of their h.s. class
64% had SAT verbal scores over 600
77% had SAT math scores over 600
74% had ACT scores over 24
18% had SAT verbal scores over 700
35% had SAT math scores over 700
20% had ACT scores over 30
73 National Merit Scholars

Graduation and After
38% graduated in 4 years
35% graduated in 5 years
5% graduated in 6 years
33% pursued further study
1400 organizations recruited on campus
15 Fulbright scholars

Financial Matters
$3698 resident tuition and fees (1999–2000)
$13,872 nonresident tuition and fees (1999–2000)
$7692 room and board
76% average percent of need met
$8596 average financial aid amount received per undergraduate (1998–99)

Academics
UCLA awards bachelor's, master's, doctoral, and first-professional **degrees**. Challenging opportunities include advanced placement, student-designed majors, an honors program, double majors, independent study, Phi Beta Kappa, and Sigma Xi. Special programs include internships, summer session for credit, off-campus study, study-abroad, and Army, Navy and Air Force ROTC.

The most frequently chosen fields are social sciences and history, psychology, and biological/life sciences. A complete listing of majors at UCLA appears in the Majors Index beginning on page 432.

The **faculty** at UCLA has 3,435 members. The student-faculty ratio is 18:1.

Students of UCLA
The student body totals 36,350, of whom 24,668 are undergraduates. 54.9% are women and 45.1% are men. Students come from 50 states and territories and 100 other countries. 97% are from California. 2.5% are international students. 4.7% are African American, 0.6% American Indian, 37% Asian American, and 14.6% Hispanic American. 97% returned for their sophomore year.

Facilities and Resources
Student rooms are linked to a campus network. The 14 **libraries** have 5,933,330 books and 94,748 subscriptions.

Campus Life
Active organizations on campus include a drama/theater group, newspaper, radio station, choral group, and marching band. 11% of eligible men and 9% of eligible women are members of national **fraternities**, national **sororities**, local fraternities, and local sororities.

UCLA is a member of the NCAA (Division I). **Intercollegiate sports** (some offering scholarships) include baseball (m), basketball, cross-country running, football (m), golf, gymnastics (w), soccer, softball (w), swimming (w), tennis, track and field, volleyball, water polo.

Campus Safety
Student safety services include late-night transport/escort service, 24-hour emergency telephone alarm devices, and student patrols.

Applying
UCLA requires an essay, SAT II: Writing Test, SAT I or ACT, SAT II Subject Test in math, third SAT II Subject Test, and a high school transcript. It recommends a minimum high school GPA of 3.5. Application deadline: 11/30; 3/2 priority date for financial aid.

UNIVERSITY OF CALIFORNIA, RIVERSIDE

URBAN SETTING ■ PUBLIC ■ STATE-SUPPORTED ■ COED
RIVERSIDE, CALIFORNIA

Web site: www.ucr.edu
Contact: Ms. Laurie Nelson, Director of Undergraduate Admission, 900
    University Avenue, Riverside, CA 92521-0102
Telephone: 909-787-3411 **Fax:** 909-787-6344
E-mail: discover@pop.ucr.edu

Academics

UCR awards bachelor's, master's, and doctoral **degrees**. Challenging opportunities
include advanced placement, accelerated degree programs, student-designed majors,
freshman honors college, an honors program, double majors, independent study, a senior
project, Phi Beta Kappa, and Sigma Xi. Special programs include cooperative education,
internships, summer session for credit, off-campus study, study-abroad, and Army and
Air Force ROTC.

The most frequently chosen fields are business/marketing, social sciences and history,
and biological/life sciences. A complete listing of majors at UCR appears in the Majors
Index beginning on page 432.

The **faculty** at UCR has 460 full-time members, 98% with terminal degrees. The
student-faculty ratio is 19:1.

Students of UCR

The student body totals 11,600, of whom 10,120 are undergraduates. 54.3% are women
and 45.7% are men. Students come from 49 states and territories and 45 other countries.
99% are from California. 1.6% are international students. 5.4% are African American,
0.5% American Indian, 40.7% Asian American, and 20.9% Hispanic American. 86%
returned for their sophomore year.

Facilities and Resources

Student rooms are linked to a campus network. 600 **computers** are available on campus
that provide access to the Internet. The 7 **libraries** have 1,851,200 books and 12,800
subscriptions.

Campus Life

There are 190 active organizations on campus, including a drama/theater group,
newspaper, radio station, and choral group. 5% of eligible men and 7% of eligible
women are members of national **fraternities**, national **sororities**, local fraternities, local
sororities, and coed fraternities.

UCR is a member of the NCAA (Division II). **Intercollegiate sports** (some offering
scholarships) include baseball (m), basketball, cross-country running, lacrosse (m),
softball (w), tennis, track and field, volleyball (w).

Campus Safety

Student safety services include late-night transport/escort service, 24-hour emergency
telephone alarm devices, 24-hour patrols by trained security personnel, student patrols,
and electronically operated dormitory entrances.

Applying

UCR requires an essay, SAT II: Writing Test, SAT I or ACT, a high school transcript,
and a minimum high school GPA of 2.82. Application deadline: 11/30; 3/2 priority date
for financial aid. Early admission is possible.

Getting in Last Year
16,316 applied
84% were accepted
2,721 enrolled (20%)
94% from top tenth of their h.s. class
3.54 average high school GPA
18% had SAT verbal scores over 600
33% had SAT math scores over 600
31% had ACT scores over 24
2% had SAT verbal scores over 700
7% had SAT math scores over 700
3% had ACT scores over 30

Graduation and After
44% graduated in 4 years
19% graduated in 5 years
4% graduated in 6 years
41% pursued further study
54% had job offers within 6 months
165 organizations recruited on campus
1 Fulbright scholar

Financial Matters
$13,930 nonresident tuition and fees (1999–
    2000)
$6579 room and board
100% average percent of need met
$8997 average financial aid amount received
    per undergraduate (1998–99)

UNIVERSITY OF CALIFORNIA, SAN DIEGO

SUBURBAN SETTING ■ PUBLIC ■ STATE-SUPPORTED ■ COED
LA JOLLA, CALIFORNIA

Web site: www.ucsd.edu
Contact: Mr. Tim Johnston, Associate Director of Admissions and Outreach, 9500 Gilman Drive, 0337, La Jolla, CA 92093-0337
Telephone: 858-534-4831
E-mail: admissionsinfo@ucsd.edu

Getting in Last Year
32,539 applied
41% were accepted
95% from top tenth of their h.s. class
3.98 average high school GPA

Graduation and After
35% pursued further study
85% had job offers within 6 months
4249 organizations recruited on campus
5 Fulbright scholars

Financial Matters
$3849 resident tuition and fees (1999–2000)
$14,023 nonresident tuition and fees (1999–2000)
$7134 room and board
$9205 average financial aid amount received per undergraduate (1999–2000 estimated)

Academics

UCSD awards bachelor's, master's, doctoral, and first-professional **degrees**. Challenging opportunities include accelerated degree programs, student-designed majors, freshman honors college, an honors program, double majors, independent study, a senior project, and Phi Beta Kappa. Special programs include cooperative education, internships, summer session for credit, off-campus study, and study-abroad. A complete listing of majors at UCSD appears in the Majors Index beginning on page 432.

The **faculty** at UCSD has 1,465 members.

Students of UCSD

The student body totals 19,918, of whom 16,230 are undergraduates. 98% are from California. 1.6% are African American, 0.7% American Indian, 34.9% Asian American, and 9.7% Hispanic American. 93% returned for their sophomore year.

Facilities and Resources

Student rooms are linked to a campus network. 1,020 **computers** are available on campus that provide access to the Internet. The 7 **libraries** have 2,500,000 books and 23,421 subscriptions.

Campus Life

There are 275 active organizations on campus, including a drama/theater group, newspaper, radio station, television station, and choral group. 10% of eligible men and 10% of eligible women are members of national **fraternities** and national **sororities**.

UCSD is a member of the NCAA (Division III). **Intercollegiate sports** include baseball (m), basketball, crew, cross-country running, fencing, golf (m), soccer, softball (w), swimming, tennis, track and field, volleyball, water polo.

Campus Safety

Student safety services include crime prevention programs, late-night transport/escort service, and 24-hour emergency telephone alarm devices.

Applying

UCSD requires an essay, SAT I or ACT, 3 SAT II Subject Tests (including SAT II: Writing Test), a high school transcript, and a minimum high school GPA of 3.3, and in some cases a minimum high school GPA of 3.4. Application deadline: 11/30; 3/2 priority date for financial aid.

UNIVERSITY OF CALIFORNIA, SANTA BARBARA

SUBURBAN SETTING ■ PUBLIC ■ STATE-SUPPORTED ■ COED

SANTA BARBARA, CALIFORNIA

Web site: www.ucsb.edu
Contact: Mr. William Villa, Director of Admissions/Relations with Schools,
    Santa Barbara, CA 93106
Telephone: 805-893-2485
E-mail: appinfo@sa.ucsb.edu

Academics

UCSB awards bachelor's, master's, and doctoral **degrees**. Challenging opportunities include advanced placement, accelerated degree programs, student-designed majors, freshman honors college, an honors program, double majors, independent study, a senior project, Phi Beta Kappa, and Sigma Xi. Special programs include internships, summer session for credit, off-campus study, study-abroad, and Army ROTC.

The most frequently chosen fields are social sciences and history, business/marketing, and biological/life sciences. A complete listing of majors at UCSB appears in the Majors Index beginning on page 432.

Students of UCSB

The student body totals 20,056, of whom 17,699 are undergraduates. 54.4% are women and 45.6% are men. Students come from 48 states and territories and 35 other countries. 96% are from California. 1.2% are international students. 2.4% are African American, 1% American Indian, 14.6% Asian American, and 13.7% Hispanic American. 89% returned for their sophomore year.

Facilities and Resources

3,000 **computers** are available on campus that provide access to the Internet. The **library** has 2,430,000 books and 18,100 subscriptions.

Campus Life

There are 250 active organizations on campus, including a drama/theater group, newspaper, radio station, and choral group. 8% of eligible men and 10% of eligible women are members of national **fraternities**, national **sororities**, local fraternities, and local sororities.

UCSB is a member of the NCAA (Division I). **Intercollegiate sports** (some offering scholarships) include baseball (m), basketball, bowling, crew, cross-country running, fencing, field hockey (w), golf, gymnastics, lacrosse, rugby (m), sailing, skiing (downhill), soccer, softball (w), swimming, tennis, track and field, volleyball, water polo.

Campus Safety

Student safety services include late-night transport/escort service and 24-hour emergency telephone alarm devices.

Applying

UCSB requires an essay, SAT II Subject Tests, SAT I or ACT, and a high school transcript, and in some cases an interview. Application deadline: 11/30; 5/31 for financial aid, with a 3/2 priority date. Early admission is possible.

Getting in Last Year

26,931 applied
53% were accepted
3,781 enrolled (26%)
3.69 average high school GPA
44% had SAT verbal scores over 600
55% had SAT math scores over 600
7% had SAT verbal scores over 700
12% had SAT math scores over 700

Graduation and After

24% pursued further study
56% had job offers within 6 months
6 Fulbright scholars

Financial Matters

$3844 resident tuition and fees (1999–2000)
$14,018 nonresident tuition and fees (1999–2000)
$7156 room and board

UNIVERSITY OF CALIFORNIA, SANTA CRUZ

SMALL-TOWN SETTING ■ PUBLIC ■ STATE-SUPPORTED ■ COED
SANTA CRUZ, CALIFORNIA

Web site: www.ucsc.edu
Contact: Mr. J. Michael Thompson, Associate Vice Chancellor, Outreach, Admissions, and Student Academic Services, Admissions Office, Cook House, Santa Cruz, CA 95064
Telephone: 831-459-4008
E-mail: admissions@cats.ucsc.edu

Getting in Last Year
13,931 applied
79% were accepted
2,365 enrolled (21%)
96% from top tenth of their h.s. class
3.53 average high school GPA
42% had SAT verbal scores over 600
41% had SAT math scores over 600
51% had ACT scores over 24
10% had SAT verbal scores over 700
7% had SAT math scores over 700
8% had ACT scores over 30

Graduation and After
38% graduated in 4 years
20% graduated in 5 years
4% graduated in 6 years
237 organizations recruited on campus
5 Fulbright scholars

Financial Matters
$4377 resident tuition and fees (1999–2000)
$14,699 nonresident tuition and fees (1999–2000)
$7337 room and board
80% average percent of need met
$9749 average financial aid amount received per undergraduate (1998–99)

Academics

UCSC awards bachelor's, master's, and doctoral **degrees**. Challenging opportunities include advanced placement, student-designed majors, freshman honors college, an honors program, double majors, independent study, a senior project, Phi Beta Kappa, and Sigma Xi. Special programs include cooperative education, internships, summer session for credit, off-campus study, study-abroad, and Army, Navy and Air Force ROTC. A complete listing of majors at UCSC appears in the Majors Index beginning on page 432.

Students of UCSC

The student body totals 11,302, of whom 10,269 are undergraduates. 57.1% are women and 42.9% are men. Students come from 48 states and territories and 62 other countries. 0.7% are international students. 2.2% are African American, 1.1% American Indian, 13.8% Asian American, and 12.9% Hispanic American. 80% returned for their sophomore year.

Facilities and Resources

Student rooms are linked to a campus network. 200 **computers** are available on campus that provide access to the Internet. The 10 **libraries** have 1,200,000 books and 10,004 subscriptions.

Campus Life

There are 100 active organizations on campus, including a drama/theater group, newspaper, radio station, and choral group. 1% of eligible men and 1% of eligible women are members of national **fraternities**, national **sororities**, local fraternities, and local sororities.

UCSC is a member of the NCAA (Division III). **Intercollegiate sports** include basketball, fencing, lacrosse, rugby (m), sailing, soccer (m), swimming, tennis, volleyball, water polo.

Campus Safety

Student safety services include evening main gate security, late-night transport/escort service, 24-hour emergency telephone alarm devices, 24-hour patrols by trained security personnel, and electronically operated dormitory entrances.

Applying

UCSC requires an essay, SAT II: Writing Test, SAT I or ACT, and a high school transcript. Application deadline: 11/30; 3/2 priority date for financial aid.

UNIVERSITY OF CHICAGO

URBAN SETTING ■ PRIVATE ■ INDEPENDENT ■ COED

CHICAGO, ILLINOIS

Web site: www.uchicago.edu
Contact: Mr. Theodore O'Neill, Dean of Admissions, 1116 East 59th Street, Chicago, IL 60637-1513
Telephone: 773-702-8650 **Fax:** 773-702-4199
E-mail: college-admissions@uchicago.edu

Academics

Chicago awards bachelor's, master's, doctoral, and first-professional **degrees**. Challenging opportunities include advanced placement, accelerated degree programs, student-designed majors, double majors, independent study, a senior project, Phi Beta Kappa, and Sigma Xi. Special programs include internships, summer session for credit, off-campus study, study-abroad, and Army and Air Force ROTC.

The most frequently chosen fields are social sciences and history, biological/life sciences, and interdisciplinary studies. A complete listing of majors at Chicago appears in the Majors Index beginning on page 432.

The **faculty** at Chicago has 1,552 full-time members. The student-faculty ratio is 4:1.

Students of Chicago

The student body totals 12,003, of whom 3,844 are undergraduates. 48.7% are women and 51.3% are men. Students come from 53 states and territories and 34 other countries. 22% are from Illinois. 5.4% are international students. 4.1% are African American, 0.2% American Indian, 20.4% Asian American, and 6% Hispanic American. 95% returned for their sophomore year.

Facilities and Resources

Student rooms are linked to a campus network. 1,000 **computers** are available on campus that provide access to the Internet. The 9 **libraries** have 5,800,000 books and 47,000 subscriptions.

Campus Life

There are 200 active organizations on campus, including a drama/theater group, newspaper, radio station, and choral group. 12% of eligible men and 5% of eligible women are members of national **fraternities** and national **sororities**.

Chicago is a member of the NCAA (Division III). **Intercollegiate sports** include baseball (m), basketball, cross-country running, football (m), soccer, softball (w), swimming, tennis, track and field, volleyball (w), wrestling (m).

Campus Safety

Student safety services include late-night transport/escort service, 24-hour emergency telephone alarm devices, 24-hour patrols by trained security personnel, and electronically operated dormitory entrances.

Applying

Chicago requires an essay, SAT I or ACT, a high school transcript, and 3 recommendations. It recommends an interview. Application deadline: 1/1; 2/1 priority date for financial aid. Early and deferred admission are possible.

Getting in Last Year

6,844 applied
48% were accepted
1,005 enrolled (31%)
79% from top tenth of their h.s. class
90% had SAT verbal scores over 600
90% had SAT math scores over 600
96% had ACT scores over 24
54% had SAT verbal scores over 700
48% had SAT math scores over 700
55% had ACT scores over 30
97 National Merit Scholars
77 valedictorians

Graduation and After

Graduates pursuing further study: 17% arts and sciences, 8% law, 8% medicine
1 Rhodes, 3 Marshall, 17 Fulbright scholars

Financial Matters

$24,234 tuition and fees (1999–2000)
$7834 room and board

UNIVERSITY OF CINCINNATI
URBAN SETTING ■ PUBLIC ■ STATE-SUPPORTED ■ COED
CINCINNATI, OHIO

Web site: www.uc.edu
Contact: Mr. James Williams, Director of Admissions, PO Box 210091, Cincinnati, OH 45221-0091
Telephone: 513-556-1100 or toll-free 800-827-8728 (in-state) **Fax:** 513-556-1105
E-mail: admissions@uc.edu

The University of Cincinnati, founded in 1819, has been consistently ranked as one of the top values in the U.S. for a 4-year undergraduate education. The University is composed of 17 individual colleges, divisions, and schools and offers more than 500 degree programs to 28,000 students from 46 states and 50 countries. UC is the birthplace of cooperative education; currently, nearly 4,000 students work in 32 states and many other countries. The University celebrates learning, diversity, and community. Its nationally recognized program, "Just Community," defines the University's values and principles. Located in one of the 10 most liveable cities in America, the University of Cincinnati offers students the opportunity for a quality education at a reasonable price.

Academics

UC awards associate, bachelor's, master's, doctoral, and first-professional **degrees**. Challenging opportunities include advanced placement, accelerated degree programs, student-designed majors, an honors program, double majors, independent study, Phi Beta Kappa, and Sigma Xi. Special programs include cooperative education, internships, summer session for credit, off-campus study, study-abroad, and Army and Air Force ROTC.

The most frequently chosen fields are (pre)law, business/marketing, and engineering/engineering technologies. A complete listing of majors at UC appears in the Majors Index beginning on page 432.

The **faculty** at UC has 1,939 full-time members, 81% with terminal degrees.

Students of UC

The student body totals 28,162, of whom 20,656 are undergraduates. 47.9% are women and 52.1% are men. Students come from 46 states and territories and 50 other countries. 0.8% are international students. 13.9% are African American, 0.3% American Indian, 2.9% Asian American, and 1% Hispanic American. 70% returned for their sophomore year.

Facilities and Resources

Student rooms are linked to a campus network. 325 **computers** are available on campus that provide access to the Internet. The 8 **libraries** have 16,363 subscriptions.

Campus Life

There are 50 active organizations on campus, including a drama/theater group, newspaper, radio station, choral group, and marching band. UC has national **fraternities**, national **sororities**, and local sororities.

UC is a member of the NCAA (Division I). **Intercollegiate sports** (some offering scholarships) include basketball, crew, cross-country running, football (m), golf (m), rugby (m), soccer, swimming, tennis, track and field, volleyball (w).

Campus Safety

Student safety services include late-night transport/escort service, 24-hour emergency telephone alarm devices, 24-hour patrols by trained security personnel, and electronically operated dormitory entrances.

Applying

UC requires SAT I or ACT and a high school transcript, and in some cases 2 recommendations and audition. It recommends an interview. Application deadline: rolling admissions.

Getting in Last Year
10,704 applied
86% were accepted
3,846 enrolled (42%)
15% from top tenth of their h.s. class
22% had SAT verbal scores over 600
28% had SAT math scores over 600
24% had ACT scores over 24
3% had SAT verbal scores over 700
6% had SAT math scores over 700
6% had ACT scores over 30

Graduation and After
14% graduated in 4 years
27% graduated in 5 years
7% graduated in 6 years
36% pursued further study
1 Fulbright scholar

Financial Matters
$4998 resident tuition and fees (1999–2000)
$12,879 nonresident tuition and fees (1999–2000)
$6399 room and board
$5087 average financial aid amount received per undergraduate (1998–99)

UNIVERSITY OF COLORADO AT BOULDER

■ URBAN SETTING ■ PUBLIC ■ STATE-SUPPORTED ■ COED
BOULDER, COLORADO

Web site: www.colorado.edu
Contact: Admission Counselor, Campus Box 30, Boulder, CO 80309-0030
Telephone: 303-492-6301 **Fax:** 303-492-7115
E-mail: apply@colorado.edu

Academics
CU-Boulder awards bachelor's, master's, doctoral, and first-professional **degrees**. Challenging opportunities include advanced placement, accelerated degree programs, student-designed majors, freshman honors college, an honors program, double majors, independent study, a senior project, Phi Beta Kappa, and Sigma Xi. Special programs include cooperative education, internships, summer session for credit, off-campus study, study-abroad, and Army, Navy and Air Force ROTC.

The most frequently chosen fields are social sciences and history, business/marketing, and communications/communication technologies. A complete listing of majors at CU-Boulder appears in the Majors Index beginning on page 432.

The **faculty** at CU-Boulder has 1,140 full-time members, 86% with terminal degrees. The student-faculty ratio is 14:1.

Students of CU-Boulder
The student body totals 28,373, of whom 22,660 are undergraduates. 48.2% are women and 51.8% are men. Students come from 56 states and territories and 88 other countries. 69% are from Colorado. 1.7% are international students. 1.9% are African American, 0.8% American Indian, 5.6% Asian American, and 5.4% Hispanic American. 84% returned for their sophomore year.

Facilities and Resources
Student rooms are linked to a campus network. 1,700 **computers** are available on campus that provide access to standard and academic software, student government voting and the Internet. The 7 **libraries** have 2,900,000 books and 25,300 subscriptions.

Campus Life
Active organizations on campus include a drama/theater group, newspaper, radio station, television station, choral group, and marching band. 10% of eligible men and 13% of eligible women are members of national **fraternities**, national **sororities**, and local sororities.

CU-Boulder is a member of the NCAA (Division I). **Intercollegiate sports** (some offering scholarships) include baseball (m), basketball, bowling, crew, cross-country running, equestrian sports, fencing, field hockey, football (m), golf, ice hockey, lacrosse, racquetball, rugby, skiing (cross-country), skiing (downhill), soccer, softball (w), squash, swimming, tennis, track and field, volleyball, water polo.

Campus Safety
Student safety services include university police department, late-night transport/escort service, 24-hour emergency telephone alarm devices, 24-hour patrols by trained security personnel, and student patrols.

Applying
CU-Boulder requires an essay, SAT I or ACT, a high school transcript, and a minimum high school GPA of 2.0, and in some cases audition for music program. It recommends recommendations and a minimum high school GPA of 3.0. Application deadline: 2/15; 4/1 priority date for financial aid. Deferred admission is possible.

The University of Colorado at Boulder, a major research and teaching university, is located in one of the most spectacular environments in the country at the foot of the Rocky Mountains. Ranking 10th among all public universities in federally funded research, the University offers tremendous academic diversity, with faculty committed to bringing their research into the classroom. Students may participate in honors programs, an undergraduate research program, and several residential programs.

Getting in Last Year
14,617 applied
85% were accepted
4,596 enrolled (37%)
24% from top tenth of their h.s. class
3.41 average high school GPA
38% had SAT verbal scores over 600
45% had SAT math scores over 600
64% had ACT scores over 24
6% had SAT verbal scores over 700
8% had SAT math scores over 700
10% had ACT scores over 30
135 valedictorians

Graduation and After
35% graduated in 4 years
24% graduated in 5 years
5% graduated in 6 years
18% pursued further study (6% arts and sciences, 5% medicine, 3% engineering)
582 organizations recruited on campus
2 Fulbright scholars

Financial Matters
$3118 resident tuition and fees (1999–2000)
$15,898 nonresident tuition and fees (1999–2000)
$5202 room and board
69% average percent of need met
$8470 average financial aid amount received per undergraduate (1998–99)

Getting in Last Year
11,781 applied
70% were accepted
2,956 enrolled (36%)
20% from top tenth of their h.s. class
31% had SAT verbal scores over 600
37% had SAT math scores over 600
5% had SAT verbal scores over 700
6% had SAT math scores over 700
12 National Merit Scholars
26 valedictorians

Graduation and After
40% graduated in 4 years
23% graduated in 5 years
4% graduated in 6 years
11% pursued further study
71% had job offers within 6 months
330 organizations recruited on campus

Financial Matters
$5404 resident tuition and fees (1999–2000)
$13,922 nonresident tuition and fees (1999–2000)
$5694 room and board

UNIVERSITY OF CONNECTICUT
RURAL SETTING ■ PUBLIC ■ STATE-SUPPORTED ■ COED
STORRS, CONNECTICUT

Web site: www.uconn.edu
Contact: Mr. Brian Usher, Associate Director of Admissions, 2131 Hillside Road, U-88, Storrs, CT 06269-3088
Telephone: 860-486-3137 **Fax:** 860-486-1476
E-mail: beahusky@uconnvm.uconn.edu

Academics
UCONN awards associate, bachelor's, master's, doctoral, and first-professional **degrees** and post-master's certificates. Challenging opportunities include advanced placement, accelerated degree programs, student-designed majors, an honors program, double majors, independent study, a senior project, Phi Beta Kappa, and Sigma Xi. Special programs include cooperative education, internships, summer session for credit, off-campus study, study-abroad, and Army and Air Force ROTC.

The most frequently chosen fields are business/marketing, social sciences and history, and health professions and related sciences. A complete listing of majors at UCONN appears in the Majors Index beginning on page 432.

The **faculty** at UCONN has 1,043 full-time members, 95% with terminal degrees. The student-faculty ratio is 15:1.

Students of UCONN
The student body totals 18,853, of whom 12,353 are undergraduates. 52.5% are women and 47.5% are men. Students come from 51 states and territories and 45 other countries. 81% are from Connecticut. 1.1% are international students. 5.1% are African American, 0.3% American Indian, 5.6% Asian American, and 4.2% Hispanic American. 86% returned for their sophomore year.

Facilities and Resources
Student rooms are linked to a campus network. 1,800 **computers** are available on campus that provide access to the Internet. The 4 **libraries** have 2,156,487 books and 13,132 subscriptions.

Campus Life
There are 226 active organizations on campus, including a drama/theater group, newspaper, radio station, television station, choral group, and marching band. 9% of eligible men and 4% of eligible women are members of national **fraternities**, national **sororities**, local fraternities, and local sororities.

UCONN is a member of the NCAA (Division I). **Intercollegiate sports** (some offering scholarships) include baseball (m), basketball (m), crew (w), cross-country running, field hockey (w), football (m), golf (m), ice hockey (m), lacrosse (w), soccer, softball (w), swimming, tennis, track and field, volleyball (w).

Campus Safety
Student safety services include late-night transport/escort service and 24-hour emergency telephone alarm devices.

Applying
UCONN requires an essay, SAT I or ACT, and a high school transcript. It recommends 1 recommendation. Application deadline: 3/1; 3/1 priority date for financial aid. Early and deferred admission are possible.

UNIVERSITY OF DALLAS

URBAN SETTING ■ PRIVATE ■ INDEPENDENT RELIGIOUS ■ COED

IRVING, TEXAS

  eAPPLY

Web site: www.udallas.edu
Contact: Mr. Larry Webb, Director of Enrollment, 1845 East Northgate
Drive, Irving, TX 75062-4799
Telephone: 972-721-5266 or toll-free 800-628-6999 **Fax:** 972-721-5017
E-mail: undadmis@acad.udallas.edu

Academics

UD awards bachelor's, master's, and doctoral **degrees**. Challenging opportunities
include advanced placement, accelerated degree programs, student-designed majors,
double majors, independent study, a senior project, and Phi Beta Kappa. Special
programs include internships, summer session for credit, off-campus study, study-abroad,
and Army and Air Force ROTC.

The most frequently chosen fields are social sciences and history, visual/performing
arts, and philosophy. A complete listing of majors at UD appears in the Majors Index
beginning on page 432.

The **faculty** at UD has 125 full-time members. The student-faculty ratio is 13:1.

Students of UD

The student body totals 3,211, of whom 1,184 are undergraduates. 58.7% are women
and 41.3% are men. Students come from 46 states and territories and 20 other countries.
59% are from Texas. 3.5% are international students. 1.6% are African American, 0.8%
American Indian, 5.6% Asian American, and 13.6% Hispanic American. 85% returned
for their sophomore year.

Facilities and Resources

Student rooms are linked to a campus network. 70 **computers** are available on campus
that provide access to the Internet. The **library** has 192,468 books and 1,819 subscriptions.

Campus Life

There are 30 active organizations on campus, including a drama/theater group,
newspaper, and choral group. No national or local **fraternities** or **sororities**.

UD is a member of the NCAA (Division III). **Intercollegiate sports** include baseball
(m), basketball, cross-country running, golf, soccer, tennis, volleyball (w).

Campus Safety

Student safety services include late-night transport/escort service, 24-hour emergency
telephone alarm devices, 24-hour patrols by trained security personnel, and electronically operated dormitory entrances.

Applying

UD requires an essay, SAT I or ACT, a high school transcript, and 1 recommendation,
and in some cases an interview. It recommends an interview. Application deadline: 2/15;
3/1 priority date for financial aid. Early and deferred admission are possible.

The University of Dallas,
the Catholic university for
independent thinkers, is
where debate and discourse are a
way of life. The professors guide
students in an environment of
intellectual inquiry that engages the
imagination. UD's distinctive and
comprehensive core curriculum
emphasizes the use of original
texts. Reading great books, sharing
a common body of knowledge with
other students, and discussing ideas
are important parts of a student's
education. UD's classical education
comes to life on its Rome campus,
where nearly 85% of sophomores
spend a semester exploring the
cities, works of art, and historic
landmarks that they have studied in
their core courses.

Getting in Last Year
1,213 applied
76% were accepted
310 enrolled (33%)
55% from top tenth of their h.s. class
3.80 average high school GPA
66% had SAT verbal scores over 600
52% had SAT math scores over 600
79% had ACT scores over 24
19% had SAT verbal scores over 700
10% had SAT math scores over 700
19% had ACT scores over 30
17 National Merit Scholars
27 valedictorians

Graduation and After
43% graduated in 4 years
15% graduated in 5 years
2% graduated in 6 years
Graduates pursuing further study: 20% arts
and sciences, 14% business, 10% medicine
50 organizations recruited on campus

Financial Matters
$14,420 tuition and fees (1999–2000)
$5446 room and board
92% average percent of need met
$13,676 average financial aid amount received
per undergraduate (1998–99)

UNIVERSITY OF DAYTON

SUBURBAN SETTING ■ PRIVATE ■ INDEPENDENT RELIGIOUS ■ COED
DAYTON, OHIO

Web site: www.udayton.edu
Contact: Mr. Myron H. Achbach, Director of Admission, 300 College Park,
   Dayton, OH 45469-1300
Telephone: 937-229-4411 or toll-free 800-837-7433 **Fax:** 937-229-4729
E-mail: admission@udayton.edu

The University of Dayton is Ohio's largest private university and a national leader in Catholic higher education. Competence, character, and commitment are hallmarks of the 80,000 alumni around the world who have called Dayton their alma mater, including 4-time Super Bowl winner Chuck Noll, ESPN anchor Dan Patrick, television star Mystro Clark, and the late humorist Erma Bombeck. University of Dayton students are encouraged to look critically at the world's problems and to become part of the solution—from joining efforts to rebuild Bosnia to boosting literacy and building housing in our own backyard. The technology-enhanced learning environment is preparing students to lead well into the next century. The University of Dayton is a place where the mind and heart serve the human community.

Getting in Last Year
6,572 applied
87% were accepted
1,800 enrolled (32%)
22% from top tenth of their h.s. class
36% had SAT verbal scores over 600
44% had SAT math scores over 600
61% had ACT scores over 24
7% had SAT verbal scores over 700
10% had SAT math scores over 700
15% had ACT scores over 30
13 National Merit Scholars
39 valedictorians

Graduation and After
51% graduated in 4 years
18% graduated in 5 years
1% graduated in 6 years
88% had job offers within 6 months
195 organizations recruited on campus
1 Fulbright scholar

Financial Matters
$15,530 tuition and fees (1999–2000)
$4870 room and board
77% average percent of need met
$11,032 average financial aid amount received
   per undergraduate (1999–2000 estimated)

Academics
UD awards bachelor's, master's, doctoral, and first-professional **degrees**. Challenging opportunities include advanced placement, accelerated degree programs, student-designed majors, freshman honors college, an honors program, double majors, independent study, a senior project, and Sigma Xi. Special programs include cooperative education, internships, summer session for credit, off-campus study, study-abroad, and Army and Air Force ROTC. A complete listing of majors at UD appears in the Majors Index beginning on page 432.

Students of UD
The student body totals 10,185, of whom 6,906 are undergraduates. 51% are women and 49% are men. Students come from 43 states and territories. 62% are from Ohio. 0.6% are international students. 3.3% are African American, 0.1% American Indian, 1.3% Asian American, and 1.6% Hispanic American. 86% returned for their sophomore year.

Facilities and Resources
Student rooms are linked to a campus network. 550 **computers** are available on campus that provide access to the Internet. The 2 **libraries** have 1,748,312 books and 4,196 subscriptions.

Campus Life
There are 160 active organizations on campus, including a drama/theater group, newspaper, radio station, television station, choral group, and marching band. 18% of eligible men and 22% of eligible women are members of national **fraternities**, national **sororities**, local fraternities, and local sororities.

   UD is a member of the NCAA (Division I). **Intercollegiate sports** (some offering scholarships) include baseball (m), basketball, crew (w), cross-country running, football (m), golf, soccer, softball (w), tennis, track and field (w), volleyball (w).

Campus Safety
Student safety services include late-night transport/escort service, 24-hour emergency telephone alarm devices, 24-hour patrols by trained security personnel, student patrols, and electronically operated dormitory entrances.

Applying
UD requires SAT I or ACT and a high school transcript, and in some cases an essay and 1 recommendation. It recommends an interview. Application deadline: rolling admissions; 3/31 priority date for financial aid. Early and deferred admission are possible.

UNIVERSITY OF DELAWARE

SMALL-TOWN SETTING ■ PUBLIC ■ STATE-RELATED ■ COED
NEWARK, DELAWARE

Web site: www.udel.edu
Contact: Mr. Larry Griffith, Director of Admissions, 116 Hullihen Hall, Newark, DE 19716
Telephone: 302-831-8123 **Fax:** 302-831-6905
E-mail: admissions@udel.edu

Academics

Delaware awards associate, bachelor's, master's, and doctoral **degrees**. Challenging opportunities include advanced placement, accelerated degree programs, student-designed majors, an honors program, double majors, independent study, a senior project, Phi Beta Kappa, and Sigma Xi. Special programs include cooperative education, internships, summer session for credit, study-abroad, and Army and Air Force ROTC.

The most frequently chosen fields are social sciences and history, business/marketing, and education. A complete listing of majors at Delaware appears in the Majors Index beginning on page 432.

The **faculty** at Delaware has 998 full-time members, 87% with terminal degrees. The student-faculty ratio is 13:1.

Students of Delaware

The student body totals 20,507, of whom 17,399 are undergraduates. 58.8% are women and 41.2% are men. Students come from 50 states and territories and 100 other countries. 40% are from Delaware. 0.9% are international students. 5.6% are African American, 0.3% American Indian, 2.6% Asian American, and 2.4% Hispanic American. 87% returned for their sophomore year.

Facilities and Resources

Student rooms are linked to a campus network. 859 **computers** are available on campus that provide access to the Internet. The 4 **libraries** have 12,220 subscriptions.

Campus Life

There are 194 active organizations on campus, including a drama/theater group, newspaper, radio station, television station, choral group, and marching band. 13% of eligible men and 15% of eligible women are members of national **fraternities**, national **sororities**, and local sororities.

Delaware is a member of the NCAA (Division I). **Intercollegiate sports** (some offering scholarships) include baseball (m), basketball, bowling, crew, cross-country running, equestrian sports, field hockey (w), football (m), golf (m), ice hockey (m), lacrosse, rugby (w), sailing, soccer, softball (w), swimming, tennis, track and field, volleyball (w), wrestling (m).

Campus Safety

Student safety services include late-night transport/escort service, 24-hour emergency telephone alarm devices, 24-hour patrols by trained security personnel, student patrols, and electronically operated dormitory entrances.

Applying

Delaware requires an essay, SAT I or ACT, a high school transcript, and 1 recommendation. It recommends SAT II Subject Tests and SAT II: Writing Test. Application deadline: 2/15; 3/15 for financial aid, with a 2/1 priority date. Early and deferred admission are possible.

Getting in Last Year

14,107 applied
63% were accepted
3,503 enrolled (39%)
26% from top tenth of their h.s. class
3.50 average high school GPA
32% had SAT verbal scores over 600
40% had SAT math scores over 600
55% had ACT scores over 24
5% had SAT verbal scores over 700
7% had SAT math scores over 700
6% had ACT scores over 30
17 National Merit Scholars
40 valedictorians

Graduation and After

51% graduated in 4 years
16% graduated in 5 years
2% graduated in 6 years
18% pursued further study (10% arts and sciences, 4% law, 3% business)
72.8% had job offers within 6 months
330 organizations recruited on campus

Financial Matters

$4858 resident tuition and fees (1999–2000)
$13,228 nonresident tuition and fees (1999–2000)
$5132 room and board
82% average percent of need met
$8200 average financial aid amount received per undergraduate (1999–2000 estimated)

Getting in Last Year
3,303 applied
82% were accepted
834 enrolled (31%)
32% from top tenth of their h.s. class
3.41 average high school GPA
31% had SAT verbal scores over 600
32% had SAT math scores over 600
58% had ACT scores over 24
4% had SAT verbal scores over 700
5% had SAT math scores over 700
9% had ACT scores over 30

Graduation and After
55% graduated in 4 years
12% graduated in 5 years
1% graduated in 6 years
24% pursued further study
67% had job offers within 6 months
242 organizations recruited on campus
3 Fulbright scholars

Financial Matters
$19,440 tuition and fees (1999–2000)
$6165 room and board

UNIVERSITY OF DENVER

SUBURBAN SETTING ■ PRIVATE ■ INDEPENDENT ■ COED
DENVER, COLORADO

Web site: www.du.edu
Contact: Mr. Morris Price, Associate Dean of Admission, University Park, Denver, CO 80208
Telephone: 303-871-3373 or toll-free 800-525-9495 (out-of-state) **Fax:** 303-871-3301
E-mail: admission@du.edu

Academics

DU awards bachelor's, master's, doctoral, and first-professional **degrees** and first-professional certificates. Challenging opportunities include advanced placement, accelerated degree programs, student-designed majors, freshman honors college, an honors program, double majors, independent study, a senior project, Phi Beta Kappa, and Sigma Xi. Special programs include cooperative education, internships, summer session for credit, study-abroad, and Army and Air Force ROTC.

The most frequently chosen fields are business/marketing, communications/communication technologies, and social sciences and history. A complete listing of majors at DU appears in the Majors Index beginning on page 432.

The **faculty** at DU has 402 full-time members, 89% with terminal degrees. The student-faculty ratio is 13:1.

Students of DU

The student body totals 9,188, of whom 3,805 are undergraduates. 57.8% are women and 42.2% are men. Students come from 52 states and territories and 54 other countries. 44% are from Colorado. 6.2% are international students. 4.1% are African American, 1.1% American Indian, 5% Asian American, and 6% Hispanic American. 84% returned for their sophomore year.

Facilities and Resources

Student rooms are linked to a campus network. 750 **computers** are available on campus that provide access to the Internet. The **library** has 1,155,981 books and 5,788 subscriptions.

Campus Life

There are 82 active organizations on campus, including a drama/theater group, newspaper, and choral group. 24% of eligible men and 23% of eligible women are members of national **fraternities** and national **sororities**.

DU is a member of the NCAA (Division I). **Intercollegiate sports** (some offering scholarships) include basketball, cross-country running, golf, gymnastics (w), ice hockey (m), lacrosse, skiing (cross-country), skiing (downhill), soccer, swimming, tennis, volleyball.

Campus Safety

Student safety services include 24-hour locked residence hall entrances, late-night transport/escort service, 24-hour emergency telephone alarm devices, 24-hour patrols by trained security personnel, and electronically operated dormitory entrances.

Applying

DU requires an essay, SAT I or ACT, a high school transcript, and 2 recommendations. It recommends an interview and a minimum high school GPA of 2.0. Application deadline: rolling admissions. Early and deferred admission are possible.

University of Detroit Mercy

Urban setting ■ Private ■ Independent Religious ■ Coed
Detroit, Michigan

Web site: www.udmercy.edu
Contact: Ms. Colleen Ezzeddine, Admissions Counselor, PO Box 19900, Detroit, MI 48219-0900
Telephone: 313-993-1245 or toll-free 800-635-5020 (out-of-state) **Fax:** 313-993-3326
E-mail: admissions@udmercy.edu

eApply

Academics

U of D Mercy awards associate, bachelor's, master's, doctoral, and first-professional **degrees** and post-bachelor's and post-master's certificates. Challenging opportunities include advanced placement, accelerated degree programs, an honors program, double majors, independent study, and a senior project. Special programs include cooperative education, internships, summer session for credit, off-campus study, study-abroad, and Army ROTC.

The most frequently chosen fields are health professions and related sciences, business/marketing, and engineering/engineering technologies. A complete listing of majors at U of D Mercy appears in the Majors Index beginning on page 432.

The **faculty** at U of D Mercy has 298 full-time members, 85% with terminal degrees. The student-faculty ratio is 16:1.

Students of U of D Mercy

The student body totals 6,212, of whom 3,932 are undergraduates. 64.7% are women and 35.3% are men. Students come from 27 states and territories and 21 other countries. 96% are from Michigan. 2.1% are international students. 35.6% are African American, 0.6% American Indian, 2.2% Asian American, and 2.8% Hispanic American. 78% returned for their sophomore year.

Facilities and Resources

Student rooms are linked to a campus network. 250 **computers** are available on campus that provide access to the Internet. The 4 **libraries** have 9,340 subscriptions.

Campus Life

Active organizations on campus include a drama/theater group, newspaper, radio station, and choral group. 22% of eligible men and 13% of eligible women are members of national **fraternities**, national **sororities**, local fraternities, and local sororities.

U of D Mercy is a member of the NCAA (Division I). **Intercollegiate sports** (some offering scholarships) include baseball (m), basketball, cross-country running, fencing, golf (m), soccer, softball (w), tennis (w), track and field.

Campus Safety

Student safety services include late-night transport/escort service, 24-hour emergency telephone alarm devices, 24-hour patrols by trained security personnel, and student patrols.

Applying

U of D Mercy requires SAT I or ACT and a high school transcript, and in some cases an interview and 1 recommendation. Application deadline: 7/1; 4/1 priority date for financial aid. Early and deferred admission are possible.

Getting in Last Year
1,414 applied
77% were accepted
448 enrolled (41%)
30% from top tenth of their h.s. class
3.25 average high school GPA
43% had ACT scores over 24
6% had ACT scores over 30

Graduation and After
29% graduated in 4 years
14% graduated in 5 years
5% graduated in 6 years
20% pursued further study (6% business, 4% engineering, 3% arts and sciences)
225 organizations recruited on campus

Financial Matters
$14,332 tuition and fees (1999–2000)
$5470 room and board
69% average percent of need met
$13,602 average financial aid amount received per undergraduate (1999–2000 estimated)

eAPPLY

UNIVERSITY OF EVANSVILLE
SUBURBAN SETTING ■ PRIVATE ■ INDEPENDENT RELIGIOUS ■ COED
EVANSVILLE, INDIANA

Web site: www.evansville.edu
Contact: Mr. Scot Schaeffer, Dean of Admission, 1800 Lincoln Avenue, Evansville, IN 47722-0002
Telephone: 812-479-2468 or toll-free 800-992-5877 (in-state), 800-423-8633 (out-of-state) **Fax:** 812-474-4076
E-mail: admission@evansville.edu

Academics
UE awards associate, bachelor's, and master's **degrees**. Challenging opportunities include advanced placement, freshman honors college, an honors program, and a senior project. Special programs include cooperative education, internships, summer session for credit, and study-abroad.

The most frequently chosen fields are business/marketing, health professions and related sciences, and engineering/engineering technologies. A complete listing of majors at UE appears in the Majors Index beginning on page 432.

The **faculty** at UE has 177 full-time members, 67% with terminal degrees. The student-faculty ratio is 13:1.

Students of UE
The student body totals 2,821, of whom 2,796 are undergraduates. 62.2% are women and 37.8% are men. Students come from 45 states and territories and 49 other countries. 60% are from Indiana. 6% are international students. 2.6% are African American, 0.2% American Indian, 1.2% Asian American, and 1% Hispanic American. 88% returned for their sophomore year.

Facilities and Resources
Student rooms are linked to a campus network. 300 **computers** are available on campus that provide access to the Internet. The 2 **libraries** have 192,061 books and 1,352 subscriptions.

Campus Life
There are 130 active organizations on campus, including a drama/theater group, newspaper, radio station, and choral group. 30% of eligible men and 20% of eligible women are members of national **fraternities** and national **sororities**.

UE is a member of the NCAA (Division I). **Intercollegiate sports** (some offering scholarships) include baseball (m), basketball, cross-country running, football (m), golf (m), soccer, softball (w), swimming, tennis, volleyball (w).

Campus Safety
Student safety services include late-night transport/escort service, 24-hour emergency telephone alarm devices, and 24-hour patrols by trained security personnel.

Applying
UE requires SAT I or ACT, a high school transcript, 1 recommendation, and a minimum high school GPA of 2.0, and in some cases an essay and an interview. It recommends an interview and a minimum high school GPA of 3.0. Application deadline: 2/15; 3/1 priority date for financial aid. Early and deferred admission are possible.

UNIVERSITY OF FLORIDA

SUBURBAN SETTING ■ PUBLIC ■ STATE-SUPPORTED ■ COED
GAINESVILLE, FLORIDA

Web site: www.ufl.edu
Contact: Office of Admissions, PO Box 114000, Gainesville, FL 32611-4000
Telephone: 352-392-1365

Academics

UF awards associate, bachelor's, master's, doctoral, and first-professional **degrees**. Challenging opportunities include advanced placement, accelerated degree programs, student-designed majors, an honors program, double majors, independent study, a senior project, Phi Beta Kappa, and Sigma Xi. Special programs include cooperative education, internships, summer session for credit, off-campus study, study-abroad, and Army, Navy and Air Force ROTC.

The most frequently chosen fields are business/marketing, engineering/engineering technologies, and social sciences and history. A complete listing of majors at UF appears in the Majors Index beginning on page 432.

The **faculty** at UF has 1,536 full-time members. The student-faculty ratio is 17:1.

Students of UF

The student body totals 43,382, of whom 31,633 are undergraduates. 52.1% are women and 47.9% are men. Students come from 52 states and territories and 114 other countries. 94% are from Florida. 1.1% are international students. 7.3% are African American, 0.4% American Indian, 6.4% Asian American, and 10.5% Hispanic American. 91% returned for their sophomore year.

Facilities and Resources

Student rooms are linked to a campus network. 447 **computers** are available on campus that provide access to the Internet. The 16 **libraries** have 3,401,279 books and 25,213 subscriptions.

Campus Life

There are 525 active organizations on campus, including a drama/theater group, newspaper, choral group, and marching band. 14% of eligible men and 15% of eligible women are members of national **fraternities** and national **sororities**.

UF is a member of the NCAA (Division I). **Intercollegiate sports** (some offering scholarships) include baseball (m), basketball, cross-country running, football (m), golf, gymnastics (w), soccer (w), softball (w), swimming, tennis, track and field, volleyball (w).

Campus Safety

Student safety services include crime and rape prevention programs, late-night transport/escort service, 24-hour emergency telephone alarm devices, 24-hour patrols by trained security personnel, student patrols, and electronically operated dormitory entrances.

Applying

UF requires SAT I or ACT and a high school transcript. Application deadline: 1/29; 3/15 priority date for financial aid. Early admission is possible.

Getting in Last Year

13,967 applied
60% were accepted
5,462 enrolled (65%)
69% from top tenth of their h.s. class
66% had SAT verbal scores over 600
75% had SAT math scores over 600
89% had ACT scores over 24
18% had SAT verbal scores over 700
22% had SAT math scores over 700
25% had ACT scores over 30
130 National Merit Scholars

Graduation and After

31% graduated in 4 years
28% graduated in 5 years
8% graduated in 6 years
27% pursued further study
920 organizations recruited on campus
1 Rhodes, 5 Fulbright scholars

Financial Matters

$2141 resident tuition and fees (1999–2000)
$9130 nonresident tuition and fees (1999–2000)
$5040 room and board
81% average percent of need met
$7908 average financial aid amount received per undergraduate (1998–99)

UNIVERSITY OF GEORGIA

SUBURBAN SETTING ■ PUBLIC ■ STATE-SUPPORTED ■ COED
ATHENS, GEORGIA

Web site: www.uga.edu
Contact: Dr. John Albright, Associate Director of Admissions, Athens, GA 30602
Telephone: 706-542-3000
E-mail: undergrad@admissions.uga.edu

T he University of Georgia (UGA) has been a leader in higher education since its founding in 1785 as America's first chartered public university. Students today live and learn in 324 buildings on a beautiful 603-acre campus surrounded by the quintessential college town of Athens. Recognized nationwide as an outstanding value because of competitive costs and high-quality lifestyle, UGA offers excellent undergraduate programs in more than 150 majors. The Honors Program, one of the oldest and largest in the nation, provides a strengthened liberal arts foundation for top undergraduates along with faculty-guided individual research and progress into graduate-level work.

Academics

UGA awards associate, bachelor's, master's, doctoral, and first-professional **degrees**. Challenging opportunities include advanced placement, accelerated degree programs, student-designed majors, an honors program, double majors, independent study, a senior project, Phi Beta Kappa, and Sigma Xi. Special programs include cooperative education, internships, summer session for credit, off-campus study, study-abroad, and Army and Air Force ROTC.

The most frequently chosen fields are business/marketing, education, and social sciences and history. A complete listing of majors at UGA appears in the Majors Index beginning on page 432.

The **faculty** at UGA has 1,809 full-time members. The student-faculty ratio is 8:1.

Students of UGA

The student body totals 30,912, of whom 24,040 are undergraduates. 54.5% are women and 45.5% are men. Students come from 53 states and territories and 131 other countries. 82% are from Georgia. 1% are international students. 5.9% are African American, 0.2% American Indian, 3.2% Asian American, and 1.3% Hispanic American. 90% returned for their sophomore year.

Facilities and Resources

Student rooms are linked to a campus network. 2,300 **computers** are available on campus that provide access to the Internet. The 3 **libraries** have 3,458,298 books and 45,258 subscriptions.

Campus Life

There are 430 active organizations on campus, including a drama/theater group, newspaper, radio station, choral group, and marching band. 16% of eligible men and 21% of eligible women are members of national **fraternities**, national **sororities**, local fraternities, and local sororities.

UGA is a member of the NCAA (Division I). **Intercollegiate sports** (some offering scholarships) include baseball (m), basketball, cross-country running, football (m), golf, gymnastics (w), soccer, swimming, tennis, track and field, volleyball.

Campus Safety

Student safety services include late-night transport/escort service, 24-hour emergency telephone alarm devices, 24-hour patrols by trained security personnel, and electronically operated dormitory entrances.

Applying

UGA requires SAT I or ACT and a high school transcript. It recommends an essay. Application deadline: 2/1; 3/1 priority date for financial aid. Early and deferred admission are possible.

Getting in Last Year
13,402 applied
63% were accepted
4,398 enrolled (52%)
3.64 average high school GPA
50% had SAT verbal scores over 600
50% had SAT math scores over 600
10% had SAT verbal scores over 700
8% had SAT math scores over 700
1 National Merit Scholar

Graduation and After
46% graduated in 4 years
16% graduated in 5 years
4% graduated in 6 years
Graduates pursuing further study: 7% business, 5% arts and sciences, 4% law
740 organizations recruited on campus
5 Fulbright scholars

Financial Matters
$3024 resident tuition and fees (1999–2000)
$10,266 nonresident tuition and fees (1999–2000)
$4902 room and board
66% average percent of need met
$5371 average financial aid amount received per undergraduate (1999–2000 estimated)

UNIVERSITY OF ILLINOIS AT URBANA–CHAMPAIGN

SMALL-TOWN SETTING ■ PUBLIC ■ STATE-SUPPORTED ■ COED
URBANA, ILLINOIS

Web site: www.uiuc.edu
Contact: Ms. Tammy Bouseman, Assistant Director of Admissions, 901 West
   Illinois, Urbana, IL 61801
Telephone: 217-333-0302
E-mail: admissions@oar.uiuc.edu

Academics

Illinois awards bachelor's, master's, doctoral, and first-professional **degrees**. Challenging opportunities include advanced placement, accelerated degree programs, student-designed majors, an honors program, double majors, a senior project, Phi Beta Kappa, and Sigma Xi. Special programs include cooperative education, internships, summer session for credit, off-campus study, study-abroad, and Army, Navy and Air Force ROTC.

The most frequently chosen fields are engineering/engineering technologies, business/marketing, and social sciences and history. A complete listing of majors at Illinois appears in the Majors Index beginning on page 432.

The **faculty** at Illinois has 2,138 full-time members, 76% with terminal degrees. The student-faculty ratio is 14:1.

Students of Illinois

The student body totals 38,851, of whom 28,916 are undergraduates. 47.8% are women and 52.2% are men. Students come from 44 states and territories and 122 other countries. 93% are from Illinois. 1.3% are international students. 7.3% are African American, 0.2% American Indian, 13.1% Asian American, and 5.4% Hispanic American. 92% returned for their sophomore year.

Facilities and Resources

Student rooms are linked to a campus network. 3,000 **computers** are available on campus that provide access to the Internet. The 40 **libraries** have 9,024,298 books and 90,985 subscriptions.

Campus Life

There are 850 active organizations on campus, including a drama/theater group, newspaper, radio station, television station, choral group, and marching band. 17% of eligible men and 22% of eligible women are members of national **fraternities**, national **sororities**, local fraternities, and local sororities.

Illinois is a member of the NCAA (Division I). **Intercollegiate sports** (some offering scholarships) include baseball (m), basketball, cross-country running, football (m), golf, gymnastics, soccer (w), swimming (w), tennis, track and field, volleyball (w), wrestling (m).

Campus Safety

Student safety services include safety training classes, ID cards with safety numbers, late-night transport/escort service, 24-hour emergency telephone alarm devices, 24-hour patrols by trained security personnel, student patrols, and electronically operated dormitory entrances.

Applying

Illinois requires an essay, SAT I or ACT, and a high school transcript, and in some cases an interview and audition, statement of professional interest. Application deadline: 1/1; 3/15 priority date for financial aid. Early and deferred admission are possible.

The University of Illinois at Urbana-Champaign is the state's premier public university, attracting top-notch students from across Illinois, the nation, and the world. Founded in 1867 as a land-grant institution, the University has grown to offer more than 4,000 courses in 150 undergraduate programs. The opportunities are endless for the 27,000 undergraduate students. From student organizations to study-abroad programs and research projects, few Illinois students can claim boredom as a problem. As one undergraduate describes her college selection process, "I wanted the education and diversity that a Big Ten university had to offer. I never expected the experience and education that I got here. It has been remarkable." Come and discover what the Illinois experience could mean to you.

Getting in Last Year
17,867 applied
71% were accepted
6,479 enrolled (51%)
50% from top tenth of their h.s. class
51% had SAT verbal scores over 600
69% had SAT math scores over 600
84% had ACT scores over 24
11% had SAT verbal scores over 700
26% had SAT math scores over 700
23% had ACT scores over 30
53 National Merit Scholars

Graduation and After
49% graduated in 4 years
23% graduated in 5 years
4% graduated in 6 years
Graduates pursuing further study: 5% business, 3% law, 3% medicine
86% had job offers within 6 months
2247 organizations recruited on campus

Financial Matters
$4752 resident tuition and fees (2000–2001)
$12,200 nonresident tuition and fees (2000–2001)
$5424 room and board
83% average percent of need met
$7800 average financial aid amount received per undergraduate (1998–99)

THE UNIVERSITY OF IOWA
SMALL-TOWN SETTING ■ PUBLIC ■ STATE-SUPPORTED ■ COED
IOWA CITY, IOWA

Web site: www.uiowa.edu
Contact: Mr. Michael Barron, Director of Admissions, 107 Calvin Hall, Iowa City, IA 52242
Telephone: 319-335-3847 or toll-free 800-553-4692 **Fax:** 319-335-1535
E-mail: admissions@uiowa.edu

Traditionally a liberal arts university, Iowa is also strong in business administration, engineering, health sciences, and the fine arts. Outstanding facilities include the University of Iowa Hospitals and Clinics, one of the largest university-owned teaching hospitals in the United States, and Hancher Auditorium, which regularly attracts nationally famous cultural events. Iowa is home to the world-renowned Writers' Workshop, International Writing Program, and Playwrights' Workshop. Popular undergraduate areas of study include engineering, communications, English, psychology, art, biological science, physics and astronomy, accounting, education, and computer science. A University-wide Honors Program is dedicated to advancing Iowa's best students.

Getting in Last Year
11,358 applied
83% were accepted
3,859 enrolled (41%)
21% from top tenth of their h.s. class
3.45 average high school GPA
45% had SAT verbal scores over 600
50% had SAT math scores over 600
61% had ACT scores over 24
14% had SAT verbal scores over 700
15% had SAT math scores over 700
10% had ACT scores over 30
30 National Merit Scholars
146 valedictorians

Graduation and After
33% graduated in 4 years
26% graduated in 5 years
5% graduated in 6 years
320 organizations recruited on campus
6 Fulbright scholars

Financial Matters
$2998 resident tuition and fees (1999–2000)
$10,440 nonresident tuition and fees (1999–2000)
$4370 room and board
75% average percent of need met
$5981 average financial aid amount received per undergraduate (1999–2000 estimated)

Academics
Iowa awards bachelor's, master's, doctoral, and first-professional **degrees**. Challenging opportunities include advanced placement, accelerated degree programs, student-designed majors, an honors program, double majors, independent study, a senior project, Phi Beta Kappa, and Sigma Xi. Special programs include cooperative education, internships, summer session for credit, off-campus study, study-abroad, and Army and Air Force ROTC.

The most frequently chosen fields are business/marketing, social sciences and history, and education. A complete listing of majors at Iowa appears in the Majors Index beginning on page 432.

The **faculty** at Iowa has 1,620 full-time members, 99% with terminal degrees. The student-faculty ratio is 14:1.

Students of Iowa
The student body totals 28,846, of whom 19,537 are undergraduates. 54.4% are women and 45.6% are men. Students come from 51 states and territories and 69 other countries. 72% are from Iowa. 1.2% are international students. 2.3% are African American, 0.5% American Indian, 3.4% Asian American, and 2.2% Hispanic American. 82% returned for their sophomore year.

Facilities and Resources
1,200 **computers** are available on campus that provide access to the Internet. The 13 **libraries** have 3,926,853 books and 47,401 subscriptions.

Campus Life
There are 357 active organizations on campus, including a drama/theater group, newspaper, radio station, choral group, and marching band. 11% of eligible men and 12% of eligible women are members of national **fraternities** and national **sororities**.

Iowa is a member of the NCAA (Division I). **Intercollegiate sports** (some offering scholarships) include badminton, baseball (m), basketball, bowling, crew, cross-country running, field hockey (w), football (m), golf, gymnastics, ice hockey, lacrosse, rugby, sailing, soccer, softball (w), swimming, table tennis, tennis, track and field, volleyball, wrestling (m).

Campus Safety
Student safety services include late-night transport/escort service, 24-hour emergency telephone alarm devices, 24-hour patrols by trained security personnel, and electronically operated dormitory entrances.

Applying
Iowa requires SAT I or ACT and a high school transcript. Application deadline: 5/15; 1/1 priority date for financial aid. Early and deferred admission are possible.

UNIVERSITY OF KANSAS

SUBURBAN SETTING ■ PUBLIC ■ STATE-SUPPORTED ■ COED
LAWRENCE, KANSAS

Web site: www.ukans.edu
Contact: Mr. Alan Cerveny, Director of Admissions and Scholarships, KU
 Visitor Center, 1502 Iowa Street, Lawrence, KS 66045-1910
Telephone: 785-864-3911 or toll-free 888-686-7323 (in-state) **Fax:**
 785-864-5006
E-mail: adm@ukans.edu

Academics

KU awards bachelor's, master's, doctoral, and first-professional **degrees** and post-master's and first-professional certificates (University of Kansas is a single institution with academic programs and facilities at two primary locations: Lawrence and Kansas City. Undergraduate, graduate, and professional education are the principal missions of the Lawrence campus, with medicine and related professional education the focus of the Kansas City campus). Challenging opportunities include advanced placement, accelerated degree programs, student-designed majors, an honors program, double majors, independent study, a senior project, Phi Beta Kappa, and Sigma Xi. Special programs include cooperative education, internships, summer session for credit, study-abroad, and Army, Navy and Air Force ROTC.

 The most frequently chosen fields are business/marketing, health professions and related sciences, and social sciences and history. A complete listing of majors at KU appears in the Majors Index beginning on page 432.

 The **faculty** at KU has 1,521 full-time members. The student-faculty ratio is 14:1.

Students of KU

The student body totals 27,838, of whom 19,477 are undergraduates. 52.8% are women and 47.2% are men. Students come from 52 states and territories and 110 other countries. 76% are from Kansas. 3.5% are international students. 2.8% are African American, 0.9% American Indian, 3.4% Asian American, and 2.4% Hispanic American.

Facilities and Resources

Student rooms are linked to a campus network. 670 **computers** are available on campus that provide access to the Internet. The 12 **libraries** have 4,304,825 books and 33,515 subscriptions.

Campus Life

There are 400 active organizations on campus, including a drama/theater group, newspaper, radio station, television station, choral group, and marching band. 19% of eligible men and 21% of eligible women are members of national **fraternities** and national **sororities**.

 KU is a member of the NCAA (Division I). **Intercollegiate sports** (some offering scholarships) include baseball (m), basketball, crew, cross-country running, fencing, football (m), golf, lacrosse (m), racquetball, rugby, soccer, softball (w), swimming, tennis, track and field, volleyball (w).

Campus Safety

Student safety services include late-night transport/escort service, 24-hour emergency telephone alarm devices, 24-hour patrols by trained security personnel, and electronically operated dormitory entrances.

Applying

KU requires SAT I or ACT, a high school transcript, and a minimum high school GPA of 2.0, and in some cases a minimum high school GPA of 2.5. Application deadline: 4/1; 3/1 priority date for financial aid. Deferred admission is possible.

The University of Kansas (KU) has a long and distinguished tradition as one of America's premier universities. Outstanding students, including more than 300 Merit Scholars, from Kansas and across the nation are attracted to KU because of its strong academic reputation, beautiful campus, affordable cost of education, and contagious school spirit. KU provides students with extraordinary opportunities in honors programs, research, internships, and study abroad. Forty minutes from Kansas City, the University is located in Lawrence, a community of 70,000 that is regarded as one of the nation's best small cities for its arts scene, live music, and historic downtown.

Getting in Last Year
8,409 applied
69% were accepted
3,878 enrolled (67%)
26% from top tenth of their h.s. class
3.40 average high school GPA
55% had ACT scores over 24
11% had ACT scores over 30
101 National Merit Scholars

Graduation and After
23% graduated in 4 years
25% graduated in 5 years
6% graduated in 6 years
32% pursued further study
400 organizations recruited on campus
1 Marshall scholar

Financial Matters
$2518 resident tuition and fees (1999–2000)
$9121 nonresident tuition and fees (1999–2000)
$3941 room and board
71% average percent of need met
$5686 average financial aid amount received per undergraduate (1998–99)

UNIVERSITY OF MARYLAND, COLLEGE PARK

SUBURBAN SETTING ■ PUBLIC ■ STATE-SUPPORTED ■ COED
COLLEGE PARK, MARYLAND

Web site: www.maryland.edu
Contact: Dr. Linda Clement, Assistant Vice President and Director of
Undergraduate Admissions, Mitchell Building, College Park, MD
20742-5235
Telephone: 301-314-8385 or toll-free 800-422-5867 **Fax:** 301-314-9693
E-mail: um-admit@uga.umd.edu

T he University of Maryland
is among the nation's
most distinguished public
research universities, attracting top
students and renowned faculty
members from around the world.
Maryland takes the lead in teaching
undergraduates, providing more than
100 innovative and challenging
academic programs, many nationally
recognized for their exceptional
quality. Opportunities for research,
internships, leadership, recreation,
and creativity abound with its
suburban location near Washington,
DC. Close-knit residence
communities, distinctive programs
for academically talented students,
and a proud multicultural community
make for an outstanding education.

Getting in Last Year
18,731 applied
54% were accepted
3,916 enrolled (39%)
45% from top tenth of their h.s. class
3.61 average high school GPA
56% had SAT verbal scores over 600
67% had SAT math scores over 600
13% had SAT verbal scores over 700
21% had SAT math scores over 700
52 National Merit Scholars

Graduation and After
32% graduated in 4 years
26% graduated in 5 years
6% graduated in 6 years
**33% pursued further study (15% arts and
   sciences, 9% law, 4% medicine)**
86% had job offers within 6 months
525 organizations recruited on campus
2 Fulbright scholars

Financial Matters
$4939 resident tuition and fees (1999–2000)
**$11,827 nonresident tuition and fees (1999–
   2000)**
$6306 room and board
67% average percent of need met
**$7019 average financial aid amount received
   per undergraduate (1998–99)**

Academics
University of Maryland, College Park awards bachelor's, master's, and doctoral **degrees**
and post-master's certificates. Challenging opportunities include advanced placement,
accelerated degree programs, student-designed majors, an honors program, double
majors, independent study, a senior project, Phi Beta Kappa, and Sigma Xi. Special
programs include cooperative education, internships, summer session for credit, off-
campus study, study-abroad, and Army, Navy and Air Force ROTC.

The most frequently chosen fields are social sciences and history, business/marketing,
and biological/life sciences. A complete listing of majors at University of Maryland, College Park appears in the Majors Index beginning on page 432.

The **faculty** at University of Maryland, College Park has 1,389 full-time members,
89% with terminal degrees. The student-faculty ratio is 14:1.

Students of University of Maryland, College Park
The student body totals 32,864, of whom 24,717 are undergraduates. 48.6% are women
and 51.4% are men. Students come from 54 states and territories and 150 other
countries. 73% are from Maryland. 2.8% are international students. 14.3% are African
American, 0.3% American Indian, 13.7% Asian American, and 5.1% Hispanic American.
90% returned for their sophomore year.

Facilities and Resources
Student rooms are linked to a campus network. 6,421 **computers** are available on
campus that provide access to student account information, financial aid summary and
the Internet. The 7 **libraries** have 2,669,919 books and 27,137 subscriptions.

Campus Life
There are 298 active organizations on campus, including a drama/theater group,
newspaper, radio station, television station, choral group, and marching band. 9% of
eligible men and 10% of eligible women are members of national **fraternities** and
national **sororities**.

University of Maryland, College Park is a member of the NCAA (Division I).
Intercollegiate sports (some offering scholarships) include baseball (m), basketball,
cross-country running, field hockey (w), football (m), golf, gymnastics (w), lacrosse, soccer, softball (w), swimming, tennis, track and field, volleyball (w), wrestling (m).

Campus Safety
Student safety services include campus police, video camera surveillance, late-night
transport/escort service, 24-hour emergency telephone alarm devices, 24-hour patrols by
trained security personnel, student patrols, and electronically operated dormitory
entrances.

Applying
University of Maryland, College Park requires an essay, SAT I or ACT, a high school
transcript, and 1 recommendation. It recommends 2 recommendations and resume of
activities. Application deadline: 2/15; 2/15 priority date for financial aid. Early admission
is possible.

University of Massachusetts Amherst

Small-town setting ■ Public ■ State-supported ■ Coed
Amherst, Massachusetts

  eApply

Web site: www.umass.edu
Contact: Mr. Joseph Marshall, Assistant Dean for Enrollment Services,
    Amherst, MA 01003
Telephone: 413-545-0222 **Fax:** 413-545-4312
E-mail: mail@admissions.umass.edu

Academics

UMass Amherst awards associate, bachelor's, master's, and doctoral **degrees** and post-master's certificates. Challenging opportunities include advanced placement, student-designed majors, an honors program, double majors, independent study, a senior project, Phi Beta Kappa, and Sigma Xi. Special programs include cooperative education, internships, summer session for credit, off-campus study, study-abroad, and Army and Air Force ROTC.

The most frequently chosen fields are business/marketing, social sciences and history, and communications/communication technologies. A complete listing of majors at UMass Amherst appears in the Majors Index beginning on page 432.

The **faculty** at UMass Amherst has 1,161 full-time members, 94% with terminal degrees. The student-faculty ratio is 18:1.

Students of UMass Amherst

The student body totals 25,031, of whom 19,372 are undergraduates. 50.6% are women and 49.4% are men. Students come from 50 states and territories and 60 other countries. 76% are from Massachusetts. 1.7% are international students. 4.7% are African American, 0.4% American Indian, 6.1% Asian American, and 4% Hispanic American. 81% returned for their sophomore year.

Facilities and Resources

Student rooms are linked to a campus network. 750 **computers** are available on campus that provide access to online course and grade information and the Internet. The 4 **libraries** have 2,882,541 books and 15,835 subscriptions.

Campus Life

There are 200 active organizations on campus, including a drama/theater group, newspaper, radio station, television station, choral group, and marching band. 5% of eligible men and 4% of eligible women are members of national **fraternities**, national **sororities**, local fraternities, and local sororities.

UMass Amherst is a member of the NCAA (Division I). **Intercollegiate sports** (some offering scholarships) include baseball (m), basketball, crew (w), cross-country running, field hockey (w), football (m), gymnastics, ice hockey (m), lacrosse, skiing (downhill), soccer, softball (w), swimming, tennis, track and field, volleyball (w), water polo.

Campus Safety

Student safety services include residence halls locked at night and during weekends, late-night transport/escort service, 24-hour emergency telephone alarm devices, 24-hour patrols by trained security personnel, student patrols, and electronically operated dormitory entrances.

Applying

UMass Amherst requires an essay, SAT I or ACT, a high school transcript, and a minimum high school GPA of 2.0. It recommends recommendations. Application deadline: 2/1; 3/1 priority date for financial aid. Early and deferred admission are possible.

The operative word for students at UMass Amherst is "choice." More than 90 academic majors, 2,000 courses per semester, the largest public school library in New England, and one of the largest university-based computing systems in the Northeast all provide for almost limitless academic exploration. For highly academically talented students, the University offers Commonwealth College, a small honors college within a nationally recognized research university. Need more? The *New York Times* calls Amherst one of the country's "Ten Best College Towns." Through the Five College Consortium, students take classes at Amherst, Hampshire, Mount Holyoke, and Smith Colleges at no extra charge.

Getting in Last Year
19,914 applied
69% were accepted
4,196 enrolled (31%)
19% from top tenth of their h.s. class
3.26 average high school GPA
34% had SAT verbal scores over 600
37% had SAT math scores over 600
6% had SAT verbal scores over 700
7% had SAT math scores over 700
40 valedictorians

Graduation and After
35% graduated in 4 years
18% graduated in 5 years
4% graduated in 6 years
13% pursued further study
97% had job offers within 6 months
568 organizations recruited on campus
3 Fulbright scholars

Financial Matters
$5212 resident tuition and fees (1999–2000)
$13,254 nonresident tuition and fees (1999–2000)
$4790 room and board
86% average percent of need met
$8069 average financial aid amount received per undergraduate (1999–2000 estimated)

eAPPLY

UNIVERSITY OF MIAMI
SUBURBAN SETTING ■ PRIVATE ■ INDEPENDENT ■ COED
CORAL GABLES, FLORIDA

Web site: www.miami.edu
Contact: Mr. Edward M. Gillis, Associate Dean of Enrollments, PO Box 248025, Ashe Building Room 132, 1252 Memorial Drive, Coral Gables, FL 33146-4616
Telephone: 305-284-4323 **Fax:** 305-284-2507
E-mail: admission@miami.edu

Getting in Last Year
12,249 applied
55% were accepted
1,859 enrolled (28%)
46% from top tenth of their h.s. class
3.86 average high school GPA
40% had SAT verbal scores over 600
44% had SAT math scores over 600
60% had ACT scores over 24
8% had SAT verbal scores over 700
11% had SAT math scores over 700
11% had ACT scores over 30
61 valedictorians

Graduation and After
45% graduated in 4 years
12% graduated in 5 years
2% graduated in 6 years
36% pursued further study (9% arts and sciences, 6% medicine, 5% law)
60% had job offers within 6 months
205 organizations recruited on campus
1 Fulbright scholar

Financial Matters
$21,344 tuition and fees (1999–2000)
$7782 room and board
85% average percent of need met
$19,537 average financial aid amount received per undergraduate (1999–2000)

Academics

UM awards bachelor's, master's, doctoral, and first-professional **degrees** and post-bachelor's and post-master's certificates. Challenging opportunities include advanced placement, accelerated degree programs, student-designed majors, an honors program, double majors, independent study, a senior project, Phi Beta Kappa, and Sigma Xi. Special programs include internships, summer session for credit, study-abroad, and Army and Air Force ROTC.

The most frequently chosen fields are business/marketing, health professions and related sciences, and visual/performing arts. A complete listing of majors at UM appears in the Majors Index beginning on page 432.

The **faculty** at UM has 752 full-time members, 86% with terminal degrees. The student-faculty ratio is 13:1.

Students of UM

The student body totals 13,715, of whom 8,628 are undergraduates. 54.8% are women and 45.2% are men. Students come from 51 states and territories and 94 other countries. 60% are from Florida. 8.7% are international students. 10.6% are African American, 0.3% American Indian, 4.7% Asian American, and 27.7% Hispanic American. 83% returned for their sophomore year.

Facilities and Resources

Student rooms are linked to a campus network. 2,000 **computers** are available on campus that provide access to the Internet. The 3 **libraries** have 1,341,296 books and 19,094 subscriptions.

Campus Life

There are 175 active organizations on campus, including a drama/theater group, newspaper, radio station, television station, choral group, and marching band. 12% of eligible men and 11% of eligible women are members of national **fraternities** and national **sororities**.

UM is a member of the NCAA (Division I). **Intercollegiate sports** (some offering scholarships) include baseball (m), basketball, crew, cross-country running, football (m), golf (w), soccer (w), swimming, tennis, track and field.

Campus Safety

Student safety services include crime prevention and safety workshops, residential college crime watch, late-night transport/escort service, 24-hour emergency telephone alarm devices, 24-hour patrols by trained security personnel, student patrols, and electronically operated dormitory entrances.

Applying

UM requires an essay, SAT I or ACT, a high school transcript, 1 recommendation, and a minimum high school GPA of 2.3, and in some cases SAT II Subject Tests. It recommends an interview. Application deadline: 3/1; 2/15 priority date for financial aid. Early and deferred admission are possible.

University of Michigan

Suburban setting ■ Public ■ State-supported ■ Coed
Ann Arbor, Michigan

Web site: www.umich.edu
Contact: Mr. Ted Spencer, Director of Undergraduate Admissions, Ann Arbor, MI 48109
Telephone: 734-764-7433 **Fax:** 734-936-0740
E-mail: ugadmiss@umich.edu

Academics

Michigan awards bachelor's, master's, doctoral, and first-professional **degrees** and post-master's certificates. Challenging opportunities include advanced placement, accelerated degree programs, student-designed majors, an honors program, double majors, independent study, a senior project, Phi Beta Kappa, and Sigma Xi. Special programs include cooperative education, internships, summer session for credit, off-campus study, study-abroad, and Army, Navy and Air Force ROTC.

The most frequently chosen fields are engineering/engineering technologies, social sciences and history, and psychology. A complete listing of majors at Michigan appears in the Majors Index beginning on page 432.

The **faculty** at Michigan has 2,993 full-time members, 95% with terminal degrees. The student-faculty ratio is 11:1.

Students of Michigan

The student body totals 37,846, of whom 24,493 are undergraduates. 49.9% are women and 50.1% are men. Students come from 53 states and territories and 90 other countries. 72% are from Michigan. 4.4% are international students. 8.1% are African American, 0.6% American Indian, 11.7% Asian American, and 4% Hispanic American. 95% returned for their sophomore year.

Facilities and Resources

Student rooms are linked to a campus network. The 21 **libraries** have 7,071,842 books and 69,280 subscriptions.

Campus Life

There are 700 active organizations on campus, including a drama/theater group, newspaper, radio station, television station, choral group, and marching band. 18% of eligible men and 18% of eligible women are members of national **fraternities**, national **sororities**, local fraternities, and local sororities.

Michigan is a member of the NCAA (Division I). **Intercollegiate sports** (some offering scholarships) include baseball (m), basketball, crew (w), cross-country running, field hockey (w), football (m), golf, gymnastics, ice hockey (m), soccer (w), softball (w), swimming, tennis, track and field, volleyball (w), wrestling (m).

Campus Safety

Student safety services include bicycle patrols, late-night transport/escort service, 24-hour emergency telephone alarm devices, 24-hour patrols by trained security personnel, student patrols, and electronically operated dormitory entrances.

Applying

Michigan requires an essay, SAT I or ACT, and a high school transcript, and in some cases SAT II Subject Tests, SAT II: Writing Test, an interview, and recommendations. Application deadline: 2/1; 9/30 for financial aid, with a 2/15 priority date. Deferred admission is possible.

The University of Michigan, Ann Arbor, is one of the nation's top-ranked public universities that is consistently rated among the top 25 academic institutions in the country. Nearly every one of the University's 17 academic schools and colleges is rated among the top in its field. Students and faculty members come from over 104 different countries and all 50 states. The academic and personal growth achieved by students is unique and diverse, and Michigan graduates are prepared to face the challenges the 21st century will have to offer. A friendly and beautiful campus, extensive resources, dedicated faculty, and exceptional students—this is the Wolverine Spirit, the Michigan tradition.

Getting in Last Year
21,324 applied
59% were accepted
5,559 enrolled (44%)
63% from top tenth of their h.s. class
3.6 average high school GPA
60% had SAT verbal scores over 600
76% had SAT math scores over 600
88% had ACT scores over 24
15% had SAT verbal scores over 700
29% had SAT math scores over 700
30% had ACT scores over 30
37 National Merit Scholars

Graduation and After
62% graduated in 4 years
19% graduated in 5 years
2% graduated in 6 years
34% pursued further study (11% arts and sciences, 5% law, 5% medicine)
950 organizations recruited on campus
17 Fulbright scholars

Financial Matters
$6333 resident tuition and fees (1999–2000)
$19,761 nonresident tuition and fees (1999–2000)
$5614 room and board
90% average percent of need met
$10,405 average financial aid amount received per undergraduate (1998–99)

UNIVERSITY OF MICHIGAN–DEARBORN

SUBURBAN SETTING ■ PUBLIC ■ STATE-SUPPORTED ■ COED
DEARBORN, MICHIGAN

Web site: www.umd.umich.edu
Contact: Mr. David Placey, Director of Admissions, 4901 Evergreen Road,
    Dearborn, MI 48128-1491
Telephone: 313-593-5100
E-mail: umdgoblu@umd.umich.edu

Getting in Last Year
2,187 applied
72% were accepted
767 enrolled (49%)

Graduation and After
23% pursued further study
24.2% had job offers within 6 months
66 organizations recruited on campus

Financial Matters
$4361 resident tuition and fees (1999–2000)
$11,849 nonresident tuition and fees (1999–2000)
84% average percent of need met
$6535 average financial aid amount received per undergraduate (1998–99)

Academics
UM-D awards bachelor's and master's **degrees**. Challenging opportunities include accelerated degree programs, student-designed majors, an honors program, independent study, and a senior project. Special programs include cooperative education, internships, summer session for credit, off-campus study, study-abroad, and Army, Navy and Air Force ROTC.

The most frequently chosen fields are engineering/engineering technologies, business/marketing, and psychology. A complete listing of majors at UM-D appears in the Majors Index beginning on page 432.

The **faculty** at UM-D has 239 full-time members, 87% with terminal degrees.

Students of UM-D
The student body totals 8,076, of whom 6,523 are undergraduates. 53.3% are women and 46.7% are men. Students come from 25 states and territories and 22 other countries. 99% are from Michigan. 0.7% are international students. 7.2% are African American, 0.5% American Indian, 5.5% Asian American, and 2.2% Hispanic American.

Facilities and Resources
350 **computers** are available on campus that provide access to the Internet. The **library** has 299,792 books and 1,169 subscriptions.

Campus Life
Active organizations on campus include a drama/theater group, newspaper, and radio station. 6% of eligible men and 5% of eligible women are members of national **fraternities** and national **sororities**.

UM-D is a member of the NAIA. **Intercollegiate sports** (some offering scholarships) include basketball, volleyball (w).

Campus Safety
Student safety services include late-night transport/escort service, 24-hour emergency telephone alarm devices, and 24-hour patrols by trained security personnel.

Applying
UM-D requires SAT I or ACT, a high school transcript, and a minimum high school GPA of 3.0, and in some cases an interview. Application deadline: rolling admissions; 4/1 priority date for financial aid.

University of Minnesota, Morris

Small-town setting ■ Public ■ State-supported ■ Coed

Morris, Minnesota

Web site: www.mrs.umn.edu

Contact: Mr. Scott K. Hagg, Acting Director of Admissions, 600 East 4th Street, Morris, MN 56267-2199

Telephone: 320-539-6036 or toll-free 800-992-8863 **Fax:** 320-589-1673

E-mail: admissions@caa.mrs.umn.edu

eApply

Academics

UMM awards bachelor's **degrees**. Challenging opportunities include advanced placement, accelerated degree programs, student-designed majors, freshman honors college, an honors program, double majors, and a senior project. Special programs include internships, summer session for credit, off-campus study, and study-abroad.

The most frequently chosen fields are social sciences and history, biological/life sciences, and business/marketing. A complete listing of majors at UMM appears in the Majors Index beginning on page 432.

The **faculty** at UMM has 122 full-time members. The student-faculty ratio is 15:1.

Students of UMM

The student body is made up of 1,867 undergraduates. 58.8% are women and 41.2% are men. Students come from 31 states and territories. 83% are from Minnesota. 0.3% are international students. 5.4% are African American, 7% American Indian, 2.6% Asian American, and 1.3% Hispanic American. 78% returned for their sophomore year.

Facilities and Resources

Student rooms are linked to a campus network. 190 **computers** are available on campus that provide access to the Internet. The **library** has 1,100 subscriptions.

Campus Life

There are 95 active organizations on campus, including a drama/theater group, newspaper, radio station, and choral group. 1% of eligible men are members of local **fraternities**.

UMM is a member of the NCAA (Division II). **Intercollegiate sports** include baseball (m), basketball, cross-country running (w), football (m), golf, soccer (w), softball (w), tennis, track and field, volleyball (w), wrestling.

Campus Safety

Student safety services include late-night transport/escort service, 24-hour emergency telephone alarm devices, 24-hour patrols by trained security personnel, and electronically operated dormitory entrances.

Applying

UMM requires an essay, SAT I or ACT, and a high school transcript, and in some cases an interview. It recommends a minimum high school GPA of 3.0. Application deadline: 3/15; 4/1 priority date for financial aid. Early and deferred admission are possible.

Getting in Last Year

994 applied
97% were accepted
457 enrolled (48%)
45% from top tenth of their h.s. class
26% had SAT verbal scores over 600
37% had SAT math scores over 600
58% had ACT scores over 24
6% had SAT verbal scores over 700
5% had SAT math scores over 700
12% had ACT scores over 30

Graduation and After

44% graduated in 4 years
13% graduated in 5 years
6% graduated in 6 years
27% pursued further study (16% arts and sciences, 3% business, 3% law)
80% had job offers within 6 months
70 organizations recruited on campus

Financial Matters

$5312 resident tuition and fees (1999–2000)
$10,014 nonresident tuition and fees (1999–2000)
$3910 room and board
92% average percent of need met
$6496 average financial aid amount received per undergraduate (1998–99)

University of Minnesota, Twin Cities Campus

Urban setting ■ Public ■ State-supported ■ Coed
Minneapolis, Minnesota

Web site: www1.umn.edu/tc
Contact: Ms. Patricia Jones Whyte, Associate Director of Admissions, 240 Williamson, Minneapolis, MN 55455-0213
Telephone: 612-625-2008 or toll-free 800-752-1000 **Fax:** 612-626-1693
E-mail: admissions@tc.umn.edu

O n this beautiful Big Ten campus in the heart of the Twin Cities of Minneapolis and St. Paul, the hallmarks are quality and opportunity. The quality of a U of M–Twin Cities education is a matter of record. And so are the opportunities—about 150 undergraduate and 180 graduate and professional degree programs, many nationally ranked; an Undergraduate Research Opportunities Program that is a national model; one of the largest study-abroad programs in the country; the fifteenth-largest university library system in the country; extraordinary opportunities for internships, employment, and personal enrichment in the culturally rich and thriving Twin Cities area; and hundreds of student organizations.

Getting in Last Year
15,319 applied
73% were accepted
5,141 enrolled (46%)
29% from top tenth of their h.s. class
52% had SAT verbal scores over 600
61% had SAT math scores over 600
61% had ACT scores over 24
13% had SAT verbal scores over 700
19% had SAT math scores over 700
11% had ACT scores over 30
223 valedictorians

Graduation and After
1 Marshall, 7 Fulbright scholars

Financial Matters
$4649 resident tuition and fees (1999–2000)
$12,789 nonresident tuition and fees (1999–2000)
$4494 room and board
85% average percent of need met
$7854 average financial aid amount received per undergraduate (1998–99)

Academics

U of M–Twin Cities Campus awards bachelor's, master's, doctoral, and first-professional **degrees** and post-bachelor's and post-master's certificates. Challenging opportunities include advanced placement, accelerated degree programs, student-designed majors, freshman honors college, an honors program, double majors, independent study, a senior project, Phi Beta Kappa, and Sigma Xi. Special programs include cooperative education, internships, summer session for credit, off-campus study, study-abroad, and Army, Navy and Air Force ROTC.

The most frequently chosen fields are social sciences and history, engineering/engineering technologies, and business/marketing. A complete listing of majors at U of M–Twin Cities Campus appears in the Majors Index beginning on page 432.

The **faculty** at U of M–Twin Cities Campus has 2,538 full-time members, 93% with terminal degrees.

Students of U of M–Twin Cities Campus

The student body totals 45,361, of whom 32,342 are undergraduates. 53.3% are women and 46.7% are men. Students come from 55 states and territories and 85 other countries. 72% are from Minnesota. 2.5% are international students. 3.9% are African American, 0.8% American Indian, 8% Asian American, and 2% Hispanic American. 82% returned for their sophomore year.

Facilities and Resources

Student rooms are linked to a campus network. The 18 **libraries** have 5,500,000 books and 48,105 subscriptions.

Campus Life

There are 350 active organizations on campus, including a drama/theater group, newspaper, radio station, television station, choral group, and marching band. 3% of eligible men and 3% of eligible women are members of national **fraternities**, national **sororities**, and local sororities.

U of M–Twin Cities Campus is a member of the NCAA (Division I). **Intercollegiate sports** (some offering scholarships) include baseball (m), basketball, cross-country running, football (m), golf, gymnastics, ice hockey, soccer (w), softball (w), swimming, tennis, track and field, volleyball (w), wrestling (m).

Campus Safety

Student safety services include safety/security orientation, security lighting, late-night transport/escort service, 24-hour emergency telephone alarm devices, 24-hour patrols by trained security personnel, student patrols, and electronically operated dormitory entrances.

Applying

U of M–Twin Cities Campus requires SAT I or ACT and a high school transcript. It recommends a minimum high school GPA of 2.0. Application deadline: rolling admissions; 2/15 priority date for financial aid. Early and deferred admission are possible.

UNIVERSITY OF MISSOURI–COLUMBIA

SMALL-TOWN SETTING ■ PUBLIC ■ STATE-SUPPORTED ■ COED
COLUMBIA, MISSOURI

Web site: www.missouri.edu
Contact: Ms. Georgeanne Porter, Director of Undergraduate Admissions, 225 Jesse Hall, Columbia, MO 65211
Telephone: 573-882-7786 or toll-free 800-225-6075 (in-state) **Fax:** 573-882-7887
E-mail: mu4u@missouri.edu

Academics

MU awards bachelor's, master's, doctoral, and first-professional **degrees**. Challenging opportunities include advanced placement, accelerated degree programs, student-designed majors, freshman honors college, an honors program, double majors, independent study, a senior project, Phi Beta Kappa, and Sigma Xi. Special programs include cooperative education, internships, summer session for credit, off-campus study, study-abroad, and Army, Navy and Air Force ROTC.

The most frequently chosen fields are business/marketing, communications/communication technologies, and education. A complete listing of majors at MU appears in the Majors Index beginning on page 432.

The **faculty** at MU has 1,669 full-time members. The student-faculty ratio is 16:1.

Students of MU

The student body totals 22,930, of whom 17,811 are undergraduates. 52.5% are women and 47.5% are men. Students come from 50 states and territories and 90 other countries. 88% are from Missouri. 1.6% are international students. 6.4% are African American, 0.5% American Indian, 2.3% Asian American, and 1.5% Hispanic American. 84% returned for their sophomore year.

Facilities and Resources

Student rooms are linked to a campus network. 1,041 **computers** are available on campus that provide access to telephone registration and the Internet. The 12 **libraries** have 2,855,615 books and 23,522 subscriptions.

Campus Life

There are 383 active organizations on campus, including a drama/theater group, newspaper, radio station, television station, choral group, and marching band. 23% of eligible men and 25% of eligible women are members of national **fraternities** and national **sororities**.

MU is a member of the NCAA (Division I). **Intercollegiate sports** (some offering scholarships) include baseball (m), basketball, cross-country running, football (m), golf, gymnastics (w), soccer (w), softball (w), swimming, tennis (w), track and field, volleyball (w), wrestling (m).

Campus Safety

Student safety services include late-night transport/escort service, 24-hour emergency telephone alarm devices, 24-hour patrols by trained security personnel, and electronically operated dormitory entrances.

Applying

MU requires ACT and a high school transcript. Application deadline: rolling admissions; 3/1 priority date for financial aid. Deferred admission is possible.

Getting in Last Year

9,091 applied
90% were accepted
3,932 enrolled (48%)
31% from top tenth of their h.s. class
69% had ACT scores over 24
17% had ACT scores over 30
33 National Merit Scholars
133 valedictorians

Graduation and After

42% graduated in 4 years
16% graduated in 5 years
2% graduated in 6 years
665 organizations recruited on campus

Financial Matters

$4581 resident tuition and fees (1999–2000)
$12,495 nonresident tuition and fees (1999–2000)
$4545 room and board
83% average percent of need met
$8244 average financial aid amount received per undergraduate (1998–99)

University of Missouri–Kansas City

Urban setting ■ Public ■ State-supported ■ Coed
Kansas City, Missouri

Web site: www.umkc.edu
Contact: Mr. Melvin C. Tyler, Director of Admissions, 5100 Rockhill Road,
Kansas City, MO 64110-2499
Telephone: 816-235-1111 **Fax:** 816-235-5544
E-mail: admit@umkc.edu

Getting in Last Year
2,583 applied
68% were accepted
688 enrolled (39%)
37% from top tenth of their h.s. class
61% had ACT scores over 24
12% had ACT scores over 30

Graduation and After
85% had job offers within 6 months
390 organizations recruited on campus

Financial Matters
$3852 resident tuition and fees (2000–2001)
$10,387 nonresident tuition and fees (2000–2001)
75% average percent of need met
$11,920 average financial aid amount received per undergraduate (1999–2000)

Academics

UMKC awards bachelor's, master's, doctoral, and first-professional **degrees** and first-professional certificates. Challenging opportunities include advanced placement, accelerated degree programs, student-designed majors, an honors program, and a senior project. Special programs include cooperative education, internships, summer session for credit, off-campus study, study-abroad, and Army ROTC.

The most frequently chosen fields are liberal arts/general studies, biological/life sciences, and business/marketing. A complete listing of majors at UMKC appears in the Majors Index beginning on page 432.

The **faculty** at UMKC has 569 full-time members, 87% with terminal degrees. The student-faculty ratio is 8:1.

Students of UMKC

The student body totals 11,518, of whom 6,790 are undergraduates. 58.2% are women and 41.8% are men. Students come from 43 states and territories and 66 other countries. 80% are from Missouri. 3.9% are international students. 12.1% are African American, 0.7% American Indian, 6.5% Asian American, and 3.9% Hispanic American. 73% returned for their sophomore year.

Facilities and Resources

Student rooms are linked to a campus network. 400 **computers** are available on campus that provide access to the Internet. The 4 **libraries** have 1,402,239 books and 12,472 subscriptions.

Campus Life

There are 75 active organizations on campus, including a drama/theater group, newspaper, and choral group. 18% of eligible men and 18% of eligible women are members of national **fraternities**, national **sororities**, and local sororities.

UMKC is a member of the NCAA (Division I). **Intercollegiate sports** (some offering scholarships) include basketball, cross-country running, golf, riflery, soccer (m), softball (w), tennis, track and field, volleyball (w).

Campus Safety

Student safety services include late-night transport/escort service, 24-hour emergency telephone alarm devices, 24-hour patrols by trained security personnel, and electronically operated dormitory entrances.

Applying

UMKC requires ACT and a high school transcript. Application deadline: rolling admissions; 3/15 priority date for financial aid. Early and deferred admission are possible.

UNIVERSITY OF MISSOURI–ROLLA

SMALL-TOWN SETTING ■ PUBLIC ■ STATE-SUPPORTED ■ COED
ROLLA, MISSOURI

Web site: www.umr.edu
Contact: Ms. Martina Hahn, Director of Admission and Student Financial
 Assistance, 102 Parker Hall, Rolla, MO 65409
Telephone: 573-341-4164 or toll-free 800-522-0938 **Fax:** 573-341-4082
E-mail: umrolla@umr.edu

Academics

UMR awards bachelor's, master's, and doctoral **degrees**. Challenging opportunities
include advanced placement, accelerated degree programs, freshman honors college, an
honors program, double majors, independent study, a senior project, and Sigma Xi.
Special programs include cooperative education, internships, summer session for credit,
off-campus study, study-abroad, and Army and Air Force ROTC.

The most frequently chosen fields are engineering/engineering technologies,
computer/information sciences, and physical sciences. A complete listing of majors at
UMR appears in the Majors Index beginning on page 432.

The **faculty** at UMR has 337 full-time members, 90% with terminal degrees.

Students of UMR

The student body totals 4,715, of whom 3,882 are undergraduates. 23.3% are women
and 76.7% are men. Students come from 46 states and territories and 35 other countries.
75% are from Missouri. 3.6% are international students. 3.9% are African American,
0.5% American Indian, 2.7% Asian American, and 1.4% Hispanic American. 84%
returned for their sophomore year.

Facilities and Resources

Student rooms are linked to a campus network. 800 **computers** are available on campus
that provide access to the Internet. The **library** has 195,089 books and 5,880 subscriptions.

Campus Life

There are 197 active organizations on campus, including a drama/theater group,
newspaper, radio station, choral group, and marching band. 28% of eligible men and
22% of eligible women are members of national **fraternities**, national **sororities**, and
local sororities.

UMR is a member of the NCAA (Division II). **Intercollegiate sports** (some offering
scholarships) include baseball (m), basketball, cross-country running, football (m), golf
(m), soccer, softball (w), swimming (m), tennis (m), track and field.

Campus Safety

Student safety services include crime prevention programs, late-night transport/escort
service, 24-hour emergency telephone alarm devices, 24-hour patrols by trained security
personnel, student patrols, and electronically operated dormitory entrances.

Applying

UMR requires SAT I or ACT and a high school transcript. Application deadline: 6/1;
3/1 priority date for financial aid. Early and deferred admission are possible.

Getting in Last Year
1,699 applied
89% were accepted
688 enrolled (46%)
48% from top tenth of their h.s. class
3.50 average high school GPA
59% had SAT verbal scores over 600
75% had SAT math scores over 600
85% had ACT scores over 24
17% had SAT verbal scores over 700
27% had SAT math scores over 700
37% had ACT scores over 30

Graduation and After
8% graduated in 4 years
34% graduated in 5 years
13% graduated in 6 years
16% pursued further study
79% had job offers within 6 months
542 organizations recruited on campus

Financial Matters
$4665 resident tuition and fees (1999–2000)
$12,579 nonresident tuition and fees (1999–2000)
$4557 room and board
81% average percent of need met
$8067 average financial aid amount received per undergraduate (1998–99)

University of New Hampshire

Small-town setting ■ Public ■ State-supported ■ Coed
Durham, New Hampshire

Web site: www.unh.edu
Contact: Mr. James Washington Jr., Director of Admissions, Grant House, 4 Garrison Avenue, Durham, NH 03824
Telephone: 603-862-1360 **Fax:** 603-862-0077
E-mail: admissions@unh.edu

Getting in Last Year

8,833 applied
81% were accepted
2,556 enrolled (36%)
21% from top tenth of their h.s. class
25% had SAT verbal scores over 600
30% had SAT math scores over 600
3% had SAT verbal scores over 700
4% had SAT math scores over 700

Graduation and After

50% graduated in 4 years
19% graduated in 5 years
4% graduated in 6 years
260 organizations recruited on campus
2 Fulbright scholars

Financial Matters

$6939 resident tuition and fees (1999–2000)
$15,829 nonresident tuition and fees (1999–2000)
$4798 room and board
85% average percent of need met
$10,405 average financial aid amount received per undergraduate (1999–2000)

Academics

UNH awards associate, bachelor's, master's, and doctoral **degrees** and post-master's certificates. Challenging opportunities include advanced placement, accelerated degree programs, student-designed majors, an honors program, double majors, independent study, a senior project, Phi Beta Kappa, and Sigma Xi. Special programs include internships, summer session for credit, off-campus study, study-abroad, and Army and Air Force ROTC.

The most frequently chosen fields are liberal arts/general studies, social sciences and history, and business/marketing. A complete listing of majors at UNH appears in the Majors Index beginning on page 432.

The **faculty** at UNH has 589 full-time members, 92% with terminal degrees. The student-faculty ratio is 14:1.

Students of UNH

The student body totals 13,591, of whom 10,877 are undergraduates. 58.6% are women and 41.4% are men. Students come from 40 states and territories and 34 other countries. 60% are from New Hampshire. 0.6% are international students. 0.7% are African American, 0.2% American Indian, 1.5% Asian American, and 0.9% Hispanic American. 84% returned for their sophomore year.

Facilities and Resources

Student rooms are linked to a campus network. 280 **computers** are available on campus that provide access to the Internet. The 5 **libraries** have 801,013 books and 9,136 subscriptions.

Campus Life

There are 156 active organizations on campus, including a drama/theater group, newspaper, radio station, choral group, and marching band. 5% of eligible men and 5% of eligible women are members of national **fraternities** and national **sororities**.

UNH is a member of the NCAA (Division I). **Intercollegiate sports** (some offering scholarships) include badminton, basketball, crew, cross-country running, equestrian sports, fencing, field hockey (w), football (m), gymnastics (w), ice hockey, lacrosse, rugby (m), sailing, skiing (cross-country), skiing (downhill), soccer, squash, swimming, tennis, track and field, volleyball.

Campus Safety

Student safety services include late-night transport/escort service, 24-hour emergency telephone alarm devices, 24-hour patrols by trained security personnel, student patrols, and electronically operated dormitory entrances.

Applying

UNH requires an essay, SAT I or ACT, a high school transcript, and 1 recommendation. It recommends SAT II Subject Tests, an interview, and a minimum high school GPA of 3.0. Application deadline: 2/1; 3/1 for financial aid. Deferred admission is possible.

THE UNIVERSITY OF NORTH CAROLINA AT ASHEVILLE

SUBURBAN SETTING ■ PUBLIC ■ STATE-SUPPORTED ■ COED
ASHEVILLE, NORTH CAROLINA

Web site: www.unca.edu
Contact: Mr. John W. White, Director of Admissions, Lipinsky Hall, CPO 2210, Asheville, NC 28804-8510
Telephone: 828-251-6481 or toll-free 800-531-9842 **Fax:** 828-251-6482
E-mail: admissions@unca.edu

Academics

UNC Asheville awards bachelor's and master's **degrees**. Challenging opportunities include advanced placement, accelerated degree programs, student-designed majors, an honors program, double majors, independent study, a senior project, and Sigma Xi. Special programs include internships, summer session for credit, off-campus study, and study-abroad.

The most frequently chosen fields are business/marketing, social sciences and history, and psychology. A complete listing of majors at UNC Asheville appears in the Majors Index beginning on page 432.

The **faculty** at UNC Asheville has 156 full-time members, 87% with terminal degrees. The student-faculty ratio is 13:1.

Students of UNC Asheville

The student body totals 3,164, of whom 3,125 are undergraduates. 58.1% are women and 41.9% are men. Students come from 43 states and territories and 23 other countries. 90% are from North Carolina. 1.3% are international students. 3% are African American, 0.4% American Indian, 0.9% Asian American, and 1.4% Hispanic American. 78% returned for their sophomore year.

Facilities and Resources

Student rooms are linked to a campus network. 249 **computers** are available on campus that provide access to online grade reports and the Internet. The **library** has 589,777 books and 2,251 subscriptions.

Campus Life

There are 80 active organizations on campus, including a drama/theater group, newspaper, and choral group. 10% of eligible men and 6% of eligible women are members of national **fraternities** and national **sororities**.

UNC Asheville is a member of the NCAA (Division I). **Intercollegiate sports** (some offering scholarships) include baseball (m), basketball, cross-country running, soccer, softball (w), tennis, track and field, volleyball (w).

Campus Safety

Student safety services include late-night transport/escort service, 24-hour patrols by trained security personnel, and electronically operated dormitory entrances.

Applying

UNC Asheville requires SAT I or ACT and a high school transcript, and in some cases an interview. It recommends an essay and a minimum high school GPA of 3.0. Application deadline: 3/15; 3/1 priority date for financial aid. Deferred admission is possible.

Getting in Last Year

1,866 applied
61% were accepted
460 enrolled (40%)
22% from top tenth of their h.s. class
3.69 average high school GPA
41% had SAT verbal scores over 600
37% had SAT math scores over 600
48% had ACT scores over 24
7% had SAT verbal scores over 700
4% had SAT math scores over 700
2% had ACT scores over 30
2 valedictorians

Graduation and After

28% graduated in 4 years
19% graduated in 5 years
5% graduated in 6 years
20% pursued further study
75% had job offers within 6 months
149 organizations recruited on campus

Financial Matters

$1960 resident tuition and fees (1999–2000)
$8580 nonresident tuition and fees (1999–2000)
$4179 room and board
78% average percent of need met
$6014 average financial aid amount received per undergraduate (1998–99)

The University of North Carolina at Chapel Hill

Suburban setting ■ Public ■ State-supported ■ Coed
Chapel Hill, North Carolina

Web site: www.unc.edu
Contact: Mr. Jerome A. Lucido, Associate Vice Chancellor/Director of Undergraduate Admissions, Office of Undergraduate Admissions, Jackson Hall 153A, Campus Box 2200, Chapel Hill, NC 27599-2200
Telephone: 919-966-3621 **Fax:** 919-962-3045
E-mail: uadm@email.unc.edu

Getting in Last Year

16,022 applied
39% were accepted
3,396 enrolled (55%)
68% from top tenth of their h.s. class
4.00 average high school GPA
61% had SAT verbal scores over 600
64% had SAT math scores over 600
18% had SAT verbal scores over 700
19% had SAT math scores over 700

Graduation and After

62% graduated in 4 years
16% graduated in 5 years
3% graduated in 6 years
72.1% had job offers within 6 months
512 organizations recruited on campus
13 Fulbright scholars

Financial Matters

$2365 resident tuition and fees (1999–2000)
$11,531 nonresident tuition and fees (1999–2000)
$5280 room and board
92% average percent of need met
$6772 average financial aid amount received per undergraduate (1998–99)

Academics

UNC Chapel Hill awards bachelor's, master's, doctoral, and first-professional **degrees** and post-master's certificates. Challenging opportunities include advanced placement, student-designed majors, freshman honors college, an honors program, double majors, independent study, Phi Beta Kappa, and Sigma Xi. Special programs include internships, summer session for credit, off-campus study, study-abroad, and Army, Navy and Air Force ROTC.

The most frequently chosen fields are social sciences and history, communications/communication technologies, and biological/life sciences. A complete listing of majors at UNC Chapel Hill appears in the Majors Index beginning on page 432.

The **faculty** at UNC Chapel Hill has 2,601 full-time members, 86% with terminal degrees.

Students of UNC Chapel Hill

The student body totals 24,353, of whom 15,434 are undergraduates. 60.6% are women and 39.4% are men. Students come from 52 states and territories and 99 other countries. 82% are from North Carolina. 0.8% are international students. 11.1% are African American, 0.7% American Indian, 5% Asian American, and 1.2% Hispanic American. 94% returned for their sophomore year.

Facilities and Resources

460 **computers** are available on campus that provide access to the Internet. The 15 **libraries** have 4,928,026 books and 44,023 subscriptions.

Campus Life

There are 406 active organizations on campus, including a drama/theater group, newspaper, radio station, television station, choral group, and marching band. 19% of eligible men and 19% of eligible women are members of national **fraternities**, national **sororities**, and local sororities.

UNC Chapel Hill is a member of the NCAA (Division I). **Intercollegiate sports** (some offering scholarships) include baseball (m), basketball (m), crew (w), cross-country running, fencing, field hockey (w), football (m), golf, gymnastics (w), lacrosse, soccer, softball (w), swimming, tennis, track and field, volleyball (w), wrestling (m).

Campus Safety

Student safety services include crime prevention programs, late-night transport/escort service, 24-hour emergency telephone alarm devices, 24-hour patrols by trained security personnel, student patrols, and electronically operated dormitory entrances.

Applying

UNC Chapel Hill requires an essay, SAT I or ACT, and a high school transcript. Application deadline: 1/15; 3/1 priority date for financial aid. Deferred admission is possible.

UNIVERSITY OF NOTRE DAME

SUBURBAN SETTING ■ PRIVATE ■ INDEPENDENT RELIGIOUS ■ COED
NOTRE DAME, INDIANA

Web site: www.nd.edu
Contact: Mr. Daniel J. Saracino, Assistant Provost for Enrollment, 220 Main
Building, Notre Dame, IN 46556-5612
Telephone: 219-631-7505 **Fax:** 219-631-8865
E-mail: admissions.admissio.1@nd.edu

Academics

Notre Dame awards bachelor's, master's, doctoral, and first-professional **degrees**. Challenging opportunities include advanced placement, student-designed majors, an honors program, double majors, independent study, a senior project, Phi Beta Kappa, and Sigma Xi. Special programs include summer session for credit, off-campus study, study-abroad, and Army, Navy and Air Force ROTC.

The most frequently chosen fields are business/marketing, social sciences and history, and engineering/engineering technologies. A complete listing of majors at Notre Dame appears in the Majors Index beginning on page 432.

Students of Notre Dame

The student body totals 10,654, of whom 8,014 are undergraduates. 45.4% are women and 54.6% are men. Students come from 54 states and territories and 46 other countries. 10% are from Indiana. 1.5% are international students. 3.2% are African American, 0.5% American Indian, 3.7% Asian American, and 6.9% Hispanic American.

Facilities and Resources

880 **computers** are available on campus that provide access to the Internet. The 9 **libraries** have 2,646,589 books and 24,106 subscriptions.

Campus Life

There are 228 active organizations on campus, including a drama/theater group, newspaper, radio station, choral group, and marching band. No national or local **fraternities** or **sororities**.

Notre Dame is a member of the NCAA (Division I). **Intercollegiate sports** (some offering scholarships) include baseball (m), basketball, bowling, crew, cross-country running, equestrian sports, fencing, field hockey, football (m), golf, gymnastics, ice hockey (m), lacrosse, sailing, skiing (downhill), soccer, softball (w), swimming, tennis, track and field, volleyball, water polo.

Campus Safety

Student safety services include late-night transport/escort service, 24-hour emergency telephone alarm devices, 24-hour patrols by trained security personnel, and electronically operated dormitory entrances.

Applying

Notre Dame requires an essay, SAT I or ACT, a high school transcript, and 1 recommendation. It recommends SAT II Subject Tests. Application deadline: 1/7; 2/15 priority date for financial aid. Deferred admission is possible.

Getting in Last Year

10,010 applied
35% were accepted
1,967 enrolled (56%)
83% from top tenth of their h.s. class
83% had SAT verbal scores over 600
89% had SAT math scores over 600
95% had ACT scores over 24
32% had SAT verbal scores over 700
42% had SAT math scores over 700
70% had ACT scores over 30
298 valedictorians

Graduation and After

87% graduated in 4 years
7% graduated in 5 years
1% graduated in 6 years
29% pursued further study (8% arts and sciences, 7% law, 6% medicine)
369 organizations recruited on campus

Financial Matters

$22,187 tuition and fees (1999–2000)
$5750 room and board
96% average percent of need met
$17,992 average financial aid amount received per undergraduate (1999–2000)

UNIVERSITY OF OKLAHOMA

SUBURBAN SETTING ■ PUBLIC ■ STATE-SUPPORTED ■ COED
NORMAN, OKLAHOMA

Web site: www.ou.edu
Contact: Mr. J. P. Audas, Director of Prospective Student Services, 1000 Asp
  Avenue, Norman, OK 73019-0390
Telephone: 405-325-2151 or toll-free 800-234-6868 **Fax:** 405-325-7478
E-mail: admission@ou.edu

Getting in Last Year
6,384 applied
89% were accepted
3,298 enrolled (58%)
32% from top tenth of their h.s. class
3.48 average high school GPA
54% had ACT scores over 24
14% had ACT scores over 30
134 National Merit Scholars
220 valedictorians

Graduation and After
16% graduated in 4 years
23% graduated in 5 years
7% graduated in 6 years
372 organizations recruited on campus
1 Rhodes, 1 Fulbright scholar

Financial Matters
$2456 resident tuition and fees (1999–2000)
$6791 nonresident tuition and fees (1999–2000)
$4384 room and board
89% average percent of need met
$5991 average financial aid amount received per undergraduate (1998–99)

Academics

OU awards bachelor's, master's, doctoral, and first-professional **degrees**. Challenging opportunities include advanced placement, accelerated degree programs, student-designed majors, freshman honors college, an honors program, double majors, independent study, a senior project, Phi Beta Kappa, and Sigma Xi. Special programs include cooperative education, internships, summer session for credit, off-campus study, study-abroad, and Army, Navy and Air Force ROTC.

The most frequently chosen fields are business/marketing, social sciences and history, and engineering/engineering technologies. A complete listing of majors at OU appears in the Majors Index beginning on page 432.

The **faculty** at OU has 914 full-time members, 88% with terminal degrees. The student-faculty ratio is 21:1.

Students of OU

The student body totals 21,320, of whom 17,245 are undergraduates. 47.9% are women and 52.1% are men. Students come from 51 states and territories and 93 other countries. 84% are from Oklahoma. 4.9% are international students. 7.2% are African American, 7.6% American Indian, 5.7% Asian American, and 3.9% Hispanic American. 80% returned for their sophomore year.

Facilities and Resources

Student rooms are linked to a campus network. 600 **computers** are available on campus that provide access to the Internet. The 8 **libraries** have 4,066,129 books and 16,890 subscriptions.

Campus Life

There are 240 active organizations on campus, including a drama/theater group, newspaper, radio station, television station, choral group, and marching band. 19% of eligible men and 22% of eligible women are members of national **fraternities**, national **sororities**, and international social clubs.

OU is a member of the NCAA (Division I). **Intercollegiate sports** (some offering scholarships) include baseball (m), basketball, cross-country running, football (m), golf, gymnastics, soccer (w), softball (w), tennis, track and field, volleyball (w), wrestling (m).

Campus Safety

Student safety services include crime prevention programs, police bicycle patrols, self-defense classes, late-night transport/escort service, 24-hour emergency telephone alarm devices, 24-hour patrols by trained security personnel, student patrols, and electronically operated dormitory entrances.

Applying

OU requires SAT I or ACT, a high school transcript, and a minimum high school GPA of 3.0, and in some cases an essay. It recommends SAT I. Application deadline: 7/15; 6/1 for financial aid, with a 3/1 priority date. Early admission is possible.

UNIVERSITY OF PENNSYLVANIA

URBAN SETTING ■ PRIVATE ■ INDEPENDENT ■ COED
PHILADELPHIA, PENNSYLVANIA

Web site: www.upenn.edu
Contact: Mr. Willis J. Stetson Jr., Dean of Admissions, 1 College Hall, Levy
Park, Philadelphia, PA 19104
Telephone: 215-898-7507

Academics

Penn awards associate, bachelor's, master's, doctoral, and first-professional **degrees** (also offers evening program with significant enrollment not reflected in profile). Challenging opportunities include advanced placement, accelerated degree programs, student-designed majors, an honors program, double majors, independent study, a senior project, Phi Beta Kappa, and Sigma Xi. Special programs include internships, summer session for credit, off-campus study, study-abroad, and Army, Navy and Air Force ROTC.

The most frequently chosen fields are social sciences and history, business/marketing, and engineering/engineering technologies. A complete listing of majors at Penn appears in the Majors Index beginning on page 432.

The **faculty** at Penn has 2,722 full-time members, 100% with terminal degrees. The student-faculty ratio is 7:1.

Students of Penn

The student body totals 18,042, of whom 9,827 are undergraduates. 48.6% are women and 51.4% are men. Students come from 50 states and territories and 91 other countries. 19% are from Pennsylvania. 8.8% are international students. 5.5% are African American, 0.2% American Indian, 19.4% Asian American, and 4.4% Hispanic American. 97% returned for their sophomore year.

Facilities and Resources

Student rooms are linked to a campus network. 1,000 **computers** are available on campus that provide access to the Internet. The 14 **libraries** have 4,672,777 books and 34,276 subscriptions.

Campus Life

There are 350 active organizations on campus, including a drama/theater group, newspaper, radio station, choral group, and marching band. Penn has national **fraternities**, national **sororities**, and local fraternities.

Penn is a member of the NCAA (Division I). **Intercollegiate sports** include baseball (m), basketball, crew, cross-country running, fencing, field hockey (w), football (m), golf (m), gymnastics (w), lacrosse, soccer, softball (w), squash, swimming, tennis, track and field, volleyball (w), wrestling (m).

Campus Safety

Student safety services include late-night transport/escort service, 24-hour emergency telephone alarm devices, 24-hour patrols by trained security personnel, and student patrols.

Applying

Penn requires an essay, SAT II: Writing Test, SAT I and SAT II or ACT, a high school transcript, and 2 recommendations. It recommends an interview. Application deadline: 1/1; 2/15 priority date for financial aid. Early and deferred admission are possible.

Getting in Last Year

17,666 applied
26% were accepted
2,507 enrolled (54%)
91% from top tenth of their h.s. class
3.79 average high school GPA
89% had SAT verbal scores over 600
96% had SAT math scores over 600
98% had ACT scores over 24
43% had SAT verbal scores over 700
62% had SAT math scores over 700
53% had ACT scores over 30
78 class presidents
235 valedictorians

Graduation and After

79% graduated in 4 years
8% graduated in 5 years
2% graduated in 6 years
20% pursued further study (7% law, 5% arts and sciences, 5% medicine)
74% had job offers within 6 months
400 organizations recruited on campus
1 Marshall, 9 Fulbright scholars

Financial Matters

$24,230 tuition and fees (1999–2000)
$7362 room and board
100% average percent of need met
$21,788 average financial aid amount received per undergraduate (1998–99)

eAPPLY

UNIVERSITY OF PITTSBURGH
URBAN SETTING ■ PUBLIC ■ STATE-RELATED ■ COED
PITTSBURGH, PENNSYLVANIA

Web site: www.pitt.edu
Contact: Dr. Betsy A. Porter, Director, Office of Admissions and Financial Aid, 4337 Fifth Avenue, First Floor, Masonic Temple, Pittsburgh, PA 115213
Telephone: 412-624-7488 **Fax:** 412-648-8815
E-mail: oafa@pitt.edu

Getting in Last Year
12,863 applied
66% were accepted
3,190 enrolled (37%)
28% from top tenth of their h.s. class
36% had SAT verbal scores over 600
39% had SAT math scores over 600
63% had ACT scores over 24
7% had SAT verbal scores over 700
7% had SAT math scores over 700
15% had ACT scores over 30
18 National Merit Scholars
64 valedictorians

Graduation and After
37% graduated in 4 years
22% graduated in 5 years
4% graduated in 6 years
36% pursued further study (6% business, 6% education, 5% arts and sciences)
400 organizations recruited on campus
1 Marshall, 4 Fulbright scholars

Financial Matters
$6698 resident tuition and fees (1999–2000)
$14,014 nonresident tuition and fees (1999–2000)
$5766 room and board

Academics

Pitt awards bachelor's, master's, doctoral, and first-professional **degrees** and post-master's certificates. Challenging opportunities include advanced placement, student-designed majors, freshman honors college, an honors program, double majors, independent study, a senior project, Phi Beta Kappa, and Sigma Xi. Special programs include cooperative education, internships, summer session for credit, off-campus study, study-abroad, and Army, Navy and Air Force ROTC.

The most frequently chosen fields are social sciences and history, English, and health professions and related sciences. A complete listing of majors at Pitt appears in the Majors Index beginning on page 432.

The **faculty** at Pitt has 1,459 full-time members, 80% with terminal degrees. The student-faculty ratio is 17:1.

Students of Pitt

The student body totals 26,162, of whom 17,168 are undergraduates. 52.7% are women and 47.3% are men. Students come from 54 states and territories and 56 other countries. 87% are from Pennsylvania. 0.9% are international students. 9.5% are African American, 0.2% American Indian, 3.7% Asian American, and 1.2% Hispanic American. 85% returned for their sophomore year.

Facilities and Resources

Student rooms are linked to a campus network. 700 **computers** are available on campus that provide access to online class listings and the Internet. The 27 **libraries** have 3,551,548 books and 22,058 subscriptions.

Campus Life

There are 500 active organizations on campus, including a drama/theater group, newspaper, radio station, television station, choral group, and marching band. Pitt has national **fraternities** and national **sororities**.

Pitt is a member of the NCAA (Division I). **Intercollegiate sports** (some offering scholarships) include baseball (m), basketball, cross-country running, football (m), gymnastics (w), soccer, softball (w), swimming, tennis (w), track and field, volleyball (w), wrestling (m).

Campus Safety

Student safety services include on-call van transportation, late-night transport/escort service, 24-hour emergency telephone alarm devices, 24-hour patrols by trained security personnel, and electronically operated dormitory entrances.

Applying

Pitt requires SAT I or ACT and a high school transcript. It recommends an essay, SAT I, an interview, and recommendations. Application deadline: rolling admissions; 3/1 priority date for financial aid. Early and deferred admission are possible.

University of Puget Sound

Suburban setting ■ Private ■ Independent ■ Coed
Tacoma, Washington

Web site: www.ups.edu
Contact: Dr. George H. Mills, Vice President for Enrollment, 1500 North
 Warner Street, Tacoma, WA 98416-0005
Telephone: 253-879-3211 or toll-free 800-396-7191 **Fax:** 253-879-3993
E-mail: admission@ups.edu

eApply

Academics
Puget Sound awards bachelor's and master's **degrees**. Challenging opportunities include
advanced placement, student-designed majors, an honors program, double majors,
independent study, a senior project, and Phi Beta Kappa. Special programs include
cooperative education, internships, summer session for credit, study-abroad, and Army
ROTC.

The most frequently chosen fields are business/marketing, social sciences and history,
and English. A complete listing of majors at Puget Sound appears in the Majors Index
beginning on page 432.

The **faculty** at Puget Sound has 211 full-time members, 82% with terminal degrees.
The student-faculty ratio is 12:1.

Students of Puget Sound
The student body totals 2,973, of whom 2,695 are undergraduates. 60.7% are women
and 39.3% are men. Students come from 48 states and territories and 16 other countries.
32% are from Washington. 0.9% are international students. 2% are African American,
1.3% American Indian, 11% Asian American, and 2.4% Hispanic American. 83%
returned for their sophomore year.

Facilities and Resources
Student rooms are linked to a campus network. 150 **computers** are available on campus
that provide access to the Internet. The **library** has 298,447 books and 1,874 subscriptions.

Campus Life
There are 40 active organizations on campus, including a drama/theater group,
newspaper, radio station, and choral group. 25% of eligible men and 24% of eligible
women are members of national **fraternities** and national **sororities**.

Puget Sound is a member of the NCAA (Division III). **Intercollegiate sports**
include baseball (m), basketball, crew, cross-country running, football (m), golf, lacrosse,
skiing (downhill), soccer, softball (w), swimming, tennis, track and field, volleyball (w).

Campus Safety
Student safety services include 24-hour locked residence hall entrances, late-night
transport/escort service, 24-hour emergency telephone alarm devices, 24-hour patrols by
trained security personnel, student patrols, and electronically operated dormitory
entrances.

Applying
Puget Sound requires an essay, SAT I or ACT, a high school transcript, and 2 recommendations. It recommends an interview and a minimum high school GPA of 3.0. Application deadline: 2/1; 2/1 priority date for financial aid. Early and deferred admission
are possible.

Getting in Last Year
4,138 applied
74% were accepted
684 enrolled (22%)
47% from top tenth of their h.s. class
3.61 average high school GPA
63% had SAT verbal scores over 600
63% had SAT math scores over 600
83% had ACT scores over 24
16% had SAT verbal scores over 700
15% had SAT math scores over 700
23% had ACT scores over 30
28 National Merit Scholars

Graduation and After
60% graduated in 4 years
10% graduated in 5 years
2% graduated in 6 years
30% pursued further study (9% arts and sciences, 5% business, 5% education)
70% had job offers within 6 months
141 organizations recruited on campus

Financial Matters
$20,605 tuition and fees (1999–2000)
$5270 room and board
88% average percent of need met
$16,939 average financial aid amount received
 per undergraduate (1999–2000 estimated)

University of Redlands

Small-town setting ■ Private ■ Independent ■ Coed
Redlands, California

Web site: www.redlands.edu
Contact: Mr. Paul Driscoll, Dean of Admissions, PO Box 3080, Redlands, CA 92373-0999
Telephone: 909-335-4074 or toll-free 800-455-5064 **Fax:** 909-335-4089
E-mail: admissions@uor.edu

Getting in Last Year
1,975 applied
80% were accepted
474 enrolled (30%)
3.46 average high school GPA
28% had SAT verbal scores over 600
30% had SAT math scores over 600
53% had ACT scores over 24
6% had SAT verbal scores over 700
2% had SAT math scores over 700
4% had ACT scores over 30
5 National Merit Scholars

Graduation and After
56% graduated in 4 years
6% graduated in 5 years
1% graduated in 6 years
30% pursued further study (3% business, 2% education, 1% law)
40% had job offers within 6 months
25 organizations recruited on campus

Financial Matters
$19,811 tuition and fees (1999–2000)
$7368 room and board
91% average percent of need met
$18,959 average financial aid amount received per undergraduate (1999–2000 estimated)

Academics
Redlands awards bachelor's and master's **degrees** and post-bachelor's and post-master's certificates. Challenging opportunities include advanced placement, student-designed majors, freshman honors college, an honors program, double majors, independent study, a senior project, and Phi Beta Kappa. Special programs include internships, off-campus study, study-abroad, and Army and Air Force ROTC.

The most frequently chosen fields are social sciences and history, business/marketing, and interdisciplinary studies. A complete listing of majors at Redlands appears in the Majors Index beginning on page 432.

The **faculty** at Redlands has 119 full-time members, 85% with terminal degrees. The student-faculty ratio is 13:1.

Students of Redlands
The student body totals 1,736, of whom 1,669 are undergraduates. 55.7% are women and 44.3% are men. Students come from 43 states and territories and 29 other countries. 69% are from California. 3.2% are international students. 3.1% are African American, 0.9% American Indian, 7.4% Asian American, and 12.1% Hispanic American. 79% returned for their sophomore year.

Facilities and Resources
Student rooms are linked to a campus network. 300 **computers** are available on campus that provide access to the Internet. The **library** has 264,385 books.

Campus Life
There are 85 active organizations on campus, including a drama/theater group, newspaper, radio station, and choral group. 18% of eligible men and 20% of eligible women are members of local **fraternities** and local **sororities**.

Redlands is a member of the NCAA (Division III). **Intercollegiate sports** include baseball (m), basketball, cross-country running, football (m), golf (m), lacrosse (w), soccer, softball (w), swimming, tennis, track and field, volleyball (w), water polo.

Campus Safety
Student safety services include safety whistles, late-night transport/escort service, 24-hour emergency telephone alarm devices, 24-hour patrols by trained security personnel, student patrols, and electronically operated dormitory entrances.

Applying
Redlands requires an essay, SAT I or ACT, a high school transcript, and 2 recommendations. It recommends an interview. Application deadline: 2/1; 2/15 priority date for financial aid. Early and deferred admission are possible.

UNIVERSITY OF RHODE ISLAND

SMALL-TOWN SETTING ■ PUBLIC ■ STATE-SUPPORTED ■ COED
KINGSTON, RHODE ISLAND

Web site: www.uri.edu
Contact: Ms. Catherine Zeiser, Assistant Dean of Admissions, 8 Ranger Road, Suite 1, Kingston, RI 02881-2020
Telephone: 401-874-7100 **Fax:** 401-874-5523
E-mail: uriadmit@uriacc.uri.edu

Academics

Rhode Island awards bachelor's, master's, doctoral, and first-professional **degrees** and post-bachelor's certificates. Challenging opportunities include advanced placement, accelerated degree programs, student-designed majors, an honors program, double majors, independent study, a senior project, Phi Beta Kappa, and Sigma Xi. Special programs include cooperative education, internships, summer session for credit, off-campus study, study-abroad, and Army ROTC.

The most frequently chosen fields are business/marketing, health professions and related sciences, and education. A complete listing of majors at Rhode Island appears in the Majors Index beginning on page 432.

Students of Rhode Island

The student body totals 14,577, of whom 10,639 are undergraduates. 55.8% are women and 44.2% are men. Students come from 44 states and territories and 47 other countries. 69% are from Rhode Island. 0.5% are international students. 3.8% are African American, 0.4% American Indian, 3.6% Asian American, and 3.6% Hispanic American. 77% returned for their sophomore year.

Facilities and Resources

552 **computers** are available on campus that provide access to the Internet. The 2 **libraries** have 783,237 books and 7,966 subscriptions.

Campus Life

There are 85 active organizations on campus, including a drama/theater group, newspaper, radio station, television station, choral group, and marching band. 6% of eligible men and 7% of eligible women are members of national **fraternities**, national **sororities**, and local sororities.

Rhode Island is a member of the NCAA (Division I). **Intercollegiate sports** (some offering scholarships) include baseball (m), basketball, crew, cross-country running, equestrian sports, fencing, field hockey (w), football (m), golf (m), gymnastics (w), ice hockey (m), lacrosse, rugby, sailing, skiing (downhill), soccer, softball (w), swimming, tennis, track and field, volleyball, water polo (m).

Campus Safety

Student safety services include late-night transport/escort service, 24-hour emergency telephone alarm devices, 24-hour patrols by trained security personnel, student patrols, and electronically operated dormitory entrances.

Applying

Rhode Island requires SAT I or ACT and a high school transcript, and in some cases a minimum high school GPA of 3.0. It recommends an interview, recommendations, and a minimum high school GPA of 3.0. Application deadline: 3/1; 3/1 priority date for financial aid. Early admission is possible.

Getting in Last Year
10,034 applied
75% were accepted
2,150 enrolled (29%)
3.2 average high school GPA
24% had SAT verbal scores over 600
27% had SAT math scores over 600
4% had SAT verbal scores over 700
4% had SAT math scores over 700

Graduation and After
155 organizations recruited on campus

Financial Matters
$4928 resident tuition and fees (1999–2000)
$13,148 nonresident tuition and fees (1999–2000)
$6378 room and board

eAPPLY

UNIVERSITY OF RICHMOND

SUBURBAN SETTING ■ PRIVATE ■ INDEPENDENT ■ COED
UNIVERSITY OF RICHMOND, VIRGINIA

Web site: www.richmond.edu
Contact: Ms. Pamela Spence, Dean of Admission, 28 Westhampton Way,
  University of Richmond, VA 23173
Telephone: 804-289-8640 or toll-free 800-700-1662 **Fax:** 804-287-6003

Academics

University of Richmond awards associate, bachelor's, master's, and first-professional
degrees. Challenging opportunities include advanced placement, accelerated degree
programs, student-designed majors, an honors program, double majors, independent
study, a senior project, Phi Beta Kappa, and Sigma Xi. Special programs include cooperative education, internships, summer session for credit, off-campus study, study-abroad,
and Army ROTC.

The most frequently chosen fields are business/marketing, social sciences and history,
and area/ethnic studies. A complete listing of majors at University of Richmond appears
in the Majors Index beginning on page 432.

The **faculty** at University of Richmond has 253 full-time members, 87% with
terminal degrees. The student-faculty ratio is 11:1.

Students of University of Richmond

The student body totals 3,777, of whom 3,034 are undergraduates. Students come from
47 states and territories and 60 other countries. 17% are from Virginia. 3.4% are international students. 5.1% are African American, 0.1% American Indian, 1.8% Asian
American, and 1.5% Hispanic American. 92% returned for their sophomore year.

Facilities and Resources

Student rooms are linked to a campus network. 500 **computers** are available on campus
that provide access to the Internet. The 5 **libraries** have 684,704 books and 4,322
subscriptions.

Campus Life

There are 225 active organizations on campus, including a drama/theater group,
newspaper, radio station, television station, and choral group. 39% of eligible men and
50% of eligible women are members of national **fraternities** and national **sororities**.

University of Richmond is a member of the NCAA (Division I). **Intercollegiate
sports** (some offering scholarships) include baseball (m), basketball, crew, cross-country
running, equestrian sports (w), fencing, field hockey (w), football (m), golf (m), lacrosse,
rugby (m), soccer, swimming, tennis, track and field, volleyball, water polo.

Campus Safety

Student safety services include campus police, late-night transport/escort service, 24-
hour emergency telephone alarm devices, 24-hour patrols by trained security personnel,
and electronically operated dormitory entrances.

Applying

University of Richmond requires an essay, SAT II: Writing Test, SAT I and SAT II or
ACT, SAT II Subject Test in math, a high school transcript, 1 recommendation, signed
character statement, and a minimum high school GPA of 2.0. Application deadline: 1/15;
2/25 for financial aid. Early and deferred admission are possible.

UNIVERSITY OF ROCHESTER

SUBURBAN SETTING ■ PRIVATE ■ INDEPENDENT ■ COED
ROCHESTER, NEW YORK

Web site: www.rochester.edu
Contact: Mr. W. Jamie Hobba, Director of Admissions, PO Box 270251,
    Rochester, NY 14627-0001
Telephone: 716-275-3221 or toll-free 888-822-2256 **Fax:** 716-461-4595
E-mail: admit@admissions.cc.rochester.edu

  eAPPLY

Academics

University of Rochester awards bachelor's, master's, doctoral, and first-professional **degrees**. Challenging opportunities include advanced placement, student-designed majors, double majors, independent study, Phi Beta Kappa, and Sigma Xi. Special programs include internships, summer session for credit, off-campus study, study-abroad, and Army, Navy and Air Force ROTC.

The most frequently chosen fields are psychology, biological/life sciences, and visual/performing arts. A complete listing of majors at University of Rochester appears in the Majors Index beginning on page 432.

The **faculty** at University of Rochester has 1,228 full-time members. The student-faculty ratio is 12:1.

Students of University of Rochester

The student body totals 7,697, of whom 4,529 are undergraduates. 48.2% are women and 51.8% are men. Students come from 52 states and territories and 45 other countries. 5.3% are international students. 5% are African American, 0.2% American Indian, 11.6% Asian American, and 4.3% Hispanic American. 93% returned for their sophomore year.

Facilities and Resources

Student rooms are linked to a campus network. 260 **computers** are available on campus that provide access to the Internet. The 6 **libraries** have 2,992,204 books and 11,254 subscriptions.

Campus Life

There are 120 active organizations on campus, including a drama/theater group, newspaper, radio station, and choral group. 20% of eligible men and 15% of eligible women are members of national **fraternities** and national **sororities**.

University of Rochester is a member of the NCAA (Division III). **Intercollegiate sports** include baseball (m), basketball, crew, cross-country running, equestrian sports, field hockey (w), football (m), golf, ice hockey (m), lacrosse, rugby (m), skiing (cross-country), skiing (downhill), soccer, softball (w), squash (m), swimming, tennis, track and field, volleyball.

Campus Safety

Student safety services include late-night transport/escort service, 24-hour emergency telephone alarm devices, 24-hour patrols by trained security personnel, and electronically operated dormitory entrances.

Applying

University of Rochester requires an essay, SAT I or ACT, a high school transcript, and 1 recommendation, and in some cases audition, portfolio. It recommends SAT II Subject Tests and 2 recommendations. Application deadline: 1/15; 2/1 priority date for financial aid. Early and deferred admission are possible.

> **F**ounded in 1850, the University of Rochester is one of the leading private universities in the country. The University of Rochester balances the choices and intellectual excitement of a major research university with the intimacy and opportunities for personal involvement of a small liberal arts college. Programs are available in 7 divisions, including Arts and Sciences, Engineering, Nursing, Education, Business, Medicine, and the Eastman School of Music. Special undergraduate opportunities include the Take Five program (fifth-year tuition free), an 8-year bachelor's/medical degree, and seminar-style Quest courses for first-year students.

Getting in Last Year
8,656 applied
66% were accepted
1,212 enrolled (21%)
57% from top tenth of their h.s. class
3.61 average high school GPA
76% had SAT verbal scores over 600
87% had SAT math scores over 600
93% had ACT scores over 24
27% had SAT verbal scores over 700
35% had SAT math scores over 700
36% had ACT scores over 30
25 National Merit Scholars
53 valedictorians

Graduation and After
65% graduated in 4 years
8% graduated in 5 years
3% graduated in 6 years
50% pursued further study (20% arts and sciences, 10% law, 9% medicine)
57% had job offers within 6 months
127 organizations recruited on campus

Financial Matters
$22,864 tuition and fees (1999–2000)
$7512 room and board
100% average percent of need met
$21,103 average financial aid amount received per undergraduate (1999–2000)

THE UNIVERSITY OF SCRANTON

URBAN SETTING ■ PRIVATE ■ INDEPENDENT RELIGIOUS ■ COED
SCRANTON, PENNSYLVANIA

Web site: www.uofs.edu
Contact: Mr. Raul A. Fonts, Director of Admissions, Scranton, PA 18510
Telephone: 570-941-7540 or toll-free 888-SCRANTON **Fax:** 570-941-4370
E-mail: admissions@uofs.edu

The Jesuit tradition at the University of Scranton focuses on care for the whole person (cura personalis). In an educational context, this means preparation not only for a career but also for life. Over the last 5 years, an average of 95% of graduates have been working or attending graduate school full-time within 6 months of graduation. Last year 49 graduates entered medical school, 40 entered law school, and 4 were named Fulbright Scholars. Scranton is truly where potential becomes achievement in the Jesuit tradition.

Getting in Last Year
3,640 applied
76% were accepted
969 enrolled (35%)
27% from top tenth of their h.s. class
3.27 average high school GPA
30% had SAT verbal scores over 600
31% had SAT math scores over 600
4% had SAT verbal scores over 700
3% had SAT math scores over 700
21 National Merit Scholars
17 class presidents
16 valedictorians

Graduation and After
70% graduated in 4 years
8% graduated in 5 years
Graduates pursuing further study: 16% arts and sciences, 5% medicine, 4% law
59% had job offers within 6 months
61 organizations recruited on campus
4 Fulbright scholars

Financial Matters
$17,740 tuition and fees (1999–2000)
$7710 room and board
74% average percent of need met
$12,539 average financial aid amount received per undergraduate (1998–99)

Academics
Scranton awards associate, bachelor's, and master's **degrees** and post-master's certificates. Challenging opportunities include advanced placement, student-designed majors, freshman honors college, an honors program, double majors, independent study, a senior project, and Sigma Xi. Special programs include internships, summer session for credit, off-campus study, and Army and Air Force ROTC.

The most frequently chosen fields are liberal arts/general studies, health professions and related sciences, and business/marketing. A complete listing of majors at Scranton appears in the Majors Index beginning on page 432.

The **faculty** at Scranton has 243 full-time members, 88% with terminal degrees. The student-faculty ratio is 14:1.

Students of Scranton
The student body totals 4,773, of whom 4,099 are undergraduates. 58.4% are women and 41.6% are men. Students come from 25 states and territories. 53% are from Pennsylvania. 0.8% are international students. 0.6% are African American, 0.1% American Indian, 1.5% Asian American, and 2% Hispanic American. 90% returned for their sophomore year.

Facilities and Resources
Student rooms are linked to a campus network. 353 **computers** are available on campus that provide access to the Internet. The 2 **libraries** have 375,701 books and 2,312 subscriptions.

Campus Life
There are 80 active organizations on campus, including a drama/theater group, newspaper, radio station, and choral group. No national or local **fraternities** or **sororities**.

Scranton is a member of the NCAA (Division III). **Intercollegiate sports** include baseball (m), basketball, bowling, crew, cross-country running, equestrian sports, field hockey (w), golf (m), ice hockey (m), lacrosse, rugby, skiing (downhill), soccer, softball (w), swimming, tennis, track and field, volleyball, wrestling (m).

Campus Safety
Student safety services include late-night transport/escort service, 24-hour emergency telephone alarm devices, 24-hour patrols by trained security personnel, student patrols, and electronically operated dormitory entrances.

Applying
Scranton requires an essay, SAT I or ACT, a high school transcript, and 2 recommendations. It recommends an interview. Application deadline: 3/1; 2/15 priority date for financial aid. Early and deferred admission are possible.

University of Southern California

Urban setting ■ Private ■ Independent ■ Coed
Los Angeles, California

Web site: www.usc.edu
Contact: Mr. Joseph Allen, Vice Provost for Enrollment, University Park Campus, Los Angeles, CA 90089
Telephone: 213-740-1111 **Fax:** 213-740-6364

As one of the country's leading private research universities, USC provides outstanding teachers, excellent facilities, and an incredible array of academic offerings, including honors programs and undergraduate research opportunities. With a student-faculty ratio of 14:1 and small classes, students work with world-acclaimed professors in every discipline as participants, not spectators. USC offers over 170 undergraduate majors in the College of Letters, Arts and Sciences and 15 professional schools. Over 450 possible combinations are available for double majors, dual majors, and major-minor programs.

Academics

USC awards bachelor's, master's, doctoral, and first-professional **degrees** and post-master's certificates. Challenging opportunities include advanced placement, accelerated degree programs, student-designed majors, an honors program, double majors, a senior project, Phi Beta Kappa, and Sigma Xi. Special programs include cooperative education, internships, summer session for credit, off-campus study, study-abroad, and Army, Navy and Air Force ROTC. A complete listing of majors at USC appears in the Majors Index beginning on page 432.

The student-faculty ratio is 13:1.

Students of USC

The student body totals 28,739, of whom 15,553 are undergraduates. 49% are women and 51% are men. Students come from 52 states and territories. 69% are from California. 7.7% are international students. 5.9% are African American, 0.8% American Indian, 23.5% Asian American, and 14.2% Hispanic American. 96% returned for their sophomore year.

Facilities and Resources

Student rooms are linked to a campus network. 5,000 **computers** are available on campus that provide access to online degree progress, grades, financial aid summary and the Internet. The 18 **libraries** have 3,300,000 books and 27,000 subscriptions.

Campus Life

There are 450 active organizations on campus, including a drama/theater group, newspaper, radio station, television station, choral group, and marching band. 20% of eligible men and 20% of eligible women are members of national **fraternities**, national **sororities**, local fraternities, and local sororities.

USC is a member of the NCAA (Division I). **Intercollegiate sports** (some offering scholarships) include baseball (m), basketball, crew (w), cross-country running (w), football (m), golf, sailing, soccer (w), swimming, tennis, track and field, volleyball, water polo.

Campus Safety

Student safety services include late-night transport/escort service, 24-hour emergency telephone alarm devices, 24-hour patrols by trained security personnel, student patrols, and electronically operated dormitory entrances.

Applying

USC requires an essay, SAT I or ACT, and a high school transcript, and in some cases recommendations. It recommends SAT II Subject Tests, an interview, and recommendations. Application deadline: 1/10. Early and deferred admission are possible.

Getting in Last Year
24,626 applied
36% were accepted
2,980 enrolled (33%)
3.80 average high school GPA
64% had SAT verbal scores over 600
75% had SAT math scores over 600
84% had ACT scores over 24
18% had SAT verbal scores over 700
25% had SAT math scores over 700
23% had ACT scores over 30
127 National Merit Scholars

Graduation and After
46% graduated in 4 years
19% graduated in 5 years
6% graduated in 6 years
85% had job offers within 6 months
500 organizations recruited on campus
1 Marshall, 2 Fulbright scholars

Financial Matters
$22,636 tuition and fees (1999–2000)
$7282 room and board

UNIVERSITY OF SOUTH FLORIDA

URBAN SETTING ■ PUBLIC ■ STATE-SUPPORTED ■ COED
TAMPA, FLORIDA

Web site: www.usf.edu
Contact: Ms. Cecelia Leslie, Director of Admissions, 4202 East Fowler
  Avenue, SVC 1036, Tampa, FL 33620-9951
Telephone: 813-974-3350 **Fax:** 813-974-9689
E-mail: bullseye@admin.usf.edu

Getting in Last Year
10,005 applied
73% were accepted
3,588 enrolled (49%)
3.5 average high school GPA
24% had SAT verbal scores over 600
24% had SAT math scores over 600
33% had ACT scores over 24
4% had SAT verbal scores over 700
3% had SAT math scores over 700
3% had ACT scores over 30
26 National Merit Scholars
20 valedictorians

Graduation and After
21% pursued further study
260 organizations recruited on campus
1 Fulbright scholar

Financial Matters
$2256 resident tuition and fees (1999–2000)
$9245 nonresident tuition and fees (1999–2000)
$4606 room and board

Academics

USF awards associate, bachelor's, master's, doctoral, and first-professional **degrees** and post-bachelor's certificates. Challenging opportunities include advanced placement, accelerated degree programs, student-designed majors, freshman honors college, an honors program, double majors, independent study, a senior project, and Sigma Xi. Special programs include cooperative education, internships, summer session for credit, off-campus study, study-abroad, and Army and Air Force ROTC.

The most frequently chosen fields are business/marketing, education, and social sciences and history. A complete listing of majors at USF appears in the Majors Index beginning on page 432.

The **faculty** at USF has 1,492 full-time members. The student-faculty ratio is 16:1.

Students of USF

The student body totals 35,118, of whom 28,916 are undergraduates. 58.8% are women and 41.2% are men. Students come from 52 states and territories and 101 other countries. 96% are from Florida. 1.7% are international students. 10.6% are African American, 0.4% American Indian, 5.5% Asian American, and 9.9% Hispanic American.

Facilities and Resources

Student rooms are linked to a campus network. 500 **computers** are available on campus that provide access to the Internet. The 3 **libraries** have 1,422,688 books and 10,155 subscriptions.

Campus Life

There are 200 active organizations on campus, including a drama/theater group, newspaper, radio station, television station, choral group, and marching band. 5% of eligible men and 4% of eligible women are members of national **fraternities** and national **sororities**.

USF is a member of the NCAA (Division I). **Intercollegiate sports** (some offering scholarships) include baseball (m), basketball, cross-country running, football (m), golf, soccer, softball (w), tennis, track and field, volleyball (w).

Campus Safety

Student safety services include residence hall lobby personnel 8 p.m.-6 a.m, late-night transport/escort service, 24-hour emergency telephone alarm devices, 24-hour patrols by trained security personnel, student patrols, and electronically operated dormitory entrances.

Applying

USF requires SAT I or ACT, a high school transcript, and a minimum high school GPA of 2.0, and in some cases recommendations. Application deadline: 3/1 priority date for financial aid. Early admission is possible.

THE UNIVERSITY OF TENNESSEE KNOXVILLE

URBAN SETTING ■ PUBLIC ■ STATE-SUPPORTED ■ COED
KNOXVILLE, TENNESSEE

Web site: www.utk.edu
Contact: Ms. Kathy Keebler, Acting Director of Admissions, 320 Student
Services Building, Knoxville, TN 37996-0230
Telephone: 865-974-2184 or toll-free 800-221-8657 (in-state) **Fax:**
865-974-6341
E-mail: admissions@utk.edu

Academics

UT Knoxville awards bachelor's, master's, doctoral, and first-professional **degrees**.
Challenging opportunities include advanced placement, accelerated degree programs,
student-designed majors, an honors program, double majors, independent study, a senior
project, Phi Beta Kappa, and Sigma Xi. Special programs include cooperative education,
internships, summer session for credit, off-campus study, study-abroad, and Army and
Air Force ROTC.

The most frequently chosen fields are business/marketing, social sciences and history,
and engineering/engineering technologies. A complete listing of majors at UT Knoxville
appears in the Majors Index beginning on page 432.

The **faculty** at UT Knoxville has 1,421 full-time members, 76% with terminal
degrees. The student-faculty ratio is 14:1.

Students of UT Knoxville

The student body totals 26,437, of whom 20,259 are undergraduates. 51.1% are women
and 48.9% are men. Students come from 50 states and territories and 100 other
countries. 89% are from Tennessee. 1.3% are international students. 5.8% are African
American, 0.3% American Indian, 2.3% Asian American, and 1% Hispanic American.
79% returned for their sophomore year.

Facilities and Resources

Student rooms are linked to a campus network. 1,000 **computers** are available on
campus that provide access to the Internet. The 7 **libraries** have 1,069,587 books and
11,156 subscriptions.

Campus Life

There are 350 active organizations on campus, including a drama/theater group,
newspaper, radio station, choral group, and marching band. 8% of eligible men and 8%
of eligible women are members of national **fraternities** and national **sororities**.

UT Knoxville is a member of the NCAA (Division I). **Intercollegiate sports** (some
offering scholarships) include baseball (m), basketball, crew (w), cross-country running,
football (m), golf, soccer (w), softball (w), swimming, tennis, track and field, volleyball
(w).

Campus Safety

Student safety services include late-night transport/escort service, 24-hour emergency
telephone alarm devices, and 24-hour patrols by trained security personnel.

Applying

UT Knoxville requires SAT I or ACT, a high school transcript, and a minimum high
school GPA of 2.0. Application deadline: 6/1; 3/1 priority date for financial aid. Early
and deferred admission are possible.

Getting in Last Year

10,605 applied
67% were accepted
4,155 enrolled (58%)
26% from top tenth of their h.s. class
3.34 average high school GPA
27% had SAT verbal scores over 600
30% had SAT math scores over 600
49% had ACT scores over 24
6% had SAT verbal scores over 700
6% had SAT math scores over 700
9% had ACT scores over 30
44 National Merit Scholars

Graduation and After

24% graduated in 4 years
26% graduated in 5 years
7% graduated in 6 years
503 organizations recruited on campus

Financial Matters

$3104 resident tuition and fees (1999–2000)
$9172 nonresident tuition and fees (1999–2000)
$4030 room and board
67% average percent of need met
$5892 average financial aid amount received per undergraduate (1999–2000)

THE UNIVERSITY OF TEXAS AT AUSTIN

URBAN SETTING ■ PUBLIC ■ STATE-SUPPORTED ■ COED
AUSTIN, TEXAS

Web site: www.utexas.edu
Contact: Freshman Admissions Center, John Hargis Hall, Austin, TX
78712-1111
Telephone: 512-475-7440 **Fax:** 512-475-7475
E-mail: frmn@uts.cc.utexas.edu

Academics

UT Austin awards bachelor's, master's, doctoral, and first-professional **degrees**. Challenging opportunities include advanced placement, accelerated degree programs, student-designed majors, an honors program, double majors, independent study, a senior project, Phi Beta Kappa, and Sigma Xi. Special programs include cooperative education, internships, summer session for credit, study-abroad, and Army, Navy and Air Force ROTC.

The most frequently chosen fields are social sciences and history, business/marketing, and communications/communication technologies. A complete listing of majors at UT Austin appears in the Majors Index beginning on page 432.

The **faculty** at UT Austin has 2,313 full-time members. The student-faculty ratio is 19:1.

Students of UT Austin

The student body totals 49,009, of whom 37,159 are undergraduates. 50.4% are women and 49.6% are men. Students come from 52 states and territories and 100 other countries. 95% are from Texas. 3% are international students. 3.4% are African American, 0.5% American Indian, 14.5% Asian American, and 13.8% Hispanic American. 89% returned for their sophomore year.

Facilities and Resources

Student rooms are linked to a campus network. 4,000 **computers** are available on campus that provide access to the Internet. The 19 **libraries** have 52,515 subscriptions.

Campus Life

There are 750 active organizations on campus, including a drama/theater group, newspaper, radio station, television station, choral group, and marching band. 10% of eligible men and 13% of eligible women are members of national **fraternities** and national **sororities**.

UT Austin is a member of the NCAA (Division I). **Intercollegiate sports** (some offering scholarships) include baseball (m), basketball, crew (w), cross-country running, football (m), golf, soccer (w), softball (w), swimming, tennis, track and field, volleyball (w).

Campus Safety

Student safety services include late-night transport/escort service, 24-hour emergency telephone alarm devices, 24-hour patrols by trained security personnel, student patrols, and electronically operated dormitory entrances.

Applying

UT Austin requires SAT I or ACT and a high school transcript, and in some cases an essay. Application deadline: 2/1; 4/1 priority date for financial aid. Deferred admission is possible.

UNIVERSITY OF THE SOUTH

SMALL-TOWN SETTING ■ PRIVATE ■ INDEPENDENT RELIGIOUS ■ COED
SEWANEE, TENNESSEE

Web site: www.sewanee.edu
Contact: Mr. Robert M. Hedrick, Director of Admission, 735 University
  Avenue, Sewanee, TN 37383-1000
Telephone: 931-598-1238 or toll-free 800-522-2234 **Fax:** 931-598-1667
E-mail: admiss@sewanee.edu

eAPPLY

Academics

Sewanee awards bachelor's, master's, doctoral, and first-professional **degrees**. Challenging opportunities include advanced placement, accelerated degree programs, student-designed majors, an honors program, double majors, a senior project, Phi Beta Kappa, and Sigma Xi. Special programs include internships, summer session for credit, and study-abroad.

The most frequently chosen fields are social sciences and history, English, and foreign language/literature. A complete listing of majors at Sewanee appears in the Majors Index beginning on page 432.

The **faculty** at Sewanee has 115 full-time members, 95% with terminal degrees. The student-faculty ratio is 11:1.

Students of Sewanee

The student body totals 1,438, of whom 1,332 are undergraduates. 54% are women and 46% are men. Students come from 46 states and territories and 20 other countries. 21% are from Tennessee. 2% are international students. 3.6% are African American, 0.2% American Indian, 0.6% Asian American, and 0.9% Hispanic American. 88% returned for their sophomore year.

Facilities and Resources

Student rooms are linked to a campus network. 92 **computers** are available on campus that provide access to the Internet. The **library** has 469,120 books and 2,478 subscriptions.

Campus Life

There are 110 active organizations on campus, including a drama/theater group, newspaper, radio station, and choral group. 65% of eligible men and 55% of eligible women are members of national **fraternities** and local **sororities**.

Sewanee is a member of the NCAA (Division III). **Intercollegiate sports** include baseball (m), basketball, crew, cross-country running, equestrian sports, fencing, field hockey (w), football (m), golf, lacrosse, rugby (m), soccer, softball (w), swimming, tennis, track and field, volleyball (w).

Campus Safety

Student safety services include security lighting, late-night transport/escort service, 24-hour emergency telephone alarm devices, and 24-hour patrols by trained security personnel.

Applying

Sewanee requires an essay, SAT I or ACT, a high school transcript, and 2 recommendations. It recommends SAT II Subject Tests and an interview. Application deadline: 2/1; 3/1 priority date for financial aid. Early and deferred admission are possible.

Getting in Last Year
1,642 applied
73% were accepted
392 enrolled (33%)
49% from top tenth of their h.s. class
3.31 average high school GPA
62% had SAT verbal scores over 600
61% had SAT math scores over 600
80% had ACT scores over 24
15% had SAT verbal scores over 700
11% had SAT math scores over 700
16% had ACT scores over 30
13 National Merit Scholars

Graduation and After
38% pursued further study (14% arts and
  sciences, 6% law, 4% business)
74% had job offers within 6 months
17 organizations recruited on campus

Financial Matters
$19,080 tuition and fees (1999–2000)
$5230 room and board
100% average percent of need met
$16,600 average financial aid amount received
  per undergraduate (1998–99)

eAPPLY

UNIVERSITY OF TULSA
URBAN SETTING ■ PRIVATE ■ INDEPENDENT RELIGIOUS ■ COED
TULSA, OKLAHOMA

Web site: www.utulsa.edu

Contact: Mr. John C. Corso, Associate VP for Administration/Dean of Admission, Office of Admission, The University of Tulsa, 600 South College Avenue, Tulsa, OK 74104

Telephone: 918-631-2307 or toll-free 800-331-3050 **Fax:** 918-631-5003

E-mail: admission@utulsa.edu

Academics

TU awards bachelor's, master's, doctoral, and first-professional **degrees**. Challenging opportunities include advanced placement, accelerated degree programs, student-designed majors, an honors program, double majors, independent study, a senior project, Phi Beta Kappa, and Sigma Xi. Special programs include internships, summer session for credit, and study-abroad.

The most frequently chosen fields are business/marketing, engineering/engineering technologies, and health professions and related sciences. A complete listing of majors at TU appears in the Majors Index beginning on page 432.

The **faculty** at TU has 310 full-time members, 96% with terminal degrees. The student-faculty ratio is 11:1.

Students of TU

The student body totals 4,192, of whom 2,924 are undergraduates. 52.2% are women and 47.8% are men. Students come from 39 states and territories and 61 other countries. 76% are from Oklahoma. 9.6% are international students. 7.5% are African American, 6.3% American Indian, 2.2% Asian American, and 3% Hispanic American. 81% returned for their sophomore year.

Facilities and Resources

Student rooms are linked to a campus network. 500 **computers** are available on campus that provide access to the Internet. The 3 **libraries** have 890,000 books and 8,850 subscriptions.

Campus Life

There are 140 active organizations on campus, including a drama/theater group, newspaper, radio station, television station, choral group, and marching band. 21% of eligible men and 23% of eligible women are members of national **fraternities** and national **sororities**.

TU is a member of the NCAA (Division I). **Intercollegiate sports** (some offering scholarships) include basketball, crew (w), cross-country running, football (m), golf, soccer, softball (w), tennis, track and field, volleyball (w).

Campus Safety

Student safety services include late-night transport/escort service, 24-hour emergency telephone alarm devices, 24-hour patrols by trained security personnel, and electronically operated dormitory entrances.

Applying

TU requires SAT I or ACT, a high school transcript, and 1 recommendation. It recommends an essay, an interview, and a minimum high school GPA of 3.0. Application deadline: 3/1 priority date for financial aid. Early and deferred admission are possible.

University of Utah

Urban setting ■ Public ■ State-supported ■ Coed
Salt Lake City, Utah

Web site: www.utah.edu
Contact: Ms. Suzanne Espinoza, Director of High School Services, 250 South Student Services Building, Salt Lake City, UT 84112
Telephone: 801-581-8761 or toll-free 800-444-8638

Academics

U of U awards bachelor's, master's, doctoral, and first-professional **degrees**. Challenging opportunities include advanced placement, accelerated degree programs, student-designed majors, an honors program, independent study, Phi Beta Kappa, and Sigma Xi. Special programs include cooperative education, internships, summer session for credit, off-campus study, study-abroad, and Army, Navy and Air Force ROTC.

The most frequently chosen fields are social sciences and history, business/marketing, and communications/communication technologies. A complete listing of majors at U of U appears in the Majors Index beginning on page 432.

Students of U of U

The student body totals 26,988, of whom 21,956 are undergraduates. 43.7% are women and 56.3% are men. Students come from 54 states and territories and 109 other countries. 83% are from Utah. 59% returned for their sophomore year.

Facilities and Resources

Student rooms are linked to a campus network. 5,000 **computers** are available on campus that provide access to the Internet. The 3 **libraries** have 3,343,734 books.

Campus Life

There are 250 active organizations on campus, including a drama/theater group, newspaper, radio station, television station, choral group, and marching band. 2% of eligible men and 3% of eligible women are members of national **fraternities**, national **sororities**, local fraternities, and local sororities.

U of U is a member of the NCAA (Division I). **Intercollegiate sports** (some offering scholarships) include baseball (m), basketball, bowling, cross-country running, football (m), golf (m), gymnastics (w), ice hockey (m), racquetball, rugby (m), skiing (cross-country), skiing (downhill), soccer, softball (w), swimming, table tennis, tennis, track and field, volleyball (w).

Campus Safety

Student safety services include late-night transport/escort service, 24-hour emergency telephone alarm devices, 24-hour patrols by trained security personnel, student patrols, and electronically operated dormitory entrances.

Applying

U of U requires SAT I or ACT, a high school transcript, and a minimum high school GPA of 2.0. It recommends a minimum high school GPA of 3.0. Application deadline: 7/1; 3/15 priority date for financial aid. Early and deferred admission are possible.

Getting in Last Year

5,328 applied
93% were accepted
27% from top tenth of their h.s. class
3.44 average high school GPA
36% had SAT verbal scores over 600
41% had SAT math scores over 600
54% had ACT scores over 24
10% had SAT verbal scores over 700
9% had SAT math scores over 700
13% had ACT scores over 30

Graduation and After

14% graduated in 4 years
14% graduated in 5 years
8% graduated in 6 years
24% pursued further study
60% had job offers within 6 months
269 organizations recruited on campus
1 Fulbright scholar

Financial Matters

$2790 resident tuition and fees (1999–2000)
$8495 nonresident tuition and fees (1999–2000)
$5179 room and board
63% average percent of need met
$7627 average financial aid amount received per undergraduate (1998–99)

UNIVERSITY OF VERMONT

SUBURBAN SETTING ■ PUBLIC ■ STATE-SUPPORTED ■ COED
BURLINGTON, VERMONT

Web site: www.uvm.edu
Contact: Mr. Donald M. Honeman, Director of Admissions, Office of
    Admissions, Burlington, VT 05401-3596
Telephone: 802-656-3370 **Fax:** 802-656-8611

Getting in Last Year
7,564 applied
80% were accepted
1,818 enrolled (30%)
16% from top tenth of their h.s. class
33% had SAT verbal scores over 600
37% had SAT math scores over 600
55% had ACT scores over 24
4% had SAT verbal scores over 700
3% had SAT math scores over 700
4% had ACT scores over 30
14 valedictorians

Graduation and After
53% graduated in 4 years
13% graduated in 5 years
3% graduated in 6 years
18% pursued further study (7% arts and sciences, 2% education, 2% law)
64% had job offers within 6 months
234 organizations recruited on campus

Financial Matters
$8044 resident tuition and fees (1999–2000)
$19,252 nonresident tuition and fees (1999–2000)
$5620 room and board
92% average percent of need met
$16,500 average financial aid amount received per undergraduate (1998–99)

Academics
UVM awards associate, bachelor's, master's, doctoral, and first-professional **degrees** and post-bachelor's and post-master's certificates. Challenging opportunities include advanced placement, student-designed majors, an honors program, double majors, independent study, a senior project, Phi Beta Kappa, and Sigma Xi. Special programs include cooperative education, internships, summer session for credit, off-campus study, study-abroad, and Army ROTC.

The most frequently chosen fields are social sciences and history, natural resources/environmental science, and business/marketing. A complete listing of majors at UVM appears in the Majors Index beginning on page 432.

The **faculty** at UVM has 554 full-time members, 85% with terminal degrees. The student-faculty ratio is 14:1.

Students of UVM
The student body totals 10,206, of whom 8,739 are undergraduates. 54.9% are women and 45.1% are men. Students come from 49 states and territories and 26 other countries. 41% are from Vermont. 1% are international students. 0.5% are African American, 0.3% American Indian, 1.6% Asian American, and 1.1% Hispanic American. 81% returned for their sophomore year.

Facilities and Resources
Student rooms are linked to a campus network. The 4 **libraries** have 1,774,077 books and 20,278 subscriptions.

Campus Life
There are 90 active organizations on campus, including a drama/theater group, newspaper, radio station, television station, and choral group. UVM has national **fraternities**, national **sororities**, and local fraternities.

UVM is a member of the NCAA (Division I). **Intercollegiate sports** (some offering scholarships) include baseball (m), basketball, crew, cross-country running, equestrian sports, field hockey (w), golf (m), gymnastics, ice hockey, lacrosse, rugby, sailing, skiing (cross-country), skiing (downhill), soccer, softball (w), swimming, tennis, track and field, volleyball, weight lifting, wrestling (m).

Campus Safety
Student safety services include late-night transport/escort service, 24-hour emergency telephone alarm devices, 24-hour patrols by trained security personnel, and electronically operated dormitory entrances.

Applying
UVM requires an essay, SAT I or ACT, and a high school transcript. It recommends an interview and 2 recommendations. Application deadline: 1/15; 2/10 priority date for financial aid. Early and deferred admission are possible.

University of Virginia

Suburban setting ■ Public ■ State-supported ■ Coed
Charlottesville, Virginia

Web site: www.virginia.edu
Contact: Mr. John A. Blackburn, Dean of Admission, PO Box 9017,
Charlottesville, VA 22906
Telephone: 804-982-3200 **Fax:** 804-924-3587
E-mail: undergrad-admission@virginia.edu

Academics

UVA awards bachelor's, master's, doctoral, and first-professional **degrees** and post-master's certificates. Challenging opportunities include advanced placement, accelerated degree programs, student-designed majors, an honors program, double majors, independent study, a senior project, Phi Beta Kappa, and Sigma Xi. Special programs include cooperative education, internships, summer session for credit, study-abroad, and Army, Navy and Air Force ROTC.

The most frequently chosen fields are social sciences and history, business/marketing, and engineering/engineering technologies. A complete listing of majors at UVA appears in the Majors Index beginning on page 432.

The **faculty** at UVA has 1,030 full-time members, 92% with terminal degrees. The student-faculty ratio is 14:1.

Students of UVA

The student body totals 22,433, of whom 13,570 are undergraduates. 54.2% are women and 45.8% are men. Students come from 52 states and territories and 106 other countries. 69% are from Virginia. 3.6% are international students. 10% are African American, 0.3% American Indian, 9.9% Asian American, and 2.1% Hispanic American. 96% returned for their sophomore year.

Facilities and Resources

Student rooms are linked to a campus network. 1,859 **computers** are available on campus that provide access to the Internet. The 15 **libraries** have 4,513,843 books and 47,479 subscriptions.

Campus Life

There are 300 active organizations on campus, including a drama/theater group, newspaper, radio station, television station, and choral group. 30% of eligible men and 30% of eligible women are members of national **fraternities**, national **sororities**, and local fraternities.

UVA is a member of the NCAA (Division I). **Intercollegiate sports** (some offering scholarships) include baseball (m), basketball, crew (w), cross-country running, field hockey (w), football (m), golf (m), lacrosse, soccer, softball (w), swimming, tennis, track and field, volleyball (w), wrestling (m).

Campus Safety

Student safety services include late-night transport/escort service, 24-hour emergency telephone alarm devices, 24-hour patrols by trained security personnel, and electronically operated dormitory entrances.

Applying

UVA requires an essay, SAT II Subject Tests, SAT II: Writing Test, SAT I or ACT, a high school transcript, and 1 recommendation. Application deadline: 1/2; 3/1 priority date for financial aid. Deferred admission is possible.

Getting in Last Year

16,461 applied
34% were accepted
2,924 enrolled (52%)
82% from top tenth of their h.s. class
3.78 average high school GPA
76% had SAT verbal scores over 600
82% had SAT math scores over 600
87% had ACT scores over 24
30% had SAT verbal scores over 700
34% had SAT math scores over 700
38% had ACT scores over 30
211 valedictorians

Graduation and After

83% graduated in 4 years
8% graduated in 5 years
1% graduated in 6 years
32% pursued further study
450 organizations recruited on campus
8 Fulbright scholars

Financial Matters

$4130 resident tuition and fees (1999–2000)
$16,603 nonresident tuition and fees (1999–2000)
$4589 room and board
92% average percent of need met
$10,042 average financial aid amount received per undergraduate (1999–2000)

UNIVERSITY OF WASHINGTON
URBAN SETTING ■ PUBLIC ■ STATE-SUPPORTED ■ COED
SEATTLE, WASHINGTON

Web site: www.washington.edu
Contact: Ms. Stephanie Preston, Assistant Director of Admissions, Office of Admissions, Box 355840, Seattle, WA 98195-5840
Telephone: 206-543-9686
E-mail: askuwadm@u.washington.edu

Getting in Last Year
12,785 applied
77% were accepted
4,353 enrolled (44%)
39% from top tenth of their h.s. class
3.63 average high school GPA
38% had SAT verbal scores over 600
49% had SAT math scores over 600
61% had ACT scores over 24
8% had SAT verbal scores over 700
10% had SAT math scores over 700
12% had ACT scores over 30

Graduation and After
37% graduated in 4 years
27% graduated in 5 years
7% graduated in 6 years
450 organizations recruited on campus
9 Fulbright scholars

Financial Matters
$3638 resident tuition and fees (1999–2000)
$12,029 nonresident tuition and fees (1999–2000)
$4905 room and board
86% average percent of need met
$8167 average financial aid amount received per undergraduate (1999–2000)

Academics
UW awards bachelor's, master's, doctoral, and first-professional **degrees**. Challenging opportunities include advanced placement, accelerated degree programs, student-designed majors, an honors program, double majors, independent study, a senior project, Phi Beta Kappa, and Sigma Xi. Special programs include cooperative education, internships, summer session for credit, study-abroad, and Army, Navy and Air Force ROTC.

The most frequently chosen fields are social sciences and history, business/marketing, and engineering/engineering technologies. A complete listing of majors at UW appears in the Majors Index beginning on page 432.

The **faculty** at UW has 2,600 full-time members, 78% with terminal degrees. The student-faculty ratio is 11:1.

Students of UW
The student body totals 35,559, of whom 25,638 are undergraduates. 52.2% are women and 47.8% are men. Students come from 52 states and territories and 59 other countries. 89% are from Washington. 2.3% are international students. 2.7% are African American, 1.3% American Indian, 22.4% Asian American, and 3.8% Hispanic American. 90% returned for their sophomore year.

Facilities and Resources
Student rooms are linked to a campus network. 285 **computers** are available on campus for student use. The 22 **libraries** have 5,820,229 books and 50,245 subscriptions.

Campus Life
There are 300 active organizations on campus, including a drama/theater group, newspaper, radio station, television station, choral group, and marching band. 12% of eligible men and 11% of eligible women are members of national **fraternities** and national **sororities**.

UW is a member of the NCAA (Division I). **Intercollegiate sports** (some offering scholarships) include baseball (m), basketball, crew, cross-country running, football (m), golf, gymnastics (w), soccer, softball (w), swimming, tennis, track and field, volleyball (w), wrestling (m).

Campus Safety
Student safety services include late-night transport/escort service, 24-hour emergency telephone alarm devices, 24-hour patrols by trained security personnel, and electronically operated dormitory entrances.

Applying
UW requires an essay, SAT I or ACT, a high school transcript, and a minimum high school GPA of 2.0. Application deadline: 1/15; 2/28 priority date for financial aid. Early admission is possible.

University of Wisconsin–Madison

Urban setting ■ Public ■ State-supported ■ Coed
Madison, Wisconsin

Web site: www.wisc.edu
Contact: Mr. Thomas Reason, Office of Admissions, 716 Langdon Street,
Madison, WI 53706-1400
Telephone: 608-262-3961 **Fax:** 608-262-7706
E-mail: on.wisconsin@mail.admin.wisc.edu

Academics

Wisconsin awards bachelor's, master's, doctoral, and first-professional **degrees**. Challenging opportunities include advanced placement, accelerated degree programs, student-designed majors, freshman honors college, an honors program, double majors, independent study, a senior project, Phi Beta Kappa, and Sigma Xi. Special programs include cooperative education, internships, summer session for credit, study-abroad, and Army, Navy and Air Force ROTC. A complete listing of majors at Wisconsin appears in the Majors Index beginning on page 432.

The student-faculty ratio is 14:1.

Students of Wisconsin

The student body is made up of 28,996 undergraduates. 52.5% are women and 47.5% are men. Students come from 52 states and territories and 99 other countries. 65% are from Wisconsin. 4% are international students. 1.9% are African American, 0.4% American Indian, 4.4% Asian American, and 2.1% Hispanic American. 96% returned for their sophomore year.

Facilities and Resources

Student rooms are linked to a campus network. 2,800 **computers** are available on campus that provide access to the Internet. The 41 **libraries** have 5,800,000 books and 62,000 subscriptions.

Campus Life

Active organizations on campus include a drama/theater group, newspaper, radio station, choral group, and marching band. 20% of eligible men and 20% of eligible women are members of national **fraternities**, national **sororities**, and eating clubs.

Wisconsin is a member of the NCAA (Division I). **Intercollegiate sports** (some offering scholarships) include basketball, crew, cross-country running, football (m), golf, ice hockey, lacrosse (w), rugby (m), sailing, soccer, softball (w), swimming, tennis, track and field, volleyball, wrestling (m).

Campus Safety

Student safety services include free cab rides throughout city, late-night transport/escort service, 24-hour emergency telephone alarm devices, 24-hour patrols by trained security personnel, and electronically operated dormitory entrances.

Applying

Wisconsin requires an essay, SAT I or ACT, and a high school transcript, and in some cases SAT II Subject Tests. Application deadline: 2/1. Early and deferred admission are possible.

Getting in Last Year
16,456 applied
73% were accepted
5,880 enrolled (49%)
47% from top tenth of their h.s. class
3.74 average high school GPA
62% had SAT verbal scores over 600
71% had SAT math scores over 600
80% had ACT scores over 24
17% had SAT verbal scores over 700
19% had SAT math scores over 700
31% had ACT scores over 30
141 National Merit Scholars
442 valedictorians

Graduation and After
69% pursued further study
1 Rhodes, 14 Fulbright scholars

Financial Matters
$3738 resident tuition and fees (1999–2000)
$13,049 nonresident tuition and fees (1999–2000)
$4206 room and board

Getting in Last Year
1,491 applied
78% were accepted
353 enrolled (30%)
43% from top tenth of their h.s. class
39% had SAT verbal scores over 600
49% had SAT math scores over 600
6% had SAT verbal scores over 700
6% had SAT math scores over 700
7 National Merit Scholars
6 valedictorians

Graduation and After
70% graduated in 4 years
4% graduated in 5 years
32% pursued further study (21% arts and sciences, 8% medicine, 2% law)
60% had job offers within 6 months
50 organizations recruited on campus

Financial Matters
$20,230 tuition and fees (1999–2000)
$5970 room and board
90% average percent of need met
$15,223 average financial aid amount received per undergraduate (1999–2000)

URSINUS COLLEGE
SUBURBAN SETTING ■ PRIVATE ■ INDEPENDENT RELIGIOUS ■ COED
COLLEGEVILLE, PENNSYLVANIA

Web site: www.ursinus.edu
Contact: Mr. Paul M. Cramer, Director of Admissions, Box 1000, Collegeville, PA 19426
Telephone: 610-409-3200 **Fax:** 610-409-3662
E-mail: admissions@ursinus.edu

Academics
Ursinus awards bachelor's **degrees**. Challenging opportunities include advanced placement, student-designed majors, an honors program, double majors, independent study, a senior project, Phi Beta Kappa, and Sigma Xi. Special programs include internships, off-campus study, and study-abroad. A complete listing of majors at Ursinus appears in the Majors Index beginning on page 432.

The **faculty** at Ursinus has 100 full-time members, 92% with terminal degrees. The student-faculty ratio is 12:1.

Students of Ursinus
The student body is made up of 1,240 undergraduates. 52.6% are women and 47.4% are men. Students come from 25 states and territories and 14 other countries. 65% are from Pennsylvania. 2.4% are international students. 6.4% are African American, 0.1% American Indian, 3.5% Asian American, and 1.9% Hispanic American. 94% returned for their sophomore year.

Facilities and Resources
Student rooms are linked to a campus network. 350 **computers** are available on campus that provide access to the Internet. The **library** has 200,000 books and 900 subscriptions.

Campus Life
There are 116 active organizations on campus, including a drama/theater group, newspaper, radio station, television station, and choral group. 35% of eligible men and 30% of eligible women are members of national **fraternities**, local fraternities, and local **sororities**.

Ursinus is a member of the NCAA (Division III). **Intercollegiate sports** include baseball (m), basketball, cross-country running, field hockey (w), football (m), golf, gymnastics (w), lacrosse, soccer, softball (w), swimming, tennis, track and field, volleyball (w), wrestling (m).

Campus Safety
Student safety services include late-night transport/escort service, 24-hour emergency telephone alarm devices, and 24-hour patrols by trained security personnel.

Applying
Ursinus requires an essay, SAT I or ACT, a high school transcript, and 2 recommendations. It recommends SAT II Subject Tests and an interview. Application deadline: 2/15; 2/15 priority date for financial aid. Early and deferred admission are possible.

VALPARAISO UNIVERSITY

SMALL-TOWN SETTING ■ PRIVATE ■ INDEPENDENT RELIGIOUS ■ COED
VALPARAISO, INDIANA

Web site: www.valpo.edu
Contact: Ms. Karen Foust, Director of Admissions, 651 South College
 Avenue, Valparaiso, IN 46383-6493
Telephone: 219-464-5011 or toll-free 888-GO-VALPO (out-of-state) **Fax:**
 219-464-6898
E-mail: undergrad_admissions@valpo.edu

Academics

Valpo awards associate, bachelor's, master's, and first-professional **degrees**. Challenging opportunities include advanced placement, accelerated degree programs, student-designed majors, freshman honors college, an honors program, double majors, independent study, and a senior project. Special programs include cooperative education, internships, summer session for credit, off-campus study, and study-abroad.

The most frequently chosen fields are business/marketing, health professions and related sciences, and trade and industry. A complete listing of majors at Valpo appears in the Majors Index beginning on page 432.

The **faculty** at Valpo has 223 full-time members, 89% with terminal degrees. The student-faculty ratio is 12:1.

Students of Valpo

The student body totals 3,650, of whom 2,986 are undergraduates. 53.3% are women and 46.7% are men. Students come from 36 states and territories and 50 other countries. 35% are from Indiana. 3.3% are international students. 3.4% are African American, 0.5% American Indian, 2.2% Asian American, and 2.5% Hispanic American. 86% returned for their sophomore year.

Facilities and Resources

Student rooms are linked to a campus network. 545 **computers** are available on campus that provide access to the Internet. The 2 **libraries** have 353,512 books and 13,984 subscriptions.

Campus Life

There are 100 active organizations on campus, including a drama/theater group, newspaper, radio station, and choral group. 30% of eligible men and 30% of eligible women are members of national **fraternities** and local **sororities**.

Valpo is a member of the NCAA (Division I). **Intercollegiate sports** (some offering scholarships) include baseball (m), basketball, cross-country running, football (m), soccer, softball (w), swimming, tennis, volleyball (w).

Campus Safety

Student safety services include late-night transport/escort service, 24-hour emergency telephone alarm devices, 24-hour patrols by trained security personnel, and electronically operated dormitory entrances.

Applying

Valpo requires SAT I or ACT and a high school transcript, and in some cases an interview. It recommends an essay and 2 recommendations. Application deadline: rolling admissions; 3/1 priority date for financial aid. Deferred admission is possible.

V alparaiso University is home to 3,700 students seeking academic excellence in the Colleges of Arts & Sciences, Business Administration, Engineering, and Nursing and Christ College—The Honors College. Nestled in a residential community of 26,000, the University offers 60 major areas of study in the liberal arts with a Christian atmosphere. America's only independent Lutheran university, "Valpo" is consistently ranked by *U.S. News & World Report* as a top regional university and best value. A low student-faculty ratio strengthens mentoring relationships. The required interdisciplinary freshman curriculum, Valpo Core, fosters a sense of true community. A nonbinding early action option allows applicants to submit applications to Valpo no later than November 1 and to receive the admission decision by December 1.

Getting in Last Year
3,494 applied
78% were accepted
734 enrolled (27%)
45% from top tenth of their h.s. class
46% had SAT verbal scores over 600
54% had SAT math scores over 600
80% had ACT scores over 24
11% had SAT verbal scores over 700
10% had SAT math scores over 700
19% had ACT scores over 30
22 National Merit Scholars
46 valedictorians

Graduation and After
Graduates pursuing further study: 6% education, 5% law, 1% engineering
71% had job offers within 6 months
63 organizations recruited on campus

Financial Matters
$17,636 tuition and fees (2000–2001)
$4660 room and board
90% average percent of need met
$16,640 average financial aid amount received per undergraduate (1999–2000 estimated)

VANDERBILT UNIVERSITY

URBAN SETTING ■ PRIVATE ■ INDEPENDENT ■ COED
NASHVILLE, TENNESSEE

Web site: www.vanderbilt.edu
Contact: Mr. Bill Shain, Dean of Undergraduate Admissions, Nashville, TN 37240-1001
Telephone: 615-322-2561 or toll-free 800-288-0432 **Fax:** 615-343-7765
E-mail: admissions@vanderbilt.edu

> **V**anderbilt University enrolls America's most talented students, who are challenged daily to expand their intellectual horizons and free their imaginations. Dialogue, service, the Honor Code, the search for knowledge and personal fulfillment—a Vanderbilt education enhances the life of every student. Vanderbilt alumni carry with them not only knowledge gained in classes, but a lifelong connection to a special community of learners. Vanderbilt is committed to enrolling talented, motivated students from diverse backgrounds. The University offers a full range of financial aid and financing options for those who need assistance.

Getting in Last Year
8,494 applied
61% were accepted
1,633 enrolled (31%)
66% from top tenth of their h.s. class
3.57 average high school GPA
75% had SAT verbal scores over 600
83% had SAT math scores over 600
95% had ACT scores over 24
22% had SAT verbal scores over 700
31% had SAT math scores over 700
34% had ACT scores over 30
85 National Merit Scholars
30 class presidents
101 valedictorians

Graduation and After
74% graduated in 4 years
6% graduated in 5 years
1% graduated in 6 years
32% pursued further study (20% arts and sciences, 7% law, 4% medicine)
63% had job offers within 6 months
250 organizations recruited on campus
2 Fulbright scholars

Financial Matters
$23,598 tuition and fees (1999–2000)
$8032 room and board
98% average percent of need met
$23,905 average financial aid amount received per undergraduate (1999–2000 estimated)

Academics
Vanderbilt awards bachelor's, master's, doctoral, and first-professional **degrees**. Challenging opportunities include advanced placement, accelerated degree programs, student-designed majors, an honors program, double majors, independent study, a senior project, Phi Beta Kappa, and Sigma Xi. Special programs include cooperative education, internships, summer session for credit, off-campus study, study-abroad, and Army, Navy and Air Force ROTC.

The most frequently chosen fields are social sciences and history, engineering/engineering technologies, and psychology. A complete listing of majors at Vanderbilt appears in the Majors Index beginning on page 432.

The **faculty** at Vanderbilt has 702 full-time members, 96% with terminal degrees. The student-faculty ratio is 8:1.

Students of Vanderbilt
The student body totals 10,022, of whom 5,780 are undergraduates. 52.7% are women and 47.3% are men. Students come from 54 states and territories and 36 other countries. 15% are from Tennessee. 3% are international students. 4.5% are African American, 0.2% American Indian, 5.8% Asian American, and 3.4% Hispanic American. 92% returned for their sophomore year.

Facilities and Resources
Student rooms are linked to a campus network. 400 **computers** are available on campus that provide access to productivity and educational software and the Internet. The 8 **libraries** have 2,512,072 books and 21,608 subscriptions.

Campus Life
There are 264 active organizations on campus, including a drama/theater group, newspaper, radio station, choral group, and marching band. 34% of eligible men and 48% of eligible women are members of national **fraternities** and national **sororities**.

Vanderbilt is a member of the NCAA (Division I). **Intercollegiate sports** (some offering scholarships) include baseball (m), basketball, crew, cross-country running, equestrian sports, fencing, field hockey, football (m), golf, ice hockey, lacrosse, rugby, sailing, soccer, squash, tennis, track and field, volleyball, water polo, wrestling.

Campus Safety
Student safety services include late-night transport/escort service, 24-hour emergency telephone alarm devices, 24-hour patrols by trained security personnel, student patrols, and electronically operated dormitory entrances.

Applying
Vanderbilt requires an essay, SAT I or ACT, a high school transcript, and 2 recommendations. It recommends SAT II Subject Tests and SAT II: Writing Test. Application deadline: 1/7; 2/1 priority date for financial aid. Early and deferred admission are possible.

VASSAR COLLEGE

SUBURBAN SETTING ■ PRIVATE ■ INDEPENDENT ■ COED
POUGHKEEPSIE, NEW YORK

Web site: www.vassar.edu
Contact: Dr. David M. Borus, Dean of Admission and Financial Aid, 124
    Raymond Avenue, Poughkeepsie, NY 12604
Telephone: 914-437-7300 or toll-free 800-827-7270 **Fax:** 914-437-7063
E-mail: admissions@vassar.edu

eAPPLY

Academics

Vassar awards bachelor's and master's **degrees**. Challenging opportunities include advanced placement, accelerated degree programs, student-designed majors, double majors, independent study, a senior project, Phi Beta Kappa, and Sigma Xi. Special programs include internships, off-campus study, and study-abroad.

The most frequently chosen fields are social sciences and history, English, and visual/performing arts. A complete listing of majors at Vassar appears in the Majors Index beginning on page 432.

The **faculty** at Vassar has 247 full-time members, 95% with terminal degrees. The student-faculty ratio is 10:1.

Students of Vassar

The student body is made up of 2,322 undergraduates. 60.8% are women and 39.2% are men. Students come from 51 states and territories and 46 other countries. 40% are from New York. 4.6% are international students. 5% are African American, 0.4% American Indian, 9% Asian American, and 5.3% Hispanic American. 92% returned for their sophomore year.

Facilities and Resources

Student rooms are linked to a campus network. 300 **computers** are available on campus that provide access to Ethernet and the Internet. The **library** has 780,651 books and 4,799 subscriptions.

Campus Life

There are 100 active organizations on campus, including a drama/theater group, newspaper, radio station, and choral group. No national or local **fraternities** or **sororities**.

Vassar is a member of the NCAA (Division III). **Intercollegiate sports** include baseball (m), basketball, crew, cross-country running, fencing, field hockey (w), golf, lacrosse, rugby, sailing, soccer, squash, swimming, tennis, volleyball.

Campus Safety

Student safety services include late-night transport/escort service, 24-hour emergency telephone alarm devices, 24-hour patrols by trained security personnel, student patrols, and electronically operated dormitory entrances.

Applying

Vassar requires an essay, SAT I and SAT II or ACT, a high school transcript, and 2 recommendations. It recommends an interview. Application deadline: 1/1; 1/10 for financial aid. Early and deferred admission are possible.

Getting in Last Year
4,777 applied
43% were accepted
635 enrolled (31%)
63% from top tenth of their h.s. class
88% had SAT verbal scores over 600
83% had SAT math scores over 600
40% had SAT verbal scores over 700
25% had SAT math scores over 700
36 class presidents
26 valedictorians

Graduation and After
81% graduated in 4 years
6% graduated in 5 years
1% graduated in 6 years
**20% pursued further study (13% arts and
    sciences, 5% law, 2% medicine)**
66% had job offers within 6 months
3 Fulbright scholars

Financial Matters
$24,030 tuition and fees (1999–2000)
$6770 room and board
100% average percent of need met
**$20,820 average financial aid amount received
    per undergraduate (1999–2000 estimated)**

VILLANOVA UNIVERSITY

SUBURBAN SETTING ■ PRIVATE ■ INDEPENDENT RELIGIOUS ■ COED
VILLANOVA, PENNSYLVANIA

Web site: www.gradartsci.villanova.edu
Contact: Mr. James Van Blunk, Director of University Admission, 800
   Lancaster Avenue, Villanova, PA 19085-1672
Telephone: 610-519-4000 or toll-free 800-338-7927 **Fax:** 610-519-6450
E-mail: gotovu@email.villanova.edu

V illanova is on the move in the new millennium. In fall 1998, the University opened its $16-million Center for Engineering Education and Research. This 88,000-square-foot structure houses an interactive multimedia center, 30 state-of-the-art laboratories, interdisciplinary student project and study rooms, and 24-hour computer workstations. In addition, fall 1999 marked the completion of a $34-million expansion and enhancement of Mendel Science Center. Construction of 4 new apartment buildings for upperclass students and the renovation of the business center, Bartley Hall, are also underway.

Getting in Last Year
9,826 applied
57% were accepted
1,680 enrolled (30%)
39% from top tenth of their h.s. class
50% had SAT verbal scores over 600
62% had SAT math scores over 600
8% had SAT verbal scores over 700
13% had SAT math scores over 700
5 National Merit Scholars
27 valedictorians

Graduation and After
76% graduated in 4 years
6% graduated in 5 years
1% graduated in 6 years
Graduates pursuing further study: 7% arts and
  sciences, 7% business, 4% law
78% had job offers within 6 months
375 organizations recruited on campus
4 Fulbright scholars

Financial Matters
$20,850 tuition and fees (1999–2000)
$8000 room and board
80% average percent of need met
$13,966 average financial aid amount received
  per undergraduate (1999–2000)

Academics
Villanova awards associate, bachelor's, master's, doctoral, and first-professional **degrees**. Challenging opportunities include advanced placement, an honors program, double majors, independent study, a senior project, Phi Beta Kappa, and Sigma Xi. Special programs include internships, summer session for credit, off-campus study, study-abroad, and Army, Navy and Air Force ROTC.

The most frequently chosen fields are business/marketing, social sciences and history, and engineering/engineering technologies. A complete listing of majors at Villanova appears in the Majors Index beginning on page 432.

The **faculty** at Villanova has 499 full-time members, 90% with terminal degrees. The student-faculty ratio is 13:1.

Students of Villanova
The student body totals 9,968, of whom 7,144 are undergraduates. 50.2% are women and 49.8% are men. Students come from 48 states and territories and 30 other countries. 31% are from Pennsylvania. 1.9% are international students. 2.9% are African American, 0.2% American Indian, 3.6% Asian American, and 3.7% Hispanic American. 93% returned for their sophomore year.

Facilities and Resources
Student rooms are linked to a campus network. 800 **computers** are available on campus that provide access to the Internet. The 2 **libraries** have 1,010,560 books and 5,338 subscriptions.

Campus Life
There are 100 active organizations on campus, including a drama/theater group, newspaper, radio station, television station, choral group, and marching band. 18% of eligible men and 34% of eligible women are members of national **fraternities** and national **sororities**.

Villanova is a member of the NCAA (Division I). **Intercollegiate sports** (some offering scholarships) include baseball (m), basketball, crew, cross-country running, field hockey (w), football (m), golf (m), ice hockey (m), lacrosse, rugby (m), sailing, soccer, softball (w), swimming, tennis, track and field, volleyball, water polo, weight lifting.

Campus Safety
Student safety services include late-night transport/escort service, 24-hour emergency telephone alarm devices, 24-hour patrols by trained security personnel, student patrols, and electronically operated dormitory entrances.

Applying
Villanova requires an essay, SAT I or ACT, and a high school transcript. Application deadline: 1/7; 2/15 priority date for financial aid. Early and deferred admission are possible.

Virginia Polytechnic Institute and State University

Small-town setting ■ Public ■ State-supported ■ Coed
Blacksburg, Virginia

Web site: www.vt.edu
Contact: Mr. Shelley Blumenthal, Associate Director for Freshmen
   Admissions, 201 Burruss Hall, Blacksburg, VA 24061-0202
Telephone: 540-231-6267 Fax: 540-231-3242
E-mail: vtadmiss@vt.edu

Academics

Virginia Tech awards associate, bachelor's, master's, doctoral, and first-professional **degrees**. Challenging opportunities include advanced placement, accelerated degree programs, an honors program, double majors, independent study, a senior project, Phi Beta Kappa, and Sigma Xi. Special programs include cooperative education, internships, summer session for credit, off-campus study, study-abroad, and Army, Navy and Air Force ROTC.

The most frequently chosen fields are business/marketing, engineering/engineering technologies, and home economics/vocational home economics. A complete listing of majors at Virginia Tech appears in the Majors Index beginning on page 432.

The **faculty** at Virginia Tech has 1,242 full-time members. The student-faculty ratio is 19:1.

Students of Virginia Tech

The student body totals 25,452, of whom 21,479 are undergraduates. 40.6% are women and 59.4% are men. Students come from 52 states and territories and 104 other countries. 75% are from Virginia. 1.9% are international students. 3.9% are African American, 0.3% American Indian, 6.5% Asian American, and 1.9% Hispanic American. 90% returned for their sophomore year.

Facilities and Resources

Student rooms are linked to a campus network. The 5 **libraries** have 2,005,765 books and 18,281 subscriptions.

Campus Life

There are 437 active organizations on campus, including a drama/theater group, newspaper, radio station, television station, choral group, and marching band. 13% of eligible men and 23% of eligible women are members of national **fraternities**, national **sororities**, and local fraternities.

Virginia Tech is a member of the NCAA (Division I). **Intercollegiate sports** (some offering scholarships) include baseball (m), basketball, bowling, crew, cross-country running, equestrian sports, fencing, field hockey, football (m), golf (m), gymnastics, ice hockey, lacrosse, rugby, skiing (downhill), soccer, softball (w), swimming, tennis, track and field, volleyball, water polo, weight lifting, wrestling (m).

Campus Safety

Student safety services include late-night transport/escort service, 24-hour emergency telephone alarm devices, 24-hour patrols by trained security personnel, student patrols, and electronically operated dormitory entrances.

Applying

Virginia Tech requires SAT I or ACT, a high school transcript, and a minimum high school GPA of 2.0. It recommends a minimum high school GPA of 3.0. Application deadline: 2/1; 3/1 priority date for financial aid. Early and deferred admission are possible.

Students wishing to learn in a high-technology environment choose Virginia Tech for several reasons. It is not only the largest university in Virginia, but it is also the commonwealth's top research university, which gives undergraduates ample opportunity to make groundbreaking discoveries. A leading magazine ranked Virginia Tech fifth in the nation in terms of best value for schools specializing in science and technical programs. Tech also was named one of the most wired colleges in America, both for its innovative use of technology in the classroom (from English to engineering) and for providing free Internet and e-mail access.

Getting in Last Year

15,883 applied
73% were accepted
4,613 enrolled (40%)
33% from top tenth of their h.s. class
3.50 average high school GPA
37% had SAT verbal scores over 600
50% had SAT math scores over 600
5% had SAT verbal scores over 700
9% had SAT math scores over 700
36 National Merit Scholars

Graduation and After

36% graduated in 4 years
31% graduated in 5 years
5% graduated in 6 years
13% pursued further study
79% had job offers within 6 months
468 organizations recruited on campus

Financial Matters

$3620 resident tuition and fees (1999–2000)
$11,844 nonresident tuition and fees (1999–2000)
$3722 room and board
63% average percent of need met
$6015 average financial aid amount received per undergraduate (1998–99)

WABASH COLLEGE

SMALL-TOWN SETTING ■ PRIVATE ■ INDEPENDENT ■ MEN ONLY
CRAWFORDSVILLE, INDIANA

Web site: www.wabash.edu
Contact: Mr. Steve Klein, Director of Admissions, PO Box 362, Crawfordsville, IN 47933-0352
Telephone: 765-361-6225 or toll-free 800-345-5385 **Fax:** 765-361-6437
E-mail: admissions@wabash.edu

Getting in Last Year
894 applied
75% were accepted
292 enrolled (44%)
36% from top tenth of their h.s. class
3.49 average high school GPA
40% had SAT verbal scores over 600
51% had SAT math scores over 600
63% had ACT scores over 24
7% had SAT verbal scores over 700
13% had SAT math scores over 700
20% had ACT scores over 30
4 National Merit Scholars
14 class presidents
12 valedictorians

Graduation and After
64% graduated in 4 years
4% graduated in 5 years
39% pursued further study (10% law, 9% theology, 7% medicine)
61% had job offers within 6 months
40 organizations recruited on campus

Financial Matters
$17,275 tuition and fees (1999–2000)
$5435 room and board
100% average percent of need met
$16,872 average financial aid amount received per undergraduate (1999–2000)

Academics
Wabash awards bachelor's **degrees**. Challenging opportunities include advanced placement, accelerated degree programs, double majors, independent study, a senior project, and Phi Beta Kappa. Special programs include cooperative education, internships, off-campus study, and study-abroad. A complete listing of majors at Wabash appears in the Majors Index beginning on page 432.

The **faculty** at Wabash has 79 full-time members, 99% with terminal degrees. The student-faculty ratio is 11:1.

Students of Wabash
The student body is made up of 861 undergraduates. Students come from 35 states and territories and 27 other countries. 74% are from Indiana. 5.2% are international students. 4.6% are African American, 3% Asian American, and 5.1% Hispanic American. 81% returned for their sophomore year.

Facilities and Resources
Student rooms are linked to a campus network. 120 **computers** are available on campus that provide access to the Internet. The **library** has 409,068 books and 1,073 subscriptions.

Campus Life
There are 54 active organizations on campus, including a drama/theater group, newspaper, radio station, and choral group. 70% of eligible undergraduates are members of national **fraternities** and language houses.

Wabash is a member of the NCAA (Division III). **Intercollegiate sports** include baseball, basketball, crew, cross-country running, football, golf, lacrosse, rugby, sailing, soccer, swimming, tennis, track and field, water polo, wrestling.

Campus Safety
Student safety services include late-night transport/escort service, 24-hour emergency telephone alarm devices, and 24-hour patrols by trained security personnel.

Applying
Wabash requires an essay, SAT I or ACT, a high school transcript, 1 recommendation, and a minimum high school GPA of 2.0. It recommends an interview and a minimum high school GPA of 3.0. Application deadline: 3/1; 3/1 for financial aid, with a 2/15 priority date. Early and deferred admission are possible.

WAKE FOREST UNIVERSITY

SUBURBAN SETTING ■ PRIVATE ■ INDEPENDENT RELIGIOUS ■ COED
WINSTON-SALEM, NORTH CAROLINA

Web site: www.wfu.edu
Contact: Mr. William G. Starling, Director of Admissions, PO Box 7305,
  Winston-Salem, NC 27109
Telephone: 336-758-5201 **Fax:** 336-758-6074
E-mail: admissions@wfu.edu

eAPPLY

Academics

Wake Forest awards bachelor's, master's, doctoral, and first-professional **degrees**. Challenging opportunities include advanced placement, accelerated degree programs, student-designed majors, an honors program, double majors, a senior project, Phi Beta Kappa, and Sigma Xi. Special programs include internships, summer session for credit, off-campus study, study-abroad, and Army ROTC.

The most frequently chosen fields are social sciences and history, business/marketing, and psychology. A complete listing of majors at Wake Forest appears in the Majors Index beginning on page 432.

The **faculty** at Wake Forest has 409 full-time members, 88% with terminal degrees. The student-faculty ratio is 11:1.

Students of Wake Forest

The student body totals 6,082, of whom 3,990 are undergraduates. 52% are women and 48% are men. Students come from 50 states and territories and 26 other countries. 28% are from North Carolina. 0.6% are international students. 8.2% are African American, 0.2% American Indian, 2% Asian American, and 0.8% Hispanic American. 91% returned for their sophomore year.

Facilities and Resources

Student rooms are linked to a campus network. 150 **computers** are available on campus that provide access to the Internet. The 4 **libraries** have 886,377 books and 16,125 subscriptions.

Campus Life

There are 125 active organizations on campus, including a drama/theater group, newspaper, radio station, television station, choral group, and marching band. 37% of eligible men and 51% of eligible women are members of national **fraternities** and national **sororities**.

Wake Forest is a member of the NCAA (Division I). **Intercollegiate sports** (some offering scholarships) include baseball (m), basketball, cross-country running, field hockey (w), football (m), golf, soccer, tennis, track and field, volleyball (w).

Campus Safety

Student safety services include late-night transport/escort service, 24-hour emergency telephone alarm devices, 24-hour patrols by trained security personnel, and electronically operated dormitory entrances.

Applying

Wake Forest requires an essay, SAT I, a high school transcript, and 1 recommendation. It recommends SAT II Subject Tests. Application deadline: 1/15; 2/1 priority date for financial aid. Early and deferred admission are possible.

Getting in Last Year

4,982 applied
49% were accepted
971 enrolled (39%)
66% from top tenth of their h.s. class
80% had SAT verbal scores over 600
83% had SAT math scores over 600
20% had SAT verbal scores over 700
26% had SAT math scores over 700
74 valedictorians

Graduation and After

70% graduated in 4 years
10% graduated in 5 years
1% graduated in 6 years
Graduates pursuing further study: 16% arts
  and sciences, 5% medicine, 5% law
62% had job offers within 6 months
180 organizations recruited on campus

Financial Matters

$21,452 tuition and fees (1999–2000)
$5900 room and board
90% average percent of need met
$17,451 average financial aid amount received
  per undergraduate (1999–2000)

WARTBURG COLLEGE

SMALL-TOWN SETTING ■ PRIVATE ■ INDEPENDENT RELIGIOUS ■ COED
WAVERLY, IOWA

Web site: www.wartburg.edu
Contact: Doug Bowman, Director of Admissions, 222 Ninth Street, NW, PO
   Box 1003, Waverly, IA 50677-1003
Telephone: 319-352-8264 or toll-free 800-772-2085 **Fax:** 319-352-8579
E-mail: admissions@wartburg.edu

Academics

Wartburg awards bachelor's **degrees**. Challenging opportunities include advanced placement, accelerated degree programs, student-designed majors, an honors program, double majors, independent study, and a senior project. Special programs include internships, summer session for credit, off-campus study, and study-abroad.

The most frequently chosen fields are education, business/marketing, and biological/life sciences. A complete listing of majors at Wartburg appears in the Majors Index beginning on page 432.

The **faculty** at Wartburg has 94 full-time members, 79% with terminal degrees. The student-faculty ratio is 14:1.

Students of Wartburg

The student body is made up of 1,546 undergraduates. 56.9% are women and 43.1% are men. Students come from 26 states and territories and 25 other countries. 78% are from Iowa. 3.9% are international students. 3.9% are African American, 0.3% American Indian, 1.1% Asian American, and 0.6% Hispanic American. 77% returned for their sophomore year.

Facilities and Resources

Student rooms are linked to a campus network. 150 **computers** are available on campus that provide access to the Internet. The **library** has 104,140 books and 732 subscriptions.

Campus Life

There are 88 active organizations on campus, including a drama/theater group, newspaper, radio station, television station, and choral group. No national or local **fraternities** or **sororities**.

Wartburg is a member of the NCAA (Division III). **Intercollegiate sports** include baseball (m), basketball, cross-country running, football (m), golf, soccer, softball (w), tennis, track and field, volleyball (w), wrestling (m).

Campus Safety

Student safety services include late-night transport/escort service, 24-hour emergency telephone alarm devices, 24-hour patrols by trained security personnel, and electronically operated dormitory entrances.

Applying

Wartburg requires a high school transcript, recommendations, and a minimum high school GPA of 2.0, and in some cases an interview. It recommends an interview. Application deadline: 6/1; 3/1 priority date for financial aid. Deferred admission is possible.

Wartburg College affirms the role of faith and values in preparing students for lives of leadership and service. It challenges students to accept responsibility and assume leadership in addressing issues facing their communities and the world. The Institute for Leadership Education provides academic course work, mentoring relationships, and practical experience to help students develop leadership skills. The College's Global and Multicultural Program offers cultural immersion for one month, a term, or an entire year in settings throughout the world. Campus life is enriched by the presence and participation of international students from more than 20 countries.

Getting in Last Year
1,385 applied
87% were accepted
411 enrolled (34%)
35% from top tenth of their h.s. class
3.50 average high school GPA
41% had SAT verbal scores over 600
43% had SAT math scores over 600
58% had ACT scores over 24
18% had SAT verbal scores over 700
10% had SAT math scores over 700
10% had ACT scores over 30
4 National Merit Scholars

Graduation and After
53% graduated in 4 years
9% graduated in 5 years
1% graduated in 6 years
74% had job offers within 6 months
15 organizations recruited on campus

Financial Matters
$14,955 tuition and fees (1999–2000)
$4360 room and board
88% average percent of need met
$14,306 average financial aid amount received
   per undergraduate (1999–2000 estimated)

WASHINGTON & JEFFERSON COLLEGE

SMALL-TOWN SETTING ■ PRIVATE ■ INDEPENDENT ■ COED
WASHINGTON, PENNSYLVANIA

Web site: www.washjeff.edu
Contact: Mr. Alton E. Newell, Dean of Enrollment, 60 South Lincoln Street, Washington, PA 15301-4601
Telephone: 724-223-6025 or toll-free 888-WANDJAY **Fax:** 724-223-5271
E-mail: admission@washjeff.edu

Academics

W & J awards associate and bachelor's **degrees**. Challenging opportunities include advanced placement, accelerated degree programs, student-designed majors, an honors program, double majors, independent study, a senior project, and Phi Beta Kappa. Special programs include internships, summer session for credit, off-campus study, study-abroad, and Army ROTC.

The most frequently chosen fields are psychology, business/marketing, and biological/life sciences. A complete listing of majors at W & J appears in the Majors Index beginning on page 432.

The **faculty** at W & J has 88 full-time members, 89% with terminal degrees. The student-faculty ratio is 12:1.

Students of W & J

The student body is made up of 1,217 undergraduates. 49.5% are women and 50.5% are men. Students come from 27 states and territories and 5 other countries. 85% are from Pennsylvania. 0.9% are international students. 2.6% are African American, 1.9% Asian American, and 0.7% Hispanic American. 88% returned for their sophomore year.

Facilities and Resources

Student rooms are linked to a campus network. 145 **computers** are available on campus that provide access to the Internet. The **library** has 176,689 books and 710 subscriptions.

Campus Life

There are 93 active organizations on campus, including a drama/theater group, newspaper, radio station, and choral group. 50% of eligible men and 40% of eligible women are members of national **fraternities** and national **sororities**.

W & J is a member of the NCAA (Division III). **Intercollegiate sports** include baseball (m), basketball, cross-country running, football (m), golf, ice hockey (m), lacrosse (m), soccer, softball (w), swimming, tennis, track and field, volleyball (w), wrestling (m).

Campus Safety

Student safety services include late-night transport/escort service, 24-hour emergency telephone alarm devices, 24-hour patrols by trained security personnel, and electronically operated dormitory entrances.

Applying

W & J requires an essay, SAT II: Writing Test, SAT I and SAT II or ACT, and a high school transcript. It recommends an interview and 3 recommendations. Application deadline: 3/1; 2/15 priority date for financial aid. Early and deferred admission are possible.

Getting in Last Year
1,261 applied
80% were accepted
327 enrolled (32%)
32% from top tenth of their h.s. class
3.4 average high school GPA
27% had SAT verbal scores over 600
26% had SAT math scores over 600
49% had ACT scores over 24
2% had SAT verbal scores over 700
4% had SAT math scores over 700
5% had ACT scores over 30

Graduation and After
73% graduated in 4 years
1% graduated in 5 years
1% graduated in 6 years
Graduates pursuing further study: 10% medicine, 8% arts and sciences, 7% law
60% had job offers within 6 months
55 organizations recruited on campus

Financial Matters
$19,000 tuition and fees (1999–2000)
$4750 room and board
76% average percent of need met
$14,489 average financial aid amount received per undergraduate (1999–2000 estimated)

eApply

Web site: www.wlu.edu
Contact: Mr. William M. Hartog, Dean of Admissions and Financial Aid,
Lexington, VA 24450-0303
Telephone: 540-463-8710 **Fax:** 540-463-8062
E-mail: admissions@wlu.edu

Getting in Last Year
3,082 applied
36% were accepted
467 enrolled (42%)
69% from top tenth of their h.s. class
90% had SAT verbal scores over 600
93% had SAT math scores over 600
100% had ACT scores over 24
33% had SAT verbal scores over 700
42% had SAT math scores over 700
33% had ACT scores over 30
36 National Merit Scholars
60 valedictorians

Graduation and After
80% graduated in 4 years
3% graduated in 5 years
1% graduated in 6 years
25% pursued further study (8% law, 5% medicine, 1% business)
1 Fulbright scholar

Financial Matters
$17,105 tuition and fees (1999–2000)
$5547 room and board
98% average percent of need met
$13,560 average financial aid amount received per undergraduate (1998–99)

Academics
W & L awards bachelor's and first-professional **degrees**. Challenging opportunities include advanced placement, accelerated degree programs, student-designed majors, an honors program, double majors, independent study, a senior project, and Phi Beta Kappa. Special programs include internships, off-campus study, study-abroad, and Army ROTC.

The most frequently chosen fields are social sciences and history, business/marketing, and biological/life sciences. A complete listing of majors at W & L appears in the Majors Index beginning on page 432.

The student-faculty ratio is 10:1.

Students of W & L
The student body totals 2,096, of whom 1,729 are undergraduates. 44% are women and 56% are men. Students come from 47 states and territories and 29 other countries. 12% are from Virginia. 3.1% are international students. 2.8% are African American, 0.1% American Indian, 1.1% Asian American, and 1% Hispanic American. 94% returned for their sophomore year.

Facilities and Resources
Student rooms are linked to a campus network. 224 **computers** are available on campus that provide access to the Internet. The 2 **libraries** have 702,532 books and 6,807 subscriptions.

Campus Life
There are 90 active organizations on campus, including a drama/theater group, newspaper, radio station, television station, and choral group. 80% of eligible men and 71% of eligible women are members of national **fraternities**, national **sororities**, and local sororities.

W & L is a member of the NCAA (Division III). **Intercollegiate sports** include baseball (m), basketball, cross-country running, equestrian sports, field hockey (w), football (m), golf (m), ice hockey, lacrosse, rugby (m), soccer, softball (w), swimming, tennis, track and field, volleyball, water polo (m), wrestling (m).

Campus Safety
Student safety services include late-night transport/escort service, 24-hour emergency telephone alarm devices, 24-hour patrols by trained security personnel, and electronically operated dormitory entrances.

Applying
W & L requires an essay, SAT I or ACT, 3 unrelated SAT II Subject Tests (including SAT II: Writing Test), a high school transcript, and 3 recommendations. It recommends an interview. Application deadline: 1/15; 2/1 priority date for financial aid. Deferred admission is possible.

WASHINGTON COLLEGE

SMALL-TOWN SETTING ■ PRIVATE ■ INDEPENDENT ■ COED
CHESTERTOWN, MARYLAND

Web site: www.washcoll.edu
Contact: Mr. Kevin Coveney, Vice President for Admissions, 300 Washington
Avenue, Chestertown, MD 21620-1197
Telephone: 410-778-7700 or toll-free 800-422-1782
E-mail: admissions_office@washcoll.edu

eAPPLY

Academics

WC awards bachelor's and master's **degrees**. Challenging opportunities include
advanced placement, student-designed majors, double majors, independent study, and a
senior project. Special programs include cooperative education, internships, off-campus
study, and study-abroad.

The most frequently chosen fields are social sciences and history, business/marketing,
and foreign language/literature. A complete listing of majors at WC appears in the
Majors Index beginning on page 432.

The **faculty** at WC has 77 full-time members, 95% with terminal degrees. The student-faculty ratio is 12:1.

Students of WC

The student body totals 1,194, of whom 1,117 are undergraduates. 60.2% are women
and 39.8% are men. Students come from 40 states and territories and 42 other countries.
50% are from Maryland. 8.6% are international students. 3.8% are African American,
0.4% American Indian, 1.7% Asian American, and 1.5% Hispanic American. 78%
returned for their sophomore year.

Facilities and Resources

Student rooms are linked to a campus network. 80 **computers** are available on campus
that provide access to the Internet. The **library** has 217,000 books and 823 subscriptions.

Campus Life

There are 50 active organizations on campus, including a drama/theater group,
newspaper, and choral group. 25% of eligible men and 25% of eligible women are
members of national **fraternities** and national **sororities**.

WC is a member of the NCAA (Division III). **Intercollegiate sports** include
baseball (m), basketball, crew, field hockey (w), ice hockey (m), lacrosse, rugby, sailing,
soccer, softball (w), swimming, tennis, volleyball (w).

Campus Safety

Student safety services include late-night transport/escort service, 24-hour emergency
telephone alarm devices, 24-hour patrols by trained security personnel, and student
patrols.

Applying

WC requires an essay, SAT I or ACT, a high school transcript, and 2 recommendations,
and in some cases an interview. It recommends an interview. Application deadline: 2/15;
2/15 priority date for financial aid. Early and deferred admission are possible.

Washington College has
initiated a $40,000
scholarship program
expressly for National Honor Society
members. Washington College NHS
Scholarships are $10,000 annual
awards renewable through the
completion of 8 semesters (full-time
enrollment and cumulative GPA of
3.0–4.0 required). To be eligible for
WC/NHS Scholarship consideration a
student must apply for freshman
admission no later than February 15
of the senior year, be admitted to
Washington College, maintain NHS
membership through graduation, and
remit a $300 enrollment deposit no
later than May 1 of the senior year.
For more information, students can
contact the Admission Office or visit
the WC Web site at http://
www.washcoll.edu

Getting in Last Year
1,479 applied
85% were accepted
282 enrolled (22%)
30% from top tenth of their h.s. class
3.2 average high school GPA
28% had SAT verbal scores over 600
29% had SAT math scores over 600
6% had SAT verbal scores over 700
3% had SAT math scores over 700

Graduation and After
58% graduated in 4 years
6% graduated in 5 years
35% pursued further study

Financial Matters
$20,200 tuition and fees (1999–2000)
$5740 room and board
89% average percent of need met
$17,977 average financial aid amount received
per undergraduate (1999–2000)

WASHINGTON UNIVERSITY IN ST. LOUIS

SUBURBAN SETTING ■ PRIVATE ■ INDEPENDENT ■ COED
ST. LOUIS, MISSOURI

Web site: www.wustl.edu
Contact: Ms. Nanette Tarbouni, Director of Admissions, Campus Box 1089, 1 Brookings Drive, St. Louis, MO 63130-4899
Telephone: 314-935-6000 or toll-free 800-638-0700 **Fax:** 314-935-4290
E-mail: admissions@wustl.edu

Getting in Last Year
17,109 applied
34% were accepted
1,384 enrolled (24%)
79% from top tenth of their h.s. class
86% had SAT verbal scores over 600
94% had SAT math scores over 600
97% had ACT scores over 24
33% had SAT verbal scores over 700
49% had SAT math scores over 700
55% had ACT scores over 30
157 National Merit Scholars
23 class presidents
138 valedictorians

Graduation and After
76% graduated in 4 years
9% graduated in 5 years
1% graduated in 6 years
Graduates pursuing further study: 13% arts and sciences, 9% medicine, 4% law
65% had job offers within 6 months
280 organizations recruited on campus

Financial Matters
$24,745 tuition and fees (2000–2001)
$7724 room and board
100% average percent of need met
$20,682 average financial aid amount received per undergraduate (1999–2000 estimated)

Academics

Washington awards bachelor's, master's, doctoral, and first-professional **degrees** and post-bachelor's certificates. Challenging opportunities include advanced placement, accelerated degree programs, student-designed majors, double majors, independent study, Phi Beta Kappa, and Sigma Xi. Special programs include cooperative education, internships, summer session for credit, off-campus study, study-abroad, and Army and Air Force ROTC.

The most frequently chosen fields are social sciences and history, engineering/ engineering technologies, and business/marketing. A complete listing of majors at Washington appears in the Majors Index beginning on page 432.

The **faculty** at Washington has 737 full-time members, 98% with terminal degrees. The student-faculty ratio is 7:1.

Students of Washington

The student body totals 12,088, of whom 6,509 are undergraduates. 51.3% are women and 48.7% are men. Students come from 52 states and territories and 86 other countries. 13% are from Missouri. 5.4% are international students. 6.6% are African American, 0.2% American Indian, 11.3% Asian American, and 2.1% Hispanic American. 96% returned for their sophomore year.

Facilities and Resources

Student rooms are linked to a campus network. 2,500 **computers** are available on campus that provide access to e-mail and the Internet. The 14 **libraries** have 1,425,034 books and 20,278 subscriptions.

Campus Life

There are 200 active organizations on campus, including a drama/theater group, newspaper, radio station, television station, and choral group. 22% of eligible men and 21% of eligible women are members of national **fraternities** and national **sororities**.

Washington is a member of the NCAA (Division III). **Intercollegiate sports** include baseball (m), basketball, crew, cross-country running, field hockey (w), football (m), golf, ice hockey (m), lacrosse, racquetball, rugby (m), soccer, softball (w), swimming, tennis, track and field, volleyball.

Campus Safety

Student safety services include late-night transport/escort service, 24-hour emergency telephone alarm devices, 24-hour patrols by trained security personnel, student patrols, and electronically operated dormitory entrances.

Applying

Washington requires an essay, SAT I or ACT, a high school transcript, and 2 recommendations. It recommends portfolio for art and architecture programs and a minimum high school GPA of 3.0. Application deadline: 1/15; 2/15 for financial aid. Early and deferred admission are possible.

WEBB INSTITUTE

SUBURBAN SETTING ■ PRIVATE ■ INDEPENDENT ■ COED
GLEN COVE, NEW YORK

Web site: www.webb-institute.edu
Contact: Mr. William G. Murray, Executive Director of Student
   Administrative Services, Crescent Beach Road, Glen Cove, NY 11542-1398
Telephone: 516-671-2213 **Fax:** 516-674-9838
E-mail: admissions@webb-institute.edu

Academics

Webb awards bachelor's **degrees**. Challenging opportunities include double majors and a senior project. Special programs include cooperative education, internships, and off-campus study.

The most frequently chosen field is engineering/engineering technologies. A complete listing of majors at Webb appears in the Majors Index beginning on page 432.

The **faculty** at Webb has 8 full-time members, 50% with terminal degrees. The student-faculty ratio is 7:1.

Students of Webb

The student body is made up of 81 undergraduates. Students come from 28 states and territories. 23% are from New York. 1.2% are Asian American. 96% returned for their sophomore year.

Facilities and Resources

28 **computers** are available on campus that provide access to the Internet. The **library** has 39,318 books and 255 subscriptions.

Campus Life

No national or local **fraternities** or **sororities**.

Intercollegiate sports include baseball, basketball, cross-country running, sailing, soccer, tennis, volleyball.

Campus Safety

Student safety services include 24-hour emergency telephone alarm devices, 24-hour patrols by trained security personnel, and electronically operated dormitory entrances.

Applying

Webb requires SAT I, SAT II: Writing Test, SAT II Subject Tests in math and either physics or chemistry, a high school transcript, an interview, 2 recommendations, proof of U.S. citizenship, and a minimum high school GPA of 3.5. Application deadline: 2/15; 7/1 priority date for financial aid.

Getting in Last Year
70 applied
46% were accepted
22 enrolled (69%)
75% from top tenth of their h.s. class
3.9 average high school GPA
95% had SAT verbal scores over 600
100% had SAT math scores over 600
30% had SAT verbal scores over 700
65% had SAT math scores over 700
1 National Merit Scholar
2 valedictorians

Graduation and After
70% graduated in 4 years
9% graduated in 5 years
38% pursued further study (38% engineering)
11 organizations recruited on campus

Financial Matters
$0 tuition and fees (2000–2001)
$6250 room and board
100% average percent of need met
$5250 average financial aid amount received
   per undergraduate (1999–2000)

WELLESLEY COLLEGE

SUBURBAN SETTING ■ PRIVATE ■ INDEPENDENT ■ WOMEN ONLY
WELLESLEY, MASSACHUSETTS

Web site: www.wellesley.edu
Contact: Ms. Janet Lavin Rapelye, Dean of Admission, 106 Central Street,
   Wellesley, MA 02481-8203
Telephone: 781-283-2270 **Fax:** 781-283-3678
E-mail: admission@wellesley.edu

Wellesley College is a liberal arts institution for exceptional women. The College provides an individualized education, with an average class size of 20 students in more than 900 courses offered. Wellesley uses technology as a vital component of classroom teaching and offers cross-registration and a double-degree program with MIT. Located just 12 miles from Boston and its 250,000 college students, Wellesley is a multicultural community in which students learn as much from each other as from their classes. Women who attend Wellesley learn the skills necessary to successfully pursue any interest; Wellesley graduates are leaders in the laboratory, the classroom, the courtroom, the boardroom, and their communities—anywhere they choose.

Getting in Last Year
2,862 applied
46% were accepted
596 enrolled (45%)
70% from top tenth of their h.s. class
85% had SAT verbal scores over 600
89% had SAT math scores over 600
42% had SAT verbal scores over 700
35% had SAT math scores over 700

Graduation and After
84% graduated in 4 years
3% graduated in 5 years
1% graduated in 6 years
28% pursued further study
71% had job offers within 6 months
124 organizations recruited on campus
1 Marshall, 3 Fulbright scholars

Financial Matters
$23,320 tuition and fees (1999–2000)
$7234 room and board
100% average percent of need met
$18,704 average financial aid amount received
   per undergraduate (1999–2000)

Academics
Wellesley awards bachelor's **degrees** (double bachelor's degree with Massachusetts Institute of Technology). Challenging opportunities include advanced placement, student-designed majors, double majors, independent study, a senior project, Phi Beta Kappa, and Sigma Xi. Special programs include internships, off-campus study, study-abroad, and Army and Air Force ROTC.

The most frequently chosen fields are social sciences and history, psychology, and English. A complete listing of majors at Wellesley appears in the Majors Index beginning on page 432.

The **faculty** at Wellesley has 224 full-time members, 94% with terminal degrees. The student-faculty ratio is 10:1.

Students of Wellesley
The student body is made up of 2,333 undergraduates. Students come from 53 states and territories and 77 other countries. 23% are from Massachusetts. 5.7% are international students. 7% are African American, 0.7% American Indian, 23.4% Asian American, and 5.6% Hispanic American. 95% returned for their sophomore year.

Facilities and Resources
Student rooms are linked to a campus network. 200 **computers** are available on campus that provide access to electronic bulletin boards and the Internet. The 4 **libraries** have 689,627 books and 4,756 subscriptions.

Campus Life
There are 160 active organizations on campus, including a drama/theater group, newspaper, radio station, and choral group. No national or local **sororities**.

Wellesley is a member of the NCAA (Division III). **Intercollegiate sports** include basketball, crew, cross-country running, fencing, field hockey, lacrosse, rugby, sailing, skiing (downhill), soccer, softball, squash, swimming, tennis, track and field, volleyball.

Campus Safety
Student safety services include late-night transport/escort service, 24-hour emergency telephone alarm devices, 24-hour patrols by trained security personnel, and electronically operated dormitory entrances.

Applying
Wellesley requires an essay, SAT I and SAT II or ACT, a high school transcript, and 3 recommendations, and in some cases an interview. It recommends an interview. Application deadline: 1/15; 1/15 priority date for financial aid. Early and deferred admission are possible.

Wells College
RURAL SETTING ■ PRIVATE ■ INDEPENDENT ■ WOMEN ONLY
AURORA, NEW YORK

Web site: www.wells.edu
Contact: Ms. Susan Raith Sloan, Director of Admissions, MacMillan Hall,
    Aurora, NY 13026
Telephone: 315-364-3264 or toll-free 800-952-9355 **Fax:** 315-364-3227
E-mail: admissions@wells.edu

Academics
Wells awards bachelor's **degrees**. Challenging opportunities include advanced placement, accelerated degree programs, student-designed majors, double majors,
independent study, a senior project, and Phi Beta Kappa. Special programs include
internships, off-campus study, study-abroad, and Air Force ROTC.

The most frequently chosen fields are social sciences and history, biological/life sciences, and visual/performing arts. A complete listing of majors at Wells appears in the
Majors Index beginning on page 432.

The **faculty** at Wells has 42 full-time members, 100% with terminal degrees. The
student-faculty ratio is 8:1.

Students of Wells
The student body is made up of 404 undergraduates. Students come from 24 states and
territories and 9 other countries. 65% are from New York. 3.1% are international
students. 3.7% are African American, 0.5% American Indian, 6% Asian American, and
2.3% Hispanic American. 80% returned for their sophomore year.

Facilities and Resources
Student rooms are linked to a campus network. 95 **computers** are available on campus
that provide access to the Internet. The **library** has 248,130 books and 412 subscriptions.

Campus Life
There are 39 active organizations on campus, including a drama/theater group,
newspaper, and choral group. No national or local **sororities**.

Wells is a member of the NCAA (Division III). **Intercollegiate sports** include field
hockey, lacrosse, soccer, softball, swimming, tennis.

Campus Safety
Student safety services include late-night transport/escort service, 24-hour emergency
telephone alarm devices, 24-hour patrols by trained security personnel, and electronically operated dormitory entrances.

Applying
Wells requires an essay, SAT I or ACT, a high school transcript, and 2 recommendations.
It recommends an interview. Application deadline: 3/1; 2/15 priority date for financial
aid. Early and deferred admission are possible.

Wells College believes that the 21st century will be a time of unprecedented opportunity for women. Women who are prepared for leadership roles will have a distinct advantage. Wells College has an integrative liberal arts curriculum to prepare women for the leadership roles they will assume in all areas of life in the next century. Wells women are being prepared to become the 21st-century leaders in a variety of fields: business, government, the arts, sciences, medicine, and education. The liberal arts curriculum, combined with a wide array of internships, outstanding study-abroad opportunities, leadership programs, and a wealth of cocurricular activities, helps Wells women realize their potential and career goals.

Getting in Last Year
410 applied
90% were accepted
135 enrolled (37%)
33% from top tenth of their h.s. class
3.50 average high school GPA
43% had SAT verbal scores over 600
26% had SAT math scores over 600
63% had ACT scores over 24
5% had SAT verbal scores over 700
2% had SAT math scores over 700
7% had ACT scores over 30
3 valedictorians

Graduation and After
56% graduated in 4 years
1% graduated in 5 years
2% graduated in 6 years
15% pursued further study (11% arts and
    sciences, 2% education, 2% medicine)
39% had job offers within 6 months

Financial Matters
$12,300 tuition and fees (1999–2000)
$6100 room and board
90% average percent of need met
$13,807 average financial aid amount received
    per undergraduate (1998–99)

WESLEYAN COLLEGE

SUBURBAN SETTING ■ PRIVATE ■ INDEPENDENT RELIGIOUS ■ WOMEN ONLY
MACON, GEORGIA

Web site: www.wesleyancollege.edu
Contact: Mr. Jonathan Stroud, Vice-President for Enrollment and Marketing,
4760 Forsyth Road, Macon, GA 31210-4462
Telephone: 912-757-5206 or toll-free 800-447-6610 **Fax:** 912-757-4030
E-mail: admissions@wesleyancollege.edu

Wesleyan College, a four-year liberal arts college for women, is a leader and an innovator in women's education. The first college in the world chartered to grant degrees to women, Wesleyan took its mission of educating women seriously in 1836, and the college continues to take that mission seriously today. It continues to maintain high standards of academic excellence and to encourage the intellectual growth of its students. Wesleyan is committed to the goals of training women to understand and appreciate the liberal and fine arts and preparing them for careers and a lifetime of learning.

Getting in Last Year
391 applied
76% were accepted
160 enrolled (54%)
42% from top tenth of their h.s. class
3.50 average high school GPA
46% had SAT verbal scores over 600
33% had SAT math scores over 600
60% had ACT scores over 24
12% had SAT verbal scores over 700
2% had SAT math scores over 700
6% had ACT scores over 30
5 National Merit Scholars
5 valedictorians

Graduation and After
42% graduated in 4 years
3% graduated in 5 years
2% graduated in 6 years
24% pursued further study (14% arts and
 sciences, 4% business, 3% education)
68% had job offers within 6 months
75 organizations recruited on campus

Financial Matters
$16,300 tuition and fees (1999–2000)
$6600 room and board
83% average percent of need met
$12,420 average financial aid amount received
 per undergraduate (1999–2000 estimated)

Academics

Wesleyan awards bachelor's and master's **degrees**. Challenging opportunities include advanced placement, accelerated degree programs, student-designed majors, an honors program, double majors, independent study, and a senior project. Special programs include internships, summer session for credit, off-campus study, and study-abroad.

The most frequently chosen fields are psychology, education, and business/marketing. A complete listing of majors at Wesleyan appears in the Majors Index beginning on page 432.

The **faculty** at Wesleyan has 44 full-time members, 100% with terminal degrees. The student-faculty ratio is 11:1.

Students of Wesleyan

The student body totals 607, of whom 585 are undergraduates. Students come from 26 states and territories and 10 other countries. 79% are from Georgia. 3.1% are international students. 30.2% are African American, 0.5% American Indian, 2.5% Asian American, and 2.9% Hispanic American. 65% returned for their sophomore year.

Facilities and Resources

Student rooms are linked to a campus network. 500 **computers** are available on campus that provide access to the Internet. The **library** has 140,579 books and 650 subscriptions.

Campus Life

There are 48 active organizations on campus, including a drama/theater group, newspaper, and choral group. No national or local **sororities**.

Wesleyan is a member of the NCAA (Division III). **Intercollegiate sports** include basketball, equestrian sports, soccer, softball, tennis, volleyball.

Campus Safety

Student safety services include late-night transport/escort service, 24-hour emergency telephone alarm devices, 24-hour patrols by trained security personnel, and electronically operated dormitory entrances.

Applying

Wesleyan requires an essay, SAT I or ACT, a high school transcript, and 1 recommendation. It recommends an interview and 2 recommendations. Application deadline: 3/1; 3/1 priority date for financial aid. Early and deferred admission are possible.

WESLEYAN UNIVERSITY

SMALL-TOWN SETTING ■ PRIVATE ■ INDEPENDENT ■ COED
MIDDLETOWN, CONNECTICUT

Web site: www.wesleyan.edu
Contact: Mrs. Nancy Hargrave Meislahn, Dean of Admissions and Financial
   Aid, Stewart M Reid House, Middletown, CT 06459-0265
Telephone: 860-685-3000 **Fax:** 860-685-3001
E-mail: admissions@wesleyan.edu

Academics

Wesleyan awards bachelor's, master's, and doctoral **degrees**. Challenging opportunities include advanced placement, accelerated degree programs, student-designed majors, double majors, independent study, a senior project, Phi Beta Kappa, and Sigma Xi. Special programs include internships, off-campus study, study-abroad, and Army, Navy and Air Force ROTC.

The most frequently chosen fields are social sciences and history, psychology, and English. A complete listing of majors at Wesleyan appears in the Majors Index beginning on page 432.

The **faculty** at Wesleyan has 279 full-time members. The student-faculty ratio is 11:1.

Students of Wesleyan

The student body totals 3,200, of whom 2,758 are undergraduates. 51.9% are women and 48.1% are men. Students come from 48 states and territories and 43 other countries. 9% are from Connecticut. 4.6% are international students. 9.1% are African American, 0.2% American Indian, 7.4% Asian American, and 6% Hispanic American. 96% returned for their sophomore year.

Facilities and Resources

Student rooms are linked to a campus network. 250 **computers** are available on campus that provide access to the Internet. The 4 **libraries** have 1,200,000 books and 3,166 subscriptions.

Campus Life

There are 200 active organizations on campus, including a drama/theater group, newspaper, radio station, and choral group. 8% of eligible men and 2% of eligible women are members of national **fraternities**, national **sororities**, local fraternities, and eating clubs.

Wesleyan is a member of the NCAA (Division III). **Intercollegiate sports** include baseball (m), basketball, crew, cross-country running, equestrian sports, field hockey (w), football (m), golf (m), ice hockey, lacrosse, rugby, sailing, soccer, softball (w), squash, swimming, tennis, track and field, volleyball, wrestling (m).

Campus Safety

Student safety services include late-night transport/escort service, 24-hour emergency telephone alarm devices, 24-hour patrols by trained security personnel, student patrols, and electronically operated dormitory entrances.

Applying

Wesleyan requires an essay, SAT II: Writing Test, SAT I and SAT II or ACT, a high school transcript, and 3 recommendations. It recommends an interview. Application deadline: 1/1; 2/1 for financial aid. Early and deferred admission are possible.

For more than 160 years, Wesleyan University has championed the values of a liberal education in the arts and sciences. It seeks to train minds and open hearts and asks students to contribute to the good of society and to the world. About 30% of the undergraduates are members of minority groups, while 12% are the first in their families to attend college. Wesleyan is committed to meeting the full demonstrated financial need of all students.

Getting in Last Year

6,402 applied
29% were accepted
732 enrolled (39%)
70% from top tenth of their h.s. class
86% had SAT verbal scores over 600
87% had SAT math scores over 600
48% had SAT verbal scores over 700
41% had SAT math scores over 700

Graduation and After

13% pursued further study (7% arts and sciences, 3% medicine, 2% law)
70% had job offers within 6 months
180 organizations recruited on campus
6 Fulbright scholars

Financial Matters

$25,120 tuition and fees (1999–2000)
$6510 room and board
100% average percent of need met
$21,135 average financial aid amount received per undergraduate (1998–99)

WESTMINSTER COLLEGE

SUBURBAN SETTING ■ PRIVATE ■ INDEPENDENT ■ COED
SALT LAKE CITY, UTAH

Web site: www.wcslc.edu

Contact: Mr. Philip J. Alletto, Vice President of Student Development and Enrollment Management, 1840 South 1300 East, Salt Lake City, UT 84105-3697

Telephone: 801-832-2200 or toll-free 800-748-4753 **Fax:** 801-484-3252

E-mail: admispub@wsclc.edu

Getting in Last Year

876 applied
86% were accepted
320 enrolled (42%)
30% from top tenth of their h.s. class
3.64 average high school GPA
33% had SAT verbal scores over 600
23% had SAT math scores over 600
52% had ACT scores over 24
10% had SAT verbal scores over 700
6% had SAT math scores over 700
8% had ACT scores over 30

Graduation and After

27% graduated in 4 years
16% graduated in 5 years
6% graduated in 6 years
48% pursued further study (14% business, 3% education, 2% arts and sciences)
80 organizations recruited on campus

Financial Matters

$12,726 tuition and fees (1999–2000)
$4750 room and board
82% average percent of need met
$10,686 average financial aid amount received per undergraduate (1998–99)

Academics

Westminster College awards bachelor's and master's **degrees** and post-bachelor's certificates. Challenging opportunities include advanced placement, student-designed majors, an honors program, double majors, independent study, and a senior project. Special programs include internships, summer session for credit, and Army, Navy and Air Force ROTC.

The most frequently chosen fields are business/marketing, education, and communications/communication technologies. A complete listing of majors at Westminster College appears in the Majors Index beginning on page 432.

The **faculty** at Westminster College has 109 full-time members, 89% with terminal degrees. The student-faculty ratio is 17:1.

Students of Westminster College

The student body totals 2,274, of whom 1,737 are undergraduates. 62.3% are women and 37.7% are men. Students come from 25 states and territories and 21 other countries. 94% are from Utah. 1.5% are international students. 0.5% are African American, 0.6% American Indian, 2.7% Asian American, and 4.6% Hispanic American. 77% returned for their sophomore year.

Facilities and Resources

Student rooms are linked to a campus network. 65 **computers** are available on campus that provide access to the Internet. The **library** has 88,086 books and 1,456 subscriptions.

Campus Life

There are 41 active organizations on campus, including a drama/theater group, newspaper, and choral group. No national or local **fraternities** or **sororities**. Westminster College is a member of the NAIA. **Intercollegiate sports** include basketball, golf, soccer (m), volleyball (w).

Campus Safety

Student safety services include late-night transport/escort service, 24-hour emergency telephone alarm devices, 24-hour patrols by trained security personnel, student patrols, and electronically operated dormitory entrances.

Applying

Westminster College requires SAT I or ACT, a high school transcript, and a minimum high school GPA of 2.5. It recommends an essay, an interview, 1 recommendation, and a minimum high school GPA of 3.0. Application deadline: rolling admissions. Early and deferred admission are possible.

WHEATON COLLEGE

SUBURBAN SETTING ■ PRIVATE ■ INDEPENDENT RELIGIOUS ■ COED
WHEATON, ILLINOIS

Web site: www.wheaton.edu
Contact: Mr. Dan Crabtree, Director of Admissions, 501 East College
Avenue, Wheaton, IL 60187-5593
Telephone: 630-752-5011 or toll-free 800-222-2419 (out-of-state) **Fax:**
630-752-5285
E-mail: admissions@wheaton.edu

Academics

Wheaton awards bachelor's, master's, and doctoral **degrees** and post-bachelor's
certificates. Challenging opportunities include advanced placement, student-designed
majors, double majors, independent study, and a senior project. Special programs include
internships, summer session for credit, off-campus study, study-abroad, and Army and
Air Force ROTC.

The most frequently chosen fields are English, philosophy, and social sciences and
history. A complete listing of majors at Wheaton appears in the Majors Index beginning
on page 432.

The **faculty** at Wheaton has 171 full-time members, 91% with terminal degrees.
The student-faculty ratio is 12:1.

Students of Wheaton

The student body totals 2,732, of whom 2,338 are undergraduates. 52.5% are women
and 47.5% are men. Students come from 50 states and territories and 13 other countries.
23% are from Illinois. 1% are international students. 1.9% are African American, 0.4%
American Indian, 3.8% Asian American, and 2.8% Hispanic American. 92% returned for
their sophomore year.

Facilities and Resources

Student rooms are linked to a campus network. 126 **computers** are available on campus
that provide access to the Internet. The 2 **libraries** have 342,746 books and 3,264
subscriptions.

Campus Life

There are 71 active organizations on campus, including a drama/theater group,
newspaper, radio station, television station, and choral group. No national or local
fraternities or **sororities**.

Wheaton is a member of the NCAA (Division III). **Intercollegiate sports** include
baseball (m), basketball, crew, cross-country running, field hockey (w), football (m), golf
(m), ice hockey (m), lacrosse, soccer, softball (w), swimming, tennis, track and field, volleyball, wrestling (m).

Campus Safety

Student safety services include late-night transport/escort service, 24-hour patrols by
trained security personnel, and electronically operated dormitory entrances.

Applying

Wheaton requires an essay, SAT I or ACT, a high school transcript, and 2 recommendations. It recommends SAT II: Writing Test and an interview. Application deadline: 1/15;
2/15 priority date for financial aid. Deferred admission is possible.

Getting in Last Year

1,964 applied
53% were accepted
583 enrolled (56%)
61% from top tenth of their h.s. class
3.66 average high school GPA
78% had SAT verbal scores over 600
77% had SAT math scores over 600
95% had ACT scores over 24
33% had SAT verbal scores over 700
27% had SAT math scores over 700
43% had ACT scores over 30
59 National Merit Scholars

Graduation and After

72% graduated in 4 years
10% graduated in 5 years
2% graduated in 6 years
25% pursued further study
179 organizations recruited on campus

Financial Matters

$14,930 tuition and fees (1999–2000)
$5080 room and board
80% average percent of need met
$13,109 average financial aid amount received
per undergraduate (1999–2000)

WHITMAN COLLEGE

SMALL-TOWN SETTING ■ PRIVATE ■ INDEPENDENT ■ COED
WALLA WALLA, WASHINGTON

Web site: www.whitman.edu
Contact: Mr. John Bogley, Dean of Admission and Financial Aid, 345 Boyer Avenue, Walla Walla, WA 99362-2083
Telephone: 509-527-5176 **Fax:** 509-527-4967
E-mail: admission@whitman.edu

Whitman College is committed to providing an excellent, well-rounded liberal arts and sciences undergraduate education. Whitman students develop capacities to analyze, interpret, criticize, communicate, and engage. A concentration on basic disciplines, combined with a supportive residential life program that encourages personal and social development, is intended to foster intellectual vitality, confidence, leadership, and the flexibility to succeed in a changing technological, multicultural world. An active student-faculty research program, required senior projects, and comprehensive examinations challenge students in all areas of the arts and sciences. Whitman's location in Walla Walla, Washington, offers an ideal setting for a rigorous education, an active campus life, and a strong sense of community in the beautiful Pacific Northwest.

Getting in Last Year
2,151 applied
50% were accepted
368 enrolled (34%)
63% from top tenth of their h.s. class
3.75 average high school GPA
80% had SAT verbal scores over 600
79% had SAT math scores over 600
95% had ACT scores over 24
35% had SAT verbal scores over 700
26% had SAT math scores over 700
39% had ACT scores over 30
22 National Merit Scholars
42 valedictorians

Graduation and After
65% graduated in 4 years
8% graduated in 5 years
1% graduated in 6 years
25 organizations recruited on campus

Financial Matters
$20,906 tuition and fees (1999–2000)
$5900 room and board
90% average percent of need met
$13,533 average financial aid amount received per undergraduate (1999–2000)

Academics
Whitman awards bachelor's **degrees**. Challenging opportunities include advanced placement, accelerated degree programs, student-designed majors, an honors program, double majors, independent study, a senior project, Phi Beta Kappa, and Sigma Xi. Special programs include cooperative education, internships, off-campus study, and study-abroad.

The most frequently chosen fields are social sciences and history, biological/life sciences, and English. A complete listing of majors at Whitman appears in the Majors Index beginning on page 432.

The **faculty** at Whitman has 107 full-time members, 94% with terminal degrees. The student-faculty ratio is 10:1.

Students of Whitman
The student body is made up of 1,400 undergraduates. 57.4% are women and 42.6% are men. Students come from 37 states and territories and 16 other countries. 47% are from Washington. 1.7% are international students. 1.2% are African American, 1% American Indian, 6.6% Asian American, and 2.9% Hispanic American. 91% returned for their sophomore year.

Facilities and Resources
Student rooms are linked to a campus network. 134 **computers** are available on campus that provide access to course registration information and the Internet. The 2 **libraries** have 282,540 books and 1,916 subscriptions.

Campus Life
There are 75 active organizations on campus, including a drama/theater group, newspaper, radio station, and choral group. 37% of eligible men and 34% of eligible women are members of national **fraternities**, national **sororities**, and local sororities.

Whitman is a member of the NCAA (Division III). **Intercollegiate sports** include baseball (m), basketball, cross-country running, fencing, golf, lacrosse, rugby, skiing (cross-country), skiing (downhill), soccer, swimming, tennis, track and field, volleyball, water polo.

Campus Safety
Student safety services include late-night transport/escort service, 24-hour emergency telephone alarm devices, 24-hour patrols by trained security personnel, student patrols, and electronically operated dormitory entrances.

Applying
Whitman requires an essay, SAT I or ACT, a high school transcript, and 1 recommendation. It recommends SAT II Subject Tests and an interview. Application deadline: 2/1; 11/15 priority date for financial aid. Early and deferred admission are possible.

WHITTIER COLLEGE

SUBURBAN SETTING ■ PRIVATE ■ INDEPENDENT ■ COED
WHITTIER, CALIFORNIA

Web site: www.whittier.edu
Contact: Ms. Urmi Kar, Dean of Enrollment, 13406 E Philadelphia Street,
    PO Box 634, Whittier, CA 90608-0634
Telephone: 562-907-4238 **Fax:** 562-907-4870
E-mail: admission@whittier.edu

Academics

Whittier awards bachelor's, master's, and first-professional **degrees**. Challenging opportunities include advanced placement, accelerated degree programs, student-designed majors, double majors, independent study, and a senior project. Special programs include internships, summer session for credit, off-campus study, study-abroad, and Army and Air Force ROTC.

The most frequently chosen fields are business/marketing, interdisciplinary studies, and biological/life sciences. A complete listing of majors at Whittier appears in the Majors Index beginning on page 432.

The **faculty** at Whittier has 96 full-time members, 96% with terminal degrees. The student-faculty ratio is 12:1.

Students of Whittier

The student body totals 2,203, of whom 1,296 are undergraduates. 56.3% are women and 43.7% are men. Students come from 33 states and territories and 20 other countries. 73% are from California. 4.3% are international students. 5.5% are African American, 1.1% American Indian, 7.8% Asian American, and 26.3% Hispanic American. 71% returned for their sophomore year.

Facilities and Resources

Student rooms are linked to a campus network. 150 **computers** are available on campus that provide access to the Internet. The 2 **libraries** have 225,337 books and 1,357 subscriptions.

Campus Life

There are 56 active organizations on campus, including a drama/theater group, newspaper, radio station, and choral group. 15% of eligible men and 15% of eligible women are members of local **fraternities** and local **sororities**.

Whittier is a member of the NCAA (Division III). **Intercollegiate sports** include baseball (m), basketball, cross-country running, football (m), golf (m), lacrosse, soccer, softball (w), swimming, tennis, track and field, volleyball (w), water polo.

Campus Safety

Student safety services include late-night transport/escort service, 24-hour patrols by trained security personnel, and electronically operated dormitory entrances.

Applying

Whittier requires an essay, SAT I or ACT, a high school transcript, 2 recommendations, and a minimum high school GPA of 2.0, and in some cases a minimum high school GPA of 3.5. It recommends SAT II Subject Tests, an interview, and a minimum high school GPA of 2.5. Application deadline: rolling admissions; 2/1 priority date for financial aid. Deferred admission is possible.

While the National Endowment for the Humanities has recognized Whittier College's curriculum as a model for liberal arts colleges, and the College has produced 4 Rhodes scholars, students are encouraged to choose Whittier not just for its recognition but also for its substance. They should explore and appreciate the College's innovative curriculum, organized around the way people actually learn; a system of resident Faculty Masters, at whose homes students exchange insights on the world's events and cultures; team-taught and "paired" courses, natural arenas for heated discussion and mind-opening challenges; and professors who claim their success only when students declare their own.

Getting in Last Year
1,345 applied
92% were accepted
381 enrolled (31%)
25% from top tenth of their h.s. class
3.12 average high school GPA
21% had SAT verbal scores over 600
23% had SAT math scores over 600
32% had ACT scores over 24
4% had SAT verbal scores over 700
5% had SAT math scores over 700
5% had ACT scores over 30
4 valedictorians

Graduation and After
22% pursued further study (10% education, 5% arts and sciences, 2% law)
61% had job offers within 6 months
25 organizations recruited on campus

Financial Matters
$20,128 tuition and fees (1999–2000)
$6736 room and board

Getting in Last Year
1,541 applied
90% were accepted
363 enrolled (26%)
48% from top tenth of their h.s. class
3.71 average high school GPA
52% had SAT verbal scores over 600
50% had SAT math scores over 600
78% had ACT scores over 24
13% had SAT verbal scores over 700
10% had SAT math scores over 700
17% had ACT scores over 30
3 National Merit Scholars
12 class presidents
26 valedictorians

Graduation and After
66% graduated in 4 years
7% graduated in 5 years
2% graduated in 6 years
150 organizations recruited on campus

Financial Matters
$21,822 tuition and fees (1999–2000)
$5700 room and board
93% average percent of need met
$18,285 average financial aid amount received per undergraduate (1999–2000 estimated)

WILLAMETTE UNIVERSITY
URBAN SETTING ■ PRIVATE ■ INDEPENDENT RELIGIOUS ■ COED
SALEM, OREGON

Web site: www.willamette.edu
Contact: Mr. James M. Sumner, Vice President for Enrollment, 900 State Street, Salem, OR 97301-3931
Telephone: 503-370-6303 or toll-free 877-542-2787 **Fax:** 503-375-5363
E-mail: undergrad-admission@willamette.edu

Academics
Willamette awards bachelor's, master's, and first-professional **degrees**. Challenging opportunities include advanced placement, accelerated degree programs, student-designed majors, an honors program, double majors, independent study, and Phi Beta Kappa. Special programs include cooperative education, internships, off-campus study, study-abroad, and Air Force ROTC.

The most frequently chosen fields are social sciences and history, biological/life sciences, and business/marketing. A complete listing of majors at Willamette appears in the Majors Index beginning on page 432.

The **faculty** at Willamette has 172 full-time members, 96% with terminal degrees. The student-faculty ratio is 11:1.

Students of Willamette
The student body totals 2,364, of whom 1,724 are undergraduates. 55.5% are women and 44.5% are men. Students come from 36 states and territories and 17 other countries. 44% are from Oregon. 1.5% are international students. 1.6% are African American, 1.1% American Indian, 6.4% Asian American, and 4.1% Hispanic American. 88% returned for their sophomore year.

Facilities and Resources
Student rooms are linked to a campus network. 200 **computers** are available on campus that provide access to the Internet. The 2 **libraries** have 279,574 books and 1,569 subscriptions.

Campus Life
There are 78 active organizations on campus, including a drama/theater group, newspaper, radio station, and choral group. 28% of eligible men and 22% of eligible women are members of national **fraternities** and national **sororities**.

Willamette is a member of the NCAA (Division III). **Intercollegiate sports** include baseball (m), basketball, crew, cross-country running, football (m), golf, lacrosse (m), rugby, soccer, softball (w), swimming, tennis, track and field, volleyball (w).

Campus Safety
Student safety services include late-night transport/escort service, 24-hour emergency telephone alarm devices, 24-hour patrols by trained security personnel, student patrols, and electronically operated dormitory entrances.

Applying
Willamette requires an essay, SAT I or ACT, a high school transcript, 1 recommendation, and a minimum high school GPA of 2.0, and in some cases an interview. It recommends an interview. Application deadline: 2/1; 2/1 priority date for financial aid. Early and deferred admission are possible.

WILLIAM JEWELL COLLEGE

SMALL-TOWN SETTING ■ PRIVATE ■ INDEPENDENT RELIGIOUS ■ COED
LIBERTY, MISSOURI

Web site: www.jewell.edu
Contact: Mr. Chad Jolly, Dean of Enrollment Development, 500 College Hill,
Liberty, MO 64068-1843
Telephone: 816-781-7700 or toll-free 800-753-7009 **Fax:** 816-415-5027
E-mail: admission@william.jewell.edu

eAPPLY

Academics

William Jewell awards bachelor's **degrees** (also offers evening program with significant
enrollment not reflected in profile). Challenging opportunities include advanced placement, accelerated degree programs, student-designed majors, an honors program,
double majors, independent study, and a senior project. Special programs include internships, summer session for credit, and study-abroad.

The most frequently chosen fields are business/marketing, psychology, and education. A complete listing of majors at William Jewell appears in the Majors Index beginning on page 432.

The **faculty** at William Jewell has 85 full-time members, 80% with terminal degrees.
The student-faculty ratio is 10:1.

Students of William Jewell

The student body is made up of 1,145 undergraduates. 58.3% are women and 41.7% are
men. Students come from 32 states and territories and 12 other countries. 77% are from
Missouri. 1.9% are international students. 2.6% are African American, 0.4% American
Indian, 0.8% Asian American, and 1.7% Hispanic American. 77% returned for their
sophomore year.

Facilities and Resources

Student rooms are linked to a campus network. 100 **computers** are available on campus
that provide access to the Internet. The 2 **libraries** have 248,310 books and 899
subscriptions.

Campus Life

There are 36 active organizations on campus, including a drama/theater group,
newspaper, radio station, and choral group. 43% of eligible men and 34% of eligible
women are members of national **fraternities** and national **sororities**.

William Jewell is a member of the NAIA. **Intercollegiate sports** (some offering
scholarships) include baseball (m), basketball, cross-country running, football (m), golf,
soccer, softball (w), tennis, track and field, volleyball (w).

Campus Safety

Student safety services include late-night transport/escort service, 24-hour emergency
telephone alarm devices, 24-hour patrols by trained security personnel, and electronically operated dormitory entrances.

Applying

William Jewell requires SAT I or ACT, a high school transcript, and a minimum high
school GPA of 2.0. It recommends an essay, ACT, an interview, 2 recommendations, and
a minimum high school GPA of 2.5. Application deadline: 3/15; 3/1 priority date for
financial aid. Early and deferred admission are possible.

Getting in Last Year

739 applied
86% were accepted
285 enrolled (45%)
31% from top tenth of their h.s. class
3.59 average high school GPA
32% had SAT verbal scores over 600
34% had SAT math scores over 600
56% had ACT scores over 24
17% had SAT verbal scores over 700
5% had SAT math scores over 700
13% had ACT scores over 30
24 valedictorians

Graduation and After

50% graduated in 4 years
6% graduated in 5 years
1% graduated in 6 years
19% pursued further study (10% arts and
sciences, 4% medicine, 3% law)
80% had job offers within 6 months
119 organizations recruited on campus

Financial Matters

$13,020 tuition and fees (1999–2000)
$4010 room and board

WILLIAMS COLLEGE

SMALL-TOWN SETTING ■ PRIVATE ■ INDEPENDENT ■ COED
WILLIAMSTOWN, MASSACHUSETTS

Web site: www.williams.edu
Contact: Mr. Thomas H. Parker, Director of Admission, 988 Main Street, Williamstown, MA 01267
Telephone: 413-597-2211
E-mail: admission@williams.edu

Williams is a tightly knit residential community with a focus on the direct educational partnership between students and faculty members. The College emphasizes the continuities between academic and extracurricular life while maintaining a firm commitment to excellence in teaching, artistic endeavor, and scholarly research. Williams admits students without regard to financial need and provides financial assistance to meet 100% of demonstrated need. The College places a high priority on fostering a multicultural community—to promote an enriched exchange of ideas and to prepare its graduates for a world of increasing diversification.

Getting in Last Year
5,007 applied
23% were accepted
544 enrolled (47%)
84% from top tenth of their h.s. class
90% had SAT verbal scores over 600
91% had SAT math scores over 600
56% had SAT verbal scores over 700
59% had SAT math scores over 700

Graduation and After
88% graduated in 4 years
5% graduated in 5 years
1% graduated in 6 years
19% pursued further study
65% had job offers within 6 months
100 organizations recruited on campus

Financial Matters
$24,790 tuition and fees (1999–2000)
$6730 room and board
100% average percent of need met
$21,955 average financial aid amount received per undergraduate (1999–2000)

Academics

Williams awards bachelor's and master's **degrees**. Challenging opportunities include advanced placement, accelerated degree programs, student-designed majors, an honors program, double majors, independent study, a senior project, Phi Beta Kappa, and Sigma Xi. Special programs include internships, off-campus study, and study-abroad.

The most frequently chosen fields are social sciences and history, biological/life sciences, and English. A complete listing of majors at Williams appears in the Majors Index beginning on page 432.

The **faculty** at Williams has 242 full-time members.

Students of Williams

The student body totals 2,162, of whom 2,113 are undergraduates. 49% are women and 51% are men. Students come from 51 states and territories and 32 other countries. 15% are from Massachusetts. 5.6% are international students. 6.7% are African American, 0.4% American Indian, 9.1% Asian American, and 6.4% Hispanic American. 98% returned for their sophomore year.

Facilities and Resources

Student rooms are linked to a campus network. 150 **computers** are available on campus that provide access to the Internet. The 10 **libraries** have 420,144 books and 2,853 subscriptions.

Campus Life

There are 110 active organizations on campus, including a drama/theater group, newspaper, radio station, choral group, and marching band. No national or local **fraternities** or **sororities**.

Williams is a member of the NCAA (Division III). **Intercollegiate sports** include baseball (m), basketball, crew, cross-country running, equestrian sports, field hockey (w), football (m), golf, ice hockey, lacrosse, rugby, sailing, skiing (cross-country), skiing (downhill), soccer, softball (w), squash, swimming, tennis, track and field, volleyball, water polo, wrestling (m).

Campus Safety

Student safety services include late-night transport/escort service, 24-hour emergency telephone alarm devices, 24-hour patrols by trained security personnel, student patrols, and electronically operated dormitory entrances.

Applying

Williams requires an essay, SAT I and SAT II or ACT, a high school transcript, and 2 recommendations. Application deadline: 1/1; 2/1 for financial aid. Early and deferred admission are possible.

WITTENBERG UNIVERSITY

SUBURBAN SETTING ■ PRIVATE ■ INDEPENDENT RELIGIOUS ■ COED
SPRINGFIELD, OHIO

Web site: www.wittenberg.edu
Contact: Mr. Kenneth G. Benne, Dean of Admissions, PO Box 720,
 Springfield, OH 45501-0720
Telephone: 937-327-6314 ext. 6366 or toll-free 800-677-7558 ext. 6314 **Fax:**
 937-327-6379
E-mail: admission@wittenberg.edu

eAPPLY

Academics

Wittenberg University awards bachelor's **degrees**. Challenging opportunities include
advanced placement, accelerated degree programs, student-designed majors, freshman
honors college, an honors program, double majors, independent study, a senior project,
Phi Beta Kappa, and Sigma Xi. Special programs include internships, summer session for
credit, off-campus study, study-abroad, and Army and Air Force ROTC. A complete
listing of majors at Wittenberg University appears in the Majors Index beginning on
page 432.

The **faculty** at Wittenberg University has 144 full-time members, 97% with terminal
degrees. The student-faculty ratio is 14:1.

Students of Wittenberg University

The student body is made up of 1,940 undergraduates. 56.1% are women and 43.9% are
men. Students come from 42 states and territories and 36 other countries. 60% are from
Ohio. 3.1% are international students. 5.7% are African American, 0.2% American
Indian, 1% Asian American, and 0.9% Hispanic American. 85% returned for their
sophomore year.

Facilities and Resources

Student rooms are linked to a campus network. 400 **computers** are available on campus
that provide access to the Internet. The 3 **libraries** have 350,000 books and 1,200
subscriptions.

Campus Life

There are 100 active organizations on campus, including a drama/theater group,
newspaper, radio station, and choral group. 15% of eligible men and 35% of eligible
women are members of national **fraternities** and national **sororities**.

Wittenberg University is a member of the NCAA (Division III). **Intercollegiate
sports** include baseball (m), basketball, cross-country running, field hockey (w), football
(m), golf, ice hockey (m), lacrosse, rugby, soccer, softball (w), swimming, tennis, track and
field, volleyball.

Campus Safety

Student safety services include crime prevention programs, late-night transport/escort
service, 24-hour emergency telephone alarm devices, 24-hour patrols by trained security
personnel, student patrols, and electronically operated dormitory entrances.

Applying

Wittenberg University requires an essay, SAT I or ACT, a high school transcript, and 1
recommendation, and in some cases an interview. It recommends SAT II Subject Tests
and an interview. Application deadline: 3/15; 3/15 for financial aid, with a 2/15 priority
date. Early and deferred admission are possible.

Getting in Last Year
2,535 applied
92% were accepted
616 enrolled (26%)
39% from top tenth of their h.s. class
3.40 average high school GPA
31% had SAT verbal scores over 600
38% had SAT math scores over 600
59% had ACT scores over 24
6% had SAT verbal scores over 700
6% had SAT math scores over 700
11% had ACT scores over 30
3 National Merit Scholars
40 class presidents

Graduation and After
63% graduated in 4 years
6% graduated in 5 years
1% graduated in 6 years
24% pursued further study (5% business, 5%
 medicine, 2% arts and sciences)
94% had job offers within 6 months
100 organizations recruited on campus
2 Fulbright scholars

Financial Matters
$20,906 tuition and fees (1999–2000)
$5206 room and board
96% average percent of need met
$19,361 average financial aid amount received
 per undergraduate (1999–2000)

Getting in Last Year
1,279 applied
85% were accepted
307 enrolled (28%)
50% from top tenth of their h.s. class
3.40 average high school GPA
49% had SAT verbal scores over 600
51% had SAT math scores over 600
50% had ACT scores over 24
7% had SAT verbal scores over 700
11% had SAT math scores over 700
5% had ACT scores over 30
4 National Merit Scholars
9 class presidents
11 valedictorians

Graduation and After
31% pursued further study (9% arts and sciences, 5% medicine, 4% business)
60% had job offers within 6 months

Financial Matters
$16,975 tuition and fees (1999–2000)
$5015 room and board

WOFFORD COLLEGE

URBAN SETTING ■ PRIVATE ■ INDEPENDENT RELIGIOUS ■ COED
SPARTANBURG, SOUTH CAROLINA

Web site: www.wofford.edu
Contact: Mr. Brand Stille, Director of Admissions, 429 North Church Street, Spartanburg, SC 29303-3663
Telephone: 864-597-4130
E-mail: admissions@wofford.edu

Academics

Wofford awards bachelor's **degrees**. Challenging opportunities include advanced placement, accelerated degree programs, student-designed majors, an honors program, double majors, independent study, a senior project, and Phi Beta Kappa. Special programs include cooperative education, internships, summer session for credit, off-campus study, study-abroad, and Army ROTC.

The most frequently chosen fields are business/marketing, social sciences and history, and biological/life sciences. A complete listing of majors at Wofford appears in the Majors Index beginning on page 432.

The **faculty** at Wofford has 71 full-time members, 92% with terminal degrees. The student-faculty ratio is 14:1.

Students of Wofford

The student body is made up of 1,100 undergraduates. 46.6% are women and 53.4% are men. Students come from 20 states and territories and 3 other countries. 0.3% are international students. 9.3% are African American, 0.5% American Indian, 1% Asian American, and 0.8% Hispanic American. 90% returned for their sophomore year.

Facilities and Resources

Student rooms are linked to a campus network. 118 **computers** are available on campus that provide access to the Internet. The **library** has 178,874 books and 642 subscriptions.

Campus Life

There are 68 active organizations on campus, including a drama/theater group, newspaper, and choral group. 50% of eligible men and 58% of eligible women are members of national **fraternities** and national **sororities**.

Wofford is a member of the NCAA (Division I). **Intercollegiate sports** (some offering scholarships) include baseball (m), basketball, cross-country running, fencing, football (m), golf, soccer, tennis, track and field, volleyball (w).

Campus Safety

Student safety services include late-night transport/escort service, 24-hour emergency telephone alarm devices, 24-hour patrols by trained security personnel, and electronically operated dormitory entrances.

Applying

Wofford requires an essay, SAT I or ACT, and a high school transcript. It recommends SAT II: Writing Test, an interview, and 2 recommendations. Application deadline: 2/1; 3/15 priority date for financial aid. Early and deferred admission are possible.

WORCESTER POLYTECHNIC INSTITUTE

SUBURBAN SETTING ■ PRIVATE ■ INDEPENDENT ■ COED
WORCESTER, MASSACHUSETTS

Web site: www.wpi.edu
Contact: Ms. Monica Inzer, Director of Admissions, 100 Institute Road,
  Worcester, MA 01609-2280
Telephone: 508-831-5286 **Fax:** 508-831-5875
E-mail: admissions@wpi.edu

eAPPLY

Academics

WPI awards bachelor's, master's, and doctoral **degrees**. Challenging opportunities
include advanced placement, accelerated degree programs, student-designed majors,
double majors, independent study, a senior project, and Sigma Xi. Special programs
include cooperative education, summer session for credit, off-campus study, study-
abroad, and Army, Navy and Air Force ROTC.

The most frequently chosen fields are engineering/engineering technologies,
biological/life sciences, and computer/information sciences. A complete listing of majors
at WPI appears in the Majors Index beginning on page 432.

The student-faculty ratio is 13:1.

Students of WPI

The student body totals 3,875, of whom 2,784 are undergraduates. 22.7% are women
and 77.3% are men. Students come from 51 states and territories and 40 other countries.
5% are international students. 1.8% are African American, 0.3% American Indian, 6.8%
Asian American, and 2.6% Hispanic American. 91% returned for their sophomore year.

Facilities and Resources

Student rooms are linked to a campus network. 1,000 **computers** are available on
campus that provide access to the Internet. The **library** has 170,000 books and 1,400
subscriptions.

Campus Life

There are 65 active organizations on campus, including a drama/theater group,
newspaper, radio station, and choral group. 35% of eligible men and 40% of eligible
women are members of national **fraternities** and national **sororities**.

WPI is a member of the NCAA (Division III). **Intercollegiate sports** include
baseball (m), basketball, bowling, crew, cross-country running, fencing, field hockey (w),
football (m), golf (m), ice hockey (m), lacrosse, rugby, sailing, skiing (downhill), soccer,
softball (w), swimming, tennis, track and field, volleyball, water polo, wrestling (m).

Campus Safety

Student safety services include late-night transport/escort service, 24-hour emergency
telephone alarm devices, 24-hour patrols by trained security personnel, and student
patrols.

Applying

WPI requires SAT I and SAT II or ACT, a high school transcript, and 1 recommendation. It recommends an essay. Application deadline: 2/1; 3/1 priority date for
financial aid. Early and deferred admission are possible.

Getting in Last Year
3,231 applied
79% were accepted
664 enrolled (26%)
43% from top tenth of their h.s. class
58% had SAT verbal scores over 600
83% had SAT math scores over 600
13% had SAT verbal scores over 700
29% had SAT math scores over 700
30 National Merit Scholars

Graduation and After
58% graduated in 4 years
16% graduated in 5 years
3% graduated in 6 years
150 organizations recruited on campus

Financial Matters
$22,108 tuition and fees (1999–2000)
$6912 room and board
90% average percent of need met
$17,122 average financial aid amount received
  per undergraduate (1999–2000 estimated)

eApply

Getting in Last Year
3,247 applied
89% were accepted
774 enrolled (27%)
31% from top tenth of their h.s. class
3.46 average high school GPA
38% had SAT verbal scores over 600
38% had SAT math scores over 600
62% had ACT scores over 24
7% had SAT verbal scores over 700
6% had SAT math scores over 700
12% had ACT scores over 30
7 National Merit Scholars
25 valedictorians

Graduation and After
54% graduated in 4 years
11% graduated in 5 years
2% graduated in 6 years
19% pursued further study (7% arts and sciences, 5% medicine, 4% law)
93% had job offers within 6 months
173 organizations recruited on campus

Financial Matters
$15,880 tuition and fees (2000–2001)
$6680 room and board
82% average percent of need met
$11,618 average financial aid amount received per undergraduate (1998–99)

XAVIER UNIVERSITY
SUBURBAN SETTING ■ PRIVATE ■ INDEPENDENT RELIGIOUS ■ COED
CINCINNATI, OHIO

Web site: www.xu.edu
Contact: Mr. Marc Camille, Dean of Admission, 3800 Victory Parkway, Cincinnati, OH 45207-2111
Telephone: 513-745-3301 or toll-free 800-344-4698 **Fax:** 513-745-4319
E-mail: xuadmit@admin.xu.edu

Academics
Xavier awards associate, bachelor's, master's, and doctoral **degrees** and post-bachelor's and post-master's certificates. Challenging opportunities include advanced placement, accelerated degree programs, an honors program, double majors, independent study, and a senior project. Special programs include cooperative education, internships, summer session for credit, off-campus study, study-abroad, and Army and Air Force ROTC.

The most frequently chosen fields are business/marketing, liberal arts/general studies, and education. A complete listing of majors at Xavier appears in the Majors Index beginning on page 432.

The **faculty** at Xavier has 254 full-time members, 78% with terminal degrees. The student-faculty ratio is 15:1.

Students of Xavier
The student body totals 6,466, of whom 3,958 are undergraduates. 60.1% are women and 39.9% are men. Students come from 43 states and territories and 39 other countries. 65% are from Ohio. 1.3% are international students. 9% are African American, 0.1% American Indian, 1.9% Asian American, and 1% Hispanic American. 88% returned for their sophomore year.

Facilities and Resources
Student rooms are linked to a campus network. 200 **computers** are available on campus that provide access to the Internet. The 3 **libraries** have 175,293 books and 1,501 subscriptions.

Campus Life
There are 90 active organizations on campus, including a drama/theater group, newspaper, radio station, and choral group. No national or local **fraternities** or **sororities**.

Xavier is a member of the NCAA (Division I). **Intercollegiate sports** (some offering scholarships) include baseball (m), basketball, crew, cross-country running, fencing, golf, lacrosse, riflery, rugby, sailing, skiing (downhill), soccer, swimming, tennis, volleyball, wrestling (m).

Campus Safety
Student safety services include campus-wide shuttle service, late-night transport/escort service, 24-hour emergency telephone alarm devices, 24-hour patrols by trained security personnel, and electronically operated dormitory entrances.

Applying
Xavier requires an essay, SAT I or ACT, a high school transcript, and recommendations. It recommends an interview. Application deadline: rolling admissions; 2/15 priority date for financial aid. Early and deferred admission are possible.

Yale University

Urban setting ■ Private ■ Independent ■ Coed
New Haven, Connecticut

Web site: www.yale.edu
Contact: Admissions Director, PO Box 208234, New Haven, CT 06520-8324
Telephone: 203-432-9300 **Fax:** 203-432-9392
E-mail: undergraduate.admissions@yale.edu

Academics

Yale awards bachelor's, master's, doctoral, and first-professional **degrees**. Challenging opportunities include advanced placement, accelerated degree programs, student-designed majors, an honors program, double majors, independent study, a senior project, Phi Beta Kappa, and Sigma Xi. Special programs include summer session for credit, study-abroad, and Army and Air Force ROTC. A complete listing of majors at Yale appears in the Majors Index beginning on page 432.

Students of Yale

The student body totals 11,032, of whom 5,440 are undergraduates. 49.8% are women and 50.2% are men. Students come from 55 states and territories and 74 other countries. 10% are from Connecticut. 6.4% are international students. 7.3% are African American, 0.7% American Indian, 16.2% Asian American, and 5.9% Hispanic American. 98% returned for their sophomore year.

Facilities and Resources

Student rooms are linked to a campus network. 350 **computers** are available on campus that provide access to the Internet. The 21 **libraries** have 10,800,000 books and 57,377 subscriptions.

Campus Life

There are 300 active organizations on campus, including a drama/theater group, newspaper, radio station, choral group, and marching band. Yale has national **fraternities** and national **sororities**.

Yale is a member of the NCAA (Division I). **Intercollegiate sports** include baseball (m), basketball, crew, cross-country running, fencing, field hockey (w), football (m), golf, gymnastics (w), ice hockey, lacrosse, soccer, softball (w), squash, swimming, table tennis (m), tennis, track and field, volleyball.

Campus Safety

Student safety services include late-night transport/escort service, 24-hour emergency telephone alarm devices, 24-hour patrols by trained security personnel, and electronically operated dormitory entrances.

Applying

Yale requires an essay, SAT I and SAT II or ACT, a high school transcript, and 3 recommendations. It recommends an interview. Application deadline: 12/31; 2/1 priority date for financial aid. Early and deferred admission are possible.

Getting in Last Year

13,270 applied
16% were accepted
1,296 enrolled (61%)
95% from top tenth of their h.s. class

Graduation and After

Graduates pursuing further study: 10% medicine, 8% law, 6% arts and sciences
62% had job offers within 6 months
3 Rhodes, 20 Fulbright scholars

Financial Matters

$24,500 tuition and fees (1999–2000)
$7440 room and board

YESHIVA UNIVERSITY

URBAN SETTING ■ PRIVATE ■ INDEPENDENT ■ COED
NEW YORK, NEW YORK

Web site: www.yu.edu
Contact: Mr. Michael Kranzler, Director of Undergraduate Admissions, 500 West 185th Street, New York, NY 10033-3201
Telephone: 212-960-5400 ext. 277 **Fax:** 212-960-0086
E-mail: yuadmit@ymail.yu.edu

Getting in Last Year
671 enrolled
3.4 average high school GPA

Graduation and After
Graduates pursuing further study: 17% law, 10% arts and sciences, 10% medicine
50 organizations recruited on campus

Financial Matters
$15,960 tuition and fees (1999–2000)
$5270 room and board

Academics

YU awards bachelor's, master's, doctoral, and first-professional **degrees** (Yeshiva College and Stern College for Women are coordinate undergraduate colleges of arts and sciences for men and women, respectively. Sy Syms School of Business offers programs at both campuses). Challenging opportunities include advanced placement, student-designed majors, an honors program, double majors, and a senior project. Special programs include internships, summer session for credit, off-campus study, and study-abroad. A complete listing of majors at YU appears in the Majors Index beginning on page 432.

Students of YU

The student body totals 5,481, of whom 2,529 are undergraduates. 43.6% are women and 56.4% are men. Students come from 31 states and territories and 30 other countries. 83% returned for their sophomore year.

Facilities and Resources

142 **computers** are available on campus that provide access to the Internet. The 7 **libraries** have 995,312 books and 9,760 subscriptions.

Campus Life

Active organizations on campus include a drama/theater group, newspaper, radio station, and choral group. No national or local **fraternities** or **sororities**.

YU is a member of the NCAA (Division III). **Intercollegiate sports** include basketball, cross-country running (m), fencing (m), tennis, volleyball (m), wrestling (m).

Campus Safety

Student safety services include late-night transport/escort service, 24-hour emergency telephone alarm devices, and 24-hour patrols by trained security personnel.

Applying

YU requires SAT I or ACT, a high school transcript, an interview, and 2 recommendations. It recommends an essay and SAT II Subject Tests. Application deadline: 2/15. Early and deferred admission are possible.

APPENDIXES

Colleges Costing $7500 or Less

Cooper Union for the Advancement of Science and Art	$0
Deep Springs College	$0
United States Air Force Academy	$0
United States Coast Guard Academy	$0
United States Merchant Marine Academy	$0
United States Military Academy	$0
United States Naval Academy	$0
Berea College	$3,885
New Mexico Institute of Mining and Technology	$5,912†
The University of North Carolina at Asheville	$6,139†
Webb Institute	$6,250‡
University of Kansas	$6,459†
The Curtis Institute of Music	$6,575*
University of Oklahoma	$6,840†
Shepherd College	$6,862†
University of South Florida	$6,862†
The University of Alabama in Huntsville	$6,892†
South Dakota School of Mines and Technology	$6,972†
North Carolina School of the Arts	$6,979†
Oklahoma State University	$6,994†
North Carolina State University	$7,074†
Louisiana State University and Agricultural and Mechanical College	$7,101†
The University of Tennessee Knoxville	$7,134†
Florida State University	$7,148†
New College of the University of South Florida	$7,155†
University of Florida	$7,181†
Brigham Young University	$7,284
Iowa State University of Science and Technology	$7,303†‡
Virginia Polytechnic Institute and State University	$7,342†
The University of Iowa	$7,368†

*Full room and board not available; estimated cost figured in.
†Cost for in-state students.
‡Figures are for 2000–2001.

Ten Largest Colleges

The University of Texas at Austin	49,009
The Ohio State University	48,003
University of Minnesota, Twin Cities Campus	45,361
Texas A&M University	43,442
University of Florida	43,382
Michigan State University	43,038
Pennsylvania State University University Park Campus	40,658
University of Illinois at Urbana–Champaign	38,851
University of Michigan	37,846
Purdue University	37,762

Ten Smallest Colleges

Deep Springs College	24
Webb Institute	81
The Curtis Institute of Music	165
San Francisco Conservatory of Music	243
Thomas Aquinas College	267
Marlboro College	290
College of the Atlantic	293
Mannes College of Music, New School University	323
Christendom College	344
College of Insurance	357

Colleges Accepting Fewer than Half of Their Applicants

Amherst College
Babson College
Bard College
Barnard College
Bates College
Berea College
Boston College
Bowdoin College
Brown University
Bucknell University
California Institute of Technology
California Institute of the Arts
California Polytechnic State University, San Luis Obispo
Carleton College
Carnegie Mellon University
Claremont McKenna College
Cleveland Institute of Music
Colby College
Colgate University
The College of St. Scholastica
College of the Holy Cross
The College of William and Mary
Columbia University, Columbia College (NY)
Columbia University, The Fu Foundation School of Engineering and Applied Science
Connecticut College
Cooper Union for the Advancement of Science and Art
Cornell University
The Curtis Institute of Music
Dartmouth College
Davidson College
Deep Springs College
Duke University
Emory University
Franklin and Marshall College
Georgetown University
The George Washington University
Grove City College
Hamilton College (NY)
Harvard University
Harvey Mudd College
Haverford College
Johns Hopkins University
The Juilliard School
Lafayette College
La Salle University
Lehigh University
Manhattan School of Music
Mannes College of Music, New School University
Massachusetts College of Art
Massachusetts Institute of Technology
Middlebury College
New England Conservatory of Music
New York University
North Carolina School of the Arts
Northwestern University
Parsons School of Design, New School University
Pennsylvania State University University Park Campus
Pepperdine University (Malibu, CA)

Pomona College
Princeton University
Rhode Island School of Design
Rice University
Rutgers, The State University of New Jersey, College of Pharmacy
Rutgers, The State University of New Jersey, Mason Gross School of the Arts
Rutgers, The State University of New Jersey, Rutgers College
Sarah Lawrence College
Skidmore College
Stanford University
State University of New York at Binghamton
State University of New York Maritime College
Swarthmore College
Trinity College (CT)
Tufts University
Union College (NY)
United States Air Force Academy
United States Coast Guard Academy
United States Merchant Marine Academy
United States Military Academy
United States Naval Academy
University of California, Berkeley
University of California, Los Angeles
University of California, San Diego
University of Chicago
The University of North Carolina at Chapel Hill
University of Notre Dame
University of Pennsylvania
University of Richmond
University of Southern California
University of Virginia
Vassar College
Wake Forest University
Washington and Lee University
Washington University in St. Louis
Webb Institute
Wellesley College
Wesleyan University
Whitman College
Williams College
Yale University

Single-Sex Colleges: Men Only
Deep Springs College
Hampden-Sydney College
Morehouse College
Saint John's University (MN)
Wabash College

Single-Sex Colleges: Women Only
Agnes Scott College
Barnard College
Bryn Mawr College
College of Saint Benedict
Mills College
Mount Holyoke College
Randolph-Macon Woman's College
Rutgers, The State University of New Jersey, Douglass College
Saint Mary's College (IN)

Scripps College
Smith College
Spelman College
Sweet Briar College
Wellesley College
Wells College
Wesleyan College

Colleges With Religious Affiliation

Baptist
Baylor University
Belmont University
Bethel College (MN)
Cedarville College
Georgetown College
Kalamazoo College
Linfield College
Ouachita Baptist University
Samford University
Union University
Wake Forest University
William Jewell College

Brethren
Elizabethtown College
Juniata College

Christian Church (Disciples of Christ)
Chapman University
Hiram College
Transylvania University

Churches of Christ
David Lipscomb University
Harding University
Pepperdine University (Malibu, CA)

Episcopal
University of the South

Friends
Earlham College
Guilford College

Interdenominational
Berry College
Illinois College
John Brown University
Messiah College
Taylor University

Jewish
List College, Jewish Theological Seminary of America

Latter-day Saints (Mormon)
Brigham Young University

Lutheran
Augustana College (IL)
Augustana College (SD)
Capital University
Concordia College (MN)
Gettysburg College
Gustavus Adolphus College

Luther College
Muhlenberg College
Pacific Lutheran University
St. Olaf College
Susquehanna University
Valparaiso University
Wartburg College
Wittenberg University

Mennonite
Goshen College

Methodist
Albion College
Albright College
Allegheny College
American University
Baldwin-Wallace College
Birmingham-Southern College
Centenary College of Louisiana
Cornell College
DePauw University
Drew University
Duke University
Emory University
Hamline University
Hendrix College
Kentucky Wesleyan College
Millsaps College
Mount Union College
Nebraska Wesleyan University
North Central College
Ohio Northern University
Ohio Wesleyan University
Randolph-Macon Woman's College
Simpson College
Southern Methodist University
Southwestern University
University of Evansville
Wesleyan College
Willamette University
Wofford College

Nondenominational
LeTourneau University
Wheaton College (IL)

Presbyterian
Agnes Scott College
Alma College
Austin College
Buena Vista University
Centre College
Coe College
The College of Wooster
Davidson College
Eckerd College
Grove City College
Hampden-Sydney College
Hastings College
King College
Lafayette College
Lyon College

Macalester College
Maryville College
Millikin University
Monmouth College
Presbyterian College
Rhodes College
Trinity University
University of Tulsa

Reformed Churches
Calvin College
Central College (IA)
Hope College
Northwestern College (IA)

Roman Catholic
Bellarmine College
Boston College
Carroll College (MT)
The Catholic University of America
Christendom College
Christian Brothers University
Clarke College
College of Saint Benedict
The College of St. Scholastica
College of the Holy Cross
Creighton University
DePaul University
Fairfield University
Fordham University
Georgetown University
John Carroll University
La Salle University
Le Moyne College
Loyola College in Maryland
Loyola University Chicago
Marquette University
Providence College
Quincy University
Rockhurst University
Saint John's University (MN)
Saint Joseph's University
Saint Louis University
Saint Mary's College (IN)
Saint Mary's College of California
St. Norbert College
Santa Clara University
Siena College
Thomas Aquinas College
University of Dallas
University of Dayton
University of Detroit Mercy
University of Notre Dame
The University of Scranton
Villanova University
Xavier University

United Church of Christ
Fisk University
Ursinus College

Wesleyan

Bartlesville Wesleyan College
Houghton College

Public Colleges

Auburn University
California Polytechnic State University, San Luis Obispo
Clemson University
The College of New Jersey
The College of William and Mary
Colorado School of Mines
Colorado State University
Fashion Institute of Technology
Florida State University
Georgia Institute of Technology
Iowa State University of Science and Technology
James Madison University
Louisiana State University and Agricultural and Mechanical College
Mary Washington College
Massachusetts College of Art
Miami University
Michigan State University
Michigan Technological University
New College of the University of South Florida
New Jersey Institute of Technology
New Mexico Institute of Mining and Technology
North Carolina School of the Arts
North Carolina State University
The Ohio State University
Ohio University
Oklahoma State University
Pennsylvania State University University Park Campus
Purdue University
Rutgers, The State University of New Jersey, School of Engineering
Rutgers, The State University of New Jersey, College of Pharmacy
Rutgers, The State University of New Jersey, Cook College
Rutgers, The State University of New Jersey, Douglass College
Rutgers, The State University of New Jersey, Mason Gross School of the Arts
Rutgers, The State University of New Jersey, Rutgers College
St. Mary's College of Maryland
Shepherd College
South Dakota School of Mines and Technology
State University of New York at Albany
State University of New York at Binghamton
State University of New York at Buffalo
State University of New York College at Geneseo
State University of New York College of Environmental Science and Forestry

State University of New York Maritime College
Texas A&M University
Truman State University
United States Air Force Academy
United States Coast Guard Academy
United States Merchant Marine Academy
United States Military Academy
United States Naval Academy
The University of Alabama in Huntsville
The University of Arizona
University of California, Berkeley
University of California, Davis
University of California, Los Angeles
University of California, Riverside
University of California, San Diego
University of California, Santa Barbara
University of California, Santa Cruz
University of Cincinnati
University of Colorado at Boulder
University of Connecticut
University of Delaware
University of Florida
University of Georgia
University of Illinois at Urbana–Champaign
The University of Iowa
University of Kansas
University of Maryland, College Park
University of Massachusetts Amherst
University of Michigan
University of Michigan–Dearborn
University of Minnesota, Morris
University of Minnesota, Twin Cities Campus
University of Missouri–Columbia
University of Missouri–Kansas City
University of Missouri–Rolla
University of New Hampshire
The University of North Carolina at Asheville
The University of North Carolina at Chapel Hill
University of Oklahoma
University of Pittsburgh
University of Rhode Island
University of South Florida
The University of Tennessee Knoxville
The University of Texas at Austin
University of Utah
University of Vermont
University of Virginia
University of Washington
University of Wisconsin–Madison
Virginia Polytechnic Institute and State University

INDEXES

Majors by College

Agnes Scott College
Anthropology, art, astrophysics, biochemistry, biology, chemistry, classics, creative writing, economics, English, French, German, history, interdisciplinary studies, international relations, literature, mathematics, music, philosophy, physics, political science, psychology, religious studies, sociology, Spanish, theater arts/drama, women's studies.

Albertson College of Idaho
Accounting, anthropology, art, biology, business administration, chemistry, computer science, creative writing, economics, elementary education, English, exercise sciences, French, history, mathematics, music, philosophy, physical education, physics, political science, (pre)law, (pre)medicine, psychology, religious studies, science education, secondary education, sociology, Spanish, sport/fitness administration, theater arts/drama.

Albion College
American studies, anthropology, art, biology, business administration, chemistry, computer science, economics, education, elementary education, English, environmental science, French, geology, German, history, human services, international relations, mass communications, mathematics, modern languages, music, philosophy, physical education, physics, political science, (pre)law, (pre)medicine, (pre)veterinary studies, psychology, public policy analysis, religious studies, secondary education, sociology, Spanish, theater arts/drama, women's studies.

Albright College
Accounting, American studies, biochemistry, biology, business administration, business marketing and marketing management, chemistry, child care/development, clothing and textiles, cognitive psychology and psycholinguistics, computer science, criminal justice/law enforcement administration, economics, elementary education, English, environmental science, fashion design/illustration, fashion merchandising, finance, forestry, French, history, interdisciplinary studies, international business, mathematics, medical technology, natural resources management, philosophy, physiological psychology/psychobiology, political science, (pre)dentistry, (pre)law, (pre)medicine, (pre)veterinary studies, psychology, religious studies, secondary education, Spanish, theater arts/drama.

Alfred University
Accounting, applied art, art, art education, art history, athletic training/sports medicine, bilingual/bicultural education, biological and physical sciences, biology, biomedical technology, business administration, business economics, business education, business marketing and marketing management, ceramic arts, ceramic sciences/engineering, chemistry, clinical psychology, computer science, criminal justice studies, drawing, earth sciences, economics, education, electrical/electronics engineering, elementary education, English, environmental science, experimental psychology, finance, fine/studio arts, French, general studies, geology, German, gerontology, graphic design/commercial art/illustration, health services administration, history, information sciences/systems, interdisciplinary studies, international business, literature, mass communications, materi-

als science, mathematics, mathematics/computer science, mechanical engineering, medical laboratory technician, modern languages, philosophy, photography, physics, political science, (pre)dentistry, (pre)law, (pre)medicine, (pre)veterinary studies, printmaking, psychology, public administration, science education, sculpture, secondary education, sociology, Spanish, theater arts/drama.

Allegheny College
Art, art history, biology, chemistry, communications, computer science, computer/information sciences, economics, English, environmental science, fine/studio arts, French, geology, German, history, international relations, mathematics, music, neuroscience, philosophy, physical sciences, physics, political science, psychology, religious studies, Spanish, theater arts/drama, women's studies.

Alma College
Accounting, art, art education, athletic training/sports medicine, biochemistry, biological and physical sciences, biology, business administration, business marketing and marketing management, chemistry, computer science, dance, drawing, early childhood education, ecology, economics, education, elementary education, English, exercise sciences, French, German, gerontology, health science, history, humanities, information sciences/systems, international business, liberal arts and studies, literature, mass communications, mathematics, medical illustrating, modern languages, music, music (voice and choral/opera performance), music education, occupational therapy, philosophy, physics, political science, (pre)dentistry, (pre)law, (pre)medicine, (pre)theology, (pre)veterinary studies, psychology, public health, religious studies, secondary education, social sciences, sociology, Spanish, stringed instruments, teaching English as a second language, theater arts/drama, wind and percussion instruments.

American University
Accounting, American studies, anthropology, applied mathematics, art, art history, arts management, audio engineering, biology, broadcast journalism, business administration, business marketing and marketing management, chemistry, computer science, criminal justice studies, criminal justice/law enforcement administration, early childhood education, economics, education, elementary education, enterprise management, environmental science, European studies, film/video production, finance, fine/studio arts, French, graphic design/commercial art/illustration, health science, history, information sciences/systems, interdisciplinary studies, international business, international business marketing, international economics, international relations, journalism, Judaic studies, Latin American studies, law and legal studies, liberal arts and studies, literature, management information systems/business data processing, mass communications, mathematical statistics, mathematics, Middle Eastern studies, modern languages, music, music (general performance), music (voice and choral/opera performance), peace and conflict studies, philosophy, physics, political science, (pre)law, (pre)medicine, psychology, public administration, public relations, radio/television broadcasting,

religious studies, Russian, Russian/Slavic area studies, social sciences, sociology, Spanish, special education, theater arts/drama, women's studies.

Amherst College

African-American (black) studies, American studies, anthropology, art, Asian studies, astronomy, biology, chemistry, classics, computer science, dance, economics, English, European studies, fine/studio arts, French, geology, German, Greek (Ancient and Medieval), history, interdisciplinary studies, Latin (Ancient and Medieval), law and legal studies, mathematics, music, neuroscience, philosophy, physics, political science, psychology, religious studies, Russian, sociology, Spanish, theater arts/drama, women's studies.

Art Center College of Design

Advertising, architectural environmental design, art, film studies, graphic design/commercial art/illustration, industrial design, photography, visual/performing arts.

Auburn University

Accounting, adult/continuing education, aerospace engineering, agricultural economics, agricultural education, agricultural engineering, agricultural sciences, animal sciences, anthropology, applied mathematics, architectural engineering, architectural environmental design, architecture, art, biochemistry, bioengineering, biology, broadcast journalism, business administration, business economics, business education, business marketing and marketing management, chemical engineering, chemistry, child care/development, civil engineering, clothing/apparel/textile studies, computer engineering, criminology, developmental/child psychology, early childhood education, economics, education of the visually handicapped, electrical/electronics engineering, elementary education, engineering, English, environmental science, finance, fine/studio arts, food sciences, forestry sciences, French, geography, geological engineering, geology, German, graphic design/commercial art/illustration, health administration, health services administration, history, home economics, home economics education, horticulture science, hotel and restaurant management, housing studies, human resources management, individual/family development, industrial design, industrial engineering, interior architecture, international business, journalism, landscape architecture, logistics and materials management, management information systems/business data processing, marine biology, mass communications, materials engineering, mathematics, mechanical engineering, medical laboratory technician, medical laboratory technologies, medical technology, microbiology/bacteriology, molecular biology, music (piano and organ performance), music education, nursing, nutrition studies, operations management, ornamental horticulture, philosophy, physical education, physics, political science, poultry science, (pre)dentistry, (pre)law, (pre)medicine, (pre)veterinary studies, psychology, public administration, public relations, radio/television broadcasting, recreation and leisure studies, science education, secondary education, social work, sociology, Spanish, speech therapy, speech-language pathology/audiology, speech/rhetorical studies, textile sciences/engineering, theater arts/drama, trade and industrial education, transportation technologies, wildlife management, zoology.

Augustana College (IL)

Accounting, anthropology, art, art education, art history, Asian studies, biology, business administration, business marketing and marketing management, chemistry, classics, computer science, creative writing, cytotechnology, earth sciences, economics, education, elementary education, engineering physics, English, environmental science, finance, fine/studio arts, French, geography, geology, German, history, jazz, Latin (Ancient and Medieval), liberal arts and studies, literature, mass communications, mathematics, music, music (piano and organ performance), music (voice and choral/opera performance), music education, occupational therapy, philosophy, physical education, physics, political science, (pre)dentistry, (pre)law, (pre)medicine, (pre)veterinary studies, psychology, public administration, religious studies, sacred music, Scandinavian languages, secondary education, sociology, Spanish, speech therapy, speech-language pathology/audiology, speech/rhetorical studies, stringed instruments, theater arts/drama, wind and percussion instruments, women's studies.

Augustana College (SD)

Accounting, art, art education, athletic training/sports medicine, biology, business administration, business communications, chemistry, computer science, economics, education of the hearing impaired, elementary education, engineering physics, English, exercise sciences, foreign languages/literatures, French, German, health services administration, history, international relations, journalism, liberal arts and studies, management information systems/business data processing, mass communications, mathematics, medical technology, music, music education, nursing, philosophy, physical education, physics, political science, (pre)dentistry, (pre)law, (pre)medicine, (pre)veterinary studies, psychology, religious studies, secondary education, social studies education, social work, sociology, Spanish, special education, speech-language pathology/audiology, sport/fitness administration, theater arts/drama.

Austin College

American studies, art, biology, business administration, chemistry, classics, economics, English, French, German, history, interdisciplinary studies, international economics, international relations, Latin (Ancient and Medieval), Latin American studies, mass communications, mathematics, music, philosophy, physical education, physics, political science, (pre)law, psychology, religious studies, sociology, Spanish, speech/rhetorical studies.

Babson College

Accounting, business administration, business communications, business marketing and marketing management, economics, entrepreneurship, finance, international business, investments and securities, management information systems/business data processing, operations research.

Baldwin-Wallace College

Accounting, art, art education, art history, arts management, athletic training/sports medicine, biology, broadcast journalism, business administration, business education, business marketing and marketing management, chemistry, computer science, criminal justice/law enforcement administration, dance, economics, education, elementary education, engineering science, English, environmental science, family/consumer studies, finance, fine/studio arts, French, geology, German, health education, history, home economics, home economics education, human services, information sciences/systems, interdisciplinary studies, international relations, mass communications, mathematics, medical technology, middle school education, music, music (piano and organ performance), music (voice and choral/opera performance), music business management and merchandising, music education, music history, music therapy, neuroscience, philosophy, physical education, physical therapy, physics, political science, (pre)dentistry, (pre)law, (pre)medicine, (pre)veterinary studies, psychology, religious studies, science education, secondary education, social work, sociology, Spanish, special education, speech-language pathology/audiology, sport/fitness administration, stringed instruments, theater arts/drama, wind and percussion instruments.

Bard College
Acting/directing, African studies, American government, American history, American studies, anthropology, archaeology, area studies, art, art history, Asian studies, biochemistry, biological and physical sciences, biology, chemistry, Chinese, city/community/regional planning, classics, comparative literature, creative writing, cultural studies, dance, drama/theater literature, drawing, Eastern European area studies, ecology, economics, English, environmental biology, environmental science, European history, European studies, film studies, film/video production, fine/studio arts, French, German, Greek (Ancient and Medieval), Greek (Modern), Hebrew, history, history of philosophy, history of science and technology, humanities, interdisciplinary studies, international economics, international relations, Italian, jazz, Judaic studies, Latin (Ancient and Medieval), Latin American studies, literature, mathematics, medieval/renaissance studies, modern languages, molecular biology, music, music (general performance), music (voice and choral/opera performance), music history, music theory and composition, natural sciences, painting, philosophy, photography, physical sciences, physics, play/screenwriting, political science, (pre)dentistry, (pre)law, (pre)medicine, (pre)veterinary studies, psychology, religious studies, Romance languages, Russian, Russian/Slavic area studies, sculpture, social sciences, sociology, Spanish, theater arts/drama, visual/performing arts, western civilization.

Barnard College
African studies, American studies, anthropology, applied mathematics, architecture, art history, Asian studies, astronomy, biochemistry, biology, biopsychology, chemistry, classics, comparative literature, computer science, dance, drama/theater literature, East Asian studies, Eastern European area studies, economics, English, environmental science, European studies, French, German, Greek (Ancient and Medieval), history, Italian, Latin (Ancient and Medieval), Latin American studies, mathematical statistics, mathematics, medieval/renaissance studies, Middle Eastern studies, music, philosophy, physics, physiological psychology/psychobiology, political science, (pre)medicine, psychology, religious studies, Russian, Russian/Slavic area studies, Slavic languages, sociology, South Asian studies, Spanish, theater arts/drama, urban studies, women's studies.

Bartlesville Wesleyan College
Accounting, athletic training/sports medicine, behavioral sciences, biological and physical sciences, biology, business

administration, business education, chemistry, divinity/ministry, education, elementary education, English, exercise sciences, history, information sciences/systems, liberal arts and studies, linguistics, mass communications, mathematics, music, music (general performance), natural sciences, nursing, physical education, physical therapy, political science, (pre)dentistry, (pre)law, (pre)medicine, (pre)veterinary studies, religious studies, science education, secondary education, secretarial science, social sciences, teaching English as a second language, theology.

Bates College
African studies, American studies, anthropology, art, biochemistry, biology, chemistry, Chinese, classics, East Asian studies, economics, English, environmental science, French, geology, German, history, interdisciplinary studies, Japanese, mathematics, medieval/renaissance studies, music, neuroscience, philosophy, physics, political science, psychology, religious studies, Russian, sociology, Spanish, speech/rhetorical studies, theater arts/drama, women's studies.

Baylor University
Accounting, acting/directing, aircraft pilot (professional), American studies, anthropology, applied mathematics, archaeology, architecture, art, art education, art history, Asian studies, biblical languages/literatures, biochemistry, biology, biology education, business, business administration, business economics, business education, business marketing and marketing management, business statistics, chemistry, chemistry education, classics, clothing/apparel/textile studies, communication disorders, communications, computer education, computer science, dietetics, drama and dance education, early childhood education, earth sciences, economics, education, education of the speech impaired, elementary education, engineering, English, English composition, English education, enterprise management, environmental science, fashion design/illustration, finance, financial planning, fine/studio arts, foreign languages education, forestry, French, French language education, geology, geophysics and seismology, German, German language education, Greek (Ancient and Medieval), health education, health/physical education, history, history education, home economics, human resources management, individual/family development, insurance and risk management, interdisciplinary studies, interior design, international business, international relations, journalism, Latin (Ancient and Medieval), Latin American studies, linguistics, management information systems/business data processing, mathematics, mathematics education, museum studies, music, music (general performance), music education, music history, music theory and composition, nursing, operations management, philosophy, physical education, physics, physics education, physiological psychology/psychobiology, political science, (pre)dentistry, (pre)law, (pre)medicine, psychology, public administration, reading education, real estate, religious studies, Russian, Russian/Slavic area studies, sacred music, science education, secondary education, social science education, social studies education, social work, sociology, Spanish, Spanish language education, special education, speech education, speech/rhetorical studies, sport/fitness administration, telecommunications, theater arts/drama, theater design, urban studies.

Bellarmine College
Accounting, actuarial science, art, arts management, biology, business administration, business economics, chemistry, com-

munications, community services, computer engineering, computer science, computer/information sciences, criminal justice studies, economics, education, elementary education, English, French, German, history, human resources management, international business, international relations, liberal arts and studies, mathematics, middle school education, music, music (voice and choral/opera performance), music business management and merchandising, musical instrument technology, nursing, painting, pastoral counseling, philosophy, political science, (pre)dentistry, (pre)law, (pre)medicine, (pre)pharmacy studies, (pre)veterinary studies, psychology, sculpture, secondary education, sociology, Spanish, special education, theology.

Belmont University

Accounting, advertising, applied mathematics, art, art education, behavioral sciences, biblical languages/literatures, biblical studies, bilingual/bicultural education, biochemistry, biological and physical sciences, biology, broadcast journalism, business administration, business economics, business education, business marketing and marketing management, chemistry, computer management, computer programming, computer science, counselor education/guidance, developmental/child psychology, divinity/ministry, early childhood education, economics, education, elementary education, engineering science, English, finance, fine/studio arts, Greek (Modern), health education, health services administration, history, hospitality management, hotel and restaurant management, information sciences/systems, international business, journalism, mass communications, mathematics, medical technology, music, music (piano and organ performance), music (voice and choral/opera performance), music business management and merchandising, music education, music history, nursing, pastoral counseling, pharmacology, philosophy, physical education, physics, political science, (pre)law, (pre)medicine, (pre)veterinary studies, psychology, radio/television broadcasting, reading education, recreation and leisure studies, retail management, sacred music, secretarial science, social work, sociology, Spanish, special education, speech/rhetorical studies, theater arts/drama, western civilization.

Beloit College

Anthropology, art education, art history, Asian studies, biochemistry, biology, business administration, business economics, cell biology, chemistry, classics, comparative literature, computer science, creative writing, economics, education, elementary education, engineering, English, environmental biology, environmental science, European studies, fine/studio arts, French, geology, German, history, interdisciplinary studies, international relations, Latin American studies, literature, mass communications, mathematics, modern languages, molecular biology, museum studies, music, music education, philosophy, physics, political science, (pre)dentistry, (pre)law, (pre)medicine, psychology, religious studies, Romance languages, Russian, Russian/Slavic area studies, science education, secondary education, sociobiology, sociology, Spanish, theater arts/drama, women's studies.

Bennington College

Anthropology, architecture, art, biochemistry, biological and physical sciences, biology, ceramic arts, chemistry, Chinese, comparative literature, computer engineering technology, computer science, creative writing, dance, developmental/child

psychology, drawing, early childhood education, ecology, economics, English, environmental biology, environmental science, European studies, film studies, fine/studio arts, French, German, history, history of philosophy, humanities, interdisciplinary studies, international relations, Japanese, jazz, liberal arts and studies, literature, mathematics, modern languages, music, music (piano and organ performance), music (voice and choral/opera performance), music history, natural sciences, philosophy, photography, physics, (pre)medicine, (pre)veterinary studies, printmaking, psychology, sculpture, social sciences, sociology, Spanish, stringed instruments, theater arts/drama, visual/performing arts.

Berea College

Agricultural business, agricultural sciences, art, art education, art history, biology, biology education, business administration, chemistry, child care/development, classics, developmental/child psychology, dietetics, early childhood education, economics, education, elementary education, English, English education, family/consumer studies, fine/studio arts, foreign languages education, French, French language education, German, German language education, history, home economics education, hotel and restaurant management, industrial arts, industrial technology, mathematics, mathematics education, middle school education, music, music education, nursing, philosophy, physical education, physics, political science, (pre)dentistry, (pre)medicine, (pre)veterinary studies, psychology, religious studies, secondary education, sociology, Spanish, Spanish language education, theater arts/drama.

Berry College

Accounting, animal sciences, anthropology, applied art, art, art education, art history, biochemistry, biology, biology education, broadcast journalism, business administration, business economics, business marketing and marketing management, chemistry, chemistry education, communications, computer science, computer/information sciences, early childhood education, economics, education, elementary education, English, English education, environmental science, finance, fine/studio arts, French, French language education, German, German language education, health education, history, history education, horticulture science, information sciences/systems, interdisciplinary studies, international relations, journalism, mass communications, mathematics, mathematics education, middle school education, music, music (piano and organ performance), music (voice and choral/opera performance), music business management and merchandising, music education, philosophy, physical education, physics, physics education, political science, (pre)dentistry, (pre)law, (pre)medicine, (pre)veterinary studies, psychology, public relations, religious studies, science education, secondary education, social sciences, sociology, Spanish, Spanish language education, speech/rhetorical studies, theater arts/drama.

Bethel College (MN)

Accounting, adult/continuing education, art, art education, art history, athletic training/sports medicine, biblical studies, biochemistry, biology, business administration, chemistry, child care/development, computer science, creative writing, cultural studies, early childhood education, economics, education, elementary education, English, environmental science, finance, fine/studio arts, health education, history, international relations, liberal arts and studies, literature, management information systems/business data processing, mass communications, mathematics, molecular biology, music, music education, nursing, philosophy, physical education, physics, political science, (pre)dentistry, (pre)law, (pre)medicine, (pre)veterinary studies, psychology, sacred music, science education, secondary education, social work, Spanish, speech/rhetorical studies, theater arts/drama.

Birmingham-Southern College

Accounting, art, art education, art history, Asian studies, biology, business administration, chemistry, computer science, dance, drawing, early childhood education, economics, education, elementary education, English, fine/studio arts, French, German, history, human resources management, interdisciplinary studies, international business, mathematics, music, music (piano and organ performance), music (voice and choral/opera performance), music education, music history, painting, philosophy, physics, political science, (pre)dentistry, (pre)law, (pre)medicine, printmaking, psychology, religious studies, sculpture, secondary education, sociology, Spanish, theater arts/drama.

Boston College

Accounting, art history, biochemistry, biology, business administration, business marketing and marketing management, chemistry, classics, computer science, early childhood education, economics, elementary education, English, environmental science, finance, fine/studio arts, French, geology, geophysics and seismology, German, Hispanic-American studies, history, human resources management, individual/family development, interdisciplinary studies, Italian, management information systems/business data processing, mass communications, mathematics, music, nursing, operations research, philosophy, physics, political science, (pre)medicine, psychology, Russian, Russian/Slavic area studies, secondary education, Slavic languages, sociology, special education, theater arts/drama, theology.

Boston University

Accounting, acting/directing, aerospace engineering, American studies, anthropology, archaeology, art education, art history, astronomy, athletic training/sports medicine, bilingual/bicultural education, biochemistry, bioengineering, biology, business administration, business marketing and marketing management, chemistry, chemistry education, classics, communication disorders, communications, computer engineering, computer science, dental laboratory technician, drama and dance education, drama/theater literature, drawing, early childhood education, earth sciences, East Asian studies, ecology, economics, education, education of the hearing impaired, electrical/electronics engineering, elementary education, engineering, English, English education, environmental science, exercise sciences, film/video production, finance, foreign languages education, foreign languages/literatures, French, geography, geology, German, graphic design/commercial art/illustration, Greek (Ancient and Medieval), Greek (Modern), health science, history, hospitality management, hotel and restaurant management, industrial engineering, information sciences/systems, interdisciplinary studies, international business, international finance, international relations, Italian, journalism, Latin (Ancient and Medieval), Latin American studies, linguistics,

management information systems/business data processing, marine biology, marketing research, mass communications, mathematics, mathematics education, mathematics/computer science, mechanical engineering, medical technology, molecular biology, music (general performance), music (piano and organ performance), music (voice and choral/opera performance), music education, music history, music theory and composition, neuroscience, nutritional sciences, occupational therapy, operations management, organizational behavior, painting, paralegal/legal assistant, philosophy, physical education, physical therapy, physics, physiology, political science, (pre)dentistry, (pre)medicine, psychology, public relations, radio/television broadcasting, recreation and leisure studies, rehabilitation therapy, religious studies, Russian, science education, sculpture, social studies education, sociology, Spanish, special education, systems engineering, theater design, urban studies.

Bowdoin College

African studies, African-American (black) studies, anthropology, archaeology, art, art history, Asian studies, biochemistry, biology, chemistry, classics, computer science, economics, English, environmental science, fine/studio arts, French, geology, German, history, interdisciplinary studies, Latin American studies, mathematics, music, neuroscience, philosophy, physics, physiological psychology/psychobiology, political science, (pre)medicine, psychology, religious studies, Romance languages, Russian, sociology, Spanish, women's studies.

Bradley University

Accounting, actuarial science, art history, biochemistry, biology, business administration, business economics, business marketing and marketing management, chemistry, civil engineering, communications, computer/information sciences, construction technology, consumer economics, criminal justice/law enforcement administration, early childhood education, ecology, economics, education of the emotionally handicapped, education of the specific learning disabled, electrical/electronics engineering, elementary education, engineering physics, English, environmental engineering, family/consumer studies, finance, fine/studio arts, French, geology, German, graphic design/commercial art/illustration, health science, history, industrial engineering, industrial technology, information sciences/systems, insurance and risk management, international business, international relations, mathematics, mechanical engineering, medical technology, molecular biology, music, music (general performance), music education, music theory and composition, nursing, nutrition studies, philosophy, photography, physical therapy, physics, political science, psychology, religious studies, social work, sociology, Spanish, theater arts/drama.

Brandeis University

African studies, African-American (black) studies, American studies, anthropology, archaeology, art, art history, biochemistry, biological and physical sciences, biology, biophysics, chemistry, classics, cognitive psychology and psycholinguistics, comparative literature, computer science, creative writing, economics, engineering physics, English, European studies, fine/studio arts, French, German, Greek (Ancient and Medieval), Hebrew, history, history of philosophy, international economics, Islamic studies, Italian, Judaic studies, Latin (Ancient and Medieval), Latin American studies, linguistics, literature, mathematics, Middle Eastern studies, music, music history, neuroscience, philosophy, physics, political science, (pre)law, (pre)medicine, psychology, Russian, Russian/Slavic area studies, sociology, Spanish, theater arts/drama.

Brigham Young University

Accounting, agronomy/crop science, American studies, animal sciences, anthropology, art, art education, art history, Asian studies, astrophysics, biochemistry, biology, botany, business administration, business marketing and marketing management, chemical engineering, chemistry, chemistry education, Chinese, civil engineering, classics, communications, comparative literature, computer engineering, computer science, construction management, dance, design/visual communications, dietetics, drama and dance education, early childhood education, earth sciences, economics, electrical/electronic engineering technology, electrical/electronics engineering, elementary education, engineering, engineering technology, English, English education, European studies, family studies, family/community studies, food sciences, foreign languages education, French, French language education, geography, geology, German, German language education, graphic design/commercial art/illustration, health science, health/physical education, hearing sciences, history, history education, horticulture science, humanities, industrial arts education, industrial design, interior design, international relations, Italian, Japanese, Latin (Ancient and Medieval), Latin American studies, linguistics, mathematical statistics, mathematics, mathematics education, mechanical engineering, microbiology/bacteriology, Middle Eastern studies, molecular biology, music, music (general performance), music education, music theory and composition, nursing, nutritional sciences, philosophy, photography, physical education, physics, physics education, plant breeding, political science, Portuguese, psychology, range management, recreation/leisure facilities management, Russian, social studies education, social work, sociology, Spanish, Spanish language education, speech-language pathology, theater arts/drama, visual/performing arts, wildlife biology, wildlife management, zoology.

Brown University

African-American (black) studies, American studies, anthropology, applied mathematics, archaeology, architecture, art, art history, Asian studies, behavioral sciences, biochemistry, bioengineering, biology, biomedical science, biophysics, chemical engineering, chemistry, civil engineering, classics, cognitive psychology and psycholinguistics, comparative literature, computer engineering, computer science, creative writing, development economics, East Asian studies, economics, education, electrical/electronics engineering, engineering, engineering science, English, environmental science, film studies, film/video production, fine/studio arts, French, geochemistry, geology, geophysics and seismology, German, Greek (Ancient and Medieval), Greek (Modern), Hispanic-American studies, history, international relations, Italian, Judaic studies, Latin (Ancient and Medieval), Latin American studies, linguistics, literature, marine biology, materials engineering, mathematics, mathematics/computer science, mechanical engineering, medieval/renaissance studies, Middle Eastern studies, modern languages, molecular biology, music, music theory and composition, musicology, neuroscience, organizational behavior, philosophy, physics, political science, Portuguese, psychology, religious studies, Russian, Russian/Slavic area stud-

ies, Slavic languages, sociology, South Asian studies, Spanish, theater arts/drama, urban studies, visual/performing arts, women's studies.

Bryn Mawr College

Anthropology, archaeology, art, art history, astronomy, biology, chemistry, city/community/regional planning, classics, comparative literature, East Asian studies, economics, English, French, geology, German, Greek (Ancient and Medieval), history, Italian, Latin (Ancient and Medieval), mathematics, music, philosophy, physics, political science, psychology, religious studies, Romance languages, Russian, sociology, Spanish.

Bucknell University

Accounting, anthropology, art, art history, biochemistry, biology, business administration, cell biology, chemical engineering, chemistry, civil engineering, classics, computer engineering, computer/information sciences, early childhood education, East Asian studies, economics, education, educational statistics/research methods, electrical/electronics engineering, elementary education, English, environmental science, French, geography, geology, German, history, international relations, Latin American studies, mathematics, mechanical engineering, music, music (piano and organ performance), music (voice and choral/opera performance), music education, music history, music theory and composition, philosophy, physics, political science, psychology, religious studies, Russian, secondary education, sociology, Spanish, theater arts/drama, women's studies.

Buena Vista University

Accounting, art, arts management, athletic training/sports medicine, biological and physical sciences, biology, business administration, business economics, business education, business marketing and marketing management, chemistry, communications, computer science, criminal justice/law enforcement administration, economics, education, elementary education, English, finance, graphic design/commercial art/illustration, history, information sciences/systems, international business, liberal arts and studies, management information systems/business data processing, mass communications, mathematics, modern languages, music, music education, natural sciences, philosophy, physical education, physics, political science, (pre)dentistry, (pre)law, (pre)medicine, (pre)veterinary studies, psychology, public administration, public relations, radio/television broadcasting, religious studies, science education, secondary education, social sciences, social work, Spanish, special education, speech/rhetorical studies, theater arts/drama.

Butler University

Accounting, actuarial science, anthropology, arts management, athletic training/sports medicine, biology, business administration, business economics, business marketing and marketing management, chemistry, computer science, criminal justice studies, dance, economics, elementary education, English, finance, French, German, Greek (Modern), history, international business, international relations, journalism, Latin (Ancient and Medieval), liberal arts and studies, mathematics, medicinal/pharmaceutical chemistry, music, music (piano and organ performance), music (voice and choral/opera performance), music business management and merchandising, music education, music history, pharmacy, philosophy, physician assistant, physics, political science, psychology, public relations, religious studies, secondary education, sociology, Spanish, speech-language pathology/audiology, speech/rhetorical studies, stringed instruments, telecommunications, theater arts/drama, wind and percussion instruments.

California Institute of Technology

Aerospace engineering, applied mathematics, astronomy, astrophysics, biochemistry, biology, cell biology, chemical engineering, chemistry, civil engineering, computer engineering, computer science, earth sciences, economics, electrical/electronics engineering, engineering, engineering physics, environmental engineering, geochemistry, geology, geophysics and seismology, history, literature, materials science, mathematics, mechanical engineering, molecular biology, neuroscience, nuclear physics, physical sciences, physics, social sciences.

California Institute of the Arts

Art, computer graphics, dance, film studies, fine/studio arts, graphic design/commercial art/illustration, jazz, music, music (piano and organ performance), music (voice and choral/opera performance), photography, sculpture, stringed instruments, theater arts/drama.

California Polytechnic State University, San Luis Obispo

Aerospace engineering, agricultural business, agricultural engineering, agricultural sciences, agronomy/crop science, animal sciences, applied art, architectural engineering, architecture, art, biochemistry, biology, business administration, chemistry, city/community/regional planning, civil engineering, computer engineering, computer science, dairy science, developmental/child psychology, early childhood education, economics, electrical/electronics engineering, engineering science, English, environmental biology, environmental engineering, farm/ranch management, food sciences, forestry, graphic design/commercial art/illustration, graphic/printing equipment, history, horticulture science, human resources management, industrial engineering, industrial technology, journalism, landscape architecture, liberal arts and studies, management information systems/business data processing, materials engineering, mathematical statistics, mathematics, mechanical engineering, mechanical engineering technology, microbiology/bacteriology, music, nutrition science, ornamental horticulture, philosophy, physical education, physical sciences, physics, political science, (pre)medicine, psychology, recreation and leisure studies, social sciences, speech/rhetorical studies, trade and industrial education.

Calvin College

Accounting, American history, art, art education, art history, athletic training/sports medicine, biblical studies, bilingual/bicultural education, biochemistry, biological and physical sciences, biology, business administration, business communications, chemical engineering, chemistry, civil engineering, classics, computer science, criminal justice/law enforcement administration, economics, electrical/electronics engineering, elementary education, engineering, English, environmental science, European history, exercise sciences, film studies, fine/studio arts, French, geography, geology, German, Greek (Modern), history, interdisciplinary studies, international relations, Latin (Ancient and Medieval), mass communications, mathematics, mechanical engineering, medical technology,

music, music (general performance), music (piano and organ performance), music (voice and choral/opera performance), music conducting, music education, music history, music theory and composition, natural sciences, nursing, occupational therapy, philosophy, physical education, physical sciences, physics, political science, (pre)dentistry, (pre)law, (pre)medicine, (pre)veterinary studies, psychology, public administration, recreation and leisure studies, religious studies, sacred music, science education, secondary education, social sciences, social work, sociology, Spanish, special education, speech-language pathology/audiology, speech/rhetorical studies, teaching English as a second language, theater arts/drama, theology.

Capital University

Accounting, art, art education, art therapy, athletic training/sports medicine, biology, business administration, business marketing and marketing management, chemistry, computer science, criminology, economics, education, elementary education, English, environmental biology, finance, fine/studio arts, French, health education, history, interdisciplinary studies, international relations, jazz, liberal arts and studies, literature, mass communications, mathematics, modern languages, music, music (general performance), music (piano and organ performance), music (voice and choral/opera performance), music business management and merchandising, music education, nursing, philosophy, physical education, political science, (pre)dentistry, (pre)law, (pre)medicine, (pre)veterinary studies, psychology, public relations, radio/television broadcasting, religious studies, science education, secondary education, social work, sociology, Spanish, speech/rhetorical studies, stringed instruments, wind and percussion instruments.

Carleton College

African studies, American studies, anthropology, art history, Asian studies, biology, chemistry, classics, computer science, economics, English, fine/studio arts, French, geology, German, Greek (Ancient and Medieval), history, interdisciplinary studies, international relations, Latin (Ancient and Medieval), Latin American studies, mathematics, music, philosophy, physics, political science, psychology, religious studies, Romance languages, Russian, sociology, Spanish, women's studies.

Carnegie Mellon University

Applied mathematics, architecture, art, biochemistry, bioengineering, biology, biophysics, business administration, business economics, ceramic arts, chemical engineering, chemistry, civil engineering, cognitive psychology and psycholinguistics, computer engineering, computer science, computer/information sciences, creative writing, economics, electrical/electronics engineering, engineering, engineering design, English, environmental engineering, European studies, fine/studio arts, French, German, graphic design/commercial art/illustration, history, humanities, industrial design, information sciences/systems, interdisciplinary studies, Japanese, liberal arts and studies, literature, mass communications, materials engineering, materials science, mathematical statistics, mathematics, mechanical engineering, modern languages, music, music (general performance), music theory and composition, philosophy, physics, political science, polymer chemistry, psychology, Russian, sculpture, social sciences, Spanish, technical writing, theater arts/drama, western civilization.

Carroll College (MT)

Accounting, acting/directing, art, biology, biology education, business administration, business economics, chemistry, civil engineering, communications, computer science, education, elementary education, engineering, English, English education, environmental science, finance, French, general studies, history, history education, international relations, Latin (Ancient and Medieval), mathematics, mathematics education, medical records administration, medical technology, nursing, philosophy, physical education, political science, (pre)dentistry, (pre)law, (pre)medicine, (pre)pharmacy studies, (pre)veterinary studies, psychology, public administration, public relations, religious education, religious studies, secondary education, social science education, social sciences, social work, sociology, Spanish, Spanish language education, sport/fitness administration, teaching English as a second language, technical writing, theater arts/drama, theater design, theology.

Case Western Reserve University

Accounting, aerospace engineering, American studies, anthropology, applied mathematics, art education, art history, Asian studies, astronomy, biochemistry, bioengineering, biological and physical sciences, biology, business administration, chemical engineering, chemistry, civil engineering, classics, communication disorders, comparative literature, computer engineering, computer science, dietetics, economics, electrical/electronics engineering, engineering, engineering physics, engineering science, English, environmental science, European studies, French, geology, German, gerontology, history, history of science and technology, international relations, materials engineering, materials science, mathematical statistics, mathematics, mechanical engineering, music, music education, nursing, nutrition science, philosophy, physics, plastics engineering, political science, psychology, religious studies, sociology, Spanish, systems engineering, theater arts/drama, women's studies.

The Catholic University of America

Accounting, anthropology, architecture, art, art education, art history, biochemistry, bioengineering, biology, biology education, business, business administration, chemical and atomic/molecular physics, chemistry, chemistry education, civil engineering, classics, communications, computer engineering, computer science, construction engineering, drama and dance education, early childhood education, economics, education, electrical/electronics engineering, elementary education, engineering, English, English education, finance, French, French language education, general studies, German, German language education, history, history education, human resources management, interdisciplinary studies, international economics, international finance, Latin (Ancient and Medieval), mathematics, mathematics education, mechanical engineering, medical technology, music, music (general performance), music (piano and organ performance), music (voice and choral/opera performance), music education, music history, music theory and composition, nursing, painting, philosophy, physics, political science, psychology, religious education, religious studies, Romance languages, sculpture, secondary education, social work, sociology, Spanish, Spanish language education, theater arts/drama.

Cedarville College

Accounting, American studies, athletic training/sports medicine, biblical studies, biological and physical sciences, biology, biology education, broadcast journalism, business administration, business marketing and marketing management, chemistry, communication equipment technology, communications, computer science, criminal justice/law enforcement administration, early childhood education, education, electrical/electronics engineering, elementary education, English, English education, environmental biology, finance, health education, health/physical education, history, information sciences/systems, international business, international relations, mathematics, mathematics education, mechanical engineering, medical technology, missionary studies, music, music (piano and organ performance), music (voice and choral/opera performance), music education, nursing, pastoral counseling, philosophy, physical education, political science, (pre)dentistry, (pre)law, (pre)medicine, (pre)veterinary studies, psychology, public administration, radio/television broadcasting, sacred music, science education, secondary education, secretarial science, social sciences, social studies education, social work, sociology, Spanish, Spanish language education, special education, speech education, speech/rhetorical studies, technical writing, theater arts/drama, theology.

Centenary College of Louisiana

Accounting, art, art education, arts management, biblical studies, biochemistry, biology, biophysics, business administration, business economics, chemistry, dance, drawing, early childhood education, earth sciences, economics, education, elementary education, engineering, English, environmental science, film studies, fine/studio arts, French, geology, German, health education, health science, history, interdisciplinary studies, Latin (Ancient and Medieval), liberal arts and studies, literature, mass communications, mathematics, middle school education, military science, music, music (piano and organ performance), music (voice and choral/opera performance), music education, occupational therapy, philosophy, physical education, physical sciences, physical therapy, physics, political science, (pre)dentistry, (pre)law, (pre)medicine, (pre)veterinary studies, psychology, religious education, religious studies, sacred music, science education, secondary education, social sciences, sociology, Spanish, speech-language pathology/audiology, speech/rhetorical studies, stringed instruments, theater arts/drama, wind and percussion instruments.

Central College (IA)

Accounting, art, biology, business administration, chemistry, communications, computer science, economics, elementary education, English, environmental science, exercise sciences, French, general studies, German, history, information sciences/systems, interdisciplinary studies, international business, Latin American studies, linguistics, mathematics, mathematics/computer science, music, music education, philosophy, physics, political science, psychology, religious studies, secondary education, social sciences, sociology, Spanish, theater arts/drama, Western European studies.

Centre College

Anthropology, art, art history, biochemistry, biology, chemistry, classics, computer science, economics, elementary education, English, French, German, history, international relations, mathematics, molecular biology, music, philosophy, physics, physiological psychology/psychobiology, political science, (pre)dentistry, (pre)law, (pre)medicine, psychology, religious studies, secondary education, sociology, Spanish, theater arts/drama.

Chapman University
Accounting, advertising, American studies, applied mathematics, art, art history, athletic training/sports medicine, biochemistry, biology, broadcast journalism, business administration, business economics, business marketing and marketing management, chemistry, comparative literature, computer science, creative writing, criminal justice/law enforcement administration, dance, economics, English, environmental science, European studies, exercise sciences, film studies, film/video production, finance, fine/studio arts, food sciences, French, graphic design/commercial art/illustration, health science, history, information sciences/systems, international business, journalism, Latin American studies, law and legal studies, liberal arts and studies, literature, mass communications, music, music (piano and organ performance), music (voice and choral/opera performance), music education, music therapy, peace and conflict studies, philosophy, physical education, political science, (pre)dentistry, (pre)law, (pre)medicine, (pre)veterinary studies, psychology, public relations, religious studies, social sciences, social work, sociology, Spanish, speech/rhetorical studies, stringed instruments, theater arts/drama, wind and percussion instruments, women's studies.

Christendom College
Classics, French, history, liberal arts and studies, literature, philosophy, political science, theology.

Christian Brothers University
Accounting, biology, biology education, business, business administration, business marketing and marketing management, chemical engineering, chemistry, chemistry education, civil engineering, computer engineering, computer science, economics, education, educational psychology, electrical/electronics engineering, elementary education, engineering physics, English, English education, environmental engineering, finance, history, history education, international business, management information systems/business data processing, mathematics, mathematics education, mechanical engineering, natural sciences, physics, physics education, (pre)dentistry, (pre)law, (pre)medicine, (pre)pharmacy studies, (pre)theology, psychology, religious studies, technical writing.

Claremont McKenna College
Accounting, African-American (black) studies, American studies, art, Asian studies, biochemistry, biology, biophysics, chemistry, Chinese, classics, computer science, economics, engineering/industrial management, English, environmental science, European studies, film studies, French, German, Greek (Modern), history, international business, international economics, international relations, Italian, Japanese, Latin (Ancient and Medieval), Latin American studies, law and legal studies, literature, mathematics, Mexican-American studies, modern languages, music, philosophy, physics, physiological psychology/psychobiology, political science, (pre)dentistry, (pre)law, (pre)medicine, psychology, religious studies, Russian, Spanish, theater arts/drama, women's studies.

Clarke College
Accounting, advertising, art, art education, art history, athletic training/sports medicine, biology, business administration, business marketing and marketing management, chemistry, computer science, early childhood education, economics, education, elementary education, English, fine/studio arts, French, history, information sciences/systems, international business, liberal arts and studies, management information systems/business data processing, mass communications, mathematics, middle school education, music, music (voice and choral/opera performance), music education, nursing science, philosophy, physical education, physical therapy, psychology, public relations, religious studies, secondary education, social work, sociology, Spanish, special education, theater arts/drama.

Clarkson University
Accounting, aerospace engineering, biochemistry, biology, biophysics, biotechnology research, business administration, business economics, business marketing and marketing management, cell biology, chemical engineering, chemistry, civil engineering, communications, computer engineering, computer science, computer/information sciences, economics, electrical/electronics engineering, engineering, entrepreneurship, environmental engineering, environmental health, environmental science, finance, history, human resources management, humanities, industrial engineering, interdisciplinary studies, liberal arts and studies, management information systems/business data processing, materials engineering, materials science, mathematics, mechanical engineering, molecular biology, operations management, organizational psychology, physics, political science, (pre)law, (pre)medicine, (pre)veterinary studies, psychology, social sciences, sociology, structural engineering, technical writing, toxicology.

Clark University
Art, art history, Asian studies, biochemistry, biology, business administration, chemistry, classics, comparative literature, computer science, cultural studies, development economics, earth sciences, ecology, economics, education, elementary education, engineering, English, environmental science, film studies, fine/studio arts, French, geography, graphic design/commercial art/illustration, history, interdisciplinary studies, international relations, Judaic studies, literature, mass communications, mathematics, middle school education, modern languages, molecular biology, music, natural resources management, neuroscience, peace and conflict studies, philosophy, physics, political science, (pre)dentistry, (pre)law, (pre)medicine, (pre)veterinary studies, psychology, secondary education, sociology, Spanish, theater arts/drama.

Clemson University
Accounting, agricultural business, agricultural economics, agricultural education, agricultural engineering, agricultural mechanization, agricultural sciences, agronomy/crop science, animal sciences, architecture, biochemistry, biology, business administration, business marketing and marketing management, ceramic sciences/engineering, chemical engineering, chemistry, city/community/regional planning, civil engineering, communications, computer engineering, computer science, construction management, dairy science, early childhood education, economics, education, electrical/electronics engineering, elementary education, engineering, English, finance, fine/studio

arts, food sciences, forestry, French, geology, German, graphic design/commercial art/illustration, health science, history, horticulture science, industrial arts, industrial engineering, information sciences/systems, landscape architecture, liberal arts and studies, mathematics, mathematics education, mechanical engineering, microbiology/bacteriology, modern languages, nursing, philosophy, physics, political science, poultry science, (pre)law, (pre)medicine, (pre)veterinary studies, psychology, reading education, recreation/leisure facilities management, science education, secondary education, sociology, Spanish, special education, textile sciences/engineering, trade and industrial education, wildlife biology.

Cleveland Institute of Music

Audio engineering, music, music (piano and organ performance), music (voice and choral/opera performance), music education, stringed instruments, wind and percussion instruments.

Coe College

Accounting, African-American (black) studies, American studies, art, art education, Asian studies, athletic training/sports medicine, biochemistry, biological and physical sciences, biology, business administration, chemistry, classics, computer science, economics, education, elementary education, English, environmental science, fine/studio arts, French, German, history, interdisciplinary studies, liberal arts and studies, literature, mathematics, medical technology, molecular biology, music, music education, nursing, philosophy, physical education, physical sciences, physics, political science, (pre)dentistry, (pre)law, (pre)medicine, (pre)veterinary studies, psychology, public relations, religious studies, science education, secondary education, sociology, Spanish, speech/rhetorical studies, theater arts/drama.

Colby College

African-American (black) studies, American studies, anthropology, art, art history, biochemistry, biology, cell biology, chemistry, classics, computer science, earth sciences, East Asian studies, economics, English, environmental science, French, geology, German, history, international relations, Latin American studies, mathematics, molecular biology, music, philosophy, physics, political science, psychology, religious studies, Russian/Slavic area studies, sociology, Spanish, theater arts/drama, women's studies.

Colgate University

African studies, African-American (black) studies, anthropology, art, art history, Asian studies, astronomy, astrophysics, biochemistry, biology, chemistry, Chinese, classics, computer science, East Asian studies, economics, education, English, environmental biology, environmental science, French, geography, geology, German, Greek (Modern), history, humanities, international relations, Japanese, Latin (Ancient and Medieval), Latin American studies, mathematics, molecular biology, music, Native American studies, natural sciences, neuroscience, peace and conflict studies, philosophy, physical sciences, physics, political science, psychology, religious studies, Romance languages, Russian, Russian/Slavic area studies, social sciences, sociology, Spanish, theater arts/drama, women's studies.

College of Insurance

Actuarial science, business administration, insurance and risk management.

The College of New Jersey

Accounting, art, art education, biology, biology education, business administration, business economics, chemistry, chemistry education, computer science, criminal justice/law enforcement administration, early childhood education, economics, education, education of the hearing impaired, elementary education, engineering science, English, English education, finance, fine/studio arts, graphic design/commercial art/illustration, history, history education, industrial arts education, international business, management information systems/business data processing, mathematical statistics, mathematics, mathematics education, music, music education, nursing, philosophy, physical education, physics, physics education, political science, (pre)law, (pre)medicine, psychology, secondary education, sociology, Spanish, Spanish language education, special education, speech/rhetorical studies.

College of Saint Benedict

Accounting, art, art education, art history, biology, business administration, chemistry, classics, computer science, dietetics, economics, education, elementary education, English, fine/studio arts, forestry, French, German, history, humanities, liberal arts and studies, mass communications, mathematics, mathematics/computer science, medical technology, music, music education, natural sciences, nursing, nutrition science, occupational therapy, peace and conflict studies, philosophy, physical therapy, physics, political science, (pre)dentistry, (pre)law, (pre)medicine, (pre)pharmacy studies, (pre)theology, (pre)veterinary studies, psychology, religious education, secondary education, social sciences, social work, sociology, Spanish, theater arts/drama, theology.

The College of St. Scholastica

Accounting, biochemistry, biology, business communications, chemistry, communications, computer/information sciences, dietetics, economics, education, English composition, exercise sciences, health science, health services administration, history, humanities, international business, liberal arts and studies, management science, mathematics, medical laboratory technologies, modern languages, music, natural sciences, nursing, occupational therapy, physical therapy, psychology, religious studies, social science education, social work.

College of the Atlantic

Architectural environmental design, art, biological and physical sciences, biology, botany, ceramic arts, computer graphics, drawing, ecology, economics, education, elementary education, English, environmental biology, environmental education, environmental science, evolutionary biology, human ecology, interdisciplinary studies, landscape architecture, law and legal studies, liberal arts and studies, literature, marine biology, maritime science, middle school education, museum studies, music, natural sciences, philosophy, (pre)veterinary studies, psychology, public policy analysis, science education, secondary education, wildlife biology, zoology.

College of the Holy Cross

Accounting, African-American (black) studies, art history, Asian studies, biochemistry, biology, biopsychology, chemistry, classics, cultural studies, economics, English, environmental science, fine/studio arts, French, German, gerontology, history, Latin American studies, literature, mathematics, Middle Eastern studies, modern languages, music, peace and conflict studies, philosophy, physics, political science, (pre)dentistry, (pre)law, (pre)medicine, psychology, religious studies, Russian, sociology, Spanish, theater arts/drama, women's studies.

The College of William and Mary

African-American (black) studies, American studies, anthropology, art, art history, biology, biopsychology, business administration, chemistry, classics, computer science, cultural studies, East Asian studies, economics, English, environmental science, European studies, French, geology, German, Greek (Modern), history, interdisciplinary studies, international relations, Latin (Ancient and Medieval), Latin American studies, linguistics, mathematics, medieval/renaissance studies, modern languages, music, philosophy, physical education, physics, political science, psychology, public policy analysis, religious studies, Russian/Slavic area studies, sociology, Spanish, theater arts/drama, women's studies.

The College of Wooster

African studies, African-American (black) studies, archaeology, art, art history, Asian studies, biochemistry, biology, business economics, chemistry, classics, communications, comparative literature, computer science, economics, English, European studies, fine/studio arts, French, geology, German, Greek (Modern), history, interdisciplinary studies, international relations, Latin (Ancient and Medieval), Latin American studies, mass communications, mathematics, music, music (voice and choral/opera performance), music education, music history, music therapy, philosophy, physics, political science, (pre)dentistry, (pre)law, (pre)medicine, (pre)veterinary studies, psychology, religious studies, Russian, sociology, South Asian studies, Spanish, speech-language pathology/audiology, speech/rhetorical studies, theater arts/drama, urban studies, women's studies.

The Colorado College

Anthropology, art history, Asian studies, biochemistry, biology, chemistry, classics, comparative literature, creative writing, dance, economics, English, environmental science, film studies, fine/studio arts, French, geology, German, history, interdisciplinary studies, liberal arts and studies, mathematics, music, neuroscience, philosophy, physics, political science, psychology, religious studies, Romance languages, Russian, sociology, Spanish, theater arts/drama, women's studies.

Colorado School of Mines

Chemical engineering, chemistry, civil engineering, computer science, economics, electrical/electronics engineering, engineering, engineering physics, engineering science, environmental engineering, geological engineering, geophysical engineering, mathematics, mechanical engineering, metallurgical engineering, mining/mineral engineering, petroleum engineering.

Colorado State University

Accounting, actuarial science, aerospace engineering, agribusiness, agricultural economics, agricultural education, agricultural engineering, agricultural sciences, agronomy/crop science, American studies, animal sciences, anthropology, applied mathematics, art, art education, art history, Asian studies, athletic training/sports medicine, biochemistry, biology, biology education, botany, business administration, business education, business marketing and marketing management, ceramic arts,

chemical engineering, chemistry, chemistry education, civil engineering, clothing/apparel/textile studies, computer engineering, computer science, construction technology, creative writing, criminal justice studies, dance, dietetics, drawing, economics, electrical/electronics engineering, engineering physics, engineering science, English, English education, entomology, environmental engineering, environmental health, equestrian studies, exercise sciences, farm/ranch management, finance, fine/studio arts, fishing sciences and management, forestry sciences, French, French language education, geology, German, German language education, graphic design/commercial art/illustration, history, home economics, home economics education, horticulture science, hotel and restaurant management, humanities, individual/family development, industrial arts, industrial technology, information sciences/systems, interior design, journalism, landscape architecture, landscaping management, Latin American studies, liberal arts and studies, marketing/distribution education, mathematical statistics, mathematics, mathematics education, mechanical engineering, metal/jewelry arts, microbiology/bacteriology, music, music (general performance), music education, music therapy, natural resources management, nursery management, nutrition science, occupational therapy, painting, philosophy, photography, physical education, physical sciences, physics, physics education, plant protection, political science, (pre)dentistry, (pre)law, (pre)medicine, (pre)veterinary studies, printmaking, psychology, public relations, radio/television broadcasting, range management, real estate, recreation/leisure facilities management, science education, sculpture, social sciences, social studies education, social work, sociology, soil conservation, soil sciences, Spanish, Spanish language education, speech education, speech/rhetorical studies, technical education, textile arts, theater arts/drama, trade and industrial education, turf management, water resources, wildlife management, zoology.

Colorado Technical University

Business administration, computer engineering, computer science, electrical/electronic engineering technology, electrical/electronics engineering, health science, human resources management, information sciences/systems, management information systems/business data processing, telecommunications.

Columbia University, Columbia College (NY)

African studies, African-American (black) studies, anthropology, archaeology, architecture, art, art history, Asian-American studies, astronomy, astrophysics, biochemistry, biology, biophysics, chemical and atomic/molecular physics, chemistry, classics, comparative literature, computer science, dance, East Asian studies, Eastern European area studies, economics, English, environmental science, film studies, French, geochemistry, geology, geophysics and seismology, German, Hispanic-American studies, history, Italian, Latin American studies, mathematical statistics, mathematics, medieval/renaissance studies, Middle Eastern studies, music, neuroscience, philosophy, physics, political science, psychology, religious studies, Russian, Russian/Slavic area studies, sociology, Spanish, theater arts/drama, urban studies, women's studies.

Columbia University, The Fu Foundation School of Engineering and Applied Science

Applied mathematics, bioengineering, chemical engineering, civil engineering, computer engineering, computer science, electrical/electronics engineering, engineering mechanics, engineering/industrial management, environmental engineering, industrial engineering, materials science, mechanical engineering, operations research, physics.

Concordia College (MN)

Accounting, advertising, apparel marketing, art, art education, art history, biology, biology education, broadcast journalism, business, business administration, business education, chemistry, chemistry education, child care/development, classics, clothing and textiles, clothing/apparel/textile, communications, computer science, creative writing, dietetics, early childhood education, economics, education, elementary education, English, English education, environmental science, exercise sciences, family/consumer studies, fine/studio arts, French, French language education, German, German language education, health education, health services administration, health/physical education, history, history education, home economics education, humanities, international business, international relations, journalism, Latin (Ancient and Medieval), mass communications, mathematics, mathematics education, medical technology, music, music (general performance), music (piano and organ performance), music (voice and choral/opera performance), music education, music theory and composition, nursing, nutrition science, office management, philosophy, physical education, physics, physics education, political science, (pre)dentistry, (pre)law, (pre)medicine, (pre)veterinary studies, psychology, public relations, radio/television broadcasting, religious studies, Russian/Slavic area studies, Scandinavian languages, science education, secondary education, social studies education, social work, sociology, Spanish, Spanish language education, speech education, speech/rhetorical studies, theater arts/drama, wind and percussion instruments.

Connecticut College

African studies, anthropology, architecture, art, art history, Asian studies, astrophysics, biochemistry, biology, botany, chemistry, Chinese, classics, dance, economics, engineering physics, English, environmental science, European studies, French, German, Hispanic-American studies, history, human services, interdisciplinary studies, international relations, Italian, Japanese, mathematics, medieval/renaissance studies, music, musical instrument technology, neuroscience, philosophy, physics, political science, psychology, religious studies, Russian, social sciences, sociology, theater arts/drama, urban studies, women's studies, zoology.

Cooper Union for the Advancement of Science and Art

Architecture, art, chemical engineering, civil engineering, electrical/electronics engineering, engineering, graphic design/commercial art/illustration, mechanical engineering.

The Corcoran College of Art and Design

Applied art, art, ceramic arts, drawing, fine/studio arts, graphic design/commercial art/illustration, photography, printmaking, sculpture.

Cornell College

Anthropology, architecture, art, art education, art history, biochemistry, biology, business economics, business education, chemistry, classics, computer science, cultural studies, economics, education, elementary education, English, environmental science, exercise sciences, French, geology, German, Greek (Modern), history, interdisciplinary studies, international business, international relations, Latin (Ancient and Medieval), Latin American studies, liberal arts and studies, mathematics, medieval/renaissance studies, modern languages, music, music education, philosophy, physical education, physics, political science, psychology, religious studies, Russian, Russian/Slavic area studies, secondary education, sociology, Spanish, speech/rhetorical studies, theater arts/drama, women's studies.

Cornell University

African studies, African-American (black) studies, agribusiness, agricultural business, agricultural economics, agricultural education, agricultural engineering, agricultural mechanization, agricultural sciences, agronomy/crop science, American studies, anatomy, animal sciences, anthropology, applied economics, archaeology, architectural engineering technology, architectural environmental design, architecture, art, art history, Asian studies, astronomy, atmospheric sciences, behavioral sciences, biochemistry, bioengineering, biology, biometrics, biostatistics, botany, business administration, cell biology, chemical engineering, chemistry, child care/development, Chinese, city/community/regional planning, civil engineering, classics, clothing and textiles, communications, community services, comparative literature, computer science, consumer services, creative writing, crop production management, dairy science, dance, developmental/child psychology, dietetics, drawing, East Asian studies, Eastern European area studies, ecology, economics, education, electrical/electronics engineering, engineering, engineering physics, engineering science, English, entomology, environmental engineering, environmental science, European studies, family resource management studies, family/community studies, family/consumer studies, farm/ranch management, fine/studio arts, food sciences, French, genetics, geological engineering, geology, German, Greek (Modern), Hebrew, Hispanic-American studies, history, history of science and technology, home economics education, horticulture science, hotel and restaurant management, human ecology, human services, individual/family development, industrial engineering, information sciences/systems, interdisciplinary studies, interior architecture, international agriculture, international relations, Italian, Japanese, Judaic studies, labor/personnel relations, landscape architecture, Latin (Ancient and Medieval), Latin American studies, liberal arts and studies, linguistics, marine science, mass communications, materials engineering, materials science, mathematical statistics, mathematics, mechanical engineering, medieval/renaissance studies, microbiology/bacteriology, Middle Eastern studies, modern languages, molecular biology, music, Native American studies, natural resources management, neuroscience, nutrition science, nutritional sciences, operations research, ornamental horticulture, philosophy, photography, physics, physiology, plant breeding, plant pathology, plant sciences, political science, poultry science, (pre)law, (pre)medicine, (pre)veterinary studies, psychology, public policy analysis, religious studies, Romance languages, Russian, Russian/Slavic area studies, science/technology and society, sculpture, Slavic languages, sociobiology, sociology, soil sciences, Southeast Asian studies, Spanish, textile arts, theater arts/drama, urban studies, women's studies, zoology.

Creighton University
Accounting, American studies, art, art education, art history, atmospheric sciences, biology, business economics, business marketing and marketing management, chemistry, classics, computer science, divinity/ministry, economics, education, elementary education, emergency medical technology, English, environmental science, exercise sciences, finance, French, German, graphic design/commercial art/illustration, Greek (Modern), health services administration, history, international business, international relations, journalism, Latin (Ancient and Medieval), management information systems/business data processing, mass communications, mathematical statistics, mathematics, modern languages, music, nursing, philosophy, physics, political science, psychology, social work, sociology, Spanish, special education, speech/rhetorical studies, theater arts/drama, theology.

The Curtis Institute of Music
Music, music (piano and organ performance), music (voice and choral/opera performance), stringed instruments, wind and percussion instruments.

Dartmouth College
African studies, African-American (black) studies, American government, anthropology, archaeology, art history, Asian studies, astronomy, biochemistry, biology, chemistry, classics, comparative literature, computer science, creative writing, earth sciences, economics, education, engineering, engineering physics, engineering science, English, environmental science, evolutionary biology, fine/studio arts, French, genetics, geography, German, Greek (Ancient and Medieval), history, Italian, Judaic studies, Latin (Ancient and Medieval), Latin American studies, linguistics, mathematics, molecular biology, music, Native American studies, philosophy, physics, psychology, religious studies, Romance languages, Russian, Russian/Slavic area studies, sociology, Spanish, theater arts/drama, women's studies.

David Lipscomb University
Accounting, American government, American studies, art, athletic training/sports medicine, biblical languages/literatures, biblical studies, biochemistry, biology, biology education, business administration, business economics, business marketing and marketing management, chemistry, computer science, dietetics, divinity/ministry, education, elementary education, engineering science, English, environmental science, exercise sciences, family/consumer studies, fashion merchandising, finance, fine/studio arts, food products retailing, French, French language education, German, graphic design/commercial art/illustration, health education, history, home economics, information sciences/systems, liberal arts and studies, mass communications, mathematics, middle school education, music, music (piano and organ performance), music (voice and choral/opera performance), music education, nursing, philosophy, physical education, physics, political science, (pre)dentistry, (pre)law, (pre)medicine, (pre)veterinary studies, psychology, public administration, public relations, secondary education, social

work, Spanish, speech/rhetorical studies, stringed instruments, theology, urban studies, wind and percussion instruments.

Davidson College
Anthropology, art history, biology, chemistry, classics, economics, English, fine/studio arts, French, German, history, mathematics, music, philosophy, physics, political science, psychology, religious studies, sociology, Spanish, theater arts/drama.

Deep Springs College
Liberal arts and studies.

Denison University
African-American (black) studies, anthropology, art, art history, biochemistry, biology, chemistry, classics, computer science, creative writing, dance, East Asian studies, economics, English, environmental science, film studies, fine/studio arts, French, geology, German, history, international relations, Latin American studies, mass communications, mathematics, music, organizational behavior, philosophy, physical education, physics, political science, psychology, religious studies, sociology, Spanish, speech/rhetorical studies, theater arts/drama, women's studies.

DePaul University
Accounting, actuarial science, adult/continuing education, advertising, African studies, African-American (black) studies, American studies, anthropology, applied art, applied mathematics, art history, arts management, audio engineering, biochemistry, biology, business administration, business economics, business marketing and marketing management, chemistry, city/community/regional planning, comparative literature, computer engineering technology, computer graphics, computer programming, computer science, computer/information sciences, counselor education/guidance, creative writing, criminal justice/law enforcement administration, drawing, early childhood education, ecology, economics, education, electrical/electronic engineering technology, elementary education, English, environmental science, finance, fine/studio arts, French, geography, German, graphic design/commercial art/illustration, history, human resources management, individual/family development, information sciences/systems, interdisciplinary studies, international business, international relations, Italian, Japanese, jazz, Judaic studies, Latin American studies, law and legal studies, linguistics, literature, management information systems/business data processing, mass communications, mathematical statistics, mathematics, medical laboratory technician, military science, modern languages, music, music (piano and organ performance), music (voice and choral/opera performance), music business management and merchandising, music education, nursing, operations research, philosophy, physical education, physics, political science, (pre)dentistry, (pre)law, (pre)medicine, (pre)veterinary studies, psychology, public policy analysis, religious education, religious studies, sculpture, secondary education, social sciences, sociology, Spanish, stringed instruments, theater arts/drama, travel-tourism management, urban studies, wind and percussion instruments, women's studies.

DePauw University
Anthropology, art history, athletic training/sports medicine, biology, chemistry, classics, computer science, earth sciences,

East Asian studies, economics, elementary education, English, English composition, fine/studio arts, French, geography, geology, German, Greek (Modern), history, interdisciplinary studies, Latin (Ancient and Medieval), mass communications, mathematics, medical technology, music, music (general performance), music business management and merchandising, music education, music theory and composition, peace and conflict studies, philosophy, physics, political science, psychology, religious studies, Romance languages, Russian/Slavic area studies, sociology, Spanish, women's studies.

Dickinson College

American studies, anthropology, biochemistry, biology, chemistry, classics, computer science, dance, East Asian studies, economics, English, environmental science, fine/studio arts, French, geology, German, Greek (Modern), history, international business, international relations, Italian, Judaic studies, Latin (Ancient and Medieval), mathematics, medieval/renaissance studies, molecular biology, music, philosophy, physics, political science, (pre)dentistry, (pre)law, (pre)medicine, psychology, public policy analysis, religious studies, Russian, Russian/Slavic area studies, sociology, Spanish, theater arts/drama, theater design.

Drake University

Accounting, actuarial science, advertising, anthropology, art, art history, astronomy, biology, broadcast journalism, business, business administration, business education, business marketing and marketing management, chemistry, computer science, drawing, economics, elementary education, English, environmental science, finance, fine/studio arts, French, German, graphic design/commercial art/illustration, history, information sciences/systems, insurance and risk management, interior design, international business, international relations, journalism, mass communications, mathematics, military science, music, music (piano and organ performance), music (voice and choral/opera performance), music business management and merchandising, music education, pharmacy, pharmacy administration and pharmaceutics, philosophy, physics, political science, (pre)dentistry, (pre)law, (pre)medicine, (pre)veterinary studies, psychology, public relations, radio/television broadcasting, religious studies, sacred music, science education, sculpture, secondary education, sociology, Spanish, speech/rhetorical studies, theater arts/drama.

Drew University

American studies, anthropology, applied mathematics, art, art history, behavioral sciences, biochemistry, biology, chemistry, classics, computer science, economics, English, French, German, history, interdisciplinary studies, Italian, liberal arts and studies, mathematics, mathematics/computer science, music, neuroscience, philosophy, physics, physiological psychology/psychobiology, political science, psychology, religious studies, Russian, Russian/Slavic area studies, sociology, Spanish, theater arts/drama, women's studies.

Drury University

Accounting, architecture, art, art education, art history, behavioral sciences, biology, business administration, chemistry, computer science, computer/information sciences, criminology, economics, education, elementary education, English, environmental science, exercise sciences, fine/studio arts, French, Ger-

man, history, mass communications, mathematics, music, music education, nursing, philosophy, physical education, physics, political science, (pre)dentistry, (pre)law, (pre)medicine, (pre)veterinary studies, psychology, religious studies, secondary education, sociology, Spanish, theater arts/drama.

Duke University

African-American (black) studies, anatomy, anthropology, art, art history, Asian studies, bioengineering, biology, chemistry, civil engineering, classics, computer science, economics, electrical/electronics engineering, English, environmental science, French, geology, German, Greek (Ancient and Medieval), history, international relations, Italian, Latin (Ancient and Medieval), linguistics, literature, materials science, mathematics, mechanical engineering, medieval/renaissance studies, music, philosophy, physics, political science, psychology, public policy analysis, religious studies, Russian, Russian/Slavic area studies, Slavic languages, sociology, Spanish, theater arts/drama, women's studies.

Earlham College

African-American (black) studies, art, Asian studies, biology, business administration, chemistry, classics, computer science, economics, education, English, environmental science, French, geology, German, history, interdisciplinary studies, international relations, Latin American studies, mathematics, music, peace and conflict studies, philosophy, physics, political science, (pre)law, (pre)medicine, psychology, religious studies, sociology, Spanish, theater arts/drama, women's studies.

Eckerd College

American studies, anthropology, art, biology, business administration, chemistry, comparative literature, computer science, creative writing, economics, English, environmental science, French, German, history, human resources management, humanities, individual/family development, interdisciplinary studies, international relations, literature, marine biology, mathematics, medical technology, modern languages, music, philosophy, physics, political science, (pre)dentistry, (pre)law, (pre)medicine, (pre)veterinary studies, psychology, religious studies, Russian, sociology, Spanish, theater arts/drama, women's studies.

Elizabethtown College

Accounting, anthropology, art, biochemistry, biology, biotechnology research, business administration, chemistry, communications, computer engineering, computer science, early childhood education, economics, education, elementary education, engineering, engineering physics, English, environmental science, French, German, history, industrial engineering, international business, mathematics, modern languages, music, music education, music therapy, occupational therapy, peace and conflict studies, philosophy, physics, political science, (pre)dentistry, (pre)law, (pre)medicine, (pre)veterinary studies, psychology, religious studies, science education, secondary education, social sciences, social work, sociology, Spanish.

Emory University

Accounting, African studies, African-American (black) studies, anthropology, art history, Asian studies, biology, biomedical science, business administration, business economics, business marketing and marketing management, chemistry, classics, comparative literature, computer science, creative writing, dance, Eastern European area studies, economics, education, elementary education, English, film studies, finance, French, German, Greek (Modern), history, human ecology, international relations, Italian, Judaic studies, Latin (Ancient and Medieval), Latin American studies, liberal arts and studies, literature, mathematics, medieval/renaissance studies, music, neuroscience, nursing, philosophy, physics, political science, psychology, religious studies, Russian, secondary education, sociology, Spanish, theater arts/drama, women's studies.

Eugene Lang College, New School University

Anthropology, creative writing, economics, education, English, history, humanities, interdisciplinary studies, international relations, liberal arts and studies, literature, music history, philosophy, political science, psychology, religious studies, social sciences, sociology, theater arts/drama, urban studies, women's studies.

Fairfield University

Accounting, American studies, art, biology, business administration, business marketing and marketing management, chemistry, clinical psychology, computer science, economics, English, finance, French, German, history, information sciences/systems, international relations, management information systems/business data processing, mass communications, mathematics, modern languages, music history, neuroscience, nursing, philosophy, physics, political science, psychology, religious studies, secondary education, sociology, Spanish.

Fashion Institute of Technology

Advertising, applied art, art, business administration, business marketing and marketing management, clothing and textiles, engineering/industrial management, fashion design/illustration, fashion merchandising, fine/studio arts, graphic design/commercial art/illustration, industrial design, industrial technology, interior design, mass communications, metal/jewelry arts, photography, retail management, textile arts.

Fisk University

Accounting, art, biology, business administration, chemistry, computer science, economics, English, finance, French, health services administration, history, mathematics, music, music education, philosophy, physics, political science, psychology, public administration, religious studies, sociology, Spanish, speech/rhetorical studies, theater arts/drama.

Florida Institute of Technology

Aerospace engineering, aircraft pilot (professional), applied mathematics, astrophysics, atmospheric sciences, aviation management, aviation/airway science, biochemistry, biology, biology education, business administration, chemical engineering, chemistry, chemistry education, civil engineering, communications, computer education, computer engineering, computer science, ecology, electrical/electronics engineering, environmental science, humanities, information sciences/systems, interdisciplinary studies, marine biology, mathematics education, mechanical engineering, molecular biology, ocean engineering, oceanography, physics, physics education, psychology, science education.

Florida State University

Accounting, acting/directing, actuarial science, advertising, American studies, analytical chemistry, anthropology, applied economics, applied mathematics, art, art education, art history, Asian studies, atmospheric sciences, biochemistry, bioengineering, biology, business, business administration, business communications, business marketing and marketing management, cell biology, chemical engineering, chemistry, child care/development, civil engineering, classics, clinical psychology, clothing and textiles, communications, community health liaison, computer engineering, computer science, computer/information sciences, creative writing, criminology, dance, dietetics, early childhood education, Eastern European area studies, ecology, economics, education of the emotionally handicapped, education of the mentally handicapped, education of the specific learning disabled, education of the visually handicapped, electrical/electronics engineering, elementary education, English, English education, entrepreneurship, environmental engineering, environmental science, evolutionary biology, experimental psychology, family/consumer studies, fashion design/illustration, fashion merchandising, film studies, film/video production, finance, fine/studio arts, foreign languages education, French, genetics, geography, geology, German, Greek (Modern), health education, history, home economics, home economics education, hospitality management, housing studies, human resources management, humanities, industrial engineering, inorganic chemistry, insurance and risk management, interior design, international business, international relations, Italian, Latin (Ancient and Medieval), Latin American studies, liberal arts and studies, library science, linguistics, literature, management information systems/business data processing, marine biology, mass communications, materials engineering, mathematical statistics, mathematics, mathematics education, mechanical engineering, molecular biology, music, music (general performance), music (piano and organ performance), music (voice and choral/opera performance), music education, music history, music theory and composition, music therapy, nursing, nutrition science, nutrition studies, oceanography, operations management, organic chemistry, philosophy, physical and theoretical chemistry, physical education, physical sciences, physics, physiology, plant sciences, political science, (pre)dentistry, (pre)law, (pre)medicine, (pre)pharmacy studies, (pre)veterinary studies, psychology, public relations, radio/television broadcasting, real estate, recreation/leisure facilities management, rehabilitation therapy, religious studies, Russian, Russian/Slavic area studies, science education, secondary education, social science education, social sciences, social work, sociology, Spanish, speech-language pathology/audiology, stringed instruments, theater arts/drama, theater design, wind and percussion instruments, women's studies, zoology.

Fordham University

Accounting, African studies, African-American (black) studies, American studies, anthropology, art, art history, bilingual/bicultural education, biological and physical sciences, biology, broadcast journalism, business administration, business economics, business marketing and marketing management, chemistry, classics, comparative literature, computer management, computer science, computer/information sciences, creative writing, criminal justice/law enforcement administration, dance, Eastern European area studies, economics, education, elementary education, English, film studies, finance, fine/studio arts, French, German, graphic design/commercial art/illustration, Greek (Modern), Hispanic-American studies, history, information sciences/systems, interdisciplinary studies, international business, international relations, Italian, journalism, Latin (Ancient and Medieval), Latin American studies, liberal arts and studies, literature, management information systems/business data processing, mass communications, mathematics, medieval/renaissance studies, Middle Eastern studies, modern languages, music, music history, natural sciences, peace and conflict studies, philosophy, photography, physical sciences, physics, political science, (pre)dentistry, (pre)law, (pre)medicine, (pre)veterinary studies, psychology, public administration, radio/television broadcasting, religious studies, Romance languages, Russian, Russian/Slavic area studies, secondary education, social sciences, social work, sociology, Spanish, theater arts/drama, theology, urban studies, women's studies.

Franklin and Marshall College
African studies, American studies, anthropology, art, biology, business administration, chemistry, classics, economics, English, film studies, French, geology, German, Greek (Ancient and Medieval), history, Latin (Ancient and Medieval), mathematics, music, neuroscience, philosophy, physics, political science, psychology, religious studies, Russian/Slavic area studies, sociology, Spanish, theater arts/drama, women's studies.

Furman University
Accounting, art, art history, Asian studies, biochemistry, biology, business administration, chemistry, communications, computer science, early childhood education, economics, education, elementary education, English, environmental science, exercise sciences, fine/studio arts, French, German, Greek (Modern), history, Latin (Ancient and Medieval), mathematics, music, music (piano and organ performance), music (voice and choral/opera performance), music education, philosophy, physics, political science, (pre)dentistry, (pre)law, (pre)medicine, (pre)veterinary studies, psychology, religious studies, sacred music, secondary education, sociology, Spanish, special education, theater arts/drama, urban studies.

Georgetown College
Accounting, American studies, art, biology, business administration, business marketing and marketing management, chemistry, computer science, early childhood education, ecology, education, elementary education, English, environmental science, European studies, finance, French, German, history, information sciences/systems, international business, management information systems/business data processing, mass communications, mathematics, medical technology, music, music (piano and organ performance), music (voice and choral/opera performance), music education, nursing science, philosophy, physical education, physics, political science, (pre)dentistry, (pre)law, (pre)medicine, psychology, recreation and leisure studies, religious studies, secondary education, sociology, Spanish, speech/rhetorical studies, theater arts/drama.

Georgetown University
Accounting, American studies, Arabic, art, biochemistry, biology, business administration, business marketing and marketing management, chemistry, Chinese, classics, comparative literature, computer science, economics, English, finance, French, German, history, interdisciplinary studies, international business, international economics, international relations, Ital-

ian, Japanese, liberal arts and studies, linguistics, mathematics, nursing, philosophy, physics, political science, Portuguese, psychology, religious studies, Russian, sociology, Spanish.

The George Washington University
Accounting, American studies, anthropology, applied mathematics, archaeology, art, art history, Asian studies, biology, business administration, business economics, business marketing and marketing management, chemistry, Chinese, civil engineering, classics, computer engineering, computer science, computer/information sciences, criminal justice/law enforcement administration, dance, East Asian studies, economics, electrical/electronics engineering, emergency medical technology, engineering, English, environmental engineering, environmental science, European studies, exercise sciences, finance, fine/studio arts, French, geography, geology, German, history, human resources management, human services, humanities, industrial radiologic technology, interdisciplinary studies, international business, international relations, journalism, Judaic studies, Latin American studies, liberal arts and studies, mass communications, mathematical statistics, mathematics, mechanical engineering, medical laboratory technician, medical laboratory technologies, medical technology, Middle Eastern studies, music, nuclear medical technology, philosophy, physician assistant, physics, political science, (pre)dentistry, (pre)law, (pre)medicine, psychology, public policy analysis, radio/television broadcasting, radiological science, religious studies, Russian, Russian/Slavic area studies, sociology, Spanish, speech-language pathology/audiology, speech/rhetorical studies, systems engineering, theater arts/drama.

Georgia Institute of Technology
Aerospace engineering, architecture, biology, business administration, business economics, chemical engineering, chemistry, civil engineering, computer engineering, computer/information sciences, construction technology, electrical/electronics engineering, history of science and technology, industrial design, industrial engineering, international relations, management science, materials engineering, mathematics, mechanical engineering, nuclear engineering, organizational psychology, physics, polymer chemistry, public policy analysis, science/technology and society, textile sciences/engineering.

Gettysburg College
Accounting, African-American (black) studies, American studies, anthropology, area studies, art, art history, biochemistry, biological and physical sciences, biology, business administration, chemistry, classics, computer science, economics, education, elementary education, English, environmental science, fine/studio arts, French, German, Greek (Modern), health science, history, interdisciplinary studies, international business, international economics, international relations, Latin (Ancient and Medieval), Latin American studies, liberal arts and studies, literature, marine biology, mathematics, modern languages, music, music education, philosophy, physical education, physics, political science, (pre)dentistry, (pre)law, (pre)medicine, (pre)veterinary studies, psychology, religious studies, Romance languages, science education, secondary education, social sciences, sociology, South Asian studies, Spanish, theater arts/drama, western civilization, women's studies.

Goshen College

Accounting, art, art education, art therapy, biblical studies, bilingual/bicultural education, biology, broadcast journalism, business administration, business education, chemistry, child care/development, computer science, early childhood education, economics, education, elementary education, English, environmental science, family/community studies, German, Hispanic-American studies, history, information sciences/systems, journalism, liberal arts and studies, mass communications, mathematics, music, music education, natural sciences, nursing, peace and conflict studies, physical education, physical sciences, physics, political science, (pre)dentistry, (pre)law, (pre)medicine, (pre)veterinary studies, psychology, religious studies, science education, secondary education, social work, sociology, Spanish, teaching English as a second language, theater arts/drama.

Goucher College

American studies, architectural history, art, biology, chemistry, computer science, dance, economics, education, elementary education, English, French, history, interdisciplinary studies, international relations, management science, mass communications, mathematics, music, philosophy, political science, psychology, religious studies, Russian, sociology, Spanish, theater arts/drama, women's studies.

Grinnell College

African-American (black) studies, American studies, anthropology, art, biological and physical sciences, biology, chemistry, Chinese, classics, computer science, economics, English, environmental science, French, German, history, interdisciplinary studies, Latin American studies, linguistics, mathematics, music, philosophy, physics, political science, psychology, religious studies, Russian, science/technology and society, sociology, Spanish, theater arts/drama, Western European studies, women's studies.

Grove City College

Accounting, biochemistry, biology, business administration, business communications, business economics, business marketing and marketing management, chemistry, computer management, divinity/ministry, early childhood education, economics, electrical/electronics engineering, elementary education, English, finance, French, history, international business, literature, mass communications, mathematics, mechanical engineering, modern languages, molecular biology, music business management and merchandising, music education, philosophy, physics, political science, (pre)dentistry, (pre)law, (pre)medicine, (pre)veterinary studies, psychology, religious studies, science education, secondary education, sociology, Spanish.

Guilford College

Accounting, African-American (black) studies, anthropology, art, athletic training/sports medicine, biology, business administration, chemistry, criminal justice/law enforcement administration, economics, education, elementary education, English, environmental science, French, geology, German, history, humanities, international relations, liberal arts and studies, mass communications, mathematics, medieval/renaissance studies, music, peace and conflict studies, philosophy, physical education, physician assistant, physics, political science, (pre)dentistry, (pre)law, (pre)medicine, (pre)veterinary studies, psychology, religious

studies, secondary education, sociology, Spanish, sport/fitness administration, theater arts/drama, women's studies.

Gustavus Adolphus College

Accounting, anthropology, art, art education, art history, athletic training/sports medicine, biochemistry, biology, biology education, business administration, business economics, chemistry, chemistry education, classics, computer science, criminal justice/law enforcement administration, dance, economics, education, elementary education, English, environmental science, French, geography, geology, German, health education, history, interdisciplinary studies, international business, Japanese, Latin American studies, mass communications, mathematics, mathematics education, music, music education, nursing, occupational therapy, philosophy, physical education, physical therapy, physics, physics education, political science, (pre)dentistry, (pre)law, (pre)medicine, (pre)veterinary studies, psychology, religious studies, Russian, Russian/Slavic area studies, sacred music, Scandinavian languages, secondary education, social sciences, social studies education, sociology, Spanish, speech/rhetorical studies, theater arts/drama, trade and industrial education.

Hamilton College (NY)

African studies, American studies, anthropology, art, art history, Asian studies, biochemistry, biology, chemistry, classics, comparative literature, computer science, creative writing, dance, East Asian studies, economics, English, fine/studio arts, French, geology, German, Greek (Modern), history, international relations, Latin (Ancient and Medieval), literature, mass communications, mathematics, modern languages, molecular biology, music, neuroscience, philosophy, physics, physiological psychology/psychobiology, political science, psychology, public policy analysis, religious studies, Russian/Slavic area studies, sociology, Spanish, theater arts/drama, women's studies.

Hamline University

Anthropology, art, art history, Asian studies, athletic training/sports medicine, biology, business administration, chemistry, criminal justice/law enforcement administration, East Asian studies, Eastern European area studies, economics, education, elementary education, English, environmental science, European studies, exercise sciences, fine/studio arts, French, German, health education, history, international business, international economics, international relations, Judaic studies, Latin American studies, law and legal studies, mass communications, mathematics, medical technology, music, music (general performance), music education, occupational therapy, paralegal/legal assistant, philosophy, physical education, physical therapy, physics, political science, (pre)dentistry, (pre)law, (pre)medicine, (pre)veterinary studies, psychology, public administration, religious studies, Russian/Slavic area studies, science education, secondary education, social sciences, sociology, Spanish, theater arts/drama, urban studies, women's studies.

Hampden-Sydney College

Biochemistry, biology, biophysics, business economics, chemistry, classics, computer science, economics, English, fine/studio arts, French, German, Greek (Modern), history, humanities, Latin (Ancient and Medieval), mathematics, philosophy, physics, political science, psychology, public policy analysis, religious studies, Spanish.

Hampshire College

African studies, African-American (black) studies, agricultural sciences, American studies, anatomy, animal sciences, anthropology, applied mathematics, archaeology, architectural environmental design, architecture, art, art history, Asian studies, astronomy, astrophysics, behavioral sciences, biochemistry, biological and physical sciences, biology, biophysics, botany, business economics, Canadian studies, cell biology, chemistry, child care/development, city/community/regional planning, cognitive psychology and psycholinguistics, community services, comparative literature, computer graphics, computer programming, computer science, computer/information sciences, creative writing, cultural studies, dance, developmental/child psychology, drawing, early childhood education, earth sciences, East Asian studies, Eastern European area studies, ecology, economics, education, elementary education, English, environmental biology, environmental health, environmental science, European studies, evolutionary biology, exercise sciences, family/consumer studies, film studies, film/video production, fine/studio arts, genetics, geochemistry, geography, geology, geophysics and seismology, graphic design/commercial art/illustration, health science, Hispanic-American studies, history, history of philosophy, history of science and technology, humanities, individual/family development, interdisciplinary studies, international business, international economics, international relations, Islamic studies, jazz, journalism, Judaic studies, labor/personnel relations, Latin American studies, law and legal studies, liberal arts and studies, linguistics, literature, marine biology, mass communications, mathematical statistics, mathematics, medieval/renaissance studies, Mexican-American studies, microbiology/bacteriology, Middle Eastern studies, molecular biology, music, music history, Native American studies, natural sciences, neuroscience, nutrition science, oceanography, peace and conflict studies, philosophy, photography, physical sciences, physics, physiological psychology/psychobiology, physiology, political science, (pre)medicine, (pre)veterinary studies, psychology, public health, public policy analysis, radio/television broadcasting, religious studies, Russian/Slavic area studies, sculpture, secondary education, social sciences, sociobiology, sociology, solar technology, South Asian studies, Southeast Asian studies, telecommunications, theater arts/drama, urban studies, women's studies.

Harding University

Accounting, advertising, American studies, art, art education, art therapy, biblical languages/literatures, biblical studies, biochemistry, biological and physical sciences, biology, business administration, business marketing and marketing management, chemistry, child care/development, communication disorders, computer engineering, computer science, criminal justice studies, data processing technology, dietetics, early childhood education, economics, education of the specific learning disabled, elementary education, English, exercise sciences, family/consumer studies, fashion merchandising, finance, French, general studies, graphic design/commercial art/illustration, health services administration, history, human resources management, humanities, interior design, international business, international relations, journalism, mass communications, mathematics, mathematics education, medical technology, missionary studies, music, music (piano and organ performance), music (voice and choral/opera performance), music education,

nursing, painting, physical education, physics, political science, (pre)dentistry, (pre)law, (pre)medicine, (pre)veterinary studies, psychology, public administration, public relations, radio/television broadcasting, religious education, religious studies, science education, social sciences, social work, sociology, Spanish, speech/rhetorical studies, sport/fitness administration, stringed instruments, theater arts/drama.

Harvard University

African languages, African studies, African-American (black) studies, American studies, anthropology, applied mathematics, Arabic, archaeology, architectural engineering, architectural environmental design, art, art history, Asian studies, astronomy, astrophysics, atmospheric sciences, behavioral sciences, biblical languages/literatures, biblical studies, biochemistry, bioengineering, biological and physical sciences, biological technology, biology, biomedical science, biometrics, biophysics, cell biology, chemical engineering, chemistry, Chinese, city/community/regional planning, civil engineering, classics, cognitive psychology and psycholinguistics, comparative literature, computer engineering, computer engineering technology, computer graphics, computer programming, computer science, computer/information sciences, creative writing, cultural studies, earth sciences, East Asian studies, Eastern European area studies, ecology, economics, electrical/electronics engineering, engineering, engineering physics, engineering science, English, entomology, environmental biology, environmental engineering, environmental science, European studies, evolutionary biology, film studies, fine/studio arts, fluid and thermal sciences, folklore, French, genetics, geochemistry, geological engineering, geology, geophysical engineering, geophysics and seismology, German, Greek (Modern), Hebrew, Hispanic-American studies, history, history of philosophy, history of science and technology, humanities, individual/family development, information sciences/systems, interdisciplinary studies, international economics, international relations, Islamic studies, Italian, Japanese, Judaic studies, Latin (Ancient and Medieval), Latin American studies, liberal arts and studies, linguistics, literature, marine biology, materials engineering, materials science, mathematical statistics, mathematics, mechanical engineering, medieval/renaissance studies, metallurgical engineering, microbiology/bacteriology, Middle Eastern studies, modern languages, molecular biology, music, music history, natural resources conservation, neuroscience, nuclear physics, philosophy, physical sciences, physics, physiological psychology/psychobiology, political science, polymer chemistry, Portuguese, (pre)dentistry, (pre)law, (pre)medicine, (pre)veterinary studies, psychology, public policy analysis, religious studies, robotics, Romance languages, Russian, Russian/Slavic area studies, Scandinavian languages, Slavic languages, social sciences, sociobiology, sociology, South Asian studies, Southeast Asian studies, Spanish, systems engineering, theater arts/drama, urban studies, western civilization, women's studies.

Harvey Mudd College

Biology, chemistry, computer science, engineering, mathematics, physics.

Hastings College

Accounting, advertising, art, art education, art history, biology, biology education, business administration, business education, business marketing and marketing management, chemistry,

chemistry education, communication equipment technology, communications, computer science, computer/information sciences, creative writing, drama and dance education, economics, education, elementary education, English, English education, foreign languages education, foreign languages/literatures, German, health services administration, health/physical education, history, history education, human resources management, human services, interdisciplinary studies, international economics, international relations, journalism, liberal arts and studies, literature, mass communications, mathematics, mathematics education, modern languages, music, music (piano and organ performance), music (voice and choral/opera performance), music education, music history, philosophy, physical education, physics, physics education, political science, (pre)dentistry, (pre)law, (pre)medicine, (pre)veterinary studies, psychology, public relations, radio/television broadcasting, religious studies, science education, secondary education, social science education, social studies education, sociology, Spanish, special education, speech education, speech/rhetorical studies, sport/fitness administration, stringed instruments, theater arts/drama.

Haverford College

African studies, anthropology, archaeology, art, art history, astronomy, biochemistry, biology, biophysics, chemistry, classics, comparative literature, computer science, East Asian studies, economics, education, English, French, geology, German, Greek (Modern), history, Italian, Latin (Ancient and Medieval), Latin American studies, mathematics, music, neuroscience, peace and conflict studies, philosophy, physics, political science, (pre)law, (pre)medicine, (pre)veterinary studies, psychology, quantitative economics, religious studies, Romance languages, Russian, sociology, Spanish, urban studies, women's studies.

Hendrix College

Accounting, anthropology, art, biology, business economics, chemistry, computer science, economics, elementary education, English, French, German, history, interdisciplinary studies, international relations, mathematics, music, philosophy, physical education, physics, political science, psychology, religious studies, sociology, Spanish, theater arts/drama.

Hillsdale College

Accounting, American studies, art, biology, business administration, business marketing and marketing management, chemistry, classics, comparative literature, computer science, early childhood education, economics, education, elementary education, English, European studies, finance, French, German, history, interdisciplinary studies, international relations, mathematics, music, philosophy, physical education, physics, political science, (pre)dentistry, (pre)medicine, (pre)veterinary studies, psychology, religious studies, secondary education, sociology, Spanish, speech/rhetorical studies, theater arts/drama.

Hiram College

Art, art history, biology, business administration, chemistry, classics, computer science, economics, elementary education, English, environmental science, fine/studio arts, French, German, health science, history, international business, international economics, mass communications, mathematics, music, philosophy, physics, physiological psychology/psychobiology, political science, (pre)dentistry, (pre)law, (pre)medicine,

(pre)veterinary studies, psychology, religious studies, secondary education, sociology, Spanish, theater arts/drama.

Hobart and William Smith Colleges

African studies, African-American (black) studies, American studies, anthropology, architecture, art, art history, Asian studies, biochemistry, biology, chemistry, Chinese, classics, comparative literature, computer science, dance, economics, English, environmental science, European studies, fine/studio arts, French, geology, Greek (Ancient and Medieval), history, interdisciplinary studies, Japanese, Latin (Ancient and Medieval), Latin American studies, mathematics, medieval/renaissance studies, modern languages, music, philosophy, physics, political science, (pre)dentistry, (pre)law, (pre)medicine, (pre)veterinary studies, psychology, religious studies, Russian, Russian/Slavic area studies, sociology, Spanish, theater arts/drama, urban studies, women's studies.

Hofstra University

Accounting, African-American (black) studies, American studies, anthropology, applied mathematics, art education, art history, Asian studies, athletic training/sports medicine, biochemistry, biological and physical sciences, biology, broadcast journalism, business administration, business education, business marketing and marketing management, chemistry, classics, community health liaison, computer science, computer/information sciences, dance, early childhood education, economics, education, electrical/electronics engineering, elementary education, engineering, engineering science, English, environmental science, exercise sciences, film studies, film/video production, finance, fine/studio arts, French, geography, geology, German, Hebrew, Hispanic-American studies, history, humanities, industrial engineering, information sciences/systems, interdisciplinary studies, international business, Italian, journalism, Judaic studies, liberal arts and studies, marine biology, mass communications, mathematics, mechanical engineering, music, music education, natural sciences, philosophy, physical education, physics, political science, psychology, radio/television broadcasting technology, Russian, secondary education, secretarial science, social sciences, sociology, Spanish, speech-language pathology/audiology, speech/rhetorical studies, theater arts/drama.

Hope College

Accounting, art history, athletic training/sports medicine, biochemistry, biology, business administration, chemistry, classics, communications, computer science, dance, economics, education of the emotionally handicapped, education of the specific learning disabled, engineering, engineering physics, English, environmental science, exercise sciences, fine/studio arts, French, geology, geophysics and seismology, German, history, humanities, interdisciplinary studies, Latin (Ancient and Medieval), mathematics, music, music education, nursing, philosophy, physical education, physics, political science, psychology, religious studies, secondary education, social work, sociology, Spanish, theater arts/drama.

Houghton College

Accounting, art, art education, biblical studies, biological and physical sciences, biology, business administration, chemistry, computer science, creative writing, divinity/ministry, education, elementary education, English, French, history, humanities, international relations, literature, mass communications, mathematics, medical technology, music, music (piano and organ performance), music (voice and choral/opera performance), music education, natural sciences, pastoral counseling, philosophy, physical education, physical sciences, physics, political science, (pre)dentistry, (pre)law, (pre)medicine, (pre)veterinary studies, psychology, recreation and leisure studies, religious education, religious studies, sacred music, science education, secondary education, social sciences, sociology, Spanish, stringed instruments, wind and percussion instruments.

Illinois College

Accounting, art, biology, business administration, business economics, chemistry, computer science, cytotechnology, economics, education, elementary education, English, finance, French, German, history, information sciences/systems, interdisciplinary studies, international relations, liberal arts and studies, management information systems/business data processing, mass communications, mathematics, medical technology, music, occupational therapy, philosophy, physical education, physics, political science, (pre)dentistry, (pre)law, (pre)medicine, (pre)veterinary studies, psychology, religious studies, secondary education, sociology, Spanish, speech/rhetorical studies, theater arts/drama.

Illinois Institute of Technology

Aerospace engineering, applied mathematics, architectural engineering, architecture, biology, biophysics, chemical engineering, chemistry, civil engineering, computer engineering, computer science, electrical/electronics engineering, environmental engineering, industrial technology, information sciences/systems, materials engineering, mechanical engineering, metallurgical engineering, physics, political science, psychology.

Illinois Wesleyan University

Accounting, applied art, art, art history, arts management, biology, business administration, chemistry, computer science, drawing, economics, education, elementary education, English, European studies, fine/studio arts, French, German, graphic design/commercial art/illustration, history, insurance and risk management, interdisciplinary studies, international business, international relations, Latin American studies, liberal arts and studies, mathematics, medical technology, music, music (piano and organ performance), music (voice and choral/opera performance), music business management and merchandising, music education, nursing, philosophy, physics, political science, (pre)dentistry, (pre)law, (pre)medicine, (pre)veterinary studies, psychology, religious studies, science education, secondary education, sociology, Spanish, stringed instruments, theater arts/drama, wind and percussion instruments.

Iowa State University of Science and Technology

Accounting, advertising, aerospace engineering, agricultural business, agricultural education, agricultural engineering, agricultural mechanization, agricultural sciences, agronomy/crop science, animal sciences, anthropology, architecture, art, atmospheric sciences, biochemistry, biology, biophysics, botany, business administration, business marketing and marketing management, ceramic sciences/engineering, chemical engineering, chemistry, city/community/regional planning, civil engineering, clothing/apparel/textile studies, community

services, computer engineering, computer science, construction engineering, consumer services, dairy science, design/visual communications, developmental/child psychology, dietetics, early childhood education, earth sciences, ecology, economics, education, electrical/electronics engineering, elementary education, engineering, engineering science, English, enterprise management, entomology, environmental science, family resource management studies, family/community studies, family/consumer studies, farm/ranch management, fashion design/illustration, finance, fish/game management, food products retailing, food services technology, forestry, French, genetics, geology, German, graphic design/commercial art/illustration, health education, health/physical education, history, home economics, home economics education, horticulture science, horticulture services, hotel and restaurant management, housing studies, industrial engineering, industrial technology, interdisciplinary studies, interior design, international agriculture, international business, international relations, journalism, landscape architecture, liberal arts and studies, linguistics, logistics and materials management, management information systems/business data processing, mass communications, mathematical statistics, mathematics, mechanical engineering, medical illustrating, metallurgical engineering, microbiology/bacteriology, music, music education, natural resources management, nutrition science, ornamental horticulture, philosophy, physics, plant protection, political science, (pre)dentistry, (pre)law, (pre)medicine, (pre)veterinary studies, psychology, public administration, religious studies, Russian, secondary education, sociology, Spanish, speech/rhetorical studies, theater arts/drama, trade and industrial education, transportation technologies, visual/performing arts, wildlife biology, women's studies, zoology.

James Madison University

Accounting, anthropology, art, art history, biology, business administration, business economics, business education, business marketing and marketing management, chemistry, communications, community health liaison, computer/information sciences, early childhood education, economics, educational media design, elementary education, English, finance, foreign languages/literatures, French, geography, geology, German, health/physical education, history, hotel and restaurant management, information sciences/systems, international business, international relations, liberal arts and studies, mathematics, music (general performance), nursing, nutrition studies, philosophy, physics, political science, psychology, public administration, religious studies, Russian, science/technology and society, social sciences, social work, sociology, Spanish, special education, speech-language pathology, technical writing, theater arts/drama.

John Brown University

Accounting, art, athletic training/sports medicine, biblical studies, biochemistry, biology, broadcast journalism, business administration, business education, chemistry, computer graphics, construction engineering, construction management, divinity/ministry, early childhood education, education, electrical/electronics engineering, elementary education, engineering, engineering technology, engineering/industrial management, English, environmental science, exercise sciences, graphic design/commercial art/illustration, health education, health services administration, history, interdisciplinary studies, international business, international relations, journalism, liberal arts and studies, mass communications, mathematics, mechanical engineering, medical technology, middle school education, missionary studies, music, music (piano and organ performance), music (voice and choral/opera performance), music education, pastoral counseling, physical education, (pre)law, (pre)medicine, (pre)veterinary studies, psychology, public relations, radio/television broadcasting, recreation/leisure facilities management, religious education, religious studies, secondary education, social sciences, special education, teaching English as a second language, theology.

John Carroll University

Accounting, art history, Asian studies, biological and physical sciences, biology, business administration, business marketing and marketing management, chemistry, classics, computer science, early childhood education, East Asian studies, economics, education, elementary education, engineering physics, English, environmental science, finance, French, German, gerontology, Greek (Modern), history, humanities, interdisciplinary studies, international economics, international relations, Latin (Ancient and Medieval), literature, mass communications, mathematics, neuroscience, philosophy, physical education, physics, political science, (pre)dentistry, (pre)law, (pre)medicine, (pre)veterinary studies, psychology, public administration, religious education, religious studies, secondary education, sociology, Spanish, special education.

Johns Hopkins University

American studies, anthropology, Arabic, art history, astronomy, astrophysics, behavioral sciences, bioengineering, biology, biophysics, chemical engineering, chemistry, civil engineering, classics, cognitive psychology and psycholinguistics, computer engineering, computer science, creative writing, earth sciences, East Asian studies, economics, electrical/electronics engineering, engineering, engineering mechanics, English, environmental engineering, environmental science, film studies, French, geography, German, Hispanic-American studies, history, history of science and technology, humanities, international relations, Italian, Latin American studies, liberal arts and studies, materials engineering, materials science, mathematics, mechanical engineering, Middle Eastern studies, music, natural sciences, neuroscience, philosophy, physics, physiological psychology/psychobiology, political science, psychology, Russian, social sciences, sociology, Spanish.

The Juilliard School

Dance, music, music (piano and organ performance), music (voice and choral/opera performance), stringed instruments, theater arts/drama, wind and percussion instruments.

Juniata College

Accounting, anthropology, art history, biochemistry, biological and physical sciences, biology, biology education, botany, business administration, business marketing and marketing management, cell biology, chemistry, chemistry education, communications, computer/information sciences, criminal justice/law enforcement administration, early childhood education, ecology, economics, education, elementary education, English, English education, environmental science, fine/studio arts, foreign languages education, French, French language education, geology, German, German language education, his-

tory, human resources management, humanities, interdisciplinary studies, international business, international relations, liberal arts and studies, management information systems/business data processing, marine biology, mathematics, mathematics education, microbiology/bacteriology, molecular biology, museum studies, natural sciences, peace and conflict studies, physics, physics education, political science, (pre)dentistry, (pre)law, (pre)medicine, (pre)pharmacy studies, (pre)veterinary studies, psychology, public administration, Russian, science education, secondary education, social sciences, social studies education, social work, sociology, Spanish, special education, zoology.

Kalamazoo College

Anthropology, art, art history, biology, business economics, chemistry, classics, computer science, English, French, German, health science, history, interdisciplinary studies, mathematics, music, philosophy, physics, political science, psychology, religious studies, sociology, Spanish, theater arts/drama.

Kentucky Wesleyan College

Accounting, art, art education, biology, business administration, chemistry, communications, computer science, criminal justice studies, elementary education, English, environmental science, history, human services, interdisciplinary studies, mathematics, medical technology, middle school education, modern languages, music, music education, nursing, philosophy, physical education, physics, political science, (pre)dentistry, (pre)law, (pre)medicine, (pre)veterinary studies, psychology, religious studies, secondary education, sociology, sport/fitness administration.

Kenyon College

African-American (black) studies, American studies, anthropology, art, art history, Asian studies, biochemistry, biology, chemistry, classics, creative writing, dance, economics, English, environmental science, fine/studio arts, French, German, Greek (Modern), history, humanities, interdisciplinary studies, international relations, Latin (Ancient and Medieval), literature, mathematics, modern languages, molecular biology, music, natural sciences, neuroscience, philosophy, physics, political science, psychology, religious studies, Romance languages, sociology, Spanish, theater arts/drama, women's studies.

Kettering University

Accounting, applied mathematics, business administration, business marketing and marketing management, chemistry, computer engineering, computer science, electrical/electronics engineering, engineering/industrial management, environmental science, finance, industrial engineering, information sciences/systems, mathematical statistics, mechanical engineering, operations management, physics, plastics engineering, systems engineering.

King College

Accounting, American studies, behavioral sciences, biblical studies, biochemistry, biological and physical sciences, biology, biology education, business administration, chemistry, chemistry education, early childhood education, economics, education, elementary education, English, English education, fine/studio arts, French, French language education, history, history education, information sciences/systems, mathematics, mathematics education, mathematics/computer science, medical technology, middle school education, modern languages, music, nursing, physics, physics education, political science, (pre)law, (pre)medicine, (pre)pharmacy studies, (pre)veterinary studies, psychology, religious studies, secondary education, Spanish, Spanish language education.

Knox College

African-American (black) studies, American studies, anthropology, art, art history, biochemistry, biology, chemistry, classics, computer/information sciences, creative writing, economics, education, English, environmental science, foreign languages/literatures, French, German, history, international relations, mathematics, music, philosophy, physics, political science, psychology, Russian, Russian/Slavic area studies, sociology, Spanish, theater arts/drama, Western European studies, women's studies.

Lafayette College

American studies, anthropology, art, art history, biochemistry, biology, business economics, chemical engineering, chemistry, civil engineering, computer science, economics, electrical/electronics engineering, engineering, English, environmental engineering, fine/studio arts, French, geology, German, history, international relations, mathematics, mechanical engineering, music, music history, philosophy, physics, political science, psychology, religious studies, Russian/Slavic area studies, sociology, Spanish.

Lake Forest College

African studies, American studies, anthropology, art history, Asian studies, biology, business economics, chemistry, communications, computer science, economics, education, elementary education, English, environmental science, European studies, finance, fine/studio arts, French, German, history, Latin American studies, mathematics, music, philosophy, physics, political science, (pre)dentistry, (pre)law, (pre)medicine, (pre)veterinary studies, psychology, secondary education, sociology, Spanish, women's studies.

La Salle University

Accounting, air science, applied mathematics, art, art history, biochemistry, biology, broadcast journalism, business administration, business economics, business education, business marketing and marketing management, chemistry, classics, computer programming, computer science, computer/information sciences, creative writing, criminal justice studies, economics, education, elementary education, English, environmental science, film studies, finance, French, geology, German, graphic design/commercial art/illustration, Greek (Modern), history, human resources management, information sciences/systems, Italian, journalism, Latin (Ancient and Medieval), liberal arts and studies, literature, management information systems/business data processing, mass communications, mathematics, military science, modern languages, music, music history, nursing, nutritional sciences, occupational therapy, philosophy, physical therapy, political science, (pre)dentistry, (pre)medicine, (pre)veterinary studies, psychology, public administration, public relations, radio/television broadcasting, religious education, religious studies, Russian, Russian/Slavic area studies, science education, secondary education, social sciences, social work, sociology, Spanish, special education, speech-language pathology/audiology, speech/rhetorical studies.

Lawrence University

Anthropology, art history, biology, chemistry, classics, cognitive psychology and psycholinguistics, computer science, East Asian studies, ecology, economics, English, environmental science, fine/studio arts, French, geology, German, history, international economics, international relations, linguistics, mathematics, music, music (piano and organ performance), music (voice and choral/opera performance), music education, neuroscience, philosophy, physics, political science, (pre)dentistry, (pre)law, (pre)medicine, (pre)veterinary studies, psychology, religious studies, Russian, Russian/Slavic area studies, secondary education, Spanish, stringed instruments, theater arts/drama, wind and percussion instruments.

Lehigh University

Accounting, African studies, American studies, anthropology, architecture, art, Asian studies, biochemistry, biology, business administration, business economics, business marketing and marketing management, chemical engineering, chemistry, civil engineering, classics, cognitive psychology and psycholinguistics, computer engineering, computer science, economics, electrical/electronics engineering, engineering, engineering mechanics, engineering physics, English, environmental science, finance, French, German, history, industrial engineering, information sciences/systems, international business, international relations, journalism, materials engineering, mathematical statistics, mathematics, mechanical engineering, molecular biology, music, natural sciences, neuroscience, philosophy, physics, political science, (pre)dentistry, (pre)medicine, psychology, religious studies, Russian/Slavic area studies, science/technology and society, sociology, Spanish, theater arts/drama, urban studies.

Le Moyne College

Accounting, applied mathematics, biological and physical sciences, biology, business administration, chemistry, communications, creative writing, economics, elementary education, English, English education, foreign languages education, French, history, international relations, labor/personnel relations, mathematics, mathematics education, philosophy, physician assistant, physics, political science, (pre)dentistry, (pre)law, (pre)medicine, (pre)pharmacy studies, (pre)veterinary studies, psychology, religious studies, science education, secondary education, social studies education, sociology, Spanish, theater arts/drama.

LeTourneau University

Accounting, aircraft mechanic/airframe, aircraft pilot (professional), aviation technology, biblical studies, biology, business administration, business marketing and marketing management, chemistry, computer engineering, computer engineering technology, computer science, drafting, electrical/electronic engineering technology, electrical/electronics engineering, elementary education, engineering, engineering technology, English, history, information sciences/systems, interdisciplinary studies, management information systems/business data processing, mathematics, mechanical engineering, mechanical engineering technology, natural sciences, physical education, (pre)dentistry, (pre)law, (pre)medicine, (pre)veterinary studies, psychology, religious studies, secondary education, sport/fitness administration, welding technology.

Lewis & Clark College

Anthropology, art, biochemistry, biology, business administration, chemistry, computer science, East Asian studies, economics, English, environmental science, French, German, Hispanic-American studies, history, international relations, mass communications, mathematics, modern languages, music, philosophy, physics, political science, (pre)dentistry, (pre)law, (pre)medicine, (pre)veterinary studies, psychology, religious studies, sociology, Spanish, theater arts/drama.

Linfield College

Accounting, anthropology, art, athletic training/sports medicine, biological and physical sciences, biology, business, chemistry, communications, computer science, creative writing, economics, elementary education, English, exercise sciences, finance, French, German, health education, history, international business, mathematics, music, philosophy, physical education, physics, political science, psychology, religious studies, sociology, Spanish, theater arts/drama.

List College, Jewish Theological Seminary of America

Biblical studies, history, Judaic studies, literature, museum studies, music, philosophy, religious studies.

Louisiana State University and Agricultural and Mechanical College

Accounting, agricultural business, animal sciences, anthropology, architectural engineering technology, architecture, biochemistry, bioengineering, biology, business administration, business economics, business marketing and marketing management, chemical engineering, chemistry, civil engineering, computer engineering, computer science, dairy science, dietetics, economics, electrical/electronics engineering, elementary education, English, environmental engineering, environmental science, fashion merchandising, finance, fine/studio arts, food sciences, forest management, French, general studies, geography, geology, German, history, individual/family development, industrial engineering, interior architecture, international business, landscape architecture, Latin (Ancient and Medieval), liberal arts and studies, management science, mass communications, mathematics, mechanical engineering, microbiology/bacteriology, music, music (general performance), music education, petroleum engineering, philosophy, physical education, physics, plant sciences, political science, poultry science, psychology, Russian/Slavic area studies, secondary education, sociology, Spanish, speech-language pathology/audiology, speech/rhetorical studies, theater arts/drama, trade and industrial education, wildlife management.

Loyola College in Maryland

Accounting, applied mathematics, art, biology, business, chemistry, classics, communications, computer/information sciences, creative writing, economics, education, electrical/electronics engineering, elementary education, engineering, English, finance, French, German, history, interdisciplinary studies, international business, mathematics, philosophy, physics, political science, psychology, religious studies, sociology, Spanish, special education, speech-language pathology.

Loyola University Chicago

Accounting, anthropology, art, biology, business administration, business economics, business marketing and marketing manage-

ment, chemistry, classics, communications, computer science, criminal justice studies, economics, elementary education, English, finance, French, German, Greek (Ancient and Medieval), history, human resources management, information sciences/systems, Italian, Latin (Ancient and Medieval), management information systems/business data processing, mathematical statistics, mathematics, music, nursing, nutrition studies, operations management, philosophy, physics, political science, (pre)dentistry, (pre)law, (pre)medicine, (pre)theology, (pre)veterinary studies, psychology, social work, sociology, Spanish, special education, theater arts/drama.

Luther College

Accounting, African studies, African-American (black) studies, anthropology, art, art education, arts management, biblical languages/literatures, biology, biology education, business, business administration, business computer programming, business marketing and marketing management, chemistry, chemistry education, classics, computer management, computer programming, computer science, computer/information sciences, cytotechnology, dance, drama and dance education, early childhood education, economics, education, elementary education, English, English composition, English education, environmental biology, foreign languages education, French, French language education, German, German language education, Greek (Modern), health education, health/physical education, Hebrew, history, history education, interdisciplinary studies, international business, international relations, Latin (Ancient and Medieval), Latin American studies, management information systems/business data processing, mass communications, mathematical statistics, mathematics, mathematics education, medical technology, middle school education, modern languages, museum studies, music, music (general performance), music (piano and organ performance), music (voice and choral/opera performance), music business management and merchandising, music conducting, music education, music history, music theory and composition, nursing, philosophy, physical education, physics, physics education, physiological psychology/psychobiology, political science, (pre)dentistry, (pre)law, (pre)medicine, (pre)theology, (pre)veterinary studies, psychology, reading education, religious studies, Scandinavian area studies, Scandinavian languages, science education, secondary education, social science education, social work, sociology, Spanish, Spanish language education, special education, sport/fitness administration, stringed instruments, theater arts/drama, theology, wind and percussion instruments.

Lyon College

Accounting, art, biology, business administration, chemistry, computer science, economics, English, history, mathematics, music, philosophy, political science, psychology, religious studies, Spanish, theater arts/drama.

Macalester College

Anthropology, art history, biology, chemistry, classics, communications, computer science, East Asian studies, economics, English, environmental science, fine/studio arts, French, geography, geology, Greek (Modern), history, humanities, interdisciplinary studies, international relations, Latin (Ancient and Medieval), Latin American studies, linguistics, mathematics, music, neuroscience, philosophy, physics, political science, psychology, religious studies, Russian, Russian/Slavic area studies, social sciences, sociology, Spanish, theater arts/drama, urban studies, women's studies.

Manhattan School of Music

Jazz, music, music (piano and organ performance), music (voice and choral/opera performance), stringed instruments, wind and percussion instruments.

Mannes College of Music, New School University

Music, music (piano and organ performance), music (voice and choral/opera performance), music conducting, music theory and composition, stringed instruments, wind and percussion instruments.

Marietta College

Accounting, advertising, art, athletic training/sports medicine, biochemistry, biology, business administration, business communications, business marketing and marketing management, chemistry, communications, computer science, economics, education, elementary education, engineering, English, environmental engineering, environmental science, fine/studio arts, French, geology, graphic design/commercial art/illustration, history, human resources management, information sciences/systems, international business, journalism, liberal arts and studies, mass communications, mathematics, modern languages, music, petroleum engineering, philosophy, physics, political science, (pre)dentistry, (pre)law, (pre)medicine, (pre)veterinary studies, psychology, public relations, radio/television broadcasting, secondary education, Spanish, speech/rhetorical studies, theater arts/drama.

Marlboro College

African studies, American studies, anthropology, applied mathematics, art, art history, Asian studies, astronomy, astrophysics, behavioral sciences, biblical studies, biochemistry, biology, botany, cell biology, ceramic arts, chemistry, classics, comparative literature, computer science, creative writing, cultural studies, dance, developmental/child psychology, drawing, East Asian studies, Eastern European area studies, ecology, economics, English, environmental biology, environmental science, European studies, experimental psychology, film studies, fine/studio arts, folklore, French, German, Greek (Modern), history, history of philosophy, human ecology, humanities, interdisciplinary studies, international economics, international relations, Italian, Latin (Ancient and Medieval), Latin American studies, linguistics, literature, marine biology, mathematics, medieval/renaissance studies, modern languages, molecular biology, music, music history, natural resources conservation, natural sciences, philosophy, photography, physics, political science, Portuguese, (pre)dentistry, (pre)law, (pre)medicine, (pre)veterinary studies, psychology, religious studies, Romance languages, Russian/Slavic area studies, sculpture, social sciences, sociology, Spanish, theater arts/drama, women's studies.

Marquette University

Accounting, advertising, African-American (black) studies, anthropology, bilingual/bicultural education, biochemistry, bioengineering, biology, biomedical science, broadcast journalism, business administration, business economics, business marketing and marketing management, chemistry, civil engineering, classics, communications, computer engineering, computer science, creative writing, criminal justice/law enforcement administration, criminology, dental hygiene, economics, education, electrical/electronics engineering, elementary education, elementary/middle/secondary education administration, engineering, English, environmental engineering, finance, French, German, history, history of philosophy, human resources management, industrial engineering, information sciences/systems, interdisciplinary studies, international business, international relations, journalism, liberal arts and studies, management information systems/business data processing, mass communications, mathematical statistics, mathematics, mechanical engineering, medical laboratory technician, middle school education, molecular biology, nursing, nursing (midwifery), philosophy, physical therapy, physician assistant, physics, political science, (pre)dentistry, (pre)law, (pre)medicine, psychology, public relations, secondary education, social work, sociology, Spanish, speech-language pathology/audiology, speech/rhetorical studies, theater arts/drama, theology, urban studies, women's studies.

Maryland Institute, College of Art

Art, art education, ceramic arts, drawing, fine/studio arts, graphic design/commercial art/illustration, interior design, intermedia, painting, photography, printmaking, sculpture, textile arts, visual/performing arts.

Maryville College

Applied art, art, art education, biochemistry, biology, biology education, business administration, chemical and atomic/molecular physics, chemistry, chemistry education, community services, computer science, developmental/child psychology, economics, education, engineering, English, English education, environmental science, fine/studio arts, history, history education, international business, international relations, mathematics, mathematics education, mathematics/computer science, music, music (piano and organ performance), music (voice and choral/opera performance), music education, nursing, physical education, physical sciences, physics education, political science, (pre)law, (pre)medicine, (pre)veterinary studies, psychology, recreation and leisure studies, religious studies, sign language interpretation, social science education, sociology, Spanish, Spanish language education, teaching English as a second language, technical writing, theater arts/drama, wind and percussion instruments.

Maryville University of Saint Louis

Accounting, actuarial science, art education, biological and physical sciences, biology, business, business administration, business marketing and marketing management, chemistry, communications, early childhood education, education, elementary education, English, environmental science, fine/studio arts, graphic design/commercial art/illustration, health science, health services administration, history, humanities, interior design, liberal arts and studies, management information systems/business data processing, mathematics, medical technology, middle school education, music, music therapy, nursing, occupational therapy, organizational psychology, paralegal/legal assistant, philosophy, physical therapy, political science, (pre)dentistry, (pre)law, (pre)medicine, psychology, religious studies, secondary education, social psychology, sociology.

Mary Washington College

American studies, architectural history, art, art history, biology, business administration, chemistry, classics, computer science, economics, elementary education, English, environmental science, fine/studio arts, French, geography, geology, German, history, interdisciplinary studies, international relations, Latin (Ancient and Medieval), liberal arts and studies, mathematics, modern languages, music, music education, philosophy, physics, political science, (pre)dentistry, (pre)law, (pre)medicine, (pre)veterinary studies, psychology, religious studies, secondary education, sociology, Spanish, theater arts/drama.

Massachusetts College of Art

Architecture, art education, art history, ceramic arts, fashion design/illustration, film/video production, fine/studio arts, graphic design/commercial art/illustration, industrial design, intermedia, metal/jewelry arts, painting, photography, printmaking, sculpture, textile arts.

Massachusetts Institute of Technology

Aerospace engineering, aerospace engineering technology, American studies, anthropology, applied mathematics, archaeology, architecture, art, bioengineering, biological and physical sciences, biology, business administration, chemical engineering, chemistry, city/community/regional planning, civil engineering, cognitive psychology and psycholinguistics, computer engineering, computer science, earth sciences, East Asian studies, economics, electrical/electronics engineering, engineering, environmental engineering, environmental health, environmental science, foreign languages/literatures, German, history, history of science and technology, humanities, interdisciplinary studies, Latin American studies, liberal arts and studies, linguistics, literature, management science, materials engineering, materials science, mathematics, mechanical engineering, music, naval architecture/marine engineering, naval science, nuclear engineering, ocean engineering, philosophy, physical sciences, physics, political science, (pre)dentistry, (pre)law, (pre)medicine, (pre)veterinary studies, Russian, Russian/Slavic area studies, science/technology and society, Spanish, theater arts/drama, urban studies, women's studies.

Messiah College

Accounting, adapted physical education, art education, art history, athletic training/sports medicine, biblical studies, biochemistry, biology, biology education, business administration, business economics, business marketing and marketing management, chemistry, chemistry education, civil engineering, communications, computer/information sciences, dietetics, early childhood education, economics, elementary education, engineering, English, English education, environmental science, exercise sciences, family/community studies, fine/studio arts, French, French language education, German, German language education, history, human resources management, humanities, information sciences/systems, international business, journalism, mathematics, mathematics education, music, music education, nursing, philosophy, physical education, physics, political science, psychology, radio/television broadcasting, recreation and leisure studies, religious education, religious studies, social studies education, social work, sociology, Spanish, Spanish language education, theater arts/drama.

Miami University

Accounting, aerospace engineering, African-American (black) studies, American studies, anthropology, architectural environmental design, architecture, art, art education, art history, athletic training/sports medicine, biochemistry, biology, biology education, botany, business, business administration, business economics, business marketing and marketing management, chemistry, child care/development, city/community/regional planning, classics, computer systems analysis, creative writing, dietetics, early childhood education, earth sciences, economics, elementary education, engineering physics, engineering technology, engineering/industrial management, English, English education, exercise sciences, family/consumer studies, finance, fine/studio arts, French, geography, geology, German, Greek (Ancient and Medieval), health education, health/physical education, history, home economics, home economics education, human resources management, individual/family development, industrial engineering, interdisciplinary studies, interior design, international relations, journalism, Latin (Ancient and Medieval), linguistics, management information systems/business data processing, management science, mass communications, mathematical statistics, mathematics, medical technology, microbiology/bacteriology, middle school education, music, music (general performance), music education, nursing, operations management, operations research, organizational behavior, philosophy, physical education, physics, political science, (pre)dentistry, (pre)law, (pre)medicine, (pre)veterinary studies, psychology, public administration, purchasing/contracts management, religious studies, Russian, science education, secondary education, social studies education, social work, sociology, Spanish, special education, speech-language pathology, speech-language pathology/audiology, speech/rhetorical studies, sport/fitness administration, systems science and theory, technical writing, theater arts/drama, wood science/paper technology, zoology.

Michigan State University

Accounting, advertising, agribusiness, agricultural and food products processing, agricultural business, agricultural economics, agricultural education, agricultural engineering, agricultural sciences, agronomy/crop science, animal sciences, anthropology, art, art education, art history, Asian studies, astrophysics, biochemistry, bioengineering, biological and physical sciences, biology, botany, business administration, business marketing and marketing management, chemical engineering, chemistry, city/community/regional planning, civil engineering, clothing/apparel/textile studies, community services, computer engineering, computer science, computer/information sciences, construction management, criminal justice/law enforcement administration, developmental/child psychology, dietetics, early childhood education, earth sciences, East Asian studies, economics, education, electrical/electronics engineering, elementary education, engineering, engineering mechanics, engineering technology, English, entomology, environmental biology, environmental science, exercise sciences, family resource management studies, family studies, family/community studies, family/consumer studies, fashion design/illustration, fashion merchandising, finance, fine/studio arts, fish/game management, food products retailing, food sciences, forestry, French, geography, geology, German, history, home economics, home economics education, horticulture science, hotel and restaurant management, human resources management, humanities, industrial design, industrial engineering, interdisciplinary studies, interior architecture, interior design, international relations, journalism, landscape architecture, Latin (Ancient and Medieval), liberal arts and studies, linguistics, mass communications, materials engineering, materials science, mathematical statistics, mathematics, mechanical engineering, medical laboratory technologies, medical technology, microbiology/bacteriology, music, music (voice and choral/opera performance), music education, music therapy, natural resources conservation, natural resources management, nursing, nutrition science, operations management, philosophy, physical education, physical sciences, physics, physiology, political science, (pre)dentistry, (pre)law, (pre)medicine, (pre)veterinary studies, psychology, public administration, public policy analysis, purchasing/contracts management, recreation/leisure facilities management, religious studies, Russian, science education, secondary education, social sciences, social work, sociology, Spanish, special education, speech-language pathology/audiology, stringed instruments, telecommunications, theater arts/drama, veterinarian assistant, veterinary technology, wildlife management, women's studies, zoology.

Michigan Technological University

Accounting, applied mathematics, biochemistry, biological technology, biology, business administration, business economics, business marketing and marketing management, chemical engineering, chemical engineering technology, chemistry, civil engineering, civil engineering technology, communications, computer engineering, computer programming, computer science, construction engineering, earth sciences, ecology, electrical/electronic engineering technology, electrical/electronics engineering, electromechanical technology, engineering, engineering mechanics, engineering physics, English, environmental engineering, finance, forest harvesting production technology, forestry, general studies, geological engineering, geology, geophysics and seismology, history, humanities, industrial engineering, information sciences/systems, management information systems/business data processing, materials engineering, mathematical statistics, mathematics, mechanical engineering, mechanical engineering technology, medical technology, metallurgical engineering, microbiology/bacteriology, mining/mineral engineering, operations management, physical sciences, physics, (pre)dentistry, (pre)medicine, (pre)veterinary studies, science education, secondary education, social sciences, surveying, technical writing.

Middlebury College

American studies, anthropology, art, art history, biochemistry, biological and physical sciences, biology, chemistry, Chinese, classics, computer science, dance, drawing, East Asian studies, Eastern European area studies, economics, education, English, environmental science, film studies, fine/studio arts, French, geography, geology, German, history, humanities, international economics, international relations, Italian, Japanese, liberal arts and studies, literature, mathematics, modern languages, molecular biology, music, natural sciences, philosophy, physical sciences, physics, political science, (pre)dentistry, (pre)law, (pre)medicine, (pre)veterinary studies, psychology, religious studies, Romance languages, Russian, Russian/Slavic area studies, secondary education, social sciences, sociology, Southeast Asian studies, Spanish, theater arts/drama, women's studies.

Millikin University

Accounting, American studies, art education, art therapy, arts management, biology, business administration, business marketing and marketing management, chemistry, communications, computer science, computer/information sciences, creative writing, economics, elementary education, English, experimental psychology, finance, fine/studio arts, foreign languages/literatures, French, German, graphic design/commercial art/illustration, history, human resources management, human services, interdisciplinary studies, international business, international relations, liberal arts and studies, management information systems/business data processing, mathematics, music, music (general performance), music (voice and choral/opera performance), music business management and merchandising, music education, nursing, operations management, philosophy, physical education, physics, political science, (pre)dentistry, (pre)law, (pre)medicine, (pre)veterinary studies, psychology, religious studies, sacred music, science education, secondary education, social science education, social work, sociology, Spanish, theater arts/drama.

Millsaps College

Accounting, anthropology, art, biology, business administration, chemistry, classics, computer science, economics, education, English, European studies, French, geology, German, history, mathematics, music, philosophy, physics, political science, psychology, religious studies, sociology, Spanish, theater arts/drama.

Mills College

American studies, anthropology, art, art history, biochemistry, biology, business economics, chemistry, comparative literature, computer science, creative writing, cultural studies, dance, developmental/child psychology, early childhood education, economics, education, elementary education, English, environmental science, fine/studio arts, French, German, Hispanic-American studies, history, interdisciplinary studies, international relations, liberal arts and studies, mass communications, mathematical statistics, mathematics, music, philosophy, (pre)medicine, psychology, social sciences, sociology, theater arts/drama, women's studies.

Milwaukee School of Engineering

Architectural engineering, bioengineering, business administration, business computer programming, computer engineering, construction management, electrical/electronic engineering technology, electrical/electronics engineering, industrial engineering, mechanical engineering, mechanical engineering technology, nursing, technical writing.

Monmouth College

Accounting, art, biology, business administration, chemistry, classics, computer science, economics, education, elementary education, English, environmental science, French, Greek (Modern), history, humanities, Latin (Ancient and Medieval), liberal arts and studies, mass communications, mathematics, military science, modern languages, music, natural sciences, philosophy, physical education, physics, political science, psychology, public relations, religious studies, secondary education, sociology, Spanish, special education, speech/rhetorical studies, theater arts/drama.

Morehouse College

Accounting, adult/continuing education, African-American (black) studies, art, biology, business administration, business marketing and marketing management, chemistry, computer/information sciences, economics, elementary education, engineering, English, finance, French, German, history, interdisciplinary studies, international relations, mathematics, middle school education, music, philosophy, physical education, physics, political science, psychology, religious studies, secondary education, sociology, Spanish, theater arts/drama, urban studies.

Mount Holyoke College

African-American (black) studies, American studies, anthropology, art history, Asian studies, astronomy, biochemistry, biology, chemistry, classics, computer science, dance, economics, education, English, environmental science, European studies, film studies, fine/studio arts, French, geography, geology, German, Greek (Modern), history, interdisciplinary studies, international relations, Italian, Judaic studies, Latin (Ancient and Medieval), Latin American studies, mathematical statistics, mathematics, medieval/renaissance studies, music, philosophy, physics, political science, psychology, religious studies, Romance languages, Russian, Russian/Slavic area studies, social sciences, sociology, Spanish, theater arts/drama, women's studies.

Mount Union College

Accounting, American studies, art, Asian studies, astronomy, athletic training/sports medicine, biology, business administration, chemistry, communications, computer science, early childhood education, economics, English, English composition, environmental biology, exercise sciences, French, geology, German, history, information sciences/systems, interdisciplinary studies, international business, Japanese, mass communications, mathematics, middle school education, music, music (general performance), music education, philosophy, physical education, physics, political science, psychology, religious studies, sociology, Spanish, sport/fitness administration, theater arts/drama.

Muhlenberg College

Accounting, American studies, art, art history, biochemistry, biology, business administration, chemistry, classics, computer science, dance, economics, elementary education, English, environmental science, fine/studio arts, French, German, Greek (Modern), history, human resources management, international economics, international relations, Latin (Ancient and Medieval), mass communications, mathematics, music, natural sciences, philosophy, physical sciences, physics, political science, (pre)dentistry, (pre)law, (pre)medicine, (pre)veterinary studies, psychology, religious studies, Russian/Slavic area studies, secondary education, social sciences, social work, sociology, Spanish, theater arts/drama.

Nebraska Wesleyan University

Art, biochemistry, biology, business administration, chemistry, computer science, economics, elementary education, English, exercise sciences, French, German, history, information sciences/systems, interdisciplinary studies, international business, international relations, mass communications, mathematics, middle school education, music, music education, nursing science, paralegal/legal assistant, philosophy, physical education, physics, physiological psychology/psychobiology, political sci-

ence, psychology, religious studies, science education, social work, sociology, Spanish, special education, sport/fitness administration, theater arts/drama, women's studies.

New College of the University of South Florida

Anthropology, art, biology, chemistry, classics, economics, environmental science, fine/studio arts, French, German, Greek (Ancient and Medieval), history, international relations, Latin (Ancient and Medieval), liberal arts and studies, literature, mathematics, medieval/renaissance studies, music, natural sciences, philosophy, physics, political science, psychology, public policy analysis, religious studies, Russian, social sciences, sociology, Spanish, urban studies.

New England Conservatory of Music

Jazz, music (piano and organ performance), music (voice and choral/opera performance), music history, music theory and composition, stringed instruments, wind and percussion instruments.

New Jersey Institute of Technology

Actuarial science, applied mathematics, architecture, business administration, chemical engineering, chemistry, civil engineering, civil engineering technology, computer engineering, computer science, computer/information sciences, electrical/electronic engineering technology, electrical/electronics engineering, engineering, engineering science, engineering technology, history, industrial engineering, industrial technology, information sciences/systems, materials engineering, materials science, mathematical statistics, mathematics, mechanical engineering, mechanical engineering technology, physics, (pre)dentistry, (pre)law, (pre)medicine, science/technology and society, surveying, systems engineering, technical writing.

New Mexico Institute of Mining and Technology

Applied mathematics, astrophysics, atmospheric sciences, behavioral sciences, biological and physical sciences, biology, business administration, chemical engineering, chemistry, computer programming, computer science, electrical/electronics engineering, engineering, engineering mechanics, environmental biology, environmental engineering, environmental science, experimental psychology, geochemistry, geology, geophysics and seismology, interdisciplinary studies, liberal arts and studies, materials engineering, mathematics, medical technology, metallurgical engineering, mining/mineral engineering, petroleum engineering, physics, (pre)dentistry, (pre)medicine, (pre)veterinary studies, psychology, science education, technical writing.

New York School of Interior Design

Interior design.

New York University

Accounting, actuarial science, African-American (black) studies, anthropology, archaeology, art, art history, behavioral sciences, biochemistry, biology, biology education, broadcast journalism, business administration, business economics, business marketing and marketing management, chemical engineering, chemistry, chemistry education, city/community/regional planning, civil engineering, classics, comparative literature, computer engineering, computer programming, computer science, computer/

information sciences, creative writing, dance, dental hygiene, diagnostic medical sonography, drama and dance education, drawing, early childhood education, East Asian studies, economics, education, education of the hearing impaired, education of the speech impaired, electrical/electronics engineering, elementary education, engineering, engineering physics, English, English education, European studies, film studies, film/video production, finance, fine/studio arts, foreign languages education, French, French language education, German, graphic design/commercial art/illustration, Greek (Modern), health services administration, Hebrew, Hispanic-American studies, history, hotel and restaurant management, humanities, information sciences/systems, interdisciplinary studies, international business, international relations, Italian, jazz, journalism, Judaic studies, Latin (Ancient and Medieval), Latin American studies, liberal arts and studies, linguistics, literature, management information systems/business data processing, mass communications, materials engineering, mathematical statistics, mathematics, mathematics education, mechanical engineering, medical radiologic technology, medical records technology, medieval/renaissance studies, Middle Eastern studies, middle school education, modern languages, music (general performance), music (piano and organ performance), music (voice and choral/opera performance), music business management and merchandising, music education, music history, music theory and composition, musical instrument technology, natural sciences, neuroscience, nursing, nutrition science, operations research, philosophy, photography, physical therapy assistant, physics, physics education, play/screenwriting, political science, Portuguese, (pre)dentistry, (pre)law, (pre)medicine, (pre)veterinary studies, psychology, radio/television broadcasting, real estate, recreation and leisure studies, religious studies, respiratory therapy, Romance languages, Russian, Russian/Slavic area studies, science education, sculpture, secondary education, social sciences, social studies education, social work, sociology, Spanish, special education, speech-language pathology/audiology, sport/fitness administration, stringed instruments, theater arts/drama, theater design, trade and industrial education, travel-tourism management, urban studies, wind and percussion instruments, women's studies.

North Carolina School of the Arts
Dance, film studies, film/video production, music, music (piano and organ performance), music (voice and choral/opera performance), theater arts/drama.

North Carolina State University
Accounting, aerospace engineering, agribusiness, agricultural and food products processing, agricultural business, agricultural education, agricultural engineering, agricultural sciences, agronomy/crop science, animal sciences, applied mathematics, architecture, arts management, atmospheric sciences, biochemistry, biology, biology education, botany, business administration, business marketing and marketing management, chemical engineering, chemistry, chemistry education, civil engineering, communications, computer engineering, computer science, construction engineering, creative writing, criminal justice/law enforcement administration, design/visual communications, economics, education, electrical/electronics engineering, engineering, English, English education, environmental engineering, environmental science, food sciences, forest management, French, French language education, geology, Ger-

man, graphic design/commercial art/illustration, health occupations education, history, horticulture science, human resources management, industrial design, industrial engineering, landscape architecture, landscaping management, liberal arts and studies, marketing/distribution education, materials engineering, mathematical statistics, mathematics, mathematics education, mechanical engineering, microbiology/bacteriology, natural resources conservation, natural resources management, nuclear engineering, oceanography, philosophy, physics, plant protection, political science, poultry science, psychology, public policy analysis, recreation/leisure facilities management, religious studies, science education, secondary education, social studies education, social work, sociology, Spanish, Spanish language education, textile sciences/engineering, travel-tourism management, turf management, wood science/paper technology, zoology.

North Central College
Accounting, actuarial science, American history, anthropology, applied mathematics, art, art education, athletic training/sports medicine, biochemistry, biology, broadcast journalism, business administration, business education, business marketing and marketing management, chemistry, classics, computer science, early childhood education, economics, education, elementary education, English, exercise sciences, finance, French, German, health education, history, humanities, international business, international relations, Japanese, jazz, liberal arts and studies, literature, management information systems/business data processing, mass communications, mathematics, modern languages, music, music (piano and organ performance), music (voice and choral/opera performance), natural sciences, philosophy, physical education, physics, political science, (pre)dentistry, (pre)law, (pre)medicine, (pre)veterinary studies, psychology, public relations, religious studies, science education, secondary education, social sciences, sociology, Spanish, speech/rhetorical studies, theater arts/drama.

Northwestern College (IA)
Accounting, art, art education, biology, business administration, business education, chemistry, computer science, economics, education, elementary education, English, environmental science, exercise sciences, history, humanities, mass communications, mathematics, medical technology, music, music education, philosophy, physical education, political science, psychology, religious education, religious studies, secondary education, secretarial science, social work, sociology, Spanish, speech/rhetorical studies, theater arts/drama, theology.

Northwestern University
African-American (black) studies, American studies, anthropology, applied mathematics, art, art history, Asian studies, astronomy, biochemistry, bioengineering, biology, cell biology, chemical engineering, chemistry, civil engineering, classics, comparative literature, computer engineering, computer science, dance, economics, electrical/electronics engineering, engineering, English, environmental science, film studies, French, geology, German, history, humanities, industrial engineering, interdisciplinary studies, international relations, Italian, journalism, Latin American studies, linguistics, materials engineering, materials science, mathematical statistics, mathematics, mechanical engineering, molecular biology, music, music (piano and organ performance), music (voice and choral/opera

performance), music education, music history, neuroscience, philosophy, physics, political science, psychology, radio/television broadcasting, religious studies, secondary education, Slavic languages, sociology, Spanish, speech therapy, speech-language pathology/audiology, speech/rhetorical studies, theater arts/drama, urban studies, wind and percussion instruments.

Oberlin College

African-American (black) studies, anthropology, archaeology, art, art history, biochemistry, biology, chemistry, classics, comparative literature, computer science, creative writing, dance, East Asian studies, ecology, economics, English, environmental science, fine/studio arts, French, geology, German, Greek (Modern), history, interdisciplinary studies, jazz, Judaic studies, Latin (Ancient and Medieval), Latin American studies, law and legal studies, mathematics, Middle Eastern studies, music, music (piano and organ performance), music (voice and choral/opera performance), music education, music history, neuroscience, philosophy, physics, physiological psychology/psychobiology, political science, psychology, religious studies, Romance languages, Russian, Russian/Slavic area studies, sociology, Spanish, stringed instruments, theater arts/drama, wind and percussion instruments, women's studies.

Occidental College

American studies, anthropology, art history, Asian studies, biochemistry, biology, business economics, chemistry, cognitive psychology and psycholinguistics, comparative literature, economics, environmental science, exercise sciences, fine/studio arts, French, geology, history, international relations, mathematics, music, philosophy, physics, physiological psychology/psychobiology, political science, psychology, public policy analysis, religious studies, sociology, Spanish, theater arts/drama, women's studies.

Oglethorpe University

Accounting, American studies, art, biology, business administration, business economics, chemistry, computer science, early childhood education, economics, education, elementary education, English, history, interdisciplinary studies, international relations, mass communications, mathematics, middle school education, philosophy, physics, political science, (pre)dentistry, (pre)law, (pre)medicine, (pre)veterinary studies, psychology, secondary education, social work, sociology, urban studies.

Ohio Northern University

Accounting, art, art education, athletic training/sports medicine, biochemistry, biology, broadcast journalism, business administration, ceramic arts, chemistry, civil engineering, computer engineering, computer science, creative writing, criminal justice/law enforcement administration, early childhood education, electrical/electronics engineering, elementary education, English, environmental science, French, graphic design/commercial art/illustration, health education, history, industrial arts, industrial technology, international business, international relations, mass communications, mathematical statistics, mathematics, mechanical engineering, medical technology, medicinal/pharmaceutical chemistry, middle school education, molecular biology, music, music business management and merchandising, music education, pharmacy, philosophy, physical education, physics, political science, psychology, public relations,

religious studies, sociology, Spanish, speech/rhetorical studies, sport/fitness administration, theater arts/drama.

The Ohio State University

Accounting, acting/directing, actuarial science, advertising, aerospace engineering, African studies, African-American (black) studies, agricultural and food products processing, agricultural business, agricultural economics, agricultural education, agricultural engineering, agricultural production, agronomy/crop science, American studies, animal sciences, anthropology, Arabic, architecture, art, art education, art history, Asian studies, Asian-American studies, astronomy, atmospheric sciences, aviation management, aviation technology, banking, biochemistry, biology, biophysics, biotechnology research, botany, broadcast journalism, business administration, business home economics, business marketing and marketing management, cartography, ceramic arts, ceramic sciences/engineering, chemical engineering, chemistry, child care/development, Chinese, city/community/regional planning, civil engineering, classics, clothing and textiles, clothing/apparel/textile studies, communications, comparative literature, computer engineering, computer programming, computer science, computer/information sciences, construction engineering, creative writing, criminal justice studies, criminology, cultural studies, dance, dental hygiene, dietetics, drama and dance education, drawing, East Asian studies, Eastern European area studies, economics, electrical/electronics engineering, engineering physics, English, entomology, environmental education, environmental engineering, environmental science, equestrian studies, exercise sciences, family studies, farm/ranch management, finance, fine/studio arts, fishing sciences and management, folklore, food sciences, forestry, French, genetics, geography, geology, geotechnical engineering, German, gerontology, graphic design/commercial art/illustration, Greek (Ancient and Medieval), Greek (Modern), Hebrew, history, horticulture science, hospitality management, human resources management, humanities, hydraulic technology, industrial arts education, industrial design, industrial engineering, information sciences/systems, insurance and risk management, interior design, international business, international relations, Islamic studies, Italian, Japanese, jazz, journalism, Judaic studies, landscape architecture, landscaping management, Latin (Ancient and Medieval), Latin American studies, linguistics, literature, logistics and materials management, marine biology, materials engineering, materials science, mathematical statistics, mathematics, mechanical engineering, medical dietician, medical records administration, medical technology, medieval/renaissance studies, metallurgical engineering, microbiology/bacteriology, Middle Eastern studies, molecular biology, music, music (general performance), music (piano and organ performance), music (voice and choral/opera performance), music education, music history, music theory and composition, natural resources management, natural resources protective services, nursing, nursing science, nutritional sciences, occupational therapy, operations management, optics, ornamental horticulture, painting, peace and conflict studies, pharmacy, philosophy, photography, physical education, physical therapy, physics, plant pathology, plant physiology, plant protection, plant sciences, political science, Portuguese, (pre)dentistry, (pre)engineering, (pre)law, (pre)medicine, (pre)pharmacy studies, (pre)veterinary studies, printmaking, psychology, public relations, purchasing/contracts management, radiological science, real estate, recreation/leisure facilities management, religious studies, respiratory therapy, robotics, Russian, Russian/Slavic area studies, science/technology and society, sculpture, social sciences, social work, sociology, soil conservation, soil sciences, Spanish, special education, speech-language pathology/audiology, structural engineering, systems engineering, technical education, telecommunications, theater arts/drama, transportation engineering, turf management, urban studies, Western European studies, wildlife management, women's studies, zoology.

Ohio University

Accounting, accounting technician, acting/directing, actuarial science, advertising, African studies, African-American (black) studies, aircraft pilot (professional), anthropology, applied mathematics, art, art education, art history, Asian studies, athletic training/sports medicine, atmospheric sciences, aviation management, aviation technology, biological and physical sciences, biology, biology education, biomedical science, botany, broadcast journalism, business administration, business economics, business education, business marketing and marketing management, cartography, cell biology, ceramic arts, chemical engineering, chemistry, chemistry education, child care/development, civil engineering, classics, communications, community services, computer engineering, computer engineering technology, computer science, creative writing, criminal justice/law enforcement administration, criminology, dance, design/visual communications, dietetics, early childhood education, economics, education of the emotionally handicapped, education of the hearing impaired, education of the multiple handicapped, education of the specific learning disabled, education of the speech impaired, electrical/electronic engineering technology, electrical/electronics engineering, elementary education, English, English education, enterprise management, environmental biology, environmental engineering, environmental health, environmental science, equestrian studies, European studies, exercise sciences, family resource management studies, family/community studies, family/consumer studies, fashion merchandising, film studies, finance, food products retailing, food services technology, forensic technology, French, French language education, general studies, geography, geology, German, German language education, Greek (Modern), health education, health facilities administration, health services administration, hearing sciences, history, home economics, housing studies, human resources management, human services, humanities, individual/family development, industrial design, information sciences/systems, interior design, international business, journalism, labor/personnel relations, Latin (Ancient and Medieval), Latin American studies, law enforcement/police science, liberal arts and studies, linguistics, management information systems/business data processing, marine biology, mass communications, mathematics, mathematics education, mechanical engineering, medical assistant, microbiology/bacteriology, middle school education, music, music (piano and organ performance), music (voice and choral/opera performance), music education, music history, music theory and composition, music therapy, nursing, nutrition science, occupational health and industrial hygiene, operations management, painting, philosophy, photography, physical education, physics, political science, (pre)dentistry, (pre)law, (pre)medicine, (pre)veterinary studies, printmaking, psychology, public health, public relations, radio/television

broadcasting, reading education, recreation and leisure studies, recreation/leisure facilities management, recreational therapy, retail management, Russian, safety and security technology, science education, sculpture, secondary education, secretarial science, social sciences, social studies education, social work, sociology, Spanish, Spanish language education, speech education, speech therapy, speech-language pathology/audiology, speech/rhetorical studies, sport/fitness administration, telecommunications, theater arts/drama, theater design, travel-tourism management, urban studies, visual/performing arts, water resources, wildlife biology.

Ohio Wesleyan University

Accounting, African-American (black) studies, anthropology, art education, art history, art therapy, astronomy, biology, botany, broadcast journalism, business administration, chemistry, classics, computer science, creative writing, cultural studies, earth sciences, East Asian studies, economics, education, elementary education, engineering science, English, environmental science, fine/studio arts, French, genetics, geography, geology, German, health education, history, humanities, international business, international relations, journalism, literature, mathematical statistics, mathematics, medieval/renaissance studies, microbiology/bacteriology, music, music education, neuroscience, philosophy, physical education, physics, political science, (pre)dentistry, (pre)law, (pre)medicine, (pre)theology, (pre)veterinary studies, psychology, public administration, religious studies, secondary education, sociology, Spanish, theater arts/drama, urban studies, women's studies, zoology.

Oklahoma State University

Accounting, advertising, agricultural business, agricultural economics, agricultural education, agricultural sciences, aircraft pilot (professional), animal sciences, architectural engineering, architecture, art, aviation management, aviation technology, biochemistry, bioengineering, biology, botany, broadcast journalism, business, business economics, business marketing and marketing management, cell biology, chemical engineering, chemistry, child care/development, civil engineering, clothing and textiles, communication disorders, computer engineering, computer management, computer programming, computer science, computer/information sciences, construction management, construction technology, consumer services, early childhood education, ecology, economics, education, electrical/electronic engineering technology, electrical/electronics engineering, elementary education, engineering, engineering technology, English, entomology, environmental science, family/community studies, family/consumer studies, farm/ranch management, fashion design/illustration, fashion merchandising, finance, fine/studio arts, fire protection/safety technology, fish/game management, forestry, French, geography, geology, German, graphic design/commercial art/illustration, health education, health science, health/physical education, history, home economics, horticulture science, hotel and restaurant management, human resources management, industrial arts, industrial engineering, industrial technology, information sciences/systems, interior design, international business, journalism, landscape architecture, management information systems/business data processing, management science, marriage and family counseling, mathematics, mechanical engineering, mechanical engineering technology, medical technology, microbiology/bacteriology, middle school education, molecular biology, music, music business management and merchandising, music education, nutrition science, philosophy, physical education, physics, plant sciences, political science, (pre)dentistry, (pre)law, (pre)medicine, (pre)veterinary studies, psychology, public relations, range management, recreation and leisure studies, Russian, science education, secondary education, sociology, Spanish, speech-language pathology/audiology, speech/rhetorical studies, technical writing, theater arts/drama, trade and industrial education, wildlife management, zoology.

Ouachita Baptist University

Accounting, art, art education, biblical studies, biology, business administration, business education, business marketing and marketing management, chemistry, computer science, dietetics, early childhood education, education, English, finance, French, history, home economics, home economics education, mass communications, mathematics, middle school education, music, music (piano and organ performance), music (voice and choral/opera performance), music education, music theory and composition, pastoral counseling, philosophy, physical education, physics, political science, (pre)dentistry, psychology, religious studies, Russian, sacred music, science education, secondary education, social sciences, sociology, Spanish, special education, speech-language pathology/audiology, speech/rhetorical studies, theater arts/drama, theology.

Pacific Lutheran University

Accounting, anthropology, art, art education, art history, biochemistry, biology, broadcast journalism, business administration, business marketing and marketing management, chemistry, Chinese, classics, computer engineering, computer science, early childhood education, earth sciences, economics, education, electrical/electronics engineering, elementary education, engineering physics, engineering science, English, environmental science, finance, fine/studio arts, French, geology, German, history, international business, international relations, journalism, literature, management information systems/business data processing, mass communications, mathematics, modern languages, music, music (piano and organ performance), music (voice and choral/opera performance), music education, nursing, philosophy, physical education, physical science, psychology, radio/television broadcasting, reading education, recreational therapy, religious studies, sacred music, Scandinavian languages, science education, secondary education, social work, sociology, Spanish, special education, theater arts/drama, women's studies.

Parsons School of Design, New School University

Architectural environmental design, architecture, art, art education, drawing, fashion design/illustration, fashion merchandising, graphic design/commercial art/illustration, industrial design, interior design, photography, sculpture.

Pennsylvania State University University Park Campus

Accounting, acting/directing, actuarial science, adult/continuing education administration, advertising, aerospace engineering, African-American (black) studies, agribusiness, agricultural business, agricultural education, agricultural engineering, agricultural mechanization, agricultural sciences, agronomy/crop science, American studies, animal sciences, anthropology,

applied economics, applied mathematics, architectural engineering, architecture, art, art education, art history, atmospheric sciences, biochemistry, biological and physical sciences, biological technology, biology, business, business administration, business economics, business marketing and marketing management, chemical engineering, chemistry, civil engineering, classics, communications, comparative literature, computer engineering, computer/information sciences, criminal justice studies, earth sciences, East Asian studies, economics, electrical/electronics engineering, elementary education, engineering science, English, environmental engineering, film studies, finance, food sciences, forestry sciences, French, geography, geology, German, graphic design/commercial art/illustration, health services administration, history, horticulture science, hospitality management, individual/family development, industrial engineering, information sciences/systems, insurance and risk management, interdisciplinary studies, international business, international relations, Italian, Japanese, journalism, Judaic studies, labor/personnel relations, landscape architecture, landscaping management, Latin American studies, liberal arts and studies, logistics and materials management, management information systems/business data processing, mathematical statistics, mathematics, mechanical engineering, medieval/renaissance studies, metallurgical engineering, microbiology/bacteriology, mining/mineral engineering, music, music (general performance), music education, natural resources conservation, nuclear engineering, nursing, nutrition science, occupational safety/health technology, operations management, petroleum engineering, philosophy, physics, political science, (pre)medicine, psychology, public administration, real estate, recreation/leisure facilities management, religious studies, Russian, secondary education, sociology, soil sciences, Spanish, special education, speech-language pathology/audiology, speech/rhetorical studies, theater design, turf management, visual/performing arts, women's studies.

Pepperdine University (Malibu, CA)

Accounting, advertising, art, athletic training/sports medicine, biology, business administration, chemistry, communications, computer science, economics, education, elementary education, English, French, German, history, humanities, interdisciplinary studies, international business, international relations, journalism, liberal arts and studies, mathematics, music, music education, natural sciences, nutrition science, philosophy, physical education, political science, (pre)dentistry, (pre)law, (pre)medicine, psychology, public relations, religious education, religious studies, secondary education, sociology, Spanish, speech/rhetorical studies, telecommunications, theater arts/drama.

Pitzer College

African-American (black) studies, American studies, anthropology, art, Asian studies, Asian-American studies, biology, business administration, chemistry, classics, economics, engineering, engineering/industrial management, English, environmental science, European studies, French, German, history, international relations, Latin American studies, linguistics, literature, mass communications, mathematics, Mexican-American studies, philosophy, physics, physiological psychology/psychobiology, political science, (pre)medicine, psychology, religious studies, Romance languages, Russian, science/technology and society, sociology, Spanish, theater arts/drama, women's studies.

Polytechnic University, Brooklyn Campus

Chemical engineering, chemistry, civil engineering, computer engineering, computer science, electrical/electronics engineering, environmental science, humanities, information sciences/systems, journalism, mathematics, mechanical engineering, physics, (pre)law, (pre)medicine, social sciences, technical writing.

Polytechnic University, Farmingdale Campus

Civil engineering, computer engineering, computer science, electrical/electronics engineering, information sciences/systems, mechanical engineering, (pre)law, (pre)medicine.

Pomona College

African-American (black) studies, American studies, anthropology, art, art history, Asian studies, astronomy, biochemistry, biology, cell biology, chemistry, Chinese, classics, computer science, dance, East Asian studies, ecology, economics, English, environmental science, film studies, fine/studio arts, French, geochemistry, geology, German, Hispanic-American studies, history, humanities, interdisciplinary studies, international relations, Japanese, liberal arts and studies, linguistics, mathematics, Mexican-American studies, microbiology/bacteriology, modern languages, molecular biology, music, neuroscience, philosophy, physics, political science, (pre)medicine, psychology, public policy analysis, religious studies, Romance languages, Russian, sociology, Spanish, theater arts/drama, women's studies.

Presbyterian College

Accounting, art, biology, business administration, chemistry, early childhood education, economics, education, elementary education, English, French, German, history, mathematics, modern languages, music, music education, philosophy, physics, political science, (pre)dentistry, (pre)law, (pre)medicine, (pre)veterinary studies, psychology, religious studies, social sciences, sociology, Spanish, special education, theater arts/drama.

Princeton University

Anthropology, architecture, art history, astrophysics, chemical engineering, chemistry, civil engineering, classics, comparative literature, computer science, East Asian studies, Eastern European area studies, ecology, economics, electrical/electronics engineering, engineering/industrial management, English, geology, German, history, mathematics, mechanical engineering, Middle Eastern studies, molecular biology, music, philosophy, physics, political science, psychology, public policy analysis, religious studies, Romance languages, sociology.

Providence College

Accounting, American studies, art history, biology, business administration, business economics, business marketing and marketing management, chemistry, community services, computer science, economics, English, environmental science, finance, fine/studio arts, fire science, French, health services administration, history, humanities, instrumentation technology, Italian, labor/personnel relations, liberal arts and studies, mathematics, music, paralegal/legal assistant, pastoral counseling, philosophy, political science, psychology, secondary education, social sciences, social work, sociology, Spanish, special education, systems science and theory, theology, visual/performing arts.

Purdue University

Accounting, aerospace engineering, aerospace engineering technology, African-American (black) studies, agricultural economics, agricultural education, agricultural engineering, agricultural mechanization, agricultural sciences, agronomy/crop science, aircraft pilot (professional), animal sciences, architectural engineering technology, art, aviation/airway science, biochemistry, biological and physical sciences, biology, botany, business administration, chemical engineering, chemistry, civil engineering, clothing/apparel/textile studies, communications, computer engineering, computer/information sciences, design/visual communications, early childhood education, economics, education, electrical/electronic engineering technology, electrical/electronics engineering, elementary education, engineering, English, entomology, food sciences, foreign languages/literatures, forestry, geology, history, home economics, horticulture science, hotel and restaurant management, humanities, individual/family development, industrial arts education, industrial engineering, industrial technology, interdisciplinary studies, landscape architecture, materials engineering, mathematical statistics, mathematics, mechanical drafting, mechanical engineering, medical technology, natural resources conservation, nuclear engineering, nursing, nutrition studies, operations management, pharmacy, philosophy, physical education, physical sciences, physics, political science, (pre)medicine, (pre)veterinary studies, psychology, robotics technology, social sciences, sociology, speech-language pathology/audiology, surveying, theater arts/drama, trade and industrial education, veterinarian assistant, wildlife management.

Quincy University

Accounting, art, art education, arts management, athletic training/sports medicine, biology, business administration, business marketing and marketing management, chemistry, communications, computer science, criminal justice/law enforcement administration, elementary education, English, environmental science, finance, fine/studio arts, history, humanities, information sciences/systems, interdisciplinary studies, journalism, mathematics, medical technology, music, music business management and merchandising, music education, nursing, philosophy, physical education, political science, (pre)dentistry, (pre)medicine, (pre)veterinary studies, psychology, public relations, radio/television broadcasting, social work, sociology, special education, sport/fitness administration, theology.

Randolph-Macon Woman's College

Art, art history, biology, chemistry, classics, creative writing, dance, economics, English, fine/studio arts, French, German, Greek (Ancient and Medieval), history, international relations, Latin (Ancient and Medieval), mass communications, mathematics, museum studies, music, music (voice and choral/opera performance), music history, philosophy, physics, political science, psychology, religious studies, Russian/Slavic area studies, sociology, Spanish, theater arts/drama.

Reed College

American studies, anthropology, art, biochemistry, biology, chemistry, Chinese, classics, dance, economics, English, fine/studio arts, French, German, history, international relations, linguistics, literature, mathematics, music, philosophy, physics, political science, psychology, religious studies, Russian, sociology, Spanish, theater arts/drama.

Rensselaer Polytechnic Institute

Aerospace engineering, air science, applied mathematics, architecture, biochemistry, bioengineering, biological and physical sciences, biology, biophysics, business administration, chemical engineering, chemistry, civil engineering, computer engineering, computer science, computer/information sciences, economics, electrical/electronics engineering, engineering, engineering physics, engineering science, engineering/industrial management, environmental engineering, environmental science, geology, German, industrial engineering, information sciences/systems, interdisciplinary studies, management information systems/business data processing, mass communications, materials engineering, mathematics, mechanical engineering, military science, natural sciences, naval science, nuclear engineering, philosophy, physical sciences, physics, (pre)dentistry, (pre)law, (pre)medicine, psychology, science education, science/technology and society, speech/rhetorical studies, systems engineering, technical writing, transportation engineering, water resources.

Rhode Island School of Design

Architecture, art, ceramic arts, clothing and textiles, drawing, fashion design/illustration, film studies, graphic design/commercial art/illustration, industrial design, interior design, landscape architecture, metal/jewelry arts, photography, printmaking, sculpture, textile arts.

Rhodes College

Anthropology, art, art history, biochemistry, biology, business administration, chemistry, classics, computer science, economics, English, fine/studio arts, French, German, Greek (Modern), history, interdisciplinary studies, international business, international economics, international relations, Latin (Ancient and Medieval), mathematics, music, philosophy, physics, political science, psychology, religious studies, Russian/Slavic area studies, sociology, Spanish, theater arts/drama, urban studies.

Rice University

Anthropology, architecture, art, art history, Asian studies, behavioral sciences, biochemistry, bioengineering, biology, business administration, chemical engineering, chemistry, civil engineering, classics, cognitive psychology and psycholinguistics, computer engineering, computer science, ecology, economics, electrical/electronics engineering, English, environmental engineering, evolutionary biology, French, geology, geophysics and seismology, German, history, linguistics, materials science, mathematical statistics, mathematics, mechanical engineering, music, neuroscience, philosophy, physical education, physics, political science, psychology, public policy analysis, religious studies, Russian/Slavic area studies, sociology, Spanish.

Ripon College

Anthropology, art, biochemistry, biology, business administration, chemistry, computer science, economics, education, elementary education, English, environmental science, French, German, history, interdisciplinary studies, Latin American studies, mathematics, music, music education, philosophy, physical education, physics, physiological psychology/psychobiology, political science, (pre)dentistry, (pre)law, (pre)medicine, (pre)veterinary studies, psychology, religious studies, Romance languages, secondary education, sociology, Spanish, speech/rhetorical studies, theater arts/drama.

Rochester Institute of Technology

Accounting, advertising, aerospace engineering, applied art, applied mathematics, art, automotive engineering technology, biochemistry, biological and physical sciences, biology, biotechnology research, business administration, business marketing and marketing management, ceramic arts, chemistry, civil engineering technology, commercial photography, communications, computer engineering, computer engineering technology, computer graphics, computer programming, computer science, computer/information sciences, craft/folk art, criminal justice studies, criminal justice/law enforcement administration, design/visual communications, diagnostic medical sonography, dietetics, economics, electrical/electronic engineering technology, electrical/electronics engineering, electromechanical technology, engineering, engineering science, engineering technology, environmental science, film/video production, finance, fine/studio arts, food products retailing, food sales operations, general studies, genetics, graphic design/commercial art/illustration, graphic/printing equipment, hospitality management, hospitality/recreation marketing, hotel and restaurant management, industrial design, industrial engineering, industrial technology, information sciences/systems, interdisciplinary studies, interior design, international business, international finance, liberal arts and studies, management information systems/business data processing, marketing research, mathematical statistics, mathematics, mathematics/computer science, mechanical engineering, mechanical engineering technology, medical illustrating, medical technology, metal/jewelry arts, natural resources management, nuclear medical technology, occupational safety/health technology, optometric/ophthalmic laboratory technician, photographic technology, photography, physician assistant, physics, polymer chemistry, (pre)dentistry, (pre)law, (pre)medicine, (pre)veterinary studies, psychology, publishing, sculpture, sign language interpretation, social work, telecommunications, tourism/travel marketing, travel-tourism management.

Rockhurst University

Accounting, biology, business administration, business marketing and marketing management, chemistry, computer programming, computer science, computer systems analysis, creative writing, cytotechnology, economics, education, elementary education, English, finance, French, history, human resources management, information sciences/systems, international relations, labor/personnel relations, management science, mass communications, mathematics, medical technology, nursing, philosophy, physics, political science, psychology, public relations, secondary education, sociology, Spanish, speech-language pathology, theater arts/drama, theology.

Rollins College

Anthropology, art, art history, biology, chemistry, classics, computer science, economics, education, elementary education, English, environmental science, fine/studio arts, French, German, history, interdisciplinary studies, international business, international relations, Latin American studies, mathematics, music, music history, philosophy, physics, political science, (pre)dentistry, (pre)law, (pre)medicine, (pre)veterinary studies, psychology, religious studies, sociology, Spanish, theater arts/drama.

Rose-Hulman Institute of Technology

Chemical engineering, chemistry, civil engineering, computer engineering, computer science, economics, electrical/electronics engineering, mathematics, mechanical engineering, optics, physics.

Rutgers, The State University of New Jersey, School of Engineering

Aerospace engineering, agricultural engineering, bioengineering, ceramic sciences/engineering, chemical engineering, civil engineering, computer engineering, electrical/electronics engineering, engineering, engineering science, industrial engineering, mechanical engineering.

Rutgers, The State University of New Jersey, College of Pharmacy

Pharmacy.

Rutgers, The State University of New Jersey, Cook College

Agricultural economics, agricultural education, agricultural engineering, agricultural sciences, animal sciences, architectural environmental design, atmospheric sciences, biochemistry, biology, biotechnology research, business economics, chemistry, communications, computer science, entomology, environmental education, environmental health, environmental science, evolutionary biology, exercise sciences, fish/game management, food sciences, forestry, geography, geology, horticulture science, interdisciplinary studies, journalism, landscape architecture, marine biology, mass communications, natural resources conservation, natural resources management, nutritional sciences, oceanography, physiology, plant sciences, (pre)dentistry, (pre)law, (pre)medicine, (pre)veterinary studies, public health, radiological science, water resources, wildlife management.

Rutgers, The State University of New Jersey, Douglass College

Accounting, African studies, American studies, anthropology, art, art history, atmospheric sciences, biology, biomedical science, biometrics, biotechnology research, business administration, business marketing and marketing management, cell biology, chemistry, Chinese, classics, communications, comparative literature, computer science, dance, East Asian studies, Eastern European area studies, ecology, economics, English, environmental science, evolutionary biology, exercise sciences, finance, food sciences, foreign languages/literatures, French, genetics, geography, geology, German, Greek (Ancient and Medieval), Hispanic-American studies, history, human ecology, interdisciplinary studies, Italian, journalism, Judaic studies, labor/personnel relations, Latin (Ancient and Medieval), Latin American studies, linguistics, management science, marine biology, mass communications, mathematical statistics, mathematics, medical technology, medieval/renaissance studies, microbiology/bacteriology, Middle Eastern studies, molecular biology, music, nutritional sciences, philosophy, physics, physiology, political science, Portuguese, (pre)dentistry, (pre)law, (pre)medicine, psychology, public health, religious studies, Russian, Russian/Slavic area studies, sociology, Spanish, theater arts/drama, urban studies, women's studies.

Rutgers, The State University of New Jersey, Mason Gross School of the Arts

Art, ceramic arts, dance, drawing, film studies, graphic design/commercial art/illustration, jazz, music, music education, painting, photography, printmaking, sculpture, theater arts/drama.

Rutgers, The State University of New Jersey, Rutgers College

Accounting, African studies, American studies, anthropology, art, art history, biology, biomedical science, biometrics, business administration, business marketing and marketing management, cell biology, chemistry, Chinese, classics, communications, comparative literature, computer science, criminal justice/law enforcement administration, dance, East Asian studies, Eastern European area studies, ecology, economics, English, evolutionary biology, exercise sciences, finance, foreign languages/literatures, French, genetics, geography, geology, German, Greek (Ancient and Medieval), Hispanic-American studies, history, interdisciplinary studies, Italian, journalism, Judaic studies, labor/personnel relations, Latin (Ancient and Medieval), Latin American studies, linguistics, management science, marine biology, mass communications, mathematical statistics, mathematics, medieval/renaissance studies, microbiology/bacteriology, Middle Eastern studies, molecular biology, music, philosophy, physics, physiology, political science, Portuguese, (pre)dentistry, (pre)law, (pre)medicine, psychology, public health, religious studies, Russian, Russian/Slavic area studies, sociology, Spanish, theater arts/drama, urban studies, women's studies.

St. John's College (MD)

Interdisciplinary studies, liberal arts and studies, western civilization.

St. John's College (NM)

Classics, history of philosophy, liberal arts and studies, literature, western civilization.

Saint John's University (MN)

Accounting, art, art education, art history, biology, business administration, chemistry, classics, computer science, dietetics, economics, education, elementary education, English, fine/studio arts, forestry, French, German, history, humanities, mass communications, mathematics, mathematics/computer science, music, music education, natural sciences, nursing, nutrition science, occupational therapy, peace and conflict studies, philosophy, physical therapy, physics, political science, (pre)dentistry, (pre)law, (pre)medicine, (pre)pharmacy studies, (pre)theology, (pre)veterinary studies, psychology, religious education, secondary education, social sciences, social work, sociology, Spanish, theater arts/drama, theology.

Saint Joseph's University

Accounting, art, biology, business administration, business marketing and marketing management, chemistry, computer programming, computer science, criminal justice/law enforcement administration, economics, education, elementary education, English, environmental science, finance, food sales operations, French, German, health services administration, history, human services, humanities, interdisciplinary studies, international relations, labor/personnel relations, liberal arts and studies, management information systems/business data processing, mathematics, philosophy, physics, political science, psychology, public administration, purchasing/contracts management, secondary education, social sciences, sociology, Spanish, theology.

St. Lawrence University

Anthropology, art, art history, Asian studies, biology, biophysics, Canadian studies, chemistry, computer science, creative writing, ecology, economics, English, environmental science, foreign languages/literatures, French, geology, geophysics and seismology, German, history, mathematics, modern languages, music, philosophy, physics, political science, psychology, religious studies, sociology, Spanish, theater arts/drama.

St. Louis College of Pharmacy

Pharmacy.

Saint Louis University

Accounting, aerospace engineering, aerospace engineering technology, aircraft mechanic/airframe, aircraft pilot (professional), American studies, art history, atmospheric sciences, aviation management, bioengineering, biology, business, business administration, business economics, business marketing and marketing management, chemistry, classics, communications, computer science, computer/information sciences, corrections, criminal justice/law enforcement administration, early childhood education, earth sciences, economics, education, electrical/electronics engineering, elementary education, engineering physics, engineering/industrial management, English, environmental science, exercise sciences, finance, fine/studio arts, French, geology, geophysics and seismology, German, Greek (Modern), history, hospitality management, human resources management, humanities, international business, international relations, Latin (Ancient and Medieval), law enforcement/police science, management information systems/business data processing, management science, mathematics, mechanical engineering, medical technology, middle school education, modern languages, music, nuclear medical technology, nursing, nutrition studies, occupational therapy, organizational behavior, organizational psychology, philosophy, physician assistant, physics, political science, Portuguese, (pre)dentistry, (pre)law, (pre)medicine, (pre)veterinary studies, psychology, public relations, Russian, secondary education, social work, sociology, Spanish, special education, speech-language pathology, speech-language pathology/audiology, theater arts/drama, theology, transportation technologies, urban studies.

Saint Mary's College (IN)

Accounting, anthropology, applied mathematics, art, art education, biochemistry, biology, business administration, business education, business marketing and marketing management, chemistry, communications, creative writing, cytotechnology, economics, education, elementary education, English, finance, French, history, humanities, interdisciplinary studies, international business, literature, management information systems/business data processing, mathematics, mathematics/computer science, medical technology, modern languages, music, music (piano and organ performance), music (voice and choral/opera performance), music education, nursing, philosophy, political science, psychology, religious studies, social work, sociology, Spanish, theater arts/drama.

Saint Mary's College of California

Accounting, anthropology, art, art education, art history, biology, business administration, chemistry, dance, economics, education, engineering, English, French, German, Greek (Modern), health education, history, interdisciplinary studies, international business, international relations, Latin (Ancient and Medieval), liberal arts and studies, literature, mass communications, mathematics, modern languages, music, nursing, philosophy, physical education, physics, political science, (pre)dentistry, (pre)law, (pre)medicine, (pre)veterinary studies, psychology, religious studies, secondary education, sociology, Spanish, theater arts/drama, theology, women's studies.

St. Mary's College of Maryland

Anthropology, art, biology, business economics, chemistry, computer science, economics, educational psychology, English, history, interdisciplinary studies, mathematics, modern languages, music, natural sciences, philosophy, physics, political science, psychology, public policy analysis, religious studies, sociology, theater arts/drama.

St. Norbert College

Accounting, art, biological and physical sciences, biology, business, business computer programming, chemistry, communications, economics, elementary education, English, French, geology, German, graphic design/commercial art/illustration, history, humanities, interdisciplinary studies, international business, international relations, management information systems/business data processing, mathematics, mathematics/computer science, medical technology, music, music education, philosophy, physics, political science, (pre)dentistry, (pre)engineering, (pre)law, (pre)medicine, (pre)veterinary studies, psychology, religious studies, sociology, Spanish.

St. Olaf College

African-American (black) studies, American studies, art, art education, art history, Asian studies, biology, chemistry, classics, cultural studies, dance, drama and dance education, economics, education, English, English education, family/consumer studies, foreign languages education, French, French language education, German, German language education, Greek (Modern), health science, Hispanic-American studies, history, Latin (Ancient and Medieval), mathematics, mathematics education, medieval/renaissance studies, music, music (piano and organ performance), music (voice and choral/opera performance), music education, nursing, philosophy, physical education, physics, political science, (pre)dentistry, (pre)law, (pre)medicine, (pre)veterinary studies, psychology, religious studies, Russian, Russian/Slavic area studies, sacred music, Scandinavian languages, science education, secondary education, social studies education, social work, sociology, Spanish, Spanish language education, speech education, speech/rhetorical studies, stringed instruments, theater arts/drama, urban studies, wind and percussion instruments, women's studies.

Samford University

Accounting, art, Asian studies, athletic training/sports medicine, biochemistry, biology, business administration, cartography, chemistry, classics, computer science, counseling psychology, dietetics, drawing, early childhood education, elementary education, engineering physics, English, environmental science, foreign languages/literatures, forestry sciences, French, geography, German, graphic design/commercial art/illustration, Greek (Ancient and Medieval), health/physical education, history, human resources management, individual/family development, interior design, international relations, journalism, Latin (Ancient and Medieval), Latin American studies, marine biology, mathematics, music (general performance), music (piano and organ performance), music (voice and choral/opera performance), music education, music theory and composition, nursing, philosophy, physical education, physics, political science, (pre)dentistry, (pre)law, (pre)medicine, (pre)pharmacy studies, (pre)veterinary studies, psychology, public administration, religious education, religious studies, sacred music, science education, social science education, sociology, Spanish, speech education, speech/rhetorical studies, theater arts/drama.

San Francisco Conservatory of Music

Music, music (general performance), music (piano and organ performance), music (voice and choral/opera performance), stringed instruments, wind and percussion instruments.

Santa Clara University

Accounting, anthropology, art, art history, biological and physical sciences, biology, business administration, business economics, business marketing and marketing management, chemistry, civil engineering, classics, communications, computer engineering, computer science, economics, electrical/electronics engineering, engineering, engineering physics, English, finance, French, Greek (Ancient and Medieval), history, interdisciplinary studies, Italian, Latin (Ancient and Medieval), liberal arts and studies, management information systems/business data processing, mathematics, mechanical engineering, music, philosophy, physics, political science, psychology, religious studies, sociology, Spanish, theater arts/drama.

Sarah Lawrence College

African-American (black) studies, American studies, anthropology, art, art history, Asian studies, biological and physical sciences, biology, chemistry, classics, comparative literature, computer science, creative writing, dance, developmental/child psychology, drawing, early childhood education, Eastern European area studies, ecology, economics, education, English, environmental science, European studies, film studies, film/video production, fine/studio arts, French, genetics, geology, German, history, humanities, individual/family development, interdisciplinary studies, international relations, Italian, Latin (Ancient and Medieval), Latin American studies, liberal arts and studies, literature, marine biology, mathematics, modern languages, music, music (piano and organ performance), music (voice and choral/opera performance), music history, natural sciences, philosophy, photography, physics, political science, (pre)dentistry, (pre)law, (pre)medicine, psychology, public policy analysis, religious studies, Romance languages, Russian, sculpture, social sciences, sociology, Spanish, stringed instruments, theater arts/drama, urban studies, western civilization, wind and percussion instruments, women's studies.

Scripps College

African-American (black) studies, American studies, anthropology, art, art history, Asian studies, Asian-American studies, biochemistry, biology, chemistry, Chinese, classics, computer science, dance, East Asian studies, economics, English, environmental science, European studies, fine/studio arts, foreign languages/literatures, French, geology, German, Hispanic-American studies, history, international relations, Italian, Japanese, Judaic studies, Latin (Ancient and Medieval), Latin

American studies, law and legal studies, linguistics, mathematics, Mexican-American studies, modern languages, molecular biology, music, neuroscience, philosophy, physics, physiological psychology/psychobiology, political science, psychology, religious studies, Russian, science/technology and society, sociology, Spanish, theater arts/drama, women's studies.

Shepherd College

Accounting, art, biology, business administration, chemistry, child care/development, computer science, criminal justice studies, culinary arts, design/visual communications, economics, electrical/electronic engineering technology, elementary education, engineering, English, environmental science, family/consumer studies, fashion merchandising, fire science, history, information sciences/systems, liberal arts and studies, mass communications, mathematics, music, nursing, occupational safety/health technology, photography, political science, psychology, recreation and leisure studies, secondary education, social work, sociology.

Siena College

Accounting, American studies, biology, business economics, business marketing and marketing management, chemistry, classics, computer science, economics, English, environmental science, finance, French, history, mathematics, philosophy, physics, political science, (pre)dentistry, (pre)law, (pre)medicine, psychology, religious studies, secondary education, social work, sociology, Spanish.

Simon's Rock College of Bard

Acting/directing, African-American (black) studies, agricultural business, American studies, anthropology, applied mathematics, art history, Asian studies, biology, ceramic arts, chemistry, cognitive psychology and psycholinguistics, computer graphics, computer science, creative writing, cultural studies, dance, developmental/child psychology, drawing, ecology, environmental science, European studies, fine/studio arts, foreign languages/literatures, French, geography, geology, German, interdisciplinary studies, jazz, Latin American studies, liberal arts and studies, literature, mathematics, metal/jewelry arts, music, music theory and composition, natural sciences, painting, philosophy, photography, physics, play/screenwriting, political science, (pre)law, (pre)medicine, printmaking, psychology, religious studies, sculpture, Spanish, theater arts/drama, visual/performing arts, women's studies.

Simpson College

Accounting, advertising, art, art education, biochemistry, biological and physical sciences, biology, business administration, business communications, chemistry, computer management, computer science, criminal justice/law enforcement administration, early childhood education, economics, education, elementary education, English, environmental biology, French, German, graphic design/commercial art/illustration, history, information sciences/systems, international business, international relations, mass communications, mathematics, medical technology, music, music (general performance), music education, philosophy, physical education, physical therapy, political science, (pre)dentistry, (pre)law, (pre)medicine, (pre)veterinary studies, psychology, religious studies, secondary education, social sciences, sociology, Spanish, speech/rhetorical studies, sport/fitness administration, theater arts/drama.

Skidmore College

American studies, anthropology, art, art history, Asian studies, biochemistry, biology, business administration, business economics, chemistry, classics, computer science, creative writing, dance, economics, elementary education, English, exercise sciences, fine/studio arts, French, geology, German, history, liberal arts and studies, literature, mathematics, music, philosophy, physics, political science, (pre)dentistry, (pre)medicine, (pre)veterinary studies, psychology, religious studies, social work, sociology, Spanish, theater arts/drama, women's studies.

Smith College

African-American (black) studies, American studies, anthropology, architecture, art, art history, astronomy, biochemistry, biology, chemistry, classics, comparative literature, computer science, dance, East Asian studies, economics, education, English, fine/studio arts, French, geology, German, Greek (Ancient and Medieval), history, interdisciplinary studies, Italian, Latin (Ancient and Medieval), Latin American studies, mathematics, medieval/renaissance studies, Middle Eastern studies, music, neuroscience, philosophy, physics, political science, Portuguese, psychology, religious studies, Russian, Russian/Slavic area studies, sociology, Spanish, theater arts/drama, women's studies.

South Dakota School of Mines and Technology

Chemical engineering, chemistry, civil engineering, computer engineering, computer science, electrical/electronics engineering, environmental engineering, geological engineering, geology, industrial engineering, interdisciplinary studies, mathematics, mechanical engineering, metallurgical engineering, mining/mineral engineering, paleontology, physics.

Southern Methodist University

Accounting, advertising, African-American (black) studies, anthropology, applied economics, art history, biochemistry, biology, broadcast journalism, business administration, business marketing and marketing management, chemistry, computer engineering, computer science, creative writing, dance, economics, electrical/electronics engineering, English, environmental engineering, environmental science, European studies, film studies, finance, fine/studio arts, foreign languages/literatures, French, geology, geophysics and seismology, German, history, humanities, international relations, journalism, Latin American studies, management information systems/business data processing, management science, mathematical statistics, mathematics, mechanical engineering, medieval/renaissance studies, Mexican-American studies, music, music (general performance), music (piano and organ performance), music education, music theory and composition, music therapy, organizational behavior, philosophy, physics, political science, psychology, public policy analysis, public relations, quantitative economics, radio/television broadcasting, real estate, religious studies, Russian, Russian/Slavic area studies, social sciences, sociology, Spanish, theater arts/drama.

Southwestern University

Accounting, American studies, animal sciences, art, art education, art history, biology, business administration, chemistry, computer science, economics, English, experimental psychology, fine/studio arts, French, German, history, international rela-

tions, literature, mass communications, mathematics, modern languages, music, music (piano and organ performance), music education, music history, philosophy, physical education, physics, political science, psychology, religious studies, sacred music, social sciences, sociology, Spanish, theater arts/drama, women's studies.

Spelman College

Art, biochemistry, biology, chemistry, computer science, developmental/child psychology, economics, engineering, English, French, history, mathematics, music, natural sciences, philosophy, physics, political science, psychology, religious studies, sociology, Spanish, theater arts/drama, women's studies.

Stanford University

African studies, African-American (black) studies, American studies, anthropology, art, Asian studies, biology, chemical engineering, chemistry, Chinese, civil engineering, classics, communications, comparative literature, computer science, earth sciences, East Asian studies, economics, electrical/electronics engineering, engineering, English, environmental engineering, environmental science, French, geology, geophysics and seismology, German, history, humanities, industrial engineering, interdisciplinary studies, international relations, Italian, Japanese, Latin American studies, linguistics, materials engineering, materials science, mathematics, mathematics/computer science, mechanical engineering, Mexican-American studies, music, Native American studies, petroleum engineering, philosophy, physics, political science, psychology, public policy analysis, religious studies, science/technology and society, Slavic languages, sociology, Spanish, systems science and theory, theater arts/drama, urban studies, women's studies.

State University of New York at Albany

Accounting, actuarial science, African-American (black) studies, anthropology, applied mathematics, art, art history, Asian studies, atmospheric sciences, biochemistry, biology, business administration, chemistry, Chinese, classics, computer science, computer/information sciences, criminal justice/law enforcement administration, earth sciences, East Asian studies, Eastern European area studies, economics, English, French, geography, geology, Hispanic-American studies, history, information sciences/systems, interdisciplinary studies, Italian, Japanese, Judaic studies, Latin (Ancient and Medieval), Latin American studies, linguistics, mass communications, mathematics, medical technology, medieval/renaissance studies, molecular biology, music, philosophy, physics, political science, psychology, public policy analysis, religious studies, Romance languages, Russian, Russian/Slavic area studies, secondary education, Slavic languages, social work, sociology, Spanish, speech/rhetorical studies, theater arts/drama, urban studies, women's studies.

State University of New York at Binghamton

Accounting, African studies, African-American (black) studies, anthropology, Arabic, art, art history, biochemistry, biology, chemistry, classics, comparative literature, computer engineering, computer science, drawing, economics, electrical/electronics engineering, English, environmental science, film studies, fine/studio arts, French, geography, geology, German, Hebrew, history, industrial engineering, information sciences/systems, interdisciplinary studies, Italian, Judaic studies, Latin American studies, linguistics, literature, management science, mathematics, mathematics/computer science, mechanical engineering, medieval/renaissance studies, music, music (general performance), nursing, philosophy, physics, physiological psychology/psychobiology, political science, (pre)law, psychology, sociology, Spanish, theater arts/drama.

State University of New York at Buffalo

Accounting, aerospace engineering, African-American (black) studies, American studies, anthropology, architectural environmental design, architecture, art, art history, biochemistry, biology, biophysics, business administration, chemical engineering, chemistry, civil engineering, classics, communication disorders, computer engineering technology, computer science, economics, electrical/electronics engineering, engineering physics, English, exercise sciences, film studies, fine/studio arts, French, geography, geology, German, history, industrial engineering, Italian, linguistics, mass communications, mathematics, mechanical engineering, medical technology, medicinal/pharmaceutical chemistry, music, music (general performance), music education, Native American studies, nuclear medical technology, nursing, occupational therapy, pharmacy, pharmacy administration and pharmaceutics, philosophy, physical therapy, physics, political science, psychology, science education, social sciences, sociology, Spanish, speech-language pathology/audiology, theater arts/drama, women's studies.

State University of New York College at Geneseo

Accounting, African-American (black) studies, American studies, anthropology, art, art history, biochemistry, biology, biophysics, business administration, chemistry, communications, comparative literature, computer science, early childhood education, economics, education, elementary education, English, fine/studio arts, French, geochemistry, geography, geology, geophysics and seismology, history, international relations, mathematics, music, natural sciences, philosophy, physics, political science, (pre)dentistry, (pre)law, (pre)medicine, (pre)veterinary studies, psychology, sociology, Spanish, special education, speech therapy, speech-language pathology/audiology, theater arts/drama.

State University of New York College of Environmental Science and Forestry

Architectural environmental design, biochemistry, biological and physical sciences, biology, biology education, biotechnology research, botany, chemical engineering, chemistry, chemistry education, city/community/regional planning, construction engineering, ecology, entomology, environmental biology, environmental education, environmental engineering, environmental science, fish/game management, fishing sciences and management, forest engineering, forest management, forestry, land use management, landscape architecture, natural resources conservation, natural resources management, plant pathology, plant physiology, plant protection, plant sciences, polymer chemistry, (pre)dentistry, (pre)law, (pre)medicine, (pre)veterinary studies, recreation and leisure studies, science education, water resources, water resources engineering, wildlife biology, wildlife management, wood science/paper technology, zoology.

State University of New York Maritime College

Atmospheric sciences, business administration, electrical/electronics engineering, environmental science, humanities, marine science, maritime science, mechanical engineering, naval architecture/marine engineering, naval science, oceanography.

Stetson University

Accounting, American studies, art, athletic training/sports medicine, biochemistry, biology, business administration, business economics, business marketing and marketing management, chemistry, computer graphics, computer science, economics, education, elementary education, English, environmental science, exercise sciences, finance, French, geography, German, history, humanities, information sciences/systems, international business, international relations, Latin American studies, marine biology, mass communications, mathematics, medical technology, molecular biology, music, music (general performance), music (piano and organ performance), music (voice and choral/opera performance), music education, music theory and composition, philosophy, physics, political science, (pre)dentistry, (pre)law, (pre)medicine, (pre)veterinary studies, psychology, religious studies, Russian/Slavic area studies, sacred music, social sciences, sociology, Spanish, speech/rhetorical studies, sport/fitness administration, theater arts/drama.

Stevens Institute of Technology

Biochemistry, bioengineering, chemical engineering, chemistry, civil engineering, computer engineering, computer science, electrical/electronics engineering, engineering/industrial management, English, environmental engineering, history, humanities, mathematical statistics, mechanical engineering, philosophy, physics, (pre)dentistry, (pre)law, (pre)medicine.

Susquehanna University

Accounting, art, art history, biochemistry, biology, broadcast journalism, business administration, business communications, business economics, business marketing and marketing management, chemistry, communications, computer science, creative writing, early childhood education, economics, elementary education, English, environmental science, finance, French, German, history, human resources management, information sciences/systems, international relations, journalism, mass communications, mathematics, music, music (piano and organ performance), music (voice and choral/opera performance), music business management and merchandising, music education, music theory and composition, musical instrument technology, philosophy, physics, political science, (pre)dentistry, (pre)law, (pre)medicine, (pre)veterinary studies, psychology, public relations, religious studies, sacred music, secondary education, sociology, Spanish, speech/rhetorical studies, stringed instruments, theater arts/drama, wind and percussion instruments.

Swarthmore College

Anthropology, art history, Asian studies, astronomy, astrophysics, biochemistry, biology, chemistry, Chinese, classics, comparative literature, computer science, dance, economics, education, engineering, English, fine/studio arts, French, German, Greek (Ancient and Medieval), history, Latin (Ancient and Medieval), linguistics, mathematics, mathematics/computer science, medieval/renaissance studies, music, philosophy, physics, physiological psychology/psychobiology, political science, psychology, religious studies, Russian, Spanish, theater arts/drama.

Sweet Briar College

Anthropology, art history, biochemistry, biology, chemistry, classics, computer science, creative writing, dance, economics, English, environmental science, fine/studio arts, French, German, Greek (Ancient and Medieval), history, interdisciplinary studies, international relations, Italian, Latin (Ancient and Medieval), mathematics, modern languages, music, philosophy, physics, political science, psychology, religious studies, sociology, Spanish, theater arts/drama.

Syracuse University

Accounting, advertising, aerospace engineering, African-American (black) studies, American studies, anthropology, applied art, architectural environmental design, architecture, art, art education, art history, behavioral sciences, biochemistry, bioengineering, biology, broadcast journalism, business administration, business marketing and marketing management, ceramic arts, chemical engineering, chemistry, child care/development, civil engineering, classics, clothing and textiles, communication disorders, computer engineering, computer graphics, computer science, computer/information sciences, consumer services, design/visual communications, dietetics, early childhood education, economics, education, electrical/electronics engineering, elementary education, engineering physics, English, English education, enterprise management, entrepreneurship, environmental engineering, environmental science, exercise sciences, family studies, family/community studies, fashion design/illustration, film studies, film/video production, finance, fine/studio arts, food products retailing, foreign languages/literatures, French, geography, geology, German, graphic design/commercial art/illustration, Greek (Modern), health education, health science, history, hospitality management, individual/family development, industrial design, information sciences/systems, interdisciplinary studies, interior design, international relations, Italian, journalism, Latin (Ancient and Medieval), Latin American studies, linguistics, literature, mathematics, mathematics education, mechanical engineering, medieval/renaissance studies, metal/jewelry arts, middle school education, modern languages, music, music (general performance), music (piano and organ performance), music (voice and choral/opera performance), music business management and merchandising, music education, music theory and composition, natural sciences, nursing, nutrition science, nutrition studies, painting, philosophy, photography, physical education, physics, political science, (pre)dentistry, (pre)law, (pre)medicine, (pre)veterinary studies, printmaking, psychology, public policy analysis, public relations, radio/television broadcasting, religious studies, retail management, Russian, Russian/Slavic area studies, science education, sculpture, secondary education, social sciences, social studies education, social work, sociology, Spanish, special education, speech-language pathology/audiology, speech/rhetorical studies, stringed instruments, telecommunications, textile arts, theater arts/drama, theater design, wind and percussion instruments, women's studies.

Taylor University

Accounting, art, art education, athletic training/sports medicine, biblical languages/literatures, biblical studies, biology, business administration, chemistry, computer engineering, computer programming, computer science, creative writing, early childhood education, economics, education, elementary education, engineering physics, English, environmental biology, environmental science, French, graphic design/commercial art/illustration, history, information sciences/systems, international business, international economics, international relations, literature, management information systems/business data processing, mass communications, mathematics, medical technology, middle school education, music, music (piano and organ performance), music (voice and choral/opera performance), music business management and merchandising, music education, natural sciences, philosophy, physical education, physics, political science, (pre)dentistry, (pre)law, (pre)medicine, (pre)veterinary studies, psychology, recreation and leisure studies, religious education, religious studies, sacred music, science education, secondary education, social sciences, social work, sociology, Spanish, sport/fitness administration, theater arts/drama, theology.

Texas A&M University

Accounting, aerospace engineering, agribusiness, agricultural and food products processing, agricultural economics, agricultural engineering, agricultural sciences, agronomy/crop science, animal sciences, anthropology, applied mathematics, architectural environmental design, atmospheric sciences, biochemistry, bioengineering, biological technology, biology, biomedical science, botany, business administration, business marketing and marketing management, cell biology, chemical engineering, chemistry, civil engineering, communications, computer engineering, computer science, construction technology, dairy science, earth sciences, economics, electrical/electronics engineering, engineering technology, engineering/industrial management, English, entomology, environmental engineering, environmental science, finance, fish/game management, fishing sciences and management, food sciences, forestry, French, genetics, geography, geology, geophysics and seismology, German, health education, history, horticulture science, industrial arts education, industrial engineering, interdisciplinary studies, international relations, journalism, landscape architecture, management information systems/business data processing, marine biology, marine science, marine technology, maritime science, mathematics, mechanical engineering, microbiology/bacteriology, molecular biology, natural resources management, naval architecture/marine engineering, nuclear engineering, nutrition science, nutritional sciences, ocean engineering, petroleum engineering, philosophy, physical education, physics, plant sciences, political science, poultry science, psychology, range management, recreation/leisure facilities management, Russian, sociology, Spanish, speech/rhetorical studies, theater arts/drama, travel-tourism management, veterinary sciences, wildlife management, zoology.

Thomas Aquinas College

Interdisciplinary studies, liberal arts and studies, western civilization.

Transylvania University

Accounting, anthropology, art, art education, biology, chemistry, computer science, economics, elementary education, English, enterprise management, exercise sciences, fine/studio arts, French, history, mathematics, middle school education, music (general performance), music education, philosophy, physical education, physics, political science, psychology, religious studies, secondary education, sociology, Spanish, theater arts/drama.

Trinity College (CT)

American studies, anthropology, art, art history, biochemistry, bioengineering, biology, chemistry, classics, comparative literature, computer science, creative writing, dance, economics, education, engineering, English, fine/studio arts, French, German, history, interdisciplinary studies, international relations, Italian, Judaic studies, mathematics, mechanical engineering, modern languages, music, neuroscience, philosophy, physics, political science, psychology, public policy analysis, religious studies, Russian, sociology, Spanish, theater arts/drama, women's studies.

Trinity University

Accounting, acting/directing, anthropology, art, art history, Asian studies, biochemistry, biology, business administration, business marketing and marketing management, chemistry, Chinese, classics, communications, computer/information sciences, economics, engineering science, English, European studies, finance, French, geology, German, history, humanities, international business, Latin American studies, management science, mathematics, music, music (general performance), music (voice and choral/opera performance), music theory and composition, philosophy, physics, political science, (pre)dentistry, (pre)law, (pre)medicine, (pre)veterinary studies, psychology, religious studies, Russian, sociology, Spanish, speech/rhetorical studies, theater arts/drama, theater design, urban studies.

Truman State University

Accounting, agricultural economics, agricultural sciences, agronomy/crop science, animal sciences, applied art, art, art history, biology, business administration, chemistry, classics, communication disorders, computer science, criminal justice/law enforcement administration, economics, English, equestrian studies, exercise sciences, finance, fine/studio arts, French, German, graphic design/commercial art/illustration, health science, history, journalism, law enforcement/police science, mass communications, mathematics, music, music (piano and organ performance), music (voice and choral/opera performance), nursing, philosophy, physics, political science, (pre)dentistry, (pre)law, (pre)medicine, (pre)veterinary studies, psychology, public health, religious studies, Russian, sociology, Spanish, speech/rhetorical studies, theater arts/drama.

Tufts University

African-American (black) studies, American studies, anthropology, archaeology, architectural engineering, art history, Asian studies, astronomy, behavioral sciences, biology, chemical engineering, chemistry, child care/development, Chinese, civil engineering, classics, computer engineering, computer science, developmental/child psychology, early childhood education, ecology, economics, electrical/electronics engineering, elementary education, engineering, engineering design, engineering physics, engineering science, English, environmental engineering, environmental science, experimental psychology, French, geology, geophysical engineering, German, Greek (Modern), history, industrial engineering, international relations, Judaic studies, Latin (Ancient and Medieval), mathematics, mechanical engineering, mental health/rehabilitation, music, philosophy, physics, political science, psychology, public health, Romance languages, Russian, Russian/Slavic area

studies, secondary education, sociobiology, sociology, Southeast Asian studies, Spanish, special education, theater arts/drama, urban studies, women's studies.

Tulane University

Accounting, African studies, American studies, anthropology, architecture, art, art history, Asian studies, biochemistry, bioengineering, biology, business administration, business marketing and marketing management, cell biology, chemical engineering, chemistry, civil engineering, classics, cognitive psychology and psycholinguistics, computer engineering, computer science, computer/information sciences, earth sciences, ecology, economics, electrical/electronics engineering, engineering science, English, environmental biology, environmental engineering, environmental science, evolutionary biology, exercise sciences, finance, fine/studio arts, French, geology, German, Greek (Modern), Hispanic-American studies, history, information sciences/systems, international relations, Italian, Judaic studies, Latin (Ancient and Medieval), Latin American studies, liberal arts and studies, linguistics, mass communications, mathematics, mechanical engineering, medical illustrating, medieval/renaissance studies, molecular biology, music, paralegal/legal assistant, philosophy, physics, political science, Portuguese, psychology, religious studies, Russian, Russian/Slavic area studies, sociology, Spanish, sport/fitness administration, theater arts/drama, women's studies.

Union College (NY)

American studies, anthropology, biochemistry, biological and physical sciences, biology, biomedical science, chemistry, civil engineering, classics, computer/information sciences, economics, electrical/electronics engineering, English, fine/studio arts, foreign languages/literatures, geology, history, humanities, liberal arts and studies, mathematics, mechanical engineering, philosophy, physics, political science, psychology, social sciences, sociology.

Union University

Accounting, advertising, art, art education, athletic training/sports medicine, biblical languages/literatures, biblical studies, biological and physical sciences, biology, broadcast journalism, business administration, business economics, business education, business marketing and marketing management, chemistry, computer science, early childhood education, economics, education, elementary education, English, family/community studies, finance, foreign languages/literatures, French, history, information sciences/systems, journalism, mass communications, mathematics, medical technology, music, music (piano and organ performance), music (voice and choral/opera performance), music business management and merchandising, music education, nursing, philosophy, physical education, physics, political science, (pre)dentistry, (pre)law, (pre)medicine, (pre)pharmacy studies, psychology, public relations, radio/television broadcasting, recreation/leisure facilities management, religious studies, sacred music, science education, secondary education, social work, sociology, Spanish, special education, speech/rhetorical studies, sport/fitness administration, teaching English as a second language, theater arts/drama, theology.

United States Air Force Academy

Aerospace engineering, area studies, atmospheric sciences, behavioral sciences, biochemistry, biological and physical sciences, biology, business administration, chemistry, civil engineering, computer science, economics, electrical/electronics engineering, engineering, engineering mechanics, engineering science, English, environmental engineering, geography, history, humanities, interdisciplinary studies, law and legal studies, materials science, mathematics, mechanical engineering, operations research, physics, political science, social sciences.

United States Coast Guard Academy
American government, civil engineering, electrical/electronics engineering, management science, marine science, mechanical engineering, naval architecture/marine engineering, operations research, political science.

United States Merchant Marine Academy
Engineering/industrial management, maritime science, naval architecture/marine engineering.

United States Military Academy
Aerospace engineering, American studies, applied mathematics, Arabic, behavioral sciences, biological and physical sciences, biology, business administration, chemical engineering, chemistry, Chinese, civil engineering, computer engineering, computer science, East Asian studies, Eastern European area studies, economics, electrical/electronics engineering, engineering, engineering physics, engineering/industrial management, environmental engineering, environmental science, European studies, French, geography, German, history, humanities, information sciences/systems, interdisciplinary studies, Latin American studies, literature, mathematics, mechanical engineering, Middle Eastern studies, military science, modern languages, nuclear engineering, operations research, philosophy, physics, political science, Portuguese, (pre)law, (pre)medicine, psychology, public policy analysis, Russian, Spanish, systems engineering.

United States Naval Academy
Aerospace engineering, chemistry, computer science, economics, electrical/electronics engineering, engineering, English, history, mathematics, mechanical engineering, naval architecture/marine engineering, ocean engineering, oceanography, physics, political science, quantitative economics, systems engineering.

The University of Alabama in Huntsville
Accounting, art, biology, business administration, business marketing and marketing management, chemical engineering, chemistry, civil engineering, computer engineering, computer/information sciences, electrical/electronics engineering, elementary education, English, finance, French, German, history, industrial engineering, management information systems/business data processing, mathematics, mechanical engineering, music, nursing, optics, philosophy, physics, political science, psychology, purchasing/contracts management, Russian/Slavic area studies, sociology, Spanish, speech/rhetorical studies.

The University of Arizona
Accounting, aerospace engineering, agricultural economics, agricultural education, agricultural engineering, agricultural mechanization, agricultural sciences, animal sciences, anthropology, architecture, art, art education, art history, astronomy, atmospheric sciences, biochemistry, biology, biology education, business, business economics, business marketing and marketing management, cell biology, chemical engineering, chemistry,

chemistry education, city/community/regional planning, civil engineering, classics, communication disorders, communications, computer engineering, computer/information sciences, consumer economics, creative writing, criminal justice/law enforcement administration, dance, drama and dance education, early childhood education, earth sciences, East Asian studies, ecology, economics, education, electrical/electronics engineering, elementary education, engineering physics, English, English education, enterprise management, environmental science, finance, fine/studio arts, foreign languages education, French, French language education, geography, geological engineering, geology, German, German language education, health education, health services administration, Hispanic-American studies, history, history education, home economics education, human resources management, humanities, individual/family development, industrial engineering, interdisciplinary studies, Italian, journalism, Judaic studies, landscape architecture, Latin American studies, linguistics, management information systems/business data processing, materials science, mathematics, mathematics education, mechanical engineering, medical technology, microbiology/bacteriology, Middle Eastern studies, mining/mineral engineering, music, music (general performance), music education, nuclear engineering, nursing, nutritional sciences, operations management, philosophy, physical education, physics, physics education, physiology, plant sciences, political science, (pre)veterinary studies, psychology, public administration, radio/television broadcasting, range management, religious studies, Russian, science education, secondary education, social science education, social sciences, social studies education, sociology, soil sciences, Spanish, Spanish language education, special education, speech education, systems engineering, theater arts/drama, theater design, veterinary sciences, visual/performing arts, wildlife management, women's studies.

University of California, Berkeley
African-American (black) studies, American studies, anthropology, applied mathematics, architecture, art, art history, Asian studies, Asian-American studies, astrophysics, bioengineering, business administration, chemical engineering, chemistry, Chinese, civil engineering, classics, comparative literature, computer/information sciences, cultural studies, earth sciences, economics, electrical/electronics engineering, engineering, engineering physics, English, environmental engineering, environmental science, film/video production, forestry sciences, French, genetics, geography, geology, geophysics and seismology, German, Greek (Ancient and Medieval), Hispanic-American studies, history, industrial engineering, interdisciplinary studies, Italian, Japanese, landscape architecture, Latin (Ancient and Medieval), Latin American studies, law and legal studies, linguistics, mass communications, materials engineering, mathematical statistics, mathematics, mechanical engineering, Middle Eastern studies, molecular biology, music, Native American studies, natural resources conservation, natural resources management, nuclear engineering, nutritional sciences, peace and conflict studies, petroleum engineering, philosophy, physical sciences, physics, political science, psychology, religious studies, Scandinavian languages, Slavic languages, social sciences, social work, sociology, Southeast Asian studies, Spanish, speech/rhetorical studies, theater arts/drama, women's studies.

University of California, Davis

Aerospace engineering, African studies, African-American (black) studies, agricultural business, agricultural economics, agricultural education, agricultural engineering, American studies, animal sciences, anthropology, art, art history, atmospheric sciences, biochemistry, bioengineering, biology, botany, cell biology, chemical engineering, chemistry, Chinese, civil engineering, clothing/apparel/textile studies, comparative literature, computer engineering, design/visual communications, early childhood education, East Asian studies, economics, electrical/electronics engineering, engineering, English, entomology, environmental biology, food sciences, French, genetics, geology, German, Hispanic-American studies, history, horticulture science, individual/family development, information sciences/systems, international agriculture, international relations, Italian, Japanese, landscape architecture, linguistics, materials engineering, mathematical statistics, mathematics, mechanical engineering, Mexican-American studies, microbiology/bacteriology, music, Native American studies, natural resources conservation, natural resources management, nutrition science, philosophy, physical education, physics, physiology, political science, poultry science, psychology, range management, religious studies, Russian, sociology, Spanish, speech/rhetorical studies, theater arts/drama, women's studies, zoology.

University of California, Los Angeles

Aerospace engineering, African languages, African-American (black) studies, American literature, anthropology, applied art, applied mathematics, Arabic, art, art history, Asian-American studies, astrophysics, atmospheric sciences, biochemistry, biology, business economics, cell biology, chemical engineering, chemistry, Chinese, civil engineering, classics, cognitive psychology and psycholinguistics, communications, comparative literature, computer engineering, computer science, design/visual communications, earth sciences, East Asian studies, ecology, economics, electrical/electronics engineering, English, European studies, exercise sciences, film studies, French, geochemistry, geography, geological engineering, geology, geophysical engineering, German, Greek (Modern), Hebrew, history, international economics, international relations, Italian, Japanese, Judaic studies, Latin (Ancient and Medieval), Latin American studies, linguistics, marine biology, materials engineering, materials science, mathematics, mechanical engineering, Mexican-American studies, microbiology/bacteriology, Middle Eastern studies, molecular biology, music, musicology, neuroscience, nursing, philosophy, physics, physiological psychology/psychobiology, plant sciences, political science, Portuguese, psychology, radio/television broadcasting, religious studies, Russian, Russian/Slavic area studies, Scandinavian languages, Slavic languages, sociology, Southeast Asian studies, Spanish, theater arts/drama, women's studies.

University of California, Riverside

African-American (black) studies, anthropology, art history, Asian studies, Asian-American studies, biochemistry, biology, biomedical science, botany, business administration, business economics, chemical engineering, chemistry, Chinese, classics, comparative literature, computer science, creative writing, cultural studies, dance, economics, electrical/electronics engineering, English, entomology, environmental engineering, environmental science, fine/studio arts, French, geography,

geology, geophysics and seismology, German, history, humanities, Latin American studies, liberal arts and studies, linguistics, mathematical statistics, mathematics, mechanical engineering, Mexican-American studies, music, Native American studies, neuroscience, philosophy, physical sciences, physics, physiological psychology/psychobiology, political science, (pre)law, psychology, public administration, religious studies, Russian, Russian/Slavic area studies, social sciences, sociology, Spanish, theater arts/drama, women's studies.

University of California, San Diego

Aerospace engineering, anthropology, applied mathematics, archaeology, art, art history, biochemistry, bioengineering, biology, biophysics, biotechnology research, cell biology, chemical and atomic/molecular physics, chemical engineering, chemistry, chemistry education, Chinese, classics, computer engineering, computer science, creative writing, cultural studies, dance, earth sciences, ecology, economics, electrical/electronics engineering, engineering, engineering physics, engineering science, English, environmental science, film studies, fine/studio arts, foreign languages/literatures, French, German, history, interdisciplinary studies, intermedia, Italian, Japanese, Judaic studies, Latin American studies, linguistics, literature, management science, mass communications, mathematics, mathematics education, mechanical engineering, medicinal/pharmaceutical chemistry, microbiology/bacteriology, molecular biology, music, music history, natural resources management, philosophy, physics, physics education, physiology, psychology, quantitative economics, religious studies, Russian, sociology, Spanish, structural engineering, systems engineering, theater arts/drama, urban studies, women's studies.

University of California, Santa Barbara

African-American (black) studies, anthropology, applied history, art history, Asian studies, Asian-American studies, biochemistry, biology, biopsychology, business economics, cell biology, chemical engineering, chemistry, Chinese, classics, communications, comparative literature, computer science, dance, ecology, economics, electrical/electronics engineering, English, environmental science, film studies, fine/studio arts, French, geography, geology, geophysics and seismology, German, history, interdisciplinary studies, Islamic studies, Italian, Japanese, Latin American studies, law and legal studies, linguistics, marine biology, mathematical statistics, mathematics, mechanical engineering, medieval/renaissance studies, Mexican-American studies, microbiology/bacteriology, Middle Eastern studies, molecular biology, music, pharmacology, philosophy, physics, physiology, political science, Portuguese, psychology, religious studies, Slavic languages, sociology, Spanish, theater arts/drama, women's studies, zoology.

University of California, Santa Cruz

American studies, anthropology, art, art history, biochemistry, biology, botany, business economics, cell biology, chemistry, Chinese, computer engineering, computer science, drawing, earth sciences, East Asian studies, ecology, economics, electrical/electronics engineering, environmental science, family/community studies, film studies, film/video production, foreign languages/literatures, French, geology, geophysics and seismology, German, history, information sciences/systems, international economics, Italian, Japanese, Latin American studies, law and legal studies, linguistics, literature, marine biology, mathematics, molecular biology, music, philosophy, photography, physics, physiological psychology/psychobiology, political science, printmaking, psychology, religious studies, Russian, Russian/Slavic area studies, sculpture, sociology, South Asian studies, Southeast Asian studies, Spanish, theater arts/drama, women's studies.

University of Chicago

African studies, African-American (black) studies, American studies, anthropology, applied mathematics, Arabic, art, art history, Asian studies, behavioral sciences, biblical languages/literatures, biochemistry, biology, chemistry, Chinese, classics, computer science, creative writing, East Asian studies, Eastern European area studies, economics, English, environmental science, film studies, fine/studio arts, French, geography, geophysics and seismology, German, Greek (Ancient and Medieval), history, history of science and technology, humanities, interdisciplinary studies, Italian, Japanese, Judaic studies, Latin (Ancient and Medieval), Latin American studies, liberal arts and studies, linguistics, mathematical statistics, mathematics, medieval/renaissance studies, Middle Eastern studies, modern languages, music, music history, philosophy, physics, political science, psychology, public policy analysis, religious studies, Romance languages, Russian, Russian/Slavic area studies, Slavic languages, social sciences, sociology, South Asian studies, Southeast Asian studies, Spanish.

University of Cincinnati

Accounting, aerospace engineering, African-American (black) studies, anthropology, architectural engineering, architectural engineering technology, architecture, art, art education, art history, Asian studies, biochemistry, biological and physical sciences, biology, broadcast journalism, business administration, business marketing and marketing management, chemical engineering, chemical engineering technology, chemistry, child care/development, city/community/regional planning, civil engineering, civil engineering technology, classics, comparative literature, computer engineering, computer engineering technology, computer management, computer programming, computer science, computer/information sciences, construction engineering, construction management, construction technology, court reporting, criminal justice/law enforcement administration, dance, data processing technology, drafting, early childhood education, economics, education, electrical/electronic engineering technology, electrical/electronics engineering, elementary education, energy management technology, engineering, engineering mechanics, engineering science, English, environmental science, environmental technology, fashion design/illustration, finance, fire protection/safety technology, fire science, French, geography, geology, German, graphic design/commercial art/illustration, health education, health services administration, heating/air conditioning/refrigeration, history, human services, humanities, industrial arts, industrial design, industrial engineering, industrial radiologic technology, industrial technology, information sciences/systems, insurance and risk management, interior design, international relations, jazz, Judaic studies, Latin American studies, law enforcement/police science, legal administrative assistant, liberal arts and studies, linguistics, literature, management information systems/business data processing, mass communications, mathematics, mechanical engineering, mechanical engineering technology, medical administrative assistant, medical laboratory technician, medical laboratory technologies, medical technology, metallurgical engineering, metallurgical technology, microbiology/bacteriology, music, music (piano and organ performance), music (voice and choral/opera performance), music education, music history, natural sciences, nuclear engineering, nuclear medical technology, nursing, nutrition science, occupational safety/health technology, operations research, paralegal/legal assistant, pharmacology, pharmacy, philosophy, physical education, physical therapy, physics, political science, (pre)law, (pre)medicine, (pre)veterinary studies, psychology, public health, public policy analysis, quality control technology, radio/television broadcasting, real estate, robotics, Romance languages, safety and security technology, science education, secondary education, secretarial science, social sciences, social work, sociology, Spanish, special education, speech-language pathology/audiology, stringed instruments, theater arts/drama, transportation technologies, urban studies, wind and percussion instruments.

University of Colorado at Boulder

Accounting, advertising, aerospace engineering, American studies, anthropology, applied mathematics, architectural engineering, architectural environmental design, art, Asian studies, biochemistry, biology, broadcast journalism, business administration, business marketing and marketing management, cell biology, chemical engineering, chemistry, Chinese, civil engineering, classics, communication disorders, communications, computer engineering, computer science, computer/information sciences, cultural studies, dance, East Asian studies, Eastern European area studies, economics, electrical/electronics engineering, engineering physics, English, environmental engineering, environmental science, film studies, finance, fine/studio arts, French, geography, geology, German, history, humanities, international relations, Italian, Japanese, journalism, Latin American studies, linguistics, management information systems/business data processing, mass communications, mathematics, mechanical engineering, molecular biology, music, music education, philosophy, physics, political science, psychology, religious studies, Russian/Slavic area studies, sociology, Spanish, theater arts/drama, women's studies.

University of Connecticut

Accounting, acting/directing, actuarial science, agricultural economics, agricultural education, agricultural sciences, agronomy/crop science, animal sciences, anthropology, applied mathematics, art history, biology, biophysics, business administration, business marketing and marketing management, cell biology, chemical engineering, chemistry, civil engineering, classics, communications, computer engineering, cytotechnology, dietetics, ecology, economics, education, electrical/electronics engineering, elementary education, English, environmental science, family resource management studies, finance, fine/studio arts, French, geography, geology, German, health services administration, history, horticulture science, individual/family development, industrial engineering, insurance and risk management, interdisciplinary studies, Italian, journalism, landscape architecture, Latin American studies, liberal arts and studies, linguistics, management information systems/business data processing, materials engineering, mathematical statistics, mathematics, mechanical engineering, medical technology, Middle Eastern studies, military science, molecular biology, music, music education, natural resources conservation, natural resources management, nursing, nutritional sciences, painting, pathology, pharmacy, philosophy, physical education, physical therapy, physics, physiology, political science, Portuguese, printmaking, psychology, real estate, recreation/leisure facilities management, Russian/Slavic area studies, sociology, Spanish, special education, theater arts/drama, theater design, urban studies, women's studies.

University of Dallas

Art, art education, art history, biochemistry, biology, ceramic arts, chemistry, classics, computer science, economics, education, elementary education, English, fine/studio arts, French, German, history, mathematics, painting, philosophy, physics, political science, (pre)dentistry, (pre)law, (pre)medicine, (pre)theology, printmaking, psychology, sculpture, secondary education, Spanish, theater arts/drama, theology.

University of Dayton

Accounting, American studies, applied art, art, art education, art history, biochemistry, biology, broadcast journalism, business administration, business economics, business marketing and marketing management, chemical engineering, chemistry, civil engineering, computer engineering, computer engineering technology, computer science, criminal justice/law enforcement administration, dietetics, early childhood education, economics, education, electrical/electronic engineering technology, electrical/electronics engineering, elementary education, English, environmental biology, environmental science, exercise sciences, finance, fine/studio arts, French, general studies, geology, German, graphic design/commercial art/illustration, health education, history, industrial technology, information sciences/systems, international business, international relations, journalism, management information systems/business data processing, mass communications, mathematics, mechanical engineering, mechanical engineering technology, music, music education, music therapy, nutrition science, philosophy, photography, physical education, physical sciences, physics, political science, (pre)dentistry, (pre)law, (pre)medicine, psychology, public relations, quantitative economics, radio/television broadcasting, religious education, religious studies, science education, secondary education, sociology, Spanish, special education, sport/fitness administration, theater arts/drama.

University of Delaware

Accounting, African-American (black) studies, agribusiness, agricultural business, agricultural economics, agricultural education, agricultural engineering, agricultural sciences, agronomy/crop science, animal sciences, anthropology, applied art, architectural history, art, art history, astronomy, astrophysics, athletic training/sports medicine, bilingual/bicultural education, biochemistry, biological technology, biology, biology education, biotechnology research, botany, business administration, business economics, business marketing and marketing management, chemical engineering, chemistry, chemistry education, child care/development, civil engineering, classics, communications, community services, comparative literature, computer engineering, computer science, computer/information sciences, consumer economics, criminal justice/law enforcement administration, developmental/child psychology, dietetics, early childhood education, East Asian studies, ecology, economics, education, electrical/electronics engineering, elementary education, engineering, English, English education, entomology,

environmental engineering, environmental science, environmental technology, exercise sciences, family/community studies, family/consumer studies, fashion design/illustration, fashion merchandising, film studies, finance, food sales operations, food sciences, foreign languages education, foreign languages/literatures, French, geography, geology, geophysics and seismology, German, graphic design/commercial art/illustration, health education, health/physical education, history, history education, horticulture science, hotel and restaurant management, individual/family development, international relations, Italian, journalism, Latin (Ancient and Medieval), Latin American studies, liberal arts and studies, linguistics, mass communications, mathematics, mathematics education, mechanical engineering, medical technology, middle school education, music, music (piano and organ performance), music (voice and choral/opera performance), music education, music theory and composition, natural resources management, neuroscience, nursing, nursing science, nutrition science, nutrition studies, nutritional sciences, operations management, ornamental horticulture, paleontology, philosophy, physical education, physics, physics education, plant protection, political science, (pre)veterinary studies, psychology, public relations, recreation/leisure facilities management, Russian, science education, secondary education, sociology, soil conservation, soil sciences, Spanish, special education, teaching English as a second language, technical writing, theater design, wildlife management, women's studies.

University of Denver

Accounting, animal sciences, anthropology, art, art education, art history, Asian-American studies, biochemistry, biological and physical sciences, biology, biopsychology, business, business administration, business economics, business marketing and marketing management, chemistry, communications, computer engineering, computer/information sciences, construction management, creative writing, economics, electrical/electronics engineering, engineering, English, environmental science, finance, fine/studio arts, French, geography, German, graphic design/commercial art/illustration, history, hospitality management, hotel and restaurant management, international business, international relations, Italian, journalism, Latin American studies, mathematical statistics, mathematics, mechanical engineering, molecular biology, music, music (general performance), musicology, operations research, philosophy, physics, political science, psychology, public administration, real estate, religious studies, Russian, social sciences, sociology, Spanish, theater arts/drama, women's studies.

University of Detroit Mercy

Accounting, alcohol/drug abuse counseling, architecture, behavioral sciences, biochemistry, biology, broadcast journalism, business administration, business marketing and marketing management, chemical engineering, chemistry, civil engineering, computer engineering, computer programming, computer science, computer/information sciences, criminal justice/law enforcement administration, dental hygiene, developmental/child psychology, early childhood education, economics, education, electrical/electronics engineering, elementary education, engineering, English, finance, health education, health services administration, history, human resources management, human services, humanities, information sciences/systems, international business, journalism, labor/personnel relations, law and legal studies, management information systems/business data processing, mass communications, mathematics, mechanical engineering, nursing, philosophy, political science, (pre)dentistry, (pre)law, (pre)medicine, psychology, public relations, radio/television broadcasting, religious studies, science education, secondary education, social work, sociology, special education, systems engineering, theater arts/drama.

University of Evansville

Accounting, anthropology, archaeology, art, art education, art history, arts management, athletic training/sports medicine, biblical studies, biochemistry, biology, business administration, business economics, business marketing and marketing management, ceramic arts, chemistry, civil engineering, classics, computer engineering, computer science, creative writing, criminal justice/law enforcement administration, drawing, economics, electrical/electronics engineering, elementary education, engineering/industrial management, English, environmental science, exercise sciences, finance, French, German, gerontology, graphic design/commercial art/illustration, health services administration, history, international business, international relations, law and legal studies, liberal arts and studies, literature, mass communications, mathematics, mechanical engineering, medical technology, music, music business management and merchandising, music education, music therapy, nursing, philosophy, physical education, physical therapy, physical therapy assistant, physics, physiological psychology/psychobiology, political science, (pre)dentistry, (pre)law, (pre)medicine, (pre)veterinary studies, psychology, religious studies, science education, sculpture, secondary education, sociology, Spanish, special education, theater arts/drama.

University of Florida

Accounting, advertising, aerospace engineering, agricultural economics, agricultural education, agricultural engineering, agronomy/crop science, American studies, animal sciences, anthropology, architecture, art education, art history, Asian studies, astronomy, botany, business administration, business marketing and marketing management, chemical engineering, chemistry, civil engineering, classics, computer engineering, computer/information sciences, construction technology, criminal justice studies, dairy science, dance, economics, electrical/electronics engineering, elementary education, engineering, English, entomology, environmental engineering, environmental science, exercise sciences, family/community studies, finance, fine/studio arts, food sciences, forestry, French, geography, geology, German, graphic design/commercial art/illustration, health education, health science, history, horticulture science, human resources management, industrial engineering, insurance and risk management, interdisciplinary studies, interior design, journalism, Judaic studies, landscape architecture, liberal arts and studies, linguistics, management science, materials engineering, mathematical statistics, mathematics, mechanical engineering, microbiology/bacteriology, music, music education, nuclear engineering, nursing, occupational therapy, pharmacy, philosophy, physical education, physical therapy, physics, plant pathology, plant sciences, political science, Portuguese, poultry science, psychology, public relations, radio/television broadcasting, real estate, recreation/leisure facilities management, rehabilitation therapy, religious studies, Russian, sociology, soil sciences, Spanish, special education, speech-language pathology/audiology, surveying, systems engineering, telecommunications, theater arts/drama, zoology.

University of Georgia

Accounting, advertising, African-American (black) studies, agricultural business, agricultural economics, agricultural education, agricultural engineering, agronomy/crop science, animal sciences, anthropology, art, art education, art history, astronomy, biochemistry, biological and physical sciences, biology, botany, broadcast journalism, business, business administration, business economics, business education, business marketing and marketing management, cell biology, chemistry, classics, clothing/apparel/textile studies, cognitive psychology and psycholinguistics, communication disorders, comparative literature, computer/information sciences, consumer economics, criminal justice studies, dairy science, dietetics, drama and dance education, early childhood education, ecology, economics, English, English education, entomology, environmental health, fashion merchandising, finance, fine/studio arts, fishing sciences and management, food sciences, foreign languages education, foreign languages/literatures, forestry, forestry sciences, French, genetics, geography, geology, German, Greek (Ancient and Medieval), health education, history, home economics education, horticulture services, housing studies, individual/family development, industrial arts education, insurance and risk management, international business, Italian, Japanese, journalism, landscape architecture, landscaping management, Latin (Ancient and Medieval), liberal arts and studies, linguistics, management information systems/business data processing, marketing/distribution education, mass communications, mathematical statistics, mathematics, mathematics education, microbiology/bacteriology, middle school education, music, music (general performance), music education, music theory and composition, music therapy, nutrition studies, pharmacy, philosophy, physical education, physics, plant protection, political science, poultry science, psychology, public relations, radio/television broadcasting technology, reading education, real estate, religious studies, Russian, science education, Slavic languages, social science education, social work, sociology, soil sciences, Spanish, special education, speech/rhetorical studies, sport/fitness administration, theater arts/drama, turf management, wildlife management, women's studies.

University of Illinois at Urbana–Champaign

Accounting, actuarial science, advertising, aerospace engineering, agribusiness, agricultural and food products processing, agricultural economics, agricultural education, agricultural engineering, agricultural mechanization, agricultural sciences, agronomy/crop science, animal sciences, anthropology, architecture, art education, art history, Asian studies, astronomy, biochemistry, bioengineering, biology, biology education, biophysics, botany, broadcast journalism, business, business administration, business education, cell biology, ceramic sciences/engineering, chemical engineering, chemistry, chemistry education, city/community/regional planning, civil engineering, classics, clothing/apparel/textile studies, comparative literature, computer education, computer engineering, computer/information sciences, consumer economics, craft/folk art, dance, dietetics, early childhood education, ecology, economics, electrical/electronics engineering, elementary education, engineering, engineering mechanics, engineering physics, English, English composition, English education, entomology, environmental science, fashion merchandising, finance, food sciences, foreign languages education, forestry, French, French language education, geography, geology, German, German language education, graphic design/commercial art/illustration, health/physical education, history, home economics, horticulture science, hotel and restaurant management, humanities, individual/family development, industrial design, Italian, journalism, landscape architecture, Latin American studies, liberal arts and studies, linguistics, mass communications, materials science, mathematical statistics, mathematics, mathematics education, mathematics/computer science, mechanical engineering, metallurgical engineering, microbiology/bacteriology, music, music (general performance), music (voice and choral/opera performance), music education, music history, music theory and composition, nuclear engineering, nutrition science, nutrition studies, ornamental horticulture, painting, philosophy, photography, physics, physics education, physiology, political science, Portuguese, (pre)veterinary studies, psychology, recreation and leisure studies, religious studies, Russian, Russian/Slavic area studies, science education, sculpture, social studies education, social work, sociology, soil sciences, Spanish, Spanish language education, special education, speech education, speech-language pathology/audiology, speech/rhetorical studies, technical education, theater arts/drama.

The University of Iowa

Accounting, actuarial science, African studies, African-American (black) studies, air science, American history, American studies, anthropology, art, art education, art history, arts management, Asian studies, astronomy, athletic training/sports medicine, biochemistry, bioengineering, biology, broadcast journalism, business administration, business economics, business marketing and marketing management, ceramic arts, chemical engineering, chemistry, chemistry education, Chinese, civil engineering, classics, comparative literature, computer engineering, computer science, creative writing, dance, drama and dance education, drawing, earth sciences, Eastern European area studies, economics, education, electrical/electronics engineering, elementary education, engineering, engineering/industrial management, English, entrepreneurship, environmental engineering, environmental science, exercise sciences, film studies, film/video production, finance, fine/studio arts, French, French language education, geography, geology, German, German language education, Greek (Modern), health education, health occupations education, history, history education, human resources management, industrial engineering, information sciences/systems, interdisciplinary studies, international business, international relations, Italian, Japanese, jazz, journalism, labor/personnel relations, Latin (Ancient and Medieval), Latin American studies, linguistics, literature, management information systems/business data processing, management science, mass communications, materials engineering, mathematical statistics, mathematics, mathematics education, mechanical engineering, medical technology, medieval/renaissance studies, metal/jewelry arts, microbiology/bacteriology, military science, museum studies, music, music (piano and organ performance), music (voice and choral/opera performance), music education, music history, music therapy, Native American studies, nuclear medical technology, nursing, painting, pharmacy, philosophy, photography, physics, political science, Portuguese, (pre)dentistry, (pre)law, (pre)medicine, (pre)pharmacy studies, (pre)veterinary studies, printmaking, psychology, public relations, radio/television broadcasting, recreation and leisure stud-

ies, recreational therapy, religious studies, Russian, science education, sculpture, secondary education, social sciences, social studies education, social work, sociology, Spanish, Spanish language education, speech education, speech therapy, speech-language pathology/audiology, speech/rhetorical studies, sport/fitness administration, stringed instruments, theater arts/drama, wind and percussion instruments, women's studies, zoology.

University of Kansas

Accounting, advertising, aerospace engineering, African studies, African-American (black) studies, American studies, anthropology, archaeology, architectural engineering, architecture, art, art education, art history, astronomy, atmospheric sciences, biochemistry, biological and physical sciences, biology, broadcast journalism, business, cell biology, chemical engineering, chemistry, Chinese, civil engineering, classics, cognitive psychology and psycholinguistics, communication disorders, computer engineering, computer/information sciences, cytotechnology, dance, design/visual communications, developmental/child psychology, ecology, economics, electrical/electronics engineering, elementary education, engineering physics, English, European studies, fine/studio arts, French, genetics, geography, geology, German, health education, health/physical education, history, humanities, international relations, Japanese, journalism, Latin American studies, liberal arts and studies, linguistics, mathematics, mechanical engineering, medical records administration, medical technology, microbiology/bacteriology, middle school education, music, music (piano and organ performance), music (voice and choral/opera performance), music education, music history, music theory and composition, music therapy, nursing science, occupational therapy, painting, petroleum engineering, philosophy, physical education, physics, physiology, political science, (pre)pharmacy studies, printmaking, psychology, radio/television broadcasting, religious studies, respiratory therapy, Russian, Russian/Slavic area studies, sculpture, secondary education, social work, sociology, Spanish, speech/rhetorical studies, stringed instruments, systems science and theory, theater arts/drama, theater design, wind and percussion instruments, women's studies.

University of Maryland, College Park

Accounting, aerospace engineering, African-American (black) studies, agricultural business, agricultural economics, agricultural engineering, agricultural sciences, agronomy/crop science, American studies, animal sciences, anthropology, architecture, art education, art history, astronomy, biochemistry, biology, broadcast journalism, business, business administration, business marketing and marketing management, cartography, cell biology, chemical engineering, chemistry, Chinese, civil engineering, classics, communications, computer engineering, computer/information sciences, criminology, dance, dietetics, drama and dance education, early childhood education, ecology, economics, education, electrical/electronics engineering, elementary education, engineering, English, English education, environmental biology, environmental science, evolutionary biology, exercise sciences, family/community studies, finance, fine/studio arts, fire protection/safety technology, food sciences, foreign languages education, French, geography, geology, German, health education, history, history education, horticulture science, human resources management, information sciences/systems, interdisciplinary studies, international business, Italian, Japanese, journalism, Judaic studies, labor/personnel relations, land use management, landscape architecture, landscaping management, linguistics, logistics and materials management, management science, marine biology, mass communications, materials engineering, materials science, mathematical statistics, mathematics, mathematics education, mechanical engineering, microbiology/bacteriology, molecular biology, music, music (general performance), music education, natural resources conservation, neuroscience, nuclear engineering, nutrition science, operations management, philosophy, physical education, physical sciences, physics, plant sciences, political science, psychology, recreation/leisure facilities management, Romance languages, Russian, Russian/Slavic area studies, science education, secondary education, social studies education, sociology, soil conservation, Spanish, special education, speech education, speech-language pathology, speech-language pathology/audiology, theater arts/drama, transportation technologies, turf management, veterinary sciences, water resources, wildlife management, women's studies, zoology.

University of Massachusetts Amherst

Accounting, African-American (black) studies, animal sciences, anthropology, apparel marketing, applied economics, architectural environmental design, art history, astronomy, biochemistry, biological and physical sciences, biology, business administration, business marketing and marketing management, chemical engineering, chemistry, Chinese, civil engineering, classics, communication disorders, communications, comparative literature, computer engineering, computer science, crop production management, dance, earth sciences, Eastern European area studies, economics, education, electrical/electronics engineering, English, environmental science, equestrian studies, exercise sciences, family resource management studies, finance, fine/studio arts, food sciences, forestry, French, general studies, geography, geology, German, history, horticulture services, hospitality management, humanities, industrial engineering, interdisciplinary studies, interior design, Italian, Japanese, journalism, Judaic studies, landscape architecture, landscaping management, law and legal studies, linguistics, mathematics, mechanical engineering, medical technology, microbiology/bacteriology, Middle Eastern studies, music, music (general performance), natural resources management, nursing, nutrition studies, ornamental horticulture, philosophy, physics, plant sciences, political science, Portuguese, (pre)dentistry, (pre)medicine, (pre)veterinary studies, psychology, Russian/Slavic area studies, sociology, Spanish, sport/fitness administration, theater arts/drama, turf management, wildlife management, women's studies, wood science/paper technology.

University of Miami

Accounting, advertising, aerospace engineering, African-American (black) studies, American studies, anthropology, architectural engineering, architecture, art, art history, atmospheric sciences, audio engineering, biochemistry, bioengineering, biology, broadcast journalism, business administration, business economics, business marketing and marketing management, ceramic arts, chemistry, civil engineering, communications, computer engineering, computer science, computer systems analysis, creative writing, criminology, electrical/electronics engineering, elementary education, engineering science, English, enterprise management, environmental engineering, environmental science, exercise sciences, film stud-

ies, film/video production, finance, French, general studies, geography, geology, German, graphic design/commercial art/illustration, health services administration, history, human resources management, industrial engineering, information sciences/systems, international business, international relations, jazz, journalism, Judaic studies, Latin American studies, law and legal studies, liberal arts and studies, marine biology, mathematics, mechanical engineering, microbiology/bacteriology, music, music (general performance), music (piano and organ performance), music (voice and choral/opera performance), music business management and merchandising, music education, music theory and composition, music therapy, natural resources management, nursing, oceanography, painting, philosophy, photography, physics, physiological psychology/psychobiology, political science, (pre)pharmacy studies, printmaking, psychology, public relations, radio/television broadcasting, real estate, religious studies, sculpture, secondary education, sociology, Spanish, special education, sport/fitness administration, stringed instruments, theater arts/drama, wind and percussion instruments, women's studies.

University of Michigan

Accounting, aerospace engineering, African studies, African-American (black) studies, American studies, anthropology, applied art, applied mathematics, Arabic, archaeology, architecture, art education, art history, Asian studies, astronomy, athletic training/sports medicine, atmospheric sciences, biblical studies, biochemistry, biology, biomedical science, biometrics, biophysics, botany, business administration, cell biology, ceramic arts, chemical engineering, chemistry, Chinese, civil engineering, classics, comparative literature, computer engineering, computer science, creative writing, dance, dental hygiene, design/visual communications, drawing, ecology, economics, education, electrical/electronics engineering, elementary education, engineering, engineering physics, engineering science, English, environmental engineering, environmental science, European studies, exercise sciences, film studies, French, general studies, geography, geology, German, graphic design/commercial art/illustration, Greek (Modern), Hebrew, Hispanic-American studies, history, humanities, industrial design, industrial engineering, interdisciplinary studies, interior design, intermedia, international relations, Islamic studies, Italian, Japanese, jazz, journalism, Judaic studies, landscape architecture, Latin (Ancient and Medieval), Latin American studies, liberal arts and studies, linguistics, literature, mass communications, materials engineering, materials science, mathematical statistics, mathematics, mechanical engineering, medical technology, medieval/renaissance studies, metal/jewelry arts, metallurgical engineering, Mexican-American studies, microbiology/bacteriology, Middle Eastern studies, molecular biology, music, music (piano and organ performance), music (voice and choral/opera performance), music education, music history, music theory and composition, natural resources management, naval architecture/marine engineering, nuclear engineering, nursing, nutrition science, oceanography, painting, pharmacy, philosophy, photography, physical education, physics, play/screenwriting, political science, printmaking, psychology, radiological science, recreation and leisure studies, religious studies, Romance languages, Russian, Russian/Slavic area studies, Scandinavian area studies, sculpture, secondary education, social sciences, sociology, South Asian studies, Southeast Asian studies, Spanish, speech/rhetorical studies, sport/fitness administration, stringed instruments, textile arts, theater arts/drama, theater design, visual/performing arts, wildlife biology, wind and percussion instruments, women's studies, zoology.

University of Michigan–Dearborn

American studies, anthropology, art education, art history, arts management, behavioral sciences, bilingual/bicultural education, biochemistry, biological and physical sciences, biology, business administration, business marketing and marketing management, chemistry, child care/development, communication equipment technology, comparative literature, computer science, computer/information sciences, developmental/child psychology, early childhood education, economics, education, electrical/electronics engineering, elementary education, engineering, English, environmental science, finance, French, German, health services administration, Hispanic-American studies, history, humanities, industrial engineering, information sciences/systems, interdisciplinary studies, international relations, liberal arts and studies, mathematics, mechanical engineering, medieval/renaissance studies, microbiology/bacteriology, middle school education, music, music history, natural sciences, philosophy, physical sciences, physics, political science, psychology, public administration, science education, secondary education, social sciences, sociology, Spanish, speech/rhetorical studies, women's studies.

University of Minnesota, Morris

Art history, biology, business administration, chemistry, computer science, economics, education, elementary education, English, European studies, fine/studio arts, French, geology, German, history, human services, Latin American studies, liberal arts and studies, management science, mass communications, mathematics, music, philosophy, physical therapy, physics, political science, (pre)dentistry, (pre)law, (pre)medicine, (pre)pharmacy studies, (pre)veterinary studies, psychology, secondary education, social sciences, sociology, Spanish, speech/rhetorical studies, theater arts/drama.

University of Minnesota, Twin Cities Campus

Accounting, actuarial science, aerospace engineering, African studies, African-American (black) studies, agricultural business, agricultural education, agricultural engineering, agricultural sciences, agronomy/crop science, American studies, animal sciences, anthropology, architecture, art, art education, art history, astronomy, astrophysics, biochemistry, biology, botany, business education, business marketing and marketing management, cell biology, chemical engineering, chemistry, Chinese, civil engineering, clothing and textiles, comparative literature, computer science, construction management, dance, dental hygiene, developmental/child psychology, early childhood education, East Asian studies, ecology, economics, education, electrical/electronics engineering, elementary education, emergency medical technology, English, English education, environmental science, European studies, family/community studies, film studies, finance, fish/game management, foreign languages education, forest management, forestry, French, genetics, geography, geological engineering, geology, geophysics and seismology, German, graphic design/commercial art/illustration, Greek (Modern), Hebrew, history, home economics education, industrial engineering, insurance and risk management, interior design, international business, international rela-

tions, Italian, Japanese, journalism, Judaic studies, landscape architecture, Latin (Ancient and Medieval), Latin American studies, linguistics, management information systems/business data processing, mass communications, materials engineering, materials science, mathematics, mathematics education, mechanical engineering, medical technology, Mexican-American studies, microbiology/bacteriology, Middle Eastern studies, mortuary science, music, music education, music therapy, Native American studies, natural resources management, neuroscience, nursing, nutrition science, occupational therapy, philosophy, physical education, physical therapy, physics, physiology, plant sciences, political science, Portuguese, (pre)dentistry, (pre)law, (pre)medicine, (pre)veterinary studies, psychology, public health, recreation/leisure facilities management, religious studies, Russian, Russian/Slavic area studies, Scandinavian languages, science education, social science education, socio-psychological sports studies, sociology, soil sciences, South Asian studies, Spanish, speech-language pathology/audiology, theater arts/drama, urban studies, women's studies, wood science/paper technology.

University of Missouri–Columbia

Accounting, advertising, agricultural business, agricultural economics, agricultural education, agricultural mechanization, agricultural sciences, animal sciences, anthropology, archaeology, art, art education, atmospheric sciences, biochemistry, bioengineering, biology, broadcast journalism, business administration, business economics, business marketing and marketing management, chemical engineering, chemistry, civil engineering, classics, clothing/apparel/textile studies, communications, computer engineering, computer science, developmental/child psychology, dietetics, early childhood education, economics, education, electrical/electronics engineering, elementary education, English, family/consumer studies, finance, fish/game management, food sciences, forestry, French, geography, geology, German, history, hotel and restaurant management, housing studies, individual/family development, industrial engineering, interdisciplinary studies, international business, journalism, liberal arts and studies, linguistics, mass communications, mathematical statistics, mathematics, mechanical engineering, microbiology/bacteriology, middle school education, music, music education, nuclear medical technology, nursing, nutrition science, occupational therapy, philosophy, physical therapy, physics, plant sciences, political science, psychology, publishing, radio/television broadcasting, radiological science, real estate, recreation and leisure studies, religious studies, respiratory therapy, Russian, Russian/Slavic area studies, science education, social work, sociology, South Asian studies, Spanish, theater arts/drama.

University of Missouri–Kansas City

Accounting, American studies, art, art history, biology, business administration, chemistry, civil engineering, computer science, criminal justice/law enforcement administration, dance, dental hygiene, early childhood education, earth sciences, economics, education, electrical/electronics engineering, elementary education, English, fine/studio arts, French, geography, geology, German, health/physical education, history, information sciences/systems, interdisciplinary studies, Judaic studies, liberal arts and studies, mass communications, mathematical statistics, mathematics, mechanical engineering, medical laboratory technician, music, music (piano and organ performance), music (voice and choral/opera performance), music education, music therapy, nursing, pharmacy, philosophy, physical education, physics, political science, psychology, secondary education, sociology, Spanish, stringed instruments, theater arts/drama, urban studies, wind and percussion instruments.

University of Missouri–Rolla

Aerospace engineering, applied mathematics, biology, ceramic sciences/engineering, chemical engineering, chemistry, civil engineering, computer engineering, computer science, economics, electrical/electronics engineering, engineering/industrial management, English, geological engineering, geology, geophysics and seismology, history, management information systems/business data processing, mechanical engineering, metallurgical engineering, mining/mineral engineering, nuclear engineering, nursing, petroleum engineering, philosophy, physics, (pre)dentistry, (pre)law, (pre)medicine, psychology.

University of New Hampshire

Accounting, adult/continuing education, agricultural business, agricultural education, agricultural sciences, agronomy/crop science, American studies, animal sciences, anthropology, art, art education, art history, athletic training/sports medicine, biochemistry, biological and physical sciences, biology, biomedical technology, botany, business administration, cell biology, chemical engineering, chemistry, child care/development, city/community/regional planning, civil engineering, civil engineering technology, classics, computer engineering, computer science, construction management, construction technology, culinary arts, dairy science, dietetics, early childhood education, earth sciences, ecology, economics, electrical/electronic engineering technology, electrical/electronics engineering, engineering technology, English, environmental engineering, environmental science, equestrian studies, evolutionary biology, exercise sciences, family/consumer studies, finance, fine/studio arts, food products retailing, forest harvesting production technology, forestry, French, geography, geology, German, Greek (Modern), health services administration, history, home economics, horticulture science, hotel and restaurant management, humanities, interdisciplinary studies, international relations, journalism, landscape architecture, landscaping management, Latin (Ancient and Medieval), liberal arts and studies, linguistics, literature, marine biology, marine science, mass communications, materials science, mathematical statistics, mathematics, mechanical engineering, mechanical engineering technology, medical laboratory technician, microbiology/bacteriology, modern languages, molecular biology, music, music (piano and organ performance), music (voice and choral/opera performance), music education, music history, natural resources conservation, natural resources management, natural sciences, nursing, nutrition science, occupational therapy, ocean engineering, oceanography, ornamental horticulture, philosophy, physical education, physics, political science, (pre)engineering, (pre)medicine, (pre)veterinary studies, psychology, recreation and leisure studies, recreation/leisure facilities management, recreational therapy, Romance languages, Russian, science education, science/technology and society, social work, sociology, soil conservation, Spanish, speech therapy, speech-language pathology/audiology, stringed instruments, surveying, theater arts/drama, trade and industrial education, travel-tourism management, water resources, wildlife biology, wildlife management, wind and percussion instruments, women's studies, zoology.

The University of North Carolina at Asheville

Accounting, art, atmospheric sciences, biology, business administration, chemistry, classics, computer science, economics, English, environmental science, fine/studio arts, French, German, history, journalism, liberal arts and studies, mass communications, mathematics, music, operations management, philosophy, physics, political science, psychology, sociology, Spanish, theater arts/drama.

The University of North Carolina at Chapel Hill

African-American (black) studies, American studies, anthropology, art history, Asian studies, biology, biostatistics, business administration, chemistry, child care/development, classics, communications, comparative literature, dental hygiene, economics, elementary education, English, English education, environmental science, European studies, family studies, fine/studio arts, French language education, geography, geology, German, German language education, health services administration, history, interdisciplinary studies, international relations, journalism, labor/personnel relations, Latin American studies, linguistics, mathematics, mathematics education, middle school education, music, music (general performance), music education, nursing, nutritional sciences, peace and conflict studies, philosophy, physical education, physics, political science, psychology, public health education/promotion, public policy analysis, radiological science, recreation and leisure studies, religious studies, Romance languages, Russian, Russian/Slavic area studies, secondary education, social sciences, social studies education, sociology, Spanish language education, speech education, theater arts/drama, women's studies.

University of Notre Dame

Accounting, aerospace engineering, American studies, anthropology, architecture, art history, biochemistry, biology, business, business marketing and marketing management, chemical engineering, chemistry, civil engineering, classics, computer engineering, computer/information sciences, design/visual communications, economics, electrical/electronics engineering, English, environmental engineering, environmental science, finance, fine/studio arts, French, geology, German, Greek (Ancient and Medieval), history, Italian, Japanese, Latin (Ancient and Medieval), liberal arts and studies, management information systems/business data processing, mathematics, mechanical engineering, medieval/renaissance studies, music, philosophy, physics, political science, (pre)medicine, psychology, religious studies, Russian, science education, sociology, Spanish, theater arts/drama, theology.

University of Oklahoma

Accounting, advertising, aerospace engineering, African-American (black) studies, aircraft pilot (professional), anthropology, architectural environmental design, architecture, area studies, art, art history, astronomy, astrophysics, atmospheric sciences, biochemistry, botany, broadcast journalism, business administration, business economics, business marketing and marketing management, ceramic arts, chemical engineering, chemistry, civil engineering, classics, communications, computer engineering, computer science, construction technology, criminology, dance, early childhood education, economics, electrical/electronics engineering, elementary education, engineering, engineering physics, English, English education, environmental engineering, film/video production, finance, fine/studio arts, foreign languages education, French, geography, geological engineering, geology, geophysics and seismology, German, health/physical education, history, humanities, industrial engineering, interior architecture, international business, journalism, liberal arts and studies, linguistics, management information systems/business data processing, mathematics, mathematics education, mechanical engineering, medical laboratory technologies, microbiology/bacteriology, music, music (piano and organ performance), music (voice and choral/opera performance), music education, Native American studies, petroleum engineering, philosophy, physics, political science, (pre)dentistry, (pre)medicine, (pre)veterinary studies, printmaking, psychology, public administration, public relations, radio/television broadcasting, real estate, religious studies, Russian, science education, secondary education, social studies education, social work, sociology, Spanish, special education, stringed instruments, theater arts/drama, wind and percussion instruments, women's studies, zoology.

University of Pennsylvania

Accounting, actuarial science, African studies, African-American (black) studies, American studies, anthropology, architectural environmental design, art, art history, behavioral sciences, biochemistry, bioengineering, biology, biophysics, business administration, business marketing and marketing management, chemical engineering, chemistry, civil engineering, classics, communications, comparative literature, computer engineering, East Asian studies, economics, education, electrical/electronics engineering, elementary education, English, entrepreneurship, environmental science, finance, folklore, French, geology, German, health facilities administration, history, history of science and technology, human resources management, humanities, insurance and risk management, interdisciplinary studies, international relations, Italian, Judaic studies, Latin American studies, law and legal studies, liberal arts and studies, linguistics, management information systems/business data processing, management science, materials engineering, mathematical statistics, mathematics, mechanical engineering, Middle Eastern studies, music, naval science, nursing, operations management, organizational behavior, peace and conflict studies, philosophy, physics, physiological psychology/psychobiology, political science, (pre)dentistry, (pre)law, (pre)medicine, (pre)veterinary studies, psychology, public policy analysis, real estate, religious studies, Romance languages, Russian, social sciences, sociology, South Asian studies, Spanish, systems engineering, theater arts/drama, transportation engineering, urban studies, women's studies.

University of Pittsburgh

Accounting, African-American (black) studies, anthropology, applied mathematics, art history, biochemistry, bioengineering, biological and physical sciences, biology, British literature, business, business education, business marketing and marketing management, chemical engineering, chemistry, child care/development, Chinese, civil engineering, classics, communications, computer engineering, computer science, corrections, creative writing, criminal justice/law enforcement administration, dental hygiene, dietetics, ecology, economics, electrical/electronics engineering, engineering physics, English, English composition, environmental education, film studies, finance, fine/studio arts, French, geology, German, health services administration, history, history of science and technology,

humanities, industrial engineering, interdisciplinary studies, Italian, Japanese, law and legal studies, liberal arts and studies, linguistics, marketing/distribution education, materials engineering, mathematical statistics, mathematics, mechanical engineering, medical records administration, medical technology, metallurgical engineering, microbiology/bacteriology, molecular biology, music, neuroscience, nursing, occupational therapy, pharmacy, philosophy, physical education, physical sciences, physics, political science, psychology, public administration, religious studies, Russian, Slavic languages, social sciences, social work, sociology, Spanish, speech/rhetorical studies, theater arts/drama, trade and industrial education, urban studies.

University of Puget Sound

Art, Asian studies, biology, business, business computer programming, chemistry, classics, communications, computer science, creative writing, economics, English, exercise sciences, French, geology, German, history, interdisciplinary studies, international business, international economics, international relations, mathematics, music, music (general performance), music business management and merchandising, music education, natural sciences, occupational therapy, philosophy, physics, political science, (pre)dentistry, (pre)law, (pre)medicine, (pre)veterinary studies, psychology, religious studies, sociology, Spanish, theater arts/drama.

University of Redlands

Accounting, anthropology, art history, Asian studies, biology, business, business administration, chemistry, computer science, creative writing, economics, education, elementary education, English, environmental science, fine/studio arts, French, German, history, interdisciplinary studies, international relations, liberal arts and studies, literature, management information systems/business data processing, mathematics, music, music (general performance), music (piano and organ performance), music (voice and choral/opera performance), music education, music history, music theory and composition, philosophy, physics, political science, psychology, religious studies, secondary education, sociology, Spanish, speech therapy, speech-language pathology/audiology.

University of Rhode Island

Accounting, animal sciences, anthropology, apparel marketing, applied economics, art, art history, bioengineering, biology, business administration, business marketing and marketing management, chemical engineering, chemistry, civil engineering, classics, clothing/apparel/textile studies, communication disorders, communications, comparative literature, computer engineering, computer/information sciences, consumer economics, dental hygiene, dietetics, economics, electrical/electronics engineering, elementary education, English, environmental science, finance, fishing sciences and management, French, geology, German, health services administration, history, human services, individual/family development, industrial engineering, interdisciplinary studies, international business, Italian, journalism, landscape architecture, Latin American studies, liberal arts and studies, management information systems/business data processing, marine biology, mathematics, mechanical engineering, medical technology, microbiology/bacteriology, music, music (general performance), music education, music theory and composition, natural resources conservation, natural resources management, nursing, nutrition studies, ocean engineering, pharmacy, philosophy, physical education, physics, political science, psychology, public policy analysis, quantitative economics, secondary education, sociology, Spanish, turf management, wildlife management, women's studies, zoology.

University of Richmond

Accounting, American studies, art, art education, art history, biology, business administration, business economics, business marketing and marketing management, chemistry, classics, computer science, criminal justice/law enforcement administration, Eastern European area studies, economics, education, elementary education, English, European studies, finance, fine/studio arts, French, German, Greek (Modern), health education, history, human resources management, interdisciplinary studies, international business, international economics, international relations, journalism, Latin (Ancient and Medieval), Latin American studies, legal administrative assistant, management information systems/business data processing, mathematics, middle school education, music, music history, philosophy, physical education, physics, political science, psychology, religious studies, secondary education, sociology, Spanish, speech/rhetorical studies, theater arts/drama, urban studies, women's studies.

University of Rochester

Anthropology, applied mathematics, art history, astronomy, biochemistry, bioengineering, biological and physical sciences, biology, cell biology, chemical engineering, chemistry, classics, cognitive psychology and psycholinguistics, comparative literature, computer engineering technology, computer science, earth sciences, economics, electrical/electronics engineering, engineering, engineering science, English, environmental science, evolutionary biology, film studies, fine/studio arts, French, genetics, geology, German, health science, history, interdisciplinary studies, Japanese, jazz, linguistics, mathematical statistics, mathematics, mechanical engineering, microbiology/bacteriology, music, music education, music history, music theory and composition, natural sciences, neuroscience, optics, philosophy, physics, political science, psychology, religious studies, Russian, Russian/Slavic area studies, sign language interpretation, Spanish, women's studies.

The University of Scranton

Accounting, biology, business administration, business marketing and marketing management, chemistry, communications, computer science, criminal justice studies, early childhood education, economics, electrical/electronics engineering, elementary education, English, environmental science, finance, foreign languages/literatures, French, German, Greek (Ancient and Medieval), health services administration, history, information sciences/systems, international business, international relations, Italian, Japanese, Latin (Ancient and Medieval), management science, mathematics, medical technology, neuroscience, nursing, occupational therapy, organic chemistry, philosophy, physical therapy, physics, political science, Portuguese, psychology, public administration, religious studies, Russian, secondary education, Slavic languages, sociology, Spanish, special education, theater arts/drama.

University of Southern California

Accounting, acting/directing, aerospace engineering, African-American (black) studies, American literature, American studies, animal sciences, anthropology, architectural engineering, architecture, art, art history, Asian-American studies, astronomy, audio engineering, biochemistry, bioengineering, biology, biophysics, British literature, broadcast journalism, business administration, business communications, business economics, business marketing and marketing management, business systems analysis and design, chemical engineering, chemistry, Chinese, city/community/regional planning, civil engineering, classics, comparative literature, computer engineering, computer science, creative writing, cultural studies, East Asian studies, economics, education, electrical/electronics engineering, engineering mechanics, engineering/industrial management, English, English education, enterprise management, environmental engineering, environmental science, exercise sciences, film studies, film/video production, finance, fine/studio arts, French, geography, geology, German, gerontology, Greek (Ancient and Medieval), health science, Hispanic-American studies, history, history of philosophy, industrial engineering, interdisciplinary studies, international business, international finance, international relations, Italian, Japanese, jazz, journalism, Judaic studies, landscape architecture, Latin (Ancient and Medieval), linguistics, management science, marine biology, mass communications, mathematics, mechanical engineering, Mexican-American studies, molecular biology, music, music (general performance), music (piano and organ performance), music (voice and choral/opera performance), music business management and merchandising, music education, music theory and composition, natural resources management, neuroscience, nursing, occupational therapy, petroleum engineering, philosophy, physical sciences, physics, physiological psychology/psychobiology, play/screenwriting, political science, psychology, public administration, public policy analysis, public relations, radio/television broadcasting, radio/television broadcasting technology, real estate, religious studies, Russian, safety and security technology, science education, social science education, sociology, Spanish, stringed instruments, structural engineering, systems engineering, theater arts/drama, theater design, urban studies, water resources, water resources engineering, wind and percussion instruments, women's studies.

University of South Florida

Accounting, African-American (black) studies, American studies, anthropology, art, art education, biological and physical sciences, biology, business, business administration, business economics, business education, business marketing and marketing management, chemical engineering, chemistry, civil engineering, classics, communications, computer engineering, computer/information sciences, criminal justice studies, dance, drama and dance education, economics, education, education of the emotionally handicapped, education of the mentally handicapped, education of the specific learning disabled, electrical/electronics engineering, elementary education, engineering, English, English education, environmental science, finance, foreign languages education, French, general studies, geography, geology, German, gerontology, history, humanities, industrial engineering, information sciences/systems, international relations, Italian, liberal arts and studies, management information systems/business data processing, management science, mathematics, mathematics education, mechanical engineering, medical technology, microbiology/bacteriology, modern languages, music (general performance), music education, nursing, philosophy, physical education, physics, political science, psychology, religious studies, Russian, science education, social science education, social sciences, social work, sociology, Spanish, special education, speech/rhetorical studies, theater arts/drama, trade and industrial education, women's studies.

The University of Tennessee Knoxville

Accounting, advertising, aerospace engineering, agribusiness, agricultural business, agricultural economics, agricultural education, agricultural engineering, animal sciences, applied art, architecture, art education, art history, biochemistry, biology, botany, business, business administration, business economics, business education, business marketing and marketing management, chemical engineering, chemistry, civil engineering, classics, computer engineering, computer science, consumer economics, cultural studies, ecology, economics, education, electrical/electronics engineering, engineering physics, engineering science, English, exercise sciences, family studies, finance, fine/studio arts, food sciences, forestry, French, geography, geology, German, graphic design/commercial art/illustration, health education, hearing sciences, history, home economics education, hotel and restaurant management, human services, industrial engineering, interior design, Italian, journalism, liberal arts and studies, logistics and materials management, materials engineering, mathematical statistics, mathematics, mechanical engineering, medical technology, metallurgical engineering, microbiology/bacteriology, music, music education, nuclear engineering, nursing, nutrition science, ornamental horticulture, philosophy, physics, plant protection, plant sciences, political science, psychology, public administration, public health, radio/television broadcasting, recreation/leisure facilities management, religious studies, Russian, social work, sociology, Spanish, special education, speech-language pathology, speech-language pathology/audiology, speech/rhetorical studies, sport/fitness administration, technical education, theater arts/drama, wildlife management, zoology.

The University of Texas at Austin

Accounting, advertising, aerospace engineering, American studies, anthropology, Arabic, archaeology, architectural engineering, architecture, art, art history, Asian studies, astronomy, biochemistry, biology, botany, business, business administration, business marketing and marketing management, chemical engineering, chemistry, civil engineering, classics, clothing/apparel/textile studies, communication disorders, community health liaison, computer/information sciences, dance, design/visual communications, ecology, economics, electrical/electronics engineering, English, evolutionary biology, finance, fine/studio arts, French, geography, geology, geophysics and seismology, German, Greek (Ancient and Medieval), health/physical education, Hebrew, history, home economics, humanities, individual/family development, interior design, Islamic studies, Italian, journalism, Latin (Ancient and Medieval), Latin American studies, liberal arts and studies, linguistics, management information systems/business data processing, mathematics, mechanical engineering, medical technology, microbiology/bacteriology, Middle Eastern studies, molecular biology, music, music (general performance), music history, music theory and composition, nursing, nutrition studies, petroleum engineering, pharmacy, philosophy, physics, political science, Portuguese, psychology, public relations, radio/television broadcasting, Russian, Russian/Slavic area studies, Scandinavian languages, Slavic

languages, social work, sociology, Spanish, speech/rhetorical studies, theater arts/drama, visual/performing arts, zoology.

University of the South

American studies, anthropology, applied art, art, art history, Asian studies, biology, chemistry, classics, comparative literature, computer science, drawing, economics, English, environmental science, European studies, fine/studio arts, forestry, French, geology, German, Greek (Modern), history, international relations, Latin (Ancient and Medieval), literature, mathematics, medieval/renaissance studies, music, music history, natural resources management, philosophy, physics, political science, psychology, religious studies, Russian, Russian/Slavic area studies, social sciences, Spanish, theater arts/drama.

University of Tulsa

Accounting, anthropology, applied mathematics, art, art history, athletic training/sports medicine, biochemistry, biological and physical sciences, biology, business administration, business marketing and marketing management, chemical engineering, chemistry, computer science, economics, electrical/electronics engineering, elementary education, engineering, engineering physics, English, English composition, environmental science, exercise sciences, finance, fine/studio arts, French, geology, geophysics and seismology, German, graphic design/commercial art/illustration, history, information sciences/systems, international business, management information systems/business data processing, mass communications, mathematics, mechanical engineering, music, music (piano and organ performance), music (voice and choral/opera performance), music education, nursing, petroleum engineering, philosophy, physics, political science, (pre)law, (pre)medicine, (pre)veterinary studies, psychology, real estate, science education, secondary education, sociology, Spanish, speech-language pathology/audiology, sport/fitness administration, theater arts/drama.

University of Utah

Accounting, anthropology, Arabic, architecture, art, art history, Asian studies, atmospheric sciences, behavioral sciences, biology, biomedical science, broadcast journalism, business administration, business marketing and marketing management, chemical engineering, chemistry, child care/development, Chinese, civil engineering, classics, computer engineering, computer science, dance, developmental/child psychology, early childhood education, economics, electrical/electronics engineering, elementary education, English, environmental engineering, environmental science, exercise sciences, family/consumer studies, film studies, finance, food sciences, French, geography, geological engineering, geology, geophysics and seismology, German, Greek (Modern), health education, history, home economics education, individual/family development, Japanese, journalism, liberal arts and studies, linguistics, mass communications, materials engineering, materials science, mathematics, mechanical engineering, medical laboratory technician, metallurgical engineering, Middle Eastern studies, mining/mineral engineering, music, music education, nursing, pharmacy, philosophy, physical education, physical therapy, physics, political science, psychology, public relations, radio/television broadcasting, recreation and leisure studies, Russian, science education, secondary education, social sciences, sociology, Spanish, speech-language pathology/audiology, speech/rhetorical studies, theater arts/drama, urban studies, women's studies.

University of Vermont

Agricultural business, agricultural economics, agricultural sciences, animal sciences, anthropology, applied mathematics, art education, art history, Asian studies, athletic training/sports medicine, biochemistry, biology, botany, business administration, Canadian studies, cell biology, chemistry, child care/development, civil engineering, classics, communication disorders, computer science, dairy science, dental hygiene, dietetics, early childhood education, Eastern European area studies, ecology, economics, education, electrical/electronics engineering, elementary education, engineering/industrial management, English, English education, environmental biology, environmental education, environmental science, European studies, family/community studies, family/consumer studies, fine/studio arts, fish/game management, foreign languages education, forestry, French, geography, geology, German, Greek (Ancient and Medieval), history, horticulture science, horticulture services, individual/family development, information sciences/systems, interdisciplinary studies, international relations, landscaping management, Latin (Ancient and Medieval), Latin American studies, mathematical statistics, mathematics, mathematics education, mechanical engineering, medical laboratory assistant, medical radiologic technology, medical technology, microbiology/bacteriology, molecular biology, music, music (general performance), music education, music history, natural resources conservation, natural resources management, nuclear medical technology, nursing, nutrition science, nutrition studies, nutritional sciences, philosophy, physical education, physics, plant sciences, political science, (pre)veterinary studies, psychology, reading education, recreation and leisure studies, recreation/leisure facilities management, religious studies, Romance languages, Russian, Russian/Slavic area studies, science education, secondary education, social science education, social work, sociology, soil sciences, Spanish, speech-language pathology/audiology, theater arts/drama, water resources, wildlife biology, wildlife management, women's studies, zoology.

University of Virginia

Aerospace engineering, African-American (black) studies, anthropology, applied mathematics, architecture, art, astronomy, biology, business, chemical engineering, chemistry, city/community/regional planning, civil engineering, classics, comparative literature, computer/information sciences, cultural studies, economics, electrical/electronics engineering, engineering, English, environmental science, French, German, history, international relations, Italian, liberal arts and studies, mathematics, mechanical engineering, music, nursing, philosophy, physical education, physics, political science, psychology, religious studies, Slavic languages, sociology, Spanish, speech-language pathology/audiology, systems engineering, theater arts/drama.

University of Washington

Accounting, aerospace engineering, African-American (black) studies, air science, anthropology, applied mathematics, architectural urban design, architecture, art, art history, Asian studies, astronomy, atmospheric sciences, bilingual/bicultural education, biochemistry, biology, biology education, biostatistics, botany, business, business administration, Canadian studies, cell biology, ceramic arts, ceramic sciences/engineering, chemical engineering, chemistry, Chinese, city/community/regional planning, civil engineering, classics, communications,

comparative literature, computer engineering, computer science, computer/information sciences, construction management, creative writing, criminal justice/law enforcement administration, cultural studies, dance, data processing technology, dental hygiene, East Asian studies, economics, education, education (multiple levels), electrical/electronics engineering, elementary education, engineering, English, environmental health, environmental science, European studies, fishing sciences and management, forest engineering, forest management, forestry, forestry sciences, French, general studies, geography, geology, geophysics and seismology, German, graphic design/commercial art/illustration, Greek (Ancient and Medieval), history, history of science and technology, humanities, industrial design, industrial engineering, information sciences/systems, interdisciplinary studies, interior architecture, international business, international relations, Italian, Japanese, Judaic studies, landscape architecture, Latin (Ancient and Medieval), Latin American studies, liberal arts and studies, linguistics, management information systems/business data processing, management science, materials engineering, mathematical statistics, mathematics, mechanical engineering, medical technology, metal/jewelry arts, metallurgical engineering, Mexican-American studies, microbiology/bacteriology, Middle Eastern studies, military science, molecular biology, music, music (general performance), music (piano and organ performance), music (voice and choral/opera performance), music education, music history, music theory and composition, musical instrument technology, musicology, Native American studies, natural resources management, naval science, nursing, nursing (maternal/child health), nursing (public health), occupational therapy, oceanography, orthotics/prosthetics, painting, pharmacy, philosophy, photography, physical therapy, physician assistant, physics, political science, printmaking, psychology, public administration, public health, religious studies, Romance languages, Russian, Russian/Slavic area studies, Scandinavian area studies, Scandinavian languages, science education, sculpture, secondary education, Slavic languages, social sciences, social work, sociology, South Asian studies, Southeast Asian studies, Spanish, speech-language pathology/audiology, speech/rhetorical studies, stringed instruments, teaching English as a second language, technical writing, textile arts, theater arts/drama, wildlife management, women's studies, wood science/paper technology, zoology.

University of Wisconsin–Madison

Accounting, actuarial science, advertising, African languages, African studies, African-American (black) studies, agricultural business, agricultural economics, agricultural education, agricultural engineering, agricultural sciences, agronomy/crop science, American studies, animal sciences, anthropology, applied art, applied mathematics, art, art education, art history, Asian studies, astronomy, biochemistry, bioengineering, biology, botany, broadcast journalism, business administration, cartography, cell biology, chemical engineering, chemistry, child care/development, Chinese, civil engineering, classics, clothing and textiles, comparative literature, computer engineering, computer science, construction management, consumer services, dairy science, developmental/child psychology, dietetics, early childhood education, earth sciences, economics, electrical/electronics engineering, elementary education, engineering, engineering mechanics, engineering physics, English, entomology, environmental engineering, experimental psychology, family/consumer studies, farm/ranch management, fashion merchandising, finance, food sciences, forestry, French, genetics, geography, geology, geophysics and seismology, German, Greek (Modern), Hebrew, Hispanic-American studies, history, history of science and technology, home economics, home economics education, horticulture science, industrial engineering, insurance and risk management, interior design, international relations, Italian, Japanese, journalism, labor/personnel relations, landscape architecture, Latin (Ancient and Medieval), Latin American studies, linguistics, mass communications, mathematical statistics, mathematics, mechanical engineering, medical technology, metallurgical engineering, microbiology/bacteriology, mining/mineral engineering, molecular biology, music, music education, natural resources management, nuclear engineering, nursing, nutrition science, occupational therapy, pharmacology, pharmacy, philosophy, physical education, physician assistant, physics, political science, Portuguese, poultry science, psychology, public relations, radio/television broadcasting, real estate, recreation and leisure studies, Russian, Scandinavian languages, science education, secondary education, Slavic languages, social sciences, social work, sociology, Southeast Asian studies, Spanish, special education, speech therapy, surveying, theater arts/drama, toxicology, urban studies, water resources, wildlife management, women's studies, zoology.

Ursinus College

Accounting, anthropology, applied mathematics, art, athletic training/sports medicine, biochemistry, biology, business administration, chemistry, classics, computer science, creative writing, East Asian studies, ecology, economics, education, English, environmental science, French, German, Greek (Modern), health education, health science, history, international relations, Japanese, Latin (Ancient and Medieval), liberal arts and studies, mass communications, mathematics, modern languages, music, philosophy, physical education, physical therapy, physics, political science, (pre)dentistry, (pre)law, (pre)medicine, (pre)veterinary studies, psychology, religious studies, Romance languages, secondary education, sociology, South Asian studies, Spanish.

Valparaiso University

Accounting, American studies, art, art education, art history, astronomy, athletic training/sports medicine, atmospheric sciences, biological and physical sciences, biology, broadcast journalism, business administration, business marketing and marketing management, chemistry, civil engineering, classics, communications, computer science, criminology, East Asian studies, economics, education, electrical/electronics engineering, elementary education, engineering, English, environmental science, European studies, finance, fine/studio arts, French, geography, geology, German, history, interdisciplinary studies, international business, international economics, international relations, journalism, Latin (Ancient and Medieval), liberal arts and studies, mathematics, mechanical engineering, music, music (general performance), music business management and merchandising, music education, nursing, philosophy, physical education, physics, political science, (pre)theology, psychology, sacred music, secondary education, social sciences, social work, sociology, Spanish, theater arts/drama, theology.

Vanderbilt University

African studies, African-American (black) studies, American studies, anthropology, art, astronomy, bioengineering, biology, chemical engineering, chemistry, civil engineering, classics, cognitive psychology and psycholinguistics, computer engineering, computer science, early childhood education, East Asian studies, ecology, economics, education, electrical/electronics engineering, elementary education, engineering, engineering science, English, European studies, French, geology, German, history, human resources management, individual/family development, interdisciplinary studies, Latin American studies, mass communications, mathematics, mechanical engineering, molecular biology, music, music (piano and organ performance), music (voice and choral/opera performance), philosophy, physics, political science, Portuguese, psychology, religious studies, Russian, secondary education, sociology, Spanish, special education, stringed instruments, theater arts/drama, urban studies, wind and percussion instruments.

Vassar College

African studies, American studies, anthropology, art history, Asian studies, astronomy, biochemistry, biology, chemistry, classics, cognitive psychology and psycholinguistics, computer science, economics, elementary education, English, environmental science, film studies, fine/studio arts, French, geography, geology, German, Hispanic-American studies, history, interdisciplinary studies, international relations, Italian, Latin (Ancient and Medieval), Latin American studies, mathematics, medieval/renaissance studies, music, philosophy, physics, physiological psychology/psychobiology, political science, psychology, religious studies, Russian, science/technology and society, sociology, theater arts/drama, urban studies, women's studies.

Villanova University

Accounting, art history, astronomy, astrophysics, biology, business administration, business economics, business marketing and marketing management, chemical engineering, chemistry, civil engineering, classics, computer engineering, computer science, criminal justice/law enforcement administration, economics, education, electrical/electronics engineering, elementary education, English, finance, French, geography, German, history, human services, information sciences/systems, international business, liberal arts and studies, management information systems/business data processing, mass communications, mathematics, mechanical engineering, natural sciences, nursing, philosophy, physics, political science, (pre)dentistry, (pre)law, (pre)medicine, (pre)veterinary studies, psychology, religious studies, secondary education, sociology, Spanish.

Virginia Polytechnic Institute and State University

Accounting, aerospace engineering, agricultural economics, agricultural education, agricultural mechanization, agronomy/crop science, animal sciences, architecture, art, biochemistry, biology, business, business administration, business education, business marketing and marketing management, chemical engineering, chemistry, civil engineering, clothing and textiles, communications, computer engineering, computer science, construction technology, consumer and homemaking education, dairy science, dietetics, early childhood education, economics, electrical/electronics engineering, engineering, engineering science, English, environmental science, finance, food sciences, forestry, French, geography, geology, German, health education, history, horticulture science, human resources management, human services, industrial arts education, industrial design, industrial engineering, information sciences/systems, interdisciplinary studies, international relations, landscape architecture, management information systems/business data processing, marketing/distribution education, materials engineering, mathematical statistics, mathematics, mechanical engineering, mining/mineral engineering, music, nutrition science, ocean engineering, philosophy, physics, political science, poultry science, psychology, sociology, Spanish, theater arts/drama, trade and industrial education, travel-tourism management, urban studies.

Wabash College

Art, biology, chemistry, classics, economics, English, French, German, Greek (Modern), history, Latin (Ancient and Medieval), mathematics, music, philosophy, physics, political science, (pre)law, (pre)medicine, (pre)veterinary studies, psychology, religious studies, Spanish, speech/rhetorical studies, theater arts/drama.

Wake Forest University

Accounting, anthropology, applied mathematics, art, art history, biology, business, chemistry, classics, communications, computer/information sciences, economics, education, elementary education, English, exercise sciences, finance, French, German, Greek (Ancient and Medieval), history, Latin (Ancient and Medieval), management science, mathematics, music, philosophy, physician assistant, physics, political science, psychology, religious studies, Russian, sociology, Spanish, theater arts/drama.

Wartburg College

Accounting, art, art education, arts management, biochemistry, biology, broadcast journalism, business administration, business marketing and marketing management, chemistry, computer science, early childhood education, economics, elementary education, English, English composition, finance, French, German, graphic design/commercial art/illustration, history, history education, information sciences/systems, international business, international relations, journalism, law enforcement/police science, mass communications, mathematics, mathematics education, medical technology, music, music (general performance), music education, music theory and composition, music therapy, occupational therapy, philosophy, physical education, physics, political science, psychology, public relations, religious studies, sacred music, secondary education, social science education, social work, sociology, Spanish, sport/fitness administration.

Washington & Jefferson College

Accounting, art, art education, biology, business administration, chemistry, economics, English, French, German, history, mathematics, philosophy, physics, political science, psychology, sociology, Spanish.

Washington and Lee University

Accounting, anthropology, archaeology, art history, biology, business administration, chemical engineering, chemistry, classics, cognitive psychology and psycholinguistics, computer science, East Asian studies, economics, engineering physics, English, fine/studio arts, foreign languages/literatures, forestry, French, geology, German, history, interdisciplinary studies, journalism, mathematics, medieval/renaissance studies, music, neuroscience, philosophy, physics, political science, psychology, public policy analysis, religious studies, Russian/Slavic area studies, sociology, Spanish, theater arts/drama.

Washington College

American studies, anthropology, art, biology, business administration, chemistry, economics, English, environmental science, French, German, history, humanities, international relations, Latin American studies, liberal arts and studies, mathematics, music, philosophy, physics, physiological psychology/psychobiology, political science, (pre)dentistry, (pre)law, (pre)medicine, (pre)veterinary studies, psychology, sociology, Spanish, theater arts/drama.

Washington University in St. Louis

Accounting, advertising, African studies, African-American (black) studies, American literature, American studies, anthropology, applied art, applied mathematics, Arabic, archaeology, architectural engineering technology, architecture, art, art education, art history, Asian studies, biochemistry, bioengineering, biology, biology education, biophysics, biopsychology, British literature, business administration, business economics, business marketing and marketing management, ceramic arts, chemical engineering, chemistry, chemistry education, Chinese, civil engineering, civil engineering technology, classics, cognitive psychology and psycholinguistics, comparative literature, computer engineering, computer science, creative writing, cultural studies, dance, design/visual communications, drama and dance education, drama/theater literature, drawing, earth sciences, East Asian studies, economics, education, electrical/electronics engineering, elementary education, engineering, engineering physics, engineering science, English, environmental science, European studies, fashion design/illustration, film studies, finance, fine/studio arts, French, French language education, German, German language education, graphic design/commercial art/illustration, Greek (Ancient and Medieval), Hebrew, history, history education, human resources management, information sciences/systems, interdisciplinary studies, international business, international economics, international finance, international relations, Islamic studies, Italian, Japanese, Judaic studies, Latin (Ancient and Medieval), Latin American studies, liberal arts and studies, literature, mathematical statistics, mathematics, mathematics education, mathematics/computer science, mechanical engineering, medieval/renaissance studies, Middle Eastern studies, middle school education, modern languages, music, music (voice and choral/opera performance), music history, music theory and composition, natural sciences, neuroscience, operations management, painting, philosophy, photography, physical sciences, physics, physics education, political science, (pre)dentistry, (pre)law, (pre)medicine, (pre)pharmacy studies, (pre)veterinary studies, printmaking, psychology, religious studies, Romance languages, Russian, Russian/Slavic area studies, science education, science/technology and society, sculpture, secondary education, social science education, social sciences, social studies education, social/philosophical foundations of education, Spanish, Spanish language education, systems engineering, systems science and theory, theater arts/drama, urban studies, women's studies.

Webb Institute

Naval architecture/marine engineering.

Wellesley College

African studies, African-American (black) studies, American studies, anthropology, archaeology, architecture, art history, astronomy, biochemistry, biology, chemistry, Chinese, classics, cognitive psychology and psycholinguistics, comparative literature, computer science, economics, English, fine/studio arts, French, geology, German, Greek (Ancient and Medieval), history, international relations, Italian, Japanese, Judaic studies, Latin (Ancient and Medieval), linguistics, mathematics, medieval/renaissance studies, music, neuroscience, peace and conflict studies, philosophy, physics, political science, psychology, religious studies, Russian, Russian/Slavic area studies, sociology, Spanish, theater arts/drama, women's studies.

Wells College

American studies, anthropology, art, art history, biochemistry, biology, business administration, chemistry, computer science, creative writing, dance, economics, education, elementary education, engineering, English, environmental science, fine/studio arts, French, German, history, international relations, mathematics, molecular biology, music, philosophy, physics, political science, (pre)dentistry, (pre)law, (pre)medicine, (pre)veterinary studies, psychology, public policy analysis, religious studies, secondary education, sociology, Spanish, theater arts/drama, women's studies.

Wesleyan College

Accounting, American studies, art history, biology, business administration, chemistry, communications, early childhood education, education, English, fine/studio arts, history, interdisciplinary studies, international business, international relations, mathematics, middle school education, music, music (piano and organ performance), music (voice and choral/opera performance), philosophy, political science, psychology, religious studies, Spanish.

Wesleyan University

African-American (black) studies, American studies, anthropology, art history, astronomy, biochemistry, biology, chemistry, classics, computer science, dance, earth sciences, East Asian studies, Eastern European area studies, economics, English, environmental science, film studies, fine/studio arts, French, German, history, humanities, interdisciplinary studies, Italian, Latin American studies, mathematics, medieval/renaissance studies, molecular biology, music, neuroscience, philosophy, physics, political science, psychology, religious studies, Romance languages, Russian, Russian/Slavic area studies, science/technology and society, social sciences, sociology, Spanish, theater arts/drama, women's studies.

Westminster Choir College of Rider University

Liberal arts and studies, music, music (piano and organ performance), music (voice and choral/opera performance), music education, music theory and composition, sacred music.

Westminster College (UT)

Accounting, aircraft pilot (professional), art, aviation management, biology, biology education, business, business administration, business economics, business marketing and marketing management, chemistry, communications, computer science, early childhood education, elementary education, English, finance, history, human resources management, interdisciplinary studies, international business, mathematics, nursing,

philosophy, physics, political science, psychology, social science education, social sciences, sociology, special education.

Wheaton College (IL)

Anthropology, archaeology, art, art history, biblical languages/literatures, biblical studies, biology, business economics, chemistry, computer science, economics, elementary education, engineering, English, environmental science, exercise sciences, French, geology, German, Greek (Ancient and Medieval), Hebrew, history, interdisciplinary studies, Latin (Ancient and Medieval), mathematics, music, music (piano and organ performance), music (voice and choral/opera performance), music business management and merchandising, music education, music history, nursing, philosophy, physical education, physical sciences, physics, political science, psychology, religious education, religious studies, social studies education, sociology, Spanish, speech/rhetorical studies, stringed instruments, wind and percussion instruments.

Whitman College

Anthropology, art, art history, Asian studies, astronomy, biology, chemistry, classics, economics, English, environmental science, French, geology, German, history, mathematics, music, philosophy, physics, political science, psychology, sociology, Spanish, theater arts/drama.

Whittier College

Art, biochemistry, biology, business administration, chemistry, developmental/child psychology, early childhood education, economics, English, French, history, international relations, liberal arts and studies, mathematics, music, philosophy, physical education, physics, political science, psychology, religious studies, social work, sociology, Spanish, theater arts/drama.

Willamette University

American studies, art, art history, Asian studies, biology, chemistry, classics, comparative literature, computer science, economics, English, environmental science, exercise sciences, fine/studio arts, French, German, Hispanic-American studies, history, humanities, international relations, mathematics, music, music education, music therapy, philosophy, physical education, physics, political science, (pre)dentistry, (pre)law, (pre)medicine, (pre)veterinary studies, psychology, religious studies, sociology, Spanish, speech/rhetorical studies, theater arts/drama.

William Jewell College

Accounting, art, biochemistry, biology, business administration, cell biology, chemistry, computer science, drama and dance education, economics, education, elementary education, English, French, history, information sciences/systems, interdisciplinary studies, international business, international relations, mathematics, medical technology, molecular biology, music, music (general performance), music education, music theory and composition, nursing, philosophy, physics, political science, (pre)dentistry, (pre)law, (pre)medicine, (pre)veterinary studies, psychology, religious studies, sacred music, secondary education, Spanish, speech education, speech/rhetorical studies, theater arts/drama.

Williams College

American studies, anthropology, art history, Asian studies, astronomy, astrophysics, biology, chemistry, Chinese, classics, computer science, economics, English, fine/studio arts, French, geology, German, history, Japanese, literature, mathematics, music, philosophy, physics, political science, psychology, religious studies, Russian, sociology, Spanish, theater arts/drama.

Wittenberg University

American studies, art, art education, art history, Asian studies, behavioral sciences, biochemistry, biological and physical sciences, biology, botany, business administration, business economics, business marketing and marketing management, cartography, cell biology, ceramic arts, chemistry, communications, comparative literature, computer graphics, computer science, creative writing, developmental/child psychology, drawing, earth sciences, East Asian studies, economics, education, elementary education, English, environmental biology, environmental science, finance, fine/studio arts, French, geography, geology, German, graphic design/commercial art/illustration, history, humanities, interdisciplinary studies, international business, international relations, liberal arts and studies, literature, marine biology, mathematics, microbiology/bacteriology, middle school education, modern languages, music, music (piano and organ performance), music (voice and choral/opera performance), music education, natural sciences, philosophy, physical sciences, physics, physiological psychology/psychobiology, political science, (pre)dentistry, (pre)law, (pre)medicine, (pre)veterinary studies, psychology, religious studies, Russian/Slavic area studies, science education, sculpture, secondary education, social sciences, sociology, Spanish, special education, theater arts/drama, theology, urban studies.

Wofford College

Accounting, art history, biology, business economics, chemistry, computer science, economics, English, finance, French, German, history, humanities, international business, international relations, mathematics, philosophy, physics, political science, (pre)dentistry, (pre)law, (pre)medicine, (pre)veterinary studies, psychology, religious studies, sociology, Spanish.

Worcester Polytechnic Institute

Actuarial science, aerospace engineering, applied mathematics, biochemistry, bioengineering, biological and physical sciences, biological technology, biology, biomedical science, business administration, cell biology, chemical engineering, chemistry, city/community/regional planning, civil engineering, computer engineering, computer management, computer science, computer/information sciences, construction engineering, construction management, economics, electrical/electronics engineering, engineering, engineering design, engineering mechanics, engineering physics, engineering science, engineering/industrial management, environmental engineering, environmental science, fire protection/safety technology, fluid and thermal sciences, genetics, geophysical engineering, history, history of science and technology, humanities, industrial engineering, information sciences/systems, interdisciplinary studies, management information systems/business data processing, materials engineering, materials science, mathematical

statistics, mathematics, mechanical engineering, metallurgical engineering, metallurgy, microbiology/bacteriology, molecular biology, music, natural sciences, nuclear engineering, nuclear physics, operations research, optics, philosophy, physics, political science, (pre)dentistry, (pre)law, (pre)medicine, (pre)veterinary studies, robotics, science/technology and society, social sciences, systems engineering, technical writing, transportation engineering.

Xavier University

Accounting, advertising, art, athletic training/sports medicine, biology, business administration, business marketing and marketing management, chemistry, classics, communication equipment technology, computer science, corrections, criminal justice/law enforcement administration, early childhood education, economics, education, English, entrepreneurship, finance, fine/studio arts, French, German, history, human resources management, humanities, information sciences/systems, international relations, liberal arts and studies, mathematics, medical radiologic technology, medical technology, middle school education, music, music education, natural sciences, nursing, occupational therapy, philosophy, physics, political science, psychology, public relations, science education, social work, sociology, Spanish, special education, sport/fitness administration, theology.

Yale University

African-American (black) studies, American studies, anthropology, applied mathematics, archaeology, architecture, art, art history, astronomy, astrophysics, bioengineering, biology, cell biology, chemical engineering, chemistry, classics, comparative literature, computer/information sciences, cultural studies, East Asian studies, ecology, economics, electrical/electronics engineering, engineering physics, engineering science, English, evolutionary biology, film studies, French, German, history, humanities, interdisciplinary studies, Italian, Judaic studies, Latin (Ancient and Medieval), Latin American studies, linguistics, literature, mathematics, mechanical engineering, molecular biology, music, philosophy, physics, political science, Portuguese, psychology, religious studies, Russian, Russian/Slavic area studies, sociology, South Asian languages, Spanish, systems science and theory, women's studies.

Yeshiva University

Accounting, biology, business administration, business marketing and marketing management, chemistry, classics, computer science, early childhood education, economics, education, elementary education, English, finance, French, Hebrew, history, interdisciplinary studies, Judaic studies, management information systems/business data processing, mass communications, mathematics, music, philosophy, physics, political science, (pre)dentistry, (pre)law, (pre)medicine, psychology, sociology, speech-language pathology/audiology, speech/rhetorical studies, theater arts/drama.

GEOGRAPHIC INDEX OF COLLEGES

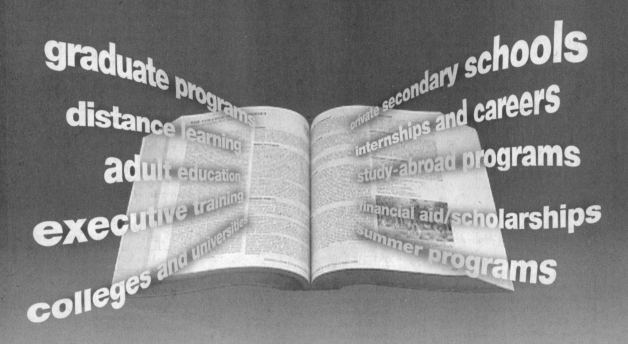